Guide to Psychological Assessment with Hispanics

Lorraine T. Benuto
Editor

Guide to Psychological Assessment with Hispanics

Springer

Editor
Lorraine T. Benuto
Department of Psychology
Victims of Crime Treatment Center
University of Nevada
Reno, NV, USA

ISBN 978-1-4614-4411-4 ISBN 978-1-4614-4412-1 (eBook)
DOI 10.1007/978-1-4614-4412-1
Springer New York Heidelberg Dordrecht London

Library of Congress Control Number: 2012946103

Printed on acid-free paper

Springer is part of Springer Science+Business Media (www.springer.com)

Para mi padre, Jorge, por haberme enseñado el valor del trabajo, la importancia de la educación, y el significado de la familia. Pero sobre todo por haber trabajado tan duro para que yo pudiera ser lo que soy hoy. Te lo agradesco.

To my mother, Lorraine, for all you've done for me (making sure I learned countless spelling words, making me "much"!) and all the things you still do today--I could not have accomplished as much as I have accomplished as much as I have without you.

Preface

Why Hispanics?

Considering that ethnocultural minority individuals who are of Hispanic/Latino origin make up the largest ethnocultural minority group in the United States, guidelines for working with this population are an absolute must. Given that a large subset of this percentage is comprised of immigrants many of whom do not speak English or who have learned English as a second language, special considerations when it comes to psychological assessment are neccessary. In fact, traditional assessments do not place much emphasis on language differences, validity of tests for ethnic minorities, or the influence of cultural or social factors. Furthermore, acculturation issues accompany many disorders in Hispanics and can influence the way in which psychological disorders are manifested. If the above are ignored, accurate diagnoses cannot be reached and psychological test results can be misinterpreted.

The above has in part contributed to the awareness of cross-cultural psychopathology as a growing concern in the field of psychology, and some researchers have indicated that cultural variations in symptom presentation exist (e.g., Ballenger et al., 2001) and others have even suggested that assessment measures do not fully capture endorsement of symptoms because of language or cultural barriers. The above calls to attention the importance of examining psychological testing and assessment practices as they relate to Hispanics. This book seeks to fill a large gap in the existing scientific literature by consolidating the research on psychological assessment with Hispanic samples into one comprehensive volume and developing simple recommendations for the psychological assessment of Hispanic clients.

Why Assessment?

Accurate assessment is the pillar of effective mental health services as correct assessment informs treatment selection and implementation via the establishment of an accurate diagnosis. In fact, when misdiagnosis occurs in the realm of clinical practice, this can lead to the selection of an inappropriate (i.e., ineffective or minimally effective) treatment to the detriment of the client.

The field of psychology has long since shifted to an evidence-based perspective and much has been written about evidence-based practice (Ollendick, 2012) with a particular focus on empirically supported treatments. With regard to psychological testing and assessment, the parallel focus is on the psychometric properties of tests, and a measure is determined to be psychometrically sound when it has been demonstrated to be reliable and valid. The crux of this book is to offer researchers and clinicians an overview of the most commonly used and/or frequently researched assessment measures and to provide research-based guidelines for the assessment of the Hispanic clients and research participants.

Organization of the Book

In terms of organization, this book is structured such that there is a chapter specific to the types of tests psychologists administer (e.g., self-report, IQ); most of the major diagnostic categories (e.g., eating disorders, mood disorders) in the Diagnostic and Statistical Manual of Mental Disorders IV-Text Revision (DSM-IV-TR: American Psychiatric Association [APA], 2000); and where appropriate chapters relevant to a certain type of psychological assessment (e.g., forensic, neuropsychological, school-based). Each chapter contains a general overview of cultural considerations that must be made when assessing the Hispanic client and then a specific exploration of the most commonly used and/or frequently researched assessment measures and the research that has been conducted on these measures with Hispanic participants. Conclusions are drawn and guidelines are provided.

The Cultural Sensitivity Movement

The cultural sensitivity movement is clearly relevant to this book. Scholars and researchers alike have been writing about ethnic differences and their relationship to mental health for decades (e.g., Cardemil, 2010; Chavez, Cornelius, & Jones, 1985) and the majority of these writings have focused on discussing ethnic differences (in attitudes, use of health care, prevalence for certain disorders, etc.), identifying barriers to access, or discussing the problems associated with the lack of cultural sensitivity with very few writers/researchers/experts proposing or implementing solutions to these problems (Benuto & Leany, 2011). This book aims to provide not only an overview of the scientific literature on psychological testing and assessment with Hispanics but also a clear set of specific, relevant, and implementable guidelines for psychological testing and assessment with this group.

What Is the Goal of This Book?

Ultimately, it should be the goal of all psychologists to use the highest quality and most psychometrically sound psychological assessment measures and procedures and to do so in a culturally sensitive manner. The goal of this book is to help facilitate the process of measure selection, administration, and interpretation for mental health professionals (clinicians, researchers, clinical supervisors, students, etc.) who work with Hispanics.

References

American Psychiatric Association. (2000). *Diagnostic and statistical manual of mental disorders* (4th ed.). Washington, DC: American Psychiatric Association.

Ballenger, J. C., Davidson, J. T., Lecrubier, Y., Nutt, D. J., Kirmayer, L. J., Lépine, J., et al. (2001). Consensus statement on transcultural issues in depression and anxiety from the International Consensus Group on Depression and Anxiety. *Journal of Clinical Psychiatry, 62*(Suppl. 13), 47–55.

Benuto, L., & Leany, B. (2011). Reforms for women and minorities. In N. Cummings & W. O'Donohue (Eds.), *21st century behavioral healthcare reforms: The promise of integrated healthcare.* New York: Routledge.

Cardemil, E. V. (2010). The complexity of cCulture: Do we embrace the challenge or avoid it?. *The Scientific Review of Mental Health Practice, 7*(2), 41–47.

Chavez, L. R., Cornelius, W. A., & Jones, O. W. (1985). Mexican immigrants and the utilization of U.S. health services: The case of San Diego. *Social Science & Medicine, 21,* 93–102.

Ollendick, T. H. (2012). The role of assessment and case conceptualization in evidence-based practice. *Psyccritiques, 57*(9). doi:10.1037/a0027211

Contents

Contributors

Saul G. Alamilla, Ph.D. Department of Psychology, Kennesaw State University, Kennesaw, GA, USA

Dana M. Alonzo, Ph.D. School of Social Work, Columbia University, New York, NY, USA

Alfredo Ardila, Ph.D. Department of Communication Sciences and Disorders, Florida International University, Miami, FL, USA

Paulina Arenas-Landgrave, Ph.D. Mental Health and Diagnosis Program, Faculty of Psychology, National Autonomous University of Mexico, Mexico City, Mexico

Danette Beitra, B.A. Center for Psychological Studies, Nova Southeastern University, Ft. Lauderdale, FL, USA

Lorraine T. Benuto, Ph.D. Department of Psychology, Victims of Crime Treatment Center, University of Nevada, Reno, NV, USA

Irene M. Bravo, Ph.D. Psychology Department, Carlos Albizu University, Miami, FL, USA

José J. Cabiya, Ph.D. Scientific Research Institute (SRI), Carlos Albizu University, San Juan, Puerto Rico

Veronica Cardenas, Ph.D. Department of Psychiatry, University of California – San Diego, La Jolla, CA, USA

Olga Cirlugea, B.A. Department of Psychology, University of Nevada, Reno, NV, USA

Maria Garrido, Psy.D. Psychology Psy.D./Ph.D. Program, Ponce School of Medicine and Health Sciences, Ponce, Puerto Rico

Paula Helu, M.S. Department of Psychiatry, University of California – San Diego, La Jolla, CA, USA

Margie Hernandez, B.A. Department of Psychology, University of North Carolina Wilmington, Wilmington, NC, USA

Jennifer Ho, B.S. Department of Psychiatry, University of California – San Diego, La Jolla, CA, USA

Tara Jackman-Venanzi, B.A. Department of Psychology, University of North Carolina Wilmington, Wilmington, NC, USA

Sarah C. Jones, B.A. Department of Psychology, University of Nevada, Las Vegas, NV, USA

Sharon Jones-Forrester, Ph.D. Department of Psychology, University of Nevada, Las Vegas, Las Vegas, NV, USA

Carolina Lara, B.A. Department of Psychology, University of Texas at El Paso, El Paso, TX, USA

Brian D. Leany, Ph.D. California Department of Corrections and Rehabilitation, Adult Division, California Correctional Health Care Services, Susanville, CA, USA

Eunice Lerma, Ph.D. Department of Educational Psychology and Leadership Studies, Brownsville, TX, USA

Jose S. Loredo, M.D., M.S., MPH, FCCP, FAASM Division of Pulmonary and Critical Care Medicine, Director of the UCSD Sleep Medicine Center, San Diego School of Medicine, University of California, San Diego, CA, USA

Esmeralda Matute, Ph.D. Neuroscience Institute, University of Guadalajara, Guadalajara, Mexico

Emilia Lucio-Gomez Maqueo, Ph.D. Mental Health and Diagnosis Program, Faculty of Psychology, National Autonomous University of Mexico, Mexico City, Mexico

Marta Meana, Ph.D. Department of Psychology, University of Nevada, Las Vegas, NV, USA

Joan Ignasi Mestre, Psy, Ph.D. IMIM (Hospital del Mar Research Institute), Parc de Salut Mar, Barcelona, Spain

Juan A. Nazario, Psy.D. Psy.D Program, Carlos Albizu University, San Juan, Puerto Rico

Taylor L. Oliver, M.A. Department of Psychology, University of Nevada, Las Vegas, NV, USA

Orlando L. Pedrosa-Roche, Ph.D. Psy.D Program, Carlos Albizu University, San Juan, Puerto Rico

Marisol Perez, Ph.D. Department of Psychology, Texas A&M University, College Station, TX, USA

Antonio E. Puente, Ph.D. Department of Psychology, University of North Carolina Wilmington, Wilmington, NC, USA

Carmen S. Roca, Ph.D. Carlos Albizu University, Miami, FL, USA

Mónica Rosselli, Ph.D. Department of Psychology, Charles E. Schmidt College of Science, Florida Atlantic University, Davie, FL, USA

Paola Clementina Rossi, M.D., Ph.D. IMIM (Hospital del Mar Research Institute), Parc de Salut Mar, Barcelona, Spain

Institute of Neuropsychiatry and Addictions, Hospital del Mar-IMIM, Parc de Salut Mar, Barcelona, Spain

John A. Sauceda, M.A. Department of Psychology, University of Texas at El Paso, El Paso, TX, USA

Cassandra Snipes, B.A. Department of Psychology, University of Nevada, Reno, NV, USA

Lourdes Suarez-Morales, Ph.D. Center for Psychological Studies, Nova Southeastern University, Ft. Lauderdale, FL, USA

Joy Lynn Suárez-Kindy, Psy.D. Psy.D Program, Carlos Albizu University, San Juan, Puerto Rico

Nicholas S. Thaler, M.A. Department of Psychology, University of Nevada, Las Vegas, Las Vegas, NV, USA

Denisse Tiznado, B.S. Department of Psychiatry, University of California – San Diego, La Jolla, CA, USA

Marta Torrens, M.D., Ph.D. IMIM (Hospital del Mar Research Institute), Parc de Salut Mar, Barcelona, Spain

Institute of Neuropsychiatry and Addictions, Hospital del Mar-IMIM, Parc de Salut Mar, Barcelona, Spain

Universitat Autònoma de Barcelona, Barcelona, Spain

Cortney S. Warren, Ph.D. Department of Psychology, University of Nevada, Las Vegas, NV, USA

John S. Wiebe, Ph.D. Department of Psychology, University of Texas at El Paso, El Paso, TX, USA

James V. Wojcik, Ph.D. Canvas Health, Oakdale, MN, USA

Manuel X. Zamarripa, Ph.D. Department of Counseling & Educational Psychology, Texas A&M-Corpus Christi, Corpus Christi, TX, USA

Davor Zink, B.S. Department of Psychology, University of North Carolina Wilmington, Wilmington, NC, USA

1 Guide to Psychological Assessment with Hispanics: An Introduction

Lorraine T. Benuto

Organization of This Book

The field of psychology has long since shifted to an evidence-based perspective, and much has been written about evidence-based practice (Ollendick, 2012). A large focus of this movement has been on interventions with heavy emphasis on empirically supported treatments (ESTs: Chambless & Ollendick, 2001) with some questioning the use of ESTs with ethnic minority individuals due to the underrepresentation of such individuals in the scientific literature (Bernal & Scharró-del-Río, 2001). In the realm of psychological testing and assessment, the parallel focus is on the psychometric properties of tests and a measure is determined to be psychometrically sound when it has been demonstrated to be reliable and valid. The crux of this book is to offer researchers and clinicians an overview of the most commonly used and/or frequently researched assessment measures and to provide research-based guidelines for the assessment of the Hispanic clients and research participants. Ultimately, it was up to each individual author to determine the most commonly used and/or frequently researched assessment measures and as each author was selected based on their expertise on the topic in question and it was at their discretion to determine what measures to review.

In terms of organization, this book is structured such that there is a chapter specific to the types of tests psychologists administer (e.g., self-report, IQ); most of the major diagnostic categories (e.g., eating disorders, mood disorders) in the *Diagnostic and Statistical Manual of Mental Disorders IV-Text Revision* (DSM-IV-TR: American Psychiatric Association, 1994); and where appropriate chapters relevant to certain types of psychological assessment (e.g., forensic, neuropsychological, school-based). Each chapter contains a general overview of cultural considerations that must be made when assessing the Hispanic client and then a specific exploration of the most commonly used and/or frequently researched assessment measures and the research that has been conducted on these measures with Hispanic participants. Conclusions are drawn and guidelines are provided.

In terms of this introductory chapter, the aims of it are to provide an overview regarding the organization of this book (see above), to discuss the mental health practitioner's role in psychological testing and assessment, and to explore how the cultural sensitivity movement relates to psychological assessment. Issues specific to Hispanics are also discussed (e.g., culture-bound syndromes).

L.T. Benuto, Ph.D. (✉)
Department of Psychology, Victims of Crime Treatment Center, University of Nevada, Reno MS 0296, Reno, NV 89557, USA
e-mail: dr.benuto@gmail.com

L.T. Benuto (ed.), *Guide to Psychological Assessment with Hispanics*,
DOI 10.1007/978-1-4614-4412-1_1, © Springer Science+Business Media New York 2013

Assessment: The Bread and Butter of the Clinical Psychologist

The Domain of the Psychologist

Psychological testing and assessment has been described as the "brightest jewel in the crown of clinical psychology," and this prestige is said to have emerged in the early 1900s with intelligence testing and was later reinforced in the 1950s with personality testing in psychiatric settings (Wood, Garb, & Nezworski 2007). This has certainly continued as even today in the majority of the United States the scope of practice of the clinical psychologist allows for the administration, scoring, and interpretation of psychological tests whereas this is not the case for other mental health practitioners (e.g., licensed clinical social workers, marriage and family therapists). Therefore, in many ways, psychological testing and assessment is what differentiates the psychologist from other mental health professionals.

Why Is Assessment Important?

Accurate assessment is the pillar of effective mental health services (Jakobsons & Buckner, 2007) as correct assessment informs treatment selection and implementation via the establishment of an accurate diagnosis (Novy, Stanley, Averill, & Daza, 2001; Therrien & Hunsley, 2012). In fact, when misdiagnosis occurs in the realm of clinical practice, this can lead to the selection of an inappropriate (i.e., ineffective or minimally effective) treatment to the detriment of the client. Consider the following. A client comes in with a clear presentation of anxiety. A clinical interview is conducted and a diagnosis of panic disorder is applied. Cognitive behavioral therapy for panic disorder is begun, and the client's anxiety does decrease although not to the extent desired. As treatment progresses, the client mentions a history of trauma and diagnostic criteria for post-traumatic stress disorder (PTSD) is evaluated and a PTSD checklist is administered. The client is then diagnosed with PTSD and prolonged exposure therapy (Foa, Hembree, & Rothbaum, 2007) is begun and the client experiences a dramatic reduction in anxiety. Clearly in clinical practice correct assessment is of utmost importance (as illustrated by the example provided above). In the context of research, accurate diagnosis is equally important as it can impact research study results, which ultimately inform the treatments that we use, and the overall progression of our field.

Psychometrics: Good Measures Make for Good Clinicians

Validity

Validity simply refers to whether or not a test measures what it is supposed to (Wood et al., 2007). For example, using a metric tape measure to measure height would theoretically be a valid means of measuring height for obvious reasons. While this definition and example may be an oversimplification of validity, defining validity becomes more complicated when we consider the different types of validity, namely, construct, content, convergent, discriminant, concurrent, and predictive and postdictive validity. See Table 1.1 for details regarding each of these types of validity. Validity is important in any discussion on psychometrics, and with regard to cultural sensitivity, it is important to consider how cultural factors could impact the various validities (e.g., if symptom presentation does in fact vary by culture, then the content of assessments should vary as well).

Table 1.1 Defining validity

Type of validity	Question related to the specific type of validity	How is this type of validity established?
Construct	Does the test measure what it is supposed to?	By examining the relationship between test scores and a variety of other measures[b]
Content	Is the content of the test appropriate for what is being measured?[a]	By showing that the behaviors sampled by the test are a representative sample of the attribute being measured[b]
Convergent	Does the test correlate with other tests that measure the same attribute or diagnosis?[a]	By showing that measures that should be related are in reality related[c]
Discriminant	Does the test show low correlations with other tests that measure the same attribute or diagnosis?[a]	By showing that measures that should *not* be related are in reality *not* related[c]
Concurrent	Does the test correlate with current non-test behaviors or symptoms?[a]	By showing the relationship between the test and behaviors and/or symptoms
Predictive and postdictive	Does the test predict relevant behaviors or symptoms in the future?[a]	By examining the relationship between test results and outcome

[a]Wood et al. (2007)
[b]Murphy and Davidshofer (2005)
[c]Trochim (2006)

Table 1.2 Defining reliability

Type of reliability	Question related to the specific type of validity	How is this type of validity established?
Test-retest reliability	Does the test yield consistent results over time?[a]	By examining the relationship between test results from an administration of a test at one point in time and an administration of the same test at a later point in time
Interrater reliability	Does the test yield consistent results among different raters?[a]	By examining the relationship between a score obtained by one test administrator and a different test administrator
Internal reliability	Are the test items that make up the test consistent with one another, i.e., are they internally consistent?[a]	By calculating odd-even reliability, spilt-half reliability, or by computing coefficient alpha[a]

[a]Wood et al. (2007)

Reliability

Similar to validity, there are different types of reliability and the most commonly discussed types include test-retest reliability, interrater reliability, and internal reliability. See Table 1.2 for the definitions of these. In the example provided in section "Validity" (see above), using a metric tape measure to measure height would likely produce reliable results (at least in the realm of test-retest reliability and interrater reliability). However, using number of books to measure height (i.e., Mr. X is 10 books tall) would be a substantially less reliable means of assessing height given that book size varies considerably across books and the books selected by the rater would also likely vary (leading to poor test-retest reliability and interrater reliability). To a large extent, language can impact the reliability of assessment measures (e.g., the language of the person administering the test; the testee). Therefore, it is important that assessments be used in the language they were developed.

Norms

Wood et al. (2007) discuss three concepts that are important in the context of norms when it comes to psychological assessment. First, there is the normative sample, which provides means and standard deviations that allow us to interpret test results based on a group of specific individuals (non-patients) who were administered the test. Second, there are normative statistics that include means and standard deviations of relevant patient groups. There are also cutoff scores between normal and disordered individuals that can help us make diagnostic decisions. Norms are very important when we consider the psychological testing and assessment of ethnic minority individuals as research has indicated that normative data derived from Euro-Americans may not be applicable to individuals from different cultural backgrounds. Nonetheless, an extant review of the literature has indicated that norms seem to be most impacted by language proficiency, educational background, economic status, and in certain instances acculturation level (as opposed to ethnic minority status in and of itself).

The Cultural Sensitivity Movement (CSM)

The cultural sensitivity movement (CSM) is clearly relevant to both this chapter and this book. Scholars and researchers alike have been writing about ethnic differences and their relationship to mental health for decades (e.g., Cardemil, 2010; Chavez, Cornelius, & Jones, 1985; Conner, Koeske, & Brown, 2009; Falicov, 1996; Givens, Houston, Van Voorhees, Ford, & Cooper, 2007; Leaf, Bruce, & Tischler, 1986; Snowden, 1998), and the majority of these writings have focused on discussing ethnic differences (in attitudes, use of health care, prevalence for certain disorders, etc.), identifying barriers to access, or discussing the problems associated with the lack of cultural sensitivity with very few writers/researchers/experts proposing or implementing solutions to these problems (Benuto & Leany, 2011). This book aims to provide not only an overview of the scientific literature on psychological testing and assessment with Hispanics but also a clear set of specific, relevant, and implementable guidelines for psychological testing and assessment with this group.

Constructs Related to the Cultural Sensitivity Movement

Despite the longstanding existence of the CSM, key constructs associated with this movement have been poorly defined (Benuto & Leany, 2011; O'Donohue, 1995). Thus, here at the outset of our discussion on the CSM, definitions pertinent to this movement and to this chapter are defined (these definitions have been largely adapted from Benuto & Leany).

The constructs we will discuss here are race and ethnicity, acculturation, and socioeconomic status. Also worth mentioning in this section is the issue of language, although language and its relationship to psychological testing and assessment will be discussed in greater detail in the section "Relevant Issues in the Assessment of Hispanics". Furthermore, there is an entire chapter in this book that provides an elaborate discussion on bilingualism and its relationship to psychological testing and assessment.

Race and Ethnicity

Race is the categorization of parts of a population based on physical appearance due to historical, social, and political forces, and determination of race is subjective as there are no genotypes to delineate categorical differences. Conversely, ethnicity refers to a subcultural group of a multicultural society usually based on a common national or tribal heritage (Heurtin-Roberts, 2003). Historically speaking, race and ethnicity have been considered to be separate entities, although as indicated above, the scientific consensus is that racial designations and ethnicity do not have scientific basis.

Specific to this chapter and book is of course the ethnic group Hispanic/Latina(o). Hispanic or Latino origin refers to the heritage, lineage, nationality group, or country of birth of the person or the person's parents or ancestors before they arrived in the United States and is often considered one of the major ethnic groups in the United States. These subgroups are many and include individuals of Cuban, Puerto Rican, Mexican, South or Central American, or other Spanish culture or origin (e.g., Spain) regardless of race (Puente, Zinik, Hernandez, Jackman-Venanzi, & Ardila, 2013). In this book, the terms Hispanic and Latino are often used interchangeably.

Acculturation

Because of the United States' melting pot phenomenon and the immigrant nature of this country, acculturation is often discussed within the CSM. Acculturation includes cultural and psychological changes resulting from intercultural contact (Berry, 2003) including changes in customs, economic status, political life, social behavior (Berry, Phinney, Sam, & Vedder, 2006), attitudes toward the acculturation process, and cultural identity (Phinney, 2003). Acculturation can be discussed in terms of unidimensionality (whereby one becomes acculturated to a new culture) or as a bidirectional construct (i.e., fusing elements of both cultures) (see Flannery, Reise, & Yu, 2001 for a theoretical and empirical overview of the various iterations of acculturation). A number of acculturation measures exist that can be used with Hispanics (e.g., the General Ethnicity Questionnaire [GEQ; Tsai, Ying, & Lee, 2000]), and many of these measures are available in both English and Spanish. Standard indices of acculturation including age of arrival, generational status, and length of residency in the United States (Marin, 1992) can also be used to help determine a person's acculturation level. Clinicians and researchers may wish to determine a client or research participant's level of acculturation as it is evident that acculturation level can confound assessment results.

Socioeconomic Status

Issues related to socioeconomic status (SES) as it pertains to mental health are also often discussed in the CSM. Benuto and Leany (2011) define socioeconomic status (SES) as an amalgam of economic, educational, racial, cultural, and/or ethnic variables. Our discussion on SES within the context of psychological testing and assessment of Hispanics will be fairly limited as far as economic impact and education level is concerned as it is important that issues related to economic status and education level not be confused with issues related to ethnic minority status (as indeed there are ethnic minority individuals who are not poor and conversely there are individuals from the majority culture who are poor; the same is true with regard to education). Suffice to say that much of the research on SES that is specific to economic limitations and education level can be generalized to nonethnic minorities who come from poor economic or limited educational backgrounds. Nonetheless, given that Hispanics do attain lower levels of education than other ethnic groups (Bauman & Graf, 2003) and are more economically limited than Whites (State Health Facts, 2010), it is important that clinicians assess for the presence of poverty and determine the client's education level (although again this applies to groups other than Hispanics) and account for these factors by using adjusted norms or interpreting test results with caution (see below for what to do when this is the case).

How Are the CSM and Psychological Testing and Assessment Related?

Generally speaking, Hispanics receive lesser and poorer quality healthcare (Guarnaccia, Martinez, & Acosta, 2005; Willerton, Dankoski, & Sevilla Martir, 2008). Reasons for this disparity may include fear of the health-care system, lack of health insurance (Guarnaccia et al., 2005; Novy et al., 2001; Willerton et al., 2008), and perceptions that mental health services are unnecessary, unwelcoming, or not useful (U.S. Department of Health and Human Services 2001). In fact, Hispanics are likely to use services mostly when in crisis and have high dropout rates and undesirable treatment outcomes (U.S. DHHS, 2001). Hispanics may also be reluctant to seek psychological services due to the lack of cultural competency of providers (Gonzales-Prendes, Hindo, & Pardo, 2011; Novy et al.).

In part due to the above, awareness of cross-cultural psychopathology is a growing concern in the field of psychology, and some researchers have indicated that cultural variations in symptom presentation exist (e.g., Ballenger et al., 2001), and others have even suggested that assessment measures do not fully capture endorsement of symptoms because of language or cultural barriers (Asnaani, Richey, Dimaite, Hinton, & Hofman, 2010) calling to attention the importance of examining psychological testing and assessment practices as they relate to Hispanics. Thus, below we explore relevant issues in the assessment of Hispanics.

Relevant Issues in the Assessment of Hispanics

When discussing psychological testing and assessment of the Hispanic client, we encounter two separate but intertwined issues. The first issue is related to language, and the second issue is that of ethnic and cultural differences among Hispanics subgroups and between Hispanics and other ethnic groups and how these differences can impact the testing and assessment process. Also of relevance (and thus discussed in this section) is the issue of culture-bound syndromes.

Language

Approximately 78% of Hispanics aged 5 and older speak Spanish as their primary language in the home (Weil, 2010), and less than half of Hispanic immigrants residing in the United States have *even* limited English language proficiency (Pew Hispanic Center, 2012). These statistics illustrate the need for the availability of psychological assessment measures in Spanish. Thus, a very salient recommendation with regard to language is that the client's language proficiency be assessed and assessments in the appropriate language be administered.

To complicate things further because the "Hispanic" ethnic group constitutes a lump of individuals from many different countries and regions, there are also idiosyncratic differences in language (and customs) between these groups. Consider the following antidote. A psychology intern who was raised in the United States within the Mexican culture relocates to Puerto Rico to complete a clinical internship. Upon arrival, she hears several words she has not ever encountered (e.g., *guagua, china, guineo*), but she is quickly able to deduce that these words mean bus, orange (as in the fruit), and banana, respectively. In Mexico, these would have been referred to as *autobús* (or simply *bús* or in certain regions *camion*), *naranja*, and *platano*.More relevant to field of psychology, let us consider this intern's clinical experiences while on internship. Upon beginning a rotation in an intensive outpatient treatment setting, she approaches clients and asks them if she can meet with them *ahorrita* which she knows to mean now. However, after consistently observing that her clients do not follow to meet with her, she learns that in Puerto Rico *ahorrita* actually means in a little while and *ahorra* is used when one wants to imply immediacy (which is different to what she is accustomed to given her Mexican upbringing). Despite these nuances that can sometimes cause confusion (or even frustration), just as there is a standard English, there is also a standard Spanish that is usually easily understood by any Spanish speaker (Puente & Ardila, 2000), and the examples above have illustrated exactly this. We can also see this if we consider the English parallel of pop vs. soda vs. soft drink vs. coke vs. cola. For the most part, we can easily interpret what is meant by these words despite regional differences within the United States that ultimately determine what you call a carbonated beverage.

These types of idiosyncratic differences in language can impact assessment results when test items include words that vary by country or region. Therefore, ideally when test items are translated (or created), having several Spanish-speaking professionals from different countries and/or regions examine the translation of test items may be useful in eliminating such idiosyncrasies. It is of course worth noting that if a single item on a test contains a word that can be interpreted to mean different things or a construct whose name is determined by region, it is not likely to cause invalid results or to make a test useless as more than likely results would still fall within less than a standard deviation of a person's true score which is typically what we expect even when such idiosyncrasies are absent. Nonetheless, in such instances, results may need to be interpreted with caution (see below on what to do in such cases).

Hispanic Cultural Characteristics

The second issue that we encounter when discussing psychological testing and assessment of the Hispanic client is that of ethnic and cultural differences among Hispanics subgroups and between Hispanics and other ethnic groups. As alluded to above, Hispanics share many cultural characteristics and there are great similarities across the subgroups that constitute the Hispanic ethnicity (although certainly there are differences as well). One of the aims of this book is to discuss and explore potentially culturally unique values that could bias assessment measures and the interpretation of assessment results—such a discussion can be found in each of the chapters of this book.

Culture-Bound Syndromes

In the original table of contents of this book, a chapter on the assessment of culture-bound syndromes was included. However, the literature on culture-bound syndromes in Hispanics is meager, and the majority of published works on culture-bound syndromes are purely descriptive and not research-focused, making it impossible to write an entire chapter on this topic. Thus, the culture-bound syndromes as they relate to Hispanics and the assessment thereof will be discussed here.

The DSM-IV-TR (APA 1994) includes several culture-bound syndromes that are specific and/or relevant to Hispanics. A summary of these syndromes can be found in Table 1.3. Of these syndromes, only research on *ataques de nervios* exists that quantifies the symptoms of this syndrome and provides evidence of its validity as a separate disorder from the anxiety disorders in the DSM-IV-TR (see San Miguel et al., 2006), making it the only culturally bound syndrome specific to Hispanics for which valid and reliable assessment practices are possible. Unfortunately, a review of the literature has yielded very few studies examining the assessment of this syndrome, e.g., Livanis and Tryon (2010) developed the 31-item Adolescent Nervios Scale; Guarnaccia, Rubio-Stipec, and Canino (1989) developed an *ataque de nervios* scale from the Somatization items of the Puerto Rican Diagnostic Interview Schedule (DIS); and San Miguel et al. have used the Explanatory Model Interview Catalogue (EMIC) to gather data on *ataque* experiences. Thus, readers are encouraged to consider measures relevant to the differential diagnoses that should be considered (see Table 1.3) to aid in attaining an accurate diagnosis when a culture-bound syndrome is suspected. Alternatively, readers may also wish to consider culture-bound syndromes when a diagnosis cannot be made due to the way in which symptoms are being presented. Other assessment practices that can prove useful in diagnosing a culture-bound syndrome include clinical interviews, collateral contacts, and record review.

Thus far we have covered the organization of this book, we have broadly talked about psychological assessment and relevant constructs, we have discussed the cultural sensitivity movement and its relevance to psychological testing and assessment, and we have explored relevant issues in the psychological assessment of Hispanics. The remainder of this chapter will focus on the provision of some general guidelines that are likely to apply the majority of the chapters in this book.

Table 1.3 Culture-bound syndromes that are specific and/or relevant to Hispanics

Name of syndrome	Syndrome characteristics	Differential diagnoses to consider
Amok (mal de pelea)	A dissociative episode that begins with brooding and is followed by violent, aggressive, or homicidal behavior[a]	Delusional, dissociative, psychotic, or impulse control disorders
Ataque de nervios	Symptoms usually arise after a distressful event and may include uncontrollable shouting, attacks of crying, trembling, heat in the chest rising into the head, verbal and physical aggression, dissociative episodes, seizure-like or fainting episodes, and suicidal gestures[a]	Anxiety, mood, dissociative, or somatoform disorders[a]
Bilis/colera	Caused by a strongly expressed anger or rage, which disturbs core body balances. Symptoms may include acute nervous tension; headache; trembling; screaming; stomach disturbances such as nausea, vomiting, or diarrhea; and loss of consciousness, and chronic fatigue may result from an acute episode[a]	Anxiety, mood, dissociative, somatoform, or adjustment disorders
Locura	Severe, chronic psychosis[a]	Delusional, dissociative, or psychotic disorders
Evil eye (mal de ojo)	Symptoms include fitful sleep, crying without apparent cause, diarrhea, vomiting, and fever. (This syndrome is most commonly observed in children)[a]	Anxiety or somatoform disorders
Nervios	Refers both to a sense of vulnerability to stressful life experiences and the symptoms produced by that vulnerability, e.g., emotional distress, somatic complaints (headaches, stomach disturbances), irritability, sleep difficulties, nervousness, inability to concentrate, tearfulness, trembling, tingling sensations, and *mareos* (dizziness)[a]	Adjustment, anxiety, depressive, dissociative, somatoform, or psychotic disorders[a]
Susto	Translated means "fright" or "soul loss" and occurs when a frightening event causes the soul to leave the body, which results in unhappiness and sickness. Symptoms include appetite disturbances, inadequate or excessive sleep, troubled sleep or dreams, sadness, lack of motivation, feelings of low self-worth or dirtiness, and somatic complaints	Mood, anxiety, somatoform,[a] delusional, dissociative, or psychotic disorders

[a]APA (2000)

Here Come the Guidelines

Interpreting with Caution

Literature related to the cultural sensitivity movement and assessment measures is replete with the recommendation to "interpret with caution." However, it is unclear specifically what is meant by this term. A simple search using Google demonstrates the difficulty in ascertaining a definition of this term, which is often used in the context of almost any situation where there are results (e.g., statistical results).

In the context of psychological assessment, this phrase does not mean that the results of an assessment are inaccurate, although it implies that they could be. Thus, where the clinician encounters tests where results should be interpreted with caution, it does not mean that the test is necessarily bad but that interpretation should be done with a few caveats.

First, the clinician is advised to examine multiple sources to try and generate an answer to their assessment/referral question (although this is not the case for Hispanics *only* and is better described as a good assessment practice that should be employed in general). For example, if the clinician is attempting to determine whether or not the results from a test aimed at assessing for dementia are valid and it is their goal to interpret the results with caution, they may wish to corroborate the test results with other test results, information provided in the clinical interview, information provided by reliable collateral contacts, clinical observations, etc. If all other measures seem to align with the results from the test in question, then the results are most likely valid. However, if the majority of other measures contradict the findings of the test, then perhaps the test results should be deemed invalid. And of course, there is always a third possibility—some data supports the findings while other data does not. In this case, additional collateral contacts can be made and tests administered to generate additional data to help answer the referral question.

Are There Times When Test Results Are More Important Than Others?

Any clinician specializing in psychological assessment knows that the crux of an assessment is answering the referral question. However, assessment procedures are not only employed when specialized testing is required. Consider the Beck Depression Inventory-II (BDI-II), for example. While the BDI-II may be administered as part of a larger assessment battery to answer some specialized question (e.g., how depressed is a client who is suing someone for damages), the BDI-II is often used as a means for assessing progress in treatment. Therefore, while there are *not* circumstances where the administration, scoring, and interpretation of tests are *unimportant*, there are circumstances where the results of such tests may carry substantially more weight than others.

If we again consider the BDI-II as a means for assessing progress in treatment, the most likely scenario to apply is as follows. A client comes to a clinician seeking treatment and reports feeling blue. The clinician, as part of the standard intake procedures, administers a BDI-II, makes note of the client's score and depression level, and ensures that the client is not suicidal. The BDI-II is then administered routinely to monitor progress in treatment. Perhaps to embellish this example a bit, let us consider that the client's level of English proficiency is moderate, and there are one or two items of the BDI-II that the client does not understand but attempts to answer to the best of his/her ability. The client opts not to mention this to the clinician and does not request forms in Spanish. In this scenario, a slight difference in scores on this measure due to cultural and/or linguistic factors may have very little implications on the client or anyone else (provided of course that the client is not suicidal). Essentially the client's score is slightly less than representative of their actual level of depression, but the client will most likely be administered cognitive behavioral therapy for depression regardless of this slight difference.

Now let us consider the following. A client suffers a tragic accident that results in a substantial head injury. As part of litigation procedures, a psychological evaluation to determine brain damage is performed. This client's level of English proficiency is also moderate. All tests are administered in English and no cultural considerations are made. Certainly one could spin this scenario a few different ways, i.e., the client could end up with a larger settlement, as due to the use of English-only testing instruments, he/she appears to have suffered greater damage than he/she actually did. However, the goal of the clinician should always be to perform the most accurate assessment procedures possible. Thus, in this second scenario, the clinician has failed to a fairly significant degree and the implication of the skewed testing results is quite grand (simply ask the insurance company paying out the settlement). We could certainly generate additional examples where the outcomes of skewed testing results have huge implications, e.g., assessing for violence risk or sexual recidivism and determining the cause of criminal behavior; however, the illustration has been made—there are in fact circumstances where more thorough and careful consideration of cultural and linguistic factors are necessary because the weight of the results for such procedures is greater.

When Is Enough Enough?

The cultural sensitivity movement often cites the limited inclusion of cultural minorities in research studies as a means for withholding evidence-based practices from these groups (Cardemil, 2010). One question worth considering within this context is, when is enough enough? More specifically, when is it okay to provide ethnic minorities with gold standard psychological services? Do we wait until we have conducted extensive research that justifies the delivery of high-quality mental health services to cultural minorities? To what extent must we stratify these hypothetical research studies (e.g., should it be minority vs. nonminority; Hispanics vs. Euro-Americans; foreign-born Hispanics vs. US-born Hispanics; Cubans vs. Mexicans vs. Puerto Ricans, etc.)? And until then, what do we do in the meantime? Do we withhold the administration of psychometrically sound assessment measures based on the premise that ethnic minorities have been underrepresented in literature?

It is the perspective of this author that high-quality mental health services should not be withheld from cultural minorities, although some experts cite the underrepresentation of such individuals in the scientific literature as a reason to do just that (Bernal & Scharró-del-Río, 2001). An alternative approach to the issue of underrepresentation of ethnic minorities in the scientific literature is that the provision of evidence-based psychological services (including scientifically sound assessment procedures) should be utilized with Hispanics (and other cultural minorities) unless there is clear evidence or a theoretical reason not to even in the absence of research on the cultural minority group in question. After all, is it not our goal to provide the best psychological services possible to our clients? Thus, it is recommended that psychometrically sound assessment measures be utilized with Hispanics even when Hispanics are underrepresented in the psychometric literature unless there is clear evidence that doing this would be a detriment to the client or there is a theoretical reason not to.

Beware of Overusing Clinical Judgment

Actuarial predictions are based on empirically validated relationships between client data and the condition to be predicted, while clinical predictions are based on the clinician's intuition, experience, and knowledge (Dawes, Faust, & Meehl, 1989). There has been a huge debate in the field (beginning with Meehl, 1954, and followed up by Holt in 1958) as to which method is more accurate. A large body of research in the domain of violence risk prediction has clearly indicated that the use of clinical judgment results in poor predictive validity (Borum, 1996; Elbogen, 2002; Litwack, 2001; Quinsey, Harris, Rice, & Cromier, 1998). More generally speaking, Grove, Zald, Lebow, Snitz, and Nelson (2000) have indicated that statistical prediction is approximately 10% more accurate than clinical prediction. In a fairly impressive meta-analysis, Ægisdóttir et al. (2006) reviewed 67 studies carried out over 56 years and found an overall greater accuracy for statistical predictions when compared to clinical methods. Interestingly, subsequent research has indicated that experience, whether educational or clinical, is positively associated with judgment accuracy (Spengler et al., 2009).

Given the above, the practicing clinician is encouraged to use actuarial predictions and to avoid the use of clinical judgment in particular when results from several tests, information from *reliable* collateral contacts, etc., contradict such judgment. After all, is it not the aim of the scholar practitioner and science practitioner to deliver psychological services that are based in science?

Summary and Conclusions

This chapter includes (1) an overview of the organization of *Guide to Psychological Assessment with Hispanics*, (2) a review of constructs relevant to psychological assessment, (3) a discussion of the cultural sensitivity movement and its relevance to psychological testing and assessment, and (4) a presentation of relevant issues in the psychological assessment of Hispanics (including a discussion on the assessment of culture-bound syndromes). This chapter also offers specific recommendations on how to interpret psychological testing or assessment results with caution; a discussion on circumstances where more thorough and careful consideration of cultural and linguistic factors are necessary because the weight of the results from the assessment and testing procedures is greater; and finally a recommendation on what to do when there is an underrepresentation of ethnic minorities in the scientific literature. Ultimately, it should be the goal of all psychologists to use the highest quality and most psychometrically sound psychological assessment measures and procedures and to do so in a culturally sensitive manner. The goal of this book is to help facilitate the process of measure selection, administration, and interpretation for psychologists who work with Hispanics.

References

Ægisdóttir, S., White, M. J., Spengler, P. M., Maugherman, A. S., Anderson, L. A., Cook, R. S., et al. (2006). The meta-analysis of clinical judgment project: Fifty-six years of accumulated research on clinical versus statistical prediction Stefanía Ægisdóttir. *The Counseling Psychologist, 34*(3), 341–382. doi: 10.1177/0011000006286696.

American Psychiatric Association. (1994). *Diagnostic and statistical manual of mental disorders* (4th ed.). Washington, DC: American Psychiatric Association.

Asnaani, A., Richey, J., Dimaite, R., Hinton, D. E., & Hofmann, S. G. (2010). A cross-ethnic comparison of lifetime prevalence rates of anxiety disorders. *The Journal of Nervous and Mental Disease, 198*(8), 551–555. doi:10.1097/NMD.0b013e3181ea169f.

Ballenger, J. C., Davidson, J. T., Lecrubier, Y., Nutt, D. J., Kirmayer, L. J., Lépine, J., et al. (2001). Consensus statement on transcultural issues in depression and anxiety from the International Consensus Group on Depression and Anxiety. *The Journal of Clinical Psychiatry, 62*(Suppl13), 47–55.

Bauman, K. J., & Graf, N. L. (2003). *Educational attainment: 2000, Census 2000 brief.* Retrieved from www.census.gov/prod/2003pubs/c2kbr-24.pdf.

Benuto, L., & Leany, B. (2011). Reforms for women and minorities. In N. Cummings & W. O'Donohue (Eds.), *21st century behavioral healthcare reforms: The promise of integrated healthcare*. New York: Routledge.

Bernal, G., & Scharró-del-Río, M. R. (2001). Are empirically supported treatments valid for ethnic minorities? Toward an alternative approach for treatment research. *Cultural Diversity and Ethnic Minority Psychology, 7*(4), 328–342. doi:10.1037/1099-9809.7.4.328.

Berry, J. W. (2003). Conceptual approaches to acculturation. In K. Chun, P. Balls-Organista, & G. Marin (Eds.), *Acculturation: Advances in theory, measurement and applied research* (pp. 17–37). Washington, DC: American Psychological Association.

Berry, J. W., Phinney, J. S., Sam, D. L., & Vedder, P. (Eds.). (2006). *Immigrant youth in cultural transition*. Mahwah, NJ: Erlbaum.

Borum, R. (1996). Improving the clinical practice of violent risk assessment. *American Psychologist, 51*, 945–956.

Cardemil, E. V. (2010). The complexity of culture: Do we embrace the challenge or avoid it? *The Scientific Review of Mental Health Practice, 7*(2), 41–47.

Chambless, D. L., & Ollendick, T. H. (2001). Empirically supported psychological interventions: Controversies and evidence. *Annual Review of Psychology, 52*, 685–716. doi:10.1146/annurev.psych.52.1.685.

Chavez, L. R., Cornelius, W. A., & Jones, O. W. (1985). Mexican immigrants and the utilization of U.S. health services: The case of San Diego. *Social Science & Medicine, 21*, 93–102.

Conner, K. O., Koeske, G., & Brown, C. (2009). Racial differences in attitudes toward professional mental health treatment: The mediating effect of stigma. *Journal of Gerontological Social Work, 52*(7), 695–712.

Dawes, R. M., Faust, D., & Meehl, P. E. (1989). Clinical versus actuarial judgment. *Science, 243*, 1668–1674.

Elbogen, E. B. (2002). The process of violence risk assessment: A review of descriptive research. *Aggression & Violent Behaviour, 7*, 591–604.

Falicov, C. (1996). Mexican families. In *Ethnicity and family therapy* (2nd ed., pp. 169–182). New York: Guilford Press.
Flannery, W., Reise, S. P., & Yu, J. (2001). An empirical comparison of acculturation models. *Personality and Social Psychology Bulletin, 27*(8), 1035–1045. doi:10.1177/0146167201278010.
Foa, E., Hembree, E. A., & Rothbaum, B. O. (2007). *Prolonged exposure therapy for PTSD: Emotional processing of traumatic experiences therapist guide*. New York: Oxford University Press.
Givens, J., Houston, T., Van Voorhees, B., Ford, D., & Cooper, L. (2007). Ethnicity and preferences for depression treatment. *General Hospital Psychiatry, 29*(3), 182–191.
Gonzales-Prendes, A., Hindo, C., & Pardo, Y. (2011). Cultural values integration in cognitive-behavioral therapy for a latino with depression. *Clinical Case Studies, 10*(5), 376–394.
Grove, W. M., Zald, D. H., Lebox, B. S., Snitz, B. E., & Nelson, C. (2000). Clinical versus mechanical prediction: A meta-analysis. *Psychological Assessment, 12*, 19–30.
Guarnaccia, P., Martinez, I., & Acosta, H. (2005). Mental health in the hispanic immigrant community: An overview. *Journal of Immigrant & Refugee Services, 3*(1), 21–46.
Guarnaccia, P., Rubio-Stipec, M., & Canino, G. (1989). Ataques de nervios in the Puerto Rican diagnostic interview schedule: The impact of cultural categories on psychiatric epidemiology. *Culture, Medicine and Psychiatry, 13*(3), 275–295.
Heurtin-Roberts, S. (2003). *Race and ethnicity in health and vital statistics*. Retrieved from www.ncvhs.hhs.gov/040902p1.pdf.
Holt, R. R. (1958). Clinical and statistical prediction: A reformulation and some new data. *Journal of Abnormal and Social Psychology, 56*, 1–12.
Jakobsons, L., & Buckner, J. (2007). The assessment, diagnosis, and treatment of psychiatric disorders in Hispanic/Latino clients. In J. Buckner, Y. Castro, J. Holm-Denoma, & T. Joiner (Eds.), *Mental health care for people of diverse backgrounds*. Abingdon: Radcliffe Publishing.
Leaf, P. J., Bruce, M. L., & Tischler, G. L. (1986). The differential effect of attitudes on the use of mental health services. *Social Psychiatry, 21*, 187–192.
Litwack, T. R. (2001). Actuarial versus clinical assessments of dangerousness. *Psychology, Public Policy, and Law, 7*, 409–443.
Livanis, A., & Tryon, G. (2010). The development of the Adolescent Nervios scale: Preliminary findings. *Cultural Diversity and Ethnic Minority Psychology, 16*(1), 9–15. doi:10.1037/a0014905.
Marin, G. (1992). Issues in the measurement of acculturation among Hispanics. In K. F. Geisinger (Ed.), *Psychological testing of Hispanics* (APA Science Volumes, pp. 235–251). Washington, DC: American Psychological Association.
Meehl, P. E. (1954). *Clinical vs. statistical prediction: A theoretical analysis and a review of the evidence*. Minneapolis, MN: University of Minnesota Press.
Murphy, K. R., & Davidshofer, C. O. (2005). *Psychological testing: Principles and applications*. Upper Saddle River, NJ: Prentice Hall.
Novy, D., Stanley, M., Averill, P., & Daza, P. (2001). Psychometric comparability of english and spanish language measures of anxiety and related affective symptoms. *Psychological Assessment, 13*(3), 347–355.
O'Donohue, W. T. (1995). Cultural sensitivity: A critical examination. In R. H. Wright & N. A. Cummings (Eds.), *Destructive trends in mental health* (pp. 29–44). New York: Routledge.
Ollendick, T. H. (2012). The role of assessment and case conceptualization in evidence-based practice. *Psyccritiques, 57*(9), 10.1037/a0027211.
Pew Hispanic Center. (2012). *Pew Hispanic Center online database*. Retrieved from http://www.pewhispanic.org/2009/03/05/statistical-portrait-of-hispanics-in-the-united-states-2007/2007-portrait-of-hispanics-22/.
Phinney, J. S. (2003). Ethnic identity and acculturation. In K. M. Chun, P. Balls Organista, G. Marín, K. M. Chun, P. Balls Organista, & G. Marín (Eds.). *Acculturation: Advances in theory, measurement, and applied research* (pp. 63–81). Washington, DC: American Psychological Association. doi:10.1037/10472-006.
Puente, A. E., & Ardila, A. (2000). Neuropsychological assessment of Hispanics. In E. Fletcher-Janzen, T. L. Strickland, & C. R. Reynolds (Eds.), *Handbook of cross-cultural neuropsychology* (pp. 87–104). Dordrecht, The Netherlands: Kluwer Academic Publishers.
Puente, A. E., Zinik, D., Hernandez, M., Jackman-Venanzi, T., & Ardila, A. (2013). Bilingualism and its impact on psychological assessment. In L. Benuto (Ed.), *Guide to psychological assessment with hispanics*. New York: Springer.
Quinsey, V. L., Harris, G. T., Rice, M. E., & Cromier, C. A. (1998). *Violent offenders: Appraising and managing risk*. Washington, DC: American Psychological Association.
San Miguel, V., Guarnaccia, P. J., Shrout, P. E., Lewis-Fernández, R., Canino, G. J., & Ramírez, R. R. (2006). A quantitative analysis of Ataque de Nervios in Puerto Rico: Further examination of a cultural syndrome. *Hispanic Journal of Behavioral Sciences, 28*(3), 313–330. doi:10.1177/0739986306291441.
Snowden, L. R. (1998). Racial differences in informal help seeking for mental health problems. *Journal of Community Psychology, 26*(5), 429–438.

Spengler, P. M., White, M. J., Ægisdóttir, S., Maugherman, A. S., Anderson, L. A., Cook, R. S., et al. (2009). The meta-analysis of clinical judgment project: Effects of experience on judgment accuracy. *The Counseling Psychologist, 37*(3), 350–399. doi:10.1177/ 0011000006295149.

State Health Facts. (2010*). United States: Poverty Rate by Race/Ethnicity, states (2009–2010), U.S. (2010).* Retrieved from http://www.statehealthfacts.org/profileind.jsp?rgn=1&cat=1&ind=14.

Therrien, Z., & Hunsley, J. (2012). Assessment of anxiety in older adults: A systematic review of commonly used measures. *Aging & Mental Health, 16*(1), 1–16.

Trochim, M. K. W. (2006). *Research methods knowledge base*. Retrieved from http://www.socialresearchmethods.net/kb/index.php.

Tsai, J. L., Ying, Y., & Lee, P. A. (2000). The meaning of "being Chinese" and "being American": Variation among Chinese American young adults. *Journal of Cross-Cultural Psychology, 31*, 302–322.

U.S. Department of Health and Human Services. (2001). *Mental health: Culture, race, and ethnicity—A Supplement to Mental Health: A report of the Surgeon General.* Rockville, MD: Author. Retrieved September 26, 2004, from: http://media.shs.net/ken/pdf/SMA-01–3613/sma-01–3613.

Weil, M. (2010). *A cultural competency program for psychologists: Clinical and supervisory practices with Latino culture and language*. Psychology Dissertations, Paper 175.

Willerton, E., Dankoski, M., & Sevilla Martir, J. (2008). Medical family therapy; A model for addressing mental health disparities among latinos. *Family, Systems, and Health, 26*(2), 196–206.

Wood, J. M., Garb, H. N., & Nezworski, M. (2007). Psychometrics: Better measurement makes better clinicians. In S. O. Lilienfeld, W. T. O'Donohue, S. O. Lilienfeld, & W. T. O'Donohue (Eds.), *The great ideas of clinical science: 17 principles that every mental health professional should understand* (pp. 77–92). New York: Routledge/Taylor & Francis Group.

2 Bilingualism and Its Impact on Psychological Assessment

Antonio E. Puente, Davor Zink, Margie Hernandez, Tara Jackman-Venanzi, and Alfredo Ardila

The psychological measurement of Spanish-speaking individuals has both a short past and a shorter history. Despite the century-long focus on testing individuals, the focus on Spanish-speaking ones is traceable back to the 1970s (Padilla, 1971). And, when the focus involves more specific assessment of bilingual Spanish speakers, it is not until much later, such as the work of Ardila and colleagues, that this issue is first attended to. Despite this recent interest, the literature is long on theory and short on empirical studies. In addition, there is a clear focus on linguistic variables to the exclusion of sociocultural ones. This chapter attempts not only to provide the history and trajectory but more important to understand bilingualism and its effect of testing Spanish speakers. In addition, emphasis is placed on considering bilingualism as an initial step in fostering the idea that the meta-construct maybe actually be sociocultural understanding and not simply appreciation of linguistic variables.

Demographics and Heterogeneity

Hispanic or Latino refers to an individual of Cuban, Puerto Rican, Mexican, South or Central American, or other Spanish culture or origin (e.g., Spain) regardless of race. Hispanic or Latino origin refers to the heritage, lineage, nationality group, or country of birth of the person or the person's parents or ancestors before they arrived in the USA. It is important to distinguish between ethnicity and race because people of Hispanic origin may be of any race. Most Latinos identify themselves as "white" or "some other race" (U.S. Census Bureau, 2012a, 2012b). In this chapter, the terms Hispanic and Latino will be used interchangeably. According to the latest census data, Hispanics account for more than half of the total US population growth in the past decade. Latinos grew 43% (15.2 million), which was four times more than the overall population growth of 10%, and accounted for most of the nation's growth (56%) (U.S. Census Bureau 2012a). Currently, Hispanics are the largest and fastest growing minority group in the country. The USA has a population of 308,745,538 of which approximately 50.5 million

A.E. Puente, Ph.D. (✉) • D. Zink, B.S. • M. Hernandez, B.A. • T. Jackman-Venanzi, B.A.
Department of Psychology, University of North Carolina Wilmington, Wilmington, NC 28403, USA
e-mail: Puente@uncw.edu; dnz6450@uncw.edu; mih8218@uncw.edu; tnj8940@alum.uncw.edu

A. Ardila, Ph.D.
Department of Communication Sciences and Disorders, Florida International University, Miami, FL, USA
e-mail: ardilaa@fiu.edu

L.T. Benuto (ed.), *Guide to Psychological Assessment with Hispanics*,
DOI 10.1007/978-1-4614-4412-1_2, © Springer Science+Business Media New York 2013

individuals or 16% are Hispanic; however, this amount does not include undocumented Hispanics (U.S. Census Bureau 2012a). The number of undocumented Latinos is estimated at 11.2 million, with 8 million being part of the workforce (Passel & Cohn, 2011). This data imply that a large number of the US population is also bilingual, and considering that the Hispanic population is growing at a faster pace than the population as a whole, it is expected that by 2050 Latinos will no longer be a minority in the USA (U.S. Census Bureau 2012b); therefore, there will be a shift from a predominant monolingual population to a mostly bilingual one. It is estimated that more than half of the world's population is bilingual or multilingual at some level of proficiency (Paradis, M., & Libben, G. (1987), and the USA will soon be a significant contributor to this number. Recent data indicates that, in the USA, of Hispanics 18 and older, 18.7% speak only English at home. Also, 3.7% of foreign-born Latinos and 37.1% of native-born Latinos speak only English at home. In contrast, 94.1% of non-Hispanic whites speak only English at home and 81.2% of Hispanics older than 18 speak a language other than English at home. Of these, 35.2% speak English very well and 46% speak English less than very well (Pew Hispanic Center, 2012a, 2012b). As it would be expected, Latinos born in the USA have considerably better English skills than foreign-born Latinos. Regarding Hispanics that are younger than 18 years, 31.7% speak only English at home, in contrast with 68.4% that speak a language other than English at home. On the other hand, 94.4% of non-Hispanic whites under 18 years speak only English at home. Of the Latinos that speak a language other than English at home, 50.3% speak English very well and 18.1% speak it less than very well (Pew Hispanic Center 2012a). This data suggests that older Hispanics tend to have more difficulties with English when compared to younger ones. This difference might partly be due the fact that language acquisition is facilitated at younger ages and that younger Hispanics have greater exposure to situations in which they have to speak English. The data also suggest that a considerable number, 64.1% or 15.715241, of Hispanics in the USA speak English poorly (Pew Hispanic Center 2012a). Even though it is common to conglomerate all Latinos into the same group, regardless of origin, there is a great degree of heterogeneity depending on the native country that should be taken into account. For example, regarding English proficiency, 46.9% of Latinos from Mexico and 40.3% from Central America speak English less than very well. In contrast, 27.6% of Hispanics from the Caribbean and 19.nfrom South America speak English less than very well (Pew Hispanic Center 2012a). These percentages suggest that English proficiency varies as a function of region of origin. At the same time, there are several characteristics that are common and shared among Latinos. Most Hispanics speak Spanish, their main religion is Roman Catholic, and they share essential values. A good example of a shared value is the importance that Latinos place in the family. The family is central, and its stability affects well-being and personal identity (Marin & Marin, 1991). However, it is important to consider that beyond the shared values and customs, there are several values, beliefs, and practices within each subgroup of Latinos that are different among subcultural groups (Cofresí & Gorman, 2004), for example, between Cubans and Argentineans. These differences usually include, but are not limited to, language, types of employment, socioeconomic status, religion, character traits, belief systems, culture, principles, and educational background (Beals & Beals, 1993).

Because of these differences, Hispanics should not be considered a unified ethnic group. There is an evident division that can be made among Hispanics living in or from the Iberian Peninsula and those living in or from the Americas. For example, in terms of customs and behaviors, Latinos from Spain are usually more similar to other Europeans than to Latin Americans; in contrast, Latinos in the USA tend to be more similar to Hispanics in the Latin American countries. Furthermore, Hispanics living in or from the Americas can be subdivided into two groups. Group number one is North America without Mexico. Group number two includes Mexico, Central, and South America. Latinos in North America and Canada are more likely to have a better knowledge of English and the American way of living. Individuals in group number 2 can be divided further according to minor language and cultural differences. In the translation and norming procedure for the Wechsler scales in Spanish, Latin

Americans were subdivided in the following subgroups: Caribbean (e.g., Cuba), Mexican, Central American (e.g., Honduras), and South American (e.g., Chilean) (Puente & Ardila, 2000).

Depending on the subcultural group, there are differences in linguistic skill and language maintenance (Sattler, 2001). Among different subcultural groups, it is common for spoken Spanish to vary in speed, intonation, and pronunciation. For example, some Spanish speakers carefully pronounce every letter and syllable in a word, while others soften or drop the final "s" in words. In addition, social class, education level, and specific region may also influence the way Spanish is spoken (Cofresí & Gorman, 2004). Regionalisms or vernacular idiosyncrasics arc common in Spanish vocabulary usage, and each country will also have its own slang terms that are used in conversational speech. Minor phonological differences are also present (Puente & Ardila, 2000). Some words and in particular slang terms that are used in one Spanish-speaking country are not understood in others. For instance, in Chile, a T-shirt is called "polera," and in Argentina it is called "remera." A Chilean would not understand "remera," and an Argentinean would not understand "polera." Another example is the word "bus." In Chile and Uruguay, bus means "bus" and "microbus," or "micro" is also used, but in Cuba, a bus is called "guagua" which would mean "baby" in Chile. However, like there is a Standard English, there is also standard Spanish that is usually easily understood by any Spanish speaker (Puente & Ardila). Nonetheless, because standard Spanish is not commonly used, it may be perceived as haughty or overly proper in an assessment situation (Cofresí & Gorman). The variability among Hispanic subcultural groups is also present in bilingual Latinos. Depending on the above-mentioned variables, the type of Spanish and type of English a bilingual individual uses will differ.

Bilingualism and Biculturalism

Like Hispanics in general, bilingual Latinos tend to be seen as a homogenous group because they share common characteristics, but it is important to acknowledge that there is also variability among bilinguals depending on the country of origin and subcultural group. Language, cultural differences, and interaction between the native culture and the new culture are some of the most important variables to consider. Most Hispanics in the USA are bilingual (Dingfilder, 2005), and beyond the interaction between the languages, there is an interaction between two cultures; therefore, most bilingual Latinos in the USA are also bicultural. Language is an essential component of any culture and with the mixture of the mother tongue and the new language; the mother culture and the new culture also become intertwined.

Historically, in the USA, in contrast with Europe, bilingualism has never been promoted or seen as a necessity. Considering that true bilingualism requires equal mastery of both languages in all areas of knowledge and functioning and also equivalent demands for the use and formal instruction in the two languages at a young age (before 10), most Americans are not true bilinguals. In a culture that discourages bilingualism, individuals whose mother language is not part of the majority culture (Latinos) tend to lose vocabulary, syntactic representation, proficiency, and grammatical mastery (Pontón & Ardila, 1999). For example, when a Spanish speaker in the USA gains new concepts and vocabulary in English, then the individual translates the newly learned concepts into Spanish in his or her mind (Manuel-Dupont, Ardila, Rosselli, & Puente, 1992). Moreover, there are culture-specific terms for which there is no appropriate translation in the culture of origin or the dominant culture. For example, Spanish does not have a word for "modem," and English does not have a word for "taco." When people are incapable of translating a word into another language because the word does not exist in that language, transliterations are produced. For example, Hispanics may say "el raite" instead of ride (Pontón & Ardila, 1999). It is common for bilingual Hispanics in the USA to adapt words and phrases in English into their Spanish vocabulary; this is typically known as "Spanglish." For example,

Latinos often say "dame una ride" which would mean "give me a ride." However, a monolingual Spanish speaker might not understand such phrases because he or she is not familiar with the English language and the American culture. The interference and mixture of the two languages can result in poor language mastery in both languages. Moreover, the Hispanic media in the USA promotes Hispanicized terms and Spanglish by using them in commercials. Latino children grow up using these terms as representations of a hybrid language that cannot be formally assessed in either English or Spanish (Pontón & Ardila, 1999).

In the USA, Spanish is not socially, academically, economically, and politically equivalent to English, and it is often viewed as a marginal language. Usually, foreign-born Latinos and Latinos in general are required to speak English at work, at school, and in general everyday activities of the mainstream culture. Spanish books and general cultural activities in Spanish are limited in the USA (Ardila et al., 2000). On the other hand, Hispanics usually use Spanish with the family, in their community, and with friends (Cofresí & Gorman, 2004). Therefore, one language or the other is used more or less depending on the context and setting. Furthermore, it is common for second-generation Latinos in the USA to speak English among themselves. There are two reasons that may explain this. First, they know English better because Spanish is only spoken at home, and, second, they have a stronger identification with the Anglo culture than the Hispanic one because they were born in it. This situation often leads to family conflict because parents may be obligated to speak English or they can force their children to speak Spanish or children can use English to confuse or bother they parents and grandparents (Manuel-Dupont et al., 1992).

Another source of conflict is language proficiency. People may become conflicted when their language ability is not sufficient to the task or they simply do not fully comprehend what is expected of them. In a bicultural context, the challenge of meeting the linguistic demand of two cultures can be very stressful (Cofresí & Gorman, 2004). Further, each language has a different culture and value system attached to it, and this may place particular constraints in an individual sense of identity (Northover, 1988). Also, Latinos may express their feelings more effectively in one language (usually Spanish) than the other (Rodriguez Gomez & Caban, 1992). People that live in a bicultural context usually maintain close relations with their mother culture, while their everyday lives occur in the dominant culture, and develop behaviors that allow them to maintain their life in both cultures (Valdez, 2000).

Types of Bilingualism

Some variables are considered crucial to pinpoint the degree of bilingualism: age and sequence of acquisition, method of acquisition, language of schooling, contexts of the two languages, patterns of use of the two languages, personal and social attitudes toward each language (e.g., Albert & Obler, 1978; Ardila, 2007; Kilborn, 1994; Paradis, 1978; Siguan, 2001; Vaid, 1986), and, it could be added, individual differences in verbal abilities. However, these are only general variables, and many variations can be found. (1) The age, sequence, and method of acquisition are not necessarily correlated with the degree of mastery of each language. (2) Language of schooling may indeed be a highly significant variable. (3) Personal and social attitudes toward the two languages can present significant variations. (4) Individual differences in the ability to learn a second language have rarely been addressed in the literature on bilingualism. But evidently, very significant differences are observed in the ability to learn and use not only a first but also a second language (Ardila, 1998).

Bilingualism can be divided according to different criteria, such as mastery of the two languages and age of acquisition of the second language.

Mastery of the Two Languages

A frequently used distinction in bilingualism refers to the mastery of both languages (Weinreich, 1953). Three situations can be distinguished:

Coordinate Bilingualism. The linguistic elements (words, phrases) are all related to their own unique concepts. That means an English-Spanish bilingual speaker of this type possesses different associations for "table" and for "mesa." There are in consequence two lexical and two semantic systems.

Compound Bilingualism. Speakers of this type attach their linguistic elements (words, phrases) to the same concepts. For them, a "table" and a "mesa" are two words for the same concept. There are in consequence two lexical systems but only one semantic system.

Subordinate Bilingualism. The linguistic elements of one of the speaker's languages are only available through elements of the speaker's other language. This type is typical of, but not restricted to, beginning L2 learners. "Mesa" means table, and table has certain semantics. There is one semantic system, and lexicon in the second language is accessed using the first-language lexicon.

It is important to note that a bilingual can simultaneously be classified in more than one category, and when learning a second language, mastery progressively increases.

Time of Acquisition of the Second Language

Bilinguals can also be distinguished according to the time of acquisition of the second language (e.g., Bialystok & Hakuta, 1999; Birdsong, 1992; DeKeyser, 2000; Flege, 1999; Genesee & Nicoladis, 1995).

Simultaneous Bilingualism. Sometimes also named *authentic bilingualism.* Learning two languages as "first languages" (two native languages). Infants who are exposed to two languages from birth will become simultaneous bilinguals. If exposure to the second language occurs after age 3–5 years, the term *sequential* bilingual is used.

Early Bilingualism. The second language is acquired before completing the acquisition of the first one; it means before the age of about 12 years.

Late Bilingualism. The second language is acquired after completing the acquisition of the first one. Second language is learned mediated by the first language. Sometimes, the term *consecutive* or *successive* bilingualism is used to refer to learning one language after already knowing another.

Some Additional Distinctions

Frequently, some additional distinctions are used in the bilingual literature (e.g., Crystal, 1987; Fabbro, 1999; Paradis, 2004; Romaine, 1989).

Balanced Bilingualism. Equal proficiency in two languages across a range of contexts. This term usually describes a native-like competence in two languages.

Dominant Language. Preferred and best-spoken language. Dominance in languages varies according to the context where those languages are used and even across time.

Receptive Bilingualism. Being able to understand two languages, but express oneself in only one.

Elective or Elitist Bilingualism. Persons who choose to study a second language.

Natural, Social, or Circumstantial Bilingualism. People who grow up in communities where several languages are spoken.

Distractive Bilingualism. When acquisition of the first language is interrupted and insufficient, or unstructured language input follows from the second language.

Subtractive Bilingualism. The addition of a second language leads to gradual erosion of competence in the first language.

Additive Bilingualism. The speaker adds a second language without any loss of competence to the first language.

Semilingualism. An individual who lacks full competence in either language.

Diglossia. A specific relationship between two or more varieties of the same language in use in a speech community in different functions.

Ambilinguism. An individual with native competency in two languages. Sometimes the term *balanced* bilingualism is used; the latter emphasizes the similar competence in both languages.

Individual Multilingualism. An individual who has access to more than one linguistic code as a means of social communication.

Societal Multilingualism. Refers to the state of a linguistic community in which two languages are in contact, with the result that two codes can be used in the same interaction and that a number of individuals are bilingual.

Pidgin. Is a communication system developed among people that do not share the same language but need to talk because of whatever reason?

Creole. Language is a pidgin that has become the native language of a community. Pidgin and Creole represent in consequence two steps in the same process (Crystal, 1987).

Dialect. Refers to a variation (usually, but not only, geographical) in a language that is understandable by other speakers of the same language.

Two Proposed Additional Classifications of Bilingualism

Strong vs. Weak Bilingualism (i.e., degree of similarity between the two languages). Most of the research on bilingualism has not distinguished the specific languages involved. However, the degree of linguistic similarity or difference between the two languages may be significant. The *interlinguistic distance* (James, 1979) between the two languages may also be included as a classification criterion in bilingualism. The linguistic distance between Spanish and Italian is minimal, whereas the linguistic distance between Spanish and Chinese is enormous. It can be proposed to name the Spanish-Italian bilingualism as a "weak bilingualism" and to name the Spanish-Chinese bilingualism as a "strong bilingualism" (Ardila, 2007). When learning Italian, a Spanish speaker is acquiring just a little bit of new language, whereas when learning Chinese, he/she is learning a large amount of new language. Of course, any degree of similarity could exist, and "weak" and "strong" bilingualism refers to a continuum. Furthermore, the relative distance could be applied to different levels of the language: phonology, lexicon, grammar, and even prosody. For instance, the phonological distance between Spanish and Greek is mild, but the grammatical distance is large. Conversely, the phonological distance between Spanish and Portuguese is large, but the grammatical distance is small.

This similarity between the two languages may impact the cerebral representation. It has been suggested that the similarity between both languages can affect the relative rate of language recovery in cases of aphasia (Galloway, 1978; Lebrun, 1976; Whitaker, 1978). It has been proposed that the proximity of structurally similar languages may require additional effort to avoid interference, leading to more separate neural structures (Albert & Obler, 1978). The opposite point of view has also been suggested: the less two languages have in common, the more they are represented separately (Paradis, 1987).

Context-Dependent vs. Context-Independent Bilingualism. Any human activity is carried out in a particular context and is associated with a specific type of cognition. Language is the major instrument of cognition. Playing chess, solving a mathematical problem, or presenting a lecture about bilingualism is associated with some perceptual information (spatial, visual, auditory, tactile, and even olfactory), some specific motor acts (moving the chess pieces, using a calculator, or writing on the blackboard), and certain cognitions. The language used is one of the elements (or the instrument) of the cognition required to carry out that activity. Quite frequently, the bilingual learns to use L1 or L2 in a specific context (e.g., for solving mathematical problems L1 is used, but for teaching L2 is the appropriate language). L1 may be the family language, and for talking about family and home issues, L1 is used; conversely, for working, L2 is the required one. Many bilinguals can use L1 or L2 mainly (and even only) within a specific context, but they have difficulties in using it in a context where usually the other language is the correct language. It means that quite frequently, bilingualism is context dependent. Rarely, a bilingual is equally capable of using either language in exactly the same contexts. For instance, few bilinguals are equally capable of solving mathematical problems in either language. Simultaneous translators may be an example of bilinguals using two languages in exactly the same context. This distinction is obviously a matter of degree and not a dichotomous distinction. This distinction could be named as "context-dependent" vs. "context-independent bilingualism" or simple "dissociated" (context-dependent) vs. "associated" (context-independent) bilingualism. Of course, a particular individual can behave as a context-independent bilingual for some activities (both languages can be used in that situation) and context-dependent for some other activities (he/she can use only one language in that situation). Different degrees of context dependency can be found.

Variables Affecting Bilingualism Acquisition

Bilingualism is a complex phenomenon, and there continues to be several theories among researchers about the processes involved in language acquisition. Manuel-Dupont et al. (1992) described that over the years, there have been several researchers that have examined strategies of acquisition used by second-language learners. On the one hand, early researchers believed that linguistic capabilities of the right hemisphere were more characteristic in the early stages of second-language acquisition. Furthermore, research findings suggest that processing in the right hemisphere is clearly evident in the early stages of learning in second-language acquisition (Manuel-Dupont et al.). On the other hand, several studies were conducted to provide evidence that the right hemisphere is dominant in the beginning stages of second-language acquisition. Manuel-Dupont et al. stated that studies continued to reveal that the left hemisphere is predominantly for functioning of language, while there was a lack of usage in the right hemisphere in the final stages of second-language acquisition (Albert & Obler, 1978). There continues to be a lack of evidence as to whether the right hemisphere is involved in later or early stages of second-language acquisition (Manuel-Dupont et al.). McLaughlin (1977) further emphasized that there are many issues unproven which include and are not limited to the following: (1) Is there a biologically based critical period for language acquisition? (2) Does bilingualism have inevitable consequences? (3) How does first-language learning differ from second-language learning? (4) Does bilingualism have positive effects on intelligence, education, or cognitive processes? To illustrate, children learn a second language more efficiently than adults, but available evidence contradicts such findings (McLaughlin). In the field, there continues to be undocumented assertions and lack of evidence about language acquisition in bilinguals.

In order to determine the variables that affect language acquisition in bilinguals, a clear understanding has to be evident in the actual biological processes of language. At present, there is a lack of available evidence in the existing literature that could create that clear understanding. An example of a recent study that demonstrates the need for clear evidence (Sebastián-Gallés & Bosch, 2002) investigated the impact of bilingualism in acquisition of phonotactic information by examining the timing and exposure to a second language. The conclusion was that it remains unclear as to whether phonotactics of a segment can be learnt by not having a segment that is clearly involved. Despite the lack of evidence-based literature, there is some research that investigates the age of language acquisition in bilinguals. Hernandez and Li (2007) concluded that sensorimotor learning is an important milestone that determines variables associated with age of language acquisition.

From the existing literature, it is clear that there is a need to further investigate how bilinguals acquire and store language. It is important to know an individual's demographic background with regards to language acquisition, for instance, but not limited to age of entry into another country, length of residency, type of exposure to second language, level of education, and dominant language usage (Bahrick, Hall, Goggin, Bahrick & Berger, 1994). This information is important as there is a need to further investigate whether these could be variables that affect language acquisition in bilingualism.

Proficiency of Bilingualism

The scientific literature addressing matters regarding bilingual individuals clearly states that proficiency is a dimension, varying among individuals, that needs to be addressed (Manuel-Dupont et al., 1992; Proctor & Silverman, 2011). The Merriam-Webster Dictionary defines the word proficiency as the "advancement in knowledge or skill" as well as "the quality or state of being proficient" (Proficiency, 2012). Moreover, the word proficient is defined as being "well advanced in an art, occupation, or branch of knowledge" (Proficient, 2012). Thus, when questioning whether someone is proficient in a language, the following two questions arise: What constitutes proficiency? Where in the continuum of proficiency does this person fall under (Proctor & Silverman)?

Determining, measuring, and assessing the degree of proficiency in bilingual individuals are complex tasks. It involves addressing several modalities of an individual's ability, including, but not limited to, grammatical knowledge and skills, aspects of communication, and the skills associated with effective communication. Aspects of communication involve learning, reading, writing, oral communication, and numeracy. As a whole, these skills are able to provide information pertaining an individual's performance ability and competence across a range of contexts. In addition to the aforementioned modalities, vocabulary and literacy development, cross-language interactions and competence in sociolinguistic discourse, and strategic skills should be assessed. Furthermore, the domain of communication is also another factor that helps determine proficiency of bilingualism (Manuel-Dupont et al., 1992). Domains of communication include home, school, work, and other areas of functioning. Though several domains and modalities are considered, it is important to note that bilingualism is a construct in which level or degree of proficiency may differ across modalities and domains. For instance, a person might be highly proficient in comprehending a certain language but unable to express his thoughts in an effective communication form. Likewise, a person may be proficient in one language in one domain (i.e., school) but not in another (i.e., home). Manuel-Dupont et al. also denote that spheres of knowledge are prevalent among bilingual individuals. They imply that it is not unusual for bilinguals to have mastered certain domains in one of their spoken languages and not the other (home-related vocabulary vs. work-related vocabulary). Cofresí and Gorman (2004) state that among Spanish-English speakers, the use of the Spanish language is an important tool in the world of family, community, and friends, whereas the use of the English language is important for the success in school and work settings.

Picture vocabulary and listening comprehension are two domains that have been used to assess the proficiency of bilingualism. In a study conducted by Archila-Suerte, Zevin, Bunta, and Hernandez (2012), a significant correlation between picture vocabulary and listening comprehension was used as a measurement of English and Spanish proficiency among bilinguals and monolinguals. Depending on when the second language was learned, bilinguals in this study were classified into three groups: early bilinguals who were exposed to the English language before the age of 5, intermediate bilinguals who were exposed to English at the age of 6 but before 9, and late bilinguals were those exposed to the English language after the age of 10. Results showed a significant difference in English proficiency between monolinguals and the three different groups of bilinguals. Further analysis revealed that the intermediate group did not significantly differ from the early or late group. Not surprisingly, the study also revealed a significant correlation between English proficiency and the use of the English language. No significant findings were found among the three bilingual groups in English proficiency. Like English proficiency, Spanish proficiency was significantly correlated with Spanish use, and significant differences among the early, intermediate, and late groups in Spanish proficiency were found. Findings indicated that the early bilingual group had a lower proficiency level than the intermediate group, and in turn the intermediate group performed lower than the late bilingual group. To illustrate an example of this finding, Sattler (2008) indicated that bilingual children may portray the following communication characteristics: (1) English words may be borrowed and incorporated into the Spanish language, (2) words may be Anglicized to develop linguistic patterns, (3) trouble with the pronunciation and enunciation of words, and (4) trouble with ordering of words. Bilingual Latino children in the USA can be fluent in English and Spanish, or they can have issues with both languages. This indicates that those bilinguals who are exposed to the second language at an earlier age (i.e., children) may experience a loss of proficiency in their native language.

Studies involving the presentation of free recall lists in both languages to bilingual individuals have demonstrated that certain skills are used to organize and store verbal information and also that the skills used vary depending on the degree of proficiency (Harris, Cullum, & Puente, 1995). In a study aimed to determine the effects of bilingualism on verbal learning and memory, bilingual individuals, whom were divided into two groups based on their level of proficiency, were compared against a group of monolingual individuals (Harris et al., 1995). Individuals who were equally proficient in the oral production of both English and Spanish were identified as "balanced." Contrarily, individuals who dominated their "mother tongue," Spanish in this case, were identified as "nonbalanced." Spanish and English list learning tests were administered to both bilingual groups. Results showed that nonbalanced bilingual speakers recalled fewer English words than either of the groups and retained fewer words compared to the monolingual group. Results also indicated that the balanced and monolingual group did not differ in performance. Alternatively, the balanced group, regardless of which list was presented, did not show significant differences in the amount of words recalled and retained in either language. The balanced group also demonstrated to use organizational strategies of semantic clustering in both languages.

A person's identity and perception of being bilingual or monolingual and their opinion of competencies is another domain that interacts with language proficiency. In a study conducted by Danzak (2011), six students between the ages of 11 and 14 who had moved to the USA within 2 years of the data collection were asked to write journal entries and to be interviewed in their language of choice. Results showed that social identity and literacy mutually interact with each other. Specifically, results showed that students, whom identified themselves as a bilingual identity with positive views of bilingualism, yielded fairly consistent scores across their Spanish and English writing. The term bilingual in this study was described as the following: (1) having an adequate level of oral language proficiency in both languages, (2) regularly speaking and feeling confident in both languages, (3) enjoying both languages, (4) and feeling content with being and living in the USA. Those students who identified themselves as a Spanish-speaking identity and who had negative views of bilingualism demonstrated higher qualities of writing in Spanish than English. Results of this study demonstrated that bilingual proficiency is the product of different factors such as literacy but also the individual's experience, motivation, and identity.

Cofresí and Gorman (2004) specified several recommendations when determining and assessing the proficiency of bilingualism. First, it is important to note that bilingual individuals may fall anywhere on the continuum of fluency in either of the languages spoken. Secondly, the dimension of cross-language flexibility needs to be assessed in the individual. Tertiary, one needs to determine whether cross-language priming occurs automatically or in a controlled fashion. Finally, because emotions have been shown to vary with language, assessing whether emotions are expressed more in one language than the other is helpful.

In sum, determining and assessing the degree or level of proficiency of bilingualism is a multifaceted construct that varies in levels among modalities and/or domains. Bilingualism proficiency is a construct that needs to evaluate aspects of communication in relation to the cultural and societal demands (Manuel-Dupont et al., 1992). It is a construct that involves (1) understanding, comprehending, expressing, and communicating both languages; (2) the strategies used with each language as well as (3) the skill to know when to use one of the languages and not the other; and (4) the level or degree of linguistic competence an individual controls each language.

Measurement of Bilingualism

Although the idea that individuals who are bilingual may actually think differently and that errors would be introduced into the measurement of an unrelated domain, Padilla (1971) was the first one to actually suggest that this could actually occur. And it is not until the 1990s that individuals (e.g., Bamford, 1991; Manuel-Dupont et al., 1992) provided specifics that address the potential confounds of bilingualism on test performance. However, it is not until the last decade that actual research has been completed that addressed how this issue plays a role in assessment.

Saenz and Huer (2003) addressed the issue of bilingual children's abilities to perform on the Clinical Evaluation of Language Fundamentals and suggested that modification of existing tests needed to occur in order to reduce measurement error. Dollaghan and Horner (2011) completed a meta-analysis of the diagnostic accuracy of bilingual assessment of Spanish-English speakers, but most studies reviewed lacked good description of standard procedures and controls. Their results indicated that there is little support for the diagnostic accuracy of these measures. Cofresí and Gorman (2004) discussed the issue of biculturalism as well as acculturation in understanding bilingualism and, in turn, how these variables affected linguistic abilities in more than one language. They suggested that problems in testing include (a) conceptual equivalence, (b) construct equivalence, (c) social equivalence, and (d) appropriate assessment metric. In addition, questions of translation were raised together with standardization of tests with bilingual individuals.

Effects of Bilingualism on Testing

As the Hispanic population increases, the need for appropriate psychological assessment instruments in Spanish also increases. Currently, the testing tools available in Spanish are limited, and this is an important problem considering how fast this population is increasing. Psychological testing of Spanish speakers is a difficult task because of the linguistic and cultural diversity of this population (e.g., Ardila et al. (1994); Ardila, Rosselli, & Puente, 1992; Pontón & Ardila, 1999). According to the cross-cultural psychology scientific literature, the main variables that affect the performance of Spanish speakers in neuropsychological tests are (a) language, (b) education, (c) socioeconomic status, and (d) acculturation (Ardila, 1995; Ardila et al. 1994; Pontón & Ardila, 1999; Puente & Perez-Garcia, 2000). In addition to these variables, Puente and Puente (2009) outlined the following as the main challenges when assessing Spanish speakers: (a) personnel problems, (b) limited tests, (c) translations, (d) copyright, (e) normative sample, (f) development of new instruments, and (g) criterion-based testing and Hispanics in North America.

Among these variables, language, and within it bilingualism, is one of the most important to consider when testing Spanish speakers because it plays a key role in the way people interact and adapt to their cultural environment. Most Latinos in the USA are bilingual, and bilingualism can have an important impact in the outcome of psychological testing. The heterogeneity, type, acquisition, and proficiency of bilingualism have to be taken into account when testing a Hispanic individual.

The heterogeneity of the language is important to consider. As it was explained before, even though most countries in South America and Central America speak Spanish, they have distinct dialects. There are important differences in words, phrases, and expressions depending on the country of origin. It might be tempting to use a psychological test that was normed in Spain to assess a Puerto Rican, Argentinean, or Cuban because they all have Spanish in common, but this practice could lead to testing error. When using psychological tests in Spanish, the country of origin of the test taker should be considered because there are important linguistic differences within the same language and the test items might not be sensitive to them. Did a study that compared the performance of Spanish-speaking individuals of four different countries (Puerto Rico, Chile, Dominican Republic, and Spain) on a series of commonly used neuropsychological tests (Verbal Serial Learning Curve, Rey-Osterrieth Complex Figure, Verbal Phonetic Fluency Test, Stroop Color and Word Test, and the Trail-Making Test). Significant differences were found in the Serial Learning Test and the Verbal Fluency Test depending on the country of origin. The authors suggested that different language abilities may produce different results.

Usually, the degree of expertise of either language varies depending on the context. For example, an individual can use Spanish to communicate with the family at home and then use English at school or work, making each language dominant in a particular setting. Bilingualism adds to the complexity of assessing Spanish speakers because it is important to determine the dominant language of the test taker and also the context has to be considered. Manuel-Dupont et al. (1992) conducted a study to assess the language usage patterns of bilingual Hispanics. Participants were Cubans that lived in the USA since early high school; they were all well educated and learned English in school but kept using Spanish at home. They were administered the BAT English version the BAT Spanish version (Paradis & Ardila, 1989), and the English-Spanish bilingualism section (Paradis & Ardila). Results indicated that participants performed significantly different in some areas of linguistic skills. Cuban Americans had poorer performance in Spanish sentence construction, number of words, morphological opposites, reading, repetition, series, semantic opposites, mental arithmetic, and dictation. In addition, fewer words, more errors, and a strong English influence were seen in the Spanish writing sample. These results can be explained by the fact that the participants learned primary literary skills in English in school because all of these areas are related to the English academic world in contrast with Spanish family world. The participants were not balanced bilinguals, and they showed strengths and weaknesses related to their linguistic and educational backgrounds.

Rosselli et al. (2002) performed a study that compared the performance of bilingual and monolingual Spanish speakers in the Stroop Test, which is a commonly used neuropsychological test. The test was administered in English and Spanish. Results showed that overall bilingual Spanish speakers performed slower than monolingual Spanish speakers in the Stroop Test, but only the difference in the color naming condition was significant. Unbalanced bilinguals performed better in their preferred language and balanced bilinguals performed similarly in both languages. Hernandez, Martinez, and Kohnert (2000) found that dominant English bilinguals performed better in English when a naming task was administered in English and Spanish.

Another study examined the effects of bilingualism on verbal learning and memory in adult Latinos. Participants were of Mexican origin and were grouped according to bilingualism type: balanced, unbalanced, and monolingual English-speaking non-Hispanics. Equivalent list learning tests in English and Spanish were developed and administered to the participants. When compared to monolinguals, nonbalanced bilinguals tested in English learned fewer words overall and obtained lower retention scores. There were no significant differences when participants were assessed in their dominant language (Harris et al., 1995).

Ardila et al. (2000) examined syntactic comprehension, verbal memory, and calculation abilities in bilingual Hispanics. All participants learned English early in life and attended English schools. In addition, for all participants L1 was Spanish. In the first study, the Spanish Syntactic Comprehension Test (Marcos & Ostrosky, 1995) was administered, and it was observed that participants comprehended the sentences better when the syntax was closer to English. Participants that learned English between 5 and 12 years of age outperformed participants that learned English before age 5. In the second study, parallel versions in English and Spanish of five subtests from the Wechsler Memory Scale (Wechsler, 1945) and the Serial Verbal Learning Test (Ardila et al., 1994) were administered. In addition, calculation ability was measured using three basic arithmetical operations and one numerical problem performed aloud in both languages. Results showed that most of the verbal memory subtests were performed better in L1. Tasks that measured speed and calculation accuracy were performed better in the participant's native language. The language that was spoken the best was a significant variable in some subtest performed in English, but not in Spanish. These results suggest that Spanish-English bilinguals may be at a disadvantage when tested in either language (Ardila et al.). In another study, English semantic and letter fluency tasks were administered to English-dominant bilinguals and English monolinguals. Bilinguals performed worse than monolinguals in both category types (Gollan, Montoya, & Werner, 2002).

Gasquoine, Croyle, Cavazos-Gonzalez, and Sandoval (2007) conducted a study that assessed the performance of adult bilingual Hispanics on neuropsychological test battery administered in English and in Spanish (Bateria Neuropsicologica and the Matrix Reasoning subtest of the WAIS-III). Participants were divided into Spanish-dominant, balanced, and English-dominant bilingual groups. Spanish- and English-dominant bilinguals were significantly affected by language of administration in tests with higher language compared to visual perceptual weighting (Woodcock-Munoz Language Survey-Revised, Letter Fluency, Story Memory, and Stroop). Language of administration did not affect the performance-balanced bilinguals. As it would be expected, the results of these studies suggest that a bilingual that is dominant in a specific language will perform better if the test is in the language of dominance; however, balanced bilinguals seem to be able to perform similarly in both languages.

Roberts, Garcia, Desrochers, and Hernandez (2002) conducted a study on the effects of bilingualism on the Boston Naming Test. There were two groups of bilingual participants (Spanish-English and French-English) that learned English as a second language since childhood and reported being highly proficient in the language. Compared to monolingual participants, bilinguals performed significantly lower. These results suggest that English norms should not be used, even when the individual claims to be proficient in English.

Another study examined the impact of bilingualism on verbal fluency and repetition skills in older adult Hispanics. It was observed that bilinguals scored equally in all tests, except for semantic verbal fluency, where they scored lower compared to Spanish and English monolinguals. Phonetic verbal fluency, free spontaneous fluency, and repetition of sentences were not affected by bilingualism. Moreover, bilinguals who learned English at an earlier age performed significantly better on English repetition test and produced a higher number of words in the description of a picture compared to bilinguals that learned English later in life (Rosselli et al., 2000). Shi and Sanchez (2010) conducted a study to determine the optimal language that should be used in speech perception tests with Spanish-English bilinguals. Word recognition tests were administered in English and Spanish, and age of language acquisition, length of immersion, daily language use, self-rated listening proficiency, and language dominance were taken into account. Results suggested that Spanish-dominant bilinguals or those that learned English after age 10 would perform better in a word recognition test administered in Spanish. In contrast, bilinguals who learned English between 7 and 10 years of age should be evaluated in English and in Spanish. In sum, it seems that the earlier the second language is acquired, the better the scores on tests will be because the individual will be more proficient in that language.

The effects of bilingualism in neuropsychological testing were examined using the Neuropsychological Screening Battery for Hispanics (NeSBHIS, Pontón et al., 1996). Participants were 300 Latinos grouped by language of choice. There were 82 bilinguals and 218 monolinguals. The participants were matched by education, and this created a third subsample of 145 participants. Results indicated that language of choice plays an important role in measures of mental control/attention (Digit Span, Digit Symbol, Color Trails I and II) and abstract nonverbal reasoning (Block Design and Raven's Standard Progressive Matrices). These findings suggest that bilingualism impacts test performance; nevertheless, in this study, bilingual participants tended to perform better on most measures even when they were matched by education. Bilingualism can have a positive effect on cognitive functioning, especially when the person is well educated and has the same degree of mastery in the two languages (Bialystok & Cummins, 1991). The main effect of bilingualism on cognitive performance seems to involve executive control; bilingual individuals consistently outperform monolinguals in tasks that involve executive control. Moreover, there is evidence for bilingualism having a protective effect against Alzheimer's disease (Bialystok, 2011). In line with these results, Yang, Yang, and Lust (2011) found that bilinguals had an advantage in attention and executive function when compared to monolinguals.

Mindt et al. (2008) presented the positive and negative effects of bilinguals. For example, they described the limitations of vocabulary size in bilinguals which could produce error in language assessment. There are some advantages, according to the authors, of having a bilingual brain. These include advantages in inhibitory control and executive function even in adults.

The difficulties of understanding the assessment of bilinguals are probably best stated by Garcia and Nanez (2011). They recently suggested that over the last 100 years, the measurement of intelligence in bilingual individuals is fraught with error. Such errors are particularly likely to be present with emergent bilinguals. The issue of appropriate measurement of a construct was once more addressed with the suggestion that extreme caution should be taken when measuring intelligence in bilinguals.

Summary and Conclusion

On the surface, it appears that bilinguals may have a distinct disadvantage in terms of cognitive functioning early in their developmental process. However, as the individual develops, this deficit evolves into a cognitive asset. Specifically, there is a growing body of evidence that indicates that as development evolves, greater efficiency in executive function develops. Hence, bilingualism is either a deterring or as a facilitating variable depending on the developmental stage when the measurement occurs. It could be that for a younger individual, then, bilingualism has a diminutive effect on cognitive functioning, whereas for the older individual, bilingualism may have a facilitating or potentiating effect on executive functioning.

When it comes to Spanish speakers, there is evidence that balanced bilinguals can and do exist. If this is the case, there is support for the notion that there are no measurement differences between balanced bilinguals and monolinguals. However, having said that, it is very difficult to be balanced universally across multiple domains. For example, Spanish is more descriptive of emotional and social issues, and English is more descriptive of technical ones. Further, the order of language acquisition is a variable of importance. Thus, it could be that if a person learns Spanish first and English second, on the surface, they could appear to be balanced, but in reality, there is a proficiency that is domain specific. In such a case, the Spanish-first balanced bilingual could develop effective strategies in emotional and social situations, and such strategies could be reflected as assets on psychological tests. In contrast, balanced bilinguals who learn English second may develop less-effective technical dominance which, in turn, may result in a reduction of scores on tests that reflect such a domain (as is the case in many standardized tests). Hence, one could erroneously conclude that the individual is "motivated" but "cognitively limited" when in reality it could both be a reflection of a true lack of a balanced bilingual person's abilities as well as simply measurement error.

The issue then becomes how to tease out the potential confounds, to be clear with what one is measuring, and to realize that Spanish and English are not "equivalent" languages, like possibly English and German as both are more technically sensitive languages. Failing to understand that Spanish is more sensitive to social and emotional issues and that English is more sensitive to technical ones would allow for an appreciation that one needs to understand that bilingualism is only the beginning of understanding biculturalism. The main issue then is to determine clearly what the construct in question is and to make sure that the linguistic issue do not dominate or supersede the careful measurement of all aspects of psychological functioning, especially social and emotional ones (where psychologists have historically lagged behind relative to cognitive assessment).

Finally, it could be that whenever the discussion begins to change from strictly bilingual assessment to understanding the effects of culture, then the focus on what construct is being measured may reconceptualize the problem. That is, if bilingualism is the first step in understanding biculturalism and its measurement, then reducing measurement error in bilingual assessment is critical. Similarly important is that once this is controlled, then the focus should shift to understanding how being bicultural (bicognitive) is more of a meta-construct that more carefully addresses how individuals from different linguistic and cultural backgrounds perform on psychological tests. And when this is addressed, one wonders whether the historic disadvantage on cognitive tests during early development indicating that Hispanics are less able will shift to understand how this initial disability eventually turns into a long-term cognitive advantage.

References

Albert, M., & Obler, L. (1978). *The bilingual brain*. New York: Academic.

Archila-Suerte, P., Zevin, J., Bunta, F., & Hernandez, A. E. (2012). Age of acquisition and proficiency in a second language independently influence the perception of non-native speech. *Bilingualism: Language and Cognition, 15*, 190–201.

Ardila, A. (1995). Directions of research in cross-cultural neuropsychology. Journal of Clinical and Experimental Neuropsychology, 17, 143–150.

Ardila, A. (1998). Bilingualism: A neglected and chaotic area. *Aphasiology, 12*, 131–134.

Ardila, A. (2007). Bilingualism in the contemporary world. In A. Ardila & E. Ramos (Eds.), *Speech and language disorders in bilinguals* (pp. 1–20). New York: Nova.

Ardila, A., Rosselli, M., & Puente, A. E. (1994). Neuropsychological Evaluation of the Spanish Speaker. New York: Premium Press.

Ardila, A., Rosselli, M., Ostrosky-Solís, F., Marcos, J., Granda, G., & Soto, M. (2000). Syntactic comprehension, verbal memory, and calculation abilities in Spanish–English bilinguals. *Applied Neuropsychology, 7*(1), Special issue: Assessment of Spanish-speaking populations, 3–16.

Ardila, A., Rosselli, M., & Puente, A. E. (1994). Neuropsychological Evaluation of the Spanish Speaker. New York: Premium Press.

Bahrick, H. P., Hall, L. K., Goggin, J. P., Bahrick, L. E., & Berger, S. A. (1994). Fifty years of language maintenance and language dominance in bilingual Hispanic immigrants. *Journal of Experimental Psychology: General, 123*(3), 264–283.

Bamford, K. W. (1991). Bilingual issues in mental health assessment and treatment. *Hispanic Journal of the Behavioral Sciences, 13*(4), 377–390.

Beals, M. J., & Beals, K. L. (1993). Transcultural counseling and the Hispanic community. In J. McFadden (Ed.), *Transcultural counseling: Bilateral and international perspectives* (pp. 213–238). Alexandria, VA: American Counseling Association.

Bialystok, E. (2011). Reshaping the mind: The benefits of bilingualism. *Canadian Journal of Experimental Psychology/Revue Canadienne De Psychologie Expérimentale, 65*(4), 229–235.

Bialystok, E., & Cummins, J. (1991). Language, cognition, and education of bilingual children. In E. Bialystok (Ed.), *Language processing in bilingual children* (pp. 222–232). Cambridge, UK: Cambridge University Press.

Bialystok, E., & Hakuta, K. (1999). Confounded age: Linguistic and cognitive factors in age differences for second language acquisition. In D. Birdsong (Ed.), *Second language acquisition and the critical period hypothesis* (pp. 161–181). Mahwah, NJ: Erlbaum.

Birdsong, D. (1992). Ultimate attainment in second language acquisition. *Language, 68*, 706–755.

Buré-Reyes, A., Hidalgo, N., Vilar-López, R., Pérez-García, M., Gontier, J., Sánchez, L., et al. Neuropsychological test performance of Spanish speakers: Is performance different across different Spanish speaking subgroups? *Archives of Clinical Neuropsychology.*

Cofresí, N. I., & Gorman, A. A. (2004). Testing and assessment issues with Spanish-English bilingual Latinos. *Journal of Counseling & Development, 82*(1), 99–106.

Crystal, D. (1987). *The Cambridge encyclopedia of language*. Cambridge, MA: Cambridge University Press.

Danzak, R. L. (2011). The interface of language proficiency and identity: A profile analysis of bilingual adolescents and their writing. *Language, Speech, and Hearing Services in Schools, 42*(4), 506–519.

DeKeyser, R. M. (2000). The robustness of critical period effects in second language acquisition. *Studies in Second Language Acquisition, 22*, 499–533.

Dingfelder, S. F. (2005). *Closing the gap for Latino patients*. Retrieved from APA monitor on psychology online database: http://www.apa.org/monitor/jan05/closingthegap.aspx.

Dollaghan, C. A., & Horner, A. A. (2011). Bilingual language assessment: A meta-analysis of diagnostic accuracy. *Journal of Speech, Language and Hearing Research, 54*(4), 1077–1088.

Fabbro, F. (1999). *The neurolinguistics of bilingualism*. Hove, UK: Psychology Press.

Flege, J. E. (1999). Age of learning and second-language speech. In D. Birdsong (Ed.), *Second language acquisition and the critical period hypothesis* (pp. 101–131). Mahwah, NJ: Erlbaum.

Galloway, L. (1978). Language impairment and recovery in polyglot aphasia: A case of a heptaglot. In M. Paradis (Ed.), *Aspects of bilingualism* (pp. 139–148). Columbia, SC: Hornbeam Press.

Garcia, E. E., & Nanez, J. E. (2011). Intelligence and bilinguals assessment. In E. G. Garcia & J. E. Nanez (Eds.), *Bilingualism and cognition: Informing research, pedagogy and policy*. Washington, DC: American Psychological Association.

Gasquoine, P., Croyle, K., Cavazos-Gonzalez, C., & Sandoval, O. (2007). Language of administration and neuropsychological test performance in neurologically intact Hispanic American bilingual adults. *Archives of Clinical Neuropsychology, 22*, 991–1001.

Genesee, F., & Nicoladis, E. (1995). Language development in preschool bilingual children. In E. Garcia & B. McLaughlin (Eds.), *Meeting the challenge of linguistic and cultural diversity in early childhood education*. New York: Teachers College Press.

Gollan, T. H., Montoya, R. I., & Werner, G. A. (2002). Semantic and letter fluency in Spanish-English bilinguals. *Neuropsychology, 16*(4), 562–576.

Harris, J. G., Cullum, C., & Puente, A. E. (1995). Effects of bilingualism on verbal learning and memory in Hispanic adults. *Journal of the International Neuropsychological Society, 1*(1), 10–16.

Hernandez, A. E., & Li, P. (2007). Age of acquisition: Its neural and computational mechanisms. *Psychological Bulletin, 133*(4), 638–650.

Hernandez, A. E., Martinez, A., & Kohnert, K. (2000). In search of the language switch: An fMRI study of picture naming in Spanish–English bilinguals. *Brain and Language, 73*, 421–431.

James, C. V. (1979). Foreign languages in school curriculum. In G. E. Perren (Ed.), *Foreign language in education* (pp. 7–28). London: CILT.

Kilborn, K. (1994). Learning a language late: Second language acquisition in adults. In M. A. Gernsbacher (Ed.), *Handbook of psycholinguistics* (pp. 917–944). New York: Academic.

Lebrun, Y. (1976). Recovery in polyglots aphasics. In Y. Lebrun & R. Hoops (Eds.), *Recovery in aphasics* (pp. 96–108). Amsterdam: Swets & Zeitlinger.

Manuel-Dupont, S., Ardila, A., Rosselli, M., & Puente, A. E. (1992). Bilingualism. In A. E. Puente, R. McCaffrey, A. E. Puente, & R. McCaffrey (Eds.), *Handbook of neuropsychological assessment: A biopsychosocial perspective* (pp. 193–210). New York: Plenum Press.

Marcos, J., & Ostrosky, F. (1995). Estrategias para la asignacion de papeles tematicos en la interpretacion de enunciados en espanol [Strategies for the assignment of thematic roles in the interpretation of Spanish statements]. In D. Pool (Ed.), *Estudios en linguistica formal* (pp. 47–62). Mexico City, Mexico: El Colegio de Mexico.

Marin, G., & Marin, B. V. (1991). *Research with Hispanic populations*. Newbury Park, CA: Sage.

McLaughlin, B. (1977). Second-language learning in children. *Psychological Bulletin, 84*(3), 438–459.

Mindt, R. M., Arendtoft, A., Germano, K. K., D'Aquila, E., Scheiner, D., Pizzirusso, M., et al. (2008). Neuropsychological, cognitive and theoretical considerations for evaluation of bilingual individuals. *Neuropsychology Review, 18*, 255–268.

Northover, M. (1988). Bilinguals or "dual linguistic identities?". In J. W. Berry & R. C. Annis (Eds.), *Ethnic psychology: Research and practice with immigrants, refugees, native peoples, ethnic groups, and sojourners* (pp. 207–216). Berwyn, PA: Swets North America.

Padilla, A. (1971). *Assessment and treatment of Hispanic individuals*. Washington, DC: US Government Printing Office.

Paradis, M. & Ardila, A. (1989) Prueba de afasia para bilingües, (American Spanish version) Hillsdale, NJ.: Lawrence Erlbaum, 26 + 127pp.

Paradis, M. (Ed.). (1978). *Aspects of bilingualism*. Columbia, SC: Hornbeam Press.

Paradis, M. (2004). *Neurolinguistic theory of bilingualism*. Amsterdam: John Benjamins.

Paradis, M., & Libben, G. (1987). *The assessment of bilingual aphasia*. Hillsdale, NJ/England, UK: Lawrence Erlbaum Associates, Inc.

Paradis, M. & Ardila, A. (1989) Prueba de afasia para bilingües, (American Spanish version) Hillsdale, NJ.: Lawrence Erlbaum, 26 + 127pp

Passel, J. S., & Cohn, D. (2011). *Unauthorized immigrant population: National and state trends, 2011*. Retrieved January 13, 2012, from Pew Hispanic Center online database: http://www.pewhispanic.org/files/reports/133.pdf.

Pew Hispanic Center. (2012a). Retrieved January 13, 2012, from Pew Hispanic Center online database: http://www.pewhispanic.org/2009/03/05/statistical-portrait-of-hispanics-in-the-united-states-2007/2007-portrait-of-hispanics-22/.

Pew Hispanic Center. (2012b). Retrieved January 13, 2012, from Pew Hispanic Center online database: http://www.pewhispanic.org/2009/03/05/statistical-portrait-of-the-foreign-born-population-in-the-united-states-2007/2007-portrait-of-foreign-born-population-27/.

Pontón, M. O., & Ardila, A. (1999). The future of neuropsychology with Hispanic populations in the United States. *Archives of Clinical Neuropsychology, 14*(7), 565–580.

Pontón, M., Satz, P., Herrera, L., Ortiz, F., Urrutia, C., Young, R., et al. (1996). Normative data stratified by age and education for the neuropsychological battery for Hispanics (NeSBHIS): Initial report. *Journal of International Neuropsychological Society, 2*, 96–104.

Proctor, C., & Silverman, R. D. (2011). Confounds in assessing the associations between biliteracy and English language proficiency. *Educational Researcher, 40*(2), 62–64.

Proficiency. (2012). *Merriam-Webster's online dictionary*. Retrieved from http://www.merriam-webster.com/dictionary/proficiency.

Proficient. (2012). *Merriam-Webster's online dictionary*. Retrieved from http://www.merriam-webster.com/dictionary/proficient.

Puente, A. E., & Ardila, A. (2000). Neuropsychological assessment of Hispanics. In E. Fletcher-Janzen, T. L. Strickland, & C. R. Reynolds (Eds.), *Handbook of cross-cultural neuropsychology* (pp. 87–104). Dordrecht, Netherlands: Kluwer Academic Publishers.

Puente, A. E., & Perez-Garcia, M. (2000). Neuropsychological assessment of ethnic minorities: Clinical issues. In I. Cuéllar & F. A. Paniagua (Eds.), *Handbook of multicultural mental health* (pp. 419–435). San Diego, CA: Academic.

Puente, A. E., & Puente, A. N. (2009). The challenge of measuring abilities and competencies in Hispanics/Latinos. In E. L. Grigorenko (Ed.) , Multicultural psychoeducational assessment (pp. 417–441). New York, NY US: Springer Publishing Co.

Roberts, P. M., Garcia, L., Desrochers, A., & Hernandez, D. (2002). English performance of proficient bilingual adults on the Boston naming test. *Aphasiology, 16*, 635–645.

Rodriguez Gomez, J. R., & Caban, M. (1992). The problem with bilingualism in psychiatric diagnoses of Hispanic patients. *Cross-Cultural Psychology Bulletin, 26*, 2–5.

Romaine, S. (1989). *Bilingualism*. Oxford, UK: Basil Blackwell.

Rosselli, M., Ardila, A., Araujo, K., Weekes, V., Caracciolo, V., Padilla, M., et al. (2000). Verbal fluency and repetition skills in healthy older Spanish English bilinguals. *Applied Neuropsychology, 7*(1), 17–24.

Rosselli, M., Ardila, A., Santisi, M., Del Rosario Arecco, M., Salvartierra, J., Conde, A., et al. (2002). Stroop effect in Spanish–English bilinguals. *Journal of the International Neuropsychological Society, 8*, 819–827.

Saenz, T. I., & Huer, M. B. (2003). Testing strategies involving least biased language assessment of bilingual children. *Communication Disorders Quarterly, 24*(4), 184–193.

Sattler, J. M. (2001). Assessment of children: Cognitive applications (4th ed.). La Mesa, CA US: Jerome M Sattler Publisher.

Sattler, J. M. (2008). *Assessment of children: Cognitive applications* (5th ed.). San Diego, CA: Author.

Sebastián-Gallés, N., & Bosch, L. (2002). Building phonotactic knowledge in bilinguals: Role of early exposure. *Journal of Experimental Psychology: Human Perception and Performance, 28*(4), 974–989.

Shi, L., & Sanchez, D. (2010). Spanish/English bilingual listeners on clinical word recognition tests: What to expect and how to predict. *Journal of Speech, Language, and Hearing Research, 53*, 1096–1110.

Siguan, M. (2001). *Bilingüismo y lenguas en contacto* [Bilingualism and languages in contact]. Madrid: Alianza Editorial.

U.S. Census Bureau. (2012a). Retrieved on January 4, 2012, from http://2010.census.gov/2010census/index.php.

U.S. Census Bureau. (2012b). *The Hispanic population: 2010*. Retrieved January 13, 2012, from U.S. Census Bureau online database: http://www.census.gov/prod/cen2010/briefs/c2010br04.pdf.

Vaid, J. (Ed.). (1986). *Language processing in bilinguals: Psycholinguistic and neuropsychological perspective*. Hillsdale, NJ: Lawrence Erlbaum Associates.

Valdez, J. N. (2000). Psychotherapy with bicultural Hispanic clients. *Psychotherapy: Theory, Research, Practice, Training, 35*, 188–196.

Wechsler, D. D. (1945). Wechsler memory scale. San Antonio, TX US: Psychological Corporation.

Weinreich, U. (1953). *Languages in contact: Findings and problems*. New York: Linguistic Circle of New York.

Whitaker, H. A. (1978). Bilingualism: A neurolinguistics perspective. In W. C. Ritchie (Ed.), *Second language acquisition research. Issues and implications* (pp. 21–32). New York: Academic.

Yang, S., Yang, H., & Lust, B. (2011). Early childhood bilingualism leads to advances in executive attention: Dissociating culture and language. *Bilingualism: Language and Cognition, 14*(3), 412–422.

The Assessment Interview: A Review of Structured and Semi-structured Clinical Interviews Available for Use Among Hispanic Clients

3

Joan Ignasi Mestre, Paola Clementina Rossi, and Marta Torrens

Overview

Diagnostic interviews are instruments designed to assess psychiatric disorders according to main diagnostic criteria (*Diagnostic and Statistical Manual of Mental Disorders* [DSM]; International Classification of Diseases Diagnostic Criteria [ICD]) in a systematic and standardized manner in order eliminate biases. Their use is aimed to reduce the variability and improve the diagnosis agreement to the key points to achieve these objectives are (1) the specific language of clinical questions, (2) the sequence of the questions, and (3) the assessment of responses. Furthermore, standardized diagnostic interviews judge systematically the relevant symptoms reducing misdiagnosis and missed diagnosed.

Both structured and semi-structured diagnostic interviews exist. Differences among them are related to the flexibility of questioning allowed to the interviewer. In a *structured interview*, all questions are standardized and must be asked verbatim, using optional probes to clarify ambiguities in how responses meet criteria. This ensures a high level of standardization even though the adherence to formulated questions cannot cover all eventualities. These interviews are especially useful for epidemiological studies, such as national surveys, since they do not need any interviewer interpretation. However, as there are questions which often involve emotional experiences, respondents doubts might become a codifying problem (training and glossary are relevant for administrators). In a *semi-structured interview*,

J.I. Mestre, Psy, Ph.D (✉)
IMIM (Hospital del Mar Research Institute), Parc de Salut Mar, Doctor Aiguader 88, 08003 Barcelona, Spain
e-mail: jmestre@imim.es

P.C. Rossi, M.D., Ph.D.
IMIM (Hospital del Mar Research Institute), Parc de Salut Mar, Doctor Aiguader 88, 08003 Barcelona, Spain

Institute of Neuropsychiatry and Addictions, Hospital del Mar-IMIM, Parc de Salut Mar,
Passeig Marítim 25-29, 08003 Barcelona, Spain
e-mail: prossi@parcdesalutmar.cat

M. Torrens, M.D., Ph.D.
IMIM (Hospital del Mar Research Institute), Parc de Salut Mar, Doctor Aiguader 88, 08003 Barcelona, Spain

Institute of Neuropsychiatry and Addictions, Hospital del Mar-IMIM, Parc de Salut Mar,
Passeig Marítim 25-29, 08003 Barcelona, Spain

Universitat Autònoma de Barcelona, Barcelona, Spain
e-mail: mtorrens@imim.es

L.T. Benuto (ed.), *Guide to Psychological Assessment with Hispanics*,
DOI 10.1007/978-1-4614-4412-1_3,

expert clinicians are also allowed to use unstructured questions to assist them in rating responses when diagnostic issues remain unresolved despite the optional probes. This can optimize criterion variance, occasionally at the expense of information variance. The *semi-structured* interviews are more suitable for clinical settings, as they allow interpretation by clinicians or interviewers, based on standardized definitions and codifications.

The main considerations in judging the usefulness of structured interviews are their psychometric qualities, such as *reliability* and *validity*. *Reliability* provides estimates regarding the reproducibility and consistency of clinical findings; this is the stability of its diagnostic outcomes. Such stability can be calculated over time (*test-retest reliability*) and at one point in time (*inter-rater reliability*). The *inter-rater reliability* is the key measure for structured interviews establishing the level of agreement between observers and interviewers rating the same interview. Kappa coefficients are the most commonly used statistic to describe *inter-rater reliability*. Yule's Y is rarely used and interclass coefficients (ICCs) are used when more than two raters are employed. *Test-retest reliability* involves the re-administration of the interview conducted by the same evaluator after a specified interval of time. Thus, the information variance due to the styles of questioning and criterion variance can be estimated. The interval may not exceed 1 month in order to minimize patient's variance that may confound results.

Most structured interviews rely on criterion-related and construct *validity*. The criterion-related *validity* evidence involves the correlation between the test and a criterion variable (or variables) taken as representative of the construct. It has two forms: the *concurrent* and *predictive validity*. The *concurrent validity* utilizes a gold standard against which to validate diagnoses and other clinical constructs. In the absence of suitable standardized measures against which to examine the validity of psychiatric diagnoses (i.e., gold standard), the longitudinal evaluation performed by an expert, using all data available (the longitudinal, expert, all data [LEAD] procedure), was conceived as a standard for validating psychiatric diagnoses (Spitzer, 1983). The LEAD procedure has been employed as a criterion for the assessment of the procedural validity of diagnostic instruments. The *predictive validity* refers to the degree in which the operationalization can predict other measures of the same construct that are assessed at some time in the future.

Structured and semi-structured clinical interviews are constantly evolving. This is due to minor or major changes necessary to adopt the novelties in the classification systems (DSM and CIE) or to modifications suggested by the different methodological procedures applied to validate them. This process leads to a wide range of different versions on heterogeneous stage of validity for each country. Consequently, clinicians and researchers should give special attention when selecting an interview or comparing results.

Structured and Semi-structured Clinical Interviews Available for Use Among Hispanic Clients

Spanish is one of the most widely spoken languages in the world, estimated to be the language of daily use between 350 and 500 million people, and growing every year. It is the official language of 21 countries and the second language in the United States. Therefore, it is not only relevant to have a valid Spanish version of the most used clinical interviews but also to harmonize it to the different traits of each regional standard variety of a language (Harkness, 2010). Moreover, a faithful translation does not ensure equivalence between the original and the cross-culturally adapted versions, nor does it guarantee the instrument reliability or validity. Achieving such equivalence is necessary to guarantee the degree of comparability needed for valid cross-cultural research (Canino et al., 1999). As the first methodological procedure, the linguistic and cultural adaptation should be conducted under some standards, which take into account matters as denotation, connotation, specificity of terms, culturally taboo topics, and equivalence of words and items (Westermeyer & Janca, 1997). The process should reduce unnecessary variance across different versions that may negatively affect measurement quality (Harkness). Efforts to improve diagnosis, like the Latin American Guide for Psychiatric Diagnosis (GLADP, 2010) which represents ICD adaptations to local realities and needs, should be encouraged (Mezzich & Salloum, 2007).

Regarding this issue, the WHO has an adaptation protocol that includes six steps: (1) forward translation, (2) expert panel review, (3) independent back-translation, (4) harmonization of vocabulary and formulation across different country versions of a shared language (if appropriate), (5) pretesting and cognitive interviewing, and (6) final version and documentation of a final version of the translated questionnaire (Harkness et al., 2008).

In this chapter, we present a review of the main used structured and semi-structured clinical interviews available for use among Hispanic clients (Table 3.1).

Structured Clinical Interview for DSM-IV Disorders (SCID)

The SCID has a long history since its initial conceptualization in 1983 until our days. Nowadays, there are two distinct clinical interviews, one for the assessment of axis I disorders (SCID-CV; First, Spitzer, Gibbon, & Williams, 1996) and one for axis II disorders (SCID-II; First, Spitzer, Gibbon, Williams, & Benjamin, 1997). Both require a trained mental health professional rater to be used. SCID can be used with adults who do not suffer severe cognitive impairment, agitation, or severe psychotic symptoms.

SCID-I

The SCID-I is available in two versions, the Clinical Version (SCID-CV), that includes the most frequent diagnoses in the clinical practice, and the Research Version (SCID-RV) which has three editions: SCID-I/P (Patient Edition; First, Spitzer, Gibbon, & Williams, 2002a), SCID-I/NP (Non-patient Edition; First, Spitzer, Gibbon, & Williams, 2002b), and SCID-I/P (w/Psychotic Screen; Patient Edition, with psychotic screening module; First, Spitzer, Gibbon, & Williams, 2002c). These are larger versions with additional diagnostic sections that can be customized by the investigators according to their needs. This chapter focuses on SCID-CV because it is probably the most often used interview in general psychiatry; it was designed for use with subjects already identified as psychiatric patients and was initially modeled on the standard clinical interview practiced by many mental health professionals. The SCID-CV is a semi-structured interview that includes two separate books: the Administration Booklet that contains the interview questions and the abridged DSM-IV diagnostic criteria. Experienced clinicians are allowed to customize questions to fit the patient's understanding. The ratings on the SCID-CV are based on both the patient's answers and the expertise of the rater (who may ask additional questions to clarify ambiguities or to assess the seriousness of symptoms). The administration time is between 1 and 2 h, depending on the presence or absence of pathology. SCID-CV comprises Module A: mood episodes, Module B: psychotic symptoms, Module C: psychotic disorders, Module D: mood disorders, Module E: substance use disorders, and Module F: anxiety and other disorders. The clinician will codify the responses of the modules as 1 = absent/false, 2 = subthreshold, or 3 = present/true and continue or skip to next module according to the instructions. There is a fourth rating option -?- used when information is insufficient.

The validity of the SCID has been assessed in several studies using approximations of the LEAD procedure. The SCID demonstrated superior validity over standard clinical interviews at intake (Basco et al., 2000; Kranzler, Kadden, Babor, Tennen, & Rounsaville, 1996). Furthermore, the last Spanish version of the SCID-I (First, Gibbon, Spitzer, Williams, & Benjamin, 1999) has been validated using

Table 3.1 Spanish version of clinical interviews

Interview	Authors	Diagnosis criteria	Structured/ semi-structured	Level of expertise and training	Uses	Time of administration (h)
SCID	First et al. (1999)	DSM	Semi-structured	Clinical experience Training	Clinical	1–2
SCAN	WHO (1998) and Vázquez-Barquero et al. (1994)	CIE DSM	Semi-structured	Clinical experience Training	Clinical	1–3
PRISM-IV	Torrens et al. (2004)	DSM	Semi-structured	Clinical experience Training	Clinical	1–3
AUDADIS	Canino et al. (1999)	DSM	Structured	Without clinical experience Training	Epidemiological	1–2
DIS-IV	Robins et al. (2000), Bravo et al. (1987), and Karno et al. (1983)	DSM	Structured	Without clinical experience Training	Epidemiological	1–2
CIDI	WHO (2004)	CIE DSM	Structured	Without clinical experience Training	Epidemiological	1–3
MINI	Bobes (1998)	CIE DSM	Structured	Without clinical experience Training	Epidemiological	1–3
DIGS	Palacio et al. (2004) and Roca et al. (2007)	DSM	Semi-structured	Clinical experience Training	Genetic studies	2–3

SCID Structured Clinical Interview for DSM Disorders, *SCAN* Schedules for Clinical Assessment in Neuropsychiatry, *PRISM-IV* Psychiatric Research Interview for Substance and Mental Disorders, *AUDADIS* Alcohol Use Disorder and Associated Disabilities Interview Schedule, *DIS-IV* Diagnostic Interview Schedule, *CIDI* Composite International Diagnostic Interview, *MINI* MINI International Neuropsychiatric Interview, *DIGS* Diagnostic Interview for Genetic Studies

LEAD procedure among substance users (Torrens, Serrano, Astals, Perez-Dominguez, & Martin-Santos, 2004). Reliability has also been assessed showing values from fair to excellent agreement in various studies (Zanarini & Frankenburg, 2001; Lobbestael, Leurgans, & Arntz, 2011), but as far as we know, no published evidence is available regarding the Spanish version yet.

SCID-II

The SCID-II is a semi-structured Axis II interview that was constructed as a complementary measure to the SCID-I in 1987, and it has incorporated changes through the years in order to adopt the DSM criteria evolution. The most relevant characteristics are its brevity (30–45 min), its friendly administration, and the modest level of training for mental health professionals. The interview is organized by diagnoses and has an identical 3-point rating system to the SCID-I.

The last Spanish version of the SCID-II was released in 1999 (First, Spitzer, Gibbon, & Williams, 1999). All versions of the interview have been used in many studies with Hispanic populations (Martin-Santos et al., 1998; Vaz Leal et al., 2005). For further information, visit www.scid4.org.

Psychometric characteristics of the Spanish version of SCID-I and SCID-II are described in Table 3.2.

Schedules for Clinical Assessment in Neuropsychiatry (SCAN)

The SCAN (World Health Organization [WHO], 1998) are a set of tools integrated into a semi-structured psychiatric interview aimed to assess, measure, and classify the psychopathology and behavior associated with the major psychiatric disorders. The core component of the SCAN Version 2.1 is the tenth version of the Patient State Examination (PSE-10) (Wing, 1998). The PSE, originally developed by Wing and colleagues, has evolved over the last four decades presenting changes in both structure and ratings. The PSE-10 is a semi-structured clinical examination and has two differentiated parts. Part I covers somatoform, dissociative, anxiety, depressive and bipolar disorders, and problems associated with eating, alcohol and other substance use, as well as a limited coverage of physical features. Part II covers psychotic and cognitive disorders and observed abnormalities of speech, affect, and behavior. The PSE covers the "current state," the month prior to the scan, and the "prior over life." The SCAN instrument has three other components: the Glossary (detailed differential definitions), the Item Group Checklist (IGC) (to rate information from other sources than the respondent), and the Clinical History Schedule (CHS) (to asses supplement PSE information). The SCAN system contains a set of computer programs (CATEGO) for processing SCAN data and providing output presented as a series of options, including a range of profiles of symptoms and IGC scores, an Index of Definition, the ICD-10 and DSM-IV categories, and a prediagnostic profile of categories.

The SCAN requires an extensive training of the interviewer prior to administration; it can be used by paraprofessionals with direct supervision but it is meant to be used by mental health professionals. The interviewer has to be familiarized with the terms of the Glossary to be able to ask the subject in detail, seeking responses according to the Glossary, and then decide whether a symptom is present, and if so, what its gravity is. After the subject's description of the symptom, the interviewer marks on the definition of the Glossary and encodes a scale attribute for the item. The administration time ranges from 1 to 2 h, and it is directly related to the absence or presence of psychopathology.

The SCAN has been widely translated into many languages following the WHO protocol. The Spanish version of the instrument also has been developed and validated, showing adequate psychometrics properties, by Vazquez-Barquero et al. (1994), member of the advisory committee. For further details, visit http://www.whoscan.org/.

Psychometric characteristics of the Spanish version of SCAN are described in Table 3.2.

Table 3.2 Psychometric characteristics of the Spanish interviews

Interview	Version	Authors	Diagnosis criteria	Translation/back-translation	Test-retest reliability	Inter-rater reliability	Validity
SCID-I	Spanish version (from original author)	First et al. (1999)	DSM	Development process	Development process	Development process	Development process and LEAD Torrens et al. (2004)
	Spanish (bilingual) version SCID-NP and SCID-P	Behavioral Sciences Research Institute at the University of Puerto Rico	DSM	Yes	Not published evidence found	Not published evidence found	Not published evidence found
SCID-II	Spanish version (from original author)	First et al. (1999)	DSM	Development process	Development process	Development process	Development process and LEAD Torrens et al. (2004)[a]
SCAN	WHO (Spanish version)	WHO (1998)	DSM/ICD	Development process	Development process	Development process	Development process
	Spanish version (Spain)	Vázquez-Barquero et al. (1994)	DSM/ICD	Yes Vázquez-Barquero et al. (1994)	Yes Vázquez-Barquero et al. (1994)	Yes Vázquez-Barquero et al. (1994)	Yes Vázquez-Barquero et al. (1994)
PRISM	Spanish version (Spain)	Torrens et al. (2004)	DSM	Yes Torrens et al. (2004)	Not published evidence found	Not published evidence found	LEAD Torrens et al. (2004)
AUDADIS	Spanish version (Puerto Rico and North America)	Canino et al. (1999)	DSM	Yes Canino et al. (1999)	Yes Canino et al. (1999)	Yes Canino et al. (1999)	LEAD Canino et al. (1999)
DIS	Spanish version (Mexico)	Anduaga et al. (1991)	DSM	Yes Karno et al. (1983)	Yes Karno et al. (1983)	Yes Karno et al. (1983), Burnam et al. (1983), and Anduaga et al. (1991)	LEAD Burnam et al. (1983)
	Spanish version (Puerto Rico)	Bravo et al. (1987)	DSM	Yes Bravo et al. (1987, 1991)	Yes Bravo et al. (1987, 1991)	Yes Canino et al. (1987)	LEAD Canino et al. (1987)
	Spanish version (Spain)	de Pablo Alcázar et al. (1992)	DSM	Development process (from original author)	Not published evidence found	Yes de Pablo Alcázar et al. (1992)	LEAD de Pablo Alcázar et al. (1992)

DISC	Spanish version (from original author)	Shaffer et al. (2000)	DSM	Development process	Development process and Kunst et al. (2009)	Development process	Development process and LEAD Kunst et al. (2009)
	Spanish version (Puerto Rico)	Bravo et al. (2001)	DSM	Yes Bravo et al. (2001)	Yes Bravo et al. (2001)	Yes Bravo et al. (2001)	Yes Bravo et al. (2001)
MINI	Spanish version (Spain)	Bobes (1998)	DSM	Development process	Not published evidence found	Not published evidence found	Yes Bobes (1998)
MINI-KID	Spanish version (Spain)	Sheehan et al. (2000)	DSM	Development process	Development process	Development process and Palacios et al. (2004) (Mexico)	Development process and Palacios et al. (2004) (Mexico)
CIDI	Spanish version	WHO (2004)	DSM/ICD	Development process	Development process and Rubio-Stipec et al. (1991)[b]	Development process	Development process
DIGS	Spanish version (Colombia)	Palacio et al. (2004)	DSM	Yes Palacio et al. (2004)	Yes Palacio et al. (2004)	Yes Palacio et al. (2004)	LEAD Palacio et al. (2004)
	Spanish version (Spain)	Roca et al. (2007)	DSM	Yes Roca et al. (2007)	Yes Roca et al. (2007)	Yes Roca et al. (2007)	Yes Roca et al. (2007)

[a]Only antisocial and borderline personality disorders
[b]Only substance abuse modules of CIDI-Auto

Psychiatric Research Interview for Substance and Mental Disorders (PRISM)

The PRISM (Hasin, Trautman, Miele, & Endicott, 1995) is a semi-structured interview developed in response to the lack of a diagnostic interview suitable for comorbidity research. Three important characteristics of the PRISM, specific to comorbidity, are (1) adding specific rating guidelines throughout the interview, including frequency and duration requirements for symptoms, explicit exclusion criteria, and decision rules for frequent sources of uncertainty; (2) positioning of the alcohol and drug sections of the PRISM near the beginning of the interview, before the mental disorder sections, so that the history of alcohol and drug use is available at the time of beginning the assessment of mental disorders; and (3) more structured alcohol and drug histories to provide a context for assessing comorbid psychiatric disorders. The first version of PRISM, based on DSM-III-R criteria, showed good to excellent reliability for many diagnoses, including affective disorders, substance use disorders, eating disorders, some anxiety disorders, and psychotic symptoms (Hasin et al., 1996). To address the changes in DSM-IV, the PRISM has been updated and revised in order to provide diagnoses of primary and substance-induced disorders and to include the expected effects of intoxication or withdrawal. In addition, the revised version of the PRISM provides a method for operationalizing the term "in excess of" the expected effects of substance in chronic substance abusers (Hasin, Trautman, & Endicott, 1998). This version also shows good test-retest reliability (Hasin et al., 2006).

The Spanish version of the PRISM (Torrens et al., 2004) was obtained after translating the original version by a bilingual research translator and back-translated by one experienced bilingual research translator. Following the back-translation, both the Spanish version and the back-translation were sent to the original authors for revision. The final version was the result of corrections for inconsistencies and problems detected by the research team. The PRISM includes the following disorders: (1) substance use disorders, including substance abuse and dependence for alcohol, cannabis, hallucinogens, licit and illicit opiates, and stimulants; (2) primary affective disorders, including major depression, manic episode (and bipolar I disorder), psychotic mood disorder, hypomanic episode (and bipolar II disorder), dysthymia, and cyclothymic disorder; (3) primary anxiety disorders, including panic, simple phobia, social phobia, agoraphobia, obsessive-compulsive disorder, generalized anxiety disorder, and posttraumatic stress disorder; (4) primary psychotic disorders, including schizophrenia, schizoaffective disorder, schizophreniform disorder, delusional disorder, and psychotic disorder not otherwise specified; (5) eating disorders, including anorexia, bulimia, and binge-eating disorder; (6) personality disorders, including antisocial and borderline personality disorders; and (7) substance-induced disorders, including major depression, mania, dysthymia, psychosis, panic disorder, and generalized anxiety disorder. The average time of administration is about 1–3 h depending on the patient clinical history.

Psychometric characteristics of the Spanish version of PRISM are described in Table 3.2.

The Alcohol Use Disorder and Associated Disabilities Interview Schedule (AUDADIS)

The AUDADIS-IV (Grant et al., 2003; Grant & Hasin, 1992) is a fully structured diagnostic interview designed to be used in general population, but it can also be used in research community samples of individuals with alcohol and drug use diagnoses (Hasin, Carpenter, McCloud, Smith, & Grant, 1997). It can be administered by either lay interviewers or clinicians after a training period. The AUDADIS-IV takes a range of 1–2 h of administration. It contains modules to measure alcohol, tobacco and drug use disorders, major mood, anxiety and personality disorders, and family histories of alcohol, drug, major depression, and antisocial personality disorder according to the DSM-IV criteria. Diagnosis time frames are the past 12 months (current) and prior to the past 12 months (past), except for lifetime diagnoses as personality disorders. Current and past time frames can be combined to create lifetime most relevant diagnoses to research.

The AUDADIS-IV has eliminated the skip-outs in order to obtain dimensional measures of psychopathology in addition to the classical categorical diagnoses, and it allows for the examination of borderline or subclinical cases often found in general population samples. Also, it was the first instrument including *(1) measures of onset recency and remission of each disorder rather than the onset and recency of the first and last symptoms of the disorder, (2) adequate measures of duration criteria (i.e., the repetitiveness of symptoms necessary to assess their clinical significance), (3) provisions for deriving hierarchical and nonhierarchical diagnoses, (4) comorbidity modules relating disorders, (5) measures of self-medication associated with anxiety and mood disorders, (6) measures of true mood and anxiety disorders and those mood and anxiety disorders that are either substance-induced or due to a general medical condition, and (7) detailed questions on the frequency, quantity, and patterning of alcohol, tobacco, and drug use (Grant et al.,* 2003*).*

The AUDADIS Spanish version (Canino et al., 1999) was validated for Hispanic populations (particularly of Puerto Rico and North America) after a translation and adaptation process. Good to excellent test-retest reliability was obtained for the diagnoses of alcohol dependence and major depression. Similarly, good to excellent agreement was obtained between the lay administered AUDADIS and other estimates of diagnoses for most diagnostic categories, with the exception of dysthymia.

Psychometric characteristics of the Spanish version of AUDADIS are described in Table 3.2.

Diagnostic Interview Schedule IV (DIS-IV)

The DIS (Robins, Helzer, Croughan, & Ratcliff, 1981) is a highly structured psychiatric interview developed at the University of Washington (starting in 1978) to be administered by both professional and lay-trained interviewers in the Epidemiologic Catchment Area Program (ECA). It was originally created based on DSM, the Feighner guidelines, and the Research Diagnostic Criteria (RDC). Its most recent version is the DIS-IV revised for DSM-IV criteria and it has a computerized version (C-DIS-IV) (Robins et al., 2000). All versions attempt to mimic a clinical interview eliminating the need for clinical judgment by using questions to determine whether psychiatric symptoms are clinically significant or not and if they are explained by medical conditions or substance use. DIS-IV assesses a lifetime history of symptoms and conditions, from childhood to the present. The interview takes between 90 and 120 min to complete in the original paper format and approximately 75 min in its computerized version. This difference is due to the difficulty of managing over 800 probe questions to ascertain clinical significance of symptoms and its correct codification that computerized version ease. All questions are written to promote closed-ended answers with responses coded "yes" or "no." The DIS provides diagnostic information about somatization/pain, specific phobia, social phobia, agoraphobia, panic disorders, generalized anxiety disorder, posttraumatic stress disorder, depression, dysthymia disorder, mania, hypomania disorders, schizophrenia, schizophreniform, schizoaffective disorders, obsessive-compulsive disorder, anorexia nervosa, bulimia disorders, attention deficit disorder, separation anxiety disorder, oppositional disorder, conduct disorder, antisocial personality disorder, nicotine dependence, abuse and dependence (alcohol, amphetamines, cannabis, cocaine, hallucinogens, opioids, PCP, sedatives, inhalants, club drugs), pathological gambling, and dementia. For more information about the interview, visit the official web page of the interview http://epidemiology.phhp.ufl.edu/assessments/c-dis-iv/.

Results on psychometric properties of the DIS-IV mostly derive from studies of earlier versions of the DIS (Rogers, 2001a). The DIS also has been widely used in research on substance use disorders (Helzer & Canino, 1992) in North America, Europe, and Asia.

The DIS has been translated into Spanish receiving extensive cross-cultural validation work. Minor modifications of the Spanish version of the DIS (Karno, Burnam, Escobar, Hough, & Eaton, 1983) for use in Mexico (Burnam, Karno, Hough, Escobar, & Forsythe, 1983) were made by Anduaga, Forteza, & Lira, 1991, obtaining good inter-rater reliability and better specificity than sensitivity. The DIS was also translated to be used in Puerto Rico samples (Bravo, Canino, & Biro, 1987; Canino et al., 1987). The sensitivity was moderately high and specificity was excellent when comparing lay interviewer results to clinical diagnoses. de Pablo Alcázar et al., 1992, obtained similar results with the Spanish version in Spain.

DIS for Children (DISC)

The first version of the DIS for children (DISC-1) appeared in 1983 for a large-scale epidemiologic survey. It has evolved during the years, and all versions underwent methodological and psychometric testing in the Cooperative Agreement for Methodologic Research for Multisite Epidemiologic Surveys of Mental Disorders in Child and Adolescent Populations (MECA study). The final result was the NIMH-DISC-IV, a highly structured diagnostic interview with a 6-month time frame, including an elective module for lifetime diagnosis, with more precise probing for episode onset, and a variety of changes in the wording of items based on data collected in the MECA study. It covers DSM-III-R, DSM-IV, and ICD-10, for over 30 of the most common diagnoses among children and adolescents. It can be administered by lay interviewers after a minimal training period (Shaffer, Fisher, Lucas, Dulcan, & Schwab-Stone, 2000). Alternative versions of the interview such as the parent version DISC-P, the Present State DISC, the Teacher DISC, the Quick DISC, and the Voice DISC are also available. Currently, the only computerized version of the NIMH-DISC-IV is the C-DISC-4.0, owned and distributed by the Division of Child and Adolescent Psychiatry at Columbia University. This program is available both in English and Spanish.

In 2001, Bravo et al. conducted a study to adapt both parent and child versions of the DISC-IV for Puerto Rico populations with the NIMH support. In 2009, Kunst, Blidner, Esrubilsky, Longarela, and Vega carried out another study to validate the Spanish version of the DISC-IV in Buenos Aires (Argentina) concluding that the DISC-IV administered by nonprofessional interviewers has the ability to discriminate between youngsters who suffer from psychiatric disorders and healthy ones, with adequate psychometric estimators except for anxiety disorders and behavior disorders that showed poor confidence levels.

Psychometric characteristics of the Spanish version of DIS-IV and DISC-IV are described in Table 3.2.

Composite International Diagnostic Interview (CIDI)

The Composite International Diagnostic Interview (CIDI) Version 1.0 was developed under the auspices of the WHO (1987). It was an expansion of the DIS-III with questions of the Patient State Examination (PSE) added to generate diagnoses based also on ICD criteria and not only on DSM criteria (Robins et al., 1988). Therefore, the CIDI was designed to encourage community epidemiological surveys in many countries around the world. These efforts were successful over the following years, and over a dozen large-scale CIDI surveys were completed during the first half of the 1990s in many countries. The WHO created the International Consortium in Psychiatric Epidemiology (ICPE) in 1997 to bring together and compare results across these surveys. One year after, in 1998, The World Health Organization officially established the WHO WMH Survey Initiative to coordinate the undertaking (Kessler & Ustun, 2004).

The last version, the CIDI 3.0, is a fully structured interview designed to be used by lay interviewers after a training course. The interviewers should only read questions as they are written without any interpretation. The first section is an introductory screening and lifetime review section to determine which sections need to be assessed. There are 22 diagnostic sections that assess mood disorders (major depression and mania), anxiety disorders (panic disorder, specific phobia, agoraphobia, generalized anxiety disorder, posttraumatic stress disorder, obsessive-compulsive disorder, and social phobia), substance use disorders (alcohol abuse and dependence, nicotine, and other drugs), childhood disorders (ADHD, oppositional-defiant disorder, conduct disorder, panic disorder, and separation anxiety disorder.), and other disorders (intermittent explosive disorder, eating disorders, premenstrual disorder, pathological gambling, neurasthenia, personality disorders, and psychotic disorders). Four additional sections assess several types of functioning and physical comorbidities. Two of them evaluate treatment of mental disorders, four assess risk factors, six sociodemographic characteristics, and the two final sections are methodological. The first of the last two includes rules for determining which respondents to select for Part II of the interview and which ones finish the interview after Part I. The second methodological section consists of interviewer observations that are recorded after the interview has ended. The entire WMH-CIDI takes an average of approximately 2 h to administer in most general populations.

The WHO WMH Survey Initiative foremost challenge was to achieve both equivalence in meaning and consistency in measurement across surveys and within surveys that had multiple language versions. As previously mentioned, the WHO established an adaptation protocol including six steps (Harkness et al., 2008). Colombia, Mexico, Peru, and Spain are WMH Initiative participating countries that have followed these steps in their Spanish versions with Spanish-language collaborators from Chile, Colombia, Mexico, Panama, Peru, Puerto Rico, Spain, and the United States as well as representatives from AMRO (Americas Regional Office) and the WHO.

At present, there are multiple versions of CIDI: in different languages, with variations in administration (computer-assisted interviews, different diagnostic standards), and results are often compared with DIS (which is its origin with PSE questions added and modified). Complete reviews of the validations conducted have been described by Rogers (2001b). For example, the reader is referred to the study conducted in Puerto Rico by Rubio-Stipec, Bravo, and Canino (1991).

Psychometric characteristics of the Spanish version of CIDI are described in Table 3.2.

Mini-International Neuropsychiatric Interview (MINI)

The MINI is a short-structured clinical Axis I interview that provides standardized data to clinicians in mental health and medical settings with a rapid and accurate evaluation of both DSM-IV and ICD-10 criteria (Lecrubier et al., 1997; Sheehan et al., 1997, 1998). It was intended to be used by trained paraprofessionals in clinical psychiatry and research settings, after a large formation process. It focuses on current disorders rather than lifetime disorders. There are four versions of the MINI: The *original MINI* is useful in clinical settings and research for its brevity (15–20 min of administration). It provides 17 Axis I disorders (major depressive disorder, dysthymic disorder, mania, panic disorder, agoraphobia, social phobia, specific phobia, obsessive-compulsive disorder, generalized anxiety disorder, alcohol abuse and dependence, drug abuse or dependence, psychotic disorder, anorexia nervosa, bulimia, and posttraumatic stress disorder), a suicidality module, and one Axis II disorder (antisocial personality disorder). The *MINI-Plus* is an extended version (45–60 min) that includes 23 disorders deeply assessed and its intended for research purposes. The *MINI-Screen* is a short version (5 min) designed for primary care settings. And finally, the MINI-KID assesses 27 diagnoses framing the questions in a language more suitable for children and adolescents. The administration time is about 40 min.

The MINI has been validated against the Structure Clinical Interview for DSM diagnoses (SCID-P) in English and French and against the Composite International Diagnostic Interview for ICD-10

(CIDI) in English, French, and Arabic. It has also been validated versus expert opinion in a large sample in four European countries (France, United Kingdom, Italy, and Spain). All resources of the MINI family can be found in www.medical-outcomes.com. The latest version of the M.I.N.I. 6.0 is dated October 10, 2010.

The Spanish translations and adaptations of the MINI 5.0.0, MINI-Plus, and MINI-Screen were conducted by L. Ferrando, J. Bobes, and J. Gibert from the IAP Institute, in Spain and by M. Soto and O. Soto from the University of South Florida, in the United States. The psychometric properties in terms of sensitivity, specificity, positive predictive value and negative predictive value of the Spanish version of the MINI have been described (Bobes, 1998). Diagnoses made by the psychiatrists were used as gold standard. The sensitivity and the specificity of the most common diagnoses were major depression (94.1 and 62.2, respectively), generalized anxiety disorder (92.3 and 64.6), and social phobia (100 and 84.2). The positive predictive and negative predictive values for these disorders were 41.0 and 97.4 for major depression, 34.2 and 97.6 for generalized anxiety disorder, and 14.2 and 100 for social phobia. The agreement between the MINI and the psychiatrist's diagnostic judgment may be considered acceptable for the most prevalent disorders at the level of primary health care.

MINI-KID

The validity and reliability of the Spanish version of the MINI-KID (Sheehan, Lecrubier, & Colón-Soto, 2000) was assessed in Mexico by Palacios, de la Peña, and Heinze (2004). It was presented at the Meeting of the American Academy of Child Psychiatry. The inter-rater reliabilities were 0.9–1 and 0.60–0.75, respectively, and concurrent validity with clinical interview was shown to be lower, from 0.35 to 0.50 (as reported in a study of the Instituto Nacional de Psiquiatría).

Psychometric characteristics of the Spanish version of the MINI are described in Table 3.2.

Diagnostic Interview for Genetic Studies (DIGS)

The DIGS (Nurnberger et al., 1994) is a specific clinical interview for genetic studies developed in the National Institute of Mental Health (NIMH) Genetics Initiative for the assessment of major mood and psychotic disorders and their spectrum conditions. It has polydiagnostic capacity and enables a detailed assessment of the course of the illness, chronology of the affective and psychotic disorders and comorbidity, an additional description of symptoms, and an algorithmic scoring capability. It is a semi-structured interview designed to be employed by trained interviewers with experience in interviewing and making judgments about manifest psychopathology. To extract the best information possible, interviewers are allowed to modify questions, but, whenever possible, questions should be read exactly as written. It is composed of 12 sections including an introduction with the Mini Mental State Examination (MMSE), demographics and a medical history, somatization, overview, mood disorders, substance abuse disorders, psychosis, comorbidity, suicidal behavior, anxiety disorders, eating disorders, and sociopathy. The average administration time is 2–3 h depending on the psychopathology of the interviewee. Reliabilities were excellent (0.73–0.95) (Nurnberger et al.), except for schizoaffective disorder. The DIGS may be useful as part of archival data gathering for genetic studies of major affective disorders, schizophrenia, and related conditions.

The DIGS 3.0 has two different Spanish versions. It was first translated into Spanish by the Departamento de Psiquiatría/Laboratorio de Genética Molecular Universidad de Antioquia, Medellín, Colombia, being validated in the Colombian population (Palacio et al., 2004). After two Spanish translations and back-translations of the original English version of DIGS, a review committee verified the linguistic and cultural equivalence of the translations. Test-retest reliability was excellent for all diagnoses (kappa>0.8). The confidence interval (CI) was excellent for schizophrenia, bipolar disorder, and major depressive disorder, and for a normal diagnosis, it was good for other psychiatric diagnosis and poor for schizoaffective disorder. The Spanish translation of the DIGS was a comprehensible and useful tool for genetic studies of psychiatric disorders in Latin America, particularly where schizophrenia and affective disorders are involved.

The other Spanish version of the DIGS (Roca et al., 2007) was created in several phases by a team of psychiatrists and psychologists from the Balearic Islands University (Palma de Mallorca, Spain). The 3.0 English version of DIGS was translated and applied in a pilot study to a small population. Minor modifications were then made to improve the comprehension of some questions. This document was back-translated and compared with the original version of DIGS. The Spanish version of DIGS incorporated some of the modifications added to the French version: (1) an optional screening question for mania was added in order to lower the threshold for entering this section by asking whether there was objective evidence of elevated mood (friends or family members have observed that the subject's mood was higher than normal); (2) optional questions were added to allow a better temporal assessment of the last episode in both the major depression and mania sections. Psychiatrists and psychologists with experience in clinical interviews were standardized in order to conduct the interviews obtaining excellent psychometric results (Roca et al.).

Psychometric characteristics of the Spanish version of the DIGS are described in Table 3.2.

Summary and Conclusions

Diagnostic interviews are helpful instruments, designed to improve agreement on psychiatric disorders assessment, according to main existing diagnostic criteria. In order to achieve satisfactory standards across different languages and cultures, interviews are validated in the different languages, such as Spanish, according to a standard protocol.

Structured interviews, such as the AUDADIS, the DIS-IV, the CIDI, and the MINI, all dispose of a validated Spanish version. The AUDADIS can be applied both to general and clinical population, to measure alcohol and drug use as well as major psychiatric disorders. The DIS-IV is a highly structured interview, aimed for eliminating the need for clinical judgment, when exploring lifetime history of symptoms and conditions. A children version is also available. The CIDI, initially developed in 1987, is now available in multiple versions, consisting of numerous sections scanning through main psychiatric disorders of adulthood and childhood, according to DSM criteria. Finally, the MINI is a short interview, providing standardized assessment of Axis I diagnosis. Different versions have been developed, to better fit different settings, such as primary care or research.

Various semi-structured interviews have a validated Spanish version. The SCID, first formulated in 1983, now consists of two interviews, for assessment of Axis I and II diagnosis, respectively. The SCAN consists of a set of tools to assess major psychiatric disorders' psychopathology and behaviors; it requires extensively trained interviewers to apply it. The PRISM is the only available interviews aimed for clinical research in comorbidity between psychiatric disorders and substance use disorders. To conclude, the DIGS is a semi-structured interview specifically developed to assess the diagnosis of major psychiatric disorder in genetic studies.

Acknowledgments This work was supported by grants from Instituto de Salud Carlos III FEDER (Red de Trastornos Adictivos-RTA RD06/001/1009 and Fondo de Investigaciones Sanitarias PS09/02121) and Ministerio de Sanidad, Politica Social e Igualdad (Plan Nacional sobre Drogas, project no. 2009I032)

References

Anduaga, J. C., Forteza, C. G., & Lira, L. R. (1991). The concurrent validity of the DIS: Experience with psychiatric patients in Mexico City. *Hispanic Journal of Behavioral Sciences, 13*, 63–77.

Basco, M. R., Bostic, J. Q., Davies, D., Rush, A. J., Witte, B., Hendrickse, W., et al. (2000). Methods to improve diagnostic accuracy in a community mental health setting. *The American Journal of Psychiatry, 157*, 1599–1605.

Bobes, J. (1998). A Spanish validation study of the mini international neuropsychiatric interview. *European Psychiatry, 13*, 198–199.

Bravo, M., Canino, G. J., & Biro, H. (1987). The diagnostic interview schedule in Spanish: Its translation and adaptation in Puerto Rico. *Acta Psiquiátrica y Psicológica de América Latina, 33*, 27–42.

Bravo, M., Canino, G. J., Rubio-Stipec, M., & Woiodbury-Fariña, M. (1991). A cross-cultural adaptation of a diagnostic instrument: the DIS adaptation in Puerto Rico. Culture, medicine and Psychiatry 15, 1–18.

Bravo, M., Ribera, J., Rubio-Stipec, M., Canino, G., Shrout, P., Ramirez, R., et al. (2001). Test-retest reliability of the Spanish version of the diagnostic interview schedule for children (DISC-IV). *Journal of Abnormal Child Psychology, 29*, 433–444.

Burnam, M. A., Karno, M., Hough, R. L., Escobar, J. I., & Forsythe, A. B. (1983). The Spanish diagnostic interview schedule. Reliability and comparison with clinical diagnoses. *Archives of General Psychiatry, 40*, 1189–1196.

Canino, G. J., Bird, H. R., Shrout, P. E., Stipec, M. R., Bravo, M., Martinez, R., et al. (1987). The Spanish diagnostic interview schedule: Reliability and concordance with clinical diagnoses in Puerto Rico. *Archives of General Psychiatry, 44*, 720–726.

Canino, G., Bravo, M., Ramirez, R., Febo, V. E., Rubio-Stipec, M., Fernandez, R. L., et al. (1999). The Spanish alcohol use disorder and associated disabilities interview schedule (AUDADIS): Reliability and concordance with clinical diagnoses in a Hispanic population. *Journal of Studies on Alcohol, 60*, 790–799.

de Pablo Alcázar, F., Albacete Belmonte, A., Meroño Méndez, A., Artiz Martínez, M., Berbell Torrecilla, F., García Peñalver, A., et al. (1992). Validity of the Spanish version of the diagnostic interview schedule. Third revision (DIS-III-R). *Actas Luso-Españolas de Neurología, Psiquiatría y Ciencias Afines, 20*, 257–262.

First, M. B., Gibbon, M., Spitzer, R. L., Williams, J. B. W., & Benjamin, L. S. (1997). *SCID-II personality questionnaire*. Washington, DC: American Psychiatric Press.

First, M. B., Gibbon, M., Spitzer, R. L., Williams, J. B. W., & Benjamin, L. S. (1999). *Entrevista clínica estructurada para los trastornos del eje II del DSM-IV*. Barcelona, Spain: Masson.

First, M. B., Spitzer, R. L., Gibbon, M., & Williams, J. B. W. (1996). *Structured clinical interview for DSM-IV axis I disorders, clinician version (SCID-CV)*. Washington, DC: American Psychiatric Press, Inc.

First, M. B., Spitzer, R. L., Gibbon, M., & Williams, J. B. W. (1999). *Entrevista Clínica Estructurada para los Trastornos del Eje I del DSM-IV*. Barcelona, Spain: Masson.

First, M. B., Spitzer, R. L., Gibbon, M., & Williams, J. B. W. (2002a). *Structured clinical interview for DSM-IV-TR axis I disorders, research version, patient edition. (SCID-I/P)*. New York: Biometrics Research, New York State Psychiatric Institute.

First, M. B., Spitzer, R. L., Gibbon, M., & Williams, J. B. W. (2002b). *Structured clinical interview for DSM-IV-TR axis I disorders, research version, non-patient edition. (SCID-I/NP)*. New York: Biometrics Research, New York State Psychiatric Institute.

First, M. B., Spitzer, R. L., Gibbon, M., & Williams, J. B. W. (2002c). *Structured clinical interview for DSM-IV-TR axis I disorders, research version, patient edition with psychotic screen (SCID-I/P W/PSY SCREEN)*. New York: Biometrics Research, New York State Psychiatric Institute.

Grant, B. F., Dawson, D. A., Stinson, F. S., Chou, P. S., Kay, W., & Pickering, R. (2003). The alcohol use disorder and associated disabilities interview schedule-IV (AUDADIS-IV): Reliability of alcohol consumption, tobacco use, family history of depression and psychiatric diagnostic modules in a general population sample. *Drug and Alcohol Dependence, 71*, 7–16.

Grant, B. F., & Hasin, D. (1992). *The alcohol Use disorder and associated disabilities interview schedule (AUDADIS)*. Rockville, MD: National Institute on Alcohol Abuse and Alcoholism.

Harkness, J. (2010). Translation: Language harmonization VIII. In *Guidelines for best practice in cross-cultural surveys*. Ann Arbor, MI: Survey Research Center, Institute for Social Research, University of Michigan. Retrieved April, 15, 2011, from http://www.ccsg.isr.umich.edu/. Revised August 2010.

Harkness, J. A., Pennell, B.-E., Villar, A., Gebler, N., Aguilar-Gaxiola, S., & Bilgen, I. (2008). Translation procedures and translation assessment in the world mental health survey initiative. In R. Kessler & T. B. Ustun (Eds.), *The World Health Organization mental health survey* (pp. 91–113). New York: Cambridge University Press.

Hasin, D., Carpenter, K. M., McCloud, S., Smith, M., & Grant, B. F. (1997). The alcohol use disorder and associated disabilities interview schedule (AUDADIS): Reliability of alcohol and drug modules in a clinical sample. *Drug and Alcohol Dependence, 44*, 133–141.

Hasin, D., Samet, S., Nunes, E., Meydan, J., Matseoane, K., & Waxman, R. (2006). Diagnosis of comorbid psychiatric disorders in substance users assessed with the psychiatric research interview for substance and mental disorders for DSM-IV. *The American Journal of Psychiatry, 163*, 689–696.

Hasin, D., Trautman, K., & Endicott, J. (1998). Psychiatric research interview for substance and mental disorders: Phenomenologically based diagnosis in patients who abuse alcohol or drugs. *Psychopharmacology Bulletin, 34*, 3–8.

Hasin, D., Trautman, K., Miele, G., & Endicott, J. (1995). *Psychiatric research interview for substance and mental disorders (PRISM)*. New York: New York State Psychiatric Institute/Columbia University.

Hasin, D. S., Trautman, K. D., Miele, G. M., Samet, S., Smith, M., & Endicott, J. (1996). Psychiatric research interview for substance and mental disorders (PRISM): Reliability for substance abusers. *The American Journal of Psychiatry, 153*, 1195–1201.

Helzer, J. E., & Canino, G. J. (Eds.). (1992). *Alcoholism in North America, Europe, and Asia*. New York: Oxford University Press.

Karno, M., Burnam, A., Escobar, J. I., Hough, R. L., & Eaton, W. W. (1983). Development of the Spanish-language version of the National Institute of Mental Health diagnostic interview schedule. *Archives of General Psychiatry, 40*, 1183–1188.

Kessler, R. C., & Ustun, T. B. (2004). The World Mental Health (WMH) survey initiative version of the World Health Organization (WHO) composite international diagnostic interview (CIDI). *International Journal of Methods in Psychiatric Research, 13*, 93–121.

Kranzler, H. R., Kadden, R. M., Babor, T. F., Tennen, H., & Rounsaville, B. J. (1996). Validity of the SCID in substance abuse patients. *Addiction, 91*, 859–868.

Kunst, G., Blidner, J., Esrubilsky, V., Longarela, H., & Vega, E. (2009). Evaluation of the validity of Diagnostic Interview Schedule for Children IV (DISC IV) in the city of Buenos Aires. *Vertex, 20*, 245–251.

Lecrubier, Y., Sheehan, D. V., Weiller, E., Amorim, P., Bonora, I., Sheehan, K. H., Janavs, J., & Dunbar, G. C. (1997). The mini international neuropsychiatric interview (MINI). A short diagnostic structured interview: Reliability and validity according to the CIDI. *European Psychiatry, 12*, 224–231.

Lobbestael, J., Leurgans, M., & Arntz, A. (2011). Inter-rater reliability of the structured clinical interview for DSM-IV axis I disorders (SCID I) and axis II disorders (SCID II). *Clinical Psychology & Psychotherapy, 18*, 75–79.

Martin-Santos, R., Bulbena, A., Porta, M., Gago, J., Molina, L., & Duro, J. C. (1998). Association between joint hypermobility syndrome and panic disorder. *The American Journal of Psychiatry, 155*, 1578–1583.

Mezzich, J. E., & Salloum, I. M. (2007). Towards innovative international classification and diagnostic systems: ICD-11 and person-centered integrative diagnosis. *Acta Psychiatrica Scandinavica, 116*, 1–5.

Nurnberger, J. I., Jr., Blehar, M. C., Kaufmann, C. A., York-Cooler, C., Simpson, S. G., Harkavy-Friedman, J., et al. (1994). Diagnostic interview for genetic studies. Rationale, unique features, and training. NIMH genetics initiative. *Archives of General Psychiatry, 51*, 849–859.

Palacio, C. A., Garcia, J., Arbelaez, M. P., Sanchez, R., Aguirre, B., Garces, I. C., et al. (2004). Validation of the diagnostic interview for genetic studies (DIGS) in Colombia. *Biomedica, 24*, 56–62.

Palacios, L., De la Peña, F., & Heinze, G. (2004). *Validez y confiabilidad del MINI KID*. Presentado en póster en el Congreso de Academia Americana de Psiquiatría Infantil. Washington, DC

Robins, L. N., Cottler, L., Bucholz, K., Compton, W., North, C., & Rourke, K. (2000). *Diagnostic interview schedule for the DSM-IV (DIS-IV)*. St. Louis, MO: Washington University School of Medicine.

Robins, L. N., Helzer, J. E., Croughan, J., & Ratcliff, K. S. (1981). National Institute of Mental Health diagnostic interview schedule. Its history, characteristics, and validity. *Archives of General Psychiatry, 38*, 381–389.

Robins, L. N., Wing, J., Wittchen, H. U., Helzer, J. E., Babor, T. F., Burke, J., et al. (1988). The composite international diagnostic interview. An epidemiologic instrument suitable for use in conjunction with different diagnostic systems and in different cultures. *Archives of General Psychiatry, 45*, 1069–1077.

Roca, M., Martin-Santos, R., Saiz, J., Obiols, J., Serrano, M. J., Torrens, M., et al. (2007). Diagnostic interview for genetic studies (DIGS): inter-rater and test-retest reliability and validity in a Spanish population. *European Psychiatry, 22*, 44–48.

Rogers, R. (2001a). Diagnostic interview schedule. In R. Rogers (Ed.), *Handbook of diagnostic and structured interviewing* (pp. 61–83). New York: Guilford press.

Rogers, R. (2001b). Composite international diagnostic interview. In R. Rogers (Ed.), *Handbook of diagnostic and structured interviewing* (pp. 135–140). New York: Guilford press.

Rubio-Stipec, M., Bravo, M., & Canino, G. (1991). The composite international diagnostic interview (CIDI): an epidemiologic instrument suitable for using in conjunction with different diagnostic systems in different cultures. *Acta Psiquiátrica y Psicológica de América Latina, 37*, 191–204.

Shaffer, D., Fisher, P., Lucas, C. P., Dulcan, M. K., & Schwab-Stone, M. E. (2000). NIMH diagnostic interview schedule for children version IV (NIMH DISC-IV): description, differences from previous versions, and reliability of some common diagnoses. *Journal of the American Academy of Child and Adolescent Psychiatry, 39*, 28–38.

Sheehan, D., Lecrubier, Y., & Colón-Soto, M. (2000). *MINI KID. Mini international neuropsychiatric interview para niños y adolescentes*. Versión en español Retrieved May, 17, 2011 from www.medical-outcomes.com

Sheehan, D. V., Lecrubier, Y., Sheehan, K. H., Amorim, P., Janavs, J., Weiller, E., et al. (1998). The mini-international neuropsychiatric interview (M.I.N.I.): the development and validation of a structured diagnostic psychiatric interview for DSM-IV and ICD-10. *The Journal of Clinical Psychiatry, 59*(Suppl 20), 22–33.

Sheehan, D. V., Lecrubier, Y., Sheehan, K. H., Janavs, J., Weiller, E., Keskiner, A., et al. (1997). The validity of the mini international neuropsychiatric interview (MINI) according to the SCID-P and its reliability. *European Psychiatry, 12*, 232–241.

Spitzer, R. L. (1983). Psychiatric diagnosis: Are clinicians still necessary? *Comprehensive Psychiatry, 24*, 399–411.

Torrens, M., Serrano, D., Astals, M., Perez-Dominguez, G., & Martin-Santos, R. (2004). Diagnosing comorbid psychiatric disorders in substance abusers: Validity of the Spanish versions of the psychiatric research interview for substance and mental disorders and the structured clinical interview for DSM-IV. *The American Journal of Psychiatry, 161*, 1231–1237.

Vaz Leal, F. J., Guisado Macias, J. A., Garcia-Herraiz, M. A., Lopez, V. B., Monge, B. M., & Bolivar, P. M. (2005). History of sexual abuse in patients with bulimia nervosa: Its influence on clinical status. *Actas Españolas de Psiquiatría, 33*, 135–140.

Vazquez-Barquero, J. L., Gaite, L., Artal, S. J., Arenal, A., Herrera, C. S., Diez Manrique, J. F., et al. (1994). Development and verification of the Spanish version of the "scanning system" psychiatric interview ("Questionnaires for clinical evaluation in neuropsychiatry"). *Actas Luso-Españolas de Neurología, Psiquiatría y Ciencias Afines, 22*, 109–120.

Westermeyer, J., & Janca, A. (1997). Language, culture and psychopathology: Conceptual and methodological issues. *Transcultural Psychiatry, 34*, 291–311.

Wing, J. K. (1998). The PSE tradition and its continuation in SCAN. In J. K. Wing, N. Sarto-rius, & T. B. Üstün (Eds.), *Diagnosis and clinical measurement in psychiatry: A reference manual for SCAN* (pp. 12–24). Cambridge, UK: Cambridge University Press.

World Health Organization. (1998). *Schedules for clinical assessment in neuropsychiatry (SCAN), version 2.1*. Geneva, Switzerland: Author.

World Health Organization – Alcohol, Drug, ad Mental Health Administration. (1987). *Composite international diagnostic interview, version 1*. Geneva, Switzerland: Author.

World Health Organization – Alcohol, Drug, and Mental Health Administration. (2004). *Composite international diagnostic interview version, 3.0*. Geneva, Switzerland: Author.

Zanarini, M. C., & Frankenburg, F. R. (2001). Attainment and maintenance of reliability of axis I and II disorders over the course of a longitudinal study. *Comprehensive Psychiatry, 42*, 369–374.

4 Using Projective Tests with Hispanic Clients

Orlando L. Pedrosa-Roche, Juan A. Nazario, and Joy Lynn Suárez-Kindy

Introduction

In order to provide mental health services to Hispanics, it is not enough to know how to speak in Spanish. The culturally sensitive clinician must also be well versed in the client's culture and the ethnic and racial variables that affect the person's development (Biever, Gómez, González, & Patrizio, 2011). It is for that reason that any mental health professional that provides services for Hispanics must acquire the necessary competencies (American Psychological Association, 2002).

Hispanics are the largest minority group in the USA (Census Bureau, 2011). As of 2011, there were 50.5 million persons of Hispanic origin and that represented a 43% increase from the year 2000. Of those, 63% are from Mexico, 9.2% from Puerto Rico, and 3.5% from Cuba. The largest concentration of Hispanics lives in the western and southern states with 41 and 36%, respectively, and tends to come from Central and South America. Interestingly, Hispanics from the Caribbean tend to live more on the eastern states (Sue & Sue, 2008; USA Census Bureau, 2011).

Hispanics are a very diverse group with different cultural backgrounds and identification with their country of origin. This diversity is due, in part, to the fact that Hispanics in the USA are the result of a blend of persons from different countries with different sociopolitical realities. But it also emanates from the cultural blend of second- and third-generation Hispanics, born and raised within a nuclear Hispanic family but also within the US culture.

Taking into consideration that Hispanics are the second largest group of habitants in the USA, and that only about 1% of psychologists are of Hispanic origin (Dingfelder, 2005), it is highly probable that at any given time any clinician may have to perform a psychological evaluation on a person from a Hispanic background. It is for this reason that it is imperative to know and understand what strategy must be followed when faced with such a challenge.

O.L. Pedrosa-Roche, Ph.D. (✉) • J.A. Nazario, Psy.D. • J.L. Suárez-Kindy, Psy.D.
Psy.D Program, Carlos Albizu University, PO Box 9023711, San Juan 00926-3711, Puerto Rico
e-mail: Opedrosa@sju.albizu.edu; Jnazario@sju.albizu.edu; Jsuarez@sju.albizu.edu

L.T. Benuto (ed.), *Guide to Psychological Assessment with Hispanics*,
DOI 10.1007/978-1-4614-4412-1_4, © Springer Science+Business Media New York 2013

Brief History on Projective Testing with Hispanics

When confronted with the situation of having to test a client that speaks Spanish, two strategies have been traditionally employed: translate an objective test or use a projective one with nonverbal stimuli. The translation of a test from English to Spanish for use with Hispanics usually produces items that may have different meaning on the target population than the one originally intended. Furthermore, since the Hispanic community is composed of persons from different countries and sociopolitical realities, different words or even the combination of words may have different meanings to persons originating from Puerto Rico, the Dominican Republic, or Mexico. The word "naranja" is used in some countries to refer to an orange, while in others the same fruit is referred to as "china."

Many nonverbal projective personality tests such as the Rorschach using John Exner's Comprehensive System, Thematic Apperception Test, and figure drawings methods such as the Draw-A-Person (DAP) or House-Tree-Person (HTP) have been touted as "culture-free" because they do not have traditional verbal items that have to be translated. For this reason, many clinicians tend to prefer those tests when faced with the task of performing a psychological evaluation on a person from another culture. However, the different kinds of stimuli used on the different tests may lend themselves to evoke different responses on a person with a Hispanic background for several reasons.

Let us take the Tell-Me-A-Story test (TEMAS) developed by Constantino, Malgady, and Rogler (1988) as an example. The TEMAS was developed to assess child and adolescent personality cognitive functioning and offers norms for African Americans, Puerto Ricans, other Hispanics, and Caucasians (Constantino, Flanagan, & Malgady, 2001). Its stimuli are similar to the TAT in which drawing depicts certain situations to which the test taker must respond. Studies by the authors show that for Puerto Rican children living in the USA, the test has better reliability and validity than for Puerto Rican children living in Puerto Rico (Constantino, Malgady, Casullo, & Castillo, 1991). Some of the differences may be due to the fact that the pictures depict scenes from communities in the USA which include buildings, animals, and scenery markedly different from that found in the island.

When using pictures such as these on tests used to assess Hispanics, the image characteristics may prove unfamiliar to the person taking the test. Features such as the scenery, clothing, furniture, or even the overall context of the image may be enough to impede the identification of the test taker with the test. Since these tests rely on that process to produce valid interpretations, the validity of the test itself may come into question.

The nonverbal nature of the Rorschach test using Exner's Comprehensive System (RCS) stimuli confers it certain immunity from attempts to manipulate the results in order to present a more or less favorable impression on the evaluator (Grossman, Wasyliw, Benn, & Gyoerkoe, 2002). At the same time, this characteristic of the blots makes the test immune to error of translation that may be due to cultural factors. Furthermore, since the Rorschach cards are totally ambiguous, the lack of identification because of image characteristics or features by the test takers is greatly minimized. This is not to say that the RCS is the perfect instrument for the assessment of personality dynamics of the Hispanic population, but the nature of its blots lacks characteristics that may be loaded with culturally relevant factors which may impair the cross-cultural validity of its inferences.

Projective Tests in Use Today

The Thematic Apperception Test (TAT) is one of the most used instruments in the USA (Watkins, Campbell, Nieberding, & Hallmark, 1995). It consists of a set of cards depicting scenes to which the test taker must provide a story. There is no standardized procedure for the administration, and the assessor may choose any number of cards to administer.

As it stands today, the TAT has many shortcomings that may hinder its use with the Hispanic population. It lacks a standardized scoring procedure with adequate psychometric properties, the pictures are not culture specific/sensitive, and it does not have culturally relevant norms as well as interpretations. Dana (2005) describes a systematic framework for high-inference TAT interpretation that represents the results of his many years of work and research on the test. However, he comments that "This rational and procedural content remains incomplete, and supplementation is required using additional low inference scores. The development and validation of new scores is imperative..." (Dana, 2005, p. 172). We could not find more recent research studying Dana's framework or the cross-cultural validity of its interpretation for specific purposes on the Hispanic population.

The TEMAS is a test derived from the tradition of the TAT storytelling format. Children from 5 and adolescents up to 18 years old can be assessed with the TEMAS. It takes a much more structured approach to projective assessment than the TAT. First, the card is colored, which tends to enhance the clinical usefulness of the test since color enhances verbal fluency and discrimination between psychiatric and normal examinees (Constantino et al., 1991). It has a standard set of instructions and an elaborated scoring procedure. It also has norms for different groups including Puerto Ricans, African Americans, and other Hispanic groups. The interpretation also takes into account the themes that each card was designed to pull.

In a study comparing the TEMAS records of Puerto Rican Children with those of New York Puerto Rican and Argentinean children (Constantino et al., 1991), the test did not perform as well as expected for the children living in Puerto Rico. The authors conclude that the reliability and validity estimates for those children were less favorable than for the mainland groups. Furthermore, some of the pictures did not pull the designated personality functions. However, for children living in New York, the reliability estimates were acceptable to good.

The Rorschach is by far the test that has received more attention and has been more researched across various cultures. With the introduction of Exner's Comprehensive System (Exner, 1993), the reliability and validity of the Rorschach, as well as its usefulness, increased dramatically. It stands as the second most taught personality assessment instrument on APA accredited programs (Childs & Eyde, 2002). It also provides norms for adults and for children for each year from 5 to 16 years of age.

Weiner (1998) pointed three issues that must be taking into consideration when studying the effect that a specific culture may have on the Rorschach. The first refers to interpretive meaning of the Rorschach variables. Many studies carried out throughout the world provide evidence that the majority of the RCS variables are not affected by cultural factors. Dana (2000, 2001) states that there is enough convincing evidence pointing that some of the constructs measured by the RCS have equivalence in other cultures. One example would be the Erlebnistypus (EB) which provides interpretations about the kind of resources that persons use when making decisions and solving problems. The dichotomy between thinking and feeling is manifested in practically every culture.

Franchi and Andronikof (1999) studied the validity of the RCS on a sample of immigrants or daughters of immigrants from West Africa. Their focus was the exploration of the use of the test in a culturally relevant manner. On their conclusion, the authors state the following:

> The Rorschach Comprehensive System proves to be an instrument capable of taping those aspects of an individual's inner referential world considered to be universal to all cultures. It captures each individual's unique "way of being in the world," including his/her referents, habitual patterns of functioning (cognitive and affective), and preferred modes of interpersonal relating (p. 130).

They end by warning that the cultural elements of those assessed with the RCS must come through in the interpretation in order to make the test culturally relevant and effective. Butcher, Nezami, and Exner (1998) performed a review of the personality assessment methods used in other cultures and concluded that the validity of the interpretations based on RCS data appears to be uniform regardless of the culture of origin of the test taker. Ritzler (1996) reviewed various protective techniques that he

Table 4.1 Selected RCS statistics from Hispanic samples

	Country				
RCS variable	Argentina (n=506)	Argentina (n=90)	Peru (n=233)	Spain (n=517)	New USA (n=450)
R	18.71	24.23	21.73	24.92	23.36
Lambda	.56	.94	.75	1.03	.58
EA	6.01	7.43	6.49	7.00	9.37
X+%	.59	.55	.52	.54	.68
Xu%	.22	.27	.30	.24	.20
X−%	.18	.17	.17	.21	.11
XA%	.81	.82	.82	.78	.88
WDA%	.83	.86	.84	.82	.91
WSum6	5.91	1.99	5.90	11.43	7.12
P	5.35	5.52	5.09	5.92	6.28
M	3.07	4.46	4.02	4.21	4.83
Sum C	3.82	3.39	3.17	3.45	5.95
Afr	.57	.45	.50	.58	.61

thought overcome the inherent problems encountered in a multicultural psychological evaluation. Regarding the RCS, he mentions that the ambiguous nature of the blots eliminates the cultural bias that may be present in other nonverbal tests that have more structured stimuli, such as the TAT.

Other studies carried out with the RCS and the MMPI-2 have provided evidence of an absence of ethnic bias when comparing the differential validity of both tests in different cultures (Meyer & Archer, 2001). In a methodologically robust study, Meyer (2002) shows evidence of the way in which several factor solutions of 59 RCS variables did not differ between ethnic groups. Various studies show that, regardless of the cultural background of the test taker, a person with an elevated X−% perceives his world in an atypical fashion and persons with low self-esteem point low on the Ego Index. In Belgium, the interpretive meaning of the depression index (DEPI), the Ego Index, the EB, and morbid responses were similar to that of the USA (Marsden, Michel, & Mormont, 1999). In Spain, persons with emotional disturbances obtain similar scores on the DEPI to those with similar characteristics in the USA (Sendín & De Felipe, 1999).

The second and third issues raised by Weiner refer to the effect that a given culture may have on the scoring of a response as well as the language effect. The Hispanic culture realities allow these two issues to be considered simultaneously. There are three types of code that may be affected by cultural variables. The first one is the Form Quality (FQ) of a response. When the response given to a blot is not on the FQ tables, the coder is required to use his or her clinical judgment in order to code the response as an unusual or minus one. If this happens frequently for a certain individual, the Xu%, which indicates that a person perceives his world in a very individualistic way, may be overestimated. Various international and cross-cultural studies, however, (Campo & Vilar, 2007; Exner, 2007; Lunazzi et al., 2007; Ráez, 2007; Sanz, 2007) have shown that this may not really be a problem after all. Table 4.1 shows various RCS indexes that may suffer from cultural variations. Among them, the Xu% shows very little variation across cultures. For a complete list of the statistics of all of the RCS indices, the reader is referred to their original studies, since these studies provide the closest data to Hispanic norms. The X+% and the X−% show more differences when comparing all of the Hispanic samples to the new US sample of nonpatients. Those indices are typically used to compare the conventionality of a person's perception to that of the norm.

Popular responses are another code category that may be influenced by culture. The same data from Table 4.1 show that such differences are very small to the point of not having interpretive significance. The variables where more variance is observed are lambda, the sum of chromatic color responses, and the experience actual (EA), which probably is directly related to the difference in the color responses since they are used in its calculation. This difference in the sum of color responses has been reported before by Dana (2005) and is one argument in favor of the use of local norms.

The index that shows the most variation is the WSum6 which is coded using the verbalizations of the examinee. Its interpretations are related to how logical is the thinking process of the test taker. It is not clear why such a great variance exists between the studies presented.

Special Considerations When Using Each Measure with Hispanic Clients

For an assessment to be culturally sensitive, the clinician/assessor, more than the test used, must be sensitive to the culture of the person being evaluated. When assessing Hispanics, it is useful to take into consideration the three broad areas of concern described by Cofresí and Gorman (2004). Those areas are client issues, test issues, and clinician/assessor issues. We provide here a brief summary of the influence those areas may have while using projective assessments.

As mentioned before, even though Spanish is spoken as a common language by the Hispanic community, the manner, process, and content in which it is spoken vary according to the country of origin of the test taker. Different words are used to refer to the same objects, situations, or feelings. At the same time, the same words may have different meanings or connotations. For instance, the word "ahorita" for a Mexican means right now whereas for a Puerto Rican means later. Since spoken language plays a major role during the administration, scoring, and interpretation of projective tests, it is imperative, if not mandatory, that the assessor is fluent in the language and its regionalisms of the test taker. Acevedo et al. (2007) make four recommendations regarding language that we feel are of paramount importance, three of which apply to projective testing. They are that the clinician makes an assessment of the test taker language of preference and conduct the assessment in that language, that a client's language proficiency be determined with a standardized instrument if necessary, and that the methods used for that determination be documented in the report.

The level of acculturation on the part of the person being assessed has been mentioned as important by many authors (Acevedo et al., 2007; Cofresí & Gorman, 2004; Cuéllar 1998; Dana, 1995, 2000). Acculturation refers to the level of assimilation of a culture's norms and mores, other than their own. Since the acculturation level may affect what is considered normal or abnormal behavior by a certain individual, an assessment via an appropriate acculturation instrument is highly recommended.

Regarding the test issues, there are two comments that we deem appropriate. First is the scarcity of research on projective measures on Hispanics for the TAT and for the TEMAS, even though we feel that the latter holds much more promise as a culturally relevant measure, at least for Hispanics living in the USA, than the former. Second, we feel that the above-mentioned research provides sufficient evidence of the validity of most indices of the RCS. More specifically, regardless of the size of the difference in any index, the clinical interpretation may be the same for both cultures.

As for the clinician/assessor issues, it is our contention that, regardless of the differences that may exist between the USA and Hispanic norms, it is the duty of the clinician to be familiar with the culture of the test taker. When this is done properly, and the information gathered from the test is treated as hypothesis that has to be corroborated with other extra test information such as the person's history and clinical observations, any bias that may be present on the test will not adversely affect the clinician's interpretation and opinion.

Recommendations

As we have tried to present in the preceding pages, when evaluating a Hispanic client with a projective test, there are four criteria that must be present. First and foremost is that the evaluation be carried out in the language that the test taker feels more conformable in. This fact alone is critical in order to avoid making incorrect interpretations and conclusions. Along with using the same language, many authors (Cofresí & Gorman, 2004; Dana, 2005) have pointed out the importance of having an assessment of the acculturation level of the assessed, take that into consideration, and include it on the report.

Third, whenever possible, we recommend that the clinician/assessor come from the same country as the person being assessed. This provides many advantages over sharing only a common language since variables such as regionalisms will be understood for exactly what they mean. Also, it allows the evaluator to understand idiosyncrasies of the client which may include, but are not limited to, religion, "familismo" (family conceptualization), worldview, and reality of the Hispanic or Latino populations. But if this is not viable, it is imperative to understand that not all Hispanics have the same cultural background, customs, and ways of behaving or even expressing themselves due to differences inherent to their different countries of origins.

We hope that these recommendations translate into more fair and culturally relevant use of projective assessment for the Hispanic community living in the USA. At the very least, this information may lead to a realization of the need for a referral on the part of clinicians working with Hispanic clients.

List of Key/Index Terms for Your Chapter

Projective assessment with Hispanics, Rorschach with Hispanics, Projective assessment with Spanish-speaking clients, Assessment with Latino clients

References

Acevedo, I., Reynaga, G., Garriott, P., Derefinko, K., Wimsatt, M., Gudonis, L., et al. (2007). Beyond instrument selection: Cultural considerations in the psychological assessment of U.S. Latinas/os. *Professional Psychology, 38*(4), 375–384.

American Psychological Association. (2002). *Guidelines on multicultural education, training, research, practice, and organizational change for psychologists*. Washington, DC: American Psychological Association.

Biever, J. L., Gómez, J. P., González, C. G., & Patrizio, N. (2011). Psychological services to Spanish-speaking populations: A model curriculum for training competent professionals. *Training and Education in Professional Psychology, 5*(2), 81–87.

Butcher, J. N., Nezami, E., & Exner, J. E., Jr. (1998). Psychological assessment of people in diverse cultures. In S. S. Kazarian & D. R. Evans (Eds.), *Cultural clinical psychology* (pp. 61–105). New York: Oxford University Press.

Campo, V., & Vilar, N. (2007). Rorschach comprehensive system data for a sample of 90 adult nonpatients from Spain (Barcelona). *Journal of Personality Assessment, 89*(1), S149–S153.

Childs, R. A., & Eyde, L. D. (2002). Assessment training in clinical psychology doctoral programs: What should we teach? What do we teach? *Journal of Personality Assessment, 78*, 130–144.

Cofresí, N., & Gorman, A. (2004). Testing and assessment issues with Spanish-English bilingual Latinos. *Journal of Counseling and Development, 82*, 99–106.

Constantino, G., Flanagan, R., & Malgady, R. (2001). Narrative assessments: TAT, CAT and TEMAS. In L. Suzuki, J. Ponterrotto, & P. Meller (Eds.), *Handbook of multicultural assessment* (pp. 217–233). San Francisco: Jossey-Bass.

Constantino, G., Malgady, R., Casullo, M., & Castillo, A. (1991). Cross-cultural standardization of TEMAS in three Hispanic subcultures. *Hispanic Journal of Behavior Sciences, 13*, 48–62.

Constantino, G., Malgady, R. G., & Rogler, L. H. (1988). *TEMAS (Tell-Me-A-Story) manual*. Los Angeles: Western Psychological Services.

Cuéllar, I. (1998). Cross-cultural clinical psychological assessment of Hispanics Americans. *Journal of Personality Assessment, 70*, 71–86.
Dana, R. (1995). Projective assessment of Latinos in the United States: Current realities, problems and prospects. *Cultural Diversity and Mental Health, 4*(3), 165–184.
Dana, R. (2000). Culture and methodology in personality assessment. In I. Cuéllar & F. A. Paniagua (Eds.), *Handbook of multicultural mental health* (pp. 97–120). San Diego, CA: Academic.
Dana, R. (2001). Clinical diagnosis of U. S. multicultural populations. In L. A. Suzuki, J. G. Ponterotto, & P. J. Meller (Eds.), *Handbook of multicultural assessment* (pp. 101–131). San Francisco: Jossey-Bass Publishers.
Dana, R. (2005). *Multicultural assessment: Principles, applications and examples*. New York: Psychology Press.
Dingfelder, S. F. (2005). Lifting as they climb: Psychology faculty and graduate students in two programs provide role models to boost Latino enrollment. *Monitor on Psychology, 36*(1), 68–69.
Exner, J. E. (1993). *The Rorschach: A comprehensive system, volume 1: Basic foundations* (3rd ed.). New York: Wiley.
Exner, J. E. (2007). A new US adult nonpatient sample. *Journal of Personality Assessment, 89*(1), S154–S158.
Franchi, V., & Andronikof, A. (1999). Methodological and epistemological issues raised by the use of the Rorschach comprehensive system in cross-cultural research. *Rorschachiana, 23*, 118–134.
Grossman, L. S., Wasyliw, O. E., Benn, A. F., & Gyoerkoe, K. L. (2002). Can sex offenders who minimize on the MMPI conceal psychopathology on the Rorschach? *Journal of Personality Assessment*, 78, 484–501.
Lunazzi, H. A., Urrutia, M. I., De la Fuente, M. G., Elias, D., Fernandez, F., & de la Fuente, S. (2007). Rorschach comprehensive system data for a sample of 506 adult nonpatients from Argentina. *Journal of Personality Assessment, 89*(1), S7–S12.
Marsden, E., Michel, A., & Mormont, C. (1999). Study of the impact of a gastroplasty on the self-image through the Rorschach. *Rorschachiana, 23*, 43–57.
Meyer, G. J. (2002). Exploring possible ethnic differences and bias in the Rorschach comprehensive system. *Journal of Personality Assessment, 78*, 104–129.
Meyer, G. J., & Archer, R. P. (2001). The hard science of Rorschach research: What do we know and where do we go? *Psychological Assessment, 13*, 486–502.
Ráez, M. (2007). Rorschach comprehensive system data for a sample of 90 adult nonpatients from Peru. *Journal of Personality Assessment, 89*(1), S119–S123.
Ritzler, B. A. (1996). Projective methods for multicultural personality assessment: Rorschach, TEMAS, and Early Memory Procedures. In L. A. Suzuki, P. J. Meller, & J. G. Ponterotto (Eds.), Handbook of Multicultural Assessment: Clinical, Psychological and educational applications (pp. 115–136). San Francisco: Jossey- Bass Publishers.
Sanz, I. A. E. (2007). Rorschach comprehensive system data for a sample of 90 adult nonpatients from Argentina. *Journal of Personality Assessment, 89*(1), S13–S19.
Sendín, C., & De Felipe, J. (1999). Rorschach and MMPI evaluation of depressive components in neurologically affected patients. *Rorschachiana, 23*, 15–27.
Sue, D. W., & Sue, D. (2008). *Counseling the culturally diverse: Theory and practice* (5th ed.). Hoboken, NJ: Wiley.
United States Census Bureau. (2011). *The Hispanic population: 2010*. Obtain of http://www.census.gov/prod/cen2010/briefs/c2010br-04.pdf.
Watkins, C. E., Campbell, V. L., Nieberding, R., & Hallmark, R. (1995). Contemporary practice of psychological assessment by clinical psychologists. *Professional Psychology, 26*, 54–60.
Weiner, I. B. (1998). *Principles of Rorschach interpretation*. New York: Lawrence Erlbaum.

5 Assessing Personality Using Self-Report Measures with Hispanic Clients

Maria Garrido and José J. Cabiya

A Context for Assessing Personality Using Self-Report Measures with Hispanic Clients

Brief Considerations on the Relationship Between Culture and Personality with Implications for Assessment, Especially Test and Scalar Equivalence

The ever-increasing cultural and linguistic diversification of the population of the United States presents mental health professionals with both challenges and opportunities in the area of psychological assessment. The development of assessment instruments with psychometric properties that enable appropriate and fair evaluation, diagnosis, and treatment planning of those whose language and cultural background are different from the Euro-American population is still a priority. In the United States, years ahead of projections, the Hispanic/Latino segment of the total population reached 16.3%, higher than any other non-Euro-American group (Ennis, Ríos-Vargas, & Albert, 2011). Information concerning language use provided by the US Census (Fernandez, Boccaccini, & Noland, 2007) indicates that approximately 48% of Hispanic individuals reported "not speaking English well," and as many as 40% were born outside the United States. While it is clear that the need for assessment instruments in Spanish is gradually being addressed (Fernandez et al., 2007), it is also critically important that those translated measures assess the same concepts across languages and are reliable.

As McCrae and Terracciano (2006) indicate in their study on national character and personality, the ability to arrive at appropriate descriptions of traits that may distinguish among groups from different national and cultural origins is contingent upon factors such as the comparability of scores obtained on translated versions of tests, whether the same traits can be used to describe personality in all cultures, and the validity of methods of measurement and assessment instruments when used in different contexts. Additionally, the authors indicate that use of a measure across cultures requires scalar evidence, where the meaning of a given score in one culture is the same or similar to its meaning in another cul-

M. Garrido, Psy.D. (✉)
Psychology Psy.D./Ph.D. Program, Ponce School of Medicine and Health Sciences, P.O. Box 7004, Ponce 00732, Puerto Rico
e-mail: mgarrido@psm.edu

J.J. Cabiya, Ph.D
Scientific Research Institute (SRI), Carlos Albizu University, Paseo Del Parque Num. 27, Los Paseos, San Juan 00926, Puerto Rico
e-mail: jcabiya@albizu.edu

L.T. Benuto (ed.), *Guide to Psychological Assessment with Hispanics*,
DOI 10.1007/978-1-4614-4412-1_5, © Springer Science+Business Media New York 2013

ture. However, they describe the challenge that translations may pose to scalar equivalence of assessment measures especially for Spanish speakers. Research reviewed by these authors indicates that translations may introduce mean level shifts, while tendencies such as acquiescence in response style may also vary across cultures. As a way to address this issue, McCrae, Terracciano, and 79 members of the Personality Profiles and Cultures Project (2005) point to the need to evaluate the construct validity of a given measure by examining the pattern of correlations between the measure and culture-level correlates. For instance, measures of a trait (e.g., extraversion or neuroticism) could be correlated to measures of subjectively rated well-being across several cultures. If meaningful correlations with the local measures of well-being emerge, it could be stated that the trait measure has scalar equivalence.

Clearly, these considerations concerning the validity of a measure across cultural and linguistic lines have significant implications for psychologists involved in the assessment of culturally diverse individuals and especially Spanish-speaking Hispanics, who themselves represent multiple nationalities and sociopolitical and historical experiences. As will be discussed next, the issues presented here face psychologists with the need for responsible test selection.

Test Selection Considerations: Availability of Translations and Equivalence

The availability of tests that have been translated to Spanish has gradually increased, making it more feasible for practitioners to employ self-report measures with Spanish monolingual clients or bilingual clients whose cultural identification is strongly Hispanic/Latino or are recent immigrants to the Unites States (Fernandez et al., 2007). As these authors indicate, however, the translation of these instruments to Spanish is not a guarantee that their original psychometric properties are preserved in the translated version. Additionally, they point out that there is scant research supporting the use of translated versions. Given the potential consequences of psychological assessment for treatment, service planning, and forensic outcomes in some cases, the authors provide ethically based guidelines for the selection of translated instruments to be used with Spanish-speaking clients.

More specifically, the authors recommend that practitioners consult directly with test publishers as to the availability of translated versions of the instrument they are planning to use and that research describing the psychometric properties of the translated test to be used is examined. The authors cite the *Standards for Educational and Psychological Testing* (American Educational Research Association, American Psychological Association, & National Council on Measurement in Education, 1999) to indicate the importance of evaluating whether there is sufficient support for the use of the test with individuals similar to the client. Nonetheless, their research led them to discover a significant gap between the number of available test translations and the number of studies describing the psychometric properties of these translations and therefore the appropriateness of their use. Additionally, they caution as to existence of different translations of the same instrument, including the MMPI-2 for which there are versions for use in Spain and Mexico and for Spanish speakers in the United States and Puerto Rico. Related to this, they point out that a practitioner's choice of a translated instrument should also take into account how similar the client is to those with whom the test was developed and indicate that test selection should consider factors such as the client's migration status. Therefore, for a recent immigrant who is bilingual but holds a strong identification with the culture of origin, it may be more appropriate to use a translated version of the test than the English version. Finally, the authors make reference to the importance of test equivalence in light of test interpretation and indicate that if a translated version is not equivalent to the original, the interpretation of the translation cannot be assumed to be similar to that of the original version. This would call, consistent with Geisinger (1998), for the development of separate norms for the translated version and to base the interpretation of the test on these norms.

With regard to practice, the same authors warn that the use of a translated version of a test that has little or no empirical support for its equivalence with the original may result in inaccurate conclusions and diagnosis concerning clients. In light of the dearth of empirically supported translations of tests, the authors recognize that practitioners are often faced with difficult decisions when they do not have appropriately validated instruments available. Therefore, they recommend if a translation that is not empirically supported for use with clients similar to the one being evaluated is employed, that scores are not reported, and that any statements derived from the evaluation are discussed in a descriptive manner similar to information derived from a clinical interview. In sum, the authors recommend a great deal of caution when interpreting results from translated versions that do have some empirical support as well as consideration of equivalence issues in the selection of translated versions of existing measures.

In the following section, we present a review of research with Spanish-speaking Hispanics in various evaluation contexts with measures that include the MMPI-2, MMPI-2 RF, MMPI-A, MCMI-III, MBMD, PAI, and the NEO. This discussion covers issues including norms, adequacy of translations, and significant extra-test correlates.

Overview of Developments in Self-Report Measures with Hispanic Clients

As the most widely applied and researched self-report personality instrument, the MMPI-2 has demonstrated its utility and clinical applicability with Spanish-speaking Hispanics in and outside the United States. This is in spite of the lack of norms for the existing Spanish version that is widely employed in the United States and Puerto Rico. It should be remembered that the existing norms for the MMPI-2 include a small and unrepresentative number of Spanish speakers ($n=73$) from one region of the United States. Historically, research studies comparing Hispanic vs. non-Hispanic White MMPI-2 differences (e.g., Lopez &Weisman, 2004; Whitworth & McBlaine, 1993) have found that while differences in profiles exist, they are considered to be small. Nevertheless, it is important to consider research where the Spanish version of the MMPI-2 has been used with Hispanics outside the United States and in diverse evaluation contexts (i.e., clinical, nonclinical, forensic, and employment) prior to reaching definitive conclusions concerning the need to develop norms for the Spanish version of the instrument. In this section, we review the main issues related to research and applications of the MMPI-2 with Spanish-speaking Hispanics.

In one of the first studies with normal college students, comparisons were made between Puerto Rican and Mexican college students (Cabiya et al., 2000). The Puerto Rican sample consisted of 271 students (149 males and 122 females), the Mexican sample of 2,174 students (929 males and 1,245 females), and the US sample combined all samples of college students with ages that ranged between 18 and 21 years. No significant differences between the two Hispanic samples were found in any of the validity and clinical scales. The sample of Puerto Rican college students was then compared with a US sample of 1,312 college students (515 males and 797 females) reported by Butcher, Graham, Dahlstrom, and Bowman (1990), and again no difference was found between the two samples except for the Mf scale. Both the Puerto Rican (mean *T*-score of 62) and the Mexican females (mean *T*-score of 64) scored much higher than US female students did (mean *T*-score of 53) as can be seen in Figs. 5.1 and 5.2.

The research summarized here suggests two main conclusions. First, that while consideration of cultural value influences in the interpretation of profile differences between Hispanics and non-Hispanic Whites is justified, such justification is likely to be more strongly supported by the existence of Hispanic normative data. Second, while profile similarity between Hispanics and non-Hispanic Whites has been observed in research conducted after the Whitworth & McBlaine, 1993 study (e.g., Cabiya

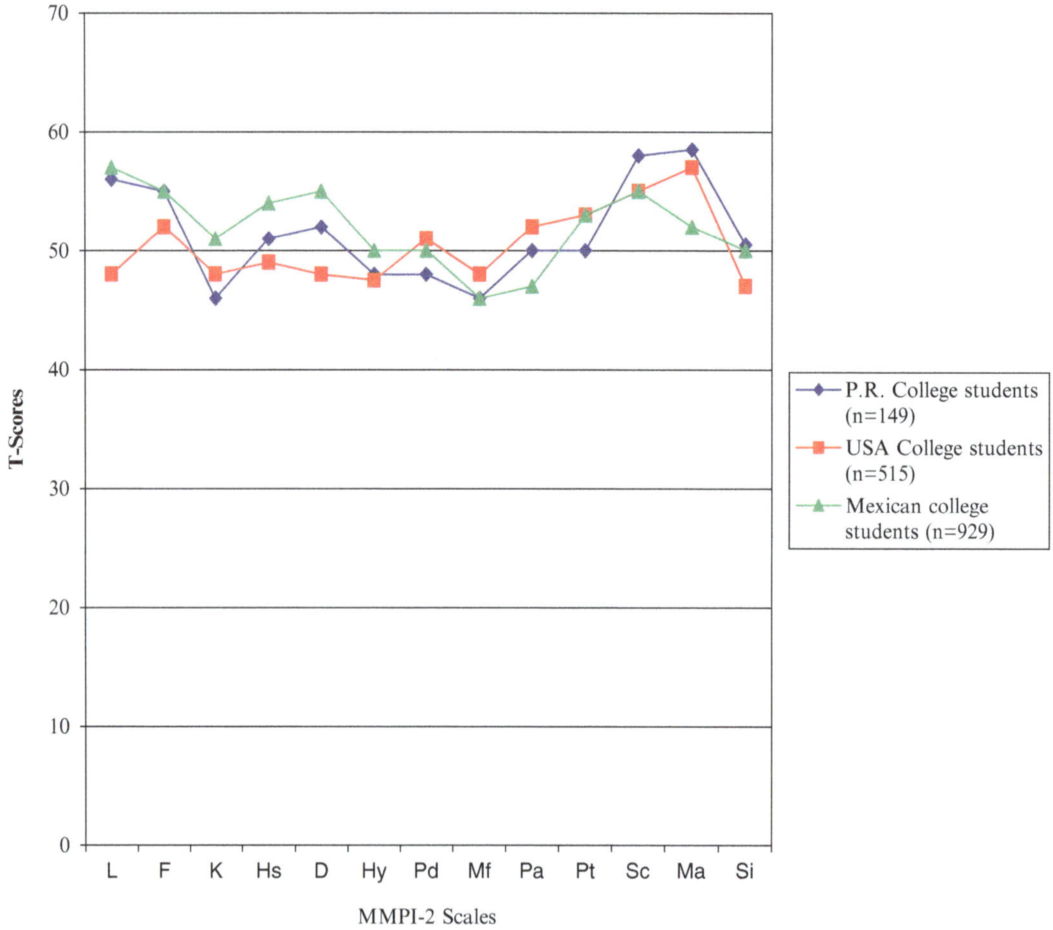

Fig. 5.1 MMPI-2 mean *T*-scores for male college students

et al., 2000), it is important to consider that this similarity has been observed when the English version of the instrument was administered to a sample of nonclinical Hispanics.

Norms-Related Issues

As recommended by Butcher (1996), translations and adaptations of the MMPI-2 should follow a standard protocol and be subject to comparisons with the original version of the instrument following back-translation procedures in order to determine the adequacy of the original version's (American) norms. Butcher cautions that if those norms are not appropriate to the translated version, the development of local norms should be considered. Additionally, while Handel and Ben-Porath (2000) support the general equivalence of existing translations of the instrument to the original, they recognize the existence of considerable variability within same-language cultures in the use of the language, with a notable example being the use of Spanish in several South American countries compared to Caribbean countries.

A significant example of the foregoing is the work of Lucio, Palacios, Duran, and Butcher (1999) and Lucio, Ampudia, Duran, Leon, and Butcher (2001) with the development of language adaptations and norms for the MMPI-2 and MMPI-A in Mexico. Specifically, these investigators examined the

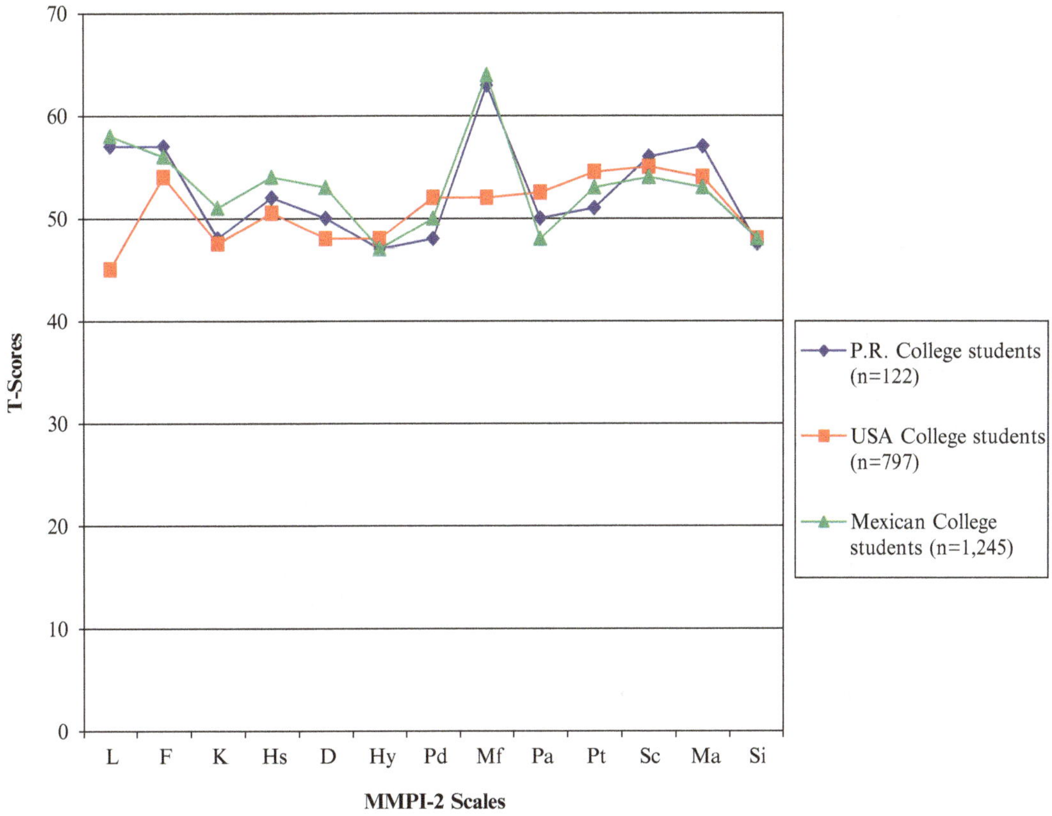

Fig. 5.2 MMPI-2 mean *T*-scores for female college students

adequacy of existing MMPI-2 norms as applied to the MMPI-2 translated for Mexico (Lucio, Reyes-Lagunes, & Scott, 1994). They found that in comparing the Mexican norms to the US norms, there were differences that were accounted for by nationality, some with effect sizes greater than 0.40. While in the end the local norms were similar to the US norms, these authors emphasize that local norms are capable of accounting for cultural factors. For instance, Hispanics may often endorse items related to spirituality and to the power and influence of spirits or saints in their lives, which may elevate scores in scales such as Sc and BIZ. Nevertheless, such item endorsements should be considered in light of culturally sanctioned beliefs and reverence toward the spiritual rather than as manifestations of psychoticism.

In an initial attempt at developing specific norms for Hispanics, the University of Minnesota Press, publisher of the MMPI-2, sponsored a study (Cabiya & Cruz, 2001) directed at establishing norms for Hispanics for the MMPI-2 using the Hispanic version in Spanish developed by García-Peltoniemi and Azán-Chaviano (1993). The sample consisted of 200 normal subjects living in Puerto Rico, including retesting 15 males and 15 females. All subjects were 18 or older and able to read Spanish at the appropriate level (6th grade or higher). The total female sample was 114 women, and the total male sample consisted of 86 men. The mean age of the participants was 40.1 years, and their level of education was 14.67 years of schooling. The sample was stratified using the 2000 Census data for the Puerto Rican population by geographical region, age, and gender. Participants were administered the MMPI-2 in their work settings, community centers, private offices, and homes. All subjects participated voluntarily. The test was administered both in groups and individually. A compensation of 20 dollars was given to each participant. The sites where volunteers were recruited included private businesses, pharmaceutical plants, senior citizen centers, public housing projects, educational institutions, car

Table 5.1 Observed and expected (in parenthesis) number of participants according to the 2000 census for the Puerto Rican population by age and gender, May 2001

Age group	Males	Females	Both genders total
20–24	17 (12)	19 (12)	36 (24)
25–34	29 (20)	30 (22)	59 (42)
35–44	16 (19)	23 (21)	39 (40)
45–54	11 (18)	18 (18)	29 (36)
55–59	3 (7)	10 (7)	13 (14)
60–64	0 (6)	0 (6)	0 (12)
65–74	5 (9)	8 (9)	13 (18)
75–80	2 (5)	2 (5)	4 (10)
80+	3 (2)	4 (2)	7 (4)
Total	86 (98)	114 (102)	200

Table 5.2 Percentages and number of participants (in parenthesis) observed and expected according to the 2000 census for the Puerto Rican population by geographical regiona May, 2001

Participants	Northeast region	Southwest region
Expected	68.32% (137)	31.68% (63)
Observed	64.5% (129)	35.5% (71)

[a]Northeast region consists of the east region, north region, central region, and metropolitan area. Southwest region consists of the south region and west region

dealerships, financing agencies, and other individual volunteers from the community. A chi-square comparison was made with actual and expected number of participants per cell according to the 2000 Census data for the Puerto Rican population. No significant differences were found in relation to group, age, gender, or geographical region using nonparametric analysis. The sociodemographic profile of the sample is presented in Tables 5.1 and 5.2, while Table 5.3 presents the mean *T*-scores for the MMPI-2 validity, clinical, and content scales for males and females. These *T*-scores were obtained using the original *T*-score tables developed for the original US sample. As seen in Table 5.3, the mean *T*-scores of all clinical scales were between half of a standard deviation (five *T*-scores) to a full standard deviation (10 *T*-points) higher than the expected normal *T*-score of 50 obtained with the original US sample except for the clinical scales Hy and Pa. The validity, Mf, and Si scales are not considered clinical scales. Therefore, it appears that applying the US norms to Puerto Ricans may lead to a tendency to overpathologize.

These findings suggest a trend toward higher scores among Puerto Ricans in several scales related to self-presentation, acknowledgment of symptomatology, health concerns, and anxiety. While it is possible to attribute these findings to cultural differences, it is also critical to examine the range of sociodemographic, life event, and cultural identity variables included in the study once the full sample is available for analysis.

MMPI-2 with Puerto Rican Clinical Groups and Prison Inmates

In Puerto Rico, Cabiya and Dávila (1999) conducted a study to compare the MMPI-2 mean *T*-scores of depressed inpatients, depressed outpatients, and matched nonclinical participants. The purpose of this study was to assess the discriminant validity of the MMPI-2 Spanish version with a Puerto Rican clinical group. The sample was obtained randomly from the patients diagnosed with major

Table 5.3 Mean *T*-scores of men and women in validity, basic, and content scales

Scale	Males (*N*=68)	Females (*N*=89)	*F*	Significance
F	64.29 (SD=64.29)	62.19 (SD=62.19)	1.078	.301
L	57.01 (SD=12.56)	61.26 (SD=11.99)	4.633	.033*
K	48.46 (SD=9.85)	49.01 (SD=10.16)	.118	.731
Hs	58.28 (SD=12.70)	59.12 (SD=11.49)	.190	.664
D	56.32 (SD=12.70)	55.58 (SD=10.29)	.178	.673
Hy	52.85 (SD=12.70)	54.16 (SD=12.70)	.499	.481
Pd	56 (SD=12.70)	54.55 (SD=12.70)	.527	.469
Mf	45.82 (SD=12.70)	58.54 (SD=12.70)	76.118	.000*
Pa	52.65 (SD=12.70)	52.42 (SD=12.70)	.016	.899
Pt	56.43 (SD=12.70)	53.79 (SD=12.70)	1.863	.174
Sc	62.28 (SD=12.70)	59.53 (SD=12.70)	1.953	.164
Ma	58.34 (SD=12.70)	56.16 (SD=12.70)	1.434	.233
Si	51.43 (SD=9.58)	51.29 (SD=9.18)	.008	.929
ANX	57.49 (SD=8.71)	54.97 (SD=10.06)	2.713	.102
FRS	57.72 (SD=12.49)	58.73 (SD=11.84)	.267	.606
OBS	53.10 (SD=10.95)	50.88 (SD=8.42)	2.074	.152
DEP	55.82 (SD=9.69)	53.56 (SD=9.80)	2.073	.152
HEA	59.35 (SD=11.48)	60.87 (SD=10.69)	.723	.396
BIZ	63.10 (SD=11.48)	59.80 (SD=10.28)	3.599	.060
ANG	58.76 (SD=11.81)	51.15 (SD=10.24)	1.158	.284
CYN	57.37 (SD=10.66)	56.73 (SD=9.83)	.151	.698
ASP	56.18 (SD=11.52)	53.97 (SD=8.39)	1.934	.166
TPA	49.97 (SD=8.86)	57.63 (SD=9.39)	.841	.361
LSE	52.93 (SD=11.39)	49.42 (SD=9.64)	4.366	.038*
SOD	49.88 (SD=10.72)	51.12 (SD=9.61)	.582	.447
FAM	55.93 (SD=9.23)	52.56 (SD=11.48)	3.905	.050*
WRK	54.41 (SD=11.25)	50.20 (SD=9.45)	6.484	.012*
TRT	57.81 (SD=11.69)	53.09 (SD=10.04)	7.386	.007*

*$p<.05$

depression, according to DSM-IV criteria for major depressive episode, in two outpatient mental health clinics and one inpatient psychiatric hospital. The final number of selected depressed inpatients was 40, depressed outpatients 35, and other psychiatric patients 35. The nonclinical sample consisted of 141 undergraduate and graduate students.

One-way analyses were performed with the mean *T*-scores for the validity, clinical, and content scales for the male and female participants. Significant differences were obtained in all scales except scales L, K, Ma, and ANG in males and scales L, Mf, ASP, and TPA in females at a .003 level of significance. Moreover, depressed outpatients scored higher than all the other groups in all scales except in scales K, Mf, and Ma in both males and females. Psychotic inpatients scored higher than the normal sample except in scales K, Mf, and ASP in both males and females. Figures 5.3, 5.4, 5.5, and 5.6 present a summary of the profiles.

In 2000, Peña, Cabiya, and Echevarria conducted a study to assess the mean MMPI-2 *T*-scores in the clinical scales of a representative sample of the total inmate population of Puerto Rico in order to develop norms for the prison inmate community. The authors were also interested in assessing the relationship between the MMPI-2 scales and several variables including history of mental health treatment, suicidal attempts, number of convictions, and drug and alcohol abuse. Three-hundred eighty-four inmates randomly from the total penal population of Puerto Rico were administered the MMPI-2 and the BARSIT (Olmo, 1958). Of this total, 361 were males and 23 were females, reflecting the

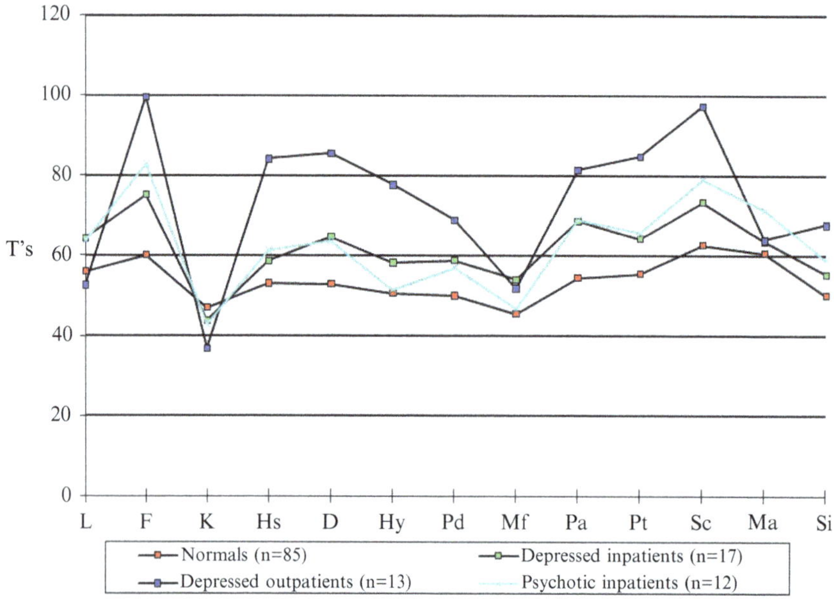

Fig. 5.3 Mean *T*-scores of males in the MMPI-2 basic scales

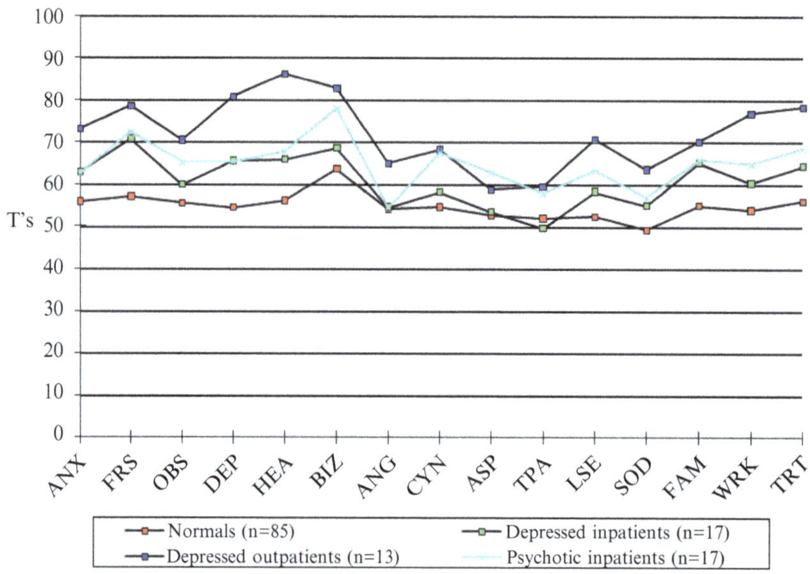

Fig. 5.4 Mean *T*-scores of males in the MMPI-2 content scales

distribution by sex of the inmate population. Of the total of participants, 321 males and 18 females had valid MMPI-2 profiles (*T*-scores below 90 in the F and VRIN scales) and were included in the analysis. Normative data for this population were subsequently developed. The mean *T*-score profile for the clinical scales of Puerto Rican inmates appears similar to that of the continental US inmates (Megargee, 1994).

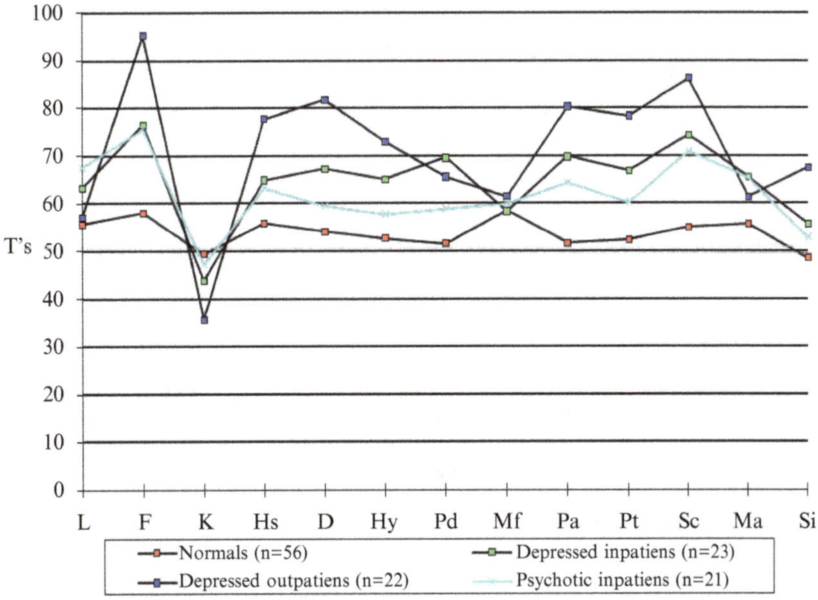

Fig. 5.5 Mean *T*-scores of females in the MMPI-2 basic scales

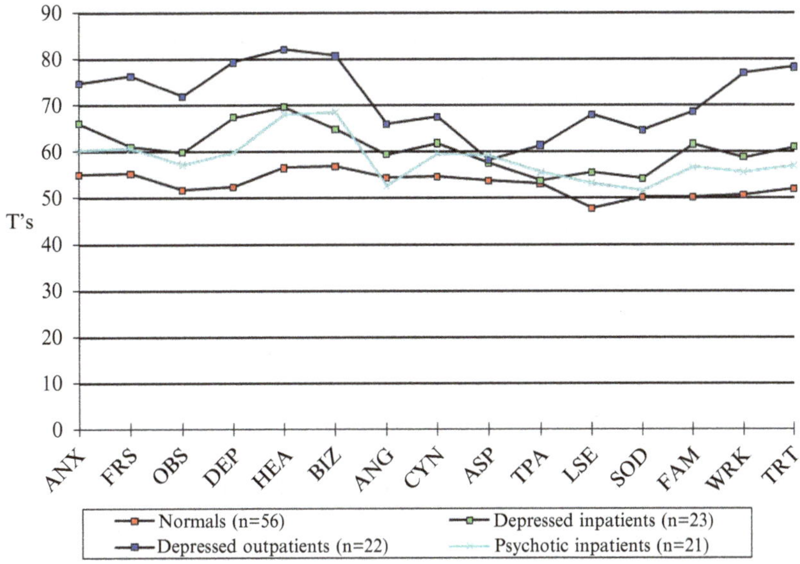

Fig. 5.6 Mean *T*-scores of females in the MMPI-2 content scales

Figures 5.7 and 5.8 present the mean *T*-scores of the present study's inmates and Megargee's (1994) reported mean *T*-scores for a sample of state male and female inmates in the continental United States. As can be seen in these figures, the main differences between the two samples appear to be in scales F, Pd, and Sc. Scales F and Sc were higher in the sample of Puerto Rican male inmates, while the state inmates scored higher in scale Pd. As can be seen in Fig. 5.8, the Puerto Rican female inmates also scored very similarly to state inmates with the main differences being in

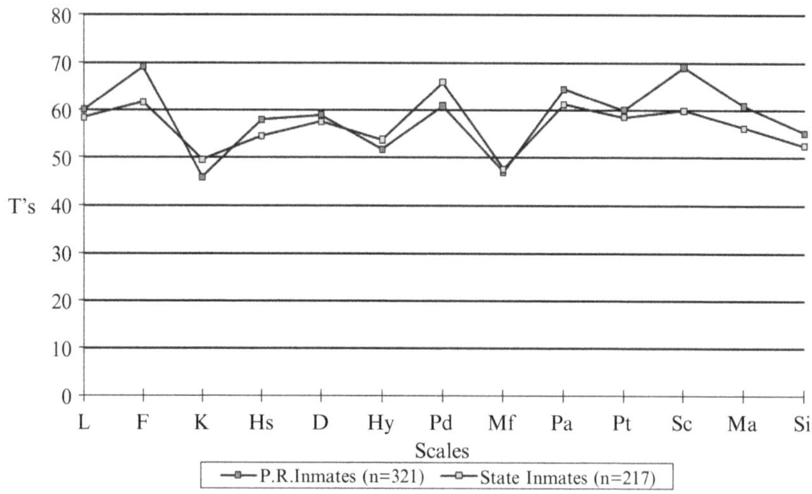

Fig. 5.7 Mean *T*-scores of male PR and state inmates

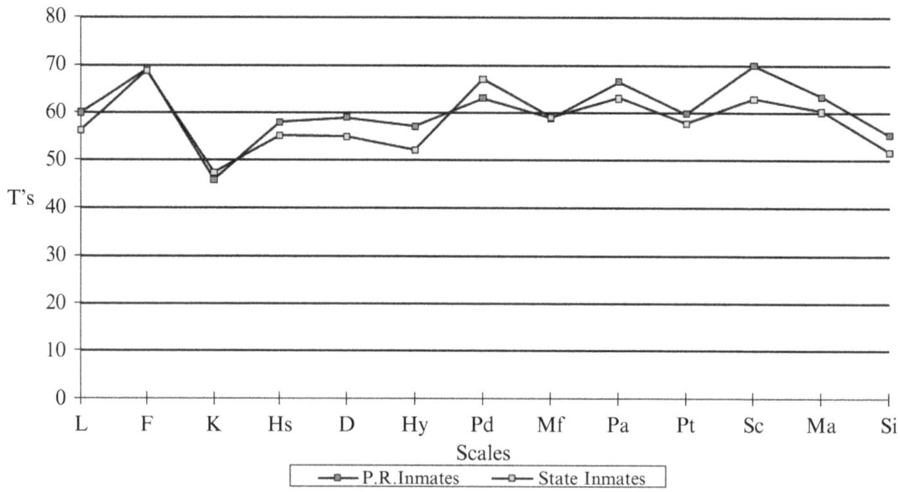

Fig. 5.8 Mean *T*-scores of female PR and state inmates

scales Hy, Pd, and Sc, where the former obtained higher scores. Finally, the content scales for both male and female inmates appear in Fig. 5.9, indicating considerable similarity in the profile pattern for both sexes.

Studies with Preemployment Candidates and Domestic Aggressors

In Puerto Rico, recently published studies using the MMPI-2 have examined the validity of MMPI-2 profiles in employment settings (e.g., Rosario-Hernández, Rovira, Álvarez, & Rodríguez, 2007; Zapata-Sola, Kreuch, Landers, Hoyt, & Butcher, 2009). Other studies have explored the profiles and emotional attachment characteristics of domestic aggressors (Figueroa, 2009). Rosario-Hernandez et al. compared candidates for employment as marshals for the Puerto Rico judiciary with experimental groups who were instructed to fake good, fake bad, and to respond honestly consistent with standard administration instructions. They found differences in most validity scales between the group

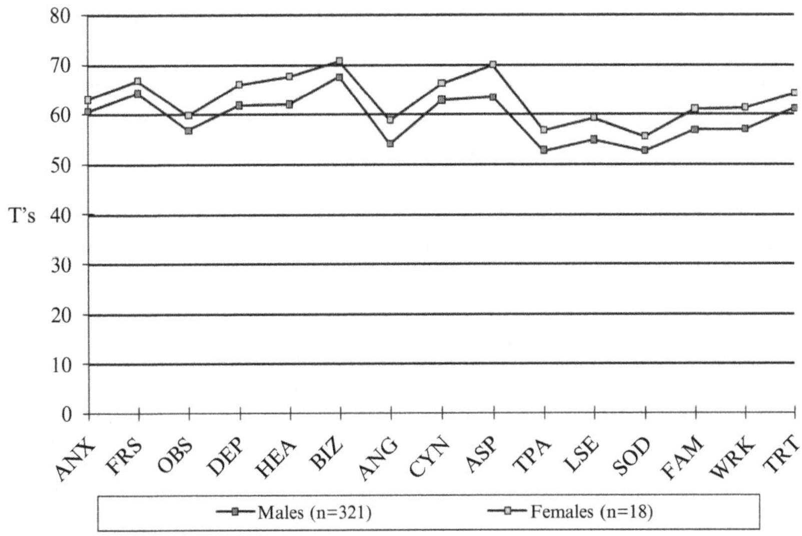

Fig. 5.9 Mean *T*-scores of male inmates and female inmates in the MMPI-2 content scales

instructed to respond honestly and the employment candidates, while there were no differences between the employment candidates and the fake good group. These findings suggest that the validity of preemployment evaluations of a Hispanic group with the MMPI-2 might be influenced by a motivation to simulate good psychological health. In another study, Zapata-Sola et al. compared Puerto Rican and American candidates for employment in sensitive positions with public power utilities. Both samples were comparable in size. No significant differences were found between both groups in their average clinical and content scales, and, in fact, the scores for both groups were similar to the norm. A noteworthy difference between both samples, however, was in the raw scores for the L scale, where the Puerto Rican sample scored higher (7.55) than their American counterparts (5.88). The findings of this study led Zapata-Sola et al. to conclude that the MMPI-2 seems not to pathologize the Puerto Rican group at least in this particular evaluation context.

In the area of domestic violence, Figueroa (2009) compared male aggressors and matched non-aggressors along MMPI-2 scales and emotional attachment characteristics. The domestic aggressors obtained clinically significant and higher scores than the non-aggressors on validity scales VRIN, F, Fb, and Fp, consistent with their reported background of psychosocial difficulties. Interestingly, on indices of positive self-presentation, non-aggressors obtained higher scores on L, K, and S. With the exception of L, which indicates that the non-aggressors sought to present themselves as unrealistically virtuous, for both groups the scores on these indices are within the normal range indicating adequate levels of openness to the evaluation.

As for the clinical scales, the domestic aggressors obtained significantly higher scores on indices of significant psychopathology such as Pd, Pa, Pt, Sc, and Ma. While their scores were at the high average level and below the clinically significant score of $T=65$, the scores suggest tendencies toward difficulties in behavioral and cognitive regulation compared to the non-aggressor counterparts. Additional significant differences in content scales between these groups lend support to the difficulties that domestic aggressors face in their behavioral, cognitive, and interpersonal functioning relative to the non-aggressors. Content scales ANX, OBS, DEP, TPA, SOD, FAM, and WRK were significantly higher for the aggressors but still within the high average range. The restructured clinical scales of aggressors also reveal difficulties related to demoralization, antisocial behavior, dysfunctional emotions, and hypomanic activation. Finally, among the supplementary scales, the domestic aggressors obtained low scores on indices of ego strength and social responsibility.

The findings also suggest that MMPI-2 scales associated with anxiety, depression, specific fears, and unusual and ruminative thinking are significantly correlated with an anxious attachment style (Bartholomew, 1990), while the strongest MMPI-2 correlation with an avoidant attachment style was observed with a scale associated with social discomfort. Generally speaking, these findings indicate that with the exception of the L scores for the non-aggressors, these participants exhibited adequate levels of openness to the evaluation. MMPI-2 findings in this study suggest that the test was sensitive to differences in indices of affective, cognitive, and behavioral functioning between the groups, thus suggesting potential avenues for intervention with domestic aggressors.

Initial Findings with the Restructured Clinical Scales (RC Scales)

More recent MMPI-2 research with Hispanic has begun to explore RC scale characteristics with this group. For instance, Velasquez and Bradley (2008) found that Hispanic/Latino college students obtained higher RC scale scores than their Anglo-Saxon counterparts. Additionally, they found that level of acculturation affected the scores on scales RCd, RC3, and RC7. These scales were significantly higher among those who reported a stronger identification with traditional Hispanic culture than among those with lower levels of Hispanic identification. These findings are suggestive as to the potential impact of migration and acculturative pressures on the emotional functioning of Hispanics and especially those who strongly adhere to their culture of origin or are recent immigrants. The findings suggest that these individuals may experience higher levels of demoralization, cynicism, and negative emotions compared to those with higher levels of acculturation. Clearly, additional study with additional and more diverse Hispanic groups is warranted in order to more conclusively establish the relationship between level of acculturation and RC scales.

In Puerto Rico et al. (under review) examined the MMPI-2 scales of employment candidates, police officers, domestic aggressors, and non-aggressors with special attention to the RC scales. Consistent with previous findings where Hispanics' L scale scores have been found to be higher than those of Anglo-Saxons (e.g., Hall, Bansal, & Lopez, 1999), mean L scale scores for the four groups compared in the study fluctuated between $T=62$ and $T=65$. According to Sellbom, Fischler, and Ben-Porath (2007), these findings could be expected among those being evaluated for employment.

The findings also indicate that the MMPI-2 validity, clinical, and RC scales detected significant differences between these groups, where consistently the domestic aggressors obtained the higher scores on most indices of affective, cognitive, and behavioral difficulties. As expected of the RC scales, given their greater distinctiveness, more significant differences were observed among the groups in their RC scale scores than among the clinical scales. Additionally, congruence between the clinical and RC scales as well as clinical and RC scales intercorrelations was explored. The findings with these Puerto Rican groups are consistent with those of, e.g., Osberg, Haseley, & Kamas, 2008; Tellegen et al., 2003; Wallace & Liljequist, 2005 and indicate that when clinical scales are compared to their RC scale counterparts, the clinical scale often reflects a higher score due to its comparatively higher item heterogeneity than the RC scale.

At the same time, clinical and RC scales intercorrelations as well as correlations between clinical and RC scales in this study reflected a trend toward higher intercorrelations among clinical scales compared to the intercorrelations among RC scales. Finally, the correlations between the clinical scales and RC scales for these samples were consistent with correlations reported in the above-referenced studies. These findings suggest that the RC scales of the MMPI-2 behave similarly with these samples as with non-Hispanic samples, yet additional research with larger samples of Hispanics is needed in order to confirm the trends observed here.

Recent norms-development efforts for the Spanish version of the MMPI-2 include a study currently in progress and led by the first author of this chapter. This study, supported by the University of Minnesota

Table 5.4 Non-gendered mean raw score comparisons between Puerto Rican (PR) and American normative (US) samples

Scale	PR mean	US mean	*t*	Cohen´s d
VR	8	5	13.6	.72
F	7	4	9.7	.52
Fp	3	1	12.3	.66
L	6	4	13.5	.72
Hs	9	5	12.7	.67
D	22	19	10.9	.59
Sc	16	10	10.7	.59
Ma	19	17	9.2	.50
RCd	5	3	9.2	.50
RC1	7	3	14.7	.80
RC3	8	6	13.4	.72
RC6	2	1	10.1	.54
RC8	4	2	12	.67

Press, involves a nonclinical sample of Puerto Rican adults ($n=436$). At the time of this writing, available findings indicate significant differences in non-gendered, non-K corrected raw scores between Puerto Rican adults and the MMPI-2 normative sample in validity, clinical, and RC scales VRIN, F, Fp, L, Hs, D, Sc, Ma, RCd, RC1, RC3, RC6, and RC8. Table 5.4 includes the raw score comparisons for both groups indicating that the raw scores tend to be higher for Puerto Ricans. Additional preliminary analyses suggest that level of Puerto Rican cultural identification has an impact on scales D, Sc, Ma, Si, RC2, RC3, and RC9. It was also observed that having experienced negative life events in the previous year has statistically significant yet small effects on most of the clinical and restructured scales.

MMPI-A

Historically, psychological tests have been employed with populations that differ considerably from the samples with which they were developed. The use of these tests to assess the emotional functioning of Hispanics is a prominent example of this and has also been the subject of numerous warnings and calls for caution about their applicability and interpretation due to questions concerning issues such as the adequacy of translations, norms, and construct equivalence (e.g., Dana, 1995; Fabrega, 1990; Malgady & Rogler, 1988; Velasquez, 1995). In the case of the adolescent version of the MMPI, the MMPI-A (Butcher et al. 1992), its development involved only the English version of the inventory, which led to the underrepresentation of Hispanic adolescents (Archer, 1992). This was subsequently addressed with the development of the Spanish-language version of the MMPI-A for use with Hispanic adolescents (Butcher, Graham, Williams, & Kaemmer, 1994).

Following publication of the MMPI-A, Garcia-Peltoniemi, Azan-Chaviano, & Lucio (1994); Lucio (1995) conducted a translation and standardization project of the MMPI-A in Mexico and found that with a few exceptions, the basic clinical scale scores of the Mexican adolescents were similar to those of the US normative sample. For both, Mexican boys and girls, L scale scores were slightly higher than for the American adolescents. Subsequently, and in response to the need for normative data that could adequately describe psychological symptomatology among Hispanic adolescents, Butcher et al. (1998) published a normative supplement for the Hispanic version of the MMPI-A. In order to ensure a representative normative sample, they included Spanish-speaking adolescents from Puerto Rico, Cuban-origin adolescents from Florida, Mexican-Americans from Los Angeles, and Mexicans from Mexico City. The majority of the scores from these groups were found to be within one standard deviation of the mean of the standard MMPI-A norms, suggesting that the standard MMPI-A norms are adequate for use with Hispanic adolescents.

Cabiya et al. (2001) evaluated the adequacy of the Spanish translation of the MMPI-A. In addition, given the importance of the MMPI-A as a diagnostic instrument, it was extremely important to obtain data concerning its capability to differentiate clinical groups from nonclinical groups. The study was conducted in two phases. The first phase was directed at assessing the psychometric properties of the Spanish translation. The second phase was directed at assessing how well the Spanish translation differentiated two clinical groups from a nonclinical sample. The data obtained with the nonclinical sample were included as part of the data used in the development of the Hispanic norms developed by Butcher et al. (1998).

The total sample of adolescents who participated in the first phase consisted of 80 students (40 males and 40 females) between the ages of 14 and 18 years enrolled in two private schools. The sample included 50 students rated as fully bilingual by their homeroom teachers using a rating scale developed by the authors. This sample of students was part of a larger sample of 247 students that will be described in the discussion of the second phase.

All the participants were administered the Spanish translation of the MMPI-A. The 50 bilingual students were administered the MMPI-A in both English and Spanish, and the order of administration of the two versions was counterbalanced. A second set of 30 randomly selected students from a sample of 247 normal students took the MMPI-A in Spanish a second time (except for one who dropped out) to determine the effect of the double administration. There was a 2-week interval between each testing for both groups.

The total sample of the second phase consisted of 247 students (122 males and 127 females) between the ages of 14 and 18 years enrolled in two private (96 students) and three public schools (151 students) in Puerto Rico. The first clinical sample used in the second phase consisted of 52 adolescents who were treated in several outpatient mental health clinics in Puerto Rico, 27 males and 25 females. A psychiatrist following DSM-IV criteria for either major depression or adjustment disorder with depressed mood diagnosed all adolescents. The second clinical sample of adolescents used in the second phase consisted of 132 juvenile delinquents who were recruited from referrals to the diagnostic clinic of the Juvenile Court of the Commonwealth of Puerto Rico ($n=87$) and from a maximum-security juvenile facility of the Administration of Juvenile Institutions of the Commonwealth of Puerto Rico ($n=45$).

In the first phase, a multivariate analysis of variance was performed with the raw scores obtained from the bilingual students in the validity and clinical scales of the English and the Spanish versions of the MMPI-A. The analysis did not reveal significant differences, $F(13,36)=.72, p\geq.05$, in the overall validity and clinical scales between the English and Spanish versions. Nor were significant overall differences found, $F(13,36)=.55$, $p\geq.05$, between males and females. Figure 5.10 presents a summary of the mean T-scores for males and females with both versions of the MMPI-A using the Hispanic norms. As shown in Fig. 5.10, all the mean T-scores hover around a T-score of 50 which suggests that the Hispanic norms are applicable to Puerto Rican adolescents.

Additionally, no significant differences were obtained in test-retest comparisons. The repeated administration of the Spanish and English versions of the MMPI-A demonstrated correspondence between the raw scores obtained with both versions. The test-retest reliability coefficients were found to be higher than .60 with the exception of the Hy scale.

In the second phase, a multivariate analysis was performed to assess if any significant differences existed among the groups that were administered the translated Spanish versions twice. No significant differences, $F(13,17)=.40, p\geq.05$, were found on an overall level between the first and second administrations in Spanish of the test. Another two sets of multivariate analysis of variance were performed with the mean raw scores obtained with the (nonclinical) student, patient, and juvenile delinquent samples in the validity, clinical, and content scales. These analyses indicated significant differences between the students and patients, $F(33,274)=4.985$, $p\leq.0001$, in scale D and between students and juvenile delinquents, $F(36,219)=4.458$, in scales Pd and Pa. The profiles of the mean T-scores, using

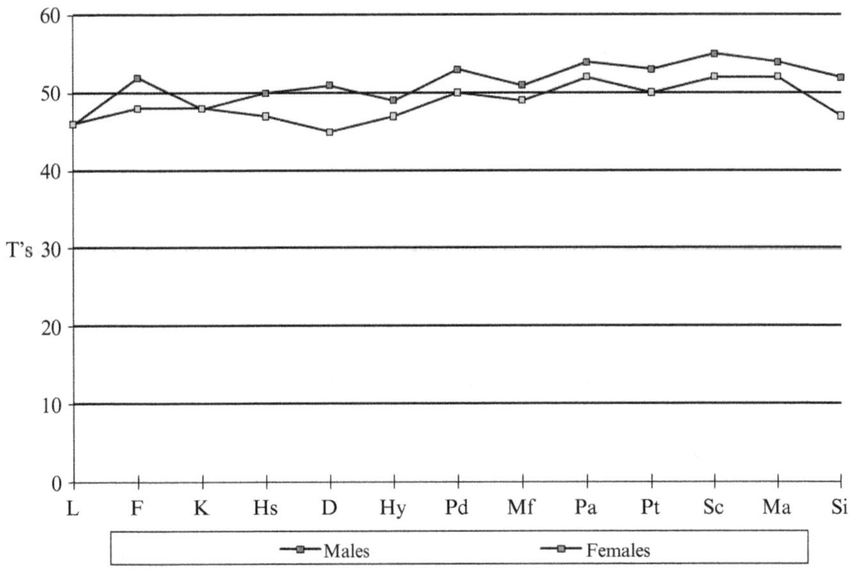

Fig. 5.10 Mean *T*-scores of males and females for the total sample in the MMPI-A basic scales

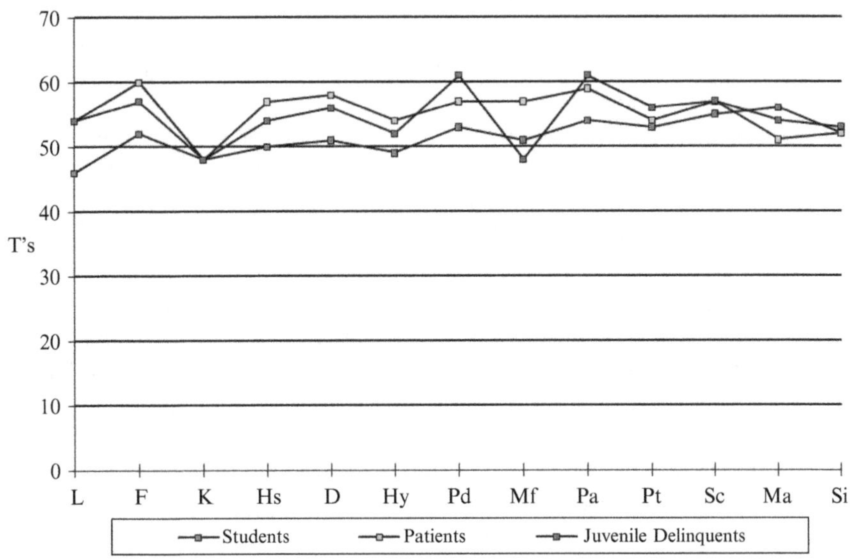

Fig. 5.11 Mean *T*-scores of students, patients and juvenile delinquents in the MMPI-A basic scales

the Hispanic norms, of the students, patients, and juvenile delinquents in the clinical scales are presented in Fig. 5.11.

All the patients in the present study were diagnosed with depressed mood. It was found that scales D and A-dep were able to differentiate the two groups, suggesting that these scales are valid tools in the assessment of depressed mood in adolescent patients.

In addition, the comparisons between the students and juvenile delinquents suggest that the Pd and Pa scales differentiated these two groups. These results are consistent with previous MMPI research with juvenile delinquents (Hathaway & Monachesi, 1963; Peña, Megargee & Brody, 1996). However, past research did find that the Sc and Ma scales also differentiated juvenile delinquents from students. In the present study, these scales did not differentiate at the .001 level.

MCMI-III

The MCMI-III (Millon, 1994; Millon, Millon, Davis, & Grossman, 2006), in contrast to the Minnesota Inventories, was developed on a rather comprehensive and complex theoretical foundation of personality development as articulated by Millon (1969) in order to describe personality and clinical pathology. The Millon Inventories rely on the use of base rates, which for purposes of test interpretation indicate how similar an individual is to those in the population who have been judged by clinicians to have a given personality characteristic or syndrome. This is different from the *T*-scores employed by the Minnesota inventories. The normative group for the inventory consisted of 998 psychiatric patients. The MCMI-III has been translated to Spanish but there are no Hispanic norms available to date. It should be noted that while the standard norms for the MCMI-III are employed with Hispanics, White participants constituted 83% of the men and 90% of the women in the sample. Hispanics only make up 1.6% of the sample for men and 0.9% for women (Millon, 1997).

Several subscales have been derived from the MMPI-2 constructed for the assessment of Axis II disorders. Morey and Waugh (1985) developed the Morey personality disorder scales (MPD), derived from the MMPI. They were later revised and standardized by Morey (1992), with only minor changes reported. The MPD consists of two basic scales which include the nonoverlapping items, and the other includes the overlapping items. These scales are composed of 11 subscales that correspond to the Axis II classifications of the DSM-IV: paranoia (PAR), schizoid (SZD), borderline (BDL), compulsive (CPS), passive-aggressive (PAG), narcissist (NAR), antisocial (ANT), histrionic (HST), schizotypal (STY), dependent (DEP), and avoidant (AVD).

The MPD has been correlated with the MCMI-II. In 1991, McCann conducted a concurrent validity study using the MPD and the MCMI-II. He correlated the 11 MPD scales with its corresponding MCMI-II personality disorder scales. McCann's findings showed significant correlations among 9 of the 11 scales, excluding the CPS and the ANT scales. These low correlations were justified due to the fact that both scales were constructed based on Millon's theory of personality and do not correspond to the diagnostic criteria of the DSM on which the MPD was based (McCann, 1989, 1991).

Fournier and Cabiya (1999) conducted a study correlating the Morey personality disorder scales (MPD), developed by Morey and Waugh (1985), with the MCMI-III, in order to explore the applicability of these instruments, in their Spanish versions, for the assessment of personality disorders with the Puerto Rican population. A sample was obtained of 130 participants between ages 18 and 51 years. Mean age was 34.67 and SD = 10.05. The subjects were divided into three independent groups: inpatients (57), outpatients (31), and nonclinical (42). All inpatients were selected from the State Psychiatric Hospital in the San Juan metropolitan area. Outpatients were selected from a psychiatric private practice also from the San Juan metropolitan area, and the nonclinical group was composed of graduate clinical psychology students and their relatives and friends. The sample was selected upon availability. Ninety-six were females and thirty four were males. A total of 35 were married and 46 were single. Seventy-three were employed and forty were unemployed. Mean level of education was 14.89 years (SD = 2.56). All participants were required a 12th grade minimum level of education, evidence of no neurological condition, and to be stable and/or free of any psychotic episode. All participants were either hospitalized for the first time or receiving psychiatric outpatient treatment for the first time. All clinical samples were referred for ruling out Axis II disorders. All MMPI-2 profiles with F scales above *T*-scores of 120 and VRIN and TRIN above 80 were eliminated. Both the overlapping and nonoverlapping scales were correlated independently with the 11 MCMI-III corresponding personality disorder scales. All raw scores were correlated using Pearson coefficient. Correlations greater than .23 were significant at the .01 level, and correlations greater than .17 were significant at the .05 level.

Significant correlation coefficients were obtained for 10 of the 11 subscales for both the overlapping and nonoverlapping scales. The only subscale that obtained a significantly low score was the CPS scale.

A descriptive analysis was conducted to observe any differences between the three independent groups by gender among the personality scales. An ANOVA was conducted to identify any differences between gender and the 11 personality disorders scales of each instrument. No significant differences were found. Results suggest a moderately high correlation among all the personality disorder scales except for the CPS scale. This last finding may be explained by the differences in theory constructs of both instruments. Previous studies using the MCMI obtained low correlations for both the ANT and CPS scales (e.g., McCann, 1989).

When the second version of the MCMI was completed, Millon revised his ANT scale to conform more adequately to the DSM-III-R criterion. This resulted in a higher and significant correlation between the ANT scales among instruments, as reported by McCann in 1991, when he replicated his original study using the revised versions of the MPD and the MCMI-II. We also found a significant correlation between the ANT scales among instruments.

Results generally suggest that the Spanish versions of the MPD and the MCMI-III may be used for the assessment and analysis of Axis II disorders. The CPS scale, however, should be interpreted with caution due to the significant differences of this personality construct among tests. The nonoverlapping scales obtained higher correlation indexes than that of the overlapping scales, which emphasizes the need of more specialized items for the description of personality.

As discussed above, the equivalence and adequacy of translated tests is of paramount importance when they are to be employed with individuals whose language and culture differ from that of the test development group. According to Muñoz and Choca (2009), existing research indicates that the factor structure of the MCMI-III is similar for Caucasians and African Americans even though African Americans have obtained higher scores on several scales when controlling for key sociodemographic variables such as gender and level of education. In order to explore whether this inventory is appropriate for use with Hispanics, the authors conducted a factor analytic study by comparing the valid records of 323 Hispanic psychiatric patients who were randomly matched to a White non-Hispanic person of similar age and gender. For both groups, four main factors emerged, showing a similar factor structure with only minor differences. According to Munoz and Choca, their finding is consistent with previous research they cite (Dyce, O'Conner, Parkins, & Janzen, 1997), suggesting that at the structural level, the MCMI-III presents no bias. The authors, nonetheless, caution that while there were not many scale-level differences between the groups, they should be documented and understood.

Additional research by Castañeda, Kjenslie, and Stiel (2006) and by Kjenslie, Castañeda, and Velasquez (2006) has explored MCMI-III characteristics of Hispanic/Latino individuals in outpatient psychiatric settings. Castañeda and colleagues examined the MCMI-III protocols of 70 Latino outpatients who met diagnostic criteria for dysthymic disorder, major depressive disorder, bipolar disorder, and schizophrenia. The authors found significant statistical differences between the four diagnostic groups on some of the MCMI-III scales. For example, persons with schizophrenia were found to obtain higher scores on the thought disorder and delusional disorder scales, while persons with major depressive disorder scored higher on the depressive and major depression scales. This finding indicates that the MCMI-III is capable of detecting differences among Latinos diagnosed with different conditions. Additionally, a tendency toward favorable self-presentation was observed as reflected by elevations in the desirability and histrionic scales. Appropriately, the authors warn that these tendencies may lead to attenuation of scale scores.

For their part, Kjenslie and colleagues compared MCMI-III profiles of Hispanic ($n = 100$) and Euro-American ($n = 50$) outpatients, most of whom met diagnostic criteria for dysthymic disorder (60%), major depressive disorder (20%), bipolar disorder (10%), and schizophrenia (10%) as well as coexisting Axis II personality disorders (50%). Among the findings, the authors observed significant differences by ethnicity on the masochistic and dependence scales, where the Euro-Americans had higher scores than their Hispanic counterparts. Also, when Hispanics were compared by linguistic version of the MCMI-III (i.e., English vs. Spanish), Spanish speakers obtained higher MCMI-III scores on the disclosure, desirability, depressive, anxiety disorder, and major depressive scales than English speakers. Finally, it was found that the disclosure and social desirability scales can be useful in evaluating the approach or demeanor taken by Hispanic patients during assessment. This finding is similar to research on the MMPI-2 that has documented that Hispanics seek to present themselves in a positive light. These findings suggest that MCMI-III can be applied in a culturally and linguistically competent manner to Hispanics as long as evaluators are aware of the client's language proficiency and preferences for purposes of assessment.

In a study that examined the comparability of the English and Spanish translations of the MMPI-2 and MCMI-III with bilingual Hispanic college students, Rossi (2003) found that there was high comparability between the English and Spanish translated versions of the MMPI-2 and MCMI-III as reflected by correlation coefficients between .50 and .95 and no major mean scale score differences. The correlations between the MMPI-2 and MCMI-III scales were moderately similar (.50–.80) to those reported by Millon (1997). There were lower rather than similar correlations on the Spanish versions of the MMPI-2 and MCMI-III (Spanish versions) when compared to those reported by Millon. The overall conclusion of the study is that comparability was found between the English and Spanish translations of the MMPI-2 and MCMI-III among bilingual college students.

Other studies of the MCMI-III that include Hispanic samples have looked at the personality and clinical syndrome characteristics of combat veterans (Ghafoori & Hierholzer, 2010), Mexican-American male batterers (Sugihara & Warner, 1999), and Puerto Rican men with histories of aggressive behavior (Santiago, 2010). In looking at the relationship between race, ethnicity, and personality characteristics among combat-exposed veterans, Ghafoori and Hierholzer used the MCMI-III along with other measures of PTSD and combat exposure and hypothesized that race and ethnicity might help explain differences in the perception and experience of distressing or traumatic experiences, which in turn may lead to the development of different forms of clinical and personality manifestations. Following examination of 96 records obtained from the Department of Veterans Affairs Central California Health Care System (VACCHCS), the authors observed that the Hispanic veterans were four times more likely to have a cluster A personality disorder, based on the American Psychiatric Association (1994) categorization of personality disorders, compared to non-Hispanic veterans. Cluster A disorders are those characterized by odd or eccentric behavior and include paranoid, schizoid, and schizotypal disorders. Indeed, after adjusting for age, education, income, PTSD symptom level, and level of combat exposure, Hispanic veterans were nearly five times as likely to have a cluster A disorder. The authors acknowledge that an assessment of acculturation level or of subjective experiences of discrimination were not included in this analysis, and they indicate that future research should take those variables into consideration in order to optimize treatment options for these individuals.

The MCMI-III has also been used to explore the personality characteristics and their relationship with behavior and coping among Hispanic men with backgrounds of aggressive behavior. For instance, Sugihara and Warner (1999) examined the personality characteristics of 60 Mexican-American male batterers in the court system in South Texas who had completed the MCMI-III. Their scores were compared with the scores of a community sample of 45 Mexican-American individuals similar in age. The batterers obtained higher scores than the non-batterers on the avoidant and passive-aggressive scales, while non-batterers frequently scored higher on the histrionic scale. The batterers scored significantly higher on 18 out of 24 MCMI-III scales, while non-batterers scored significantly higher on 2 scales. These findings suggest that the MCMI-III is capable of detecting differences in personality characteristics of individuals within the same ethnic group with different behavioral adjustment profiles.

More recently, Santiago (2010) examined the relationship between personality characteristics and coping styles among Puerto Rican men with histories of interpersonally aggressive behavior. A total of 59 men who had been court-referred to a violence prevention program participated in the study where they voluntarily completed a sociodemographic data sheet, the Spanish version of the MCMI-III, and the coping inventory (Carver & Scheier, 1989). Several significant correlations were observed between coping styles and personality. For instance, coping styles characterized by religious/spiritual inclinations were negatively correlated with antisocial personality features; coping characterized by behavioral inhibition was related to avoidant and depressive personality styles, major depression, and PTSD; a cognitively disconnected manner of coping was also associated with avoidant and schizotypal features; planning and problem solving were associated with compulsive tendencies and negatively associated with dependent, antisocial, negativistic, and depressive tendencies; finally, venting and focusing on emotions are associated with borderline, avoidant, and depressive features as well as with major depression. While these findings were obtained with a relatively small sample, they provide potentially valuable information particularly as to the kinds of intervention strategies that might be most effective according to personality characteristics. Clearly, interventions that may emphasize behaviors contrary to relatively stable personality and coping styles may not be effective and may require modification or change if they are to be effective.

MBMD

In an effort to assist medical clinical personnel develop a broad psychological understanding of their patients and consequently contribute to the development of effective treatment and management plans, the Millon Behavioral Health Inventory (MBHI) (Millon, Green, & Meagher, 1979, 1982) and subsequently the Millon Behavioral Medicine Diagnostic (MBMD) (Millon, Antoni, Millon, Minor, & Grossman, 2001) were developed. In this section, only the MBMD will be discussed as it is considered a significant development from its predecessor, the MBHI. In addition to having been developed exclusively with a clinical medical population, which makes it more sensitive to the detection of psychological and behavioral concerns of medical patients compared to the MBHI, the MBMD was developed for screening, treatment planning, and monitoring of patients facing medical and surgical conditions (Millon et al., 2001). A Spanish translation of the MBMD is available.

The MBMD developmental sample consisted of 720 medical patients with various conditions including cancer, cardiovascular disease, diabetes, HIV, pain, and neurological conditions. The development sample was 19% Hispanic ($n=135$), 16% African American, and 61% White, with the rest being represented by other groups. The authors attribute the relatively high proportions of Hispanics and African Americans in the developmental sample to the fact that much of their normative data were collected at university medical centers and public clinics, rather than at private practices. Ironically, these proportions might be more realistic of the population today.

To our knowledge, there are no published studies using the Spanish version of the MBMD where large Hispanic samples are explored or where the psychometric properties of the translated version are evaluated. However, a study to explore the coping and psychological profile of Puerto Rican patients with hypertension was conducted using the Spanish translation of the MBMD (Magraner, 2011). The sample in this study involved 80 Puerto Rican adults aged 21–75 diagnosed with hypertension and under the care of a primary care physician. Individuals with medical conditions including diabetes, cancer, history of cardiovascular surgery, or neurological conditions were excluded from the study.

Initial findings indicate age-related differences in coping strategies measured by the MBMD, where people in the 61–80 age group tend to use a respectful coping style (characterized by generally high levels of cooperation, compliance, responsibility, and conformity with the medical orders) compared to people in the 21–40 age group.

The NEO

According to McCrae (2001), the long-term study of personality traits has led to their conceptualization as endogenous basic tendencies that are expressed according to a given cultural context. McCrae et al. (2000) indicate that longitudinal studies have shown that traits are stable over long periods despite intervening life events, and that while culture may have some detectable influence on personality traits, they tend to significantly transcend the influence of culture. In a comprehensive analysis of NEO-R-PI results from 23,031 adults representing 26 cultures, McCrae (2001) found that age and gender differences resembled those found in American samples, different subsamples from each culture showed similar levels of personality traits, intercultural factor analysis yielded a close approximation to the five-factor model, and factor scores were meaningfully related to other culture-level variables.

As for the application of the Spanish version of the NEO-R-PI to a Hispanic group, a study by Lugo (2009) explored the personality traits of a sample of Puerto Rican couples. Additionally, the existence of traits was related to participants' wished-for characteristics of their partners. The findings of this largely descriptive study indicate that the Puerto Rican couples obtained scores near the norm on all traits (N, E, A, and C) except openness to experience, where their scores were lower than the norm. Likewise, for the couples in the study, the N facet scales generally correlated in the negative direction with A and C facet scales. This suggests that vulnerability to experience negative emotions is inversely related to impulse control and pro-social behavior.

Lastly, among those who wished their partner changed their personality, at least one of the partners had a high score on N. Those who wished their partner were less introverted had high E scores. According to Lugo, these findings suggest that when there are trait differences in a couple (i.e., the existence of opposite traits in the partners), their incompatibilities can be expressed using the language of traits as proposed by Raggatt (2006).

PAI

The PAI (Morey, 1991, 2007) is a 344-item self-report measure of personality and psychopathology that includes 11 clinical scales that are designed to correspond with major mental disorder diagnoses, five treatment consideration scales, and two interpersonal scales (Morey, 1991). It contains two scales that are designed to detect random responding, and it also contains six measures that are designed to detect feigned response styles.

The Personality Assessment Inventory is also among the self-report measures that were translated and made available prior to the completion of validation studies for the Spanish version (Rogers, Flores, Ustad, & Sewell, 1995). These authors explored the correspondence between the Spanish and English versions of the PAI as well as the test-retest reliability of the Spanish version with a largely Mexican-American sample (total $n=69$). The findings indicate moderate to good correlations in the clinical scales ($M\ r=.71$) between the English and Spanish versions, good stability (test-retest) for the clinical scales in Spanish version ($M\ r=.78$), and modest-to-good internal consistency for Hispanics on the Spanish and English versions. The authors caution, however, of the existence of considerable variations in the correspondence and consistency scores of the validity, treatment, and interpersonal scales of the inventory which led them to warn against interpreting the results of these scales.

Based on the limited correspondence found between the English and Spanish versions of the validity scales of the PAI, Fernandez, Boccaccini, and Noland (2008) further explored the ability of the PAI validity scales to identify under and overreporting of pathology in both language versions. They administered both language versions to 72 bilinguals under instructions to respond honestly, to overreport psychopathology for an insanity case, or to underreport psychopathology for an employment evaluation. The authors took care to carefully assess their participants' reading level, and, in general, the participants had higher levels of education than the participants in the Rogers et al. (1995) study. Together, findings from the correlation and mean difference analyses suggested that NIM and PIM were the measures with the highest level of correspondence between English and Spanish versions of the PAI. Each of the other measures showed either a significant mean difference or low correlation across language versions. There was a trend for underreporting measures to be elevated when participants responded honestly to the PAI in Spanish. The authors consider their findings to be generally supportive of the Spanish-language translation of the PAI, at least with respect to validity scale performance in a simulation study. Nevertheless, they suggest additional study of these validity scales in clinical and forensic settings before asserting the appropriateness of their use and ultimately the use of the Spanish-language PAI as an equivalent form in clinical practice.

Conclusions and Recommendations

This review of research and applications of the existing Spanish versions of self-report personality inventories with Hispanic clients leads us to the following conclusions and recommendations for test use:

1. Appropriate and fair use of tests with Spanish-speaking Hispanics requires the user's attention not only to adequacy of translations but of critical importance to equivalence of constructs. Users should ask whether a score on a given measure applied to a Hispanic client means or should be interpreted similarly to the same score obtained by the normative group for that measure. Also, if a test score were correlated with another measure of, for instance, well-being, will the pattern of correlations be similar for the normative group and for the Hispanic or other group under study? If so, then the measure could be considered equivalent across groups.
2. If there is no evidence of equivalence as described in #1, test users are cautioned not to report the results and instead use them in a descriptive manner, always emphasizing the limitations that a given measure may have in evaluating Hispanics.
3. A widely used and translated measure with Hispanics, such as the MMPI-2, has been useful in distinguishing between clinical and nonclinical groups and in various settings including preemployment assessment and forensic settings. Raw score differences between the US normative and nonclinical Hispanic groups (e.g., Puerto Ricans) continue to be identified which require consideration of cultural and contextual factors when interpreting the scores. Recent norms-development research with the Spanish version of the MMPI-2 suggests this.
4. As new scales and instruments are developed (e.g., the restructured clinical scales of the MMPI-2 and the MMPI-2-Restructured Form), research on their adequacy for the evaluation of Hispanics should also continue. Initial findings with the restructured clinical scales of the MMPI-2 suggest that culture and experiences such as migration may have an impact on scores.
5. As is the case with measures such as the MMPI-2, the results of measures of Axis II pathology such as the MCMI-III must be interpreted in light of self-presentation profiles, especially disclosure and desirability indicators.

References

American Educational Research Association, American Psychological Association, & National Council on Measurement in Education. (1999). *Standards for educational and psychological testing*. Washington, DC: American Educational Research Association.

American Psychiatric Association. (1994). *Diagnostic and statistical manual of mental disorders: DSM-IV*. Washington, DC: American Psychiatric Association.

Archer, R. P. (1992). *Assessing adolescent Psychopathology*. Hillsdale, NJ: Lawrence Erlbaum.

Bartholomew, K. (1990). Avoidance of intimacy: An attachment styles among young adults: A test of four category model. *Journal of Social and Personal Relationship, 7*, 147–178.

Butcher, J. N. (Ed.). (1996). *International adaptations of the MMPI-2: Research and clinical applications*. Minneapolis, MN: University of Minnesota Press.

Butcher, J. N., Cabiya, J. J., Lucio, G. M. E., Peña, L., Reuben, D. L., & Scott, R. (1998). *MMPI-A manual supplement for the Hispanic version of the MMPI-A for the United States*. Minneapolis, MN: University of Minnesota Press.

Butcher, J. N., Graham, J. R., Dahlstrom, W. G., & Bowman, E. (1990). The MMPI-2 with college students. *Journal of Personality Assessment, 54*, 1–15.

Butcher, J. N., Graham, J. R., Williams, C. L., & Kaemmer, B. (1994). *Inventario Multifasico de la Personalidad para Adolescentes (MMPI-A)*. Minneapolis, MN: University of Minnesota Press.

Butcher, J. N., Williams, C. L., Graham, J. R., Archer, R. P., Tellegen, A., Ben-Porath, Y., et al. (1992). *MMPI-A (Minnesota Multiphasic Personality Inventory-Adolescent): Manual for administration, scoring, and interpretation*. Minneapolis, MN: University of Minnesota Press.

Cabiya, J. J., Chavira, D., Gómez, F., Lucio, E., Castellanos, J., & Velázquez, R. (2000). MMPI-2 scores of Puerto Rican, Mexican and U.S. Latino college students. *Psychological Reports, 87*, 266–268.

Cabiya, J. J., & Cruz, R. (2001). *Estudio del MMPI-2 con una muestra de puertorriqueños normales*. Paper presented at the Annual Convention of the Puerto Rican Psychological Association, San Juan, Puerto Rico.

Cabiya, J. J., & Dávila, G. (1999). Cultural differences in MMPI-2 scores between North Americans and Puerto Ricans. *Revista Puertorriqueña de Psicologia, 12*, 144–158.

Cabiya, J. J., Lucio, E., Chavira, D. A., Castellanos, J., Gomez, F. C., & Velasquez, R. J. (2000). MMPI-2 scores of Puerto Rican, Mexican, and U.S. Latino college students: A research note. *Psychological Reports, 87*, 266–268.

Cabiya, J.J., Reuben, D., Garcia, O., Alvarado, C., Sayers, S., Lyons, M., et al. (2001). *Preliminary study of the adequacy of the Spanish translation of the MMPI-A with Puerto Rican adolescents*. Unpublished manuscript.

Carver, C., & Scheir, M. F. (1989). Assessing coping strategies: A theoretically based approach. *Journal of Personality and Social Psychology, 54*, 267–283.

Castañeda, G., Kjenslie, T. A., & Steil, A. K. (2006). *MCMI-III and Latino psychiatric outpatients: Implications for international research*. Washington, DC: American Psychological Association, 2006 Conference Abstract. Database: Psych Extra.

Dana, R. H. (1995). Culturally competent MMPI assessment of Hispanics populations. *Hispanic Journal of Behavioral Sciences, 17*, 305–319.

Dyce, J. A., O'Conner, B. P., Parkins, S. Y., & Janzen, H. L. (1997). Correlation structure of facet-level predictions. *Journal of Personality Disorders, 12*, 31–45.

Ennis, S. R., Ríos-Vargas, M., & Albert, N. G. (2011). *The Hispanic population: 2010* (2010-Census briefs). Washington, DC: U.S. Census Bureau.

Fabrega, H. (1990). Hispanic mental health research: A case for cultural psychiatry. *Hispanic Journal of Behavioral Sciences, 12*, 339–365.

Fernandez, K., Boccaccini, M. T., & Noland, R. M. (2007). Professionally responsible test selection for Spanish-speaking clients: A four-step approach for identifying and selecting translated tests. *Professional Psychology: Research and Practice, 38*, 363–374.

Fernandez, K., Boccaccini, M. T., & Noland, R. M. (2008). Detecting over- and underreporting of psychopathology with the Spanish-language personality assessment inventory: Findings from a simulation study with bilingual speakers. *Psychological Assessment, 20*, 189–194.

Figueroa, J. (2009). *Relación entre los rasgos de apego y las manifestaciones clínicas en el MMPI-2 en agresores*. Unpublished doctoral dissertation, Ponce School of Medicine, Ponce, Puerto Rico.

Fournier, M., & Cabiya, J. (1999). *Concurrent validity of MMPI-2 and MCMI-3 personality disorder scales in their Spanish versions*. Paper presented at the MMPI-2/MMPI-A 34th annual symposium, Minneapolis, MN.

García-Peltoniemi, R., & Azan-Chaviano, A. (1993). *MMPI-2: Inventario Multifasico de la Personalidad Minnesota, Versión Hispana*. Minneapolis, MN: University of Minnesota Press.

García-Peltoniemi, R., Azan-Chaviano, A., & Lucio, E. G. M. (1994). *MMPI-A: Inventario Multifásico de la Personalidad para Minnesota – Versión para adolescentes*. Minneapolis, MN: Regents of the University of Minnesota.

Garrido, M., Rosario-Hernández, E., Figueroa, J., Padovani, C., & Medina, G. (under review). *Comparación de las Escalas Clínicas y Reestructuradas del MMPI-2 en una Muestra Puertorriqueña.*

Garrido, M., Rosario-Hernandez, E., & The PSM MMPI-2 Research Group (2011, May). *Towards the development of MMPI-2 Spanish norms in Puerto Rico: Report of data tendencies.* Poster session presented at the 46th annual symposium on recent MMPI-2, MMPI-2-RF, & MMPI-A Research, Minneapolis, MN.

Geisinger, K. F. (1998). Psychometric issues in test interpretation. In J. S. Sandoval, C. L. Frisby, K. F. Geisinger, J. D. Scheuneman, & J. R. Grenier (Eds.), *Test interpretation and diversity: Achieving equity in assessment* (pp. 17–30). Washington, DC: American Psychological Association.

Ghafoori, B., & Hierholzer, R. W. (2010). Personality patterns among Black, White, and Hispanic combat veterans. *Psychological Trauma: Theory, Research, Practice, and Policy, 2*, 12–18.

Hall, G. C. N., Bansal, A., & Lopez, S. R. (1999). Ethnicity and psychopathology: A meta analytic review of 31 years of comparative MMPI/MMPI-2 research. *Psychological Assessment, 11*, 186–197.

Handel, R. W., & Ben-Porath, Y. S. (2000). Multicultural assessment with the MMPI-2: Issues for research and practice. In R. H. Dana (Ed.), *Handbook of cross cultural and multicultural personality assessment.* Mahwah, NJ: Lawrence Erlbaum Associates.

Hathaway, S. R., & Monachesi, E. D. (1963). *Adolescent personality and behavior: MMPI patterns of normal, delinquent, dropout, and other outcomes.* Minneapolis, MN: University of Minnesota Press.

Kjenslie, T. A., Castañeda, G., & Velasquez, R. J. (2006). *MCMI-III performance of Latino and Euroamerican outpatients: Role of culture.* Washington, DC: American Psychological Association, 2006 Conference Abstract. Database: Psych Extra.

Lopez, S. R., & Weisman, A. (2004). Integrating a cultural perspective in psychological test development. In R. J. Velasquez, L. M. Arellano, & B. W. McNeill (Eds.), *The handbook of Chicana/o psychology and mental health* (pp. 129–152). Mahwah, NJ: Lawrence Erlbaum Associates.

Lucio, E. (1995). *Manual para la administracion y calificacion del MMPI-A* [Minnesota Multiphasic Personality Inventory-Adolescent (MMPI-A) manual for administration, scoring and interpretation]. Mexico City, Mexico: Editorial El Manual Moderno.

Lucio, E. M., Ampudia, A., Duran, C., Leon, I., & Butcher, J. N. (2001). Comparisons of Mexican and American norms of the MMPI-2. *Journal of Clinical Psychology, 57*, 1459–1468.

Lucio, E. M., Palacios, H., Duran, C., & Butcher, J. N. (1999). MMPI-2 with Mexican psychiatric inpatients. *Journal of Clinical Psychology, 55*, 1541–1552.

Lucio, E. M., Reyes-Lagunes, I., & Scott, R. L. (1994). MMPI-2 for Mexico: Translation and adaptation. *Journal of Personality Assessment, 63*, 105–116.

Lugo, J. (2009). *Rasgos de personalidad en una muestra de parejas, utilizando el NEO-PI-R.* Unpublished doctoral dissertation, Ponce School of Medicine, Ponce, Puerto Rico.

Magraner, M. C. (2011). *Hábitos de salud, destrezas de afrontamiento, moderadores de estrés e indicadores de comorbilidades psiquiátricas en adultos puertorriqueños con hipertensión arterial.* Unpublished doctoral dissertation, Ponce School of Medicine, Ponce, Puerto Rico.

Malgady, R. G., & Rogler, L. (1988). Reply to "The empirical basis of ethnocultural and linguistic bias in mental health evaluation of Hispanics". *The American Psychologist, 43*, 1097.

McCann, J. T. (1989). MMPI personality disorder scales and the MCMI: Convergent validity. *Journal of Clinical Psychology, 45*, 365–369.

McCann, J. T. (1991). Convergent and discriminant validity of the MCMI-II and MMPI personality disorder scales. *Journal of Psychological Assessment: A Journal of Consulting and Clinical Psychology, 3*, 9–18.

McCrae, R. R. (2001). Trait psychology and culture: Exploring intercultural comparisons. *Journal of Personality, 69*, 819–846.

McCrae, R. R., Costa, P. T., Jr., Ostendorf, F., Angleitner, A., Hrebrícková, M., Avia, M. D., et al. (2000). Nature over nurture: Temperament, personality, and lifespan development. *Journal of Personality and Social Psychology, 78*, 173–186.

McCrae, R. R., & Terraciano, A. (2006). National character and personality. *Current Directions in Psychological Sciences, 15*, 156–161.

McCrae, R. R., Terracciano, A., & 79 Members of the Personality Profiles of Cultures Project. (2005). Personality profiles of cultures: Aggregate personality traits. *Journal of Personality and Social Psychology, 89*, 407–425.

Megargee, E. I. (1994). Using the Megargee MMPI-based classification system with MMPI-2 s of male prison inmates. *Psychological Assessment, 6*, 337–344.

Millon, T. (1969). *Modern psychopathology: A biosocial approach to maladaptive learning and functioning.* Philadelphia: W.B. Saunders.

Millon, T. (1994). *The Millon clinical multiaxial inventory-III.* Minneapolis, MN: NCS Pearson.

Millon, T. (1997). *Manual for the Millon clinical multiaxial inventory-III.* Minneapolis, MN: National Computer Systems, Inc.

Millon, T., Antoni, M., Millon, C., Minor, S., & Grossman, S. (2001). *The Millon behavioral medicine diagnostic (MBMD).* Minneapolis, MN: Pearson Assessments.

Millon, T., Green, C., & Meagher, R. (1979). A new inventory for the psychodiagnostician in medical settings. *Professional Psychology, 10*, 529–539.

Millon, T., Green, C., & Meagher, R. (1982). *Manual for the MBHI (Millon Behavioral Health Inventory)* (3rd ed.). Minneapolis, MN: NCS Pearson.

Millon, T., Millon, C., Davis, R., & Grossman, S. (2006). *Manual for the Millon clinical multiaxial inventory-III* (3rd ed.). Minneapolis, MN: NCS Pearson.

Morey, L. C. (1991). *The personality assessment inventory: Professional manual*. Odessa, FL: Psychological Assessment Resources.

Morey, L. C. (1992). *MMPI-2 personality scales. MMPI-2/MMPI-A news profile.*

Morey, L. C. (2007). *The personality assessment inventory: Professional manual* (2nd ed.). Odessa, FL: Psychological Assessment Resources.

Morey, L. C., & Waugh, M. H. (1985). MMPI scales for DSM-III personality disorders: Their deviations and correlates. *Journal of Personality Assessment, 49*, 245–251.

Muñoz, C., & Choca, J. P. (2009, August). *MCMI-III and Hispanics: Factor structures with Hispanic and non-Hispanic samples*. Washington, DC: American Psychological Association, 2009 Conference Abstract. Database: Psych Extra.

Olmo, F. (1958). *Manual for the BARSIT-Barranquilla rapid survey intelligence test*. New York: The Psychological Corporation.

Osberg, T. M., Haseley, E. N., & Kamas, M. M. (2008). The MMPI-2 clinical scales and restructured clinical (RC) scales: Comparative psychometric properties and relative diagnostic efficiency in young adults. *Journal of Personality Assessment, 90*, 81–92.

Peña, C., Cabiya, J. J., & Echevarria, N. (2000). MMPI-2 scores of a representative sample of state inmates in Puerto Rico. *Revista Ciencias de la Conducta, 15*, 39–52.

Peña, L. M., Megargee, E. I., & Brody, E. (1996). MMPI-A patterns of male juvenile delinquents. *Psychological Assessment, 8*, 388–397.

Raggatt, P. (2006). Putting the five-factor model into context: Evidence linking big five traits to narrative identity. *Journal of Personality, 74*, 1321–1348.

Rogers, R., Flores, J., Ustad, K., & Sewell, K. W. (1995). Initial validation of the personality assessment inventory—Spanish version with clients from Mexican American communities. *Journal of Personality Assessment, 64*, 340–348.

Rosario-Hernández, E., Rovira, L. V., Álvarez, C. I., & Rodríguez, A. (2007). Efectividad de las escalas clínicas y de validez del MMPI-2 en detectar patrones de contestación honesto, simulación y engaño en el contexto de selección de personal. *Revista Interamericana de Psicología Ocupacional, 26*, 128–139.

Rossi, L. E. (2003). Comparability of the English and Spanish translations of the MMPI-2 and MCMI-III. *DAI: Section B The Sciences and Engineering, 63*(10-B), 4961.

Santiago, E. (2010). *Relación entre estilos de afrontamiento y rasgos de personalidad en hombres que han sido agresivos*. Unpublished doctoral dissertation, Ponce School of Medicine, Ponce, Puerto Rico.

Sellbom, M., Fischler, G. L., & Ben-Porath, Y. S. (2007). Identifying MMPI-2 predictors of police officer integrity and misconduct. *Criminal Justice and Behavior, 34*, 985–1004.

Sugihara, Y., & Warner, J. A. (1999). Mexican-American male batterers on the MCMI-III. *Psychological Reports, 85*, 163–169.

Tellegen, A., Ben-Porath, Y. S., McNulty, J. L., Arbisi, P. A., Graham, J. R., & Kaemmer, B. (2003). *MMPI-2 restructured clinical (RC) scales: Development, validation, and interpretation*. Minneapolis, MN: University of Minnesota Press.

Velasquez, R. J. (1995). Personality assessment of Hispanic clients. In J. N. Butcher (Ed.), *Clinical personality assessment: Practical approaches* (pp. 120–139). New York: Oxford University Press.

Velasquez, R. J., & Bradley, V. (2008, August). *Acculturation and MMPI-2 RC scores for Latino university students*. Washington, DC: American Psychological Association, 2008 Conference Abstract. Database: Psych Extra.

Wallace, A., & Liljequist, L. (2005). A comparison of the correlational structures and elevation patterns of the MMPI-2 restructured clinical (RC) and clinical scales. *Assessment, 12*, 290–294.

Whitworth, R. H., & McBlaine, D. D. (1993). Comparison of the MMPI and MMPI 2 administered to Anglo- and Hispanic-American university students. *Journal of Personality Assessment, 61*, 19–27.

Zapata-Sola, A., Kreuch, T., Landers, R. N., Hoyt, T., & Butcher, J. N. (2009). Personality assessment in personnel selection using the MMPI-2: A cross-cultural comparison. *International Journal of Clinical and Health Psychology, 9*, 287–298.

6 IQ Testing and the Hispanic Client

Nicholas S. Thaler and Sharon Jones-Forrester

Intelligence is a controversial topic in psychology. The concept of an inherent general intellectual ability brings with it numerous assumptions about individuals including their character, judgment, and potential for success in life. This becomes all the more contentious when paired with claims that there are racial and ethnic differences in IQ scores among people (e.g., Herrnstein & Murray, 1994). While an in-depth and detailed discussion regarding the debate as to what IQ is and whether or not it is a culturally biased construct is beyond the scope of this chapter, suffice to say IQ is generally a European-Western conceptualization, is not a universally fair assessment of cognitive aptitude across populations, and is influenced by environmental factors (Brooks, Holdnack, & Iverson, 2011; Nisbett et al., 2012; Thomsen, Gallup, & Llorente, 2008). When assessing IQ with the Hispanic client a number of considerations must be made, such as the client's level of acculturation, country of origin, English language proficiency, quality and quantity of education, income, and sources of cultural bias within the test itself (Table 6.1).

There are several guidelines to be mindful of when assessing intellectual functioning within Hispanic populations, including knowledge of the generalizability and limitations of normative samples with the individual's demographic and clinical characteristics, issues of language proficiency and communication, understanding the comfort level of the examinee with the examiner's sociocultural and ethnic background (and vice-versa), cross-cultural differences in manifestations of psychopathology, and awareness of the individual's specific cultural, ethnic, and racial identity and level of acculturation. Neurological and psychological factors may also interact with demographic variables in unique manners. For example, a child who is raised in a primarily Spanish-speaking household and suffers a brain injury may exhibit substantial impairment in an English-based vocabulary test after she spends several months recovering at home, both due to the neurological insult, delayed academic achievement, and the cultural milieu of her convalescence. This, in turn, may underestimate her crystallized intelligence when undergoing intellectual assessment. A clinician or psychometrician who is unaware of these factors may therefore erroneously interpret her scores, which can then have a substantial impact on her diagnosis and treatment plan.

N.S. Thaler, M.A. (✉) • S. Jones-Forrester, Ph.D.
Department of Psychology, University of Nevada, 4505 S. Maryland Pkwy, Box 455030, Las Vegas, NV 89154-5030, USA
e-mail: nick.thaler@gmail.com; guiness3@cox.net

L.T. Benuto (ed.), *Guide to Psychological Assessment with Hispanics*,
DOI 10.1007/978-1-4614-4412-1_6, © Springer Science+Business Media New York 2013

Table 6.1 IQ tests available for Hispanic clients

Test name	Original language	Structure of test	Country of norms	Age range (years)	Notes
Wechsler Adult Intelligence Scale – Third Edition	English	Four-factor scale assessing verbal comprehension, perceptual organization, working memory, and processing speed as well as a Verbal, Performance, and Full Scale IQ	USA	16–89	All indexes influenced by language proficiency, often underestimates IQ in Hispanic populations
Wechsler Adult Intelligence Scale – Fourth Edition	English	Four-factor scale assessing verbal comprehension, perceptual reasoning, working memory, and processing speed as well as a Full Scale IQ	USA	16–90	Limited research available, but little in the battery suggests that it is dramatically different from the WAIS-III in terms of bias toward language proficiency
Escala de Inteligencia de Wechsler para Adultos	Spanish	Verbal and Performance IQ scores and a Full Scale IQ	Puerto Rico	16–64	Overestimates IQ when compared to the WAIS, no longer recommended for clinical use
Escala de Inteligencia de Wechsler para Adultos – Tercera Edicion	Spanish	Four-factor scale assessing verbal comprehension, perceptual organization, working memory, and processing speed as well as a Verbal, Performance, and Full Scale IQ	Puerto Rico	16–64	No published studies available in regard to whether or not it overcomes the limitations of the EIWA
Spanish Wechsler Adult Intelligence Scale – Third Edition	Spanish	Four-factor scale assessing verbal comprehension, perceptual organization, working memory, and processing speed as well as a Verbal, Performance, and Full Scale IQ	Spain	16–94	Appears adequate when administered to Spanish-speaking individuals from Spain, may underestimate IQ in other Spanish-speaking populations
Mexican Wechsler Adult Intelligence Scale – Third Edition	Spanish	Four-factor scale assessing verbal comprehension, perceptual organization, working memory, and processing speed as well as a Verbal, Performance, and Full Scale IQ	Mexico	16–70+	Some criticisms on its norming procedures, little validity data available
Wechsler Intelligence Scale for Children – Fourth Edition	English	Four-factor scale assessing verbal comprehension, perceptual reasoning, working memory, and processing speed as well as a Full Scale IQ	USA	6–16	Underestimates IQ in Spanish-speaking children, which appears to be primarily related to acculturation factors and language proficiency
Wechsler Intelligence Scale for Children – Fourth Edition – Spanish	Spanish	Four-factor scale assessing verbal comprehension, perceptual reasoning, working memory, and processing speed as well as a Full Scale IQ	USA	6–16	Notable for being designed specifically for Spanish-speaking children in the United States. Appears sensitive to clinical disorders

Kaufman Assessment Battery for Children – Second Edition	English	Based on CHC model and has factors of crystallized intelligence, fluid reasoning, visual processing, short-term memory, and long-term retrieval	USA	3–18	Research studies by the test publishers suggest the KABC-II is culturally neutral and with the exception of *Gc*, resilient to language barriers. *Gc* responses given in Spanish are assigned full credit
Universal Nonverbal Intelligence Test	English	Produces Reasoning, Memory, Symbolic, and Nonsymbolic Quotient scores as well as a Full Scale IQ	USA	5–17	May circumnavigate limitations of tests that rely on verbal ability, though still susceptible to errors in nonverbal communication. Criticized for having factors that may not capture intellectual functioning
Naglieri Nonverbal Ability Test	English	Test relies on progressive matrices and produces a single IQ score	USA	5–17	Large standardization sample (57,000 students grades K-12) and a study by the test author indicates it is free of cultural and language biases. NNAT-2 has a computerized adaptation
Reynolds Intellectual Assessment Scales	English	Forms verbal intelligence and nonverbal intelligence indexes as well as a Full Scale IQ	USA	3–94	Minimizes reliance on reading proficiency. An adaptation normed in Spain is now available
Batería III Woodcock-Muñoz	Spanish	Based on CHC model and has factors of crystallized intelligence, fluid reasoning, visual processing, short-term memory, long-term retrieval, processing speed, and auditory processing	Mexico, Central America, Spain, USA	2–90+	Has an achievement counterpart and theoretically appears to be a Spanish equivalent to the WJ-III
Wechsler Abbreviated Scale of Intelligence	English	Forms Verbal, Performance, and Full Scale IQ scores	USA	6–89	Short form of the WAIS-III that appears to underestimate IQ scores in minorities who are not acculturated to the USA
Kaufman Brief Intelligence Test – Second Edition	English	Forms crystallized intelligence, fluid reasoning, and Full Scale IQ scores	USA	4–90	Short form of the Kaufman scales. Verbal answers can be given in Spanish or English with different scoring procedures are provided for both
Stanford-Binet Intelligence Scales – Fifth Edition	English	Based on CHC model and has factors of crystallized intelligence, fluid reasoning, visual processing, short-term memory, and quantitative knowledge	USA	2–90+	Very little research available on its applicability toward Hispanic clients or minorities in general

The environmental context is particularly critical to consider when assessing the intellectual functioning of Hispanic clients. As defined by the US Census Bureau (2006), the "Hispanic" ethnicity incorporates an immense range of cultural, racial, and national classifications which exhibit considerable variation within the panethnic label, and it would be impossible to assume that general assessment considerations would be definitively relevant to any one individual. As might be expected, there are substantial differences among Hispanic subgroups, which include individuals from Mexico, South America, Cuba, Spain, Puerto Rico, Central America, and the Caribbean Islands. Country and community of origin may provide initial guidelines when administering and interpreting IQ tests. For instance, Hispanics born in rural areas generally have less access to health care services and may be more reluctant to be serviced by Westernized practitioners, including psychologists, due to language and cultural barriers (Sherrill et al., 2005). This has enormous implications on IQ scores, which are very much dependent on effective communication and rapport between the examiner and client. In practical application then, a client raised in a Western country may more easily obtain higher IQ scores than one born in an underdeveloped nation, even if their actual intellectual aptitude is equivalent. Psychologists must factor in their clients' background before conducting an evaluation to better understand the clients' level of comfort and familiarity with the testing environment, their prejudices or misconceptions, and their ability to effectively communicate with the examiner when they relate their histories and presenting problems, respond to test items, and voice any questions or concerns.

Differences in early nutrition, quality of health care, quality of education, and other issues relating to socioeconomic status (SES) exist and often impact performance during IQ evaluations (Artiola i Fortuny, Heaton, & Hermosillo, 1998). Hispanics in the United States are, on average, less educated compared to the general population, with 24.5% of men and 23.3% of women having less than a ninth grade education (U.S. Census Bureau, 2006), and 21.9% live below the poverty line in comparison to 8.6% of the general population (Judd et al., 2009). These socioeconomic factors are crucial to consider for their potential impact on intellectual assessment as IQ scores are heavily affected by level of education and other SES factors. Hispanic individuals also have high levels of bilingualism with English and Spanish, to varying degrees of proficiency, which is also an issue when administering an IQ test that is in English.

Proficiency in the dominant language (i.e., English) is therefore an extremely important factor to assess for when working with the Hispanic client. In the same way, psychologists should be aware of the cultural and linguistic limitations of specific tests and subtests within a larger battery to minimize biases (Ortiz, 2001). When working with a client who cannot speak English at all, psychologists should refer out to a colleague who is proficient in communicating in the client's native language. If the client is able to effectively speak English, though it is not his or her first language, the issue becomes more muddled. It is our stance that psychologists must take care during the assessment to use batteries that demonstrate good cross-cultural generalizability to Hispanic populations, several of which will be discussed later in this chapter. If such batteries are unavailable, psychologists should be aware of the biases present in their available measures and interpret results with caution. The written report should qualify any quantitative data and at best, should state that the interpretation's validity is guarded, citing scientific references addressing the measures' limitations. Even when using tests that demonstrate adequate generalizability, the psychologist should take care to report any qualitative or behavioral issues that they believe may have impacted the results. In addition, the use of translators should generally be avoided unless no other options are present, and if used, this must be stated within the report with hypotheses on how this might have impacted test results.

When assessing Hispanic children, clinicians should take into account both the child and parents' level of acculturation and education within the United States. Hispanic children are often bilingual though their degree of language proficiency between languages can greatly vary. There are ethical issues to be mindful of when communicating with parents who may not be as proficient in English as their children, and clinicians should never rely on family members to interpret feedback. Due to SES restrictions, schools are often of poorer quality, and even Hispanic youth who are meeting grade milestones may have less academic achievement compared to their grade-level European American peers. There is also some evidence that uncooperative behavior, which is an issue of concern when assessing children in general, may particularly impact Hispanic children's IQ scores (Glutting & Oakland, 1993), due to interactions with degree of language proficiency, familiarity and rapport with the examiner, and attitudes of the child's family members and the child himself toward the testing situation. This highlights the importance of using appropriately normed measures to not only minimize bias but also to minimize the impact that oppositional and uncooperative behavior may have on test performance.

Older persons of Hispanic decent also pose unique cultural considerations during intellectual assessment. Such individuals face the stresses of being an underrepresented minority population and coping with advanced age. When assessing intellectual ability, psychologists are tasked to differentiate between normal and abnormal cognitive decline. There are interactions with ethnicity regarding the onset of certain dementias such as Alzheimer's disease (AD) which are not fully understood (Clark et al., 2005) while bilingualism may stave off dementia in some subsets of the population (Gollan, Salmon, Montoya, & Galasko, 2011). Elderly Hispanics are less likely to be educated in the United States, less proficient in English, and less acculturated than their younger peers. Immigration patterns triggered by societal unrest may further impact the general level of education and English proficiency of certain age cohorts (Choca, Krueger, De La Torre, Corral, & Garside, 2009). Norms for elderly Hispanic populations are less available than those of children and younger adults, though as discussed below, some Spanish editions of IQ tests do extend up to 90 years of age. As with other Hispanic populations, the geriatric subset represents a vast and diverse population that is impossible to summate as a single group. Rather, psychologists must separately consider individual factors relating to each client in regard to the impact of age, ethnicity, education, and other cultural and demographic considerations that may impact test performance.

IQ Tests for Adult Populations

Wechsler Adult Intelligence Scale – Third Edition (WAIS-III; Wechsler, 1997a)

The WAIS-III is a commonly administered intelligence battery that was normed for adults between 16 and 89 years of age. The standardization sample consisted of 2,450 adults who were selected to match the demographics of the United States at that time. This battery also was reported as the single most frequently used IQ assessment battery by neuropsychologists for Hispanic populations in 1994 (Echemendia & Harris, 2004). The WAIS-III has been recently replaced by the Wechsler Adult Intelligence Scale – Fourth Edition (WAIS-IV; Wechsler, 2008a) but has over 15 years of research on it which can serve as guidelines for the WAIS-IV. Therefore, the WAIS-III remains relevant when considering cross-cultural issues of IQ assessment.

Although the constructs of Verbal and Performance IQ are considered outdated by most psychologists, the WAIS-III also includes the empirically derived four-factor model that is predominant with current Wechsler cognitive measures today. These factors include the Verbal Comprehension Index (VCI), the Perceptual Organization Index (POI) which was renamed in later batteries the Perceptual Reasoning Index (PRI), the Freedom from Distractibility Index (FDI) which was renamed in later batteries as the Working Memory Index (WMI), and the Processing Speed Index (PSI). Index and IQ scores are derived from 14 subtests that measure a range of cognitive abilities. It is worth exploring the modalities of each subtest as these can generalize to other Wechsler batteries and other IQ measures in terms of what they measure and how this might be influenced by cultural considerations.

The Vocabulary (VO), Information (IN), Similarities (SI), and Comprehension (CO) are four subtests with a heavy verbal component. All four subtests require both receptive and expressive language abilities, which as mentioned previously are heavily determined by proficiency with the dominant language. Three of these subtests (VO, IN, SI) form the VCI with the CO subtest serving as a supplemental subtest. Heaton, Taylor, and Manly (2003) ran a factor analysis of WAIS-III and Wechsler Memory Scale – Third Edition (WMS-III; Wechsler, 1997b) and derived from these VCI, POI, FDI, and PSI factor scores. They demonstrated that Hispanics had a VCI factor z-score that was .30 below European Americans after correcting for age, education, and gender. As might be expected, the VCI was shown to be heavily associated with acculturation as measured by language preference and education in the United States (Harris, Tulsky, & Schultheis, 2003). Although the CO subtest is not part of the VCI, it is a core subtest on other Wechsler batteries and has been criticized by others as being particularly dependent on acculturated values (Kaufman, 1994). The VO subtest has also been demonstrated to be particularly influenced by acculturation, given the interplay between fund of vocabulary knowledge, educational history, and language fluency (Gonzales & Roll, 1985).

The Block Design (BD), Matrix Reasoning (MR), Picture Completion (PC), Picture Arrangement (PA), and Object Assembly (OA) require perceptual and fluid reasoning skills. Three subtests (BD, MR, PC) comprise the POI. Although nonverbal tests were at first theoretically conceived to be more resilient against cultural factors, level of acculturation is nonetheless predictive of test performance on the POI, (Harris et al. 2003). In line with this, Heaton et al. (2003) found that Hispanics on average had a POI factor z-score that was .24 below European Americans after correcting for other demographic variables. The BD subtest in particular requires extensive communication between the examiner and examinee and so are vulnerable to language and cultural barriers. Even the MR subtest has shown to be influenced by performance depending on instructional cues (Knight, 2003). Therefore, psychologists are urged to be especially mindful of their clients' acculturation level, and particularly language proficiency and education within the United States, when administering subtests that tap into both crystallized and fluid intelligence to Hispanic clients.

At a glance, the subtests that comprised the FDI including Digit Span (DS), Letter-Number Sequencing (LN), and Arithmetic (AR) might appear to be less impacted by cultural values. This is not the case. Heaton et al. (2003) found a .41 factor z-score discrepancy favoring European Americans over Hispanics, and Harris et al. (2003) indicated that the FDI was influenced by levels of acculturation at a comparable degree to the POI. The AR subtest has a heavy load on comprehension of verbal instructions and has been shown to be influenced by verbal intellectual functioning as well as working memory (Egeland, Bosnes, & Johansen, 2009; Karzmark, 2009). Both the DS and LN are vulnerable to differences in phoneme/grapheme relationships between Spanish and English, which accounts for poorer performance on these subtests in Hispanic populations (Olazaran, Jacobs, & Stern, 1996), and DS has been found to associate with age that English was first learned and years spent in the United States (Boone, Victor, Wen, Razani, & Pontón, 2007). It is therefore clear that the FDI, and the subtests that constitute it, are as vulnerable to language and cultural discrimination as the VCI and POI.

Of interest, the PSI appears to be more resilient to cultural barriers. Only a .12 factor z-score discrepancy between European Americans and Hispanics were identified by Heaton et al. (2003). However, Harris et al. (2003) still demonstrated that level of acculturation influences PSI scores. Both the Symbol Search (SS) and Coding (CD) subtests require complex instructions which may not be followed properly if there is an error in communication; for example, a client who does not understand that he is to work as quickly as possible may choose accuracy over speed.

In summary, the English version of the WAIS-III is not adequately standardized for Hispanic populations, particularly those for whom English is not the primary language. Verbal subtests and the VCI are the most influenced by language fluency and education, but it is of significance that all four index scores demonstrate bias after accounting for these variables. Demonstrative of this, 15–25% of Hispanic individuals were misclassified as impaired on the factor scores after correcting for age, gender, and level of education, compared to 15% of European American individuals (Heaton et al. 2003). Clinicians are urged to take caution when interpreting the WAIS-III when working with Hispanic individuals.

Wechsler Adult Intelligence Scale – Fourth Edition (WAIS-IV, Wechsler, 2008a)

The WAIS-IV is the newest Wechsler intellectual scale for adults. Like the WAIS-III, it was standardized on an English-speaking population that was stratified to match current United States demographics. The standardization sample consisted of 2,200 adults between 16 and 90 years of age. The WAIS-IV removes the Verbal and Performance IQ scores and relies entirely on the VCI, PRI, WMI, and PSI as well as an overall FSIQ for interpretation. Many of the subtests from the WAIS-III were retained for the WAIS-IV, though index composition was restructured. The VCI continues to be composed of the VO, SI, and IN subtests with the CO subtest remaining supplemental. The PRI has the BD and MR subtests as core subtests, as well as the new Visual Puzzles (VP) subtest. The PC and the new Figure Weights (FW) subtests are supplemental. The WMI has the DS and AR subtests as core, and the LN subtest as supplemental. Finally, the PSI has the SS and CD subtests as core, and a new Cancellation (CA) subtest that was adapted from the WISC-IV. Some items within each subtest were revised and updated for content, and discontinue criteria were made more stringent.

As of this publication, few articles have examined the impact of acculturation on WAIS-IV performance, and virtually none examined its validity in Hispanic populations. Weiss, Saklofske, Coalson, and Raiford (2010) do report some preliminary data that suggests that WAIS-IV scores are less discrepant by ethnicity than the WAIS-III and appear to be more impacted by education. However, Western education remains a key facet of acculturation, and the increase in scores may simply reflect that more minorities were raised in a Western educational environment, granting them similar privileges as European Americans. It is likely that other minority groups, including Hispanics who have not fully acculturated to the United States, will exhibit similar score discrepancies as those observed in the WAIS-III. The new VP and FW subtests require complex instructions and timed responses much like the BD subtest, and it is unlikely that they would be resilient to cultural and language barriers. In addition, the stringent discontinue rules allow less room for errors that are not directly due to cognitive aptitude, which may further bias scores. Unless contradictory research is published, clinicians are therefore urged to take similar measures of caution with the WAIS-IV as they would with the WAIS-III.

Escala de Inteligencia de Wechsler para Adultos (EIWA; The Psychological Corporation, 1968)

The EIWA is one of the oldest and most rigorously researched Spanish adaptations of the WAIS. This measure was standardized on 1,127 native Puerto Ricans between the ages of 16 and 64 and stratified to represent the total population of Puerto Rico. Subtests mimic those of the WAIS and WAIS-III, although content was changed as needed; for example, the IN subtest has an item asking test takers to name three spoken Latin American languages. Psychometrically, the EIWA was found to be reliable with coefficient alphas ranging from .65 to .96 for subtests and .95 to .98 for IQ scores, which are rates comparable to the WAIS. In addition, the factor structure of the EIWA replicated the same dimensions of its WAIS counterpart (Gómez, Piedmont, & Fleming, 1992). Subtest differences between VIQ and PIQ measures were also found to be comparable to WAIS subtest differences (Demsky, Gass, & Golden, 1998).

Despite these promising findings, other researchers identified serious concerns regarding the EIWA's validity. López and Romero (1988) compared WAIS and EIWA equivalencies when converting raw scores to scaled scores and found significant differences. For example, the same DS raw score can lead to a scaled score discrepancy of up to five points between the two batteries favoring the EIWA. No one subtest was found to have equivalent conversions, with the EIWA overestimating scores every time, which suggests that there are differences in the level of difficulty among subtests. In other words, the EIWA standardization sample in general had lower raw scores than the WAIS sample, which necessitated inflation of scaled and index scores when the data was standardized. The authors posit that different characteristics between the two standardization samples, such as the presence of more individuals from rural communities in the Puerto Rican sample, likely account for the discrepancies in performance and the subsequent overestimation of scaled and index scores on the EIWA. Corroborating this, Melendez (1994) compared WAIS and EIWA scores with bilingual Spanish speakers and found that the EIWA can overestimate the FSIQ by an average of 20 points, calling into question its ethical use for clinical assessments within the United States.

The EIWA therefore represents a historical attempt to produce a Spanish version of the original WAIS that was found to have equivalent factor structure and reliability, though overestimating IQ scores. It can be used in research settings to evaluate cognitive processes but should not be used as a clinical tool. Even if the EIWA was equivalent in IQ scores to the WAIS, it was standardized on a Puerto Rican population, which raises the issue of its validity with other Hispanic populations. Unfortunately, this appears to be a common concern with most IQ tests designed specifically for Hispanics, given the inherent heterogeneity of this population.

Escala de Inteligencia de Wechsler para Adultos – Tercera Edicion (EIWA-III; Wechsler, 2008b)

The EIWA-III is the second revision of the EIWA and was designed to be a Spanish equivalent to the WAIS-III. Like the EIWA, the EIWA-III was standardized on a Puerto Rican population and designed for adults between 16 and 64 years of age. It produces Verbal and Performance IQ scores, as well as four index scores and an FSIQ. To date, no validation studies of the EIWA-III have been conducted, which is a concern given the EIWA's tendency to overestimate IQ scores. In addition, the EIWA-III may not be appropriate to administer outside of Puerto Rico.

Spanish Wechsler Adult Intelligence Scale – Third Edition (Spanish WAIS-III; TEA Ediciones, 2001)

The Spanish WAIS-III is an adaptation of the WAIS-III that was developed, normed, and published in Spain. The standardization sample consists of 1,369 adults from Spain between 16 and 94 years of age. According to the test publishers, this battery was designed to have verbal content that was as free as possible from regional vocabulary and cultural differences to minimize its bias across different Hispanic populations. Factor analysis demonstrated that the Spanish WAIS-III is similar in structure with the original WAIS-III (García, Ruiz, & Abad, 2003). Renteria, Li, and Plisken (2008) tested the external validity of the Spanish-III on a sample of urban and American Spanish-speaking Hispanics and generally found that the internal consistency and criterion validity were generally adequate, but some sources of bias remained. Specifically, the LN subtest demonstrated inadequate reliability, suggesting that the items within this subtest do not measure the same construct. The researchers posit that differences in phoneme/grapheme pronunciation between Latin American and European Spanish-speaking individuals may be the source of this. The Spanish WAIS-III also underestimated performance with other cognitive measures assessing attention, and some subtests with verbal content appear to be biased in favor of individuals educated in Spain. As such, although the Spanish WAIS-III appears to hold up better than the EIWA, it may underestimate IQ scores when administered to Hispanics outside the normative sample.

When WAIS-III and Spanish WAIS-III raw scores are directly compared, they appear to be roughly equivalent up to the age of 35, at which point the norms begin to differ in favor of the WAIS-III (Krueger, de la Torre, Fuentes, & Choca, 2005). Choca and colleagues (2009) hypothesized that this may be due to historical events which may have impeded education in older cohorts who grew up in unstable periods. In response to this, they have provided adjustments for the Spanish WAIS-III when it is administered to older Hispanics, though it is unclear if these adjustments are appropriate for Hispanics outside of Spain.

Mexican Wechsler Adult Intelligence Scale – Third Edition (Mexican WAIS-III; Tulsky & Zhu, 2003)

The Mexican WAIS-III was normed over a 4-year period between 2001 and 2004 on 970 individuals of Mexican descent. Both United States and Mexican norms are available for clinicians to interpret. This measure has been criticized for lacking a representative norming sample, low reliability for subtests, lack of psychometric score normalization, lack of representation for groups, statistical errors and miscalculations, and for being a direct translation of WAIS-III content (Suen & Greenspan, 2009). Escobedo and Hollingworth (2009) provide justification for using the Mexican WAIS-III specifically in regard to a death penalty case but do acknowledge several limitations to its psychometric reliability and validity. As there has yet to be rigorous research comparing the Mexican WAIS-III's psychometric properties to that of the WAIS-III, clinicians should use caution in using the Mexican WAIS-III in practice.

IQ Tests for Pediatric Populations

Wechsler Intelligence Scale for Children – Fourth Edition (WISC-IV; Wechsler, 2003)

The WISC-IV is the most recently revised edition of the original Wechsler Intelligence Scale for Children (WISC) and normed on 2,200 children between 6 and 16 years of age and stratified demographically to represent the United States population. Like the WAIS-IV, the WISC-IV removed Verbal and Performance IQ scores. Ten core and five supplemental subtests are available and in general are similar in content to their WAIS-IV counterparts. The VO, SI, and CO core subtests and the IN and Word Reasoning (WR) supplemental subtests form the VCI; the BD, Picture Concepts (PCo), and MR core subtests and PC supplemental subtest form the PRI; the DS and LN core subtests and the AR supplemental subtest form the WMI; and the CD and SS core subtests and CA supplemental subtest form the PSI. Factor analysis of the WISC-IV confirms its four-factor index structure, and additional research suggests that the WISC-IV may be interpreted through a CHC model of intelligence (Keith, Fine, Taub, Reynolds, & Kranzler, 2006).

Many of the issues with the WAIS in testing minority populations are apparent with the WISC-IV as well. Prifitera, Saklofske, Weiss, and Rolfhus (2005) reported that on average, African-American children score 11.5 points lower on the VCI, 11 points lower on the PRI, 5.2 points lower on the WMI, and 6.4 points lower on the PSI compared to their European American peers. Hispanic children score on average 10.1 points lower on the VCI, 11.4 points lower on the PRI, 7.1 points lower on the WMI, and 3.7 points lower on the PSI compared to their European American peers. When demographic variables of age, region, sex, parental SES, and number of parents in the household are controlled, these differences substantially reduce with no greater than a 6-point difference between Hispanic and European American children on all indexes. The PSI in particular had only a 1.7-point difference between groups when other variables were controlled, and both the PSI and PRI were slightly higher in Hispanic children than European American children in the younger cohorts and consistently remained the highest index scores across all age groups.

A study by Harris and Llorente (2005) examined the impact of language fluency on WISC-IV performance in Hispanic and European American children. A 10-point difference in Full Scale IQ (FSIQ) points emerged between the two groups, which reduced down to 5 points after controlling for demographic factors. The remaining 5 points were found to be primarily contained in a subsample of the Hispanic children whose native language was reported as Spanish, confirming that language proficiency is a mediator of WISC-IV performance in Hispanic children.

Wechsler Intelligence Scale for Children – Fourth Edition – Spanish (WISC-IV Spanish; Wechsler, 2005)

The WISC-IV Spanish edition was standardized on a nationally stratified sample of 851 Spanish-speaking children in the United States. Of significance, this is perhaps the first comprehensive intellectual battery normed on Spanish-speaking children in the United States' schools. Test items were revised to minimize any cultural bias and full credit is given for correct answers in either Spanish or English. Norms were derived from four major geographic regions that include Puerto Rico. Reliability of the WISC-IV Spanish appears to be comparable to the English version (Braden & Iribarren, 2007), and an early validity study reports that its WMI and PSI are sensitive to clinical populations (San Miguel Montes, Allen, Puente, & Neblina, 2010). The WISC-IV Spanish is therefore a promising battery that circumnavigates some of the standardization issues of the EIWA and Spanish WAIS-III, but additional studies on its use in clinical and other populations are needed.

Kaufman Assessment Battery for Children – Second Edition (KABC-II; Kaufman & Kaufman, 2004a)

The KABC-II is a battery of cognitive abilities for children between 3 and 18 years of age and the second edition of the Kaufman Assessment Battery for Children (KABC; Kaufman & Kaufman, 1983). The original KABC developed a reputation for being culturally neutral and sensitive to underrepresented ethnic and SES populations with studies demonstrating that profile differences between European Americans and minorities were less than that of other pediatric IQ batteries (Krohn & Lamp, 1989; Lichtenberger, Broadbooks, & Kaufman, 2000; Naglieri & Hill, 1986). Original validity pilot data demonstrated that Hispanic children outperformed European American children on the Mental Processing Composite, performed equally well on the Sequential and Simultaneous Processing Composites, and overall had only a 2-point difference on the FSIQ. As such, the KABC appears to have been an attractive intellectual battery in both clinical and research settings when working with Hispanic populations.

Like the KABC, the KABC-II was designed to be culturally neutral by minimizing verbal instructions and cueing and reducing cultural content within items. Subtest scores can be interpreted either through Luria's neuropsychological theory or the CHC model. Multiple subtests converge to form factors of crystallized intelligence (*Gc*), fluid reasoning (*Gf*), visual processing (*Gv*), short-term memory (*Gsm*), and long-term retrieval (*Glr*). Unlike the original KABC, an achievement scale is not available. Clinicians are also cautioned by the test publishers to interpret the *Gc* subtests only if they feel it is clinically relevant, given that this construct is heavily influenced by language skills. Despite this potential confound, the KABC-II does allow for responses given in Spanish to be deemed correct on these subtests. At least one study shows the KABC-II's potential of minimizing cultural bias in preschool children of African-American and European American descent (Dale, McIntosh, Rothlisberg, Ward, & Bradley, 2011). Another study demonstrated that 46 Taos Pueblo Indian children from New Mexico performed comparably to European American children on nearly all subtests except those from the *Gc* composite, though even the *Gc* subtests only differed by one to two standard scores (Fletcher-Janzen, 2003). This was an important finding, given that the Taos children come from a markedly different environment from children raised in a non-Pueblo environment. Additional data from the test manual suggests only a 2-point difference on KABC-II *Gf* construct and a 5-point difference on the *Gc* construct between Hispanic and European American children after adjusting for gender and SES (Kaufman & Kaufman, 2004a). From these findings, it appears that the second edition of the KABC remains a choice assessment measure for Hispanic children.

Universal Nonverbal Intelligence Test (UNIT; Bracken & McCallum, 1998)

The UNIT is a nonverbal assessment of intelligence standardized on 2,100 children between 5 and 17 years of age. Six subtests form an FSIQ and additional quotients including a Reasoning Quotient, Memory Quotient, Symbolic Quotient, and Nonsymbolic Quotient. Subtests include block design, analogies, mazes, and spatial and symbolic memory tasks. Reliability coefficients range from .87 to .93, and factor studies suggest a two-factor structure of memory and reasoning (Reed & McCallum, 1995). The UNIT was conceived to minimize cultural bias associated with language-loaded tests while still capturing the broad psychometric concept of *g*. One study supported the UNIT's success in this with Hispanic youth, in that it was found to have high correlations with the WISC's Verbal IQ and FSIQ scores in a sample of Mexican-American schoolchildren (Borghese & Gronau, 2005). However, as discussed earlier, nonverbal tests can still be biased by miscommunication errors between the examiner and examinee through both verbal instructions and nonverbal cues, and so psychologists should still use caution in administering the UNIT when working with Hispanic children. In addition, the memory and reasoning factors have been criticized as not truly reflecting *g* and have psychometric issues when equally weighted, though alternative scoring procedures have been identified (Caruso & Witkiewitz, 2001).

Naglieri Nonverbal Ability Test (NNAT; Naglieri, 1997)

The NNAT is a brief nonverbal measure of cognitive ability that eschews the need for the examinee to read, write, or speak. Test content is comprised of a series of progressive matrices that increase in difficulty, similar in modality to the WISC-IV Matrix Reasoning subtest. The NNAT is notable for its impressive standardization sample that included 89,600 children from the United States between kindergarten and Grade 12. One study by the author found few differences between European American, African-American, Asian, and Hispanic children on NNAT scores suggesting that it is reasonably free of cultural bias and English proficiency (Naglieri, Booth, & Winsler, 2004). The NNAT was recently updated (Naglieri Nonverbal Ability Test – Second Edition (NNAT-2); Naglieri, 2007) though few published studies have examined whether the NNAT-2 retains similar validity. Like the UNIT, the NNAT appears promising as a culturally fair assessment.

IQ Tests for Both Pediatric and Adult Populations

Reynolds Intellectual Assessment Scales (RIAS; Reynolds & Kamphaus, 2003)

The RIAS is a test of intelligence for individuals between 3 and 94 years of age designed to assess fluid and crystallized abilities and was in part conceived as a measure that avoids cultural bias. This battery was standardized on 2,438 individuals matched with the 2001 US Census Bureau. Four IQ subtests, including two verbal and two nonverbal, as well as two memory subtests are available. The two verbal subtests include Guess What (GWH) and Verbal Reasoning (VRZ) and combine to form the Verbal Intelligence Index (VIX). The GWH subtest provides two to three clues and task examinees to guess the concept being described, while the VRZ subtest is an oral test of analogies. The two nonverbal subtests include Odd-Item Out (OIO) and What's Missing (WHM) and combine to form the Nonverbal Intelligence Index (NIX). The OIO subtest requires examinees to identify which picture in a series of pictures does not belong with the others, while What's Missing is similar to the Wechsler Picture Completion subtest in structure. These four subtests combine for a Composite Intelligence Index (CIX). The memory subtests tap into verbal and nonverbal memory performance and form a Composite Memory Index (CMX). The Reynolds Intellectual Screening Test (RIST), a brief 10–15-min version of the RIAS, can also be administered and is comprised solely of the OIO and GWH subtests.

The RIAS was developed to minimize cultural bias through a rigorous evaluation of individual items through both statistical methods (e.g., differential item functioning) and an expert review by ethnic minority panels. It also eliminates a reliance on reading proficiency on test items. Initial validity studies by the test's authors confirm that there is little difference on test performance by ethnicity, though it remains possible that years and quality of education, along with other acculturation variables, may impact test performance. A European Spanish version of the RIAS was recently published (Escala de Inteligencia de Reynolds; Reynolds & Kamphaus, 2009) and normed on 2,065 Spanish-speaking children and adults from Spain with additional normative data drawn from Latin American countries. The RIAS Spanish likely has similar obstacles as the WAIS-III Spanish in its generalizability outside of European Spanish-speaking individuals, though the supplemental normative data may in part address this.

Batería III Woodcock-Muñoz (Batería III; Muñoz-Sandoval, Woodcock, McGrew, & Mather, 2005)

The Batería III is the Spanish adaptation of the Woodcock-Johnson III (WJ-III; Woodcock, McGrew, & Mather, 2001) normed on 1,413 native Spanish-speaking individuals from different regions of the world including Mexico, Central America, Spain, and the United States. Administrators of the test must be fluent in Spanish. Like the WJ-III, the Batería III has both cognitive and achievement batteries and was designed for use with individuals between 2 and 90 years of age. Subtests, examiner's manuals, technical manuals, and, for the Batería III COG, a diagnostic supplement manual are all directly translated from their WJ-III editions with minor revisions. A brief screening questionnaire is available at the beginning of assessment to determine the examinee's language proficiency.

The WJ-III and Batería III were both developed based on the CHC theory of cognitive abilities. Broad cognitive abilities including *Gc, Gf, Gsm, Gs, Gv, Glr,* and auditory processing (*Ga*) are measured by both batteries. The Batería III COG includes 31 subtests including ten core subtests of the Standard Battery, ten subtests of the Extended Battery, and an additional eleven subtests of the Diagnostic Supplement. Subtests measure both broad and narrow range of abilities which can be grouped into the seven cognitive factors described above. Reliability and factor structure of Batería III approximates that of the WJ-III. Of significance, the Batería III's normative data was equated with the norms of the WJ-III, facilitating the option of comparing both scores for a single individual to understand how language proficiency may impact performance.

Wechsler Abbreviated Scale of Intelligence (WASI; Wechsler, 1999)

The WASI was developed to be a brief and psychometrically sound version of the WAIS-III that can be administered to children and adults. The standardization sample consisted of 2,245 individuals between the ages of 6 and 89 years of age stratified to represent the United States population. The test has four subtests which were all adapted from the WAIS-III, including the VO, SI, BD, and MR subtests. Like the WAIS-III, the WASI has been found to be influenced by acculturation. Razani, Murcia, Tabares, and Wong (2007) compared WASI scores between an ethnically diverse sample and English-speaking European Americans and found that the European American group outperformed the ethnic sample on the VO and SI subtests. Level of acculturation and proficiency in English correlated with these subtests, while years of education correlated with all subtests. Given that the WASI's subtests are identical in administration and format and similar in content to the WAIS-III's subtests, it is not surprising that the same issues with the WAIS-III also pertain to the WASI.

Kaufman Brief Intelligence Test – Second Edition (K-BIT 2; Kaufman & Kaufman, 2004b)

The K-BIT 2 is a brief intelligence test designed for individuals between 4 and 90 years of age. Two of the subtests tap into verbal ability including Verbal Knowledge, which measures receptive vocabulary and general information about the world, and Riddles, which tasks individuals to solve riddles. The third subtest, Matrices, measures nonverbal intelligence and is similar in content to the Wechsler Matrix Reasoning subtest. Like the KABC-II, the K-BIT 2 was conceived to be assessed on bilingual Spanish- and English-speaking individuals. Spanish translations of test items and different scoring options for Spanish language responses are available. However, the Spanish-speaking individuals are not part of the standardization sample, making interpretation of performance difficult. Research examining Hispanic individuals' performance on the K-BIT 2, as well as the normative data for Spanish items and scoring options, are currently lacking and needed.

Stanford-Binet Intelligence Scales – Fifth Edition (SB5; Roid, 2003)

The SB5 is the most recently and substantially revised version of the Stanford-Binet IQ scales. This battery was normed on 4,800 individuals in the United States between 2 and 85 years of age and was designed to match the 2001 United States Census Bureau in demographics. Along with retaining an FSIQ, the SB5 was designed to map directly on the CHC theory of intelligence with constructs of *Gf,*

Gc, quantitative knowledge (*Gq*), *Gv*, and *Gsm*. Each domain has a verbal and nonverbal component and performance on subtests can influence the structure of test administration. Although historically there have been efforts to standardize and compare earlier editions of the Stanford-Binet scales (Gaw, 1950; Manuel, 1935), no Spanish editions of the SB5 are currently available. In addition, research on the SB5 in Hispanic populations is lacking although at least one study on the fourth edition suggests that its verbal intelligence score is influenced by lower SES in Hispanic children with spina bifida meningomyelocele (Swartwout, Garnaat, Myszka, Fletcher, & Dennis, 2010).

Summary and Recommendations

The assessment of inherent intellectual abilities remains a key part of the psychodiagnostic and neuropsychological evaluation in spite of its limitations. A review of the literature indicates that language proficiency and level of acculturation to the United States heavily influence scores on IQ tests, particularly with those tapping into verbal or crystallized intelligence, but still impacting other types including nonverbal measures (Flanagan, Ortiz, & Alfonso, 2007). This is of particular pertinence to Hispanic individuals, who often are bilingual or speak English with limited proficiency, and many of whom have recently immigrated to the United States. Hispanics raised in the United States have on average less education, poorer quality of education, lower-income jobs, and live in lower-income housing compared to European American peers, which also impacts test performance.

These influences become apparent when Hispanic individuals are compared to their European American peers and underperform on many standard IQ measures. Such discrepancies are reduced when controlled for level of education and SES, though the gap remains on classic measures such as the WAIS-III and WISC-IV. This is likely due to issues of language proficiency, verbal and nonverbal miscommunication between the examiner and examinee, and culturally biased test items. More nefarious examples, such as the use of directly translated but unstandardized measures, or the inherent biases of the examiner that may lead to poor rapport or unconscious misdirection, are also possible sources of test discrepancy though it is hoped that such events are infrequent and, when they occur, addressed. Unfortunately, there are still clinicians who continue to inappropriately use IQ tests on Hispanic individuals who are not within the scope of the normative sample. Clinicians who are proficient in Spanish also have an ethical responsibility to have their proficiency objectively evaluated. Artiola i Fortuny and colleagues have recommended that one should be able to communicate at a university level to effectively work with monolingual Spanish-speaking clients, or otherwise refer out (Artiola i Fortuny et al., 2005; Artiola i Fortuny & Mullaney, 1998).

Spanish adaptations of common intellectual measures are available. The early EIWA overestimated IQ in Hispanic adults and was not truly generalizable outside the Puerto Rican population, and little empirical evidence is available on the EIWA-III. A European Spanish form of the WAIS-III is now available and has promise, though it was primarily normed for individuals from Spain. The WISC-IV Spanish edition is unique in having been normed in the United States for Hispanic-American children and may prove extremely useful, though further research is required to confirm its validity. The KABC-II and RIAS are examples of standard IQ batteries that were designed to be as culturally neutral and language free as possible, and at least in the case of the KABC-II, the research has supported this goal. It remains to be seen if the RIAS demonstrates similar success. The UNIT and NNAT also show promise in minimizing cultural bias with Hispanic children, as they primarily rely on nonverbal communication and assessment. However, clinicians should not simply assume that administering a nonverbal test of intelligence will be sufficient in controlling for bias. It is the responsibility of the psychologist to observe and determine how any cultural barriers, whether related to language, acculturation, education, or otherwise, may impact both test-taking behavior and performance.

IQ assessment has historically not been favorable toward minority groups, but the recent publication of several Spanish language and culturally neutral IQ batteries is encouraging. Spanish language neuropsychology batteries are also available (e.g., Batería Neuropsicológica en Español; Artiola i Fortuny, Hermosillo, Heaton, & Pardee, 1999) and allow clinicians the opportunity to provide comprehensive neurocognitive evaluations on their Spanish-speaking clients. It is the authors' opinions that the additional research examining the psychometric properties of such batteries across subpopulations of Hispanic individuals, including those with psychological and medical disorders, is needed to add to the literature on cognitive functioning in minority and, indeed, dominant populations. Validity studies remain few and far between, and many that do exist were published by the test authors themselves. If and when additional validity studies come out, they will allow clinicians and researchers to reliably interpret test scores in a meaningful and clinically useful manner. In the meantime, clinicians and researchers are encouraged to make use of the current measures that exist with the caveat that depending on the circumstances (e.g., acculturation level, language proficiency), results should be interpreted with caution.

References

Artiola i Fortuny, L., Garolera, M., Romo, D., Feldman, E., Barillas, H., Keefe, R., et al. (2005). Research with Spanish-speaking populations in the United States: Lost in the translation: A commentary and a plea. *Journal of Clinical and Experimental Neuropsychology, 27*(5), 555–564. doi:10.1080/13803390490918282.

Artiola i Fortuny, L., Heaton, R. K., & Hermosillo, D. (1998). Neuropsychological comparisons of Spanish-speaking participants from the US–Mexico border region versus Spain. *Journal of the International Neuropsychological Society, 4*(4), 363–379.

Artiola i Fortuny, L., Hermosillo, D., Heaton, R. K., & Pardee, R. E. (1999). *Manual de normas y procedimientos para la Batería Neuropsicológica en Español.* Tucson, AZ: m Press.

Artiola i Fortuny, L., & Mullaney, H. A. (1998). Assessing patients whose language you do not know: Can the absurd be ethical? *Clinical Neuropsychologist, 12*(1), 113–126. doi:10.1076/clin.12.1.113.1727.

Boone, K., Victor, T. L., Wen, J., Razani, J., & Pontón, M. (2007). The association between neuropsychological scores and ethnicity, language, and acculturation variables in a large patient population. *Archives of Clinical Neuropsychology, 22*(3), 355–365. doi:10.1016/j.acn.2007.01.010.

Borghese, P., & Gronau, R. C. (2005). Convergent and discriminant validity of the universal nonverbal intelligence test with limited English proficient Mexican-American elementary students. *Journal of Psychoeducational Assessment, 23*(2), 128–139. doi:10.1177/073428290502300202.

Bracken, B. A., & McCallum, R. S. (1998). *Universal nonverbal intelligence test examiner's manual.* Itsaka, IL: Riverside.

Braden, J. P., & Iribarren, J. A. (2007). Test review: Wechsler, D. (2005). Wechsler intelligence scale for children—Fourth edition Spanish. San Antonio, TX: Harcourt Assessment. *Journal of Psychoeducational Assessment, 25*, 292–299.

Brooks, B. L., Holdnack, J. A., & Iverson, G. L. (2011). Advanced clinical interpretation of the WAIS-IV and WMS-IV: Prevalence of low scores varies by level of intelligence and years of education. *Assessment, 18*(2), 156–167. doi:10.1177/1073191110385316.

Caruso, J. C., & Witkiewitz, K. (2001). Memory and reasoning abilities assessed by the universal nonverbal intelligence test: A reliable component analysis (RCA) study. *Educational and Psychological Measurement, 61*(1), 5–22. doi:10.1177/00131640121971031.

Choca, J. P., Krueger, K. R., De La Torre, G. G., Corral, S. S., & Garside, D. (2009). Demographic adjustments for the Spanish version of the WAIS-III. *Archives of Clinical Neuropsychology, 24*(6), 619–629. doi:10.1093/arclin/acp049.

Clark, C. M., DeCarli, C., Mungas, D., Chui, H. I., Higdon, R., Nuñez, J., et al. (2005). Earlier onset of Alzheimer disease symptoms in Latino individuals compared with Anglo individuals. *Archives of Neurology, 62*(5), 774–778. doi:10.1001/archneur.62.5.774.

Dale, B. A., McIntosh, D. E., Rothlisberg, B. A., Ward, K. E., & Bradley, M. (2011). Profile analysis of the Kaufman assessment battery for children, second edition, with African American and Caucasian preschool children. *Psychology in the Schools, 48*(5), 476–487. doi:10.1002/pits.20571.

Demsky, Y. I., Gass, C., & Golden, C. J. (1998). Interpretation of VIQ–PIQ and intersubset differences on the Spanish version of the WAIS (EIWA). *Assessment, 5*(1), 25–29. doi:10.1177/107319119800500105.

Echemendia, R. J., & Harris, J. G. (2004). Neuropsychological test use with Hispanic/Latino populations in the United States: Part II of a national survey. *Applied Neuropsychology, 11*(1), 4–12. doi:10.1207/s15324826an1101_2.

Egeland, J., Bosnes, O., & Johansen, H. (2009). Factor structure of the Norwegian version of the WAIS-III in a clinical sample: The arithmetic problem. *Assessment, 16*(3), 292–300. doi:10.1177/1073191108324464.

Escobedo, P., & Hollingworth, L. (2009). Annotations on the use of the Mexican norms for the WAIS-III. *Applied Neuropsychology, 16*(3), 223–227. doi:10.1080/09084280903098851.

Flanagan, D. P., Ortiz, S. O., & Alfonso, V. C. (2007). *Essentials of cross-battery assessment – Second Edition*. Hoboken, NJ: Wiley.

Fletcher-Janzen, E. (2003). *A validity study of the KABC-II and the Taos Pueblo Indian children of New Mexico*. Circle Pines, MN: American Guidance Service.

García, L. F., Ruiz, M., & Abad, F. (2003). Factor structure of the Spanish WAIS-III. *Psicothema, 15*(1), 155–160.

Gaw, E. (1950). El vocabulario de la prueba Stanford-Binet en El Salvador. *Revista De Psicología General Y Aplicada, 5*, 5701–5730.

Glutting, J., & Oakland, T. (1993). *Guide to the assessment of test session behavior*. San Antonio, TX: The Psychological Corporation.

Gollan, T. H., Salmon, D. P., Montoya, R. I., & Galasko, D. R. (2011). Degree of bilingualism predicts age of diagnosis of Alzheimer's disease in low-education but not in highly educated Hispanics. *Neuropsychologia, 49*(14), 3826–3830. doi:10.1016/j.neuropsychologia. 2011.09.041.

Gómez, F. C., Piedmont, R. L., & Fleming, M. Z. (1992). Factor analysis of the Spanish version of the WAIS: The Escala de Inteligencia Wechsler para Adultos (EIWA). *Psychological Assessment, 4*(3), 317–321. doi:10.1037/1040-3590.4.3.317.

Gonzales, R. R., & Roll, S. (1985). Relationship between acculturation, cognitive style, and intelligence. *Journal of Cross-Cultural Psychology, 16*(2), 190–205.

Harris, J. G., & Llorente, A. M. (2005). Cultural considerations in the use of the Wechsler intelligence scale for children – fourth edition (WISC-IV). In A. Prifitera, D. H. Saklofske, L. G. Weiss, A. Prifitera, D. H. Saklofske, & L. G. Weiss (Eds.), *WISC-IV clinical use and interpretation: Scientist-practitioner perspectives* (pp. 381–413). San Diego, CA: Elsevier Academic Press. doi:10.1016/B978-012564931-5/50013-X.

Harris, J. G., Tulsky, D. S., & Schultheis, M. T. (2003). Assessment of the non-native English speaker: Assimilating history and research findings to guide clinical practice. In D. S. Tulsky, D. H. Saklofske, G. J. Chelune, R. K. Heaton, R. J. Ivnik, R. Bornstein, A. Prifitera, & M. F. Ledbetter (Eds.), *Clinical interpretation of the WAIS-III and WMS-III* (pp. 343–390). San Diego, CA: Academic. doi:10.1016/B978-012703570-3/50015-8.

Heaton, R. K., Taylor, M. J., & Manly, J. (2003). Demographic effects and use of demographically corrected norms with the WAIS-III and WMS-III. In D. S. Tulsky, D. H. Saklofske, G. J. Chelune, R. K. Heaton, R. J. Ivnik, R. Bornstein, A. Prifitera, & M. F. Ledbetter (Eds.), *Clinical interpretation of the WAIS-III and WMS-III* (pp. 181–210). San Diego, CA: Academic. doi:10.1016/B978-012703570-3/50010-9.

Herrnstein, R. J., & Murray, C. A. (1994). *The bell curve: Intelligence and class structure in American life*. New York: Free Press.

Judd, T., Capetillo, D., Carrión-Baralt, J., Mármol, L. M., San Miguel-Montes, L., Navarrete, M., et al. (2009). Professional considerations for improving the neuropsychological evaluation of Hispanics: A National Academy of Neuropsychology education paper. *Archives of Clinical Neuropsychology, 24*(2), 127–135.

Karzmark, P. (2009). The effect of cognitive, personality, and background factors on the WAIS-III arithmetic subtest. *Applied Neuropsychology, 16*(1), 49–53. doi:10.1080/09084280802644144.

Kaufman, A. S. (1994). *Intelligent testing with the WISC-III*. New York: Wiley.

Kaufman, A. S., & Kaufman, N. L. (1983). *Kaufman assessment battery for children. Interpretive manual*. Circle Pines, MN: American Guidance Service.

Kaufman, A. S., & Kaufman, N. L. (2004a). *Kaufman assessment battery for children* (2nd ed.). Circle Pines, MN: AGS Publishing.

Kaufman, A. S., & Kaufman, N. L. (2004b). *Kaufman brief intelligence test* (2nd ed.). Circle Pines, MN: AGS Publishing.

Keith, T. Z., Fine, J., Taub, G. E., Reynolds, M. R., & Kranzler, J. H. (2006). Higher order, multisample, confirmatory factor analysis of the Wechsler intelligence scale for children – Fourth edition: What does it measure? *School Psychology Review, 35*(1), 108–127.

Knight, T. A. (2003). WAIS-III matrix reasoning: Instruction effects on task perception and performance. *Psychological Reports, 93*(1), 66–68. doi:10.2466/PR0.93.5.66-68.

Krohn, E. J., & Lamp, R. E. (1989). Concurrent validity of the Stanford-Binet fourth edition and K-ABC for head start children. *Journal of School Psychology, 27*(1), 59–67. doi:10.1016/0022-4405(89)90031-9.

Krueger, K. R., de la Torre, G. G., Fuentes, H., & Choca, J. P. (2005). Comparing Spanish and English norms for the WAIS and WMS. In J. Choca (Chair), *Spanish language adaptations of the Wechsler scales—WISC-IV, WAIS-III/WMS-III*. Symposium at the annual convention of the American Psychological Association, Washington, DC.

Lichtenberger, E. O., Broadbooks, D. Y., & Kaufman, A. S. (2000). *Essentials of cognitive assessment with KAIT and other Kaufman measures*. New York: Wiley.

López, S., & Romero, A. (1988). Assessing the intellectual functioning of Spanish-speaking adults: Comparison of the EIWA and the WAIS. *Professional Psychology: Research and Practice, 19*(3), 263–270. doi:10.1037/0735-7028.19.3.263.

Manuel, H. T. (1935). *Spanish and English editions of the Stanford-Binet in relation to the abilities of Mexican children* (University of Texas Bulletin, 3532). Austin, TX: University of Texas.

Melendez, F. (1994). The Spanish version of the WAIS: Some ethical considerations. *Clinical Neuropsychologist, 8*(4), 388–393. doi:10.1080/13854049408402041.

Muñoz-Sandoval, A. F., Woodcock, R. W., McGrew, K. S., & Mather, N. (2005). *Bateria-III Woodcock-Muñoz*. Itasca, IL: Riverside.

Naglieri, J. A. (1997). *Naglieri nonverbal ability test*. San Antonio, TX: The Psychological Corporation.

Naglieri, J. A. (2007). *Naglieri nonverbal ability test – Second Edition*. San Antonio, TX: The Psychological Corporation.

Naglieri, J. A., Booth, A. L., & Winsler, A. (2004). Comparison of Hispanic children with and without limited English proficiency on the Naglieri nonverbal ability test. *Psychological Assessment, 16*(1), 81–84. doi:10.1037/1040-3590.16.1.81.

Naglieri, J. A., & Hill, D. S. (1986). Comparison of WISC-R and K-ABC regression lines for academic prediction with Black and White children. *Journal of Clinical Child Psychology, 15*, 352–355.

Nisbett, R. E., Aronson, J., Blair, C., Dickens, W., Flynn, J., Halpern, D. F., et al. (2012). Intelligence: New findings and theoretical developments. *American Psychologist*. doi:10.1037/a0026699.

Olazaran, J., Jacobs, D. M., & Stern, Y. (1996). Comparative study of visual and verbal short-term memory in English and Spanish speakers: Testing a linguistic hypothesis. *Journal of the International Neuropsychological Society, 2*(2), 105–110. doi:10.1017/S1355617700000953.

Ortiz, S. O. (2001). Assessment of cognitive abilities in Hispanic children. *Seminars in Speech and Language, 22*(1), 17–36.

Prifitera, A., Saklofske, D. H., Weiss, L. G., & Rolfhus, E. (2005). The WISC-IV in the clinical assessment context. In A. Prifitera, D. H. Saklofske, L. G. Weiss, A. Prifitera, D. H. Saklofske, & L. G. Weiss (Eds.), *WISC-IV clinical use and interpretation: Scientist-practitioner perspectives* (pp. 3–32). San Diego, CA: Elsevier Academic Press. doi:10.1016/B978-012564931-5/50002-5.

Razani, J., Murcia, G., Tabares, J., & Wong, J. (2007). The effects of culture on WASI test performance in ethnically diverse individuals. *The Clinical Neuropsychologist, 21*(5), 776–788. doi:10.1080/13854040701437481.

Reed, M., & McCallum, R. (1995). Construct validity of the universal nonverbal intelligence test (UNIT). *Psychology in the Schools, 32*(4), 277–290. doi:10.1002/1520-6807(199510)32:4<277::AID-PITS2310320406>3.0.CO;2-M.

Renteria, L., Li, S., & Pliskin, N. H. (2008). Reliability and validity of the Spanish language Wechsler adult intelligence scale (3rd edition) in a sample of American, urban, Spanish-speaking Hispanics. *The Clinical Neuropsychologist, 22*(3), 455–470. doi:10.1080/13854040701336428.

Reynolds, C. R., & Kamphaus, R. W. (2003). *Reynolds intellectual assessment scales: Professional manual*. Lutz, FL: PAR.

Reynolds, C. R., & Kamphaus, R. W. (2009). *Escalas de Inteligencia de Reynolds*. Madrid, Spain: TEA Ediciones.

Roid, G. H. (2003). *Stanford-Binet intelligence scales, fifth edition, examiner's manual*. Itasca, IL: Riverside.

San Miguel Montes, L. E., Allen, D. N., Puente, A. E., & Neblina, C. (2010). Validity of the WISC–IV Spanish for a clinically referred sample of Hispanic children. *Psychological Assessment, 22*(2), 465–469. doi:10.1037/a0018895.

Sherrill, W. W., Crew, L., Mayo, R. M., Mayo, W. F., Rogers, B. L., & Haynes, D. F. (2005). Educational and health services innovation to improve care for rural Hispanic communities in the US. *Education for Health: Change in Learning & Practice, 18*(3), 356–367. doi:10.1080/13576280500312850.

Suen, H. K., & Greenspan, S. (2009). Serious problems with the Mexican norms for the WAIS-III when assessing mental retardation in capital cases. *Applied Neuropsychology, 16*(3), 214–222. doi:10.1080/09084280903098786.

Swartwout, M. D., Garnaat, S. L., Myszka, K. A., Fletcher, J. M., & Dennis, M. (2010). Associations of ethnicity and SES with IQ and achievement in spina bifida meningomyelocele. *Journal of Pediatric Psychology, 35*(9), 927–936. doi:10.1093/jpepsy/jsq001.

TEA Ediciones. (2001). *WAIS-III Escala de Inteligencia de Wechsler para Adultos-III; Manual tecnico*. Madrid, Spain: TEA Ediciones.

The Psychological Corporation. (1968). *Escala de Inteligencia Wechsler para Adultos*. New York: Author.

Thomsen, C., Gallup, L., & Llorente, A. M. (2008). Intellectual abilities: Theoretical and applied assessment considerations. In A. M. Llorente (Ed.), *Principles of neuropsychological assessment with Hispanics: Theoretical foundations and clinical practice* (pp. 57–77). New York: Springer. doi:10.1007/978-0-387-71758-6_4.

Tulsky, D., & Zhu, J. (2003). *Escala Wechsler de Inteligencia para adultos-III*. Cuauhtémoc, Mexico: Manual Moderno.

U.S. Census Bureau. (2006). *Hispanic population of the United States*. Retrieved January 7, 2012, from http://www.census.gov/population/www/socdemo/hispanic/files/Internet_Hispanic_in_US_2006.pdf

Wechsler, D. (1997a). *Wechsler adult intelligence scale – Third edition*. San Antonio, TX: The Psychological Corporation.

Wechsler, D. (1997b). *Wechsler Memory Scale – Third Edition. (WMS-III)*. San Antonio, TX: The Psychological Corporation.

Wechsler, D. (1999). *Wechsler abbreviated scale of intelligence*. San Antonio, TX: The Psychological Corporation.

Wechsler, D. (2003). *Wechsler intelligence scale for children—Fourth edition*. San Antonio, TX: The Psychological Corporation.

Wechsler, D. (2005). *Wechsler intelligence scale for children—Fourth edition—Spanish*. San Antonio, TX: Harcourt Assessment.

Wechsler, D. (2008a). *Wechsler adult intelligence scale–Fourth edition*. San Antonio, TX: Pearson.

Wechsler, D. (2008b). *Escala de Inteligencia de Wechsler para Adultos-Tercera Edicion (EIWA-III)*. San Antonio, TX: NCS Pearson.

Weiss, L. G., Saklofske, D. H., Coalson, D., & Raiford, S. E. (2010). *WAIS-IV clinical use and interpretation: Scientist-practitioner perspectives*. London: Academic.

Woodcock, R. W., McGrew, K. S., & Mather, N. (2001). *Woodcock-Johnson III*. Itasca, IL: Riverside.

Assessing Effort and Malingering with the Hispanic Client

7

Lorraine T. Benuto and Brian D. Leany

What Is Malingering and Effort?

The DSM-IV defines malingering as "…the intentional production of false or grossly exaggerated physical or psychological symptoms, motivated by external incentives…" and specifies that malingering should be strongly suspected if any combination of the following is observed: medicolegal context of presentation, marked discrepancy between self-reported stress or disability and objective findings, lack of cooperation during diagnostic evaluation or with prescribed treatment, or presence of antisocial personality disorder (American Psychiatric Association, 2000). It is important to note that malingering may occur in many forms including the feigning of cognitive difficulties, psychiatric complications, or somatic problems (e.g., chronic pain) (Vilar-Lopez et al., 2007).

Recently, a debate has ensued regarding the term "malingering," and many professionals prefer the use of the term "effort" (sometime specified as "poor" or "suboptimal") to describe what previously would have simply been termed malingering. It is important to note that within the context of this chapter, the term "malinger" will be used. The main differentiation between "effort" and "malingering" has to do with motivation. In theory, one could exhibit poor effort for any number of reasons (e.g., fatigue, disinterest in the testing process, etc.), whereas with malingering, there is intentional production of symptoms that are motivated by an external incentive. Certainly, it is impossible to know for certain a client's intention and motivation (i.e., clients can and do lie); however, the majority of tests discussed within this chapter aim to assess for symptoms that are feigned. From there, the individual clinician must explore through the use of other tests, collaterals, scientific research, etc., whether or not the client may be producing symptoms due to an external incentive with special attention being paid to whether or not any of the following are apparent: medicolegal context of presentation, marked discrepancy between self-reported stress or disability and objective findings, lack of cooperation during diagnostic evaluation or with prescribed treatment, or presence of antisocial personality disorder (APA, 2000).

L.T. Benuto, Ph.D. (✉)
Department of Psychology, Victims of Crime Treatment Center, University of Nevada, Reno MS 0296, Reno, NV 89557, USA
e-mail: dr.benuto@gmail.com

B.D. Leany, Ph.D.
California Department of Corrections and Rehabilitation, Adult Division, California Correctional Health Care Services, PO Box 750, Susanville, CA 96127, USA
e-mail: leanyb@gmail.com

L.T. Benuto (ed.), *Guide to Psychological Assessment with Hispanics*,
DOI 10.1007/978-1-4614-4412-1_7,

Why Assessment Is Important?

Accurate assessment of malingering is important for a number of reasons. First, malingering can cause harm to the individual who is malingering via several avenues, i.e., he or she may receive unnecessary treatment, he or she may not receive necessary treatment or may receive a contraindicated treatment, extraordinary amounts of time and effort may be dedicated to feigning as opposed to more constructive and healthy activities, future claims of an illness may be met with skepticism, etc. In fact, clinicians may encounter malingering via referrals from frustrated health professionals who have a client with a history of unsuccessful treatment and a spectrum of diagnoses usually with some co-occurring personal problem or familial discord. Accordingly, the financial costs of malingering are thought to be high (consider all the medical attention somebody who is malingering receives), and fraud (which broadly includes malingering) costs the insurance industry $150 billion annually and costs families approximately $1,800 per year in increased insurance costs (Garriga, 2007). Others have estimated that malingering specifically runs the United States a $5.36 billion per year, which does not include working days lost or the cost of substituting for the individual who is absent as a result of their malingering endeavors (Gouvier, Lees-Haley, & Hammer, 2003).

Occasionally, the clinician may feel ethically conflicted when it becomes apparent that a V-code of malingering is merited. This may result from the apparent repercussions that the individual being tested may face if such a diagnosis is applied, e.g., in the context of the Veteran's Administration, the individual could lose access to benefits; in a personal injury litigation, the individual could be exempt from receiving financial compensation; in the context of an educational evaluation, the individual would not receive academic accommodations, etc. However, for the reasons discussed above, the APA code of ethics by which psychologists are bound, and the stance of other professional organizations on the topic (see discussion below on the National Academy of Neuropsychology), if a V-code of malingering is merited, it must be applied.

Certainly, accurate and early identification of malingering is of utmost importance (for the reasons discussed above), although this goal is not met without certain challenges and may be even more complicated when assessing specific populations, e.g., Hispanics. In fact, some research has demonstrated differences in performance that are associated with cultural differences when psychological tests are used with other ethnic groups than the tests were designed for (Puente & Perez-Garcia, 2000). Furthermore, the National Academy of Neuropsychology Policy and Planning Committee (Bush et al., 2005) has asserted that the use of Symptom Validity Tests (SVTs) with culturally diverse populations for whom validation data do not exist must be carefully considered and experts have illustrated that the Hispanic client may be difficult to assess given the low development of forensic neuropsychology in Spanish-speaking countries (Verdejo-García, Alcázar-Córcoles, Gómez-Jarabo-García, & Pérez-García, 2004). However, Bush et al. do not preclude the use of SVTs for these populations but only reiterate the APA's stance that any practitioner must be able to justify their use of such tests and determination based on these tests must be supported by science. In fact, this chapter goes on to state that neuropsychologists who suspect secondary gain as an incentive for feigning have an ethical obligation to assess for malingering.

Aims of the Chapter

Thus, the aim of this chapter is to explore the most commonly used and/or researched measures that strive to assess for malingering specifically in the context of their use with Hispanics and to generate evidence-based recommendations for the assessment of malingering with the Hispanic client.

Test of Memory Malingering (TOMM: Tombaugh, 1996)

Overview of the TOMM

The TOMM specifically assesses for false symptoms of memory impairment and consists of two learning trials and an optional retention trial. The client is first presented with 50 pictures of common objects. After the presentation of the 50 pictures, the client is presented with two pictures and must identify which of the two he or she has previously viewed. Results are based on two cutoff scores: (1) below chance and (2) criterion based on head injured and cognitively impaired clients. Research has indicated that over half (55.6%) of participants in nonclinical populations score 49 or 50 on the TOMM and only 8.4% score lower than 45 (Tombaugh, 1996), and as alluded to above, from a purely chance perspective at worst, one would expect the client to score 50% on the TOMM although research has demonstrated that even individuals with actual cognitive impairment tend to score higher than chance. Certainly, a score of less than chance would suggest deliberate feigning of memory impairment.

The TOMM and the Hispanic Client

The TOMM has been researched specifically with Hispanics. For example, Prieto De Estebecorena (2007) administered the TOMM to a group of 120 foreign-born Hispanics of varying levels of education and acculturation. While Prieto De Estebecorena did find some associations between scores on trial 1 of the TOMM and education and acculturation levels, the average score of participants on trial 1 of the TOMM was 45.59 (SD=3.35) (trial 2: M=48.57; SD=1.54; trial 3: M=49.26; SD=1.23). While these means are slightly lower than what Tombaugh (1996) has reported in nonclinical samples, they are still substantially above chance, and, thus, the interpretation of the scores would essentially be the same.

Vilar-Lopez and colleagues (2007) have also researched the TOMM and specifically examined differences in performance between Hispanics and their North American counterparts. They studied three groups (all of which were 6 months post-injury): a group of patients with Post-Concussion Syndrome (PCS) not involved in any PCS-related litigation (PCS-NLI), a group of patients with PCS involved in PCS-related litigation (PCS-LI), and a group of analog malingerers (AN). The assessment of the PCS-NLI and PCS-LI groups comprised a functional neuroimaging study (SPECT) and, on a different day, a neuropsychological battery of tests (of which the TOMM was a part of). Using the TOMM, 88.6% of the AN group were classified as malingerers, suggesting that the TOMM does a good job at identifying malingering (although it is important to note that no significant differences were found between litigants and non-litigants with PCS). Most relevant to this chapter is that no differences in the performance on the TOMM were identified between the Spanish and North American samples. However, in this same study, a statistically significant difference was observed between the group with brain damage (PCS) and a group with a high probability of malingering (PCS-LI). Vilar-Lopez and colleagues suggest that this difference may be explained by the heterogeneity of the groups considered to have a high probability of malingering, leading to varying percentages of malingering subjects in the different studies. Specifically, the authors assert that just because one would assume that a group has a high probability to malinger (e.g., they are involved in litigation as was the case for this study), does not mean that they are malingering. Therefore, one could reasonably deduce that the group contained non-malingers as well as malingers. Thus, the recommendation based upon the equivalency between Spanish and North American samples is that this test be utilized in neuropsychological and cognitive assessments, to rule out feigning with Hispanic clients.

Word Memory Test (WMT) and Medical Symptom Validity Test (MSVT)

Overview of the WMT and MSVT

The Word Memory Test (WMT; Green, 2003; Green & Astner, 1995) and the Medical Symptom Validity Test (MSVT; Green, 2004) are computerized memory tests with multiple subtests measuring verbal and nonverbal memory that contain hidden measures, which serve to check the validity of the patient's test scores. There is also a nonverbal version of the MSVT, which consists of artist-drawn colored images that appear on the computer screen (as opposed to words).

The WMT and MSVT and the Hispanic Client

Both the WMT and the MSVT are available in Spanish and have been researched with a Hispanic sample. Specifically, Green, Montijo, and Brockhaus (2011) cross-validated the proposed easy–hard difference cutoffs for the WMT and the MSVT with a sample of patients with probable dementia tested in Spanish in Puerto Rico. They chose to focus on samples of patients with probable dementia because such patients tend to have as much cognitive impairment or more impairment than almost any other category of patients. Results demonstrated that it is possible to achieve very high specificity for poor effort in groups with dementia who have severe impairment of verbal memory, as shown by their very low free recall scores on both tests, i.e., it is possible to determine from the test results on the WMT or MSVT whether failure on the easy subtests is likely to reflect actual impairment despite severe memory impairment or poor effort.

MMPI-2 and A

Overview of the MMPI

The MMPI is one of the most frequently used measures in psychology to assess for personality and psychopathology. Extensive information regarding the MMPI can be found in self-report personality assessment chapter of this book. As it pertains to this chapter, the MMPI as a tool for assessing for malingering will be discussed.

Generally speaking, there are a number of scales that can be examined to detect malingering although the MMPI-2 Fake Bad Scale (FBS; Lees-Haley, English, & Glenn, 1991) was specifically developed to detect response bias in personal injury cases and to some extent measures "somatic malingering" (Larrabee, 1998) as the scale items consist largely of items relating to physical distress and it overlaps with other MMPI-2 scales of somatic over-endorsement (scales 1, 3; Nelson, Sweet, & Demakis, 2006). In addition to its use with personal injury litigants, research has also demonstrated good discriminate validity for this scale in the context of traumatic brain injury litigants (Greiffenstein, Baker, Gola, Donders, & Miller, 2002; Larrabee, 2003; Martens, Donders, & Millis, 2001; Ross, Millis, Krukowski, Putnam, & Adams, 2004). Furthermore, a number of meta-analyses have indicated that several scales beyond the FBS are good at detecting malingering. For example, Berry, Baer, and Harris (1991) conducted a meta-analysis of 28 MMPI studies of faking bad in adults and found that both the F (Infrequency) scale and the F-K (Infrequency minus Defensiveness) index were effective at detecting fake-bad profiles. Subsequently, Rogers, Sewell, and Salekin (1994) also conducted a meta-analysis of 15 studies of malingering and found that the F scale, F-K index, Fb (Back Infrequency Scale) scale, the revised Social Desirability Scale, and the obvious-subtle index were good at detecting malingering. In addition to the above, research has demonstrated good discriminate validity for the F and Fb scales and the F-K index (Bagby, Nicholson, Buis, & Bacchiochi, 2000; Cramer, 1995; Lim & Butcher, 1996).

The MMPI-2 and the Hispanic Client

Certainly, a large portion of the personality assessment chapter was dedicated to the MMPI-2 and the Hispanic client. Thus, this section will only focus on the MMPI-2 and the Hispanic client as the MMPI-2 relates to malingering.

Some researchers have indicated that Hispanics tend to endorse more somatic symptoms than Caucasians on both the MMPI-2 (Hall, Bansal, & Lopez, 1999) and other measures (e.g., Angel & Guarnaccia, 1989; Haberman, 1970, 1976; Srole et al., 1978) although meta-analysis has not indicated this to be the case (Hall et al. 1999). Specific to malingering, Dean et al. (2008) found results that a systematic bias against ethnic minorities on the FBS was absent and suggested that the FBS is appropriate for use with Hispanics in clinical settings. However, Hall et al. found that when examined via meta-analysis Latino-American males had higher scores than European Americans on the three validity scales (*L, F,* and *K*) although a large effect sizes was only observed for the L scale (Latinos scored higher than Euro-Americans). Lucio and Valencia (1997) found that the Mexican version of the MMPI-2 was able to distinguish those who were asked to fake good, as well as those who were asked to fake symptoms of schizophrenia, paranoid type, from students provided normal instructions for the MMPI-2 (assumed to respond normally), and genuine psychiatric patients. The scales most relevant across genders were F, Fp, L, and K. Here the response pattern was similar to what you would see in the normative sample for North Americans. Mexican-Americans asked to fake schizophrenia showed T-scores for infrequency (F-120T) that would invalidate the profiles. However, Mexican-Americans who faked good were indistinguishable from normal controls. Thus, the Spanish version of the MMPI-2 appears to be useful for identifying those faking severe mental illness, but the reverse (identifying those faking good) would seem impossible with this test.

The MMPI-A and the Hispanic Client

The Minnesota Multiphasic Personality Inventory—Adolescent (MMPI-A) (Butcher & Pope, 1992) was developed in the United States to assess issues specific to adolescents, using a current age-appropriate normative sample. The Mexican version of the MMPI-A was developed using a stringent methodology to adapt the test to the Mexican population (Lucio, Ampudia, Duran, Gallegos, & Leon, 1999). Lucio, Durán, Graham, and Ben-Porath (2002) examined the extent to which the validity scales of the MMPI-A identified Mexican adolescents who were instructed to fake bad. The results of this study indicate that the validity scales and indexes of the MMPI-A (F, F1, F2, and F-K) can accurately detect adolescents who complete the test with instructions to fake bad.

Higher optimal cutoff scores were required for boys than for girls for discriminating the standard and fake-bad conditions for nonclinical adolescents, and the opposite was true for discriminating the fake-bad and clinical groups. In addition, higher cutoff scores were required for optimal discrimination between fake-bad and standard condition groups for base rates lower than that in the present study (50%). Although Stein, Graham, and Williams (1995) found lower cut off scores than in the current study, the authors indicated that the scores that they reported seemed to be atypically low. The higher cutoff scores in the current study could also indicate cultural differences between Mexican and US adolescents. This factor should be taken into account when Hispanic adolescents are tested in the United States. It is possible that clinical Mexican adolescents are more likely to exaggerate their symptoms or admit them more openly than Hispanic adolescents living in the United States. Thus, one should be very cautious in generalizing the findings of the above study to Hispanic adolescents in the United States. Similar to the recommendations of Lucio, Valencia, and Butcher (2001), for Mexican-American adults, one may wish to consider utilizing both the Mexican-American norms as well as the North American norms to rule out socially appropriate, gender-appropriate responses.

Digit Span

Overview of Digit Span and Malingering and Effort

Digit Span (DS) is used in many psychological tests designed to assess various aspects of cognitive function (e.g., Wechsler Adult Intelligence Scale-IV; Montreal Cognitive Assessment) and specifically assesses auditory attention. It may be administered forward and/or backward depending on the assessment measure. Reliable Digit Span (RDS; Greiffenstein, Baker, & Gola, 1994) has been used as a means to assess for effort or feigning of cognitive or other symptoms. RDS is calculated by summing the longest forward and backward digit strings from the Digit Span test. Because Digit Span performance tends to be preserved in persons with brain dysfunction (e.g., Greiffenstein et al., 1994; Heinly, Greve, Bianchini, Love, & Brennan, 2005; Iverson & Tulsky, 2003), it serves as good indicator of feigned cognitive impairment, and there is substantial research to support its validity (Suhr & Barrash, 2007).

Digit Span and the Hispanic Client

Traditionally, it has been found that Hispanics recall, on average, fewer numbers on Digit Span than do their non-Hispanic counterparts (Kaufman, 1990). More recent research supports these earlier findings particularly in the context of administration in English vs. Spanish (Boone, Victor, Wen, Razani, & Ponton, 2007; Gasquoine, Croyle, Cavazos-Gonzalez, & Sandoval, 2007; Wheeler, 2010), and it has been purported that these differences are a result of the differences in the phonological length of digits (e.g., Ardila et al., 2000). That being said, research specifically assessing Reliable Digit Span with Hispanics in either English or Spanish appears to be absent. In fact, a review of the literature has indicated that in many studies examining RDS demographic data is not mentioned (e.g., Axelrod, Fichtenberg, Millis, & Wertheimer, 2006; Babikian, Boone, Lu, & Arnold, 2006; Heinly et al., 2005; Larrabee, 2003); thus, it is unknown if Hispanics were included as part of the sample or alternatively in many studies that do report ethnicity, Hispanics were not part of the sample (e.g., Greve et al., 2007; Strauss et al., 2002). In the few studies where ethnicity was mentioned and Hispanics were included, they constituted between 1 and 1.6% of the samples (Greve et al. 2010; Marshall & Happe, 2007). Because RDS is essentially based on DS performance and ethnic and language differences exist in terms of DS performance, the RDS may require an adjustment although it appears that such differences primarily exist as a result of English vs. Spanish language administration. Thus, while RDS is traditionally used as an implicit measure of malingering, current research does not seem to support this use for Hispanic clients, in particular those whose primary language is Spanish.

The Structured Interview of Reported Symptoms (SIRS; Rogers, Bagby, & Dickens, 1992)

Overview of the SIRS

The original SIRS has been referred to as the gold standard for assessing for feigned mental disorders (Rogers, 2008) and is the most commonly used feigning measure in forensic practice (Archer, Buffington-Vollum, Stredny, & Handel, 2006). The SIRS is currently in its second edition, referred to as the Structured Interview of Reported Symptoms, Second Edition (SIRS-2; Rogers, Sewell, & Gillard, 2010a), and contains significant changes designed to prevent false-positive and false-negative classification errors (Rubenzer, 2010). The Spanish translation of the SIRS (Spanish SIRS: based on the original SIRS) consists of 172 items (organized into eight primary scales: rare symptoms [RS], symptom combinations [SC], improbable and absurd symptoms [IA], blatant symptoms [BL], subtle symptoms [SU], selectivity of symptoms [SEL], severity of symptoms [SEV], and reported versus observed symptoms [RO]) administered in a structured interview format. Questions are mostly scored using a "no," "qualified yes" (e.g., "sometimes"), or "yes" format, and 32 items are asked twice as a means to assess response consistency (Rogers et al., 1992).

The SIRS and the Hispanic Client

The Spanish SIRS has undergone a rigorous process of translation and back translation, which has resulted in a linguistically equivalent measure for the Spanish translation. Initial research with bilingual Hispanics showed similar scores between the Spanish and English versions of the SIRS (Rogers, Sewell, & Gillard, 2010b). Correa, Rogers, and Hoersting (2010) also investigated the Spanish SIRS with 80 Spanish-speaking Hispanic-American outpatients, and results indicated favorable reliability and validity. Therefore, the SIRS-2 administered in Spanish would be a good screening item to suggest further assessment for malingering with the Hispanic client.

The Sentence Completion Task-75 (SCT-75)

Overview of the SCT-75

The Sentence Completion Task-75 (SCT-75) is a revised version of the Sentence Completion Task-136 (SCT-136; Timmons, Lanyon, Almer, & Curran, 1993) which compares responses of individuals instructed to malinger with MMPI profiles and identifies three specific patterns of responding for malingering. The original version of this measure consisted of 136 items, and the revised version consists of 75 items. The Spanish version of the SCT-75 was created via the back-translation method (Saavedra, 1999).

The SCT-75 and the Hispanic Client

A single research study has examined the Spanish version of the SCT-75. Saavedra (1999) administered the Spanish version of the SCT-75 to 80 Hispanic participants who were foreign-born, 18 or older, who had been living in the United States for at least 1 year, and who considered Spanish to be their native language. Half of the participants (the experimental group) were involved in personal injury litigation and reported suffering from physical and/or psychological injuries and difficulties due to accidents they incurred. The other half of the participants (the control group) also reported suffering from chronic physical and/or psychological injuries and difficulties but were not involved in personal injury litigation or seeking any type of financial compensation. The experimental group also completed the Spanish version of the MMPI-2. Results indicated that the S-SCT-75 had overall poor internal consistency although certain significant differences were found between both groups on some of the S-SCT-75 variables, such as problem focus and disability exaggeration, no significant differences were found between groups on the other S-SCT-75 subscales. Results also indicated that the S-SCT-75 had limited concurrent validity with the Spanish MMPI-2, although some significant correlations between tests were found, such as between the MMPI-2's depression scale and the S-SCT-75's domain of angry negativity and its subscales of denigration of doctors and depressive outlook. Thus, this measure is not recommended for use in the assessment of malingering with the Hispanic client, particularly considering the availability of psychometrically superior assessment measures.

Miller-Forensic Assessment of Symptoms Test (M-FAST; Miller, 2001)

Overview of the M-FAST

The Miller-Forensic Assessment of Symptoms Test (M-FAST; Miller, 2001) is a 25-item structured interview intended to help identify malingered psychopathology. A total score corresponds with seven strategies frequently used among individuals who malinger: unusual hallucinations, reported versus observed, rare combinations, extreme symptomatology, negative image, unusual symptom course, and suggestibility. The M-FAST has been shown to have good psychometric properties (Miller, 2001).

The M-FAST and the Hispanic Client

Guy and Miller (2004) have examined the utility of the M-FAST among Hispanics and other ethnic minority groups. Specifically, they examined this measure with a sample of incarcerated males ($N=50$) who had applied for mental health services in a maximum-security prison and a small portion of the sample were Hispanic (12%, $n=6$). Results from this study indicated that accurate classification was best achieved with an M-FAST total cutoff score of 6 (which is consistent with past research), and results across ethnic groups were practically identical, suggesting preliminary generalizability of the M-FAST for African-American, Hispanic, and Caucasian inmates. Other studies not specifically examining ethnic differences in terms of performance on the M-FAST but exploring reliability and or validity have not excluded Hispanics from their samples, and the inclusion of Hispanics has ranged from 5 (Messer, & Fremouw, 2007) to 16% (Veazey, Wagner, Hays, & Miller, 2005). This suggests that the M-FAST has great utility as a screening for malingering across cultures, and that the clinician working with the Hispanic client, who suspects malingering, could screen their client using this measure with a good deal of confidence.

Fig. 7.1 Rey-Ostrich 15 Items

A	B	C
1	2	3
a	b	c
○	□	△
I	II	III

Rey 15 Items

Overview of the Rey-Ostrich 15 Items

The Rey-Ostrich 15-Item Test is a simple test that consists of two parts. First, the client is briefly exposed to a page that contains 15 items (numbers, letters, and geometrical figures—see Fig. 7.1) and asked to reproduce items. Subsequently, in a recognition trial, the client is presented with a page containing all target items plus 15 new items and asked to identify which of the items they were not presented with earlier (Salazar, Lu, Wen, & Boone, 2007).

The Rey 15 Items and the Hispanic Client

Salazar et al. (2007) discuss findings from a study presented by Salazar, Lopez, Peña, and Mitrushina (2003) who administered the Rey 15-Item Test plus recognition (Boone, Salazar, Lu, Warner-Chacon, & Razani, 2002) and the Dot Counting Test (see below for results specific to the DCT) to 108 Spanish-speaking males. The results of this study showed a statistically significant difference between both levels of education (less than 6 years or greater than 6 years), as well as language spoken (English or Spanish). These results suggest that those with less than 6 years of education are more likely to score lower than educated or English-speaking individuals, and, thus, a lower cutoff would be necessary for this group to detect malingering, while a higher cutoff would be necessary for those who speak English or those who have greater than 6 years of education. However, the variability among the groups comes with a less than optimal yet adequate level of specificity (e.g., the ability to detect approximately 82% of malingers, with a cutoff of <9 in the less than 6 years of education group and approximately 90% of malingering with a cutoff of <17 in the greater than 6 years of education group). Thus, as long as educational level of the individual being assessed is known and the appropriate adjustment to the cut score is made, the Rey 15-Item Test acts as a suitable measure of malingering in the Hispanic client.

Dot Counting Test (DCT; Boone, Lu, & Herzberg, 2002)

Overview of the Dot Counting Test

The Dot Counting Test (DCT; Boone et al., 2002) consists of the administration of 24 4×6 cards (presented one at a time) that contain a variable number of dots. On the first half of the cards, the dots are arranged in a standardized random order (with 11, 19, 15, 23, 27, and 7 dots, respectively, on each card). On the other half of the cards, the dots are arranged in easily recognizable symmetrical groups (containing 12, 20, 16, 24, 28, and 8 dots, respectively). The client is instructed as follows: "I'm going to show you cards with dots on them. I want you to count the dots as quickly as you can" (Boone et al., 1995). Lezak (1983) has offered recommendations on how to score and interpret the test results. Specifically, he identified that a mean grouped dot counting time in excess of the mean time for brain-damaged subjects (4.8″) and a mean grouped dot counting time that was not at least twice as fast as the mean ungrouped dot counting time (ungrouped/grouped = <2) are indicative of malingering. Boon et al. have indicated that the failure on this test can be computed as follows:

$$\text{Score} = \text{M Grouped Time} - \left\{ \frac{\text{M Ungrouped Time}}{\text{M Grouped Time}} \right\}$$

The Dot Counting Test (DCT) and the Hispanic Client

As described in the "Rey 15 Items" section of this chapter, Salazar et al. (2007) discuss findings from a study presented by Salazar et al. (2003). Relative to the Hispanic client, participants performed at a comparable level to English speakers on the DCT. Thus, the standard DCT test cutoff (e.g., use of the standard E-score cutoff of ≥17) can be used with monolingual Spanish speakers of low educational level with no loss in specificity (Salazar et al.2007).

Summary and Recommendations

In this chapter, we have reviewed some of the most commonly used and well-researched tests that aim to assess for malingering and/or effort. A summary of these measures with appropriate recommendations can be found in Table 7.1. This review has revealed that there are several useful measures that can be used to assess for malingering with good psychometric properties available to for use with the Hispanic client. These measures, when administered appropriately and under the considerations described above, should serve as useful tools in discerning genuine psychological symptoms from symptoms of malingering. Thus, the inclusion of these measures in an assessment battery, particularly when feigning of symptoms is or could be expected, should aid in proper diagnosis and corresponding interventions for the Hispanic client. When administering a test that requires that results be interpreted with caution, this may be achieved by gathering additional data, i.e., administering additional tests that assess for malingering, corroborating the information provided with reliable collateral contacts, etc.

In sum, a clinician should not be reluctant to diagnose their client with malingering. In fact, it is much more detrimental to the client to treat them for a disorder that does not exist and likely diverts resources from individuals with genuine mental illness. Thus, if there is substantial evidence to suggest that a V-code of malingering is merited, it is the ethical responsibility of the clinician to include this as part of a 5-axis diagnosis, and there are several reliable and valid assessment measures that can be used with the Hispanic client to help ascertain this information.

Table 7.1 Malingering and effort tests

Test name	Original language	Available in Spanish	Research conducted with Hispanics	Are cultural modifications necessary?
Test of Memory Malingering	English	Since this test is essentially a nonverbal test, it can be utilized with Spanish-speaking clients	Several studies have supported the use of this measure with Hispanics	No
The Word Memory Test and the Medical Symptom Validity Test	English	Yes	Research with a Puerto Rican sample has supported the use of this measure with Hispanics	No
MMPI-II and MMPI-A	English	Yes	Extensive research has been conducted with Hispanic samples	Yes—please see the section on the "MMPI-2 and A" for specifics
Reliable Digit Span	English	Easily administered in Spanish	Research on the RDS and Hispanics is essentially absent and research on Digit Span indicates that language appears to impact results	Yes
The Structured Interview of Reported Symptoms	English	Spanish translation available	Yes, limited research has been conducted	No
The Sentence Completion Task-75 (SCT-75)	English	Spanish translation available	Yes, although the research suggests that this is not a good measure to use with Hispanics	This measure should not be used with Hispanics due to its poor psychometric properties
Miller-Forensic Assessment of Symptoms Test (M-FAST)	English	No	Yes, limited research has been conducted	No
Rey 15 Items	English	Easily administered in Spanish	Yes, limited research has been conducted	No
Dot Counting Test	English	Easily administered in Spanish	Yes, limited research has been conducted	No

References

American Psychiatric Association. (2000). *Diagnostic and statistical manual of mental disorders* (4th ed., Text rev.). Washington, DC: APA.

Angel, R., & Guarnaccia, P. J. (1989). Mind, body, and culture: Somatization among Hispanics. *Social Science & Medicine, 28*, 1229–1238.

Archer, R. P., Buffington-Vollum, J. K., Stredny, R. V., & Handel, R. W. (2006). A survey of psychological test use patterns among forensic psychologists. *Journal of Personality Assessment, 87*(1), 84–94 & 11.

Ardila, A., Monica, R., Feggy, O. S., Jose, M., Gladys, G., & Migue, S. (2000). Syntactic comprehension, verbal memory, and calculation abilities in Spanish-English bilinguals. *Applied Neurospychology, 7*(1), 3–16 & 14.

Axelrod, B. N., Fichtenberg, N. L., Millis, S. R., & Wertheimer, J. C. (2006). Detecting incomplete effort with digit span from the Wechsler adult intelligence scale—Third edition. *The Clinical Neuropsychologist, 20*(3), 513–523.

Babikian, T., Boone, K., Lu, P., & Arnold, G. (2006). Sensitivity and specificity of various digit span scores in the detection of suspect effort. *The Clinical Neuropsychologist, 20*(1), 145–159.

Bagby, R. M., Nicholson, R. A., Buis, T., & Bacchiochi, J. R. (2000). Can the MMIP-2 validity scales detect depression feigned by experts? *Assessment, 7*(1), 55–62.

Berry, D. T. R., Baer, R. A., & Harris, M. J. (1991). Detection of malingering on the MMPI: A meta-analysis. *Clinical Psychology Review, 11*(5), 585–598.

Boone, K. B., Lu, P., & Herzberg, D. (2002). *The dot counting test*. Los Angeles: Western Psychological Services.

Boone, K. B., Salazar, X., Lu, P., Warner-Chacon, K., & Razani, J. (2002). The Rey 15-item recognition trial: A technique to enhance sensitivity of the Rey 15-item memorization test. *Journal of Clinical and Experimental Neuropsychology, 24*(5), 561–573.

Boone, K. B., Savodnik, I., Ghaffarian, S., Lee, A., Freeman, D., & Berman, N. G. (1995). Key 15-item memorization and dot counting scores in a "stress" claim worker's compensation population: Relationship to personality (MCMI) scores. *Journal of Clinical Psychology, 51*(3), 457–463.

Boone, K. B., Victor, T. L., Wen, J., Razani, J., & Ponton, M. (2007). The association between neuropsychological scores and ethnicity, language, and acculturation variables in a large patient population. *Archives of Clinical Neuropsychology, 22*(3), 355–365.

Bush, S. S., Ruff, R. M., Troster, A. I., Barth, J. T., Koffler, S. P., Pliskin, N. H., et al. (2005). Symptom validity assessment: Practice issues and medical necessity: NAN Policy & Planning Committee. *Archives of Clinical Science, 20*(4), 419–426.

Butcher, J. N., & Pope, K. S. (1992). The research base, psychometric properties, and clinical uses of the MMPI-2 and MMPI-A. *Canadian Psychology/Psychologie canadienne, 33*, 61–78.

Correa, A. A., Rogers, R., & Hoersting, R. (2010). Validation of the Spanish SIRS with monolingual Hispanic outpatients. *Journal of Personality Assessment, 92*(5), 458–464.

Cramer, K. M. (1995). Comparing three new MMPI-2 randomness indices in a novel procedure for random profile derivation. *Journal of Personality Assessment, 63*(3), 514.

Dean, A. C., Boone, K. B., Kim, M. S., Curiel, A. R., Martin, D. J., Victor, T. L., et al. (2008). Examination of the impact of ethnicity on the Minnesota multiple personality inventory-2 (MMPI-2) fake bad scale. *The Clinical Neuropsychologist, 22*, 1054–1060.

Garriga (2007). Malingering in the Clinical Setting. Psychiatric Times, 24(3), 1–4.

Gasquoine, P. G., Croyle, K. L., Cavazos-Gonzalez, C., & Sandoval, O. (2007). Language of administration and neuropsychological test performance in neurologically intact Hispanic American bilingual adults. *Archives of Clinical Neuropsychology, 22*(8), 991–1001.

Gouvier, W. D., Lees-Haley, P. R., & Hammer, J. H. (2003). The neuropsychological examination in the detection of malingering in the forensic arena: Costs and benefits. In G. P. Prigatano & N. H. Pliskin (Eds.), *Clinical neuropsychology and cost outcome research* (pp. 405–424). New York: Taylor and Francis.

Green, P. (2003). *Green's word memory test for windows: User's manual*. Edmonton, Canada: Green's Publishing.

Green, P. (2004). *Green's medical symptom validity test (MSVT): User's manual*. Edmonton, Canada: Green's Publishing.

Green, P., & Astner, K. (1995). *Manual for the oral word memory test*. Edmonton, Canada: Neurobehavioural Associates.

Green, P., Montijo, J., & Brockhaus, R. (2011). High specificity of the word memory test and medical symptoms validity test in groups with severe verbal memory impairment. *Applied Neuropsychology: Adult, 18*(2), 86–94.

Greiffenstein, M. F., Baker, W. J., & Gola, T. (1994). Validation of malingered amnesia measures with a large clinical sample. *Psychological Assessment, 6*(3), 218–224.

Greiffenstein, M. F., Baker, W. J., Gola, T., Donders, J., & Miller, L. (2002). The fake bad scale in atypical and severe closed head injury litigants. *Journal of Clinical Psychology, 58*(12), 1591–1600.

Greve, K. W., Bianchini, K. J., Etherton, J. L., Meyers, J. E., Curtis, K. L., & Ord, J. S. (2010). The reliable digit span test in chronic pain: Classification accuracy in detecting malingered pain-related disabilities. *The Clinical Neuropsychologist, 24*(1), 137–152.

Greve, K. W., Springer, S., Bianchini, K. J., Black, F. W., Heinly, M. T., Love, J. M., et al. (2007). Malingering in toxic exposure: Classification accuracy of reliable digit span and WAISS-III digit span scaled scores. *Assessment, 14*(1), 12–21.

Guy, L., & Miller, H. (2004). Screening for malingered psychopathology in a correctional setting: Utility of the Miller-forensic assessment of symptoms test (M-FAST). *Criminal Justice and Behavior, 31*(6), 695–716.

Haberman, P. W. (1970). Ethnic differences in psychiatric symptoms reported in community surveys. *Public Health Reports, 85*, 495–502.

Haberman, P. W. (1976). Psychiatric symptoms among Puerto Ricans in Puerto Rico and New York City. *Ethnicity, 3*, 133–144.

Hall, G. C. N., Bansal, A., & Lopez, I. R. (1999). Ethnicity and psychopathology: A meta-analytic review of 31 years of comparative MMPI-MMPI-2 research. *Psychological Assessment, 11*(2), 186–197.

Heinly, M. T., Greve, K. W., Bianchini, K. J., Love, J. M., & Brennan, A. (2005). WAIS digit span-based indicators of malingered neurocognitive dysfunction classification accuracy in traumatic brain injury. *Assessment, 12*(4), 429–442.

Iverson, G. L., & Tulsky, D. S. (2003). Detecting malingering on the WAIS-III unusual digit span performance patterns in the normal population and in clinical groups. *Archives of Clinical Neuropsychology, 18*(1), 1–9.
Kaufman, A. S. (1990). *Assessing adolescent and adult intelligence*. Boston: Allyn and Bacon.
Larrabee, G. J. (1998). Somatic malingering on the MMPI and MMPI-2 in personal injury litigants. *The Clinical Neuropsychologist, 12*(2), 179–188.
Larrabee, G. (2003). Detection of malingering using atypical performance patterns on standard neuropsychological tests. *The Clinical Neuropsychologist, 17*(3), 410–425.
Lees-Haley, P. R., English, L. T., & Glenn, V. J. (1991). A fake bad scale on the MMPI-2 for personal injury claimants. *Psychological Reports, 68*, 203–210.
Lezak, M. (1983). *Neuropsychological assessment* (2nd ed.). New York: Oxford University Press.
Lim, J., & Butcher, J. N. (1996). Detection of faking on the MMPI-2: Differentiation among faking-bad, denial, and claiming extreme virtue. *Journal of Personality Assessment, 67*(1), 1 & 25.
Lucio, E., Ampudia, A., Duran, C., Gallegos, L., & Leon, I. (1999). La Nueva version del Inventario Multifasico de la Personalidad de Minnesota para Adolescents: MMPI-A [The new version of the Minnesota multiphasic personality inventory for Mexican adolescents]. *Revista Mexicana de Psicología, 16*, 217–226.
Lucio, E., Durán, C., Graham, J. R., & Ben-Porath, Y. S. (2002). Identifying faking bad on the Minnesota multiphasic personality inventory-adolescent with Mexican adolescents. *Assessment, 9*(1), 62–69. doi:10.1177/1073191102009001008.
Lucio, E., & Valencia, M. (1997). Detección del perfil de los sujetos simuladores y de los sujetos honestos por medio de las escalas del MMPI-2. *Salud Mental, 20*(4), 23–33.
Marshall, P., & Happe, M. (2007). The performance of individuals with mental retardation on cognitive tests assessing effort and motivation. *The Clinical Neuropsychologist, 21*(5), 826–840.
Martens, M., Donders, J., & Millis, S. R. (2001). Evaluation of invalid response sets after traumatic head injury. *Journal of Forensic Neuropsychology, 2*(1), 1–18.
Messer, J. M., & Fremouw, W. J. (2007). Detecting malingered posttraumatic stress disorder using the morel emotional numbing test-revised (MENT-R) and the Miller forensic assessment of symptoms test (M-FAST). *Journal of Forensic Psychological Practice, 7*(3), 33–57.
Miller, H. A. (2001). *MFAST: Miller forensic assessment of symptoms test professional manual*. Odessa, FL: Psychological Assessment Resources, Inc.
Nelson, N. W., Sweet, J. J., & Demakis, G. J. (2006). Meta-analysis of the MMPI-2 fake bad scale: Utility in forensic practice. *The Clinical Neuropsychologist, 20*, 39–58.
Prieto De Estebecorena, M. J. (2007). *Evaluating the role of education and acculturation in the performance of Hispanics on a non-verbal test*. ProQuest dissertations and theses, Fielding Graduate University, 123 p. Retrieved from http://search.proquest.com/docview/304704860?accountid=452.
Puente, A. E., & Perez-Garcia, M. (2000). Neuropsychological assessment of ethnic minorities: Clinical issues. In I. Cuéllar & F. A. Paniagua (Eds.), *Handbook of multicultural mental health* (pp. 419–435). San Diego, CA: Academic. doi:10.1016/B978-012199370-2/50021-3.
Rogers, R. (Ed.). (2008). *Clinical assessment of malingering and deception*. New York: The Guilford Press.
Rogers, R., Bagby, R. M., & Dickens, S. E. (1992). *Structured interview of reported symptoms (SIRS) and professional manual*. Odessa, FL: Psychological Assessment Resources, Inc.
Rogers, R., Sewell, K. W., & Gillard, N. (2010a). *Structured interview of reported symptoms-2 (SIRS-2) and professional manual*. Odessa, FL: Psychological Assessment Resources, Inc.
Rogers, R., Sewell, K. W., & Gillard, N. D. (2010b). *SIRS professional manual* (2nd ed.). Lutz, FL: Psychological Assessment Resources, Inc.
Rogers, R., Sewell, K. W., & Salekin, R. T. (1994). A meta-analysis of malingering on the MMPI-2. *Assessment, 1*(3), 227–237.
Ross, S. R., Millis, S. R., Krukowski, R. A., Putnam, S. H., & Adams, K. M. (2004). Detecting incomplete effort on the MMPI-2: An examination of the fake-bad scale in mild head injury. *Journal of Clinical & Experimental Neuropsychology, 26*(1), 115–124 & 10.
Rubenzer, S. (2010). Review of the structured inventory of reported symptoms-2 (SIRS-2). *Open Access Journal of Forensic Psychology, 2*, 273–286.
Saavedra, L. T. (1999). *The translation and validation of the SCT-75 for assessing malingering among Hispanics involved in personal injury litigation.* ProQuest dissertations and theses, Miami Institute of Psychology of the Caribbean Center for Advanced Studies, 99 p. Retrieved from http://search.proquest.com/docview/304569267?accountid=452.
Salazar, X. D., Lopez, E., Peña, R., & Mitrushina, M. (2003). *Datos normativos y validez de tres pruebad para la evaluación de bajo esfuerzo/simulación en personas con educación limitada.* [Validation and preliminary normative data for three effort measures within a limited education, Spanish-speaking sample living in the United States]. Poster session presented at the annual international meeting of the Sociedad Lationamericana de Neuropsicología, Montreal, Canada.

Salazar, X. F., Lu, P. H., Wen, J., & Boone, K. (2007). The use of effort tests in ethnic minorities and in non-English-speaking and English as a second language populations. In K. Boone (Ed.), *Assessment of feigned cognitive impairment: A neuropsychological perspective* (pp. 405–427). New York: Guilford Press.

Srole, L., Langner, T. S., Michael, S. T., Kirkpatrick, P. O., Marvin, K., & Rennie, T. A. C. (1978). *Mental health in the metropolis: The midtown Manhattan study*. New York: McGraw-Hill.

Stein, L. A. R., Graham, J. R., & Williams, C. L. (1995). Detecting fake-bad MMPI-A profiles. *Journal of Personality Assessment, 65*(3), 415–427.

Strauss, E., Slick, D. J., Levy-Bencheton, J., Hunter, M., MacDonald, S. W., & Hultsch, D. F. (2002). Intraindividual variability as an indicator of malingering in head injury. *Archives of Clinical Neuropsychology, 17*(5), 423–444.

Suhr, J. A., & Barrash, J. (2007). Performance on standard attention, memory, and psychomotor speed tasks as indicators of malingering. In G. L. Larrabee (Ed.), *Assessment of malingered neuropsychological deficits* (pp. 131–170). New York: Oxford University Press.

Timmons, L. A., Lanyon, R. I., Almer, E. R., & Curran, P. J. (1993). Development and validation of sentence completion test indices of malingering during examination for disability. *American Journal of Forensic Psychology, 11*(3), 23–38.

Tombaugh, T. N. (1996). *The test of memory malingering (TOMM)*. Toronto, Canada: Multi-Health Systems.

Veazey, C. H., Wagner, A. L., Hays, J. R., & Miller, H. A. (2005). Validity of the Miller forensic assessment of symptoms test in psychiatric inpatients. *Psychological Reports, 96*(3), 771–774.

Verdejo-García, A., Alcázar-Córcoles, M. A., Gómez-Jarabo-García, G. A., & Pérez-García, M. (2004). Guidelines for the scientific and professional development of forensic neuropsychology. *Revista de Neurologia, 39*(01), 60–73.

Vilar-Lopez, R., Santiago-ramajo, S., Gomez-Rio, M., Verdejo-Garcia, A., Llamas, J. M., & Perez-Garcia, M. (2007). Detection of malingering in a Spanish population using three specific malingering tests. *Archives of Clinical Neuropsychology, 22*(3), 379–388.

Wheeler, D. K. (2010). *Digit span with a linguistically diverse Latina/Latino population: A cross-language study*. ProQuest dissertations and theses, Fielding Graduate University. Retrieved from http://search.proquest.com/docview/855633123?accountid=452.

Assessing Mood Disorders and Suicidality in Hispanics

8

John S. Wiebe, John A. Sauceda, and Carolina Lara

Epidemiology of Mood Disorders in Hispanics

Early epidemiological research on mood disorders among Hispanics in the USA produced equivocal results. Often, the focus of epidemiological studies was on symptomatology, rather than on clinical diagnoses (e.g., Roberts, 1981; Vega, Warheit, Buhl-Auth, & Meinhardt, 1984), and different Hispanic subgroups were infrequently distinguished in analyses (e.g., Frerichs, Aneshensel, & Clark, 1981; Vernon & Roberts, 1982). Such strategies led to ambiguity in the interpretation of results. Since mood symptom measures typically detect general psychological distress in addition to diagnosable mood disorders, recent immigrants and members of underprivileged minority groups might be expected to show elevated scores on symptom measures even without any history of psychiatric disorder. In addition, the lack of subgroup analyses obscured potentially important differences between those originating from very different cultural backgrounds and subjected to very different migratory pressures and influences.

Even with the advent of more comprehensive epidemiological research using standardized diagnostic interviews, data were not necessarily collected in Spanish. For example, the National Comorbidity Study (NCS) included a sample of 719 US Hispanic participants (Kessler et al., 1994), surveyed only in English. This led to a restriction of range on important variables linked to language proficiency, such as acculturation and for some Hispanic subgroups, socioeconomic status. Not surprisingly, results of this study were quite different than those of other epidemiological work, indicating that Hispanics were twice as likely as African Americans to report current depression.

Given the inconsistent results of epidemiological studies, Mendelson, Rehkopf, and Kubzansky (2008) completed a major meta-analysis on the topic. Combining eight large studies with a total *N* of 76,270, they found no significant difference in lifetime prevalence of depression between Hispanics and non-Hispanic Whites. However, when analyzing 23 studies of depressive symptoms comprising 38,997 participants, they found a slightly (though clinically insignificantly) greater rate of symptom reporting among Hispanics. In addition, while women reported substantially greater rates of depression regardless of ethnicity, the gender difference was slightly larger among Hispanics than among non-Hispanic Whites. Although the Mendelson et al. meta-analysis did not conduct analyses by eth-

J.S. Wiebe, Ph.D. (✉) • J.A. Sauceda, M.A. • C. Lara, B.A.
Department of Psychology, University of Texas at El Paso, 500 West University Avenue, El Paso, TX 79968, USA
e-mail: jwiebe@utep.edu; jasauceda@miners.utep.edu; clara3@miners.utep.edu

L.T. Benuto (ed.), *Guide to Psychological Assessment with Hispanics*,
DOI 10.1007/978-1-4614-4412-1_8, © Springer Science+Business Media New York 2013

nic subgroup, Alegría et al. (2007) analyzed data from the carefully sampled National Latino and Asian American Study, which included 577 Cuban Americans, 868 Mexican Americans, 495 Puerto Ricans, and 614 Hispanics who described their ethnic subgroup as "other." They found lower rates of depressive disorders among Mexican Americans than among the other groups and greater distress among Puerto Ricans. In general, the results mirrored past research (e.g., Vega et al., 1998), finding a strong negative association between mental health and acculturation to US culture, referenced by English fluency, years in the USA, and age at migration.

Less work has been done on bipolar disorders among Hispanics. In addition, due to the lower base rates of bipolar disorders, the data are more difficult to interpret even in studies with large community samples. Perron, Fries, Kilbourne, Vaughn, and Bauer (2010) analyzed data from a representative US sample of 43,093 individuals participating in the 2001–2002 National Epidemiologic Survey on Alcohol and Related Conditions (NESARC). They found no significant differences in the rates of bipolar I disorder across racial and ethnic groups, with 3.8% of African Americans, 3.6% of non-Hispanic Whites, and 3.4% of Hispanics meeting criteria for the diagnosis. However, they did find a lower prevalence of depressive episodes in their Hispanic subsample.

Somatization of Depression

Anecdotal reports of somatization of depression among Hispanics abound. Indeed, the DSM-IV TR suggests that Hispanics (and those of Mediterranean descent) are particularly likely to express somatic symptoms of depression, such as "nerves" or headaches, in place of affective symptoms, though the manual leaves the diagnostic implications of this information entirely to the professional judgment of the diagnostician. Early ideas arising from psychoanalytic theory suggest that expression of psychological distress through physical symptoms is characteristic of those who are less psychologically mature or sophisticated. Taking this concept a step further, Leff (1981) discussed an "evolutionary" model of cultural development, suggesting that somatization of depression is associated with less advanced cultures. Proponents of the concept (e.g., Escobar, 1987) make reference to the practice in "developing societies."

However, empirical work has been less than persuasive on the association of somatization of depression with Hispanic ethnicity. An early study frequently cited as support for Hispanic somatization (Escobar, Gomez, & Tuason, 1983) compared 41 depressed Colombian patients to 32 non-Hispanics from the USA. While there was a significant difference between the groups on the "anxiety-somatization" score from the Hamilton Rating Scale for Depression, there was no difference in frequency of somatic symptoms of depression (sleep problems, loss of appetite, physical complaints, and loss of interest in sex); indeed, three of these were reported less often (though nonsignificantly so) by the Columbian sample. Larger and more recent studies have also failed to achieve consensus on the topic. For example, data from 4,222 Mexican American adults and 1,063 non-Hispanic Whites involved in the Los Angeles Epidemiological Catchment Area (LAECA) Study and the National Center for Health Statistics' Hispanic Health and the Nutrition Examination Survey (HHANES) showed no consistent ethnic differences in somatic symptoms of depression. In fact, Mexican Americans born in the USA reported significantly *more* somatic symptoms than those born in Mexico (Golding, Aneshensel, & Hough, 1991).

Very few studies in which somatization has been reported as a function of ethnicity or acculturation have controlled for socioeconomic status as a potentially confounding variable. In addition, Villaseñor and Waitkin (1999) point out that several factors limit the validity of modern structured interviews in detecting somatization among US Hispanics. For example, it is possible that physical symptoms categorized by researchers as "medically unexplained" may simply reflect poor access to health care services by minority populations, language barriers in understanding physicians' diagnoses, or folk understandings of physiological processes. The topic of somatization of depression among Hispanics remains a complex topic that is not sufficiently understood. While clinicians should always be alert to non-affective symptoms of depression when conducting evaluations, a tendency to interpret somatic symptoms expressed by Hispanic patients as reflections of emotional distress may not serve those patients well.

Measures of Depressive Symptoms

Many self-report measures used to assist with the evaluation of depressive symptoms in clinical and community settings have been used extensively with Hispanic samples. Spanish translations have been undertaken for many instruments in various dialects and with varying degrees of care and validation. We will review data here on the most frequently employed self-report questionnaires. In addition to these measures, many semi-structured and structured interviews have been very useful in the diagnosis of mood disorders in both clinical and research settings, and they are reviewed in an earlier chapter (Mestre, Rossi, & Torrens, 2012).

The Beck Depression Inventory (BDI)

The BDI, a 21-item scale originally published by Beck, Ward, Mendelson, Mock, and Erbaugh in 1961, has long been the most widely used self-report questionnaire measure of depressive symptoms. The BDI and its scoring criteria have been revised multiple times (e.g., BDI-I – Beck, Rush, Shaw, & Emery, 1979; BDI-IA – Beck & Steer, 1993; BDI-II – Beck, Steer, & Brown, 1996). The first version to be widely used in Spanish was the BDI-IA (Sanz & Vázquez, 1998; Vázquez & Sanz, 1997). Reports have shown that the psychometric properties of the Spanish translation compare favorably to those of the original English BDI-IA (Bonicatto, Dew, & Soria, 1998; Suárez-Mendoza, Cardiel, Caballero-Uribe, Ortega-Soto, & Márquez-Marín, 1997). Although factor analyses of the Spanish BDI-IA have shown different structures (e.g., Ibáñez, González, & Peñate, 1997; Jurado et al., 1998), most have yielded essentially the same Cognitive/Somatic two-factor structure as is frequently seen with the English version (e.g., Aragón Ramírez, Bragado Alvarez, & Carrasco Galán, 1999; Bonicatto et al., 1998). However, the items tapping irritability, crying, and indecisiveness, which have consistently loaded on the Cognitive/Affective scale in English, have tended instead to load on the Somatic scale in Spanish. The scoring guidelines proposed for the BDI-IA by Beck and Steer (1993) have been used interchangeably with the English and Spanish versions: 0–9 (minimal depression), 10–16 (mild depression), 17–29 (moderate depression), and 30–63 (severe depression).

The BDI-II was introduced by Beck and colleagues in 1996 in an effort to increase content validity, mapping more closely to DSM criteria for major depression. It is a proprietary instrument available only through Pearson/PsychCorp, which produced a Spanish-language version translated and back-translated by a group of psychologists from the USA, Central and South America, Cuba, Mexico, and Puerto Rico. Carmody (2005) found the English-language BDI-II to yield similar results across different ethnic groups in a diverse college student sample. Hispanic students did report lower scores on the worthlessness and irritability items in simple tests of the 21-item mean differences with no control for type I error. However, there were no significant differences in overall scores.

When evaluated in a substantial sample of bilingual college students, primarily of Mexican descent, the Spanish-language BDI-II showed evidence of metric invariance from the English version, with not only the same basic factor structure but with similar item loadings, and no significant mean differences between languages either between subjects or within individuals who took both versions in counterbalanced order with a 1-week interval (Wiebe & Penley, 2005). A study of the

Spanish BDI-I in end-stage renal disease patients of Mexican descent also showed a similar factor structure, with no significant difference between the scores of bilinguals who took the measure in both languages (Penley, Wiebe, & Nwosu, 2003). Thus, no different cutoff scores have been recommended for the Spanish BDI-II. The scoring guidelines recommended by Beck et al. (1996) are 0–13 (minimal depression), 14–19 (mild depression), 20–28 (moderate depression), and 29–63 (severe depression).

The BDI-II is a widely recognized instrument that has amassed a strong literature to aid in its interpretation. Both the English and Spanish versions have good reliability and validity, and the BDI-II has been updated to reflect current diagnostic standards. The clear anchors associated with each response option on the various versions of the BDI are clinically useful, and the instrument is frequently used to track patient progress in therapy. However, the anchors also introduce complexity for researchers, as they represent only an ordinal, rather than an interval or ratio, scale of measurement. Finally, the expense of a proprietary instrument may cause many clinicians or researchers to select one of the many measures available free of charge (e.g., PHQ-9, CES-D, HADS).

Patient Health Questionnaire-9 (PHQ-9)

The PHQ-9 is a nine-item instrument that follows the nine symptoms of the *DSM-IV-TR* diagnostic criteria for major depression (Kroenke, Spitzer, & Williams, 2001). It is a derivative of the more general Patient Health Questionnaire for depression and other common mental disorders encountered in primary care (Spitzer, Kroenke, & Williams, 1999; Spitzer, Williams, Kroenke, Hornyak, & McMurray, 2000) as well as the original clinician-administered Primary Care Evaluation of Mental Disorders (PRIME-MD; Spitzer et al., 1994). The PHQ-9 is a self-report questionnaire that can be used to tentatively diagnose and depression and monitor the condition over time due to its criterion-based, continuous scoring format. The instructions specify a 2-week reporting period, with each item using a four-point response scale: *not at all*, *several days*, *more than half the days*, and *nearly every day*. The first two questions (one assessing depressed mood and the second assessing anhedonia) from the PHQ-9, known as the PHQ-2, (Kroenke, Spitzer, & Williams, 2003) are also used as a depression screen in lieu of the longer 9-item form.

Initial internal consistency reliability estimates for the PHQ-9 were $\alpha=.89$ and $\alpha=.86$ in the original Primary Care and Obstetrics-Gynecology Studies (Kroenke et al., 2001). Huang, Chung, Kroenke, Delucchi, and Spitzer (2006) used data from the original validation studies (Spitzer et al., 1999, 2000) to estimate internal consistency in a sample of 974 Hispanics (97.8% of whom were female; no ethnic subgroup identified). Internal consistency for this group was $\alpha=.80$. In Hispanic samples, construct validity with the PHQ-9 has been assessed with subscales from the Short-Form Health Survey (SF-20 and SF-36; Gross et al., 2005; Kroenke et al., 2001; Spitzer et al., 1999; Spitzer et al., 2000; Stewart, Hays, & Ware, 1988). Correlations between SF-20 mental health, social functioning, and general health subscales and PHQ-9 total scores are high, ranging from .51 to .78.

Several studies have investigated depression in Spanish-speaking populations using translations of the PHQ-9. Diez-Quevedo, Rangil, Sanchez-Planell, Kroenke, and Spitzer (2001) translated the entire PHQ for use in Spain, validating the instrument in a large sample of inpatients from a university hospital. They correlated PHQ scores with the presence of symptoms detected by a blind face-to-face interview with a mental health professional ($r=.71$) and scores on the Beck Depression Inventory ($r=.76$). Overall, the authors note the Spanish PHQ showed good-to-strong agreement with other self-report instruments and clinician-administered interview and results compared favorably to those with the English version. This translation remains one of the most popular, although even the translators note that its Castellano dialect is inappropriate for use with US Hispanics.

Starting with the Diez-Quevedo et al. (2001) version, Schmaling and Hernandez (2005) used a back-translation strategy to develop a PHQ that could be used successfully on the Texas-Mexico border. Four hundred eighty-six patients at a two local health clinics participated in their study; a majority (97.4%) were of Mexican origin. Use of the PHQ and PRIME-MD as a diagnostic tool resulted in 39% of the Mexican Americans in their primary care setting meeting criteria for one or more depressive disorders. However, they noted that only 21% of those cases detected by the PHQ had been identified by the patients' primary care physicians, whose methods had achieved good specificity (90%), but poor sensitivity. Thus, Schmaling and Hernandez (2005) point out the value of using the Spanish-language PHQ as a screening tool in primary care to avoid missing mood disorder cases. Other Spanish translations have been developed by the MAPI Research Institute for Spanish-speaking subgroups (e.g., Mexican, Puerto Rican). However, many have not been independently validated or psychometrically evaluated.

Kroenke et al. (2001) established cut points and categories to optimize operating characteristics in two separate samples of 3,000 participants. Starting with a cut point of 10 to indicate clinically significant depression (with both sensitivity and specificity of 88%), they further categorized scores of 5–9 as mild depression, 10–14 as moderate, 15–19 as moderately severe, and 20–27 as severe. A later meta-analysis by Gilbody, Richards, Brealy, and Hewitt (2007) demonstrated that optimal screening cut points for the PHQ-9 have ranged across studies from 9 to 13 with no significant differences in performance, though the original cut point of 10 is most frequently applied. Using that cut point, the Spanish validation study conducted by Diez-Quevedo et al. (2001) found similar operating characteristics to those reported in English-speaking samples for any mood disorder (89% sensitivity, 87% specificity). However, Gross et al. (2005) studied Hispanic diabetics (mainly of Caribbean descent; no other ethnicity-specific information reported) using the translation by Diez-Quevedo et al. and found that a cutoff score of 12 for depression optimized operating characteristics (83% sensitivity; 92% specificity). Gilbody et al. (2007) note that cut points may be adjusted depending on population characteristics in order to optimize sensitivity and specificity.

Huang et al. (2006) conducted tests of differential item functioning on the PHQ-9 across ethnic and racial groups with the data from the original validation studies. They found that Hispanics, when compared to Chinese-Americans and non-Hispanic Whites, had higher scores on the anhedonia and appetite items and lower scores on items referring to disturbances of sleep and feelings of guilt. However, no differences were found in overall mean scores or factor structure among Chinese, Hispanic, African, and European Americans. Also, after controlling for socioeconomic status, no differences were seen the endorsement of somatic or negative affect items. Data from this study suggest that no difference in cutoff scores is needed for Hispanics.

The PHQ for adolescence (PHQ-A) has been developed to focus on disorders most common among adolescents in primary care settings. It was validated in a sample of 403 English speakers (12.4% Hispanic) between the ages of 13 and 18 (Johnson, Harris, Spitzer, & Williams, 2002) with results generally equivalent to those for the original PHQ. In addition, Richardson et al. (2010) found the PHQ-2 screening tool valid for screening for depression in a sample of 2,291 youth between the ages of 13 and 17. However, these studies did not focus on work with Hispanic youth or involve Spanish-language administration of the measures.

The PHQ-9 has demonstrated strong reliability and validity across multiple studies and has been used extensively with US Hispanics. Evidence for equivalent factor structures and mean scores across ethnicity has also been reported (Huang et al., 2006), with some minimal differential item functioning by ethnicity. Although translations are available for various Spanish regional dialects, few of the translations have been rigorously evaluated. The criterion-referenced nature of the instrument (i.e., correspondence to DSM-IV) aids in clinical interpretation and can permit diagnostic estimates in community studies. The brevity and free availability of the PHQ-9 contributes to its popularity with clinicians and researchers alike.

Center for Epidemiologic Studies Depression Scale (CES-D)

The CES-D is a 20-item measure of depressive symptomatology developed by the National Institute of Mental Health for use with community samples (Radloff, 1977). More of a measure of general distress rather than a diagnostic tool, it was shown to comprise four factors in the standardization samples: depressed affect, positive affect, somatic and retarded activity, and interpersonal issues. However, the samples for Radloff's (1977) initial studies were all White participants from the East Coast and Midwest, except for a small African American subsample; Hispanics were not represented.

Translations of the measure and work with Hispanics did soon follow. Roberts (1980) did an initial study of different ethnic groups with the CES-D. After using a translation/backtranslation approach, he administered the instrument to Anglos, African Americans, and a sample of 181 Mexican Americans, 21% of whom took the measure in Spanish. He replicated Radloff's four-factor structure across all three samples and found no differences in internal consistency reliability as a function of ethnicity or language; Cronbach's alpha for the Anglos was .85, for the Mexican Americans interviewed in English it was 0.83, and for those interviewed in Spanish it was 0.88. Masten, Caldwell-Colbert, Alcala, and Mijares (1986) used the Roberts translation with 148 students in Mexico, obtaining substantial correlations with the Spanish BDI ($r = .59$) and the Spanish Depression Adjectives Checklist (Lubin, Millham, & Paredes, 1980; $r=.49$–$.64$) in two subsamples. They found a 1-week test-retest reliability coefficient of .49.

Direct comparisons between English and Spanish-language versions of the instrument come from a more recent translation by Perczek, Carver, Price, and Pozo-Kaderma (2000). They also used a backtranslation strategy, with "neutral" Spanish and teams of translators from South America and Cuba. They then gathered data from a sample of 142 Spanish-English bilingual undergraduate students (largely of Cuban descent) and a sample of 60 women recovering from breast cancer. In the undergraduate sample, measures were given in both languages during a single administration, with counterbalanced order. Internal consistency of the Spanish translation ($\alpha=.89$) was comparable to that in English ($\alpha=.92$), the two versions were highly correlated ($r=.88$; $p<.01$), and the mean scores were not significantly different from one another in either sample.

One of the largest studies of the CES-D in Hispanics made use of data from the Hispanic Health and Nutrition Examination Survey (Hispanic HANES; Guarnaccia, Angel, & Worobey, 1989). With substantial subgroup representation (3,117 Mexican Americans, 808 Cuban Americans, and 1,266 Puerto Ricans), Guarnaccia et al. used confirmatory factor analysis to determine that Radloff's original four factors were not a good fit to the data. Turning to an exploratory approach, they instead found a three-factor solution, with affective and somatic items loading on the same first factor, rather than different factors. Further breaking the sample down by ethnicity, gender, and language, the researchers found that the factor structure of the instrument varied greatly across subgroups. For example, they noted that the results for English-speaking Mexican American men tended to resemble those for Anglos, while for Mexican American women, affective and somatic symptoms tended to load together regardless of preferred language. The factor structure among Cuban Americans reflected an "isolation" factor that the authors associated with immigration patterns unique to this subgroup, and Puerto Rican men showed a different pattern of loadings on the first factor, which the authors termed "demoralization" and linked conceptually to greater patterns of unemployment and marital disruption. The Guarnaccia et al. (1989) study did not test for statistical significance in differential model fit and did not account for differences in socioeconomic status and other potentially confounding variables. However, later studies with substantial Hispanic samples (e.g., Posner, Stewart, Marín, & Pérez-Stable, 2001; Rivera-Medina, Caraballo, Rodríguez-Cordero, Bernal, & Dávila-Marrero, 2010) have done so and continue to show widely divergent factor structures across subgroups for the CES-D.

A number of short forms of the CES-D have been introduced, and Grzywacz, Hovey, Seligman, Arcury, and Quandt (2006) studied Spanish versions of three popular forms among seven samples of Mexican immigrants to the USA (total $N=685$). They used an independent backtranslation approach to develop the short forms, which varied substantially in content and response format. The alpha coefficients for the three forms ranged from .719 to .789, and they accounted for between 78.6 and 89.5% of the variance in scores from the complete CES-D. While all short forms tested appeared appropriate for use with Mexican immigrants, the ten-item, four response-option Boston form (Kohout et al., 1993) offered the strongest reliability and content validity and yielded the same factor structure as the full CES-D.

Grzywacz et al. (2006) point out that complexity and colloquialisms in the wording of the CES-D may limit its utility for non-English speakers. For example, the item "I felt I could not shake off the blues" does not have a clear Spanish equivalent. Even among English-speaking Hispanics, the instrument should be used with caution, due to the instability of its factor structure across groups. Finally, the lack of the criterion referencing limits its usefulness in clinical settings and for diagnostic purposes.

The Hospital Anxiety and Depression Scale (HADS)

The HADS is a 14-item self-report measure developed by Zigmond and Snaith (1983) in an attempt to clinically differentiate between anxiety and depression disorders. It was meant for use in nonpsychiatric medical settings, but it has been successfully employed in community samples, as well. Initially introduced in Europe, it was first translated using standardized procedures for use in Spain by Bulbena and Berrios, in collaboration with one of the instrument's authors, Snaith. Tejero Pociello, Guimerá Querol, Farré Martí, and Peri (1986) then administered this version of the Hospital Anxiety and Depression Scale to a group of 66 Spanish psychiatric patients, finding acceptable internal consistency, with coefficient alpha scores of 0.81 for anxiety and 0.82 for depression.

More comprehensive validation studies of the Castellano HADS were completed by Herrero et al. (2003) and Quintana et al. (2003). Quintana et al. included 685 Spanish participants in their study, demonstrating alpha coefficients of .86 for both depression and anxiety and test-retest reliability (Pearson and Spearman correlations and kappas for categorical ratings) of .85–.91 for an unspecified follow-up period. They found a strong two-factor structure (anxiety and depression), and modest evidence of discriminant validity, with the depression scale preferentially predicting BDI scores and the anxiety scale predicting scores on the State Trait Anxiety Inventory, though the scales were heavily overlapping. Herrero et al. used a sample of 385 adult outpatients with severe medical pathology in Barcelona. Internal consistency was strong for the subscales, but the coefficient alpha for the full 14-item measure was even greater (.90), suggesting overlap among the subscales which was confirmed by a correlation of .68 between depression and anxiety scores. Herrero et al. used cutoff scores of 5 for depression (72% sensitivity/87% specificity) and 8 for anxiety (80% sensitivity/85% specificity), though they noted that these figures were lower than for other studies.

The Castellano version was later edited for use in a Mexican sample by López-Alvarenga et al. (2002), who collected data from 75 obese, nondiabetic adults. Although a pilot study with the Spanish translation showed poor results, rewording items and eliminating idioms improved validity of the questionnaire, achieving alpha coefficients of .86 for each scale and increasing kappas for concordance with a structured interview to .68 for anxiety and .73 for depression. However, the anxiety and depression subscales were highly correlated in this study ($r=.70$) limiting the ability to discriminate between the two constructs. Based on a series of unpublished masters theses, López-Alvarenga et al. cited a series of unpublished masters theses establishing cutoffs for the Spanish version of 7 for depression and 8 for anxiety, but with rather poorer psychometric performance than has been observed for either the English or the Castello version (76% sensitivity/45% specificity for depression and 62% sensitivity/58% specificity for anxiety).

While the HADS was developed for use with adults, there have been some efforts to adapt it for use with adolescents (e.g., White, Leach, Sims, Atkinson, & Cottrell, 1999). Results have been favorable but reflect a need to adjust cut scores to reflect the lower incidence of depression and anxiety disorders among children. As yet, there is no substantial work with the instrument in Hispanic or Spanish-speaking children.

The HADS has been used across many different languages and cultures. Its brevity and generally strong psychometric properties have contributed to its popularity. Surprisingly, it has not been widely used with Latinos in the USA, and initial data from Mexico (López-Alvarenga et al., 2002) raise some concern regarding its predictive value. The two-factor structure of the instrument is appealing to clinicians and researchers who wish to assess both depressive and anxious symptoms, but the high intercorrelation of the scales reflects the well-known difficulty of distinguishing reliably between these highly related constructs.

Measures of Bipolar Symptoms

Due to the obvious difficulties inherent in assessing mania through performance on self-report measures, most questionnaires meant to detect the presence of bipolar disorders have focused on hypomanic symptoms or on lifetime history of manic symptoms. Some of these measures also tap depressive symptoms. Several of the measures reviewed take the perspective, still controversial among bipolar disorder researchers, of assessing a "hypomanic personality" or variation on a hypomanic trait in normal populations.

The Mood Disorder Questionnaire (MDQ)

The Mood Disorder Questionnaire (Hirschfeld et al., 2000) is a 13-item self-report measure of hypomanic and manic symptoms. The MDQ was designed as a screening measure for bipolar spectrum disorders. Individuals read 13 statements describing manic symptoms and respond to each dichotomously by indicating whether they have experienced the symptom during their lifetime. The MDQ items were developed from DSM diagnostic criteria and clinical experience. Those who endorse any of the 13 symptoms then report whether more than one symptom was experienced during the same period of time, and the severity of these symptoms on a four-point response scale (no problems, minor problem, moderate problem, and serious problem). An individual screens positive for bipolar spectrum disorder by endorsing seven or more of the 13 symptoms, indicating temporal overlap of at least two symptoms, and reporting that these symptoms have caused moderate or severe problems. Of course, all positive screens must be confirmed by a full differential diagnostic interview.

Various Spanish translations of the MDQ are available, most of which have been adapted and tested in Spain using a standard backtranslation method (Sanchez-Moreno et al., 2008). Therefore, linguistic equivalence and use of the MDQ in other Spanish-speaking populations outside of Europe must be carefully examined. A Spanish version of the MDQ has been adapted and validated in a Mexican sample (Corona, Berlanga, Gutiérrez-Mora, & Fresán, 2007). The process involved having four bilingual psychiatrists with experience treating bipolar disorder develop four separate translations. The translations were then discussed and merged together by consensus. This merged version was then backtranslated into English and discrepancies were resolved in the development of a final Spanish-language form (Corona et al., 2007).

The original English version demonstrated good internal consistency (alpha = .90; Hirschfeld et al., 2000) and was validated with a follow-up diagnostic interview using the Structured Clinical Interview for DSM-IV, administered by a social worker blind to MDQ results. Operating characteristics were .73 for sensitivity and .90 for specificity. In their Mexican sample, Corona et al. (2007) found that operating characteristics were optimized (.71 sensitivity and .92 specificity) with a cutoff score of 10, which is higher than that used with other Spanish versions (Sanchez-Moreno et al., 2008; Zaratiegui et al., 2011).

The MDQ is brief and reliable when used in psychiatric settings but has been shown to be less sensitive in the detection of bipolar disorder II or bipolar disorder, not otherwise specified (Zimmerman, Galione, Chelminski, Young, & Ruggero, 2010). More research is needed in testing the MDQ in nonpsychiatric settings and optimizing its ability to detect milder forms of bipolar disorder. Furthermore, additional research is needed to develop appropriate translations for other Spanish dialects and cultural contexts.

Internal State Scale (ISS) and the Hypomanic Personality Scale (HPS)

A study by Ruggero, Johnson, and Cuellar (2004) involved the translation and validation of the Internal State Scale (Bauer et al., 1991) and the Hypomanic Personality Scale (Eckblad & Chapman, 1986) in a sample of Hispanic college students. The ISS is a self-report assessment of current manic and depressive symptoms comprising four subscales. Individuals respond to all 16 statements (e.g., "today I feel restless") on a Likert-type response scale ranging from 1 ("not at all") to 10 ("extremely"). The HPS is a 48-item measure of "hypomanic personality," meant to capture individuals at risk for developing bipolar disorder. Individuals respond to descriptive statements, such as "I often feel excited and happy for no apparent reason," using a true-or-false format.

The original scoring algorithm for the ISS was developed for differentiating between three states: euthymic, depressed, and hypomanic. Therefore, combinations of scores on two of the four subscales (Well-being and Activation) can be used as indicators of mood states. For scoring information, see Bauer et al. (1991) and Bauer, Vojta, Kinosian, Altshuler, and Glick (2000). The original validation studies showed that the ISS had adequate internal consistency reliability across each of the four subscales (alphas > .81) and good criterion-related validity when testing against the Young Mania Rating Scale (activations subscale; $r = .60$, $p < .01$; Bauer et al., 1991). In a separate study at an outpatient clinic, optimal operating characteristics were achieved with an activation subscale range of scores between 155 and 199 (Bauer et al., 2000). The 155–199 range yields a mean sensitivity of .80 and specificity mean of .71. Increasing cutoff scores above 200 reduces specificity to .57 and reduces specificity to .84.

In the original validation study of the HPS, Eckblad, and Chapman (1986) constructed contrasting groups based on high and low HPS scores, demonstrating that the groups differed on measures tapping hypomanic personality characteristics, depressive symptoms, alcohol and drug use, and schizotypal features. Indeed, when the groups were compared on blind clinician interviews (the SADS-L), 78% of the high-scoring group were diagnosed with hypomanic episodes, while none of the low-scoring group received such a diagnosis. Schalet, Durbin, and Revelle (2011) conducted a factor analysis of the HPS in a large sample of young adults and found a weak common factor, undergirded by subscales tapping constructs he labeled Social Vitality, Mood Volatility, and Excitement. While the authors acknowledged that higher scores overall scores on the HPS were indicative of greater risk for developing bipolar disorders, they noted that the subscales were not strongly intercorrelated and predicted other variables differentially, suggesting caution when interpreting global scores and selecting subscale scores based on specific research questions.

Test name	Original language	Type of assessment	Country of norms	Age range (years)
Beck Depression Inventory – Second Edition (BDI-II), 1996	English	Self-report questionnaire assessing depressive symptoms; modeled after DSM-IV diagnostic criteria	USA, Mexico, Puerto Rico, Spain	13 to adult
Patient Health Questionnaire-9 (PHQ-9)	English	Self-report questionnaire reflecting the nine DSM-IV criteria for depression; designed for use in primary care settings	USA, Mexico, Spain	13 to adult
Center for Epidemiologic Studies Depression Scale (CES-D)	English	Self-report questionnaire tapping general distress related to depressive disorders; frequently used in community studies	USA, Mexico, Puerto Rico, Spain	14 to adult
The Hospital Anxiety and Depression Scale (HADS)	English	Self-report questionnaire assessing depression and anxiety symptoms; has been used effectively in both clinical settings and the community	USA, Mexico, Spain	12 to adult
Mood Disorder Questionnaire (MDQ)	English	Self-report screening measure for bipolar spectrum disorders	USA, Mexico, Spain	13 to adult
Internal State Scale (ISS)	English	Self-report assessment of current manic and depressive symptoms	USA	16 to adult
Hypomanic Personality Scale (HPS)	English	Self-report instrument meant to assess a personality trait hypothesized to underlie hypomania	USA	14 to adult

The careful translation process followed by Ruggero et al. (2004) involved having a medical translator create initial Spanish-language versions of the ISS and HPS. Then, to ensure language equivalence across regional Hispanic dialects, a group of translators who had lived in various Spanish-speaking countries reviewed the initial translation and replaced words and phrases that were region-specific with words and phrases deemed to be neutral to various Hispanic cultures and groups. The final steps involved a backtranslation process and a review for reconciling differences across English and Spanish versions. When administered to a Hispanic college student sample, Ruggero et al. found that the Spanish-language measures demonstrated psychometric properties that were very similar to those previously observed among English speakers.

Other Measures of Bipolar Symptoms

Several scales assessing bipolar symptoms have been translated into Spanish by Spanish researchers for use in Europe. The most common translated scales include the Bech-Rafaelsen Mania Scale (Bech, Bolwig, Kramp, & Rafaelsen, 1979), the Bipolar Spectrum Diagnostic Scale (Ghaemi et al., 2005), and the Bipolar Inventory of Symptoms Scale (Bowden et al., 2007). The differences between scales lie in their research purposes; some are designed provide a comprehensive assessment of behavioral and cognitive symptoms of bipolar disorder, some are designed to detect changes due to treatment, and others are meant to detect less severe symptoms of bipolar spectrum disorders. However, cultural and linguistic differences between North, Central, and South American Hispanics and European Spanish speakers should be examined before adopting a translation.

Suicidality Among Hispanics

When approaching the issue of suicidality in US Hispanics, it is important to note vast differences between ethnic subgroups. Data from smaller early studies were inconsistent on the topic, but more recent data from larger epidemiological studies have shown clearer patterns of results. For example, Oquendo, Lizardi, Greenwald, Weissman, and Mann (2004) summarized data from the ECA studies as well as the HHANES, comprising thousands of carefully sampled Hispanic participants and non-Hispanic Whites. They showed similar rates of suicide attempts among Mexican Americans and non-Hispanic Whites, but much higher rates among Puerto Ricans. These results were largely replicated by an analysis of the NLAAS data by Fortuna, Pérez, Canino, Sribney, and Alegría (2007). In both studies, Cuban Americans reported the lowest rates of suicide attempts, though their reports were not significantly different from those of Mexican Americans. While very high rates of suicide attempts are frequently recorded in Puerto Rican samples, analysis of data from Puerto Rican inpatients admitted after attempting suicide show relatively mild depressive symptoms and low medical lethality and suicidal intent (Fernandez-Pol, 1986). Indeed, Oquendo et al. (2004) point out that while Puerto Ricans report approximately three times the number of suicide attempts of non-Hispanic Whites, non-Hispanic Whites have higher rates of completed suicide than all Hispanic subgroups, including Puerto Ricans, likely because they tend to select more lethal means. Among Puerto Ricans, suicide attempts appear to be especially closely tied to heavy use of alcohol or other substances (Fernandez-Pol, 1986; Reyes et al., 2011).

In general, Hispanic culture appears to be a protective factor against suicidality. As with depression, suicide attempts and ideation among Hispanics are positively associated with acculturation, as referenced by English proficiency and US nativity (Fortuna et al., 2007; Oquendo et al., 2004), and this association holds true even among the higher-risk Puerto Rican subgroup (Monk & Warshauer, 1974). Also, among Hispanics, high levels of family conflict are particularly predictive of suicide attempts, and familism may be a mediator of the protective effect of Hispanic culture (e.g., Fortuna et al., 2007; Peña et al., 2011).

Assessment of Suicidality

Many depression scales include a single suicidality item (e.g., the BDI, the PHQ-9). Although there is virtually no research validating the predictive validity of these single items from questionnaires, they certainly serve as a starting point for clinical assessment and should trigger a complete evaluation of risk factors (see American Psychiatric Association, 2003 for a detailed review of suicide assessment). There have been many attempts to create more detailed measures of suicidality for clinical purposes. However, the challenges associated with such a task are obvious. The prediction of low base rate behaviors such as suicide requires extremely large samples and prospective designs over substantial periods of time.

The development of most suicidality scales has involved the collection of data on internal consistency and concurrent validity, but rarely predictive validity. Among the instruments with evidence of predictive validity are the Beck Scale for Suicide Ideation (BSS; Beck, Kovacs, & Weissman, 1979) and the Beck Hopelessness Scale (BHS; Beck, Weissman, Lester, & Trexler, 1974). A cutoff score of 2 on the SSI has been shown to predict a sevenfold increase in suicide over a 20-year follow-up period in a sample of 6,891 psychiatric outpatients (Brown, Beck, Steer, & Grisham, 2000). Beck, Steer, Kovacs, and Garrison (1985) used the BHS in a sample of hospitalized patients with suicidal ideation, demonstrating that a cutoff score of 9 accurately predicted 91% of suicides in over the next 10 years. However, other long-term studies have not replicated these results (e.g., Beck & Steer, 1989).

Both the BSS and BHS are commercially available in English and Spanish. However, there are no data on the psychometric properties of the translations. In addition, there is virtually no literature on use of suicide assessment instruments with Hispanics in the USA. While there has been some attention to the role of family dynamics and other culturally relevant psychosocial factors in the suicide of adolescent Hispanic girls in the USA (e.g., Zayas, Lester, Cabassa, & Fortuna, 2005), the area of Hispanic suicide in general remains an understudied field.

References

Alegría, M., Mulvaney-Day, N., Torres, M., Polo, A., Cao, Z., & Canino, G. (2007). Prevalence of psychiatric disorders across Latinos subgroups in the United States. *American Journal of Public Health, 97*, 68–75.

American Psychiatric Association. (2003). Practice guideline for the assessment and treatment of patients with suicidal behaviors. *The American Journal of Psychiatry, 160*(Nov suppl.), 1–60.

Aragón Ramírez, N., Bragado Alvarez, M. C., & Carrasco Galán, I. (1999). Análisis factorial del B.D.I. (Beck Depression Inventory) en padres de niños con trastornos psicopathológicos [Factorial analysis of BDI (Beck Depression Inventory) in parents of children with psychopathological disorders]. *Analisis y Modificacion De Conducta, 25*, 81–102.

Bauer, M. S., Crits-Christoph, P., Ball, W. A., Dewees, E., McAllister, T., Alahi, P., et al. (1991). Independent assessment of manic and depressive symptoms by self-rating: Scale characteristics and implications for the study of mania. *Archives of General Psychiatry, 48*, 807–812.

Bauer, M. S., Vojta, C., Kinosian, B., Altshuler, L., & Glick, H. (2000). The internal state scale: Replication of its discriminating abilities in a multisite, public sector sample. *Bipolar Disorders, 2*, 340–346. doi:10.1034/j.1399-5618.2000.020409.x.

Bech, P., Bolwig, T. G., Kramp, P., & Rafaelsen, O. J. (1979). The Bech-Rafaelsen Mania Scale and the Hamilton Depression Scale. *Acta Psychiatrica Scandinavica, 59*, 420–430. doi:10.1111/j.1600-0447. 1979.tb04484.x.

Beck, A. T., Kovacs, M., & Weissman, A. (1979). Assessment of suicidal intention: The scale for suicide ideation. *Journal of Consulting and Clinical Psychology, 47*(2), 343–352.

Beck, A. T., Rush, A. J., Shaw, B. F., & Emery, G. (1979). *Cognitive therapy of depression*. New York: Guilford Press.

Beck, A. T., & Steer, R. A. (1989). Clinical predictors of eventual suicide: A five to ten year prospective study of suicide attempters. *Journal of Affective Disorders, 17*, 203–209.

Beck, A. T., & Steer, R. A. (1993). *Manual for the Beck Depression Inventory*. San Antonio, TX: Psychological Corporation.

Beck, A. T., Steer, R. A., & Brown, G. K. (1996). *Manual for the Beck Depression Inventory-II*. San Antonio, TX: Psychological Corporation.

Beck, A. T., Steer, R. A., Kovacs, M., & Garrison, B. (1985). Hopelessness and eventual suicide: A 10-year prospective study of patients hospitalized with suicidal ideation. *The American Journal of Psychiatry, 142*, 559–563.

Beck, A. T., Ward, C. H., Mendelson, M., Mock, J., & Erbaugh, J. (1961). An inventory for measuring depression. *Archives of General Psychiatry, 4*, 53–63.

Beck, A. T., Weissman, A., Lester, D., & Trexler, L. (1974). The measurement of pessimism: The hopelessness scale. *Journal of Consulting and Clinical Psychology, 42*, 861–865.

Bonicatto, S., Dew, A. M., & Soria, J. J. (1998). Analysis of the psychometric properties of the Spanish version of the Beck Depression Inventory in Argentina. *Psychiatry Research, 79*, 277–285.

Bowden, C. L., Singh, V., Thompson, P., Gonzalez, J. M., Katz, M. M., Dahl, M., et al. (2007). Development of the bipolar inventory of symptoms scale. *Acta Psychiatrica Scandinavica, 116*, 189–194. doi:10.1111/j.1600-0447.2006.00955.x.

Brown, G. K., Beck, A. T., Steer, R. A., & Grisham, J. R. (2000). Risk factors for suicide in psychiatric outpatients: A 20-year prospective study. *Journal of Consulting and Clinical Psychology, 68*, 371–377.

Carmody, D. P. (2005). Psychometric characteristics of the Beck Depression Inventory-II with college students of diverse ethnicity. *International Journal of Psychiatry in Clinical Practice, 9*(1), 22–28. doi:10.1080/13651500510014800.

Corona, R., Berlanga, C., Gutiérrez-Mora, D., & Fresán, A. (2007). La detección de casos de trastorno bipolar por medio de un instrumento de tamizaje: El cuestionario de trastornos del animo versión en español. *Salud Mental, 30*, 50–57.

Diez-Quevedo, C., Rangil, T., Sanchez-Planell, L., Kroenke, K., & Spitzer, R. L. (2001). Validation and utility of the patient health questionnaire in diagnosing mental disorders in 1003 general hospital Spanish inpatients. *Psychosomatic Medicine, 63*, 679–686.

Eckblad, M., & Chapman, L. J. (1986). Development and validation of a scale for hypomanic personality. *Journal of Abnormal Psychology, 95*, 214–222. doi:10.1037/0021-843X.95.3.214.

Escobar, J. I. (1987). Cross-cultural aspects of the somatization trait. *Hospital & Community Psychiatry, 38*(2), 174–180.

Escobar, J. I., Gomez, J., & Tuason, V. B. (1983). Depressive phenomenology in North and South American patients. *The American Journal of Psychiatry, 140*(1), 47–51.

Fernandez-Pol, B. (1986). Characteristics of 77 Puerto Ricans who attempted suicide. *The American Journal of Psychiatry, 143*, 1460–1463.

Fortuna, L. R., Perez, D. J., Canino, G., Sribney, W., & Alegria, M. (2007). Prevalence and correlates of lifetime suicidal ideation and suicide attempts among Latino subgroups in the United States. *The Journal of Clinical Psychiatry, 68*, 572–581. doi:10.4088/JCP.v68n0413.

Frerichs, R. R., Aneshensel, C. S., & Clark, V. A. (1981). Prevalence of depression in Los Angeles County. *American Journal of Epidemiology, 113*, 691–699.

Ghaemi, S. N., Miller, C. J., Berv, D. A., Klugman, J., Rosenquist, K. J., & Pies, R. W. (2005). Sensitivity and specificity of a new bipolar spectrum diagnostic scale. *Journal of Affective Disorders, 84*, 273–277. doi:10.1016/S0165-0327(03)00196-4.

Gilbody, S., Richards, D., Brealey, S., & Hewitt, C. (2007). Screening for depression in medical settings with the patient health questionnaire (PHQ): A diagnostic meta-analysis. *Journal of General Internal Medicine, 22*, 1596–1602. doi:10.1007/s11606-007-0333-y.

Golding, J. M., Aneshensel, C. S., & Hough, R. L. (1991). Responses to depression scale items among Mexican-Americans and non-Hispanic Whites. *Journal of Clinical Psychology, 47*, 61–75. doi:10.1002/1097-4679(199101)47:1<61::AID-JCLP2270470110>3.0.CO;2-E.

Gross, R., Olfson, M., Gameroff, M. J., Carasquillo, O., Shea, S., Feder, A., et al. (2005). Depression and glycemic control in Hispanic primary care patients with diabetes. *Journal of General Internal Medicine, 20*, 460–466. doi:10.1111/j.1525-1497.2005.30003.x.

Grzywacz, J. G., Hovey, J. D., Seligman, L. D., Arcury, T. A., & Quandt, S. A. (2006). Evaluating short-form versions of the CES-D for measuring depressive symptoms among immigrants from Mexico. *Hispanic Journal of Behavioral Sciences, 28*, 404–424. doi:10.1177/0739986306290645.

Guarnaccia, P. J., Angel, R., & Worobey, J. L. (1989). The factor structure of the CES-D in the Hispanic health and nutrition examination survey: The influences of ethnicity, gender and language. *Social Science & Medicine, 29*, 85–94. doi:10.1016/0277-9536(89)90131-7.

Herrero, M. J., Blanch, J., Peri, J. M., De Pablo, J., Pintor, L., & Bulbena, A. (2003). A validation study of the hospital anxiety and depression scale (HADS) in a Spanish population. *General Hospital Psychiatry, 25*, 277–283. doi:10.1016/S0163-8343(03)00043-4.

Hirschfeld, R. M., Williams, J. B., Spitzer, R. L., Calabrese, J. R., Flynn, L., Keck, P. E., et al. (2000). Development and validation of a screening instrument for bipolar spectrum disorder: The mood disorder questionnaire. *The American Journal of Psychiatry, 157*, 1873–1875. doi:10.1176/appi.ajp. 157.11.1873.

Huang, F. Y., Chung, H., Kroenke, K., Delucchi, K. L., & Spitzer, R. L. (2006). Using the patient health questionnaire-9 to measure depression among racially and ethnically diverse primary care patients. *Journal of General Internal Medicine, 21*, 547–552. doi:10.1111/j.1525-1497.2006.00409.x.

Ibáñez, I., González, M., & Peñate, W. (1997). Comparación de modelos factoriales alternativos para la versión española del Inventario de Depresión de Beck [Comparison of factorial models for the Spanish version of the Beck Depression Inventory]. *Analisis y Modificacion De Conducta, 23*, 283–303.

Johnson, J. G., Harris, E. S., Spitzer, R. L., & Williams, J. B. W. (2002). The patient health questionnaire for adolescents: Validation of an instrument for the assessment of mental disorders among adolescent primary care patients. *The Journal of Adolescent Health, 30*, 196–204.

Jurado, S., Villegas, M. E., Méndez, L., Rodríguez, F., Loperena, V., & Varela, R. (1998). La estandarización del Inventario de Depresión de Beck para los residentes de la Ciudad de México [Standardization of Beck's Depression Inventory for Mexico City inhabitants]. *Salud Mental, 21*, 26–31.

Kessler, R. C., McGonagle, K. A., Zhao, S., Nelson, C. B., Hughes, M., Eshleman, S., et al. (1994). Lifetime and 12-month prevalence of DSM-III-R psychiatric disorders in the United States: Results from the National Comorbidity Survey. *Archives of General Psychiatry, 51*(1), 8–19.

Kohout, F. J., Berkman, L. F., Evans, D. A., & Cornoni-Huntley, J. (1993). Two shorter forms of the CES-D Depression Symptoms Index. Journal of Aging and Health, 5, 179–193. doi:10.1177/089826439300500202.

Kroenke, K., Spitzer, R. L., & Williams, J. B. (2001). The PHQ-9: Validity of a brief depression severity measure. *Journal of General Internal Medicine, 16*, 606–613. doi:10.1046/j.1525-1497.2001.016009606.x.

Kroenke, K., Spitzer, R. L., & Williams, J. B. W. (2003). The patient health questionnaire-2: Validity of a two-item depression screener. *Medical Care, 41*, 1284–1292. doi:10.1097/01.MLR.0000093487.78664.3C.

Leff, J. P. (1981). *Psychiatry around the globe: A transcultural view*. New York: Marcel Dekker.

López-Alvarenga, J. C., Vázquez-Velázquez, V., Arcila-Martínez, D., Sierra-Ovando, A. E., González-Barranco, J., & Salín-Pascual, R. J. (2002). Accuracy and diagnostic utility of the hospital anxiety and depression scale (HADS) in a sample of obese Mexican patients. *Revista De Investigación Clínica; Organo Del Hospital De Enfermedades De La Nutrición, 54*, 403–409.

Lubin, B., Millham, J., & Paredes, F. (1980). Spanish language versions of the depression adjective check lists. *Hispanic Journal of Behavioral Sciences, 2*, 51–57.

Masten, W. G., Caldwell-Colbert, A. T., Alcala, S. J., & Mijares, B. E. (1986). Confiabilidad y validez de la escala de depresión del Centro de Estudios Epidemiologicos. *Hispanic Journal of Behavioral Sciences, 8*, 77–84. doi:10.1177/07399863860081003.

Mendelson, T., Rehkopf, D. H., & Kubzansky, L. D. (2008). Depression among Latinos in the United States: A meta-analytic review. *Journal of Consulting and Clinical Psychology, 76*(3), 355–366.

Mestre, J. I., Rossi, P. C., & Torrens, M. (2012). The assessment interview: A review of structured and semi-structured clinical interviews available for use among Hispanic clients. In L. Benuto (Ed.), *Guide to psychological assessment with Hispanics*. New York: Springer.

Monk, M., & Warshauer, M. E. (1974). Completed and attempted suicide in three ethnic groups. *American Journal of Epidemiology, 100*, 333–345.

Oquendo, M. A., Lizardi, D., Greenwald, S., Weissman, M. M., & Mann, J. J. (2004). Rates of lifetime suicide attempt and rates of lifetime major depression in different ethnic groups in the United States. *Acta Psychiatrica Scandinavica, 110*, 446–451. doi:10.1111/j.1600-0447.2004.00404.x.

Peña, J. B., Kuhlberg, J. A., Zayas, L. H., Baumann, A. A., Gulbas, L., Hausmann-Stabile, C., et al. (2011). Familism, family environment, and suicide attempts among Latina youth. *Suicide & Life-Threatening Behavior, 41*(3), 330–341. doi:10.1111/j.1943-278X. 2011.00032.x.

Penley, J. A., Wiebe, J. S., & Nwosu, A. (2003). Psychometric properties of the Spanish Beck Depression Inventory-II in a medical sample. *Psychological Assessment, 15*, 569–577.

Perczek, R., Carver, C. S., Price, A. A., & Pozo-Kaderman, C. (2000). Coping, mood, and aspects of personality in Spanish translation and evidence of convergence with English versions. *Journal of Personality Assessment, 74*, 63–87. doi:10.1207/S15327752JPA740105.

Perron, B. E., Fries, L. E., Kilbourne, A. M., Vaughn, M. G., & Bauer, M. S. (2010). Racial/ethnic group differences in bipolar symptomatology in a community sample of persons with bipolar I disorder. *The Journal of Nervous and Mental Disease, 198*(1), 16–21. doi:10.1097/NMD.0b013e3181c818c5.

Posner, S. F., Stewart, A. L., Marín, G., & Pérez-Stable, E. J. (2001). Factor variability of the Center for Epidemiological Studies Depression Scale (CES-D) among urban Latinos. *Ethnicity and Health, 6*, 137–144. doi:10.1080/13557850120068469.

Quintana, J. M., Padierna, A., Esteban, C., Arostegui, I., Bilbao, A., & Ruiz, I. (2003). Evaluation of the psychometric characteristics of the Spanish version of the Hospital Anxiety and Depression Scale. *Acta Psychiatrica Scandinavica, 107*, 216–221.

Radloff, L. S. (1977). The CES-D scale: A self-report depression scale for research in the general population. *Applied Psychological Measurement, 1*, 385–401. doi:10.1177/014662167700100306.

Reyes, J. C., Robles, R. R., Colón, H. M., Negrón, J. L., Matos, T. D., & Calderón, J. M. (2011). Polydrug use and attempted suicide among Hispanic adolescents in Puerto Rico. *Archives of Suicide Research, 15*(2), 151–159. doi:10.1080/13811118.2011.565274.

Richardson, L. P., Rockhill, C., Russo, J. E., Grossman, D. C., Richards, J., McCarty, C., et al. (2010). Evaluation of the PHQ-2 as a brief screen for detecting major depression among adolescents. *Pediatrics, 125*, e1097–e1103. doi:10.1542/peds.2009-2712.

Rivera-Medina, C. L., Caraballo, J. N., Rodríguez-Cordero, E. R., Bernal, G., & Dávila-Marrero, E. (2010). Factor structure of the CES-D and measurement invariance across gender for low-income Puerto Ricans in a probability sample. *Journal of Consulting and Clinical Psychology, 78*, 398–408. doi:10.1037/a0019054.

Roberts, R. E. (1980). Reliability of the CES-D scale in different ethnic contexts. *Psychiatry Research, 2*, 125–134. doi:10.1016/0165-1781(80)90069-4.

Roberts, R. E. (1981). Prevalence of depressive symptoms among Mexican Americans. *The Journal of Nervous and Mental Disease, 169*(213), 219.

Ruggero, C. J., Johnson, S. L., & Cuellar, A. K. (2004). Spanish-language measures of mania and depression. *Psychological Assessment, 16*, 381–385. doi:10.1037/1040-3590.16.4.381.

Sanchez-Moreno, J., Villagran, J. M., Gutierrez, J. R., Camacho, M., Ocio, S., Palao, D., et al. (2008). Adaptation and validation of the Spanish version of the mood disorder questionnaire for the detection of bipolar disorder. *Bipolar Disorders, 10*, 400–412. doi:10.1111/j.1399-5618.2007.00571.x.

Sanz, J., & Vázquez, C. (1998). Fiabilidad, validez y datos normativos del inventario para la depresión de Beck [Reliability, validity, and normative data of the Beck Depression Inventory]. *Psicothema, 10*, 303–318.

Schalet, B. D., Durbin, C. E., & Revelle, W. (2011). Multidimensional structure of the hypomanic personality scale. *Psychological Assessment, 23*, 504–522. doi:10.1037/a0022301.

Schmaling, K. B., & Hernandez, D. V. (2005). Detection of depression among low-income Mexican Americans in primary care. *Journal of Health Care for the Poor and Underserved, 16*, 780–790. doi:10.1353/hpu.2005.0105.

Spitzer, R. L., Kroenke, K., & Williams, J. B. (1999). Validation and utility of a self-report version of PRIME-MD: The PHQ primary care study. *Journal of the American Medical Association, 282*, 1737–1744. doi:10.1001/jama.282.18.1737.

Spitzer, R., Williams, J. B., Kroenke, K., Hornyak, R., & McMurray, J. (2000). Validity and utility of the PRIME-MD patient health questionnaire in assessment of 3000 obstetric-gynecologic patients: The PRIME-MD Patient Health Questionnaire Obstetrics-Gynecology Study. *American Journal of Obstetrics and Gynecology, 183*, 759–769. doi:10.1067/mob.2000.106580.

Spitzer, R. L., Williams, J. B., Kroenke, K., Linzer, M., deGruy, F. V., III, Hahn, S. R., et al. (1994). Utility of a new procedure for diagnosing mental disorders in primary care The PRIME-MD 1000 Study. *Journal of the American Medical Association, 272*, 1749–1756. doi:10.1001/jama.272.22.1749.

Stewart, A. L., Hays, R. D., & Ware, J. E., Jr. (1988). The MOS short-form general health survey. Reliability and validity in a patient population. *Medical Care, 26*, 724–735.

Suárez-Mendoza, A. A., Cardiel, M. H., Caballero-Uribe, C. V., Ortega-Soto, H. A., & Márquez-Marín, M. (1997). Measurement of depression in Mexican patients with rheumatoid arthritis: Validity of the Beck Depression Inventory. *Arthritis Care and Research, 10*, 194–199.

Tejero Pociello, A. A., Guimerá Querol, E. M., Farré Martí, J. M., & Peri, J. M. (1986). Uso clínico del HAD (Hospital Anxiety and Depression Scale) en población psychiátrica: Un estudio de sensibilidad, fiabilidad y validez. *Revista del Departamento de Psiquiatría de la Facultad de Medicina de Barcelona, 13*(5), 233–238.

Vázquez, C., & Sanz, J. (1997). Fiabilidad y valores normativos de la versión española del inventario para la depresión de Beck de 1978 [Reliability and normative data of the Spanish version of the 1978 Beck's Depression Inventory]. *Clínica y Salud, 8*, 403–422.

Vega, W. A., Kolody, B., Aguilar-Gaxiola, S., Alderete, E., Catalano, R., & Caraveo-Anduaga, J. (1998). Lifetime prevalence of *DSM-III-R* psychiatric disorders among urban and rural Mexican Americans in California. *Archives of General Psychiatry, 55*, 771–778.

Vega, W., Warheit, G., Buhl-Auth, J., & Meinhardt, K. (1984). The prevalence of depressive symptoms among Mexican Americans and Anglos. *American Journal of Epidemiology, 120*, 592–607.

Vernon, S. W., & Roberts, R. E. (1982). Prevalence of treated and untreated psychiatric disorders in three ethnic groups. *Social Science & Medicine, 16*, 1575–1582.

Villaseñor, Y., & Waitzkin, H. (1999). Limitations of a structured psychiatric diagnostic instrument in assessing somatization among Latino patients in primary care. *Medical Care, 37*(7), 637–646.

White, D., Leach, C., Sims, R., Atkinson, M., & Cottrell, D. (1999). Validation of the hospital anxiety and depression scale for use with adolescents. *The British Journal of Psychiatry, 175*, 452–454. doi:10.1192/bjp. 175.5.452.

Wiebe, J. S., & Penley, J. A. (2005). A psychometric comparison of the Beck Depression Inventory-II in English and Spanish. *Psychological Assessment, 17*(4), 481–485.

Zaratiegui, R. M., Vázquez, G. H., Lorenzo, L. S., Marinelli, M., Aguayo, S., Strejilevich, S. A., et al. (2011). Sensitivity and specificity of the mood disorder questionnaire and the bipolar spectrum diagnostic scale in Argentinean patients with mood disorders. *Journal of Affective Disorders, 132*, 445–449. doi:10.1016/j.jad.2011.03.014.

Zayas, L. H., Lester, R. J., Cabassa, L. J., & Fortuna, L. R. (2005). Why do so many Latina teens attempt suicide? A conceptual model for research. *The American Journal of Orthopsychiatry, 75*, 275–287. doi:10.1037/0002-9432.75.2.275.

Zigmond, A. S., & Snaith, R. P. (1983). The hospital anxiety and depression scale. *Acta Psychiatrica Scandinavica, 67*, 361–370. doi:10.1111/j.1600-0447. 1983.tb09716.x.

Zimmerman, M., Galione, J. N., Chelminski, I., Young, D., & Ruggero, C. J. (2010). Performance of the bipolar spectrum diagnostic scale in psychiatric outpatients. *Bipolar Disorders, 12*, 528–538. doi:10.1111/ j.1399-5618.2010.00840.x.

9 Special Considerations When Assessing the Hispanic Adolescent: Examining Suicide Risk

Emilia Lucio-Gomez Maqueo
and Paulina Arenas-Landgrave

Considerations When Assessing the Adolescent

Human development is a continuous process in which there can be critical periods where adaptive success or failure has an important influence on the subsequent life course (Archer, 2005). Considering that beginning in childhood people face numerous threatening and challenging situations that require action and adaptation, a central feature of human development assumes the ability to adapt to stress and adversity (Compas, Connor-Smith, Saltzman, Thomsen, & Wadsworth, 2001). Adolescence is a developmental stage that requires considerable adjustment. Every teenager has to deal not only with biological and cognitive changes but also with a series of complex and interrelated sociopsychological tasks such as shifts in relationships with family, friends, the peer group, and the wider world (Coleman & Hagell, 2007; Seiffge-Krenke, 2009). Although adolescents are considered an at-risk population, most of them go through adolescence without significant difficulties. However, the presence of non-normative stressors, such as critical life events, exerts a cumulative adverse effect on adolescent emotional and behavioral symptoms, increasing the likelihood of maladaptive outcomes in this population (Compas, 1987; Seiffge-Krenke, 2000).

Stress is a major factor that affects the way people manage their lives; it is intimately tied to mental health and is very possibly linked to physical health problems (Compas, 1998; Frydenberg, 2008; Hobfoll, Schwarzer, & Chon, 1996). Similarly, stressful life events have a great influence in the course and development of a wide variety of psychological and behavioral problems (Connor-Smith & Compas, 2004). Due to the fact that stress is common and affects health and causes people to be more vulnerable to emotional distress, research on primary prevention and intervention on adolescents in risky situations is of evident concern, particularly when we consider that young people face a considerable number of changes (including personal, social, and family changes) that may lead to many stressful situations.

Adolescent health is essential for social, economical, and political progress in all countries (Maddaleno, Morello, & Infante-Espínola, 2003), so effective attention on health status in this group is of great interest not only to members of several professions (e.g., health professionals, teachers) but

E. Lucio-G. Maqueo, Ph.D (✉) • P. Arenas-Landgrave, Ph.D.
Mental Health and Diagnosis Program, Faculty of Psychology, National Autonomous University of Mexico, Ciudad Universitaria 3000. Col. Copilco-Universidad, 04360 Mexico City, Mexico
e-mail: melgm@unam.mx; paudani@yahoo.com

L.T. Benuto (ed.), *Guide to Psychological Assessment with Hispanics*,
DOI 10.1007/978-1-4614-4412-1_9, © Springer Science+Business Media New York 2013

also to parents and even society at large as adolescents are more vulnerable to risky behaviors during this period. Some of the injurious health habits acquired during adolescence do not present morbidity at this development stage, but they do so during adulthood (Coleman, Hendry, & Kloep, 2007). In this regard, risk behaviors in adolescence are important themes in clinical psychological research.

Hispanic Adolescents: A Brief Review of the Literature

While the main focus of this chapter will be on suicide risk and relevant assessment with the Hispanic adolescent, we must first address a few things. While the literature is not 100 % in accord with whether the Hispanic adolescent fairs better or worse than nonminority adolescents, it is apparent that Hispanics perceive mental health services as unnecessary, unwelcoming, or not useful; are likely to use services mostly when in crisis; and have high dropout rates and undesirable treatment outcomes (U.S. Department of Health and Human Services, 2001). Lack of insurance coverage can also contribute to underutilization of services (Iniguez & Palinkas, 2003). This may be of particular concern considering that at least some of the literature cites Hispanic adolescents at higher risk for certain mental health conditions than other adolescent groups, e.g., Whites and Hispanics are more commonly diagnosed with eating disordered behavior than other ethnic groups (Davis & Yager, 1992), and Hispanic adolescents have been reported to use alcohol and illicit drugs at a higher rate than their White counterparts (Martinez, Eddy, & DeGarmo, 2003). Because stressors have been discussed as a contributing factor to suicide risk, we thought it is necessary to mention the above. The following includes an overview of patterns or risk behaviors in the Hispanic adolescent.

Suicide Risk in Adolescents

To assess adolescents, health is of great concern as patterns of risk behaviors such as smoking, overeating, alcohol, and drug use can have long-term health consequences. One way to assess the health status of adolescents is to examine behaviors that increase the risk for morbidity and mortality (Rew, 2005) and risk factors that have a negative influence on youths' well-being. Specific to this chapter is suicidal behavior which tends to increase during adolescence in part due to the stressors that serve to aggravate the adolescent's feelings of distress and despair (Spirito & Overholser, 2003). Thus, stressful life events may play an important role in the development of suicidal tendencies among adolescents by serving as a trigger to the suicidal act. In fact, it has been reported that different types of stressful life events are related to suicide risk, with the most common stressors involving interpersonal conflict and loss or failure (Hernandez, 2007; Lewinsohn, Rohde, & Seeley, 1996). Nonetheless, before we proceed, we would like to reiterate (as stated above) that while adolescents are considered an at-risk population, most of them go through adolescence without significant difficulties.

Incidence

Nowadays, one of the main health problems with respect to adolescents is self-inflicted violence. The prevalence of both suicide attempts and completed suicide has risen dramatically in many countries during the last years (e.g., Borges et al., 2009; O'Connor, Rasmussen, Miles, & Hawton, 2009; Friedmann and Kohn (2008); Portzky & van Heeringen, 2007). With respect to the increase of suicide mortality in adolescents, the study of suicide related behaviors (e.g., ideation, plans, attempts) is of important concern as is the need to prevent and reduce self-inflicted violence. This is particularly important if we consider that self-harm behavior may be potentially life-threatening and can lead to serious, long-term consequences in the adolescent's physical health and may act as a cause of psychological distress and anxiety. Moreover, it can be a risk factor of subsequent suicide attempts and completed suicide in this population.

According to the World Health Organization, at least 100,000 youths kill themselves each year worldwide. While many age groups are showing a decline in suicide rates, rates of youths committing suicide have risen in both developing and developed countries. Indeed, the numbers may be an underestimate as deaths are only attributed to suicide where proof of intent is established (Wasserman, Cheng, & Jiang, 2005).

Data on suicidality includes suicidal ideation, suicide plan(s), and suicide attempt(s). It is important to note that nonlethal suicidal thoughts and behaviors are strong risk factors for subsequent suicide attempts and death, and the prevalence of these behaviors in young people is increasing worldwide. In fact, suicide is the second or third leading cause of death among adolescents between the ages of 15 and 24 in many countries (e.g., Anderson, 2002; Everall, Altrows, & Paulson, 2006; Instituto Nacional de Estadística, Geografía e Informática (INEGI), 2006; Rew, 2005). In the United States, death by suicide is the third leading cause of death for adolescents, accounting for 14.6 % of deaths in this age group (Centers for Disease Control and Prevention (CDC), 2006), and in Canada, it is the second highest cause of death for youth aged 10–24, while in other American countries such as Guyana (28.8 %), Cuba (17.6 %), and Uruguay (14.6 %), suicide rates are above 10 deaths per 100,000 among this population (World Health Organization (WHO), 2008). Attempted suicide is much more common in females than in males, with Hispanic females and Native American females showing the highest rates of suicide attempts (Spirito & Hernandez-Cervantes, 2009).

Despite the above, in certain Latin-American countries, it is apparent that changes in suicide trends are occurring. For example, despite that the Mexican suicide rate among youths is low when compared to countries such as Finland, Japan, or the United States, Mexico has one of the largest *increases* in suicide (61.9 %) among 28 countries examined (WHO, 2002, 2008). Specifically the increase between 1990 and 2000 was 150 % for Mexican youths ages 5–14 years and 74 % for those 15–24 years old (Bridge, Goldstein, & Brent, 2006). Nonetheless, it is worth noting that generally speaking Hispanics tend to have lower rates of suicide attempts than other ethnic groups. This, however, does not exempt this group from meriting evidence-based assessment procedures. Thus, a discussion regarding the risk factors associated with suicide follows followed by a discussion of assessment measures that are likely to be useful when assessing for suicide risk in the Hispanic adolescent.

Risk Factors Associated with Suicide

During the last few decades, there has been a considerable research and interest in determining the risk factors of suicide among adolescents. Much of this research has focused on studying prior suicide attempts, psychiatric disorders, and substance abuse among adolescent suicide victims (e.g., Beautrais, 2000; Fergusson, Beautrais, & Horwood, 2003; Pfeffer, 1998; Shaffer, Gould, Fisher, Trautman, & Moreau, 1996). Some other studies have also examined the role that childhood adversities like physical, sexual, or emotional abuse; a family history of suicidal behavior; and adverse life circumstances may play (Brent, Bridge, Johnson, & Connolly, 1996; Ellis & Trumpower, 2008; Johnson et al., 2002; Lucio, Loza, & Duran, 2000).

In relation to stressful life events, some studies (Johnson et al., 2002) have reported that individuals who are exposed to a series of adversities during childhood and adolescence are at a particularly high risk for suicide. During adolescence, many youths can show psychological distress and some are also exposed to several types of traumatic experiences with severe consequences (e.g., physical illness, accidents, arrest, neglect), among which hopelessness and anxiety stand out (Kirk, 1993).

Duarté-Vélez and Bernal (2007) have asserted that in order to identify risk and protective factors of suicide in Latinos youths, studies of Hispanic subgroups should be conducted. Furthermore, recent data show that the largest legal permanent resident flow to the United States comes from Mexico, representing the 64 % of Hispanic population in the United States, including a significant number of Mexican adolescents (U.S. Department of Homeland Security, 2007) calling to light the importance of improved suicide risk assessment for Hispanics both internationally and within the United States.

Instruments for Suicide Risk Assessment

There are several instruments for screening suicide risk in adolescents developed and used in the United States and these will be reviewed below. However, it is important to first note that teenagers tend to respond differently to the instruments adapted or developed for use with Hispanics than they do to instruments developed for use with other cultures. This may be due in part to varying reading levels, not liking to respond to impersonal lists, preference for items written in the first person (e.g., "My father has died" instead of "Father died"), etc. Thus, culture-specific instruments may be particularly suitable for Hispanic adolescents who do not have a high educational level and also for those who do.

Columbia Suicide Screen

The Columbia Suicide Screen (CSS: Shaffer et al., 2004) is an 11-item instrument that assesses symptoms of depression, substance abuse, suicidal ideation, and past suicide attempts. These screening items are embedded within 32 general health questions and 4 items on relationship and family concerns. This instrument has been used in a Teen Screen Program in which there are seven steps for risk assessment of which psychiatric referrals are a part of. Published research on the CSS with Hispanics is not available; thus, this may not be the best alternative for assessing suicide risk with Hispanic adolescents.

Suicidal Ideation Questionnaire (SIQ)

The Suicidal Ideation Questionnaire (SIQ: Reynolds, 1987, 1991) assesses the frequency of suicidal thoughts in adolescents and can be used to evaluate or monitor troubled youths. Two versions of the SIQ are available: a 30-item format for adolescents in grades 10–12 and a 15-item format for adolescents in grades 7–9 (SIQ-JR). Both forms use a 7-point scale to assess the frequency of suicidal thoughts and ideas. The reliability coefficients are .97 for the SIQ and .93–.94 for the SIQ-JR. A review of the literature has indicated that the SIQ has been used with Hispanic adolescents (e.g., Muehlenkamp, Cowles, & Gutierrez, 2010), although it does not appear that a translated version of this measure exists; therefore, this measure may be good for use with the English-speaking Hispanic adolescent only.

Beck Suicidal Ideation Scale (BSI)

Another very frequently used instrument is the Beck Suicidal Ideation Scale (BSI; Beck & Steer, 1991). This instrument is a 21-item self-report measure based on a semi-structured interview that may be used to identify the presence and severity of suicidal ideation. Items on this measure also assess the respondent's suicidal plans, deterrents to suicide, and the level of openness to revealing suicidal thoughts. The BSI was designed to quantify and assess suicidal intention. The English version of this measure includes items related to suicidal ideation and attitude toward ideation: wish to die – live magnitude, desire to make an active suicide attempt, and control over suicidal action. The total score yields a severity score for suicidal ideation and attempt. There are published studies on the Spanish adaptations of this instrument (Artasanchez, 1999; Gonzalez-Macip, Diaz, Ortiz, Gonzalez-Forteza, & Gonzalez-Nuñez, 2000) although it is important to note that youths have reported that this instrument is quite repetitive and have expressed that a 7-point scale was not easy to answer. Thus, while this measure is available in Spanish, it may not be the ideal measure to use with the Hispanic adolescent.

Self-Harm Behavior Questionnaire

The Self-Harm Behavior Questionnaire (SHBQ; Gutierrez et al. 2001) is a combined forced-choice and free-response questionnaire that aims to assess the extent to which adolescents have engaged in self-harm activities over their lifetime and currently. Research has indicated that the SHBQ is internally consistent and has adequate evidence for convergent validity for use with Caucasian, African American, and Hispanic adolescents (Muehlenkamp et al., 2010), although it does not appear that a translated version of this measure exists; therefore, this measure may be good for use with the English-speaking Hispanic adolescent only.

The Suicide Risk Inventory for Adolescents

The IRIS (Inventario de Riesgo Suicida para Adolescentes "Suicide Risk Inventory for Adolescents") (Hernandez & Lucio, 2006a, 2006b) is a screening test aimed at detecting risk for suicidal behavior. It includes 50 items, which are divided into 3 subscales and an index (emotional difficulties associated with suicidal risk [26 items]). The subscales are (a) Suicidal Ideation, Attempt, and Intent (7 items); (b) Depression and Hopelessness (8 items); and (c) Lack of Protective Circumstances (6 items). For each of the items, the respondent is asked to rate their response on a 5-point frequency scale (A – "All the time" to E – "Never") specifically with regard to how he/she has felt during the last year. The reliability of the inventory is acceptable (Cronbach's alpha=0.95) and convergent validity was established using the Beck Suicide Scale.

The IRIS is intended for use within a model of suicide assessment whereby the objective is to first identify suicidal behavior and second to place the suicidal adolescent in an intervention program and is based in some parameters of suicide risk in adolescents developed by other authors (Goldston, 2000; Jacobs, 1999; Shaffer, Garland, Gould, Fisher, & Trautman, 1998). Further research has been conducted to further establish validity as well as to develop items that take into account cultural issues and are phrased into a familiar language for Hispanic adolescents (Lucio et al., 2000). While this instrument was developed with a Mexican population, it has been used in other Latin-American countries (Copari, 2006) and is considered a sound means of assessing suicidality with Hispanic/Latino adolescents.

With the IRIS, adolescents can be classified in four levels of suicide risk:

1. High risk (priority 1): Defined as endorsing the three critical items (25, 49, 50) and obtaining a T-score higher than 60 in the first 3 subscales.
2. Risk for attempt (priority 2): Defined as endorsing item 50, which refers to previous attempts, having a T-score higher than 60 on one of the other subscales, or as endorsing item 25 or 49 (critical items).

Table 9.1 Examples of items of the adolescent suicide risk inventory (IRIS) (Hernandez & Lucio, 2006a, 2006b)

49 I've planned my own death	He planeado mi propia muerte
50 I've attempted to take my own life	He intentado quitarme la vida
25 I've thought of committing suicide	He pensado en suicidarme
32 I believe or feel my own death might be a solution to my troubled life	Creo o siento que mi muerte podría ser una solución a los problemas en mi vida
27 I have or I know of a place where I'd like to die	Conozco o tengo un lugar donde me gustaría morir
16 I've felt or believed that my existence is horrible, hideous	He creído o sentido que mi existencia es horrible, odiosa
43 I've felt disappointed in life	Me he sentido desilusionado (a) de la vida
23 I feel angry and/or frustrated	Me siento enojado (a) y/o frustrado (a)

3. Risk for ideation (priority 3): Defined as reporting recurrent suicidal ideation via the endorsement of item 25 (suicide ideation) or item 49 (suicide planning) and obtaining a score higher than 60 in one of the other subscales.
4. Low risk (priority 4): Defined as presenting emotional difficulties associated with suicidal risk. This may include the endorsement of item 49 and obtaining a T-score higher than 60 in one of the first three subscales.
5. Without risk: Defined as not fulfilling any of the criteria mentioned above.

Some examples of IRIS items are presented in Table 9.1.

Beyond a Single Test: A Model for Suicide Risk Assessment

Accurate assessment of suicide risk demands knowledge of factors that may put an adolescent at risk as well as the symptoms the at-risk adolescent may display. It also requires different clinical and interpersonal skills to communicate with the adolescent in a sensitive and therapeutically firm manner.

Adolescent suicide is a multifactorial problem, and Shaffer et al. (2001) have proposed that the following factors must be taken into account to assess suicidal risk:

- Biological and genetic
- Demographical factors
- Family and childhood
- Mental disorders
- Previous suicide attempts
- Personality and cognitive styles
- Adverse or stressful events

Considering the multifactorial nature of suicide, it is recommended that the IRIS be used as part of an assessment model for suicide risk detection and also as part of a prevention strategy. This assessment model includes the use of different instruments developed specially for Spanish-speaking Hispanic clients, which have been validated and have adequate reliability. The instruments to be used in the model include the IRIS (Hernandez & Lucio, 2006a, 2006b), the Life-Events Questionnaire (Lucio & Duran, 2003), and the Minnesota Multiphasic Personality Inventory for Adolescents (MMPI-A) which has been validated and adapted for use with a Hispanic population (Lucio, Ampudia-Rueda, Duran-patino, Gallegos-Mejia, & Leon-Guzman, 1999).

The assessment model can be applied to adolescents who are at risk for suicide and who still have some protective factors, e.g., being in school. The model includes two stages: first, a screening task that is conducted whereby the client is administered the IRIS and the Life-Events Questionnaire and general demographical information is collected. The results are then evaluated, and it is determined if the adolescent is at risk of suicide from a clinical-epidemiological perspective. The second stage involves a referral system for individual or group treatment in the school or at an external psychological center. Adolescents are then assessed via the MMPI-A to further the suicide risk assessment process.

Life-Events Questionnaire

The Life-Events Questionnaire (Lucio & Duran, 2003) is included in the model because life stressors have been recognized as suicide conduct detonators in adolescents (Barrera et al., 1993; Farmer & Creed, 1989; Gisper, Wheeler, Marsh, & Davis, 1985). Stressful life events are factors that have a negative influence on the patterns of development (Compas, 1998). It has also been shown that they contribute to a better understanding of suicidal adolescent as their recent life is essential in the clinical treatment of this group (Marttunen, 1994; Spirito & Overholser, 2003). The Life-Events Questionnaire (Lucio & Duran, 2003) is a 130-item questionnaire which evaluates normative and nonnormative events during the last year, in seven areas of adolescents' life: family, school, achievement and failure, social, personal, behavioral problems, and health. This questionnaire captures the evaluation that the adolescent makes of each situation according to the following scales: (a) it happened to me and was good, (b) it happened to me and was bad, and (c) it happened to me and was not important.

The model discussed above has been appraised in several studies with adolescents at senior and junior high schools (Lucio & Hernandez, 2009; Lucio, Linaje, Perez, & Arenas, 2009; Lucio et al., 2000; Lucio-Gomez Maqueo, Plascencia, & Zamarron, 2005). In the above referenced studies, the predictive value of the IRIS and Life-Events Questionnaire has been tested as a significant group of adolescents who were screened were also interviewed. While the intervention portion of this model is beyond the scope of this chapter (which is focused on assessment), it is worth noting that prevention strategies and relevant interventions have been successful at reducing suicide risk. The following is a case example that is used to illustrate the above:

> Ferdinand was an adolescent who came to a Psychological Center because he had attempted against his life twice. He was referred to the center by one of his schoolteachers. His first suicide attempt involved him trying to hang himself from a water tank; this was unsuccessful as a neighbor found him. The second time he tried to cut himself with a razor blade, but her mother noticed it. On both occasions he downplayed his actions saying that he was playing. Ferdinand was a fairly lonely teenager, reticent especially about his mother, and an average achiever in school. He had few close friends at school and at home only his grandfather was a real support to him (they were very close). When Ferdinand´s grandfather died it was unexpected and stressful as he did not know his grandfather was seriously ill. When Ferdinand found out that his grandfather had died he became very nervous and anxious, and he started to hit himself but his godfather calmed him down. In that moment Ferdinand said *"I should have died and not my grandpa."* Ferdinand became very sad and he did not want to eat and his school grades dropped significantly. After this major event, Ferdinand began to feel as though nobody loved or understood him anymore, and he got angry and undisciplined about everything. His grandfather's death was an overwhelming loss to Ferdinand. and he felt an intense threat to his existence. At home, once he tried to beat his grandmother. During therapy, Ferdinand said that his only support was his grandfather and that he missed him a lot. He had a good attitude and disposition to treatment. With respect to his mother, she appeared collaborative at the beginning of treatment but later was quite tired and despaired by her son and would say *"I really do not know what to do with him anymore"*.This case example raises the question *is it possible to reduce the apparent suicidal ideation that Ferdinand was experiencing even though he was not overtly expressing it?* Over the course of 30 sessions, Ferdinand achieved substantial change. The IRIS questionnaire was administered to him as a pre- and posttreatment. With respect to the level of suicide risk, he was initially classified as at risk for attempt (priority 2), and in posttreatment, he was classified as without risk. This case example illustrates the way in which a measure such as the IRIS can assess for the presence of suicide risk in a multifactorial manner and when risk is identified, an evidence-based intervention can be applied and the IRIS provides information regarding a reduction in risk as well.

Summary

Young people face a multitude of ongoing life stressors that can contribute to an increased risk of emotional, behavioral, and health difficulties. In fact, they might become predisposed to suicidal thoughts and actions after a succession of traumatic events (e.g., major losses, depression, personality disturbances). These factors can create emotional states that evoke feelings of hopelessness and despair.

Taking into consideration that emotional dysregulation and unexpected or extreme stressors are highly related to suicide risk in young people (Brezo et al., 2008; Kirk, 1993); it is quite useful to assess not only suicide risk but also the number and type of stressors the adolescents is dealing with. This information can prove useful in the context of suicide risk assessment and also in the context of general assessment and can prove useful in the context of choosing appropriate interventions for the adolescent.

It is also important to note that the presence of stress is considered a risk factor not only for the adolescent but also for their family. One major aim of our field is to work on health promotion by providing psychological attention to adolescents and their families with the goal being to enhance stress management and to improve relationships within the family. Better than resolving problems is preventing them, as prevention can be more effective than universal intervention. In fact, primary intervention can counteract against difficulties even before problems appear (Durlak & Wells, 1997). It is necessary to assess suicidality among adolescents in order to stop suicide rates from increasing. From the data presented in this chapter, it is clear that suicidality in Hispanic adolescents should be assessed when risk facts are apparent so that preventative actions can be taken and treatment provided.

References

Anderson, R. (2002). *Deaths: Leading causes for 2000* (National vital statistics reports, 50 (16)). Hyattsville, MD: National Center for Health Statistics.

Archer, R. (2005). Adolescent development and psychopathology. In *MMPI-A. Assessing adolescent psychopathology* (pp. 1–25). Mahwah, NJ: Lawrence Erlbaum Associates.

Artasanchez, F. (1999). *Factores de riesgo para la ideación suicida: análisis retrospectivo para los factores de interacción y crianza* [Risk factors for suicidal ideation: Retrospective analysis for interaction and upbringing factors]. Unpublished master thesis, Psychology School, National Autonomous University of Mexico, Mexico City.

Barrera, P., Gomez, C., Jaar, H., Nuñez, C., Orellana, G., & Lolas, F. (1993). Percibirse sin apoyo social predispone al intento Suicida [Not perceiving social support predispose to suicidal attempts]. *Anales de Salud Mental, 9*, 75–81.

Beautrais, A. (2000). Risk factors for suicide and attempted suicide among young people. *The Australian and New Zealand Journal of Psychiatry, 34*, 420–436.

Beck, A., & Steer, R. (1991). *Manual for Beck scale for suicide*. New York: Psychological Corporation.

Borges, G., Medina-Mora, M. E., Orozco, R., Ouéda, C., Villatoro, J., & Fleiz, C. (2009). Distribución y determinantes sociodemográficos de la conducta suicida en Mexico [Socio-demographic elements and distribution of suicide behavior in Mexico]. *Salud Mental, 32*, 413–425.

Brent, D., Bridge, J., Johnson, B., & Connolly, J. (1996). Suicidal behavior runs in families: A controlled family study of adolescent suicide victims. *Archives of General Psychiatry, 53*, 1145–1152.

Brezo, J., Barker, E., Paris, J., Hébert, M., Vitaro, F., Tremblay, R., et al. (2008). Childhood trajectories of anxiousness and disruptiveness as predictors of suicide attempts. *Archives of Pediatrics & Adolescent Medicine, 162*(11), 1015–1021.

Bridge, J., Goldstein, T., & Brent, D. (2006). Adolescent suicide and suicidal behavior. *Journal of Child Psychological Psychiatry, 47*, 372–394.

Centers for Disease Control and Prevention (CDC). (2006). *Web-based injury statistics query and reporting system (WISQARS)*. www.cdc.gov/ncipc/wisqars. Accessed 12 Mar 2010.

Coleman, J., & Hagell, A. (2007). *Adolescence, risk and resilience. Against the odds*. West Sussex, England: Wiley.

Coleman, J., Hendry, L., & Kloep, M. (2007). *Adolescence and health*. West Sussex, England: Willey.

Compas, B. (1987). Coping with stress during childhood and adolescence. *Psychological Bulletin, 101*(3), 393–403.

Compas, B. (1998). An agenda for coping research and theory: Basic and applied developmental issues. *International Journal of Behavioral Development, 22*(2), 231–237.

Compas, B., Connor-Smith, J., Saltzman, H., Thomsen, A., & Wadsworth, M. (2001). Coping with stress during childhood and adolescence: Problems, progress, and potential in theory and research. *Psychological Bulletin, 127*(1), 87–127.

Connor-Smith, J., & Compas, B. (2004). Coping as a moderator of relations between reactivity to interpersonal stress, health status, and internalizing problems. *Cognitive Therapy and Research, 28*, 347–368.

Copari, N. (2006). Estrategias de Detección y Prevención de Factores de Riesgo de Problemas Emocionales en Adolescentes Paraguayos [Detection and prevention strategies of emotional risk factors in Paraguayan adolescents]. *Revista Eureka, 3*(3), 6–14.

Davis, C., & Yager, J. (1992). Transcultural aspects of eating disorders: A critical literature review. *Culture, Medicine and Psychiatry, 16*, 377–394.

Duarté-Vélez, Y., & Bernal, G. (2007). Suicide behavior among Latino and Latina adolescents: Conceptual and methodological issues. *Death Studies, 31*, 435–455.

Durlak, J., & Wells, A. (1997). Primary preventions mental health programs for children and adolescents. A meta-analytic review. *American Journal of Community Psychology, 25*, 115–152.

Ellis, T., & Trumpower, D. (2008). Health-risk behaviors and suicidal ideation: A preliminary study of cognitive and developmental factors. *Suicide & Life-Threatening Behavior, 38*(3), 251–259.

Everall, R., Altrows, J., & Paulson, B. (2006). Creating a future: A study of resilience in suicidal female adolescents. *Journal of Counseling and Development, 84*, 461–470.

Farmer, R., & Creed, F. (1989). Life events and hostility in self-poisoning. *The British Journal of Psychiatry, 154*, 390–395.

Fergusson, D. M., Beautrais, A. L., & Horwood, L. J. (2003). Vulnerability and resiliency to suicidal behaviours in young people. *Psychological Medicine, 33*(1), 61–73.

Friedmann, H., & Kohn, R. (2008). Mortality, or probability of death, from a suicidal act in the United States. *Suicide & Life-Threatening Behavior, 38*(3), 287–301.

Frydenberg, E. (Ed.). (2008). *Adolescent coping. Advances in theory, research and practice*. London: Routledge.

Gisper, M., Wheeler, K., Marsh, L., & Davis, M. (1985). Suicidal adolescents: Factors in evaluation. *Adolescence, 20*, 753–762.

Goldston, D. (2000). *Assessment of suicidal behaviors and risk among children and adolescents*. Technical report submitted to NIMH under Contract No. 263-MD-909995.

Gonzalez-Macip, S., Diaz, A., Ortiz, S., Gonzalez-Forteza, C., & Gonzalez, J. J. (2000). Características psicométricas de la Escala de Ideación Suicida de Beck (ISB) en estudiantes universitarios de la Ciudad de México [Psychometric properties of the Beck suicide ideation scale in University Students of Mexico City]. *Salud Mental, 23*(2), 21–30.

Gutierrez, P., Osman, A., Barrios, F., Kopper., B. (2001). Development and Initial Validation of the Self-Harm Behavior Questionnaire. Journal of Personality Assessment 77 (3) 475–490 doi:10.207/S15327752jpa7703_08.

Hernandez, Q. (2007). *Estrategia de intervención para adolescentes en riesgo suicida* [Intervention Strategy for adolescents at risk of suicide]. Unpublished doctoral dissertation, Facultad de Psicología, UNAM, Mexico City.

Hernandez, Q., & Lucio, E. (2006a). *Inventario de Riesgo Suicida para Adolescentes, IRIS* [Inventory for suicidal risk in adolescents]. México City, México. Facultad de Psicología, UNAM.

Hernandez, Q., & Lucio, E. (2006b). Evaluación del riesgo suicida y estrés asociado en adolescentes estudiantes mexicanos [Stress and suicide risk assessment in Mexican adolescents]. *Revista Mexicana de Psicología, 23*(1), 45–52.

Hobfoll, S., Schwazer, R., & Chon, K. (1996). Disentangling the stress labyrinth: Interpreting the meaning of the term stress as it is studied. *Japanese Health Psychology, 4*, 1–22.

Iniguez, E., & Palinkas, L. A. (2003). Varieties of health services utilization by underserved Mexican American women. *Journal of Health Care for the Poor and Underserved, 14*, 52–69. doi:10.1177/1049208902238823.

Instituto Nacional de Estadística, Geografía e Informática (INEGI). (2006). *Estadísticas a propósito del día Internacional de la Juventud. Datos nacionales* [Statistics in relation to Youth International Day. National data]. México: INEGI.

Jacobs, D. (1999). *The Harvard Medical School guide to suicide assessment and intervention*. San Francisco, CA.: Jossey-Bass.

Johnson, G., Cohen, P., Gould, M., Kasen, S., Brown, J., & Brook, J. (2002). Childhood adversities, interpersonal difficulties, and risk for suicide attempts during late adolescence and early adulthood. *Archives of General Psychiatry, 59*, 741–749.

Kirk, W. (Ed.). (1993). *Adolescent suicide: A school-based approach to assessment & intervention*. Champaign, IL: Research Press.

Lewinsohn, P., Rohde, P., & Seeley, J. (1996). Adolescent suicidal ideation and attempts: Prevalence, risk factors and clinical implications. *Clinical Psychology, Suicide and Practice, 3*, 25–46.

Lucio, E. & Duran, C. (2003). *Cuestionario de Sucesos de Vida* [Life-events questionnaire]. México City, Mexico: El Manual Moderno.

Lucio, E., Ampudia-Rueda, A., Duran-Patino, C., Gallegos-Mejia, L., & Leon-Guzman, I. (1999). The new version of the Minnesota Multiphasic Personality Inventory for Mexican adolescents. *Revista Mexicana de Psicologia, 16*, 217–226.

Lucio, E., & Hernandez, Q. (2009). Personalidad y riesgo suicida en adolescentes estudiantes [Personality and suicide risk in adolescents]. *Revista Médica del Instituto Mexicano del Seguro Social, 47*(1), 33–40.

Lucio, E., Linaje, M., Perez, M., & Arenas, P. (2009). Una estrategia preventiva para adolescentes con riesgo de suicidio y consumo de sustancias en el escenario escolar [A prevention strategy for adolescents with suicide and substance abuse adolescents]. *Revista española de drogodependencia, 34*(3), 323–330.

Lucio, E., Loza, G., & Duran, C. (2000). Los sucesos de vida estresantes y la personalidad de adolescentes con intento suicida [Stressful life events and personality configuration in suicidal adolescents]. *Psicología Contemporánea, 7*(2), 58–65.

Lucio-Gomez Maqueo, E., Plascencia, M., & Zamarron, G. (2005). Detección del riesgo suicida y otros problemas emocionales en una muestra de adolescentes de Aguascalientes [Detection of suicidal risk and other emotional problems in a group of adolescents from Aguscalientes]. *Investigación y Ciencia, 32*, 29–36.

Maddaleno, M., Morello, P., & Infante-Espínola, F. (2003). Salud y desarrollo de adolescentes y jóvenes en Latinoamérica y el Caribe: desafíos para la próxima década [Health and development of young in Latin America and the Caribean: Challenges for the next decade]. *Salud Pública de México, 45*(1), 132–139.

Martinez, C. R., Jr., Eddy, J. M., & DeGarmo, D. S. (2003). Preventing substance use among Latino youth. In Z. Sloboda & W. J. Bukoski (Eds.), *Handbook of drug abuse prevention: Theory, science, and practice* (pp. 365–380). New York: Plenum.

Marttunen, M. (1994). Psychosocial maladjustment, mental disorders and stressful life events precede adolescent suicide. *Psychiatria Fennica, 25*, 39–51.

Muehlenkamp, J. J., Cowles, M. L., & Gutierrez, P. M. (2010). Validity of the self-harm behavior questionnaire with diverse adolescents. *Journal of Psychopathology and Behavioral Assessment, 32*(2), 236–245. doi:10.1007/s10862-009-9131-7.

O'Connor, R., Rasmussen, S., Miles, J., & Hawton, K. (2009). Self-harm in adolescents: Self-report survey in schools in Scotland. *The British Journal of Psychiatry, 194*, 68–72.

Pfeffer, C. (1998). Risk factors associated with youth suicide: A clinical perspective. *Psychiatric Annals, 18*, 652–656.

Portzky, G., & van Heeringen, K. (2007). Deliberate self-harm in adolescents. *Child and Adolescent Psychiatry, 20*, 337–342.

Rew, L. (2005). *Adolescent health. A multidisciplinary approach to theory, research and intervention*. Thousand Oaks, CA: Sage.

Reynolds, W. (1987). *Suicidal ideation questionnaire (SIQ): Professional manual*. Odessa, FL: Psychological Assessment Resources.

Reynolds, W. (1991). A school-based procedure for the identification of adolescents at risk for suicidal behavior. *Family & Community Health, 14*, 64–75.

Seiffge-Krenke, I. (2000). Causal links between stressful events, coping style, and adolescent symptomatology. *Journal of Adolescence, 23*, 675–691.

Seiffge-Krenke, I. (2009). Changes in stress perception and coping during adolescence: The role of situational and personal factors. *Child Development, 80*, 259–279.

Shaffer, D., Garland, A., Gould, M., Fisher, P., & Trautman, P. (1998). Preventing teenage suicide: A critical review. *Journal of the American Academy of Child and Adolescent Psychiatry, 27*, 675–687.

Shaffer, D., Gould, M., Fisher, P., Trautman, P., & Moreau, D. (1996). Psychiatric diagnosis in child and adolescent suicide. *Archives of General Psychiatry, 53*, 339–348.

Shaffer, D., Pfeffer, C. R., Bernet, W., Arnold, V., Beitchman, J., Benson, S., et al. (2001). Practice parameter for the assessment and treatment of children and adolescents with suicidal behavior. *Journal of the American Academy of Child and Adolescent Psychiatry, 40*(7), 24–51.

Shaffer, D., Scott, M., Wilcox, H., Maslow, C., Hicks, R., Lucas, C. P., et al. (2004). The Columbia suicide screen: Validity and reliability of a screen for youth suicide and depression. *Journal of the American Academy of Child and Adolescent Psychiatry, 43*(1), 71–79.

Spirito, A., & Hernandez-Cervantes, Q. (2009). Prevention of suicidal behavior during adolescence. In R. J. DiClemente, R. A. Crosby, & J. S. Santelli (Eds.), *Adolescent health: Understanding and preventing risk behaviors* (pp. 233–247). San Francisco, CA: Jossey-Bass.

Spirito, A., & Overholser, J. (2003). *Evaluating and treating adolescent suicide attempters: From research to practice*. New York: Academic.

U.S. Department of Health and Human Services. (2001). *Mental health: Culture, race, and ethnicity—A supplement to mental health: A report of the surgeon general*. Rockville, MD: U.S. Department of Health and Human Services.

U.S. Department of Homeland Security, Office of Immigration Statistics. (2007). *Yearbook of immigration statistics: 2006 (Annual flow report, March 2008)*. Washington, DC: U.S. Government Printing Office.

Wasserman, D., Cheng, Q., & Jiang, G. (2005). Global suicide rates among young people aged 15–19. *World Psychiatry, 4*(2), 114–120.

World Health Organization (WHO). (2002). Taken from http://www.who.int/child-adolescent-health/OVERVIEW/AHD/adh over.htm. Feb 2007.

World Health Organization (WHO). (2008). Taken from http://www.who.int/mental_health/prevention/suicide/country_reports/en/index.html. Jan 2011.

Assessing Suicidality with the Hispanic Adult

10

Dana M. Alonzo

Cultural Considerations in Suicide Risk Assessment of Hispanic Clients

The Hispanic adult client at risk for suicidal behavior poses a unique challenge to clinicians. A number of important issues need to be considered in order to conduct an effective assessment with this population. The most fundamental issue is that the client must actually be attending treatment in order for a risk assessment to be conducted. As simple as this sounds, it is often most difficult to achieve with Hispanic clients. The ability to maintain suicidal individuals in treatment has eluded practitioners (Lizardi, Stanley, & Oquendo, 2010). Of those who do attend treatment, studies have shown that, 3 months after being hospitalized for a suicide attempt, 38% of attempters will not be attending outpatient treatment (Monti, Cedereke, & Ojehagen, 2003), and, that after a year, 73% of attempters will no longer be in treatment (Krulee & Hayes, 1988). In addition to the overall problem of suicide attempters having a low rate of treatment engagement and adherence, studies have demonstrated that, as a group, Hispanics, in particular, have a very low rate of mental health service utilization. In fact, several studies have found that the lower rates of entry into psychiatric treatment by Hispanics relative to Whites persist even after controlling for sociodemographic factors and presence of psychiatric diagnosis (Hough et al., 1987; Vega & Lopez, 2001; Wells, Hough Golding, Burnam, & Karno, 1987). Several studies have also shown that Hispanics not only have lower rates of initial entry into mental health care compared to non-Hispanic Whites but also have poorer treatment retention once care has been accessed, with higher rates of premature termination of care ("dropout") (Marcos & Cancros, 1982; Sánchez-Lacay et al., 2001; Sue, 1977). Barriers to service utilization for the Hispanic client tend to involve access barriers such as limited awareness of mental disorders, limited understanding of the mental health system, lack of information, language barriers, and lack of insurance (Sadavoy, Meier, Ong, Yuk, 2004; Strug & Mason, 2001). Interestingly, however, research has indicated that Hispanics attend significantly fewer overall outpatient psychiatric appointments (Hough et al., 1987; Sue, 1977), even after controlling for rates of insurance and other SES variables (Padgett, Patrick, Burns, & Schlesinger, 1994; Temkin-Greener & Clark, 1988).

D.M. Alonzo Ph.D. (✉)
School of Social Work, Columbia University,
1255 Amsterdam Avenue, New York, NY 10027, USA
e-mail: dl2298@columbia.edu

L.T. Benuto (ed.), *Guide to Psychological Assessment with Hispanics*,
DOI 10.1007/978-1-4614-4412-1_10, © Springer Science+Business Media New York 2013

To address this, Snowden (2003) recommends paying close attention to historical provider and individual characteristics that may serve as sources of bias and may contribute to lack of engagement in treatment among minority populations. Furthermore, a three-pronged approach has been suggested for managing Hispanic suicidal behavior and mental health issues in general (Rios-Ellis, 2005). Such an approach emphasizes (1) addressing clients' presenting complaints and reducing associated symptomatology, (2) utilizing empowerment-focused strategies based on comprehensive assessment of clients' histories which tend to include experiences of trauma and social isolation, and (3) utilizing a life-course approach that includes examination of the effects of racism, discrimination, and resource disparities (Rios-Ellis, 2005).

Immigration status and the immigration process are also factors that greatly impact suicide risk among Hispanic clients and should be included of any risk assessment with this population. The process of immigrating is a stressful life event (Worchel & Gearing, 2010) and is associated with increased levels of mental health illnesses (Shoval, Schoen, Vardi, & Zalsman, 2007), including suicide (Hjern & Allebeck, 2002; Kposowa, McElvain, & Breault, 2008; Kushner, 1991; Lester, 1997, 1998; Wadsworth & Kubrin, 2007). At least 50% of Hispanics in the United States are immigrants (Porter, 2003). Hispanics have been shown to experience a different process of immigration and assimilation from other ethnic minority groups (Wadsworth & Kubrin, 2007), perhaps the result of withdrawal of previously established protective factors (Worchel & Gearing, 2010). For example, immigrants not only lack a well-developed support system in their new country but also experience the loss of their previously established support network in their country of origin (Sorenson & Shen, 1996). Immigrants have also been found to earn less money, be less likely to seek mental health services, suffer from linguistic barriers, and be faced with prejudice and discrimination (Sorenson & Shen, 1996; Shoval et al., 2007). Immigrants at greatest risk for suicide include those who were unhappy with the decision to migrate, have low expectations for the future, experience social isolation in their host country, have low socioeconomic status, and encounter language barriers (Ferrada-Noli, Asberg, Ormstad, & Nordstrom, 1995). Immigrants living in areas with high immigrant populations may be at lower suicide risk as they may experience less isolation and alienation (Wadsworth & Kubrin, 2007).

However, research in this area is somewhat inconsistent. According to the theory of migration selectivity, only individuals with a high likelihood of achieving in the new country are chosen or supported in their decision to immigrate (Sorenson & Shen, 1996; Wadsworth & Kubrin, 2007; Worchel & Gearing, 2010). Therefore, one might expect that stronger, healthier individuals are more likely to immigrate and, as such, the levels of suicide among immigrants would be lower (Hayes-Batista, Schink, & Chapa, 1988; Stephen, Foote, Hendershot, & Schoenborn, 1994). Examination of the nature of a client's immigration experience is fundamental to the accurate assessment of suicide risk of Hispanics.

Equally as important as the consideration of immigration factors in conducting a suicide risk assessment with Hispanic clients is the assessment of acculturation. Acculturation is the process through which immigrants pass as they move to a new country and is characterized by the struggle to maintain one's cultural identity, traditions, values, and customs while adapting to their host culture. For some immigrants, this process can cause great conflict, resulting in increased risk of suicidal behavior, among other mental health problems (Hovey & King, 1997). This ensuing conflict is known as acculturative stress (Berry & Kim, 1988; Hovey & King, 1996, 1997; Padilla, Cervantes, Maldonado, & Garcia, 1988; Williams & Berry, 1991). Overall, suicide rates have been found to be positively associated with acculturative stress among Hispanics (Gutierrez, Osman, Kopper, & Barrios, 2000; Vega, Gil, Warheit, Apospori, & Zimmerman, 1993). High levels of acculturative stress have been found to be a risk factor for suicide among Mexican-Americans (Sorenson & Golding, 1988; Swanson et al., 1992), Central Americans (Hovey, 2000), and Puerto Ricans (Monk & Warshauer, 1974; Oquendo, Lizardi, Greenwald, Weissman, & Mann, 2004). Availability of social supports in the host culture, degree of support from primary and extended family members, socioeconomic status, mastery of the language of the host culture, expectations for the future, and pre-immigration level of adjustment have been found to contribute to the degree of acculturative stress experienced (Hovey & King, 1997; Williams & Berry, 1991).

Another key factor to consider in the assessment of suicide risk among Hispanics is the quality of family relationships of the client (Kirmayer, Groleau, Guzder, Blake, & Jarvis, 2003). As compared to non-Hispanics, Hispanics tend to place greater value on family relationships and cohesiveness. *Familismo* (familism), which emphasizes close relationships with immediate and extended family networks, has been shown to serve as a protective factor against suicide for Hispanics (Hovey & King, 1997; Oquendo et al., 2005). Additionally, Hispanics have been shown to endorse greater responsibility toward family than their non-Hispanic counterparts (Oquendo et al., 2005). However, when expectations for familial support are not met or when friction exists between family members, mental health problems, including suicidal behavior, may be increased.

Also important to consider is *fatalismo* (fatalism), the belief that life is predetermined by fate. Fatalismo has been found to be a risk factor for suicide among Hispanics (Hoppe and Martin, 1986; Hovey & King, 1997; Sorenson & Golding, 1988). Evidence suggests that because the locus of control is seen as outside of the individual, it may serve to reduce an individual's desire to cope with and manage stressors (Hoppe and Martin, 1986; Hovey & King, 1997; Sorenson & Golding, 1988). Others, however, have found that endorsement of fatalismo may be a protective factor, an adaptive worldview. It may be that it encourages a healthy response to uncontrollable life events (Oquendo et al., 2001). Rather than struggling with trying to control all events and situations, Hispanics endorsing a fatalistic approach may be more accepting of difficulty situations, attributing them to fate, luck, or "God's will." As degree of adherence to fatalismo varies among Hispanic ethnic subgroups, it is essential to assess the Hispanic client's level of endorsement of this belief structure in order to accurately assess suicide risk.

Historical Trends in Suicide Rates in the Hispanic Community

Suicide attempt and completed suicide are major problems among the Hispanic population. Suicide is the 12th leading cause of death among Hispanics (Center for Disease Control and Prevention, 2011). When examined by age group, suicide is the third leading cause of death among Hispanic young adults aged 25–34. However, the highest rate of suicide (21.96 per 100,000) was found among older males aged 85 and older (Center for Disease Control and Prevention, 2007).

Some studies have shown that Hispanics have elevated rates of suicide attempt when compared to their Caucasian and African-American counterparts. The National Comorbidity Study (NCS) found that when compared to Blacks and Whites, Hispanics had significantly greater odds of making a suicide attempt (1.2 for Hispanics vs. 1.0 for Whites and .6 for Blacks) (Kessler, Borges, & Walters, 1999). Likewise, Oquendo et al. (2004) found elevated rates of suicide among Hispanics as compared to Caucasians and African-Americans. However, it has been noted that findings in this area are inconsistent (Worchel & Gearing, 2010). When examined as a group, some have found that Hispanics have a lower rate of suicide than Caucasians and a higher rate than African-Americans (Oquendo et al., 2005). As per the US Census Bureau (2005), for Hispanics, the suicide rate for all ages was 5.4 per 100,000 as compared to 12.53 for non-Hispanics of all ages. Furthermore, evidence shows that Hispanics report less suicidal ideation and make fewer lethal attempts than non-Hispanics despite having similar suicide intent (Oquendo et al.). For example, 3.3% of Hispanic adults aged 18 and over report having serious thoughts of suicide over the past year, which is lower than the overall rate for adults in the United States (3.7).

Table 10.1 Tests available in Spanish for the assessment of Hispanic adults

Test name	Original language	Type of assessment	Country of norms	Age range (years)
Spanish Reasons for Living Inventory	English	A 48-item self-report measure assessing 6 domains of adaptive beliefs and expectations (survival and coping beliefs, responsibility toward family, child-related concerns, fear of suicide, fear of social disapproval, moral objections) that serve as reasons to resist acting on suicidal urges	Colombia, USA	18+
Spanish Modified Scale for Suicidal Ideation	English	Clinician-rated scale assessing suicidal symptoms over a 1-year period. Higher scores reflect more severe suicidal ideation	USA	18+
Beck Depression Inventory	English	21-item self-report measure in which patients rate symptoms associated with depression according to their intensity	Argentina, Puerto Rico, Spain	18+

Rates of Suicide Attempt Vary Among Hispanic Adults

Studies have also demonstrated that rates of lifetime suicide attempt vary according to Hispanic ethnic subgroups, with evidence indicating that certain groups of Hispanics may have lower rates of suicide attempt than their Black and White counterparts. Sorenson and Golding (1988) examined suicide attempt among Mexican-Americans and found that this group has a lower rate of suicide attempt than Whites. Oquendo et al. (2004) found that Cuban Americans have the lowest rate of suicide attempt when compared to Whites, Blacks, Puerto Ricans, and Mexican-Americans. Oquendo et al. (2004) and Baca-Garcia et al. (2011) also found that Puerto Ricans had the highest rate of suicide attempt across ethnic groups, a finding consistent with several other studies. For example, one study found that the rate of lifetime suicide attempt among Puerto Ricans is approximately threefold the rate among Mexican-Americans and Cuban Americans (Oquendo et al., 2004; Ungemack & Guarnaccia, 1998). Another study that examined the rate of suicide attempt across nine different countries found that Puerto Ricans living on the island of Puerto Rico had the highest rate of suicide attempt by more than fivefold (Weissman et al., 1999). Yet, the completed suicide rate for Puerto Ricans is lower than the completed suicide rates for other Hispanic ethnic subgroups and for Caucasians (Oquendo et al., 2001). The findings of these studies emphasize that there are differences between Hispanic ethnicities. Failure to consider these differences may result in inaccurate assessment of suicide risk among Hispanic clients. Only by understanding and examining the unique risk and protective factors for suicide for the specific Hispanic ethnicity of the client can prevention and intervention efforts be effective (Worchel & Gearing, 2010).

Suicide Assessment Measures

Although psychological testing companies are creating and selling Spanish translations of many psychological tests, rarely do these tests have sufficient research, if any, to support the appropriateness of their use with Hispanics in the United States (Table 10.1) (Fernandez, Boccaccini, & Noland, 2007). Some research has been conducted on assessment tools measuring constructs related to suicide, such as depression. However, there is a dearth of research examining the reliability and validity of suicide assessment measures for use with adult Hispanics in the United States. The Reasons for Living Inventory (RFLI; Linehan, Goodstein, Nielsen, & Chiles, 1983), however, is one such suicide-specific measure that has received the attention in terms of studies of cultural relevancy and psychometric properties of the Spanish language version of the measure.

The Reasons for Living Inventory (RFLI) (Linehan et al., 1983) is a frequently used measure in studies examining suicidal behavior. The RFLI assesses six domains of beliefs and expectations that are suggested to serve as motivations for resisting suicidal urges. These domains include survival and coping beliefs (e.g., I believe I can learn to adjust or cope with my problems), responsibility toward family (e.g., I have a responsibility and commitment to my family), child-related concerns (e.g., I want to watch my children as they grow), fear of suicide (e.g., I am afraid of the unknown), fear of social disapproval (e.g., I am concerned about what others would think of me), and moral objections (e.g., I believe only God has the right to end a life). Individuals who endorse these beliefs and expectations are thought to be less likely to attempt suicide than those who do not. The 48 items are rated according to a 6-point Likert-type scale ranging from 1 (not at all) to 6 (extremely important). Scores are generated by calculating the mean rating for each subscale, and a score for the total scale is generated by summing the scores of all of the items (Linehan et al.). Linehan et al. reported Cronbach's alphas ranging from .72 to .89 for the subscales of the RFLI, indicating moderately high reliability (Linehan et al.). Osman et al. (1993) found alphas ranging from .79 to .92 for the six subscales, with an alpha of .89 for the RFL as a whole. Neither study examined ethnicity of study participants.

Recently, a Spanish translation of the Reasons for Living Inventory (RFLI) was adapted by Oquendo et al. (2000). The study was conducted with 29 bilingual Dominican, Puerto Rican, and Cuban participants living in a large urban city of the United States. All participants were fluent in both spoken and written English and Spanish. The Spanish translation was conducted by a psychiatrist with knowledge of the language as spoken in Spain and Puerto Rico and a bilingual committee of clinicians from Cuba, Dominican Republic, and Mexico (Oquendo et al.). A six-step process was used to complete the translation of the instrument. Oquendo et al. determined that the linguistic, scale, and conceptual equivalence of the measure was moderate to high. However, they found that four subscales were not semantically equivalent. Overall, the scale development was methodologically inadequate for several reasons. They utilized a small sample size ($n=29$), they lacked a sound rationale, and the psychometric evaluation was poor.

Another translation of the RFLI into Spanish developed in Colombia has shown acceptable psychometric properties (García-Valencia et al., 2007, 2009). Acceptable internal consistency has been found for the overall score, and the Colombian translation has also been found to yield significant variance in predicting suicide risk. This version of the SRFLI also retains four of the six factors from the English version of the RFLI (survival and coping beliefs, responsibility to family, child-related concerns, and moral objections related to suicide) as well as two new factors that emerged (fear of death and social disapproval and perception of incapacity for suicide).

Another major suicide assessment measure, the Modified Scale for Suicidal Ideation (Miller, Norman, Bishop, & Dow, 1986), has been translated into Spanish and has been examined for the psychometric properties of the Spanish language version. The MSSI is a modified version of Beck, Kovacs, and Weissman's (1979) Scale for Suicidal Ideation (SSI). Modifications included the addition of prompt questions, modification of the rating points, and the development of initial screening scores. The Spanish Modified Scale for Suicidal Ideation (SMSSI) is an interviewer-rated scale designed to assess suicidal symptoms over a 1-year period. Each item is rated on a 0- to 3-point scale. The ratings are summed to yield a total score ranging from 0 to 54, with higher scores reflecting more severe suicidal ideation. The psychometric properties and validity of the MSSI have been well supported (Garza et al., 2009; Garza & Pettit, 2010; Miller et al., 1986; Pettit et al., 2009; Rudd et al., 1996). MSSI scores have been shown to agree with expert clinician's judgments regarding suicidal ideation. Validity data also indicates that the MSSI discriminates between suicide attempters and non-attempters and correlates with measures of depression and hopelessness in a similar manner to the original SSI scale (Miller et al.).

Garza and Pettit (2010) report on the psychometric properties of the SMMSI. They conducted a study with 73 Spanish-speaking Mexican and Mexican-American women in the United States. They report a Cronbach's alpha of 0.92.

Depression is the psychiatric illness most often associated with suicidal behavior (Bostwick & Pankratz, 2000). Therefore, most studies of suicide include some measure for assessing severity of depression. The Beck Depression Inventory (BDI) (Beck, Ward, Mendelson, Mock, & Erbaugh, 1961) has been widely used not only to assess severity of depression in a clinical population but also to detect depression in the general population and has been acknowledged as being multidimensional (Boyle, 1985). Emery, Steer, and Beck (1981), Silver, Bohnert, Beck, and Marcus (1971), and Fine and Steer (1977) have indicated that depression as measured by the BDI has a positive relationship with suicidal behavior.

The items composing the BDI were generated from clinical observations regarding the attitudes and symptoms typically found in depressed psychiatric patients (Beck et al., 1961). The inventory consists of 21 items, each comprised of four statements which respondents rate on a scale of 0–3 according to intensity. The 21 items were chosen to reflect symptomatology and attitudes and specifically address mood, pessimism, sense of failure, lack of satisfaction, guilt feelings, sense of punishment, self-dislike, self-accusation, suicidal wishes, crying, irritability, social withdrawal, indecisiveness, distortion of body image, work inhibition, sleep disturbance, fatigability, loss of appetite, weight loss, somatic preoccupation, and loss of libido (Beck et al.). The Center for Cognitive Therapy has recommended the following guidelines: a score of less than 10 represents minimal depression, between 10 and 18 represents mild to moderate depression, 19–29 represents moderate to severe depression, and 30–63 represents severe depression (Beck, Steer, & Garbin, 1988).

Internal consistency of the BDI has been examined in multiple studies using clinical and nonclinical populations. Working with adult psychiatric patients, Beck et al. (1961) assessed 139 inpatients and 270 outpatients and yielded a reliability coefficient of .93. Beck and Steer (1984) yielded a Cronbach's alpha of .86 from a sample of 248 adult outpatients. Byerly and Carlson (1982), using a mixed sample of adults, yielded an alpha of .86 for 68 inpatients and an alpha of .81 for 63 outpatients.

Stability of the BDI over time has also been assessed. Beck (1967) conducted a test-retest study that also used clinical ratings and determined that changes in ratings on the BDI were consistent with changes in clinical ratings, suggesting consistency between clinicians' perceptions and patients' self-reports.

Validity of the BDI has also been explored. Approximately 15 studies using samples of adult psychiatric patients were conducted between the years of 1961 and 1983 to examine the BDI'S validity. For example, convergent validity of the BDI has been examined by comparing the BDI with the Hamilton Depression Rating Scale. The correlations yielded ranged from .61 to .86 with a mean correlation coefficient of .73 (Bailey & Coppen, 1976; Rounesville, Weissman, Rosenberger, Wilber, & Kleber, 1979; Schnurr, Hoaken, & Jarrett, 1976; Steer, McElroy, & Beck, 1982). Convergent validity has also been established using the Zung Self-Rating Scale with correlation coefficients ranging from .73 to .81 (Blatt, Quinlan, Chevron, McDonald, & Zuroff, 1982; Hesslbrock, Hesslbrock, Tenmen, Meyer, & Workman, 1983; Mendels, Secunda, & Dyson, 1972; Seitz, 1970; Schaefer et al., 1985).

Several studies have examined the reliability and validity of Spanish translations of the BDI. Five were conducted in Spain; hence, their generalizability to Hispanic populations in the United States remains questionable (Conde-Lopez, Chamorro, & Useros-Serrano, 1976; Ramos-Brieva, 1986; Torres-Castillo, Hernandez-Malpica, & Ortega-Soto, 1991). Similarly, another study validated the BDI on a community sample of 608 participants in Argentina and reported high internal consistency (Chronbach's alpha of .87) (Bonicatto, Dew, & Soria, 1998), yet its appropriateness for use with US Hispanics was not established. Another study conducted with a clinical sample in Puerto Rico examined the internal consistency and construct validity of a Spanish-translated version of the BDI and reported an alpha coefficient of .89 (Bernal, Bonilla, & Santiago, 1995). These studies all suggest appropriateness of the use of the BDI with Hispanic populations to assess for the severity of depression. However, given that these studies were conducted on international populations, further research is necessary to validate its use with US Hispanics.

Azocar, Areán, Miranda, and Muñoz (2001) conducted a seminal study with 292 medical outpatients to develop a Spanish version of the BDI. As there was no official version of the BDI in Spanish at the time the study was conducted, the authors created a Spanish version using translation and back-translation methods. Participants completed an English- or a Spanish-translated and back-translated version of the Beck Depression Inventory. Items were analyzed for bias between Spanish and English-speaking patients to determine scale equivalence. Differential item functioning (DIF), utilizing the Mantel Haenszel method, was used to examine differences in the endorsement of Beck Depression Inventory (BDI) items.

Ethnic differences were found, with Hispanics being more likely to endorse items reflecting tearfulness and punishment. The endorsement of inability to work was less likely among Hispanics than among non-Hispanics. Overall, however, the study reported an alpha coefficient of .97 and concluded that the BDI is an adequate measure of depression that could appropriately be used with Hispanic clients (Azocar et al., 2001). The study does have methodological limitations. Only 55 of the subjects were Spanish-speaking, and bilingual fluency was not assessed. Furthermore, psychometric properties for scale construction, inter-rater and test-retest reliability, and content and predictive validity were not reported.

Recommendations

Research

Culturally competent practice is increasingly being recognized as essential as the minority population in the United States continues to grow at a rapid rate. In order to conduct an effective, culturally competent suicide risk assessment with Hispanic clients, reliable and valid Spanish language assessment tools are necessary. Future research should focus on validation of Spanish language translations of the major suicide assessment measures (i.e., Suicide Intent Scale (SIS, Beck, Schuyler, & Herman, 1974)). Future research should also examine how Hispanic cultural factors may impact the reporting of suicidal behaviors as a means of improving the engagement of Hispanic suicidal clients in treatment.

Practice

In order to improve the assessment of suicidal behavior of Hispanic clients, it is imperative for clinicians practice from a culturally competent, evidence-based practice perspective. This requires clinicians to (1) recognize their biases and values, (2) avoid making assumptions regarding their understanding of the client's presenting problem based on shared ethnic identity, (3) acknowledge that their worldview may differ from their clients, (4) seek to elicit the client's expectations for treatment, and (5) employ relevant engagement, assessment, and intervention strategies.

Key Terms

Access barriers: Limited awareness of mental disorders, limited understanding of the mental health system, lack of information, language barriers, and lack of insurance.

Acculturation is the process through which immigrants pass as they move to a new country characterized by the struggle to maintain one's cultural identity, traditions, values and customs while adapting to their host culture.

Acculturative stress: The conflict that some individual's experience as a result of the struggle to maintain one's cultural identity, traditions, values, and customs while adapting to their host culture.

BDI: Beck Depression Inventory.

Familismo (familism): It emphasizes close relationships with immediate and extended family networks common among Hispanic ethnic subgroups.

Fatalismo (fatalism), the belief that life is predetermined by fate.

Migration selectivity: Only individuals with a high likelihood of achieving in the new country are chosen to or supported in their decision to immigrate.

RFLI: Reasons for Living Inventory.

SMSSI: Spanish Modified Scale for Suicidal Ideation.

SRFLI: Spanish Reasons for Living Inventory.

References

Azocar, F., Areán, P., Miranda, J., & Muñoz, R. F. (2001). Differential item functioning in a Spanish translation of the Beck Depression Inventory. *Journal of Clinical Psychology, 57*, 355–365.

Baca-Garcia, E., Perez-Rodriguez, M. M., Keyes, K. M., Oquendo, M. A., Hasin, D. S., Grant, B. F., et al. (2011). Suicidal ideation and suicide attempts among Hispanic subgroups in the United States: 1991–1992 and 2001–2002. *Journal of Psychiatric Research, 45*(4), 512–518.

Bailey, J., & Coppen, A. (1976). A comparison between the Hamilton rating Scale and the Beck inventory in measurement of depression. *The British Journal of Psychiatry, 128*, 486–489.

Beck, A. T. (1967). *Depression: Causes and treatment*. Philadelphia: University of Pennsylvania Press.

Beck, A. T., Kovacs, M., & Weissman, A. (1979). Assessment of suicidal intention: The scale for suicide ideation. *Journal of Consulting and Clinical Psychology, 47*(2), 343–352.

Beck, A. T., Schuyler, D., & Herman, I. (1974). Development of suicidal intent scales. In A. T. Beck, H. L. P. Resnick, & D. J. Lettieri (Eds.), *In the prediction of suicide* (pp. 45–56). Bowie, MD: Charles Press.

Beck, A. T., & Steer, R. A. (1984). Internal consistencies of the original and revised Beck Depression Inventory. *Journal of Clinical Psychology, 40*, 136501367.

Beck, A. T., Steer, R. A., & Garbin, M. G. (1988). Psychometric properties of the Beck Depression Inventory: Twenty-five years of evaluation. *Clinical Psychology Review, 8*, 77–100.

Beck, A. T., Ward, C. H., Mendelson, M., Mock, J., & Erbaugh, J. (1961). An inventory for measuring depression. *Archives of General Psychiatry, 4*, 561–571.

Bernal, G., Bonilla, J., Santiago, E. (1995). Psychometric properties of the BDI and SCL-36 in a Puerto Rican sample (in Spanish). *Revista Latinoamericana de Psicología, 27*, 207–230.

Berry, J. W., & Kim, U. (1988). *Acculturation and mental health*. London: Sage.

Blatt, S. J., Quinlan, D. M., Chevron, E. S., McDonald, C., & Zuroff, D. (1982). Dependency and self-criticism: Psychological dimensions of depression. *Journal of Consulting and Clinical Psychology, 50*, 113–115.

Bonicatto, S., Dew, A. M., Soria, J. J. (1998). Analysis of the psychometric properties of the Spanish version of the Beck Depression Inventory in Argentina. *Psychiatry Research, 79*(3), 277–285.

Bostwick, J. M., & Pankratz, V. S. (2000). Affective disorders and suicide risk: A reexamination. *The American Journal of Psychiatry, 157*, 1925–1932.

Boyle, G. J. (1985). Self-report measures of depression: Some psychometric considerations. *British Journal of Clinical Psychology, 24*, 45–59.

Byerly, F. C., & Carlson, W. A. (1982). Comparison among inpatients, outpatients, and normals on three self-report depression inventories. *Journal of Clinical Psychology, 38*, 797–804.

Center for Disease Control and Prevention. (2007). *Injury mortality reports*. Retrieved from http://webappa.cdc.gov/sasweb/ncipc/mortrate10_sy.

Center for Disease Control and Prevention (CDC). (2011). *Web-based injury statistics query and reporting*. Retrieved from http://www.cdc.gov/ncipc/wisqars.

Conde-Lopez, V., Chamorro, T. E., Useros-Serrano, E. (1976). Estudio crítico de la fiabilidad y validez de la E.E.C. de Beck para la medida de la depresiön. *Archives of Neurology, 39*, 313–338.

Emery, G. D., Steer, R. A., & Beck, A. T. (1981). Depression, hopelessness, and suicidal intent among heroin addicts. *The International Journal of the Addictions, 16*, 425–429.

Fernandez, K., Boccaccini, M. T., & Noland, R. M. (2007). Professionally responsible test selection for Spanish-speaking clients: A four-step approach for identifying and selecting translated tests. *Professional Psychology: Research and Practice, 38*(4), 363–374.

Ferrada-Noli, M., Asberg, M., Ormstad, K., & Nordstrom, P. (1995). Definite and undetermined forensic diagnoses of suicide among immigrants in Sweden. *Acta Psychiatrica Scandinavica, 91*, 130–135.

Fine, W., & Steer, R. A. (1977). The relationship between alcoholism and depression in black men. *Currents in Alcoholism, 2*, 35–43.

García-Valencia, J., Palacio-Acosta, C., Arias, S., Ocampo, M., Calle, J., Restrepo, D., Vargas, G., & López, C. (2007). Clinical assessment of suicidal risk in subjects with a recent suicide attempt. *Revista Colombiana de Psiquiatría, 36*(4), 610–627.

Garcia-Valencia, J., Palacio Acosta, C. A., & Vargas, G. (2009). Validation of the Reasons for Living Inventory (Rfl) in subjects with suicidal behavior in Colombia. *rev.colomb.psiquiatr, 38*(1), 66–84.

Garza, M. J., Pettit, J. W., Perez, M., & Garnaat, S. L. (2009). *Psychometric Properties and Convergent Validity of Spanish Translations of Self- Report and Interview-Based Measures of Suicidal Ideation*. Unpublished manuscript.

Garza, M. J., & Pettit, J. W. (2010). Perceived burdensomeness, familism, and suicidal ideation among Mexican women: Enhancing understanding of risk and protective factors. *Suicide & Life-Threatening Behavior, 40*(6), 56–573.

Gutierrez, P. M., Osman, A., Kopper, B. A., & Barrios, F. X. (2000). Why young people do not kill themselves: The reasons for living inventory for adolescents. *Journal of Clinical Child Psychology, 29*, 177–187.

Hayes-Batista, D. F., Schink, W. O., & Chapa, J. (1988). *The burden of support: Young Latinos in an aging society*. Stanford, CA: Stanford University Press.

Hesslbrock, M. M., Hesslbrock, V. M., Tenmen, H., Meyer, R. E., & Workman, K. L. (1983). Methodological considerations in the assessment of depression in alcoholics. *Journal of Consulting and Clinical Psychology, 51*, 399–405.

Hjern, A., & Allebeck, P. (2002). Suicide in first- and second-generation immigrants in Sweden: A comparative study. *Social Psychiatry and Psychiatric Epidemiology, 37*, 423–429.

Hoppe, S. K., & Martin, H. W. (1986). Patterns of suicide among Mexican Americans and Anglos, 1960–1980. *Social Psychiatry, 21*, 83–88.

Hough, R., Landsverk, J., Karno, M., Burnam, A., Timbers, D., Escobar, J., et al. (1987). Utilization of health and mental health services by Los Angeles Mexican Americans and non-Hispanic Whites. *Archives of General Psychiatry, 44*, 702–709.

Hovey, J. D. (2000). Acculturative stress, depression, and suicidal ideation among Central American immigrants. *Suicide & Life Threatening Behavior, 30*, 125–139.

Hovey, J. D., & King, C. A. (1996). Acculturative stress, depression, and suicidal ideation among immigrant and second-generation Latino adolescents. *Journal of the American Academy of Child and Adolescent Psychiatry, 35*(9), 1183–1192.

Hovey, J. D., & King, C. A. (1997). Suicidality among acculturating Mexican Americans: Current knowledge and directions for research. *Suicide & Life-Threatening Behavior, 27*(1), 92–103.

Kessler, R. C., Borges, G., & Walters, E. E. (1999). Prevalence of and risk factors for lifetime suicide attempts in the National Comorbidity Survey. *Archives of General Psychiatry, 56*(7), 617–626.

Kirmayer, L. J., Groleau, D., Guzder, J., Blake, C., & Jarvis, E. (2003). Cultural consultation: A model of mental health service for multicultural societies. *Canadian Journal of Psychiatry, 48*(3), 145–153.

Kposowa, A. J., McElvain, J. P., & Breault, K. D. (2008). Immigration and suicide: the role of marital status, duration of residence, and social integration. *Archives of Suicide Research, 12*(1), 82–92.

Krulee, D., & Hayes, R. (1988). Compliance with psychiatric referrals from a general hospital psychiatry outpatient clinic. *General Hospital Psychiatry, 10*, 339–345.

Kushner, H. I. (1991). *American suicide: A psychocultural exploration*. New Brunswick, NJ: Rutdger University Press.

Lester, D. (1997). Suicide in America: A nation of immigrants. *Suicide & Life Threatening Behavior, 27*, 50–59.

Lester, D. (1998). Suicide rates of immigrants. *Psychological Reports, 82*, 50.

Linehan, M. M., Goodstein, J. L., Nielsen, S. L., & Chiles, J. A. (1983). Reasons for staying alive when you are thinking of killing yourself: The reasons for living inventory. *Journal of Consulting and Clinical Psychiatry, 42*(6), 861–865.

Lizardi, D., Stanley, B., & Oquendo, M. (2010). Treatment engagement and suicide attempters: A review. *Psychiatric Services, 61*, 1183–1191.

Marcos, L. R., & Cancro, R. (1982). Pharmacotherapy of Hispanic depressed patients: Clinical observations. *American Journal of Psychotherapy, 36*(4), 505–512.

Mendels, J., Secunda, S.K., Dyson, W. L. A. (1972). Controlled study of the antidepressant effects of lithium carbonate. *Archives of General Psychiatry, 26*, 154–157.

Miller, I. W., Norman, W. H., Bishop, S. B., & Dow, M. G. (1986). The modified scale for suicidal ideation: Reliability and validity. *Journal of Consulting and Clinical Psychology, 54*, 724–725.

Monk, M., & Warshauer, M. E. (1974). Completed and attempted suicide in three ethnic groups. *American Journal of Epidemiology, 130*, 348–360.

Monti, K., Cedereke, M., & Ojehagen, A. (2003). Treatment attendance and suicidal behavior 1 month and 3 months after a suicide attempt: A comparison between two samples. *Archives of Suicide Research, 7*, 167–174.

Oquendo, M. A., Baca-Garcia, E., Graver, R., Mora, M., Montalvan, V., & Mann, J. J. (2000). Spanish adaptation of the reasons for living inventory. *Hispanic Journal of Behavioral Sciences, 22*, 369–381.

Oquendo, M. A., Dragatsi, D., Harkavy-Friedman, J., Dervic, K., Currier, D., Burke, A. K., et al. (2005). Protective factors against suicidal behavior in Latinos. *The Journal of Nervous and Mental Disease, 193*(7), 438–443.

Oquendo, M. A., Ellis, S. P., Greenwald, S., Malone, K. M., Weiss-man, M. M., & Mann, J. J. (2001). Ethnic and sex differences in rates of suicide completion relative to major depression in the United States. *The American Journal of Psychiatry, 158*, 1652–1658.

Oquendo, M. A., Lizardi, D., Greenwald, S., Weissman, M., & Mann, J. (2004). Rates of lifetime suicide attempt relative to rates of lifetime major depression in different ethnic groups in the United States. *Acta Psychiatrica Scandinavica, 110*, 446–451.

Osman, A., Gifford, J., Jones, T., Lickiss, L., Osman, J., & Wenzel, R. (1993). Psychometric evaluation of the reasons for living inventory. *Psychological Assessment, 5*(2), 154–158.

Padgett, D. K., Patrick, C., Burns, B. J., & Schlesinger, H. J. (1994). Ethnicity and the use of outpatient mental health services in a national insured population. *American Journal of Public Health, 84*(2), 222–226.

Padilla, A. M., Cervantes, R. C., Maldonado, M., & Garcia, R. E. (1988). Coping responses to psychosocial stressors among Mexican and Central American immigrants. *Journal of Community Psychology, 16*, 418–427.

Pettit, J. W., Garza, M. J., Grover, K. E., Schatte, D. J., Morgan, S. T., Harper, A., et al. (2009). Factor structure and psychometric properties of the Modified Scale for Suicidal Ide- ation among suicidal youth. *Depression and Anxiety, 26*, 769–774.

Porter, E. (2003, March 25). Hispanics gain amid overall decline in U.S. jobs. *Wall Street Journal.*

Ramos-Brieva, J. A. (1986). Validez predictiva del Beck Depression Inventory (BDI) en castellano. *Actas Luso-Esp Neurol Psiquiatr, 14*, 47–51.

Rios-Ellis, B. (2005). *Critical disparities in Latino mental health: Transforming research into action.* Retrieved September 29, 2011, from www.nclr.org

Rounesville, B. J., Weissman, M. M., Rosenberger, P. H., Wilber, C. H., & Kleber, H. D. (1979). Detecting depressive disorders in drug abusers. *Journal of Affective Disorders, 1*, 255–267.

Rudd, M. D., Rajab, H., Orman, D. T., Stulman, D. A., Joiner, T., & Dixon, W. (1996). Effectiveness of an outpatient problem-solving in- tervention targeting suicidal young adults: Prelim- inary results. *Journal of Consulting and Clinical Psy- chology, 64*, 179–190.

Sadavoy, J., Meier, R., Ong, A., & Yuk, M. (2004). Barriers to access to mental health services for ethnic seniors: The Toronto study. *Canadian Journal of Psychiatry, 49*(3), 192–199.

Sánchez-Lacay, J. A., Lewis-Fernández, R., Goetz, D., Blanco, C., Salmán, E., Davies, S., et al. (2001). Open trial of nefazodone among Hispanics with major depression: Efficacy, tolerability, and adherence issues. *Depression and Anxiety, 13*, 118–124.

SBDI: Azocar, F., Areán, P., Miranda, J., & Muñoz, R. F. (2001). Differential item functioning in a Spanish translation of the Beck Depression Inventory. *Journal of Clinical Psychology*, 57, 355–365.

Schaefer, A., Brown, J., Watson, C. G., Plemel, D., DeMotts, J., Howard, M. T., et al. (1985). Comparison of the validities of the Beck, Zung, and MMPI depression scales. *Journal of Consulting and Clinical Psychology, 53*, 415–418.

Schnurr, R., Hoaken, P. C. S., & Jarrett, F. J. (1976). Comparison of depression inventories in a clinical population. *Canadian Psychiatric Association Journal, 21*, 473–476.

Seitz, F. C. (1970). Five psychological measures of neurotic depression: A correlation study. *Journal of Clinical Psychology, 26*, 504–550.

Shoval, G., Schoen, G., Vardi, N., & Zalsman, G. (2007). Suicide in Ethiopian immigrants in Israel: A case for study of the genetic-environmental relation in suicide. *Archives of Suicide Research, 11*, 247–253.

Silver, M. A., Bohnert, M., Beck, A. T., & Marcus, D. (1971). Relation of depression to attempted suicide and seriousness of attempt. *Archives of General Psychiatry, 25*, 573–576.

SMMSI: Garza, M. J., & Pettit, J. W. (2010). Perceived burdensomeness, familism, and suicidal ideation among Mexican women: 342 Enhancing understanding of risk and protective factors. *Suicide & Life-Threatening Behavior*, 40(6), 56–573.

Snowden, L. R. (2003). Bias in mental health assessment and intervention: Theory and evidence. *American Journal of Public Health, 93*, 239–243.

Sorenson, S. B., & Golding, J. M. (1988). Suicide ideation and attempts in Hispanics and non-Hispanic whites: demographic and psychiatric disorder issues. *Suicide & Life-Threatening Behavior, 18*, 205–219.

Sorenson, S. B., & Shen, H. (1996). Youth suicide trends in California: An examination of immigrant and ethnic group risk. *Suicide & Life-Threatening Behavior, 26*, 143–154.

SRFLI: Oquendo, M. A., Baca-Garcia, E., Graver, R., Mora, M., Montalvan, V., & Mann, J. J. (2000). Spanish adaptation of the 383 reasons for living inventory. *Hispanic Journal of Behavioral Sciences*, 22, 369–381

Steer, R. A., McElroy, M. G., & Beck, A. T. (1982). Structure of depression in alcoholic men: A partial replication. *Psychological Reports, 50*, 723–728.

Stephen, E. H., Foote, K., Hendershot, G. E., & Schoenborn, C. A. (1994). Health of the foreign-born population: United States, 1989–1990. *Advance Data, 14*, 1–12.

Strug, D., & Mason, S. (2001). Social service needs of Hispanic immigrants: An exploratory study of the Washington Heights community. *Journal of Ethnic & Cultural Diversity in Social Work, 10*(3), 69–88.

Sue, S. (1977). Community mental health services to minority groups: Some optimism, some pessimism. *American Psychologist, 32*(8), 616–624.

Swanson, J. W., Linskey, A. O., Quintero-Salinas, R., Pumariega, A. J., & Holzer, C. E. (1992). A binational school survey of depressive symptoms, drug use, and suicidal ideation. *Journal of the American Academy of Child and Adolescent Psychiatry, 31*, 669–678.

Temkin-Greener, H., & Clark, K. T. (1988). Ethnicity, gender, and utilization of mental health services in a Medicaid population. *Social Science & Medicine, 26*(10), 989–996.

Ungemack, J. A., & Guarnaccia, P. J. (1998). Suicidal ideation and suicide attempts among Mexican Americans, Puerto Ricans and Cuban Americans. *Transcultural Psychiatry, 35*, 307–327.

US Bureau of the Census. (2005). *Educational attainment of the population 15 years and over, by age, sex, race, and Hispanic origin: 2004.*

Vega, W. A., Gil, A., Warheit, G., Apospori, E., & Zimmerman, R. (1993). The relationship of drug use to suicide ideation and attempts among African American, Hispanic, and white non-Hispanic male adolescents. *Suicide & Life Threatening Behavior, 23*, 110–119.

Vega, W. A., & Lopez, S. R. (2001). Priority issues in Latino mental health services research. *Mental Health Services Research, 3*(4), 189–200.

Wadsworth, T., & Kubrin, C. E. (2007). Hispanic suicide in U.S. metropolitan areas: Examining the effects of immigration, assimilation, affluence, and disadvantage. *American Journal of Sociology, 12*(6), 1848–1885.

Weissman, M. M., Bland, R. C., Canino, G. J., Greenwald, S., Hwu, H. G., Joyce, P. R., et al. (1999). Prevalence of suicide ideation and suicide attempts in nine countries. *Psychological Medicine, 29*, 9–17.

Wells, K. B., Hough, R. L., Golding, J. M., Burnam, M. A., & Karno, M. (1987). Which Mexican-Americans underutilize health services? *The American Journal of Psychiatry, 144*(7), 918–922.

Williams, C. L., & Berry, J. W. (1991). Primary prevention of acculturative stress among refugees: Application of psychological theory and practice. *The American Psychologist, 46*, 632–664.

Worchel, D., & Gearing, R. E. (2010). *Suicide assessment: Empirical and evidence-based practices.* New York: Springer.

11 Assessment of Anxiety with Hispanics

Cassandra Snipes

Anxiety and the Hispanic Client

The Hispanic population is the largest and fastest growing minority group in the United States and will comprise 50% of the total US population by 2050 (Jakobsons & Buckner, 2007; Willerton, Dankoski, & Sevilla Martir, 2008), and some evidence suggests that Hispanics are at an increased risk for the development of anxiety disorders. Specifically, research has indicated that Hispanics either born in the United States or those who have lived in the country for more than thirteen years report higher rates of anxiety disorders than non-Hispanic Whites (Cintron, Carter, Suchday, Sbrocco, & Gray, 2005; Guarnaccia, Martinez, & Acosta, 2005; Novy, Stanley, Averill, & Daza, 2001). Moreover, Vega and colleagues (1998) have identified lifetime prevalence for anxiety disorders in Mexican American immigrants of 18% for women and 9% for men and of 27% for women and 20% for men among Mexican Americans born in the United States (Vega et al., 1998). This high prevalence of anxiety in the Hispanic population has been attributed to family dysfunction and larger household size (Blume, Resor, Villanueva, & Braddy, 2009). Low social support, low self-esteem, and religious beliefs can also contribute to anxiety in this population (Blume et al., 2009).

In addition to experiencing high rates of anxiety disorders in general, evidence suggests that Hispanic Americans may be at greater risk for experiencing posttraumatic stress disorder (PTSD) (Blume et al., 2009). This greater risk may be due to increased exposure to potentially traumatic events (PTEs). For example, Hein and Bukszpan (1999) found that 25% of low-income Latina and African American women met criteria for PTSD and that more than 10% had witnessed violence (Blume et al.). Research has also indicated that Hispanic American Vietnam veterans exhibited high rates of PTSD and more severe symptoms than non-Hispanic Whites (Ortega & Rosenheck, 2000 in Blume et al.).

Despite the research cited above, whether or not Hispanics truly have higher rates of anxiety disorders than their Caucasian counterparts is unclear. Some studies find higher level of symptom severity and higher prevalence rates of anxiety disorders among Hispanics (Asnaani, Richey, Dimaite, Hinton, & Hofman, 2010; Novy et al., 2001), others find that rates of mental illness are comparable between Hispanics and the general US population (Jakobsons & Buckner, 2007). Despite the fact

C. Snipes, B.A. (✉)
Department of Psychology, University of Nevada, Reno, NV 89512, USA
e-mail: snipes.cassandra@gmail.com

L.T. Benuto (ed.), *Guide to Psychological Assessment with Hispanics*,
DOI 10.1007/978-1-4614-4412-1_11, © Springer Science+Business Media New York 2013

that evidence is mixed regarding rates of anxiety disorders between Hispanic and Caucasian samples, it is still imperative to conduct effective assessment of these disorders as assessment has important implications in terms of treatment.

Cultural Sensitivity

Awareness of cross-cultural psychopathology is a growing concern in the field of psychology, and variation in symptom presentation is becoming apparent between groups (Robinson, Klenck, & Norton, 2010). Some findings indicate that symptoms typically associated with anxiety differ for Hispanic and Anglo individuals (Cintron et al., 2005). Furthermore, some have suggested that assessment measures do not fully capture endorsement of these diagnoses because of language or cultural barriers (Asnaani et al., 2010). The above calls to light the need to investigate the validity and reliability of assessment measures as they pertain to the Hispanic client.

Regardless of whether or not Hispanics experience more disability as a result of anxiety, evidence consistently shows that Hispanics receive lesser and poorer quality health care (Guarnaccia et al., 2005; Willerton et al., 2008). This disparity results in a greater mental health-related disability in this population. Many explanations for this disparity in mental health care have been posited, e.g., fear of the health care system and lack of health insurance (Guarnaccia et al., 2005; Novy et al., 2001; Willerton et al., 2008). Although these health care system concerns may contribute to the lack of equity of Hispanic mental health care, this population may be reluctant to seek psychotherapy services due to the lack of cultural competency of providers (Gonzales-Prendes, Hindo, & Pardo, 2011; Novy et al.). Effective and culturally competent assessment of mental health disorders (and particularly anxiety disorders) is a crucial step in properly serving the Hispanic population.

Assessment of Hispanics

Correct assessment is the backbone of providing efficient and successful delivery of mental health services (Jakobsons & Buckner, 2007). Efficient assessment informs treatment selection and implementation, and without this information, informed treatment decisions are not possible (Novy et al., 2001; Therrien & Hunsley, 2012). Two issues are of particular importance when assessing anxiety in Hispanic individuals: language and the interpretation equivalence for measures largely standardized on the Caucasian population (Jakobsons & Buckner, 2007). Although large portions of Hispanic Americans are bilingual, many report Spanish as the primary or preferred language (Daza, Novy, Stanley, & Averill, 2002). Approximately 78% of Latinos, age 5 and older speak Spanish as their primary language in the home (Weil, 2010). Evidence also suggests that service utilization is increased (through reduced dropout rates) for Mexican Americans when services are available in Spanish (Novy et al.). This phenomenon requires that Spanish-language assessment be made available.

The Goals of This Chapter

First, it is necessary to identify which measures (1) are most commonly used to assess anxiety in English-speaking populations and (2) have good psychometric properties and then to specify their utility with Hispanics. Although many Hispanics identify Spanish as their primary language, the shortage of Spanish-speaking clinicians (Novy et al., 2001) necessitates that reliable English measures be available for use with this population. Thus, this chapter will consist of a review of assessment measure for generalized anxiety disorder, panic disorder, specific phobias, and posttraumatic stress disorder as they relate to both English- and Spanish-speaking Hispanics. Furthermore, because evidence shows that Hispanics often express mental health symptoms through somatization and experts suggest that this is an important cultural consideration when assessing anxiety disorders (Cintron et al., 2005; Cucciare, Gray, Azar, Jimenez, & Gallagher-Thompson, 2010; Willerton et al., 2008), this chapter will also emphasize the importance of administering assessments that assess somatic symptoms of anxiety.

Psychological assessment measures have been in routine clinical use for many decades; however, it is just within the last 10 years that measures have begun to be standardized for use in Hispanic populations. As is presented below, there are still a limited number of assessments that have been validated on Hispanic samples. This excludes several measures that have excellent psychometric properties and are widely used in clinical practice (e.g., the SCID-I). That being said, there is significant debate in the field regarding whether it is ethical to reserve using a reliable and well-validated assessment (and behavioral health interventions, for that matter) measure simply because it has not been validated with the individual patient's cultural group (Cardemil, 2010).

It is clear from the evidence reviewed below that although this population may be underrepresented in research, Hispanics have not been excluded. Therefore, it is the view of this author that measures should be utilized with Hispanics unless there is clear evidence or a theoretical reason not to. The goal of this chapter is to present the current best practices in anxiety assessment in a Hispanic population in order to ensure access to quality behavioral health care.

Assessment of Anxiety as a Domain

Structured Clinical Interview for DSM-IV Axis I Disorders (SCID-I)

The Structured Clinical Interview for DSM-IV Axis I Disorders (SCID-I) is a clinician-administered, semi-structured interview for use with individuals who are undergoing evaluation for psychopathology. The entirety of the measure takes between 1 and 2 h to administer, and its main body consists of nine diagnostic modules, anxiety disorders included. The interviewer may choose to selectively focus only on areas of the greatest diagnostic interest (e.g., panic disorder). The measure provides probe questions and suggested follow-up questions. The interviewer codes responses as 1 = absent/false, 2 = subthreshold, or 3 = present/true. There is a fourth rating option [?] used when information is insufficient. Skip directions are employed when a subject fails to meet a critical criterion required for a particular disorder (Sanchez-Villegas et al., 2008). The SCID demonstrated validity over standard clinical interviews at intake (Zanarini et al., 2000).

The SCID-I and the Hispanic Client

Although a review of extant literature yielded no studies focused on standardizing the SCID-I with a Hispanic sample, bilingual interviewers in a research setting have still successfully administered this measure to Hispanics in English (Cucciare et al., 2010). This suggests that the measure may be of acceptable use with Hispanics in a clinical setting. Furthermore, an examination of the sample constellation of studies that have examined the reliability and validity of the SCID-I has demonstrated that Hispanics have not been excluded from research on the English version of the SCID-I (e.g., Alegria et al.; 2009; Lewis-Fernandez et al., 2008). Further supporting the validity and reliability of the Spanish version of the SCID-I is research on its use among substance users (Torrens, Serrano, Astals, Perez-Dominguez, & Martin-Santos, 2004).

In sum, Hispanics have not been excluded from research on the SCID-I (English version), and there is certainly no empirical evidence (or anecdotal evidence to the knowledge of this author) that suggests

Table 11.1 Anxiety disorder assessment measures with Hispanics

Measure	Constructs assessed	Availability in Spanish	Recommended use
Structured Clinical Interview for DSM-IV Axis I Disorders (SCID-I)	Assess the presence of DSM-IV anxiety disorders	Yes	Although this measure has not been standardized on a Hispanic population, bilingual interviewers in a research setting have still successfully administered the measure, and it is recommended for use with the Hispanic population
Anxiety Disorder Interview Schedule (ADIS-IV)	Assesses the presence of anxiety and mood disorders	No	While the ADIS-IV has not been exclusively researched with Hispanics, an examination of the samples of the studies that have utilized the ADIS-IV with this population has indicated that it is a viable diagnostic measure and it is recommended for use
Beck Anxiety Inventory (BAI)	Consists of 21 items that primarily measure physiological symptoms of anxiety	Yes	Both the English- and Spanish-language versions of the BAI have strong psychometric properties and are highly recommended for use with the Hispanic population
Anxiety Severity Index (ASI)	Measures anxiety sensitivity, e.g., the fear of anxiety and anxiety-related somatic symptoms	Yes	The English-language ASI has sound psychometric properties in both clinical and nonclinical Hispanic samples. The ASI has also been successfully translated into Spanish and demonstrates good psychometric properties. Both versions are recommended for use with the Hispanic population
State-Trait Anxiety Inventory (STAI)	Examines two dimensions of anxiety: state and trait anxiety	Yes	Both the English-language version and the Spanish-language version (IDARE) have sound psychometric properties and are recommended for use
Clinician-Administered PTSD Scale (CAPS)	Assesses 17 symptoms associated with PTSD	Yes	Both the English-language and the Spanish-language CAPS have adequate psychometric properties and are recommended for use with this population
Posttraumatic Stress Disorder Checklist (PCL)	Assesses the 17 core PTSD symptoms	Yes	Both the English-language version and the Spanish-language version are recommended for use with the Latino population
Generalized Anxiety Disorder Questionnaire-IV (GAD-Q-IV)	Full diagnostic criteria of GAD	No	This measure has sound psychometric properties and is recommended for use with the Hispanic population

that the use of the Spanish version of the SCID-I is problematic. Therefore, while ideally research examining the psychometric properties of the SCID-I Spanish version should be conducted, until this research is available, there is no reason for clinicians to use subpar assessment measures or measures that otherwise lack good psychometric properties with Hispanics.

Anxiety Disorder Interview Schedule (ADIS-IV)

The Anxiety Disorder Interview Schedule (ADIS-IV; is a semi-structured interview that assesses the presence of anxiety and mood disorders. Clinician severity ratings are made on a 0–8 Likert-type scale, with higher ratings indicating more severe symptoms and impairment in life functioning. Evidence suggests good reliability of the ADIS-IV (Table 11.1).

The ADIS-IV and the Hispanic Client

While the ADIS-IV has not been exclusively researched with Hispanics, an examination of the samples of the studies that have utilized the ADIS-IV with this population has indicated that it is a viable diagnostic measure (Brown, Campbell, Lehman, Grisham, & Mancill, 2001; Buckner & Schmidt, 2009; Street et al., 1997). Despite the fact that the psychometric properties of the ADIS-IV as administered to a Hispanic population are unknown, the measure can still be used in both research and clinical settings until relevant data is available as there are no apparent reasons that this measure should be used with Hispanics.

Beck Anxiety Inventory (BAI)

The Beck Anxiety Inventory (BAI) is one of the most frequently used self-report measures to assess anxious symptomology in clinical settings (Magan, Sanz, & Garcia-Vera, 2008). It consists of 21 items that primarily measure physiological symptoms of anxiety. Fourteen of the items refer to somatic symptoms, and the remaining seven items reflect specific cognitions associated with anxiety and panic. Respondents use a 4-point severity scale to note symptoms experienced during the past week with responses ranging from "Not all" to "Severely- I could barely stand it" (Steer, Ranieri, Beck, & Clark, 1993). Total scores range from 0 to 63. The BAI is typically used to assess response to treatment and to determine the most effective treatment; therefore, it is routinely administered before and after intervention. A statistically significant reduction in the BAI score is considered a successful response to treatment, in regard to anxious symptomology (Magan et al., 2008). This measure has also been shown to successfully discriminate the construct of anxiety from depression (Beck, Epstein, Brown, & Steer, 1988).

The BAI and the Hispanic Client

In accordance with the English-language version of the BAI, the Spanish translation of the BAI is a 21-item self-report measure designed to assess the severity of anxiety symptomology (Beck et al., 1988). Respondents are asked to rate the degree to which they were affected by each item in the past week on a Likert-type scale, ranging from 0 (*not at all*) to 3 (*severely; I could barely stand it*). Each item is assigned a score from 0 to 3, depending on the participant's response, and then the items are totaled. A possible score of 0 to 63 can be obtained.

Research on the use of the BAI with Hispanics has been conducted, and internal consistency of the BAI in Spanish-speaking populations is strong (alpha = .92), and both convergent and divergent validity have been demonstrated (Novy et al., 2001; Steer et al., 1993). In fact, many studies have found the BAI to be valid and reliable in diverse samples, and data suggest that the use of the Spanish-language BAI yields psychometric properties comparable with those exhibited in Caucasian samples (Jakobsons & Buckner, 2007; Magan et al., 2008). Internal consistency estimates for the Spanish version of the BAI is high (.93) and similar to levels found in other populations (Magan et al., 2008; Novy et al., 2001; Sanz & Navarro, 2003). The mean BAI score for the general Spanish population has been identified as 11; therefore, it is proposed that a score equal to or lower than 11 represents clinically significant recovery from anxious symptomology for a Spanish-speaking adult patient (Magan et al.). This mean BAI score is comparable to means found in the general adult population in several other countries (Magan et al.). In conclusion, the BAI is a useful measure to aid in the detection of an anxiety disorder in a clinical intake process and is also a helpful way as assessing anxiety symptomology throughout the course of treatment.

Anxiety Severity Index (ASI)

Anxiety sensitivity refers to the fear of anxiety and anxiety-related somatic symptoms; this construct has been proposed as a risk factor for both anxiety disorders in general and specifically for panic disorder (Sandin, Chorot, & Mc Nally, 2001). The Anxiety Severity Index (ASI) is a 16-item measure of fear of anxiety and possible consequences of anxiety. Ratings are made on a 4-point scale ranging from *very little* to *very much,* with the total scores ranging from 0 to 64. Fear of anxiety symptoms can be categorized into five subtypes: (a) catastrophic cognitions-caused anxiety sensitivity, (b) trauma associations-caused anxiety sensitivity, (c) metaphor-caused anxiety sensitivity, (d) direct conditioning-caused anxiety sensitivity, and (e) other-caused anxiety sensitivity (Hinton, Chong, Pollack, Barlow, & McNally, 2008).

The ASI and the Hispanic Client

The English-language ASI has sound psychometric properties in both clinical and nonclinical Hispanic samples (Borden & Lister, 1994; Novy et al., 2001). The ASI has also been successfully translated into Spanish, and the Spanish-language ASI has good psychometric properties (e.g., alpha=.85: Sandin et al., 2001; alpha=.93: Novy et al., 2001) with a mean and standard deviation that are comparable to those found in the general population (Sandin et al.). In summary, the Spanish version of the ASI has sound psychometric properties that are comparable to ones reported for the general English-speaking population and is viable clinical assessment option.

State-Trait Anxiety Inventory (STAI)

The State-Trait Anxiety Inventory (STAI) is a self-report measure that examines two dimensions of anxiety: state and trait anxiety (Virella, Arbona, & Novy, 1994). State anxiety is considered to be nervousness or worry that is highly related to situational or contextual factors. Trait anxiety refers to more stable dispositional anxiety. Each of the two dimensions is assessed using a separate 20-item scale that is comprised of anxiety-present or anxiety-absent items (Virella et al., 1994).

The STAI and the Hispanic Client

The English-language version of the STAI has been found to have similar psychometric properties when administered to a Hispanic and a Caucasian sample (Virella et al., 1994). The STAI has also been successfully translated into a Spanish-language measure: the Inventario de Ansiedad Rasgo-Estado (IDARE). Psychologists, psychiatrists, and professional translators from ten different Spanish-speaking countries completed the translation (Virella et al.). The measure has a high degree of internal consistency (alpha=.92) and supports the construct of the IDARE. The Spanish-language version of the STAI has strong psychometric properties and is a viable resource to evaluate state and trait anxiety among Hispanics (Virella et al.).

Assessment of Posttraumatic Stress Disorder

Clinician-Administered PTSD Scale (CAPS)

The Clinician-Administered PTSD Scale (CAPS) is commonly used in PTSD research and clinical settings (Benuto, Olmo-Terrasa, & Reyes-Rabanillo, 2011). It is semi-structured diagnostic interview for assessing the 17 symptoms associated with PTSD (Blake et al., 1990). The frequency and intensity of each of the 17 symptoms are rated (e. g., distress or functional impairment), thus resulting in 34 items.

Each question is followed by prompt questions and suggested follow-up questions that aim at clarifying the frequency and intensity of the symptom (Blake et al., 1995). Using a 5-point (0–4) Likert-type rating scale, frequency and intensity ratings are summed for each symptom to yield a severity score (0–8) and across symptoms to yield scores for the three symptom clusters (reexperiencing, avoidance and numbing, and hyperarousal). The CAPS acts as both a dichotomous diagnostic tool (presence or absence of PTSD) and provides a fine-grained analysis of severity. The CAPS has been demonstrated to be quite psychometrically sound with test–retest reliability ranging from .90 to .98 and an internal consistency of .94 for the total score (Blake et al., 1995).

The CAPS and the Hispanic Client

Specific to Hispanics, research has been successfully conducted with this population on the CAPS (Lieberman, Van Horn & Ghosh Ippen, 2005; Palmieri, Weathers, Difede & King, 2007). In a sample of veterans referred to VA PTSD clinic, the Spanish-language CAPS was found to have adequate internal consistency (alpha = .84) and to be able to differentiate between those diagnosed with PTSD (vs. those who were not) with a moderate effect size (.36) (Benuto et al., 2011). At least one other study has found the Spanish-language version of the CAPS to have sound psychometric properties (Bobes et al., 2000). Based on this literature, as well as the fact that Spanish translation of the CAPS is routinely used in a research context, this measure is recommended for use with the Hispanic population.

Posttraumatic Stress Disorder Checklist (PCL)

The Posttraumatic Stress Disorder Checklist (PCL) is a 17-item self-report rating scale and is used as a self-report screening measure for PTSD symptoms (Weathers, Litz, Herman, Huska, & Keane, 1993). The PCL-C is a general civilian version of the Posttraumatic Stress Disorder Checklist and with symptoms written generally to apply to any traumatic event (Benuto et al., 2011; Weathers et al., 1993). Each item corresponds to one of the 17 core DSM-IV symptoms. Examinees indicate how much they were bothered by each of the 17 symptoms during the past month with severity ratings ranging from "Not at all" to "Extremely" (Weathers et al.). The English version of this measure has high internal consistency (alpha = .85–.98) (Wilkins, Lang & Norman, 2011) and has been found to correlate well with the Mississippi Scale (.93) and the PK scale (.77) of the MMPI-2 (Weathers et al.), thus supporting its validity (Benuto et al.).

The PCL and the Hispanic Client

There is surprisingly little known regarding the effect of race on an individual's PCL performance (McDonald & Calhoun, 2010). However, two papers have reported general equivalence of the English- and Spanish-language versions of the PCL (Marshall, 2004; Orlando & Marshall, 2002). The Spanish-language version of this measure was created using double translation procedures (Orlando & Marshall, 2002). Although the measures were not completely equivalent on an item-by-item basis, no bias was detected at the PCL composite score level (Marshall, 2004). This suggests that the two measures are equivalent in regard to the total PCL score. In conclusion, the Spanish-language version of the PCL is recommended for use in clinical practice and research settings (Benuto et al., 2011).

Assessment of Generalized Anxiety Disorder

Generalized anxiety disorder (GAD) is one of the most common anxiety disorders, marked by excessive and uncontrollable worry as well as associated physical symptoms such as fatigue and muscle tension (Robinson et al., 2010). In general, findings support the fact that Hispanics do not experience greater prevalence of GAD than other racial groups, with some studies demonstrating that Hispanics experience a decreased prevalence when compared with a Caucasian population (Breslau et al., 2006; Robinson et al., 2010).

Generalized Anxiety Disorder Questionnaire-IV (GAD-Q-IV)

The Generalized Anxiety Disorder Questionnaire-IV (GAD-Q-IV) is a self-report diagnostic measure of generalized anxiety disorder and is the only English-language measure that assesses the full diagnostic criteria of GAD. The measure is composed of nine items that assess the presence, frequency, and controllability of excessive worry, the number of endorsed worry themes and physical symptoms, and the interference and distressed caused by worry and its symptoms.

The GAD-Q-IV and the Hispanic Client

Studies have established the psychometric properties of the GAD-Q-IV for the Hispanic population with demonstrated sensitivity (83%) and specificity (89%), adequate test–rest reliability ($k = .67$), as well as both convergent and discriminant validity (Newman et al., 2002; Robinson et al., 2010). In a study examining the use of the GAD-Q-IV across racial groups, Robinson and colleagues also demonstrated the similar factor structures and similar psychometric properties between Caucasians and Hispanic populations (Robinson et al.). Therefore, this measure is recommended for use in the Hispanic population.

Recommendations

It is imperative that an evidence-based assessment approach be employed with Hispanics due to the high prevalence of anxiety disorders among this group and also because correct assessment is the backbone of providing efficient and successful delivery of mental health services. Without effective and accurate assessment, treatment planning is at a disadvantage and research methodology may be hindered. Although Hispanics are underrepresented in research examining the psychometric properties of some assessment measures, from the data that does exist, it is apparent that there are a number of measures that can be employed for use in the assessment of anxiety in both clinical and research settings.

Specifically, measures such as the Beck Anxiety Inventory (BAI) and the Anxiety Severity Index (ASI) have been very well researched with Hispanic samples and are specifically recommended for assessing physiological symptoms of anxiety and anxiety sensitivity, respectively. Administration of the BAI may have particular relevance to Hispanics as Hispanics may display anxiety symptoms through somatization and the BAI assesses for the physiological components of anxiety. Furthermore, both the State-Trait Anxiety Inventory (STAI) and Generalized Anxiety Disorder Questionnaire-IV (GAD-Q-IV) have also been sufficiently studied and standardized with Hispanics and are recommended for assessment of both state and trait anxiety and as well as for the assessment GAD.

With regard to PTSD, both the Clinician-Administered PTSD Scale (CAPS) and the Posttraumatic Stress Disorder Checklist (PCL) are viable assessment measures for Hispanic clients. Each measure is available in both English and Spanish, and research has been conducted with Hispanics for both of these measures.

Finally, while widely used and well-regarded measures, such as the Structured Clinical Interview for DSM-IV Axis I Disorders (SCID-I) and the Anxiety Disorder Interview Schedule (ADIS-IV), have not been exclusively researched with Hispanics, these measures are commonly used in research with Hispanic participants. Furthermore, Hispanics have not been excluded from research on the SCID-I (English version), and there is certainly no empirical evidence to suggest that the use of the Spanish version of the SCID-I or ADIS-IV is problematic. Therefore, both of these measures are recommended for use with this population.

While ideally research examining the psychometric properties of each measure should be conducted, until this research is available, there is no reason for clinicians to use a non-evidence-based assessment approach or for clinicians or researchers to use measures that otherwise lack good psychometric properties with Hispanics. In this chapter, we have presented many measures that are viable for use with this the Hispanic client or research participant. These measures should be utilized when assessing for the presence of an anxiety disorder with Hispanics in order to ensure accurate treatment planning and provision of quality behavioral health care.

References

Alegria, M., Shrout, P. E., Torres, M., Lewis-Fernandez, R., Abelson, J. M., & Powell, M. (2009). Lessons learned from the clinical reappraisal study of the composite international diagnostic interview with latinos. *International Journal of Methods in Psychiatric Research, 18*(2), 84–95.

Asnaani, A., Richey, J., Dimaite, R., Hinton, D., & Hofman, S. (2010). A cross-ethnic comparison of lifetime prevalence rates of anxiety disorders. *The Journal of Nervous and Mental Disease, 198*(8), 551–555.

Beck, A., Epstein, N., Brown, G., & Steer, R. (1988). An inventory for measuring clinical anxiety: Psychometric properties. *Journal of Counseling and Clinical Psychology, 56*, 893–897.

Benuto, L., Olmo-Terrasa, A., & Reyes-Rabanillo, M. (2011). Exploring the factor structure and psychometric properties of a spanish translation of the clinician-administered PTSD scale. *The International Journal of Educational and Psychological Assessment, 9*(1), 14–26.

Blake, D., Weathers, F., Nagy, L., Kaloupek, D., Gusman, F., Charney, D., et al. (1995). The development of a clinician-administered PTSD scale. *Journal of Traumatic Stress, 8*(1), 75–90.

Blake, D., Weathers, F., Nagy, L., Kaloupek, D., Klauminzer, G., Charney, D., et al. (1990). A clinician rating scale for assessing current and lifetime PTSD: The CAPS-I. *Behavior Therapist, 18*, 187–188.

Blume, A. W., Resor, M., Villanueva, M. R., & Braddy, L. D. (2009). Alcohol use and comorbid anxiety, traumatic stress, and hopeless among Hispanics. *Addictive Behaviors, 34*(9), 709–713.

Bobes, J., Calcedo-Barba, A., Garcia, M., Francois, M., Rico-Villademoros, F., Gonzales, M. P., et al. (2000). Evaluation of the psychometric properties of the Spanish version of 5 questionnaires for the evaluation of post-traumatic stress syndrome. *Actas Esq Psiquiatr, 28*(4), 207–18.

Borden, J. W., & Lister, S. C. (1994). The anxiety sensitivity construct: Cognitive reactions to physiological change. *Journal of Anxiety Disorders, 8*(4), 311–321.

Breslau, J., Aguilar-Gaxiola, S., Kendler, K., Su, M., Williams, D., & Kessler, R. (2006). Specify race-ethnic differences in risk for psychiatric disorder in a USA national sample. *Psychological Medicine, 36*(1), 57–68.

Brown, T. A., Campbell, L. A., Lehman, C. L., Grisham, J. R., & Mancill, R. B. (2001). Current and lifetime comorbidity of the DSM-IV anxiety and mood disorders in a large clinical sample. *Journal of Abnormal Psychology, 110*(4), 585–599.

Buckner, J. D., & Schmidt, N. B. (2009). Social anxiety disorder and marijuana use problems: the mediating role of marijuana effect expectancies. *Depression and Anxiety, 26*(9), 864–870.

Cardemil, E. (2010). The complexity of culture: Do we embrace the challenge or avoid it? *The Scientific Review of Mental Health Practice, 7*(2), 41–47.

Cintron, J., Carter, C., Suchday, S., Sbrocco, T., & Gray, J. (2005). Factor structure and construct validity of anxiety se index among island puerto ricans. *Journal of Anxiety Disorders, 19*, 51–68.

Cucciare, M., Gray, H., Azar, A., Jimenez, D., & Gallagher-Thompson, D. (2010). Exploring the relationship between physical health, depressive symptoms, and depression diagnoses in hispanic dementia caregivers. *Aging & Mental Health, 14*(3), 274–282.

Daza, P., Novy, D., Stanley, M., & Averill, P. (2002). The depression anxiety stress scale-21: Spanish translation and validation with a hispanic sample. *Journal of Psychopathology and Behavioral Assessment, 24*(3), 195–205.

Gonzales-Prendes, A., Hindo, C., & Pardo, Y. (2011). Cultural values integration in cognitive-behavioral therapy for a latino with depression. *Clinical Case Studies, 10*(5), 376–394.

Guarnaccia, P., Martinez, I., & Acosta, H. (2005). Mental health in the hispanic immigrant community: An overview. *Journal of Immigrant & Refugee Services, 3*(1), 21–46.

Hein, D. & Bukszpan, C. (1999). Interpersonal violence in "normal" low-income groups. *Women and Health, 29*, 1–16.

Hinton, D., Chong, R., Pollack, M., Barlow, D., & McNally, R. (2008). Ataque de nervios: Relationship to anxiety sensitivity and dissociation predisposition. *Depression and Anxiety, 25*, 489–495.

Jakobsons, L., & Buckner, J. (2007). The assessment, diagnosis, and treatment of psychiatric disorders in hispanic/latino clients. In J. Buckner, Y. Castro, J. Holm-Denoma, & T. Joiner (Eds.), *Mental health care for people of diverse backgrounds*. Oxford/Seattle: Radcliffe Publishing.

Lewis-Fernandez, R., Turner, J. B., Marshall, R., Turse, N., Neria, Y., & Dohrenwend, B. P. (2008). Elevated rates of current PTSD among Hispanic veterans in the NVVRS: True prevalence or methodological artifact? *Journal of Traumatic Stress, 21*(2), 123–132.
Lieberman, A. F., Van Horn, P., & Ghosh Ippen, C. (2005). Toward evidence-based treatment: Child–parent psychotherapy with preschoolers exposed to marital violence. *American Academy of Child and Adolescent Psychiatry, 44*(12), 1241–1247.
Magan, I., Sanz, J., & Garcia-Vera, M. (2008). Psychometric properties of a spanish version of the beck anxiety inventory (BAI) in general population. *The Spanish Journal of Psychology, 11*(2), 626–640.
Marshall, G. N. (2004). Posttraumatic stress disorder symptom checklist: Factor structure and English-Spanish measurement invariance. *Journal of Traumatic Stress, 17*(3), 223–23.
McDonald, S. D., & Calhoun, P. S. (2010). The diagnostic accuracy of the PTSD checklist: A critical review. *Clinical Psychology Review, 30*(8), 976–987.
Newman, M., Zuellig, A., Kachin, K., Constantino, M., Przeworkski, A., Erickson, T., et al. (2002). Preliminary reliability and validity of the generalized anxiety disorder questionnaire-IV: A revised self-report diagnostic measure of generalized anxiety disorder. *Behavior Therapy, 33*, 215–233.
Novy, D., Stanley, M., Averill, P., & Daza, P. (2001). Psychometric comparability of English and Spanish language measures of anxiety and related affective symptoms. *Psychological Assessment, 13*(3), 347–355.
Orlando, M., & Marshall, G. N. (2002). Differential item functioning in a Spanish translation of the PTSD checklist: Detection and evaluation of impact. *Psychological Assessment, 14*(1), 50–59.
Palmieri, P. A., Weathers, F. W., Difede, J., & King, D. W. (2007). Confirmatory factor analysis of the PTSD Checklist and the clinician-administered PTSD scale in disaster workers exposed to the world trade center ground zero. *Journal of Abnormal Psychology, 116*(2), 239–341.
Robinson, C., Klenck, S., & Norton, P. (2010). Psychometric properties of the generalized anxiety disorder questionnaire for DSM-IV among four racial groups. *Cognitive Behaviour Therapy, 39*(4), 25–261.
Sanchez-Villegas, A., Schlatter, J., Ortuno, J., Lahortiga, F., Pla, J., Benito, S., et al. (2008). Validity of a self-reported diagnosis of depression among participants in a cohort study using the Structure Clinical Interview for DSM-IV (SCID). *BMC Psychiatry, 8*(43).
Sandin, B., Chorot, P., & Mc Nally, R. (2001). Anxiety sensitivity index: Normative data and its differentiation from state anxiety. *Behaviour Research and Therapy, 39*(2), 213–219.
Sanz, J., & Navarro, M. (2003). Propiedades psicometricas de una version espanola del Inventario de Ansiedad de Beck (BAI) en estudiantes universitarios. *Ansiedad y Estres, 9*, 59–84.
Steer, R., Ranieri, W., Beck, A., & Clark, D. (1993). Further evidence for the validity of the anxiety inventory with psychiatric outpatients. *Journal of Anxiety Disorders, 7*, 195–205.
Street, L. L., Salman, E., Garfinkle, R., Silvestri, J., Carrasco, J., Cardenas, D., et al. (1997). Discriminating between generalized anxiety disorder and anxiety disorder not otherwise specified in a Hispanic population: Is it only a matter of worry? *Depression and Anxiety, 5*, 1–6.
Therrien, Z., & Hunsley, J. (2012). Assessment of anxiety in older adults: A systematic review of commonly used measures. *Aging & Mental Health, 16*(1), 1–16.
Torrens, M., Serrano, D., Astals, M., Perez-Dominguez, G., & Martin-Santos, R. (2004). Diagnosing comorbid psychiatric disorders in substance abuser: Validity of the spanish versions of the psychiatric research interview for substance abuse and mental disorders and the structured clinical interview for DSM-IV. *The American Journal of Psychiatry, 161*, 1231–1237.
Vega, W. A., Kolody, B., Aguilar-Gaxiola, S., Aldrete, E., Catalano, R., & Caraveo-Anduaga, J. (1998). Lifetime prevalence of DSM-IIR psychiatric disorders among urban and rural Mexican Americans in California. *Archives of General Psychiatry, 55*, 771–778.
Virella, B., Arbona, C., & Novy, D. (1994). Psychometric properties and factor structure of the spanish version of the state-trait anxiety inventory. *Journal of Personality Assessment, 63*(3), 401–412.
Weathers, F., Litz, B., Herman, D., Huska, J., & Keane, T. (1993). *The PTSD checklist (PCL): Reliability, validity, and diagnostic utility*. Paper Presented at The Annual Meeting of International Society for Posttraumatic Stress Studies, San Antonio, TX.
Weil, M. (2010). A cultural competency program for psychologists: Clinical and supervisory practices with Latino culture and language. *Psychology Dissertations, Paper 175.*
Wilkins, K. C., Lang, A. J., & Norman, S. B. (2011). Synthesis of the psychometric properties of the PTSD checklist (PCL) military, civilian, and specific versions. *Depression and Anxiety, 28*(7), 596–606.
Willerton, E., Dankoski, M., & Sevilla Martir, J. (2008). Medical family therapy; A model for addressing mental health disparities among latinos. *Family, Systems, and Health, 26*(2), 196–206.
Zanarini, M., Skodol, A., Bender, D., Dolan, R., Sanislow, C., Shaefer, E., et al. (2000). The collaborative longitudinal personality disorders study: Reliability of axis I and axis II diagnoses. *Journal of Personality Disorders, 14*(4), 291–299.

12 Assessing Substance-Related Disorders in Hispanic Clients

Lourdes Suarez-Morales and Danette Beitra

Introduction

Substance abuse is a significant problem among Hispanics. The National Survey on Drug Abuse and Health reveals that 35% of Hispanics 12 years or older have used illicit drugs in their lifetime SAMHSA, (2005) and 72% have used alcohol SAMHSA, (2007). Despite the great need for services, Hispanics do not generally seek treatment for mental health and substance abuse problems when compared to other ethnic groups in the United States (Wells, Klap, Koike, & Sherbourne, 2001). Among the many barriers contributing to poor treatment participation and low research involvement, difficulty completing assessment instruments written in English has been identified as a significant limiting factor. This likely affects a significant number of Hispanics, given estimates that 55% of the Hispanic adult population in the United States have limited English proficiency (U.S. Census, 2000).

In the following paragraphs, we discuss some of the more relevant issues regarding how culture may affect assessment of substance abuse in Hispanic populations. After discussing the interplay between cultural considerations and assessment, we provide detailed descriptions of the major assessment instruments used in the field of substance abuse, their psychometric properties, and the availability of these instruments in the Spanish language. We also summarize the scarce evidence for the psychometric properties of the Spanish version of these instruments. The aim of this chapter is to provide a tool for clinicians and/or researchers interested in working with Hispanic minorities to identify potential instruments for their clinical or research work, as well as stimulate further epidemiological, clinical, or psychometric studies utilizing Spanish-language instruments for substance abuse.

Cultural Considerations When Assessing Substance Use in Hispanic Populations

In the field of substance use, cultural considerations when assessing Hispanic clients include issues regarding the availability of translated and validated instruments in Spanish, response patterns of this ethnic minority population, and interpretation of the data collected.

L. Suarez-Morales, Ph.D. (✉) • D. Beitra, B.A.
Center for Psychological Studies, Nova Southeastern University, 3301 College Ave., Ft. Lauderdale, FL 33314, USA
e-mail: lsuarezmorales@nova.edu

L.T. Benuto (ed.), *Guide to Psychological Assessment with Hispanics*,
DOI 10.1007/978-1-4614-4412-1_12, © Springer Science+Business Media New York 2013

Several instruments of alcohol and drug abuse have been translated into Spanish. However, the fact that an instrument has been translated and used with Hispanic populations does not necessarily imply that its psychometric properties are appropriate to warrant its use with Hispanic populations. On the other hand, because the process of adapting and testing an instrument can be time-consuming and costly, the benefit of using translated instruments despite the lack of validity information may be that previous data is available which provides an opportunity for comparison (Freeman, Lewis, & Colon, 2002). The instruments that will be discussed in this chapter have all been translated into Spanish. However, many of these translations and evaluations of the instruments' psychometric properties have been done in foreign, Spanish-speaking countries; thus, caution needs to be exercised when using these instruments with Hispanics residing in the United States, as they may not possess cross-cultural equivalence.

The process to establish cross-cultural equivalence is complex and includes evaluating the instrument's content, technical, and criterion equivalence (Flaherty, 1987). Content equivalence refers to whether each item is equally relevant to each culture. For example, an item referring to family problems as a result of substance use may be more relevant in nonimmigrant cultures than in immigrant or migrant cultures, in which family members are dispersed or in the country of origin. In addition, technical equivalence refers to obtaining similar effects when using the same measuring strategy in different cultures. As Marin and Marin (1991) pointed out, because Hispanics place greater importance on personal contact and establishing a relationship, interviews may result in more personal disclosure than a telephone survey. Finally, criterion equivalence is established when a measure is evaluated according to each culture's norms and similar results are obtained. In the substance use field, problem drinking, for example, can vary according to the culturally accepted patterns and social situations of alcohol consumption (Annis et al., 1996). This is particularly relevant for Hispanics in the United States, given research findings indicating a relationship between drug use and socioeconomic status (Arroyo, Miller, & Tonigan, 2003), acculturation level (Alegria et al., 2008; Ortega, Rosenheck, Alegria, & Desai, 2000; Vega, Alderete, Kolody, & Aguilar-Gaxiola, 1998), as well as varying patterns of drug use in Hispanic subgroups (e.g., Mexican, Puerto Rican, Cuban; SAMHSA, 2005). However, many of the instruments available in Spanish, for which psychometric properties have been evaluated, have been conducted in Spain, where the culture and nationality is more homogenous than the Hispanic culture in the United States. For a more thorough discussion of the issues involved in cultural equivalence and translation of instruments for Hispanic populations, the reader is referred to Marin and Marin (1991) and Freeman and colleagues (2002).

In addition to availability of appropriate instruments, response patterns among Hispanic populations may affect the information gathered from these instruments. Research suggests that Hispanics, in general, have a tendency to disclose limited personal information, including drug use to strangers, have preference for extreme response categories on scaled responses, and have a tendency for providing socially desirable responses among others (Freeman et al., 2002). Using culturally appropriate instruments is one way to counteract these response tendencies. Another suggestion includes matching the interviewer and client in terms of ethnic characteristics. This strategy has worked well in research with Hispanic minorities (Sue, Fujino, Hu, Takeuchi, & Zane, 1991; Sullivan & Lasso, 1992) and should work as well in clinical settings. The problem about extreme response responding is more difficult to address when using self-report questionnaires that have a 5-point scale or less. For this reason, an interview format may be more conducive to obtaining accurate information as well as provide an opportunity to develop rapport with the client, which is culturally congruent with the value of personalismo (i.e., preference for personal associations) (Marin & Marin, 1991). However, some research suggests that interviews may lead to less disclosure when compared to self-report questionnaires, given that the client may attempt to minimize socially undesirable or illegal behavior, as is the case of drug use (Aquilino, 1994; Rogers, Miller, & Turner, 1998). In general, the researcher or clinician

Table 12.1 Substance-related assessment instruments and their availability in Spanish

			Language availability	
Instrument	Type of assessment	Age range	English	Spanish
Addiction Severity Index (ASI)	Semi-structured interview Computer administration	Adults: (18+)	Yes	Yes
Teen Addiction Severity Index (T-ASI)	Semi-structured interview	Adolescents: (12–17)	Yes	Yes
CAGE questionnaire	Structured interview Self-report	Adults: (18+) Adolescents: (12–17)	Yes	Yes
Alcohol Use Disorders Identification Test (AUDIT)	Interview Self-report	Adults: (18+) Adolescents: (14–18)	Yes	Yes
Michigan Alcoholism Screening Test (MAST)	Self-report Structured interview	Adults: (18+) Adolescents: (13–17)	Yes	Yes
Drug Abuse Screening Test (DAST)	Self-report Structured interview	Adults: (18+)	Yes	Yes
Drug Abuse Screening Test-Adolescent (DAST-A)	Self-report Structured interview	Adolescents: (13–17)	Yes	Yes
Substance Abuse Subtle Screening Inventory (SASSI)	Self-report: Pencil-paper Computer administration Web-based administration	Adults: (18+)	Yes	Yes
Substance Abuse Subtle Screening Inventory-Adolescent (SASSI-A2)	Self-report: Pencil-paper Computer administration Web-based administration	Children and adolescents: (10–17)	Yes	Yes

should be aware of these issues when working with Hispanic ethnic minorities and choose the most appropriate method to gather information based on the reason for collecting the information, in the first place. For example, for information collected for research purposes, anonymity and/or confidentiality of the information should be stressed. On the other hand, for information collected for clinical purposes, the establishment of trust and rapport with the client should be emphasized prior to collecting the information.

Once the information is collected, caution should be given to the way it is interpreted. Factors discussed before, including acculturation level, socioeconomic status, and national origin, all come into play when interpreting information from assessment instruments with Hispanic clients. In particular, acculturation, which refers to the process of adaptation when a person comes into contact with another culture (Berry, 1997), is not commonly considered in the clinical assessment of Hispanic clients. However, as research suggests, it is a significant modifier of behavior, including illicit drug use and alcohol use, in Hispanic populations in the United States (Alegria et al., 2008; Ortega et al., 2000; Vega et al., 1998). In addition, the available Spanish and validated instruments for alcohol and drug use do not currently have norms for Hispanic subgroups residing in the United States based on country of origin. The studies conducted in the United States typically treat Hispanics as a homogeneous group and ignore the extensive heterogeneity in this ethnic minority group. On the other hand, the psychometric studies for Spanish-language instruments conducted abroad may employ samples from populations that have dissimilar cultural, immigration, and socioeconomic experiences to those of US Hispanic populations. Until more research is conducted with Hispanic samples in the United States, the currently available and validated instruments in Spanish should be used with caution.

The next section of this chapter provides an overview of the major assessment instruments used in the field of substance abuse, with a special focus on screening and multidimensional instruments that examine alcohol or drug using patterns, as well as associated problems. Table 12.1 provides a summary of these assessment instruments, their availability in Spanish, and for use with younger populations. Although other instruments exist that may be useful for diagnostic purposes (e.g., Composite International Diagnostic Interview (CIDI; Robins et al., 1988)) of substance abuse or dependence, assessment of clinical diagnoses is the focus of another chapter in this book, and we refer the reader to that chapter. We summarize the psychometric evidence for the original version of the assessment instruments, all of which is based on data from majority samples from the population. Next, we provide information about the availability of these instruments in the Spanish language. The scarce evidence for the psychometric properties of the Spanish version of these instruments is also discussed. Finally, information on adaptations for assessment instruments of substance use with younger populations and the information available for translated versions of these instruments are summarized.

Addiction Severity Index (ASI)

The Addiction Severity Index (ASI) is the most widely used assessment instrument in the substance use field. The ASI is a semi-structured interview that assesses current (i.e., last 30 days) and lifetime problems in seven areas in the individual's life that may be impacted by substance use (McLellan, Luborsky, Woody, & O'Brien, 1980). It is used in treatment of substance abuse/dependence to determine the severity of the client's substance use on the client's functioning for treatment planning, as well as to monitor the client's progress throughout treatment. The ASI may be administered by a trained clinician and takes approximately 30–45 minutes to complete. The original version of the ASI was developed by A. Thomas McLellan and his collaborators from the University of Pennsylvania's Center for the Studies of Addiction. It has undergone several revisions over the years, and a "Lite," shorter version, and a computerized version are also available. The ASI has been translated into many languages. In particular, the Spanish translation of the instrument was developed originally by the World Health Organization. However, several versions in Spanish exist developed in Spain, Costa Rica, and the United States. The "Lite" version of the ASI and the computerized version are also available in Spanish.

The areas covered by the ASI include medical, employment/support, drug and alcohol use, legal, family/social relationships, and psychiatric problems. The ASI yields two summary indices in each area: the interviewer severity ratings (ISRs) and the composite scores (CSs). The ISRs represent a "need for additional treatment" rating, based on historical information provided by the client. The ISR ranges in severity from *no problem* (0) to *most severe* (9) (McLellan et al., 1980). This estimate is further refined based on the client's subjective rating of the current importance of the problem and the need for treatment (Alterman, Brown, Zaballero, & McKay, 1994). The CSs, on the other hand, are arithmetically weighted summary scores based on a set of items referring to recent functioning in the past month. The CSs range from *no problem* (0.00) to *most severe* (1.00). The number of items included in each composite score varies from three in the medical status to 13 in the family/social relationships area.

Criterion Validity

Interrelationship among scores on ASI scales. Emphasis on the independence of the seven problem areas of the ASI has been examined in studies to establish the discriminant validity of the subscales. The findings suggest that intercorrelations of the subscales using the severity ratings and composite scores are usually low, with the exception of the drug and legal scales (Appleby, Dyson, Altman, & Luchins, 1997) and the psychiatric and family/social scales, which have been found to be moderately related (Appleby et al., 1997; Hendriks, Kaplan, van Limbeek, & Geerlings, 1989; Zanis, McLellan, Cnaan, & Randall, 1994).

Association between ASI and external criterion variables. To establish concurrent validity of the ASI, scores on each subscale have been compared to similar criterion measures at the same point in time. An early study conducted by Kosten, Rounsaville, and Kleber (1983) examined the severity ratings with criterion variables in a sample of opiate addicts and found that correlation coefficients varied widely (e.g., ranging between –0.05 for the alcohol and drug scale with the Michigan Alcoholism Screening Test (MAST) and 0.55 between the psychiatric scale and Maudsley neuroticism). Another study by Zanis et al. (1994) provided concurrent validity coefficients in the moderate range for three composite scores of the ASI (i.e., alcohol scale, drug scale, and psychiatric scale) in a homeless sample of substance users. Moderate to high concurrent validity coefficients have been found for the alcohol scale and drug scale of the ASI when compared to other instruments screening for alcohol or drug use (e.g., CAGE, MAST, Clinical Use, Abuse, and Dependence Scale) in a sample of patients admitted to a mental health hospital (Appleby et al., 1997). Evidence of discriminant validity of the ASI has been established in these studies by demonstrating that the ASI subscales do not correlate with constructs not measured by these subscales.

Reliability

Internal consistency. Studies examining the internal consistency of the ASI have been conducted with various populations using the composite scores. Interviewer severity ratings are not used, given that these ratings are based on subjective and clinical judgments of the interviewer as well as the patient. In general, high Cronbach's alpha coefficients have been reported for three of the seven composite scales (e.g., medical status, alcohol use, psychiatric status) of the ASI (Makela, 2004). Initially, McLellan and colleagues (1980) reported an internal reliability estimate of 0.73 with a sample of patients with alcohol and drug use problems. In addition, in a sample of opiate-dependent patients, coefficients ranging between 0.58 for the employment scale and 0.92 for the alcohol scale were found (Hendriks et al., 1989). Medium-sized coefficients have been reported in dual diagnosis populations (Hodgins & El-Guebaly, 1992) and a sample of homeless substance users (Zanis et al., 1994).

Inter-rater reliability. High inter-rater reliabilities were obtained for severity ratings (McLellan et al., 1980). In later studies, some instability of severity ratings in some problem areas, specifically employment, drugs, family/social, and psychiatric areas, has been found (Alterman et al., 1994; Zanis et al., 1994). Because composite scores rely less on subjective judgment than severity ratings, higher inter-rater reliabilities have been reported for these indices.

Test-retest reliability. The original authors of the ASI reported good test-retest reliabilities (McLellan et al., 1985). However, the literature on short-term test-retest reliability varies from excellent to unsatisfactory depending on the sample, with problematic values stemming from mental health patient or homeless populations (Makela, 2004).

Utility Information

To determine the utility of the ASI for clinical decisions, data supporting the sensitivity and specificity of this instrument are required. Sensitivity refers to how well an instrument will identify individuals with a problem, in this case alcohol or drug use problem. Specificity, on the other hand, indicates how well it screens out individuals who do not have a problem. In inpatient samples, a value of 1 or more on the alcohol severity rating had a sensitivity of 93% with respect to current alcohol abuse and a corresponding specificity of 59%, with similar values for drug severity rating when using the Structured Clinical Interview for *DSM-III-R* (Appleby et al., 1997).

Spanish Versions of the ASI

Validity. Psychometric studies examining the criterion validity of the Spanish version of the ASI have been conducted in Spain and Costa Rica (Gonzalez-Saiz, Salvador Carulla, Martinez Delgado, Lopez Cardenas, & Ruz Franzi, 2002; Sandí Esquivel & Avila Corrales, 1990). Higher scores obtained in a sample of drug users in Costa Rica in comparison to a sample of university students were taken as an indication of discriminant validity (Sandí Esquivel & Avila Corrales, 1990). On the other hand, Gonzalez-Saiz (1997) found using an opiate-dependent sample from Spain that the scales of family/social relations, drug use, and employment were statistically related to clinical scores of global client functioning from a structured interview of *DSM-IV* criteria, thus supporting its concurrent validity. More recently, an evaluation of the sixth version of the ASI in Spain found low correlations between ASI-6 subscale scores and the Clinical Global Impression scores (Diaz Mesa et al., 2010).

Reliability. Using the Spanish version used in Spain, Gonzalez-Saiz (1997) found that the ASI's employment scale had the smallest Cronbach's coefficient of 0.55, whereas the alcohol scale had the largest (0.75). Higher internal reliability coefficients have been reported for the last version of the ASI-6, ranging from 0.70 to 0.93, with the lowest coefficients for the family subscale. The alcohol and drug subscales were found to have Cronbach's alpha coefficients of 0.88 and 0.93, respectively (Diaz Mesa et al., 2010).

Other indexes of reliability have also been reported for the Spanish version of the ASI. For example, the inter-rater reliability coefficient of the Spanish ASI examined by Gonzalez-Saiz (1997) was reported to be 0.95 for composite scores and 0.80 for severity ratings. In addition, test-retest reliability coefficient of 0.78 for the composite scores and 0.79 for the severity ratings were reported (González-Saiz, 1997).

Utility. The study conducted in Costa Rica attempted to distinguish between alcoholic and nonalcoholic male patients. It was found that a value of 4 or more on the alcohol severity rating had a sensitivity of 98% and specificity of 100% (Sandí Esquivel & Avila Corrales, 1990).

In general, the Spanish versions of the ASI seem to be valid and reliable. However, because the psychometric studies were conducted in foreign countries, caution should be exercised when used with Hispanic populations in the United States, as they may not possess cultural equivalence. Although the ASI has been translated for use in the United States and a long and "Lite" version is available, to our knowledge, psychometric studies have not been conducted. An exception is a study conducted to examine the psychometric properties of the computer-administered version, which supported the instrument's convergent/discriminant validity, factorial validity, and reliability (Butler, Redondo, Fernandez, & Villapiano, 2009).

Application with Younger Populations

Two similar versions adapted from the adult version of the ASI have been developed: the Teen Addiction Severity Index (T-ASI; Kaminer, Bukstein, & Tarter, 1991) and the Comprehensive Addiction Severity Index for Adolescents (CASI-A; Meyers, McLellan, Jaeger, & Pettinati, 1995). Because a Spanish version of the T-ASI is available, our discussion will focus on the T-ASI's psychometric properties for the English and Spanish versions.

The T-ASI can be used with 12- to 17-year-olds (Kaminer et al., 1991; Kaminer, Wagner, Plummer, & Seifer, 1993). The T-ASI includes 142 items, which assess the severity of addiction in seven domains: substance use, school status, employment status, family function, peer-social relationships, legal status, and psychiatric status. The severity of the problem in each domain is assessed in a 5-point scale. Good concurrent validity of the T-ASI's substance use scale with a clinical interview of substance abuse diagnosis, as well as for the psychiatric scale, and a self-report of internalizing and externalizing problems have been reported for the English version (Kaminer et al., 1993).

A team of researchers in Spain working in collaboration with Dr. Kaminer translated the T-ASI and examined its psychometric properties in a sample of 80 Spanish youths admitted for psychological treatment. The concurrent validity of the T-ASI substance use scale was examined with two external measures of substance use, one objective and one subjective measure, finding correlation coefficients of 0.90 and 0.69, respectively. Appropriate concurrent validity for the school and family scales was also reported. Discriminant validity was examined by comparing the scores on the T-ASI scales for a clinical sample and a nonclinical sample. Except for the psychiatric status scale, all the other scales were found to discriminate between the two samples (Diaz et al., 2008).

Cut Down, Annoyed, Guilty, and Eye-Opener (CAGE)

Often used in clinical settings to detect alcoholism, the CAGE screening tool (Mayfield, McLeod, & Hall, 1974) is a brief questionnaire with four items that refer to the idea of drinking cessation, criticism, feelings of guilt associated with drinking, and drinking behaviors in the morning. The CAGE acronym stands for Cut Down, Annoyed, Guilty, and Eye-Opener. Each component of the acronym corresponds to the information in each question. The CAGE is considered a useful tool for the diagnosis of alcoholism in primary care. Given the ease of administration, it is recommended that the CAGE be used during the first interview to detect alcoholism. Although the open-ended responses associated with the items may suggest the possibility that the answers given are false, validation studies have shown that 90% of alcoholism cases can be correctly identified. The work carried out in different populations concerning the validity of the CAGE demonstrates high sensitivity, but specificity decreases in hospital settings. The CAGE total score ranges from 0 to 4, with scores over 2 indicative of alcoholism. Ewing (1984) considers that the cutoff of scores in the range of 2–3 provides the most favorable outcome in detecting alcoholism. Other works (Rydon, Redman, Sanson-Fisher, & Reid, 1992) found that the results of the CAGE are not conclusive and suggest that the detection of alcoholism by this instrument is questionable. Given these weaknesses, the CAGE has the advantage that it does not require specialized training and is quick to administer.

Validity and Utility of the CAGE with Hispanics

A study evaluating the sensitivity and validity of the English and Spanish version of the CAGE instrument in a large Hispanic sample utilizing both ICD-10 and *DSM-IV* criteria for alcohol abuse and dependence found that the sensitivity of this screening instrument was limited in some respects (Cherpitel, 1998). Specifically, the CAGE was less sensitive in identifying problematic drinking in females than in males, for participants in the low acculturation group, or for nondependent drinkers (Cherpitel, 1998). The CAGE had adequate sensitivity in detecting alcohol dependence (88%) and harmful drinking or abuse (71%) in this Hispanic sample (Cherpitel, 1998). In addition, the specificity was also adequate for alcohol dependence (81%) and harmful drinking or abuse (87%) (Cherpitel, 1998). Among Hispanic males, the CAGE performed optimally at detecting alcohol problems at a standard cutoff of 2, while for women, performance was improved considerably when the cutoff was lowered to 1 (Cherpitel, 1998).

The CAGE screening instrument has also been validated in detecting alcohol use disorders in a cross-sectional study with Hispanic participants from hospital-based primary care practice (Saitz, Lepore, Sullivan, Amaro, & Samet, 1999). The results from this study suggest that while utilizing a cutoff point of 1 or more, the sensitivity and specificity of the CAGE in Hispanics were 92 and 74%, respectively (Saitz et al., 1999). When utilizing cutoff points of 2 or more, the sensitivity and specificity of the CAGE in Hispanics was 80 and 93%, respectively (Saitz et al., 1999). CAGE scores of 0, 2, 3, and 4 were associated with substance abuse or dependence likelihood ratios in Hispanics of 0.1, 4.8, 18.5, and 36.8, respectively (Saitz et al., 1999). Overall, researchers suggest that the CAGE instrument is a valid screening tool for detecting alcohol use disorders in Hispanic populations.

Reliability

An examination of the reliability of the CAGE instrument resulted in a high internal consistency (Cronbach's α=.73) with a 95% confidence interval of .67–.79 and very high test-retest reliability coefficients (Martinez-Delgado, Fernandez-Repeto, & Gonzalez-Saiz, 2002).

Application with Younger Populations

The positive predictive value, negative predictive value, sensitivity, and specificity of the CAGE instrument were evaluated in an ethnically diverse adolescent population (i.e., White, Black, other races) ranging in ages from 12 to 20 years of age. Results from the study demonstrated the greatest levels of sensitivity and specificity for the CAGE instrument at a cutoff point of 1 (Kelly, Donovan, Chung, Cook, & DelBridge, 2004). At a cutoff point of 1, the sensitivity, specificity, positive predictive value, and negative predictive value of the CAGE instrument in adolescents were .66, .58, .52, and .71, respectively (Kelly et al., 2004). The internal consistency for CAGE in this adolescent sample was found to be low (Cronbach α=.56) (Kelly et al., 2004). Overall, researchers cautioned the use of the CAGE instrument in adolescents because it did not perform well in identifying alcohol use problems or disorders in this sample (Kelly et al., 2004). The CAGE was only able to correctly identify two thirds of participants with alcohol use disorders (Kelly et al., 2004).

Alcohol Use Disorders Identification Test (AUDIT)

Alcohol Use Disorders Identification Test (AUDIT) is used as a screening instrument for alcohol-related problems. The AUDIT was developed by the World Health Organization and was first made available in 1989, as a brief assessment tool to screen for excessive drinking in primary medical settings and to identify drinking as the cause of presenting illness. It can also be useful in other settings, including substance abuse treatment agencies and research settings, to identify hazardous and harmful patterns of alcohol consumption. After its development, it has received widespread international use and has been translated into several foreign languages and validated in six countries, including Mexico and the United States (Babor, Higgins-Biddle, Saunders, & Monteiro, 2001).

The AUDIT contains ten questions that may be administered as an interview or as a self-report questionnaire and usually takes 2–4 minutes. The individual answers questions about frequency of alcohol use (questions 1–3), alcohol dependence symptoms (questions 4–6), and alcohol-related problems (questions 7–10) in a scale of 0–4, with anchors that vary by question. Research indicates that a cutoff score of 8 indicates hazardous or harmful alcohol use, especially in medical settings (Babor et al., 2001). The manual suggests that a score of 1 or more on questions 2 or 3 indicates hazardous consumption of alcohol. Scores above 0 on questions 4–6 indicate the presence of alcohol dependence. Endorsing questions 7–10 indicates that alcohol-related harm is already being experienced. In a study of treatment matching for persons who had a wide range of alcohol problem severity, AUDIT scores were compared with diagnostic data reflecting low, medium, and high degrees of alcohol dependence. It was found that AUDIT scores in the range of 8–15 represented a medium level of alcohol problems, whereas scores of 16 and above represented a high level of alcohol problems (Miller, Zweben, DiClemente, & Rychtarik, 1992), which would warrant treatment for an alcohol use disorder.

Validity

The relationship of the AUDIT to other screening tools for alcohol use problems has been examined to demonstrate its concurrent validity. Bohn, Babor, and Kranzler (1995) found a strong correlation between the AUDIT and the MAST (r=.88) for both males and females and correlations of .47 and .46 for males and females, respectively, on a covert content alcoholism screening test. A high correlation coefficient (.78) was also found between the AUDIT and the CAGE in ambulatory care patients (Hays, Merz, & Nicholas, 1995). AUDIT scores were found to correlate well with measures of drinking consequences, attitudes toward drinking, vulnerability to alcohol dependence, negative mood states after drinking, and reasons for drinking (Bohn et al., 1995).

Reliability

Internal consistency. A review of studies examining the psychometric properties of the AUDIT identified at least ten independent studies examining the instrument's internal consistency. In general, the mean value of Cronbach's alpha coefficient reported in these studies was .80, suggesting high internal consistency (de Meneses-Gaya, Zuardi, Loureiro, & Crippa, 2009).

Test-retest reliability. One study examined one-month interval between administrations and found a test-retest coefficient of .84 for the total scores. However, when examining each item separately, item 9, referring to someone being injured as a result of the individual's drinking, was found to have the lowest correlation between administrations (r=.29) (Selin, 2003). Another study examining a 30-day interval also reported adequate test-retest reliability, with item 9 having the lowest correlation (Dybek et al., 2006).

Inter-rater reliability. No studies were identified examining the AUDIT's inter-rater reliability when it is administered as an interview (de Meneses-Gaya et al., 2009).

Spanish Versions of the AUDIT

The AUDIT is available and readily used in Spain. A Spanish version and a Catalan version of the AUDIT were compared in an early study and were found to be comparable. However, the cutoffs suggested by the authors varied from the recommended cutoff. Specifically, a cutoff of 9 to detect drinkers at risk and of 10 to identify alcohol dependence was recommended for men, whereas the cutoff for females was suggested to be 10 or 11 for alcohol dependence and no identifiable cutoff for female drinkers at risk was found (Contel Guillamón, Gual Solé, & Colom Farran, 1999). More recently, the sensitivity of the AUDIT was further examined in a sample of female patients. It was found that a cutoff of 6 provides the highest sensitivity and specificity values for women. The internal consistency of the AUDIT in this sample was found to be 0.93 (Cronbach's alpha) (Perula-de-Torres et al., 2005). In another study also conducted in Spain by Gomez and colleagues (2005) in a primary health care clinic, the cutoff for men was found to be 8, which is consistent with the recommended cutoff. These researchers also examined the validity of shorter versions of the AUDIT. Using the first three questions of the AUDIT, referred to in the literature as AUDIT-C, sensitivity of .98 and specificity of .91 were reported, with a cutoff score of 3 (Gomez, Conde, Santana, & Jorrin, 2005).

Application with Younger Populations

Although the AUDIT was originally developed for use with adult populations, its utility with adolescent populations has been evaluated in two studies. One study comparing the ability of the AUDIT to identify adolescents with alcohol problems versus two other screening instruments found that a score of 9 yielded sensitivity of .76 and specificity of .79 and was better than the other two instruments at identifying alcohol-related problems (Cook, Chung, Kelly, & Clark, 2005). On the other hand, a study conducted by Knight and colleagues (2003) with a sample of 14- to 18-year-olds found the AUDIT to be insensitive at the recommended cutoff of 8. Authors recommended a cutoff of 2 for identifying problematic use and of 3 or more for misuse and dependence. These findings were attributed to developmental factors and the lower prevalence of alcohol use in this age group. To our knowledge, a Spanish version of the AUDIT for use with youth is not available.

Michigan Alcoholism Screening Test (MAST)

The Michigan Alcoholism Screening Test (MAST) (Selzer, 1971) is a highly used instrument developed in order to identify alcohol problems. The MAST consists of 25 items rated as true/false and can be administered as a self-report or structured interview. When used as a structured interview, the MAST takes approximately 15–20 minutes to administer. The MAST includes questions related to alcohol use and the negative consequences associated with it. The MAST also assesses functioning in the domains of family, occupational, physical, and legal problems, as well as a sense of loss of control and experience with previous treatments. The MAST total score ranges from 0 to 53, with scores over 5 indicative of alcoholism as the traditional cutoff (Iraugi, Gonzalez Saiz, & Gisbert, 2002). This instrument is criticized for the lack of sensitivity and specificity of the traditional cutoff.

Validity

The validity of the MAST was examined by comparing its profile to that of the SASSI-3 (described later in this chapter) in terms of participant demographic variables and social desirability variables (Laux, Newman, & Brown, 2004). Results from this study found that MAST and SASSI-3 scores agreed in their classification rates (e.g., nondependent, dependent) in a sample of 94 participants from a community mental health and addiction treatment center. These findings did not differ in terms of demographic variables. Results from the study also pointed out that as participants' level of defensiveness increased, their MAST scores decreased, indicating that defensiveness accounted for approximately

23.6% of the total variance in MAST scores (Laux et al., 2004). As a result, researchers and clinicians should be sensitive and aware of the presence of patient defensiveness and denial when utilizing the MAST instrument. The researchers also report that there was no influence of item endorsement frequency on the internal consistency of MAST scores (Laux et al., 2004).

Reliability

Internal consistency. A meta-analytic study by Shields, Howell, Potter, and Weiss (2007) examined the reliability of the MAST based on weighed reliability and internal consistency estimates. The meta-analysis, which examined 62 studies, resulted in an internal consistency reliability estimate for the MAST between .78 and .84 (Shields et al., 2007). Results also indicated that there was no substantial difference in reliability estimates between the MAST and Short MAST (SMAST, a shorter version of the MAST, comprised of 13 items) (Shields et al., 2007). Shields et al. also report that the MAST produced equally reliable scores across samples with average ages ranging from 19.6 to 40.6 years. This means that reliability estimates are not likely to suffer due to the age of the sample if it falls within this adult age range.

Neither sample ethnicity (e.g., Caucasian, Black, and Hispanic) nor language of administration (e.g., English, Spanish) had any significant association with the variation in the MAST reliability coefficients (Shields et al., 2007). Results of the meta-analysis indicated a statistically significant relationship between sample sex and reliability, which suggests that males tend to generate more reliable scores than females when utilizing the MAST instrument (Shields et al., 2007). The MAST instrument produced adequately reliable scores for samples drawn from clinical populations, but not for nonclinical samples, which suggests that this instrument may not be ideally suited for use in nonclinical populations (Shields et al., 2007).

Utility

The clinical utility of the MAST instrument has been examined in a variety of populations. One study investigated the utility of the MAST instrument in identifying alcohol problems by comparing a high-risk sample (i.e., relatives of alcoholics) and a community sample without a history of alcoholism (Crowe, Kramer, Hesselbrock, Manos, & Bucholz, 1997). Results from the Semi-Structured Assessment for the Genetics of Alcoholism (SSAGA) and the MAST were compared on their positive predictive validity, sensitivity, specificity, and percentage of the sample that screened positive. Researchers found that the MAST is an effective instrument to screen for significant alcohol problems in both community and high-risk patients (Crowe et al., 1997). As the base rate of alcoholism in the population being screened increases, the positive predictive value of the MAST instrument also increases (Crowe et al., 1997). Results from this study suggest that the predictive utility of the MAST is more pronounced in males than in females. Overall, the authors conclude that the MAST instrument can detect most cases of alcoholism with acceptable specificity in patient populations at a high risk for alcoholism and caution clinicians about using this screening instrument in patient populations with a base-rate representative of the general population (Crowe et al., 1997).

Validity and Utility of the MAST with Hispanics

The sensitivity and specificity of the English and Spanish version of the MAST were evaluated in a sample of emergency department Hispanic patients in the United States. The results of this study suggest that the sensitivity of the MAST in accurately detecting alcohol dependence or harmful drinking and abuse was lower than other screening instruments examined in this population (Cherpitel, 1998). Specifically, the sensitivity of the MAST for alcohol dependence and harmful drinking or abuse was 71 and 51%, respectively (Cherpitel, 1998). On the other hand, the specificity of the MAST was found to be adequate in accurately identifying participants who did not have an alcohol problem (Cherpitel, 1998). The specificity for alcohol dependence and harmful drinking and abuse was found to be 94 and 98%, respectively (Cherpitel, 1998). Overall, researchers noted that the MAST did not work as well as other screening instruments evaluated in Hispanics for identifying individuals who met criteria for a current alcohol disorder (Cherpitel, 1998).

The psychometric evaluation of the MAST in Spain with a sample of 137 male alcohol users attending community treatment indicated that this instrument possesses good internal consistency (i.e., KR-20 coefficient of .81). A factor analysis of the MAST performed in this sample yielded three factors, the first related to recognition of alcohol abuse or dependence, the second factor describing social problems related to alcohol consumption, and the third factor related to clinical problems. Each subscale had adequate internal consistency (ranging from .76 to .67) (Ballesteros & Ariño, 1995).

Application with Younger Populations

The MAST instrument was modified in order to make it more appropriate for use with young persons. The modification involved making item-content changes consistent with the life experiences of adolescents. A study with an ethnically diverse sample (e.g., Caucasian, Hispanic, Native American) by Snow, Thurber, and Hodson (2002) revealed that the adolescent version of the MAST did not demonstrate homogeneity of items congruent with that of the adult version (inter-item correlation coefficient = .12). However, it did have adequate internal consistency with Cronbach's alpha reliability coefficient of 0.73. Although the authors of this study agree that it is worthwhile to reliably differentiate adolescents in need of further assessment for substance abuse, they caution clinicians from relying heavily on information gathered from this instrument because of the need for improvements in psychometric properties (Snow et al., 2002).

Drug Abuse Screening Test (DAST)

The Drug Abuse Screening Test (DAST; Skinner, 1982) was developed in order to provide a brief instrument for the clinical detection of problems related to drug use and the evaluation of treatment. It consists of 20 items and provides a quantitative index of the extent of consequences related to drug use. The DAST can be administered in two formats (self-report or interview) and requires approximately 5 minutes to complete it. The original DAST contained 28 items and was constructed following the model of the Michigan Alcoholism Screening Test (MAST). A shorter version of the DAST was derived at a later date, composed of 20 items that best discriminated and mediated the same original construct. Each of the questions in the DAST contains two options to choose from in a yes/no answer format. The DAST total score ranges from 0 to 20 and places the individual on a continuum that represents the degree of problems with drugs (Iraugi et al., 2002).

Validity

The DAST has moderate to high levels of validity, sensitivity, and specificity (Yudko, Lozhkina, & Fouts, 2007). Yudko and colleagues (2007) reviewed all the studies that addressed the reliability and validity of the DAST between the years of 1982 and 2005 and found that the DAST is a highly face-valid instrument. The instrument appears to measure what it purports to assess, problematic drug use. Although good face validity is generally associated with feasibility of use in certain populations, researchers warn that this might not be the case when assessing socially undesirable traits, such as drug use.

Criterion validity. The DAST has been found to have adequate criterion validity, as it positively correlated with other instruments that measure the same construct (Yudko et al., 2007). The DAST total score was highly correlated with the frequency of drug use, number of drugs used, and number of drug-related treatments (Yudko et al., 2007).

Construct and discriminative validity. The DAST instrument was found to have satisfactory construct and discriminative validity, both in terms of specificity and sensitivity. Specifically, the sensitivity of the DAST instrument varied according to the group being studied. Therefore, researchers suggest that in order for clinicians to obtain maximum sensitivity, a lower cutoff score should be utilized when screening for drug abusers, and a higher cutoff score is recommended when screening for nondrug abusers (Yudko et al., 2007). Unfortunately, DAST cutoffs for specific populations have not yet been developed.

Reliability

The DAST items have high internal consistency, and most of the variance associated with the instrument has been accounted for by a single factor (Yudko et al., 2007).

Test-retest reliability. Results from test-retest reliability analyses also suggest that the DAST yields relatively stable results over time (Yudko et al., 2007). Although these findings support the usefulness of the DAST in terms of validity and reliability, further validation work is needed in other populations and settings.

Spanish Version

The psychometric properties of the Spanish version of the DAST (DAST-20) and brief DAST (DAST-10) have been evaluated in several studies conducted in Spain. One such study examined these properties in 259 adult participants (121 drug users, 138 healthy controls) using the *DSM-IV TR* criteria (Perez-Galvez, Garcia-Fernandez, de Vicente Manzanaro, Oliveras-Valenzuela, & Lahoz-Lafuente, 2010). Both versions of the Spanish DAST were found to have high internal reliability. Results of an exploratory factor analysis extracted five factors in the original DAST (accounting for 74.12% of the variance) and two factors in the brief DAST version (accounting for 62.18% of the variance) (Pérez Gálvez et al., 2010). In addition, cutoffs of ≥ 5 for the DAST-20 and ≥ 3 for the DAST-10 were found to have high agreement with *DSM-IV TR* diagnosis in the Spanish population (Pérez Gálvez et al., 2010). Utilizing the cutoff for the original DAST-20 classified correctly 98.07% of the cases, while utilizing the cutoff for the brief DAST-10 classified correctly 95.36% of the cases (Pérez Gálvez et al., 2010). Another study conducted with Hispanic in the United States also found the Spanish version of the DAST-10 to be reliable and differentiated among drug abusers and nonsubstance abusers (Bedregal, Sobell, Sobell, & Simco, 2006). However, this latter study found an unidimensional factor structure for the DAST-10 (Bedregal et al., 2006), which is different from the factor structure found in the Spanish sample. In general, based on the available studies, it appears that the Spanish versions of the DAST-20 and the DAST-10 can be considered valid and reliable instruments for drug abuse detection in Hispanic adult populations.

Application with Younger Populations

A modified version of the DAST for adolescents (DAST-A) was psychometrically evaluated in a group of adolescent inpatients and demonstrated high test-retest reliability, an unidimensional factor structure, good internal consistency, and good concurrent validity (Martino, Grilo, & Fehon, 2000). While utilizing the *DSM-IV* classification system, DAST-A scores greater than 6 yielded specificity of 84.5%, sensitivity of 78.6%, and positive predictive validity (82.3%) in differentiating adolescent inpatient clients with and without drug-related disorders (Martino et al., 2000).

Substance Abuse Subtle Screening Inventory (SASSI)

The Substance Abuse Subtle Screening Inventory (SASSI) is a brief self-report psychological screening instrument that helps identify individuals who have a high probability of having a substance abuse or dependence disorder (Miller, 1985/1999). The SASSI includes both face-valid and subtle items that have no apparent relationship to substance abuse to identify individuals who are unwilling or unable to acknowledge substance abuse symptoms (Miller, 1985/1999). The SASSI is available in an adult version (SASSI-3) that contains 67 true/false subtle items, 12 items directly related to alcohol use, and 14 items directly related to drug use with four response choices (e.g., never, once or twice, several times, repeatedly). The SASSI takes about 10–15 minutes to administer and is available in pencil-paper, computer self-administered, or web-based administration versions. Although the SASSI does not yield an overall score, various subscales aimed at identifying individuals in treatment for alcohol and/or drug dependence, individuals with substance misuse, individuals with high levels of defensiveness, family systems that are affected by substance use, correctional factors, and random answering patterns are derived (Miller, 1985/1999). Each subscale contains descriptors for low and high T-scores.

Validity

In a meta-analytic review of 36 peer-reviewed empirical studies by Feldstein and Miller (2006), the validity of the SASSI was examined. It was found that the SASSI classifications converged with those from other direct screening instruments and were also correlated with general distress, ethnicity, and social deviance (Feldstein & Miller, 2006).

Reliability

In a study with a sample of 254 college students (Clements, 2002), the SASSI-3 was found to have high internal consistency for the face-valid subscales. However, the author concluded that the usefulness of the scales using the subtle items of the SASSI-3 was questionable (Clements, 2002).

Utility

The study conducted by Clements (2002) indicated a low degree of clinical utility for the subtle items of the SASSI for detecting alcohol dependence. In addition, results of the meta-analytic review suggested that the sensitivity of the SASSI instrument was similar to screening instruments used in the public domain, but that the specificity of the instrument yielded a high rate of false positives (Feldstein &

Miller, 2006). These authors concluded that clinicians need to be cautious while utilizing the SASSI due to high specificity coefficients, which have suggested an overclassification bias when used with ethnic minorities.

Spanish Version

The SASSI-3 has been developed and validated in Spanish for use with Hispanic populations. In a study by Lazowski, Boye, Miller, and Miller (2002), a Spanish version of the SASSI was created and administered to 1,744 respondents from multiple treatment programs throughout the United States, who were classified as either having or not having a substance use disorder. Findings indicated a high overall internal consistency for the Spanish version. Test-retest reliability was examined after approximately a 1-month interval between administrations and yielded the same result in 86% of participants (Lazowski et al., 2002). Cutoff scores for the Spanish version of the SASSI were also analyzed for stability, and the percentage of consistent decision rule results ranged between 82 and 100% (Lazowski et al., 2002). Validity analyses resulted in a 76.7% correspondence rate with clinical diagnoses. The cutoff scores accurately identified 83% of respondents diagnosed with substance dependence, 62% of respondents diagnosed with substance abuse, and 61% of respondents who were not classified as having a substance use disorder (Lazowski et al., 2002). This study also evaluated the accuracy of the SASSI as a function of demographic variables (e.g., age, education level, marital status, occupational status) and found a significant association only between occupational status and the accuracy of SASSI test classifications (Lazowski et al., 2002). Participants who identified as having full- or part-time employment were accurately classified by the SASSI instrument 83% of the time, while participants who identified as unemployed were accurately classified 100% of the time (Lazowski et al., 2002). The authors conclude that the Spanish SASSI is a moderately adequate instrument that is likely to be useful in clinical contexts for screening purposes. Given the differences among Spanish-speaking cultures, researchers caution that these results may not generalize to all Hispanic populations. Due to the small sample of women and individuals under the age of 18 in the study, it is difficult to ascertain the degree to which the obtained results from the Spanish SASSI will generalize to women and adolescents (Lazowski et al., 2002).

Application with Younger Populations

The adolescent version (SASSI-A2) contains 100 items in which the individual rates subtle items on a true/false scale and other direct items about alcohol or drug use on a Likert scale. The SASSI adolescent version has been identified as having reasonable convergent validity and moderate utility for identifying substance dependence among youth offenders, aged 10–17, in a juvenile detention center (Sweet & Suales, 2003). However, the clinical utility examined in this study was only relevant to the face-valid items on the instrument (Sweet & Suales, 2003). The authors conclude that the adolescent version of the SASSI needs to be used with caution by clinicians because of issues with poor construct validity within the subtle scales of the instrument (Sweet & Suales, 2003).

Summary and Recommendations

This chapter summarized the most widely used instruments for assessment of substance abuse disorders and related problems for use with Hispanic populations. It provided some general cultural considerations that should be taken into account when working with this ethnic minority group. It also described in great detail the available psychometric data for the corresponding instruments for both English and Spanish versions.

Compared to a decade ago, the field of substance use has made great strides in improving assessment instruments, evaluating their psychometric properties, and providing parallel versions in Spanish for use with Hispanic populations. The latter effort has been mostly achieved by foreign collaborators and researchers interested in this clinical and research area. However, future efforts are needed in the United States to continue the work that has been pioneered by our foreign colleagues to examine the validity, reliability, and utility of substance use instruments with Hispanic samples of the population. Of particular interest would be to examine how Hispanic subgroups in the United States compare to each other, as most of the available literature compares Hispanics, as a homogeneous group, to other ethnic minority and majority groups. Because the experiences of each Hispanic subgroup are unique in terms of their socioeconomic status, immigration and acculturation experiences, and cultural views about alcohol and drug use, it is important to determine whether the available instruments are sensitive enough to capture these differences and make appropriate diagnosis or classifications.

Until more research is available, we recommend that the available instruments be evaluated for potential use in clinical and research settings with Hispanic populations. Particularly for Spanish-language instruments, one strategy that has been used with success in clinical research with Hispanic substance users is submitting the instrument for review by bilingual individuals from the same populations where the instrument will be ultimately used. These consultants then provide local variations for terms or words included in the items of the test that may be incorporated into the final revised instrument (Suarez-Morales et al., 2007). The data collected using the revised instrument may then be used to compare the responses between the US sample and other Spanish-speaking populations with whom the instrument has been used. Finally, preliminary psychometric data for the instrument with a US sample may be provided.

References

Alegria, M., Canino, G., Shrout, P. E., Woo, M., Duan, N., Vila, D., et al. (2008). Prevalence of mental illness in immigrant and non-immigrant U.S. Latino groups. *American Journal of Psychiatry, 165*, 359–369. doi:10.1176/appi.ajp.2007.07040704.

Alterman, A. I., Brown, L. S., Zaballero, A., & McKay, J. R. (1994). Interviewer severity ratings and composite scores of the ASI: A further look. *Drug and Alcohol Dependence, 34*(3), 201–209. doi:10.1016/0376-8716(94)90157-0.

Annis, H. M., Sobell, L. C., Ayala-Velazquez, H., Rybakowski, J. K., Sandahl, C., Saunders, B., et al. (1996). Drinking-related assessment instruments: Cross-cultural studies. *Substance Use & Misuse, 31*, 1525–1546. doi:10.3109/10826089609063990.

Appleby, L., Dyson, V., Altman, E., & Luchins, D. J. (1997). Assessing substance use in multiproblem patients: Reliability and validity of the Addiction Severity Index in a mental hospital population. *The Journal of Nervous and Mental Disease, 185*, 159–165.

Aquilino, W. S. (1994). Interview mode effects in surveys of drug and alcohol use: A field experiment. *Public Opinion Quarterly, 54*, 71–91. doi:10.1086/269419.

Arroyo, J. A., Miller, W. R., & Tonigan, J. S. (2003). The influence of Hispanic ethnicity on long-term outcome in three alcohol-treatment modalities. *Journal of Studies on Alcohol, 64*, 98–104.

Babor, T. F., Higgins-Biddle, J. C., Saunders, J. B., & Monteiro, M. G. (2001). *The Alcohol Use Disorders Identification Test: Guidelines for use in primary care* (2nd ed.). Geneva, Switzerland: World Health Organization, Department of Mental Health and Substance Dependence.

Ballesteros, J., & Ariño, J. (1995). Utilidad del Michigan Alcoholism Screening Test (MAST) en la evaluación del alcoholismo. In F. Rodriguez Pulido & A. Sierra Lopez (Eds.), *La investigación epidemiológica de drogodepencias*. Las Palmas,Spain: ICEPSS.

Bedregal, L. E., Sobell, L. C., Sobell, M. B., & Simco, E. (2006). Psychometric characteristics of a Spanish version of the DAST-10 and the RAGS. *Addictive Behaviors, 31*, 309–319. doi:10.1016/j.addbeh.2005.05.012.

Berry, J. W. (1997). Immigration, acculturation, and adaptation. *Applied Psychology: An International Review, 46*(1), 5–68. doi:10.1111/j.1464-0597.1997.tb01087.x.

Bohn, M. J., Babor, T. F., & Kranzler, H. R. (1995). The Alcohol Use Disorders Identification Test (AUDIT): Validation of a screening instrument for use in medical settings. *Journal of Studies on Alcohol, 56*, 423–432.

Butler, S. F., Redondo, J. P., Fernandez, K. C., & Villapiano, A. (2009). Validation of the Spanish Addiction Severity Index Multimedia Version (S-ASI-MV). *Drug and Alcohol Dependence, 99*, 18–27. doi:10.1016/j.drugalcdep.2008.06.012.

Cherpitel, C. J. (1998). Gender, injury status and acculturation differences in performance of screening instruments for alcohol problems among US Hispanic emergency department patients. *Drug and Alcohol Dependence, 53*, 147–157. doi:10.1016/S0376-8716(98)00122-7.

Clements, R. (2002). Psychometric properties of the Substance Abuse Subtle Screening Inventory-3. *Journal of Substance Abuse Treatment, 23*, 419–423. doi:10.1016/S0740-5472(02)00279-9.

Contel Guillamón, M., Gual Solé, A., & Colom Farran, J. (1999). Test para la identificación de transtornos por uso de alcohol (AUDIT): Traducción y validación del AUDIT al catalán y castellano. *Adicciones, 11*(4), 337–347.

Cook, R. L., Chung, T., Kelly, T. M., & Clark, D. B. (2005). Alcohol screening in young persons attending a sexually transmitted disease clinic: Comparison of AUDIT, CRAFFT, and CAGE instruments. *Journal of General Internal Medicine, 20*, 96–97.

Crowe, R. R., Kramer, J. R., Hesselbrock, V., Manos, G., & Bucholz, K. K. (1997). The utility of the Brief MAST and the CAGE in identifying alcohol problems. *Archives of Family Medicine, 6*, 477–483. doi:10.1001/archfami.6.5.477.

de Meneses-Gaya, C., Zuardi, A. W., Loureiro, S. R., & Crippa, A. S. (2009). Alcohol Use Disorders Identification Test (AUDIT): An updated systematic review of psychometric properties. *Psychology & Neuroscience, 2*(1), 83–97. doi:10.3922/j.psns.2009.1.12.

Diaz, R., Castro-Fornieles, J., Serrano, L., Gonzalez, L., Calvo, R., Goti, J., et al. (2008). Clinical and research utility of Spanish Teen-Addiction Severity Index (T-ASI). *Addictive Behaviors, 33*, 188–195. doi:10.1016/j.addbeh.2007.06.002.

Diaz Mesa, E. M., Garcia-Portilla, P., Saiz, P. A., Bobes Bascaran, T., Casares, M. J., Fonseca, E., et al. (2010). Rendimiento psicométrico de la sexta versión del Addiction Severity Index en español (ASI-6). *Psicothema, 22*(3), 513–519.

Dybek, I., Bischof, G., Grothues, J., Reinhardt, S., Meyer, C., Hapke, U., et al. (2006). The reliability and validity of the Alcohol Use Disorders Identification Test (AUDIT) in a German general practice population sample. *Journal of Studies on Alcohol, 67*, 473–481.

Ewing, J. A. (1984). Detecting alcoholism: The CAGE questionnaire. *Journal of the American Medical Association, 252*, 1905–1907. doi:10.1001/jama.252.14.1905.

Feldstein, S. W., & Miller, W. R. (2006). Does subtle screening for substance abuse work? A review of the Substance Abuse Subtle Screening Inventory (SASSI). *Addiction, 102*, 41–50. doi:10.1111/j.1360-0443.2006.01634.x.

Flaherty, J. A. (1987). Appropriate and inappropriate research methodologies for Hispanic mental health. In M. Gaviria (Ed.), *Health and behavior: Research agenda for Hispanics* (pp. 177–186). Chicago: University of Illinois Press.

Freeman, R. C., Lewis, Y. P., & Colon, H. M. (2002). Instrumentation, data collection, and analysis issues. In R. C. Freeman, Y. P. Lewis, & H. M. Colon (Eds.), *Handbook for conducting drug abuse research with Hispanic populations* (pp. 167–188). Westport, CT: Praeger.

Gomez, A., Conde, A., Santana, J. M., & Jorrin, A. (2005). Diagnostic usefulness of brief versions of Alcohol Use Disorders Identification Test (AUDIT) for detecting hazardous drinkers in primary care settings. *Journal of Alcohol Studies, 66*, 305–308.

González-Saiz, F. (1997). Estandarización de un instrumento de evaluación multidimensional en los trastornos adictivos. (Tesis doctoral). Universidad de Cádiz, Spain. In J. Iraurgi Castillo & F. Gonzalez-Saiz (Eds.), *Instrumentos de Evaluacion en Drogodependencia* (pp. 255–261). Madrid, Spain: Aula Médica.

Gonzalez-Saiz, F., Salvador Carulla, L., Martinez Delgado, J. M., Lopez Cardenas, A., & Ruz Franzi, I. (2002). Estudio de fiabilidad y validez de la versión española de la entrevista clinica Addiction Severity Index (ASI). In J. Iraurgi Castillo & F. Gonzalez-Saiz (Eds.), *Instrumentos de Evaluacion en Drogodependencia* (pp. 271–307). Madrid, Spain: Aula Médica.

Hays, R. D., Merz, J. F., & Nicholas, R. (1995). Response burden, reliability, and validity of the CAGE, Short MAST, and AUDIT alcohol screening measures. *Behavioral Research Methods, Instruments & Computers, 27*, 277–280. doi:10.3758/BF03204745.

Hendriks, V. M., Kaplan, C. D., van Limbeek, J., & Geerlings, P. (1989). The Addiction Severity Index: Reliability and validity in a Dutch addict population. *Journal of Substance Abuse Treatment, 6*, 133–141.

Hodgins, V. M., & El-Guebaly, N. (1992). More data on the Addiction Severity Index: Reliability and validity with the mentally ill substance abuser. *The Journal of Nervous and Mental Disease, 180*, 197–201.

Iraugi, I., Gonzalez Saiz, F., & Gisbert, J. (2002). Instumentos de evaluación utilizados en la investigación clínica de las toxicomanías: Una guía de los instrumentos adaptados al castellano. In I. Castillo & F. Gonzalez-Saiz (Eds.), *Instrumentos de evaluación en drogodependencias* (pp. 79–120). Madrid, Spain: Aula Médica.

Kaminer, Y., Bukstein, O., & Tarter, R. E. (1991). The Teen-Addiction Severity Index: Rationale and reliability. *The International Journal of the Addictions, 26*(2), 219–226. doi:10.3109/10826089109053184.

Kaminer, Y., Wagner, E., Plummer, B., & Seifer, R. (1993). Validation of the Teen Addiction Severity Index (T-ASI): Preliminary findings. *The American Journal on Addictions, 2*(3), 250–254. doi:10.3109/10550499309113946.

Kelly, T. M., Donovan, J. E., Chung, T., Cook, R. L., & Delbridge, T. R. (2004). Alcohol use disorders among emergency department-treated older adolescents: A new brief screen (RUFT-Cut) using the AUDIT, CAGE, CRAFFT, and RAPS-QF. *Alcoholism, Clinical and Experimental Research, 28*(5), 746–753. doi:10.1097/01.ALC.0000125346.37075.85.

Knight, J. R., Sherritt, L., Harris, S. K., Gates, E. C., & Chang, G. (2003). Validity of brief alcohol screening tests among adolescents: A comparison of the AUDIT, POSIT, CAGE, and CRAFFT. *Alcoholism, Clinical and Experimental Research, 27*, 67–73.

Kosten, T. R., Rounsaville, B. J., & Kleber, H. D. (1983). Concurrent validity of the Addiction Severity Index. *Journal of Nervous and Mental Disorders, 171*, 606–610.

Laux, J. M., Newman, I., & Brown, R. (2004). The Michigan Alcoholism Screening Test (MAST): A statistical validation analysis. *Measurement and Evaluation in Counseling and Development, 36*, 209–225.

Lazowski, L. E., Boye, M. W., Miller, G. A., & Miller, F. G. (2002). *The development and validation of the Spanish SASSI*. Springville, IN: The SASSI Institute.

Makela, K. (2004). Studies of the reliability and validity of the Addiction Severity Index. *Addiction, 99*, 398–410. doi:10.1111/j.1360-0443.2004.00665.x.

Marin, G., & Marin, B. V. (1991). *Research with Hispanic populations*. Newbury Park, CA: Sage.

Martinez Delgado, J. M., Fernandez Repeto, M., & Gonzalez Saiz, F. (2002). Instumentos e indicadores para el cribado (screening) de problemas relacionados con el consumo de sustancias. In I. Castillo & F. Gonzalez-Saiz (Eds.), *Instrumentos de evaluación en drogodependencias* (pp. 79–120). Madrid, Spain: Aula Médica.

Martino, S., Grilo, C. M., & Fehon, D. C. (2000). Development of the Drug Abuse Screening Test for Adolescents (DAST-A). *Addictive Behaviors, 25*(1), 57–70. doi:10.1016/S0306-4603(99)00030-1.

Mayfield, R. L., McLeod, G., & Hall, P. (1974). The CAGE questionnaire: Validation of a new alcoholism screening instrument. *The American Journal of Psychiatry, 131*(10), 1121–1123.

McLellan, A. T., Luborsky, L., Cacciola, J., Griffith, J., Evans, F., Barr, H. L., et al. (1985). New data from the Addiction Severity Index reliability and validity in three centers. *The Journal of Nervous and Mental Disease, 173*(7), 412–423. doi:10.1097/00005053-198507000-00005.

McLellan, A. T., Luborsky, L., Woody, G. E., & O'Brien, C. P. (1980). An improved diagnostic evaluation instrument for substance abuse patients: The Addiction Severity Index. *The Journal of Nervous and Mental Disease, 168*(1), 26–33. doi:10.1097/00005053-198001000-00006.

Meyers, K., McLellan, A. T., Jaeger, J. L., & Pettinati, H. M. (1995). The development of the Comprehensive Addiction Severity Index for Adolescents (CASI-A). *Journal of Substance Abuse Treatment, 12*(3), 181–193. doi:10.1016/0740-5472(95)00009-T.

Miller, G. A. (1999). *The Substance Abuse Subtle Screening Inventory (SASSI) manual, Second Edition*. Springville, IN: The SASSI Institute. (Original work published 1985).

Miller, W. R., Zweben, A., DiClemente, C. C., & Rychtarik, R. G. (1992). *Motivational enhancement therapy manual: A clinical research guide for therapists treating individuals with alcohol abuse and dependence* (Project MATCH monograph series, Vol. 2). Rockville, MD: NIAAA.

Ortega, A. N., Rosenheck, R., Alegria, M., & Desai, R. A. (2000). Acculturation and the lifetime risk of psychiatric and substance use disorders among Hispanics. *The Journal of Nervous and Mental Disease, 188*, 728–735. doi:10.1097/00005053-200011000-00002.

Pérez Gálvez, B., García Fernández, L., de Vicente Manzanaro, M., Oliveras Valenzuela, M., & Lahoz Lafuente, M. (2010). Validación española del Drug Abuse Screening Test (DAST-20 y DAST-10). *Salud y Drogas, 10*(1), 35–50.

Perula-de-Torres, L. A., Fernandez-Garcia, J. A., Arias-Vega, R., Muriel-Palomino, M., Marquez-Rebollo, E., & Ruiz-Moral, R. (2005). Validity of AUDIT test for detection of disorders related with alcohol consumption in women. *Medicina Clínica (Barcelona), 125*, 727–730.

Robins, L. N., Wing, J., Wittchen, H. U., Helzer, J. E., Babor, T. F., Burke, J., et al. (1988). The Composite International Diagnostic Interview: An epidemiologic instrument suitable for use in conjunction with different diagnostic systems and in different cultures. *Archives of General Psychiatry, 45*, 1069–1077. doi:10.1001/archpsyc.1988.01800360017003.

Rogers, S. M., Miller, H. G., & Turner, C. F. (1998). Effects of interview mode on bias in survey measurements of drug use: Do respondent characteristics make a difference? *Substance Use & Misuse, 33*, 2179–2200. doi:10.3109/10826089809069820.

Rydon, P. H., Redman, S., Sanson-Fisher, R. W., & Reid, A. L. (1992). Detection of alcohol related problems in general practice. *Journal of Studies on Alcohol, 5*(3), 197–201.

Saitz, R., Lepore, M. F., Sullivan, L. M., Amaro, H., & Samet, J. H. (1999). Alcohol abuse and dependence in Latinos living in the United States. *Archives of Internal Medicine, 159*, 718–724. doi:10.1001/archinte.159.7.718.

Sandí Esquivel, L. E., & Avila Corrales, K. (1990). Validity of the Addiction Severity Index (adapted version) in a Costa Rican population group. *Bulletin of the Pan American Health Organization, 24*(1), 70–76.

Selin, K. H. (2003). Test-retest reliability of the Alcohol Use Disorder Identification Test in a general population sample. *Alcoholism, Clinical and Experimental Research, 27*, 1428–1435.

Selzer, M. L. (1971). The Michigan Alcoholism Screening Test: The quest for a new diagnostic instrument. *The American Journal of Psychiatry, 127*, 1653–1658.

Shields, A. L., Howell, R. T., Potter, J. S., & Weiss, R. D. (2007). The Michigan Alcoholism Screening Test and its shortened form: A meta-analytic inquiry into score reliability. *Substance Use & Misuse, 42*, 1783–1800.

Skinner, H. A. (1982). The drug abuse screening test. *Addictive Behaviors, 7*(4), 839–845. doi:10.1016/0306-4603(82)90005-3.

Snow, M., Thurber, S., & Hodson, J. M. (2002). An adolescent version of the Michigan Alcoholism Screening Test. *Adolescence, 37*(148), 835–840.

Suarez-Morales, L., Matthews, J., Martino, S., Ball, S., Rosa, C., Farentinos, C., et al. (2007). Issues in designing and implementing a Spanish-language multisite clinical trial. *The American Journal on Addictions, 16*(3), 206–215.

Substance Abuse and Mental Health Services Administration. National Survey on Drug Use and Health, 2003 and 2004. Office of Applied Studies. (2005). Available at: www.oas.samhsa.gov/nsduh. Accessed 10 Nov 2011.

Substance Abuse and Mental Health Services Administration. National Survey on Drug Use and Health, 2006 and 2007. Office of Applied Studies. (2007). Available at: www.oas.samhsa.gov/nsduh. Accessed 10 Nov 2011.

Sue, S., Fujino, D., Hu, L., Takeuchi, D., & Zane, N. (1991). Community mental health services for ethnic minority groups: A test of the cultural responsiveness hypothesis. *Journal of Consulting and Clinical Psychology, 59*, 533–540. doi:10.1037//0022-006X.59.4.533.

Sullivan, M., & Lasso, B. (1992). Community mental health services for Hispanics: A test of the cultural compatibility hypothesis. *Hispanic Journal of Behavioral Sciences, 14*, 455–468.

Sweet, R. I., & Suales, K. K. (2003). Validity of the Substance Abuse Subtle Screening Inventory-Adolescent version (SASSI-a). *Journal of Substance Abuse Treatment, 24*, 331–340. doi:10.1016/S0740-5472(03)00049-7.

U.S. Census Bureau. Language Use. (2000). Available at: http://www.census.gov/population/www/socdemo/lang_use.html. Accessed 6 Nov 2011.

Vega, W. A., Alderete, E., Kolody, B., & Aguilar-Gaxiola, S. (1998). Illicit drug use among Mexicans and Mexican Americans in California: The effects of gender and acculturation. *Addiction, 93*, 1839–1850. doi:10.1046/j.1360-0443.1998.931218399.x.

Wells, K., Klap, R., Koike, A., & Sherbourne, C. (2001). Ethnic disparities in unmet need for alcoholism, drug abuse, and mental health care. *The American Journal of Psychiatry, 158*, 2027–2032. doi:10.1176/appi.ajp. 158.12.2027.

Yudko, E., Lozhkina, O., & Fouts, A. (2007). A comprehensive review of the psychometric properties of the Drug Abuse Screening Test. *Journal of Substance Abuse Treatment, 32*, 189–198.

Zanis, D. A., McLellan, A. T., Cnaan, R. A., & Randall, M. (1994). Reliability and validity of the Addiction Severity Index with homeless sample. *Journal of Substance Abuse Treatment, 11*(6), 541–548. doi:10.1016/0740-5472(94)90005-1.

Assessing Sexual Dysfunction in Hispanic Clients

13

Marta Meana, Taylor L. Oliver, and Sarah C. Jones

Introduction

Over 40 years ago, Masters and Johnson (1966) introduced their highly influential sexual response model. Focused primarily on physiological processes, the model described the sexual response as consisting of four distinct stages: excitement, plateau, orgasm, and resolution. Kaplan (1974) later added sexual desire as the motivational state that preceded excitement. These models formed the basis for the classification and description of sexual dysfunctions in the various editions of the American Psychiatric Association's *Diagnostic and Statistical Manual of Mental Disorders* (DSM). Since the introduction of these early models, research has increasingly pointed to a more complex sexual response and to multiple factors that can contribute to the development/maintenance of sexual problems. Consequently, a systemic and multidisciplinary approach to the assessment and treatment of sexual dysfunction has been argued to constitute best practice (Binik & Meana, 2009; Weeks & Cross, 2004). Within this approach, culture is no longer considered a backdrop to sexual function, but rather a potentially important influence in its construction and in the ways that sexual satisfaction is facilitated or hindered. Some have argued that cultural factors may even be primary determinants of sexual well-being, especially in groups that are disempowered (Tiefer, 1991). Unfortunately, research lags well behind theories that assert the centrality of culture in the sexual functioning of men and women.

Within an American context, the paucity of the said research is striking. Hispanics are no exception, despite the fact that they number over 50 million, representing one in every six Americans (U.S. Census Bureau, 2011). As Lewis (2004) has pointed out, it is telling that there is no shortage of studies on high-risk sexual behaviors in ethnic minorities, but precious little attention on sexual function. Wiederman, Maynard, and Fretz (1996) reviewed over 1,000 papers published in two major sexuality journals between 1971 and 1995 and found that ethnicity was reported in only 26% of them. The number of non-European-American participants in these and the majority of recent studies also tend to be too small to generalize to the population. In addition, ethnic groups are broadly defined, often collapsing cultures with significantly different values and histories into a single category (e.g., Asian or Hispanic). Finally, the tendency is to compare the sexual function of ethnic minorities to that of

M. Meana, Ph.D. (✉) • T.L. Oliver, M.A. • S.C. Jones, B.A.
Department of Psychology, University of Nevada, 4505 Maryland Parkway, Las Vegas, NV 89154, USA
e-mail: marta.meana@unlv.edu; tayloroliver4@gmail.com; sarahcjones94@gmail.com

L.T. Benuto (ed.), *Guide to Psychological Assessment with Hispanics*,
DOI 10.1007/978-1-4614-4412-1_13,

European-Americans without reference to the possibility that the assessment methods themselves may be more valid for one group than for another. Between-group differences are consequently hard to interpret as they may actually reflect variation in the way cultural groups respond to instruments. Validation of sexual function measures on Hispanic-Americans is practically nonexistent, although an increasing number are being translated into Spanish. Translation, however, is not validation.

Regardless of the slow pace of research on the sexual function of ethnic minorities, clinicians cannot wait for the empirical validation and standardization of instruments before attending to their clients. In an attempt to promote the assessment and treatment of sexual difficulties in individuals of Hispanic descent, this chapter will propose the best available options. To that end, we will first present an overview of the sexual dysfunctions (and likely revisions in the next edition of the DSM), followed by the little data available on their prevalence in Hispanic-Americans. We will then describe the best measures available for the assessment of sexual dysfunction in men and women and conclude with a review of cultural issues that should inform assessment and compensate, if only partially, for the lack of Hispanic norms.

The Sexual Dysfunctions

There are nine sexual dysfunctions listed in the DSM-IV-TR (American Psychiatric Association, 2000). Three are applicable to both men and women: hypoactive sexual desire disorder (HSDD), sexual aversion disorder (SAD), and dyspareunia; three are specific to women: female sexual arousal disorder (FSAD), female orgasmic disorder (FOD), and vaginismus; and three are specific to men: erectile disorder (ED), male orgasmic disorder (MOD), and premature ejaculation (PE). In order for sexual difficulties to rise to the level of DSM-defined dysfunction, symptoms must cause marked distress or interpersonal difficulty. Each dysfunction is also accompanied by three specifiers relating to onset (lifelong/acquired), situationality (generalized/situational), and etiology (due to psychological factors or a combination of physical and psychological factors). All but the sexual pain disorders (dyspareunia and vaginismus) map onto the desire, arousal, and orgasm phases of the Masters and Johnson/Kaplan model of the sexual response. A brief description of each sexual dysfunction, with prevalence estimates, follows. It is important to keep in mind that comorbidity is high among the sexual dysfunctions, especially for women. When one dimension of sexual function becomes problematic, there is often a domino effect.

Disorders of Desire

There are two dysfunctions that correspond to the desire phase of the sexual response: HSDD and SAD. HSDD is defined as the absence or deficiency of sexual fantasies and desire for sexual activity. It is the most common presenting problem in therapy for sexual problems and is considerably more prevalent in women than in men (Meana, 2010). Low desire accompanied by distress has been estimated at 10–26% of women across studies (Brotto, 2010a). While low desire estimates that include the distress criterion are not available for men, speculation from studies that did not include the distress criterion is that the prevalence of HSDD in men might range from 1 to 20% (Brotto, 2010b). Reports of low desire regardless of distress generally result in a doubling of prevalence estimates. This indicates that there are many individuals with low desire who do not consider it a problem. SAD is diagnosed in individuals who experience extreme aversion to sexual activity and who are consequently highly avoidant of sexual contact with partners. Sometimes hidden under the presentation of low desire, SAD has a significant phobic/anxiety component that differentiates it from HSDD. Prevalence is unknown but it is generally believed to be more common in women than in men (Meana, Binik, & Thaler, 2008).

Disorders of Arousal

Dysfunctions mapping onto the arousal phase are FSAD and ED. FSAD is diagnosed when a woman complains of persistent/recurrent inability to attain/maintain an adequate lubrication-swelling response during sexual activity. It is uncommon for premenopausal, healthy women to present with FSAD alone. Difficulty with arousal tends to co-occur with desire difficulties, in which case the HSDD generally takes precedence in most clinical presentations. Prevalence estimates are thus unreliable and highly dependent on the age of the sample (the range in the literature is 2.6–33%) (Graham, 2010a). ED, the male equivalent, refers to the persistent/recurrent partial or complete inability to attain or maintain an erection sufficient for penetration. This disorder appears to be highly age and health dependent, with prevalence estimates also varying significantly as a function of whether the distress criterion is applied (Segraves, 2010a). Prevalence estimates have ranged from 5% in men under 60, to 17% in 40-year-olds, to 34% at age 70 (Meana et al., 2008).

Disorders of Orgasm

Orgasm phase disorders include FOD, MOD, and PE. Female orgasmic disorder (FOD) is described as a persistent delay in, or absence of, orgasm following a normal excitement phase, given competent stimulation (left to clinician judgment). A recent review found a prevalence of 10–34% for complete inability to achieve orgasm (with or/and without a partner) and 11–30% for difficulty reaching orgasm (Graham, 2010b). Male orgasmic disorder (MOD) is diagnosed when men present with delayed, absent, incomplete, or anhedonic ejaculation. Age and health variables appear to be as central as in ED, and the prevalence range is low, only occasionally rising above 3% (Rowland et al., 2010). The DSM-IV-TR defines PE as persistent/recurrent ejaculation with minimal stimulation before, on, or shortly after penetration and before the man wishes it would happen. Because of difficulties in operationalizing what constitutes rapid or early ejaculation, there are no reliable estimates of its prevalence. Depending on the criteria used, the range has varied from 1 to 3% in some studies and up to 30% in others (Rowland et al.).

Disorders of Pain During Sex

The sexual pain disorders stand outside of the sexual response model as they are not directly related to any particular phase. They do, however, often negatively affect all of them. Although men can also experience pain with penetration, dyspareunia is primarily a female sexual dysfunction. It is defined as the experience of recurrent or persistent genital pain associated with penetrative sex, and its prevalence in women has been estimated to be anywhere from 12 to 21% (Landry & Bergeron, 2009). Vaginismus is described as a spasm in the outer third of the vagina that interferes dramatically with sexual intercourse (usually making penetration impossible). Although it can be difficult to distinguish dyspareunia from vaginismus, the latter appears to have phobic anxiety and avoidance components that exceed the more moderate trepidation of women with dyspareunia (Binik, 2010a). Vaginismus is also less common than dyspareunia, with population-based estimates at 1% or less (Fugl-Meyer & Fugl-Meyer, 1999).

Proposed Changes in the DSM-5

The explosion of sexual dysfunction research in the last two decades has resulted in serious reconsiderations of the description and classification of sexual problems. Significant changes are being proposed for the fifth edition of the DSM. It is beyond the scope of this chapter to detail the currently proposed changes. However, it is important to summarize them as they reflect research findings and future directions.

In terms of women, the movement is toward the consolidation of dysfunctions and the integration of multiple specifiers that more accurately reflect the diversity of factors that can influence female sexual function. Because of the rarity of SAD and the difficulty teasing apart HSDD from FSAD, a new category of sexual interest/arousal disorder is being proposed. This new category would collapse HSDD, SAD, and FSAD (Brotto, 2010a; Graham, 2010a). It would also include an expanded set of specifiers that would more comprehensively cover the multiple biopsychosocial and relational influences on women's sexual function. There is also a proposal to collapse dyspareunia and vaginismus into a new diagnostic category currently termed genito-pelvic pain/penetration disorder (Binik, 2010a, 2010b). Driving this initiative is (1) the lack of empirical validation for a categorical distinction between dyspareunia and vaginismus and (2) research that supports a conceptualization of dyspareunia as a pain disorder rather than as a psychosexual disturbance. In summary, the DSM-5 could be halving the number of female sexual dysfunctions from the current six (HSDD, SAD, FSAD, FOD, dyspareunia, vaginismus) to three (sexual interest/arousal disorder, FOD, genito-pelvic pain/penetration disorder).

Proposals for changes in the male sexual dysfunctions also include more nuanced descriptions of dysfunctions and a longer list of specifiers. However, the male sexual dysfunctions are likely to remain the same in number, if not name. In addition to hypoactive sexual desire disorder in men, delayed ejaculation disorder (DED) is being proposed as an alternative to MOD, and early ejaculation disorder (EED) is being proposed as an alternative to PE (Segraves, 2010a, 2010b, 2010c). Another change being considered is the elimination of the "marked distress" criterion from some dysfunctions (ED) and its demotion to "discomfort or worry" for others (DED and EED).

Sexual Difficulties in Hispanic-Americans

There is scarce data on the sexual function of Hispanic-Americans. Although the ethnic composition of participants is now reported in most manuscripts, the number of Hispanics in clinical studies generally remains too small to analyze and interpret. A handful of large epidemiologically sound studies on nonclinical populations do, however, give us a comparative glimpse into their sexual complaints, if not technically their sexual dysfunction.

The current limited data indicates that Hispanic-Americans report levels of sexual difficulty similar to those of Euro-Americans. Until further data is collected, the aforementioned general prevalence figures for the sexual dysfunctions should be considered our best prevalence estimates within a Hispanic-American population. In fact, in the National Health and Social Life Survey (NHSLS), with its national probability sample of 1,749 women and 1,410 men aged 18–59, Hispanic-Americans were the group least likely to report sexual problems (Laumann, Paik, & Rosen, 1999). Similarly, in Cain et al.'s (2003) study of 3,262 midlife women, Hispanic-Americans reported the lowest levels of sexual complaints. In a younger sample of both Latinas and Spanish women, prevalence rates did not differ between the two groups and the overall proportion of women with sexual complaints (41%) was similar to that of women in the NHSLS study (43%) (Hullfish et al., 2009). In regard to men, Kupelian, Link, Rosen, and McKinlay's (2008) report of the Boston Area Community Health Survey found that socioeconomic status rather than race/ethnicity contributed to the variance in erectile dysfunction in a stratified random sample of 2,301 men aged 30–79.

In contrast, the California Men's Health Study involving 78,445 men aged 45–69 found the prevalence of moderate to severe erectile dysfunction to be higher in Hispanic-Americans than in Euro-Americans (Smith et al., 2009). One small study ($N=102$) of Hispanic women in an inner-city menopause clinic found elevated rates of sexual dysfunction in comparison to Euro-Americans (Schnatz, Whitehurst, & O'Sullivan, 2010). This latter result may be more informative about socioeconomic status than ethnicity. Large epidemiological studies tend to control for socioeconomic variables when reporting ethnicity comparisons because low socioeconomic status and related stress is consistently found to be a predictor of sexual difficulties (Kupelian et al., 2008; Laumann et al., 1999). From a clinical standpoint, socioeconomic stress needs to be adequately assessed in Hispanic and all other populations seeking treatment for sexual concerns.

While most studies to date have found no difference in sexual function between Hispanics and Euro-Americans, it is hard to know how ethnic groups respond to and react to survey questions and measures standardized on Euro-Americans. Perhaps Hispanics have comparable levels of sexual function, but it is also possible that they are more reticent to report sexual problems for cultural reasons. Aside from prevalence estimates, there are some interesting sexuality-related group differences likely to be relevant to assessment and treatment. For example, Cain et al. (2003) found that Hispanic women were the least likely to report that they engaged in sex for pleasure, as well as the most likely to report that the desire to conceive was the primary motivator for their sexual behavior. Compared with other ethnic groups, the Hispanic women in that study were also very likely to report engaging in sexual relations in order to please a partner. In Hispanic men, there is some evidence suggesting that depression may be more strongly linked to erectile dysfunction than it is in Euro-American men (DeFronzo Dobkin, Leiblum, Rosen, Menza, & Marin, 2006). In any case, the assessment and treatment of sexual dysfunction in Hispanic men and women are important as Hispanics evidence the same high prevalence rates that we find in the general population. Until research catches up on the validation of measures with Hispanic populations, we are limited to existing assessment methods, a selection of which will be presented in the next section. Administered with an eye toward cultural factors, these interviews, instruments, and questionnaires are still likely to provide clinicians with helpful information.

Assessment Tools

The Clinical Interview

Regardless of the presenting sexual complaint, the clinical interview remains the mainstay of the clinician's assessment toolbox. It is also likely to be the method most likely to reveal cultural influences on sexual function. Unlike in the case of other Axis I disorders, there is no validated, standardized interview for sexual dysfunctions. A number of authors, however, have proposed guidelines here summarized (Pukall, Meana, & Fernandez, 2010).

The interview typically starts with the client's open-ended characterization of the sexual difficulty. This characterization is likely to be rich in culturally relevant information. The clinician can at this point ask more operationally specific questions about the problem, the conditions under which it occurs, and the biopsychosociocultural dimensions that might be implicated. Knowledge about the client's culture will be helpful in guiding the clinician to gather pertinent information in ways that are sensitive to sociocultural sexual attitudes.

Biological factors important to consider are age, general health status (e.g., body mass index), lifestyle factors (e.g., exercise, diet), hormone levels, chronic pain syndromes (e.g., provoked vestibulodynia, chronic prostatitis), conditions affecting the vascular and nervous systems, and pelvic or perineum trauma. Potentially iatrogenic surgeries that may interfere with the musculature and innervation of the genital area, as well as its cosmetic appearance, are also important to rule out. Medications such as antidepressants, antipsychotics, and antihypertensives often have a negative impact on sexual function and should be inquired about. Assessment of some of these factors may require a medical referral.

In terms of individual cognitive-affective factors, depression and anxiety are often comorbid with sexual dysfunction. Substance abuse disorders can also complicate treatment and cannot be ignored or glossed over. Misinformation, lack of knowledge about physiology and the sexual response, unrealistic expectations, emotional dysregulation, and maladaptive cognitive sets have all been implicated in sexual function and satisfaction. Some of these cognitive-affective factors may arise from past sexual trauma, negative experiences, and/or learned sexual scripts. Sexual scripts tend to be highly culturally determined.

It is also central to assess the quality of the individual's current relationship. Even when sexual difficulties do not arise from relationship conflict, sexual dysfunction can severely impact even the happiest of couples. Discrepancies in sexual desire and preferences, anger, distrust, and ineffective communication are some of the important relational issues to assess. Ideally, both partners should be interviewed together and/or separately to gather as much information as possible. Partner sexual dysfunction is common and should be investigated. Finally, the assessment of family of origin factors, as well as ethnocultural and religious attitudes and beliefs, are important as they can be implicated in the development and maintenance of sexual difficulties. Beliefs need to be respected to successfully treat the individual or the couple.

Self-Report Measures of Global Sexual Function (and Relationship)

Table 13.1 provides a select listing and psychometric evaluation of empirically validated, clinically useful self-report measures of sexual function, with an indication of which are available in Spanish. A number of them also address relational factors. Although in isolation none of these instruments are sufficient to determine a diagnosis, they can be helpful in diagnostic assessment and case conceptualization. A description of the measures follows.

Measures Applicable to Both Men and Women

The *Dyadic Adjustment Scale* (DAS: Spanier, 1976) is the most widely used instrument for the assessment of relationship quality. It consists of 32 items in a variety of response formats. These are summed to yield a total score ranging from 0 to 151, with higher scores indicating better dyadic adjustment. The items also break down into four subscales which can be used independently: dyadic consensus (13 items), dyadic satisfaction (10 items), dyadic cohesion (5 items), and affective expression (4 items). It is easy to administer (10–15 min) and provides information about the marital context within which the sexual dysfunction exists.

The *Changes in Sexual Functioning Questionnaire* (CSFQ, CSFQ-14: Clayton, McGarvey, & Clavet, 1997) can be clinician-administered as a structured interview (CSFQ-I) or self-administered as a gender-specific questionnaire (CSFQ-F or CSFQ-M). It measures five dimensions of sexual functioning (frequency of sexual activity, desire, pleasure, arousal, orgasmic capacity), as well as comorbid conditions, medications, alcohol and substance use, and relationship status. The first 21 items of the questionnaire apply to both men and women and are followed by 36 male-specific and 35 female-specific items, answered primarily on 5-point Likert-type scales. Recently abbreviated into a short form, the CSFQ-14 is self-administered.

The *Derogatis Interview for Sexual Functioning* (DISF/DISF-R; Derogatis, 1997) is a 26-item interview assessing global sexual functioning and five domains: sexual cognition/fantasy, sexual arousal, sexual behavior/experience, orgasm, and sexual drive/relationship. There is a distinct self-administered version (DISF-R) also consisting of 26 items. Items are responded to on 9- and 5-point adjectival scales, and both formats take 15–20 min to complete.

Table 13.1 Ratings of sexual function measures with adequate clinical utility

Instrument	Norms	Internal consistency	Test-retest reliability	Content validity	Construct validity	Validity generalization	Spanish version
Global sexual function							
Applicable to men and women							
DAS	G	G	A	G	G	G	X
DISF	L	A	A	A	A	A	X
CSFQ/ CSFQ-14	G	A	A	G	G	A	X
GRISS	G	A	A	A	G	G	
ISS	G	E	A	A	A	A	X
SII	A	G	A	A	A	A	X
Applicable to women only							
BISF-W	A	A	A	A	A	A	
FSDS	G	G	A	G	G	A	
FSFI	G	E	A	G	G	G	X
MFSQ	G	A	A	G	G	G	
SFQ	G	G	A	E	G	G	X
SSS-W	G	G	A	G	A	U	
Applicable to men only							
BSFI-M	A	G	A	G	A	A	
IIEF/IIEF-5	G	G	A	G	G	G	X
MSHQ	G	G	A	G	A	U	
Dysfunction-specific							
DSDS	U	NA	U	G	G	U	
PFSF	G	G	A	G	A	G	X
MSIQ	G	G	A	G	A	U	
SDI	A	G	A	G	A	A	
SIDI-F	G	E	U	G	A	U	
SAS	L	G	A	A	U	U	
VPCQ	L	A	A	G	G	U	
(cont'd)							

Note: Some of the psychometric evaluations in this table are from Meana, Binik, and Thaler (2008). As translation of measures is an ongoing effort, clinicians should check to see if the measure in question has been translated since the publication of this chapter. Norms are not specific to Hispanic populations

Abbreviations for instruments in alphabetical order: *BISF-W* Brief Index of Sexual Functioning for Women, *BSFI-M* Brief Sexual Function Inventory-Male, *CSFQ* Changes in Sexual Functioning Questionnaire, *DAS* Dyadic Adjustment Scale, *DSDS* Decreased Sexual Desire Screener, *DISF* Derogatis Interview for Sexual Functioning, *FSDS* Female Sexual Distress Scale, *FSFI* Female Sexual Function Index, *GRISS* Golombok-Rust Inventory of Sexual Satisfaction, *ISS* Index of Sexual Satisfaction, *IIEF/IIEF-5* International Index of Erectile Function, *MFSQ* McCoy Female Sexuality Questionnaire, *MSHQ* Male Sexual Health Questionnaire, *MSIQ* Menopausal Sexual Interest Questionnaire, *PFSF* Profile of Female Sexual Function, *SAS* Sexual Aversion Scale, *SDI* Sexual Desire Inventory, *SFQ* Sexual Function Questionnaire, *SII* Sexual Interaction Inventory, *SIDI-F* Sexual Interest and Desire Inventory-Female, *SSS-W* Sexual Satisfaction Scale for Women, *VPCQ* Vaginal Penetration Cognition Questionnaire

A adequate, *G* good, *E* excellent, *NA* not applicable, *L* less than acceptable, *U* unavailable

The *Golombok-Rust Inventory of Sexual Satisfaction* (GRISS; Rust & Golombok, 1986) is 56-item self-administered measure of sexual function and relationship quality in heterosexual relationships. The GRISS has 28 items each for men and women and yields scores on the following dimensions: for women – orgasmic difficulties, vaginismus, non-sensuality, avoidance, and dissatisfaction; for men – erectile dysfunction, premature ejaculation, non-sensuality, avoidance, and dissatisfaction. There are also two common dimensions that pertain to infrequency and noncommunication. Items are responded to on 5-point adjectival scales, and it takes approximately 10 min to complete.

The *Index of Sexual Satisfaction* (ISS: Hudson, Harrison, & Crossup, 1981) is a self-administered measure of dissatisfaction in the sexual aspects of a couple's relationship from the perspective of the respondent. In the original measure, 25 items were responded to on 5-point adjectival scales describing relative frequency. A newer version has 7-point scales and minor item revisions. The measure takes 5–7 min to complete.

The *Sexual Interaction Inventory* (SII: Lopiccolo & Steger, 1974) is a self-report inventory assessing the heterosexual couple's sexual functioning and satisfaction. The SII requires responses from both partners. At 102 questions, it is a lengthy measure covering 17 behaviors. It is divided into 11 scales: frequency dissatisfaction-male, female; self acceptance-male, female; pleasure-male, female; perceptual accuracy-male of female, female of male; mate acceptance-male of female, female of male; and total disagreement. Some of the 6-point adjectival scale items inquire about frequency and others about pleasure. It takes approximately 30 min to complete.

Measures for Women

The *Brief Index of Sexual Functioning for Women* (BISF-W: Rosen, Taylor, & Leiblum, 1998) consists of 22 items measuring sexual function globally and on seven dimensions: thoughts/desire, arousal, frequency of sexual activity, receptivity/initiation, pleasure/orgasm, relationship satisfaction, and problems affecting sexual function. Items are responded to in a variety of formats, and it takes 15–20 min to administer.

The *Female Sexual Distress Scale* (FSDS: Derogatis, Rosen, Leiblum, Burnett, & Heiman, 2002) assesses sexually related distress in women. It is a 12-item measure with 4-point adjectival scales that takes a handful of minutes to administer.

The *Female Sexual Function Index* (FSFI: Rosen et al., 2000) is the most widely used measure of global sexual function in women. It is a brief, 19-item self-administered measure of female sexual function yielding a total score, as well as scores on five domains: desire, and subjective arousal, lubrication, orgasm, satisfaction, and pain. Items are responded to on 5–6-point adjectival scales and in reference to the past 4 weeks. The FSFI takes approximately 15 min to administer and is scored such that lower scores denote more difficulty.

The *McCoy Female Sexuality Questionnaire* (MFSQ: McCoy & Matyas, 1998) consists of 19 items assessing a woman's general level of sexual interest and response over the past month. Answered on a 7-point adjectival scale, the first 11 questions inquire about general sexual enjoyment, arousal, interest, satisfaction with partner, and feelings of attractiveness; the remaining eight questions relate to intercourse frequency and enjoyment, orgasm frequency and pleasure, lubrication, pain with intercourse, and the impact of partner's potential erectile difficulties. Time to administer is approximately 10 min.

The *Sexual Function Questionnaire* (SFQ: Quirk et al., 2002) is a 34-item self-administered instrument assessing eight dimensions of female sexual function and sexual satisfaction for women; desire, arousal-sensation, arousal-lubrication, subjective arousal, enjoyment, orgasm, pain, and partner relationship. Items are answered in reference to the preceding 4 weeks on 5-point adjectival scales, and it takes 15–20 min to complete.

The *Sexual Satisfaction Scale for Women* (SSS-W; Meston & Trapnell, 2005) measures sexual satisfaction in women along personal and relational dimensions. It consists of 30 items divided into five domains of satisfaction; communication, compatibility, contentment, relational concern, and personal concern. Items are responded to on 5-point scales anchored at "strongly agree" and "strongly disagree" in reference to the respondent's situation at the time of administration.

Measures for Men

The *Brief Sexual Function Inventory-M* (BSFI-M; O'Leary et al., 1995) is a brief 11-item measure of male sexual function covering sexual drive, erection, ejaculation, subjective problem assessment of drive, erection and ejaculation, and overall satisfaction. Responses are given on 5-point adjectival scales in reference to the past month, with higher scores indicating better function.

The *International Index of Erectile Function* (IIEF; Rosen et al., 1997; IIEF-5; Rosen, Cappelleri, Smith, Lipsky, & Pena, 1999) consists of 15 items addressing five domains of sexual function: erectile function, orgasmic function, sexual desire, intercourse, and overall satisfaction. Response options consist of 5- or 6-point adjectival scales, and the time reference is the prior 4 weeks. The IIEF-5 is the shorter version consisting of five items from the IIEF that specifically measure erectile function and intercourse satisfaction. It takes less than 5 min to complete.

The *Male Sexual Health Questionnaire* (MSHQ; Rosen et al., 2004) is a 25-item self-administered measure designed to assess sexual function and satisfaction in older men with urogenital concerns often associated with heart disease, prostate cancer, and benign prostatic hyperplasia/lower urinary tract symptoms. The MSHQ addresses three domains of sexual function: erection, ejaculation, and satisfaction with the sexual relationship.

Dysfunction-Specific Assessment

With the exception of measures assessing sexual desire, there are few dysfunction-specific self-administered measures. On the other hand, physiological assessment methods abound. The latter have the advantage of being more culture-neutral than self-report measures.

Hypoactive Sexual Desire Disorder (HSDD)

The diagnosis of HSDD is usually based on the presenting complaint of distress about sexual desire level, taking into account natural discrepancies between partners. However, self-administered measures can help with the operationalization of severity, as well as with the tracking of treatment-related changes. Global sexual function measures for use with men or women that have desire-specific domains are the CFSQ, DISF, and GRISS. Female-specific global measures that address desire levels are the BISF-W, FSFI, MFSQ, and SFQ. Male-specific measures with desire scales are the BSFI-M and the IIEF. The following are desire-specific measures.

The *Decreased Sexual Desire Screener* (DSDS; Clayton et al., 2009) is a brief female HSDD screener that combines five patient "yes/no" questions with specific instructions for the clinician to verify/investigate answers and apply a diagnostic algorithm. As the title implies, it is intended specifically for the diagnosis of acquired HSDD in women.

The *Profile of Female Sexual Function* (PFSP: Derogatis et al., 2004) is a 37-item self-report instrument specific to the measurement of sexual desire and associated symptoms in naturally and surgically menopausal women with HSDD. It covers seven domains of sexual function; desire, arousal, orgasm, pleasure, sexual concerns, responsiveness, and self-image.

The *Menopausal Sexual Interest Questionnaire* (MSIQ: Rosen, Lobo, Block, Yang, & Zipfel, 2004) is a 10-item scale designed to assess desire, responsiveness, and satisfaction in postmenopausal women. Four questions assessing whether the woman perceives a decline in her level of sexual desire as a consequence of menopause precede the items. Questions are asked in reference to the past week and are responded to on 7-point adjectival scales.

The *Sexual Desire Inventory* (SDI; Spector, Carey, & Steinberg, 1996) is a 14-item self-administered measure of dyadic and solitary desire. Equally applicable to men and women, its focus is primarily on cognitive rather than behavioral dimensions of desire. Each item is responded to according to the intensity of feeling or frequency of occurrence on 7- or 8-point adjectival scales and yields scores for dyadic desire, solitary desire, as well as a total score.

The *Sexual Interest and Desire Inventory* (SIDI-F: Clayton et al., 2006; Sills et al., 2005) is a clinician-administered instrument quantifying the severity of symptoms in premenopausal women diagnosed with HSDD. The 13 items cover the following areas: relationship-sexual, receptivity, initiation, desire-frequency, affection, desire-satisfaction, desire-distress, thoughts-positive, erotica, arousal-frequency, arousal-ease, arousal-continuation, and orgasm.

When the desire problem cannot be linked to psychological, relational, situational, or disease-related factors, hormones may be worth investigating while seriously considering risks. It is important to keep in mind though that no single estrogen or androgen level has been found predictive of low desire in either sex (Davis, Davison, Donath, & Bell, 2005; Schiavi, White, Mandeli, & Levine, 1997).

Sexual Aversion Disorder (SAD)

In terms of self-report measures, clients with SAD will generally show low desire on the desire-specific domains of global sexual function and desire measures. It is unlikely, however, that these will detect the severity of the problem. The only measure specific to SAD is the *Sexual Aversion Scale* (SAS; Katz, Gipson, Kearly, & Kriskovich, 1989). Its 30 items assess fear and phobic avoidance of sexual contact theorized to be associated to trauma, guilt, social inhibitions, and fear of sexually transmitted diseases (STDs).

Female Sexual Arousal Disorder (FSAD)

The CSFQ, BISF-W, and MFSQ all inquire about arousal generally and in terms of lubrication. Arousal questions can also be found in desire-specific measures such as the PFSF and the SIDI-F, but the assessment remains relatively brief. The FSFI and the SFQ are two measures whose coverage of arousal problems is more extensive. Physiological measures of female sexual arousal appear to be limited to research studies. They have centered on changes in vaginal and clitoral blood flow, vaginal temperature, vulvar temperature, vulvar blood flow, and brain activation (Pukall et al., 2010). None have been validated, and they do not appear to be gaining much ground in clinical settings.

Male Erectile Disorder (ED)

Because of the strong link between ED and health, its comprehensive assessment usually requires a thorough clinical interview including medical and psychosexual history, physical examination, and laboratory testing. More specialized diagnostic tests may be required in some cases. Although self-administered measures may be helpful, they are rarely sufficient. Global sexual function measures that inquire about ED are CSFQ, DISF-R, and GRISS. Male-specific measures that explore ED in more detail are the BSFI-M and the IIEF-5. Nocturnal penile tumescence (NPT), penile strain gauges, RigiScan monitor, and Doppler ultrasound are some of the specialized assessments for ED. Intracavernosal injection testing and penile duplex ultrasonography have been found clinically useful in the detection of arterial inflow abnormalities and veno-occlusions (Meana et al., 2008).

Female Orgasmic Disorder (FOD)

There are no widely used, clinically helpful measures specific to FOD. Within a clinical interview, women will typically report never having had an orgasm (or not being sure), difficulty attaining one, or loss of orgasm-related pleasure or intensity. Almost all of the self-administered measures of general and female-specific sexual function covered in this chapter inquire directly about orgasm.

Male Orgasmic Disorder (MOD)

Although most global sexual function measures inquire about orgasm and satisfaction with ejaculatory latency and sensation, the most comprehensive coverage of orgasmic problems in men is provided by the MSHQ which has seven questions devoted to ejaculation, its occurrence, delay, volume, force, pain or discomfort, and pleasure, as well as retrograde ejaculation. Retrograde ejaculation and emission phase disorders will likely have a physiological cause. As in the case of ED, a careful medical history and physician referral are likely to be important.

Premature Ejaculation (PE)

There is no self-administered measure that taps directly into PE in sufficient detail to be helpful in assessment. As aforementioned, the diagnosis of PE is complicated by variations in what is considered an adequate intravaginal ejaculation latency time (IELT). Most clinicians do not use IELT cutoff points to assess for PE. Assessment usually relies more on clinical impression and client distress, although evidence now points to 1 min as the IELT cutoff (McMahon et al., 2008). Metz and Pryor (2000) provide a useful decision tree to consider potential PE etiologic pathways.

Dyspareunia and Vaginismus

The assessment of sexual function and pain is necessary in cases of dyspareunia and/or vaginismus. The BISF-W, CSFQ, FSFI, GRISS, MFSQ, and SFQ all contain questions assessing pain with intercourse. The only measure focused exclusively on problematic vaginal penetration is the *Vaginal Penetration Cognition Questionnaire* (VPCQ; Klaassen & ter Kuile, 2009). The measure taps into maladaptive cognitions about intercourse, including concerns about control, genital incompatibility, and self-image. It is not a diagnostic tool but rather one that explores cognitions in women who have difficulties with penetration. The *McGill Pain Questionnaire* (MPQ; Melzack, 1975), the *Pain Catastrophizing Scale* (PCS; Sullivan, Bishop, & Pivik, 1995), as well as visual analog scales and pain diaries can all be useful in the assessment of pain and pain-related cognition and affect. The diagnosis of dyspareunia and vaginismus generally requires a physical examination that includes cotton-swab palpation of the vulva and a pelvic exam. Assessment of vulvar or pelvic diseases is another important reason for a medical referral. The assessment of pelvic floor tonicity by a physical therapist is now considered best practice (Rosenbaum & Owens, 2008).

Cultural Considerations in the Assessment of Sexual Dysfunction in Hispanic-Americans

Given the state of research and literature on the assessment of sexual difficulties in Hispanic-Americans, clinicians have little choice but to use current instruments and capitalize on the flexibility of the clinical interview. In some cases, reviewing client responses to questionnaires to delve further into underlying meanings can be a helpful strategy to confirm or disconfirm that the measure captured the client's lived reality. Generally, both the clinical interview and the administration and interpretation of instruments can be greatly enhanced by an understanding of the ways in which culture may be impacting on the sexual function of Hispanic-Americans. This involves the clinician self-educating about the client's heritage. With this understanding in hand, the clinician can compensate for the lack of instruments validated with this population. The following are a handful of culturally relevant issues to keep in mind throughout assessment and treatment of Hispanic clients with sexual difficulties. As a comprehensive review of Hispanic cultural values is beyond the scope of this chapter, coverage will center on cultural values and issues with the most obvious connections to sexuality.

Universality or Cultural Relativism?

While some well-meaning clinicians remain insufficiently aware of cultural factors, others may focus on cultural differences where none or few exist. The data we have indicates that Hispanic-Americans may suffer from similar levels of sexual dysfunction as Euro-Americans. We do not know whether this is an artifact of culturally inadequate methodology or whether it is real. It does appear that across much of the world, individuals assert the importance of intimacy and sexual satisfaction (Laumann et al., 2005). In line with this universal value, the World Health Organization (2011) has asserted the primacy of sexual health as "a state of physical, mental and social well-being in relation to sexuality. It requires a positive and respectful approach to sexuality and sexual relationships, as well as the possibility of having pleasurable and safe sexual experiences, free of coercion, discrimination and violence." Sexuality may be conceptualized differently across cultures, but it remains a central aspect of all cultures. Consequently, the assessment of sexual difficulties is as important to Hispanic-American clients as to any other clients. Clinicians should thus not hesitate to assess suspected sexual problems in Hispanic clients. They do, however, need to be informed about the ways in which culture may shape that assessment.

Verguenza (Shame)

Many clients, regardless of ethnicity, find it difficult to approach health professionals about a sexual problem (e.g., Shifren et al., 2009). This may be particularly pronounced in Hispanic groups who uphold religious and cultural values wherein sexuality is considered a particularly sensitive issue. Cultural expectations of modesty for women and of virility for men can complicate assessment as the latter may involve disclosing attitudes and behaviors that counter these values. The "verguenza" may be about having a sexual problem, but it may also be about discussing sexuality in general. Research on Hispanic adolescents has shown that sexuality is rarely discussed within their family of origin, even less than among other ethnic groups (DuRant, Pendergrast, & Seymore, 1990). Clinically, the difficulty may be particularly pronounced if the client and therapist are of the opposite sex. Acknowledging the client's discomfort and normalizing it can go a long way toward building the trust necessary for comprehensive disclosure. It is also important to let clients disclose at their own pace. Most clients are ultimately relieved to be able to discuss their sexual concerns freely, but it may take them a while to realize that it is safe to do so.

Religion and Conservatism

Although strict adherence to religious systems has been linked to sexual conservatism (in Ahrold & Meston, 2010), this may be truer of Euro-Americans than of Hispanic-Americans. In many Hispanic cultures, religion and spirituality may constitute a blend of traditional and indigenous religious attitudes that are in fact more sex-positive than those found in Euro-American Christianity (Musgrave, Allen, & Allen, 2002). Working with clients who have sexual difficulties always requires attention to and respect for their religious beliefs. However, it would be a mistake to assume that because a client is Hispanic-American, they would necessarily espouse particularly conservative sexual values. In fact, in some instances, those very values result in pockets of sexual permissiveness, such as the greater likelihood of extramarital affairs found in Hispanic men. This behavior is generally connected to machismo, which is a complex construction of masculinity that combines both double-standard sexual values (e.g., more sexual freedom for men than for women) with a strong sense of responsibility for the welfare of the family. Letting the client know that you will be asking them questions about attitudes and behaviors that may not be condoned by their belief systems communicates an understanding of their cultural and religious context, while acknowledging that individuals do not always adhere to these. Again, it is crucial that the client's ethnicity not result in assumptions about how they will react. There is simply too much within-group variance to characterize Hispanics monolithically and to make culture-based assumptions without checking in with the client.

Gender Roles

Often touted as the most striking aspect of Hispanic cultures are gender roles. The most broadly drawn gender roles are those of *marianismo* for women and *machismo* for men.

Marianismo is a gender-specific value that applies to women from a number of Hispanic cultures, although it is particularly prominent in Mexican culture. *Marianismo* encourages a woman to emulate the Virgin Mary by being submissive and self-abnegating, prioritizing the welfare of her husband and children above her own needs (Lopez-Baez, 1999). It is not difficult to see how this cultural value might influence sexual function or the willingness to report sexual problems. The model for women is an iconic figure (Virgin Mary) who supposedly conceived without having had sex. Within this context, the very idea that a woman asserts her individual needs, enjoys sex, or complains about it stands well outside the female ideal of self-abnegation and sexual "purity." As aforementioned, Hispanic-American women in one large study were the least likely to report having sex for pleasure and the most likely to have sex for procreation (Cain et al., 2003). On the other hand, being sexually receptive is likely to be considered an important marital and familial obligation. Cain et al. also found that Hispanic women were highly likely to report having sex to please their partners. Not surprisingly, feelings of inadequacy when they have difficulty becoming aroused have been reported by Latinas (Santos-Ortiz & Vazquez, 1989).

Inadequacy is likely to also feature prominently in Hispanic men with sexual dysfunction. This may be related to certain aspects of the masculine cultural ideology known as *machismo*. There is some debate about the positive and negative aspects of *machismo*, but most would agree that it involves both the responsibility to protect and provide for the family, as well as a certain level of domination and sexual assertiveness/aggression (Morales, 1996). This hyper-masculine ideal can place a burden on sexual function, as problems can easily be internalized as weakness or a loss of virility. Research has shown that sexually dysfunctional men are more likely to espouse certain myths about male sexuality (Baker & De Silva, 1988). Some of these include that men should not express certain emotions, that performance is what counts in sex, and that a man always wants and is ready to have sex. These and other myths about male sexuality align closely with machismo. They are thus likely to be espoused by a significant number of Hispanic men. In addition to affecting sexual function by instating unreasonable performance demands, hyper-masculine beliefs are also likely to result in high levels of defensiveness around sexual difficulties. The willingness to seek help for and to fully disclose a sexual problem to a health professional may be particularly challenging for some Hispanic men. As in the case with women, clinicians aware of these values can then directly or indirectly address the culturally specific cognitive-affective schema that may accompany sexual dysfunction.

The Impact of Ethnic Stereotypes

The theme of sexuality runs through the heart of most dominant culture stereotypes of disadvantaged groups. Lewis (2004) powerfully argued that branding the sexuality of minority groups as "dangerous" has been the modus operandi. Threatened by difference and potential loss of power, the dominant culture has traditionally engaged in discourses about the rampant sexuality of minority groups and engaged in multiple, not to mention horrifying, attempts to control it. Out of these discourses, stereotypes emerge that can then be internalized by the group in question and wreak havoc on many quality of life dimensions, including sexual function.

The most common sexuality-related stereotype for Hispanics is that of the "Latin lover." Although Lewis (2004) focuses on the male version of the stereotype, one just needs to scan over current media and television to see that the "hot Latina" has also become common stereotype currency. Although on the surface this seems a sex-positive image, it is just another example of the sexualization of minority groups, with attendant negative repercussions. The most obvious one is that it sets up expectations for sexual performance than can have a negative impact on sexual function and on the dynamics of sexual relationships. The stereotype of immigrants "over-reproducing" is another sexualizing stereotype with direct impact on Hispanic-Americans. The study of sexuality in the context of immigration stress has had no research attention to speak of (Fourcroy, 2006). It is thus important to investigate the extent to which Hispanic clients presenting with sexual problems have internalized damaging stereotypes as there may be sexual and relational consequences to this internalized stigmatization.

Beware of Monolithic Cultural Assumptions

We are increasingly becoming aware that the term "Hispanic" includes multiple cultures with significant between-group differences. Assessing the exact origin of Hispanic clients is thus important. However, there is other within-group diversity with potential impact on sexual scripts and function that may need to be assessed. Acculturation, ethnic identity, rural/urban distinctions, and socioeconomic status are all important components of client histories with empirically supported links to sexuality. Dismissing the variation within a minority group can feel as prejudicial (and sometimes more) as dismissing the fact that a client has a Hispanic heritage. It is also likely to diminish assessment accuracy and treatment efficacy.

Conclusion

The current literature generally indicates that Hispanic-Americans have a similar prevalence of sexual dysfunction to that of Euro-Americans. That prevalence, however, is high. As clinicians, we cannot let the paucity of research specific to the sexual lives of Hispanic-Americans delay the delivery of much needed services for such individuals with sexual problems. A clinical interview conducted with an informed awareness of cultural factors and values likely to impact client disclosure and experience remains our most powerful assessment tool. The addition of self-report measures can augment our assessment capabilities. The interpretation of results, however, needs to remain cautious in light of the general lack of validation of sexual function measures with Hispanic populations. Reviewing self-report questions and answers with the Hispanic client can partly compensate for this lack. Importantly, clinicians also need to self-educate about cultural factors that may impact their client's sexual function and satisfaction. Within a number of Hispanic cultures, some of these factors are likely to include verguenza, religious beliefs, gender roles, and the impact of sexualized and other stereotypes. Keeping these and other cultural pressures in mind will enhance the assessment, the treatment, and the well-being of Hispanic clients experiencing sexual difficulties.

References

Ahrold, T. K., & Meston, C. M. (2010). Ethnic differences in sexual attitudes of U.S. college students: Gender, acculturation, and religiosity factors. *Archives of Sexual Behavior, 39*, 190–202.

American Psychiatric Association. (2000). *Diagnostic and statistical manual of mental disorders* (4th ed., Text revision). Washington DC: Author.

Baker, C. D., & De Silva, P. (1988). The relationship between male sexual dysfunction and belief in Zilbergeld's myths: An empirical investigation. *Sexual and Marital Therapy, 3*, 229–238.

Binik, Y. M. (2010a). The DSM diagnostic criteria for vaginismus. *Archives of Sexual Behavior, 39*, 278–291.

Binik, Y. M. (2010b). The DSM diagnostic criteria for dyspareunia. *Archives of Sexual Behavior, 39*, 292–303.

Binik, Y. M., & Meana, M. (2009). The future of sex therapy: Specialization or marginalization? *Archives of Sexual Behavior, 38*, 1016–1027.

Brotto, L. A. (2010a). The DSM diagnostic criteria for hypoactive sexual desire disorder in women. *Archives of Sexual Behavior, 39*, 221–239.

Brotto, L. A. (2010b). The DSM diagnostic criteria for hypoactive sexual desire disorder in men. *The Journal of Sexual Medicine, 7*, 2015–2030.

Cain, V. S., Johannes, C. B., Avis, N. E., Mohr, B., Schocken, M., Skurnick, J., et al. (2003). Sexual functioning and practices in a multi-ethnic study of midlife women: Baseline results from SWAN. *Journal of Sex Research, 40*, 266–276.

Clayton, A. H., Goldfischer, E. R., Goldstein, I., Derogatis, L., Lewis-D'Agostino, D. J., & Pyke, R. (2009). Validation of the Decreased Sexual Desire Screener (DSDS): A brief diagnostic instrument for generalized acquired female hypoactive sexual desire disorder (HSDD). *The Journal of Sexual Medicine, 6*, 730–738.

Clayton, A. H., McGarvey, E. L., & Clavet, G. J. (1997). The Changes in Sexual Functioning Questionnaire (CSFQ): Development, reliability, and validity. *Psychopharmacology Bulletin, 33*, 731–745.

Clayton, A. H., Segraves, R. T., Leiblum, S., Basson, R., Pyke, R., Cotton, D., et al. (2006). Reliability and validity of the Sexual Interest and Desire Inventory-Female (SIDI-F), a scale designed to measure severity of female hypoactive sexual desire disorder. *Journal of Sex & Marital Therapy, 12*, 115–135.

Davis, S. R., Davison, S. L., Donath, S., & Bell, R. J. (2005). Circulating androgen levels and self-reported sexual function in women. *Journal of the American Medical Association, 294*, 91–96.

DeFronzo Dobkin, R., Leiblum, S. R., Rosen, R. C., Menza, M., & Marin, H. (2006). Depression and sexual functioning in minority women: Current status and future directions. *Journal of Sex & Marital Therapy, 32*, 23–36.

Derogatis, L. R. (1997). The Derogatis Interview for Sexual Functioning (DISF/DISF-SR): An introductory report. *Journal of Sex & Marital Therapy, 23*, 291–304.

Derogatis, L. R., Rosen, R., Leiblum, S., Burnett, A., & Heiman, J. (2002). The Female Sexual Distress Scale (FSDS): Initial validation of a standardized scale for assessment of sexually related personal distress in women. *Journal of Sex & Marital Therapy, 28*, 317–330.

Derogatis, L. R., Rust, J., Golombok, S., Bouchard, C., Nachtigall, L., Rodenberg, C., et al. (2004). Validation of the Profile of Female Sexual Function (PFSF) in surgically and naturally menopausal women. *Journal of Sex & Marital Therapy, 30*, 25–36.

DuRant, R. H., Pendergrast, R., & Seymore, C. (1990). Sexual behavior among Hispanic female adolescents in the United States. *Pediatrics, 85*, 1051–1058.

Fourcroy, J. L. (2006). Customs, culture, and tradition – What role do they play in a woman's sexuality? *The Journal of Sexual Medicine, 3*, 954–959.

Fugl-Meyer, A. R., & Fugl-Meyer, K. S. (1999). Sexual disabilities, problems and satisfaction in 18–74 year old Swedes. *Scandinavian Journal of Sexology, 2*, 79–105.

Graham, C. A. (2010a). The DSM diagnostic criteria for female sexual arousal disorder. *Archives of Sexual Behavior, 39*, 240–255.

Graham, C. A. (2010b). The DSM diagnostic criteria for female orgasmic disorder. *Archives of Sexual Behavior, 39*, 256–270.

Hudson, W. W., Harrison, D. F., & Crossup, P. C. (1981). A short form scale to measure sexual discord in dyadic relationships. *Journal of Sex Research, 17*, 157–174.

Hullfish, K. L., Pastore, L. M., Mormon, A. J. A., Wernecke, Y., Bovbjerg, V. E., & Clayton, A. H. (2009). Sexual functioning of Latino women seeking outpatient gynecologic care. *The Journal of Sexual Medicine, 6*, 61–69.

Kaplan, H. (1974). *The new sex therapy*. New York: Brunner/Mazel.

Katz, R. C., Gipson, M. T., Kearly, A., & Kriskovich, M. (1989). Assessing sexual aversion in college students: The sexual aversion scale. *Journal of Sex & Marital Therapy, 15*, 135–140.

Klaassen, M., & ter Kuile, M. M. (2009). Development and initial validation of the Vaginal Penetration Cognition Questionnaire (VPCQ) in a sample of women with vaginismus and dyspareunia. *The Journal of Sexual Medicine, 6*, 1617–1627.

Kupelian, V., Link, C. L., Rosen, R. C., & McKinlay, J. B. (2008). Socioeconomic status, not race/ethnicity, contributes to variation in the prevalence of erectile dysfunction: Results from the Boston Areas Community Health (BACH) Survey. *The Journal of Sexual Medicine, 5*, 1325–1333.

Landry, T., & Bergeron, S. (2009). How young does vulvo-vaginal pain begin? Prevalence and characteristics of dyspareunia in adolescents. The Journal of Sexual Medicine, 6, 927–935.

Laumann, E. O., Nicolosi, A., Glasser, D. B., Paik, A., Gingell, C., Moreira, E., et al. (2005). Sexual problems among women and men aged 40–80 years: Prevalence and correlates identified by the Global Study of Sexual Attitudes and Behaviors. *International Journal of Impotence Research, 17*, 39–57.

Laumann, E. O., Paik, A., & Rosen, R. C. (1999). Sexual dysfunction in the United States: Prevalence and predictors. *Journal of the American Medical Association, 281*, 537–544.

Lewis, L. J. (2004). Examining sexual health discourses in a racial/ethnic context. *Archives of Sexual Behavior, 33*, 223–234.

Lopez-Baez, S. (1999). Marianismo. In J. S. Mio, J. E. Trimble, P. Arredondo, H. E. Cheatham, & D. Sue (Eds.), *Key words in multicultural interventions: A dictionary* (p. 183). Westport, CT: Greenwood.

LoPiccolo, J., & Steger, J. C. (1974). The Sexual Interaction Inventory: A new instrument for assessment of sexual dysfunction. *Archives of Sexual Behavior, 3*, 585–595.

Masters, J., & Johnson, V. (1966). *Human sexual response*. Boston: Little Brown.

McCoy, N. L., & Matyas, J. R. (1998). McCoy Female Sexuality Questionnaire. In C. M. Davis, W. L. Yarber, R. Bauserman, G. Schreer, & S. L. Davis (Eds.), *Handbook of sexuality related measures* (pp. 249–251). Thousand Oaks, CA: Sage.

McMahon, C. G., Waldinger, M. D., Porst, H., Dean, J., Sharlip, I., Adaikan, P. G., et al. (2008). An evidence-based definition of lifelong premature ejaculation: Report of the International Society for Sexual Medicine (ISSM) Ad Hoc Committee for the Definition of Premature Ejaculation. *The Journal of Sexual Medicine, 5*, 1590–1606.

Meana, M. (2010). Elucidating women's (hetero)sexual desire: Definitional challenges and content expansion. *Journal of Sex Research, 47*, 104–122.

Meana, M., Binik, Y. M., & Thaler, L. (2008). Sexual dysfunction. In J. Hunsley & E. Mash (Eds.), *A guide to assessments that work* (pp. 464–487). New York: Oxford University.

Melzack, R. (1975). The McGill Pain Questionnaire: Major properties and scoring methods. *Pain, 1*, 277–299.

Meston, C. M., & Trapnell, P. (2005). Development and validation of a five-factor sexual satisfaction and distress scale for women: The Sexual Satisfaction Scale for Women. *The Journal of Sexual Medicine, 2*, 66–81.

Metz, M. E., & Pryor, J. L. (2000). Premature ejaculation: A psychophysiological approach for assessment and management. *Journal of Sex & Marital Therapy, 26*, 293–320.

Morales, E. (1996). Gender roles among Latino gay and bisexual men: Implications for family and couple relationships. In J. Laird & R. J. Green (Eds.), *Lesbians and gays in couples and families: A handbook for therapists* (pp. 272–297). San Francisco: Jossey-Bass.

Musgrave, C. F., Allen, C. E., & Allen, G. J. (2002). Spirituality and health for women of color. *American Journal of Public Health, 92*, 557–560.

O'Leary, M. P., Fowler, F. J., Lenderking, W. R., Barber, B., Sagnier, P. P., Guess, H. A., et al. (1995). A brief male sexual function inventory for urology. *Urology, 46*, 697–706.

Pukall, C., Meana, M., & Fernandez, Y. (2010). Sexual dysfunctions and deviations. In D. L. Segal & M. Hersen (Eds.), *Diagnostic interviewing* (4th ed., pp. 283–314). New York: Springer.

Quirk, F. H., Heiman, J. R., Rosen, R. C., Laan, E., Smith, M. D., & Boolell, M. (2002). Development of a sexual function questionnaire for clinical trials of female sexual dysfunction. *Journal of Women's Health & Gender-Based Medicine, 11*, 277–289.

Rosen, R., Brown, C., Heiman, J., Leiblum, S., Meston, C., Shabsigh, R., et al. (2000). The Female Sexual Function Index (FSFI): A multidimensional self-report instrument for the assessment of female sexual function. *Journal of Sex & Marital Therapy, 26*, 191–208.

Rosen, R. C., Cappelleri, J. C., Smith, M. D., Lipsky, J., & Pena, B. M. (1999). Development and evaluation of an abridged, 5-item version of the International Index of Erectile Function (IIEF-5) as a diagnostic tool for erectile dysfunction. *International Journal of Impotence Research, 11*, 319–326.

Rosen, R. C., Catania, J., Pollack, L., Althof, S., O'Leary, M., & Seftel, A. D. (2004). Male Sexual Health Questionnaire (MSHQ): Scale development and psychometric validation. *Urology, 64*, 777–782.

Rosen, R. C., Lobo, R. A., Block, B. A., Yang, H.-M., & Zipfel, L. M. (2004). Menopausal Sexual Interest Questionnaire (MSIQ): A unidimensional scale for the assessment of sexual interest in postmenopausal women. *Journal of Sex & Marital Therapy, 30*, 235–250.

Rosen, R. C., Riley, A., Wagner, G., Osterloh, I. H., Kirkpatrick, J., & Mishra, A. (1997). The International Index of Erectile Function (IIEF): A multidimensional scale for assessment of erectile dysfunction. *Urology, 49*, 822–830.

Rosen, R. C., Taylor, J. E., & Leiblum, S. (1998). Brief Index of Sexual Functioning for Women. In C. M. Davis, W. L. Yarber, R. Bauserman, G. Schreer, & S. L. Davis (Eds.), *Handbook of sexuality-related measures* (pp. 251–255). Thousand Oaks, CA: Sage.

Rosenbaum, T. Y., & Owens, A. (2008). The role of pelvic floor physical therapy in the treatment of pelvic and genital pain-related sexual dysfunction. *The Journal of Sexual Medicine, 5*, 513–523.

Rowland, D., McMahon, C. G., Abdo, C., Chen, J., Jannini, E., Waldinger, M. D., et al. (2010). Disorders of orgasm and ejaculation in men. *The Journal of Sexual Medicine, 7*, 1668–1686.

Rust, J., & Golombok, S. (1986). The GRISS: A psychometric instrument for the assessment of sexual dysfunction. *Archives of Sexual Behavior, 15*, 157–165.

Santos-Ortiz, M., & Vazquez, M. M. (1989). An exploratory study of the expression of female sexuality: The experience of two groups of Puerto Rican women from different social backgrounds. In C. T. Garcia Coll & M. de Lourdes Mattei (Eds.), *The psychosocial development of Puerto Rican women* (pp. 141–165). New York: Praeger.

Schiavi, R. C., White, D., Mandeli, J., & Levine, A. C. (1997). Effect of testosterone administration on sexual behavior and mood in men with erectile dysfunction. *Archives of Sexual Behavior, 26*, 231–241.

Schnatz, P. F., Whitehurst, S. K., & O'Sullivan, D. M. (2010). Sexual dysfunction, depression, and anxiety among patients of an inner-city menopause clinic. *Journal of Women's Health, 19*, 1843–1849.

Segraves, R. T. (2010a). Considerations for diagnostic criteria for erectile dysfunction in DSM-V. *The Journal of Sexual Medicine, 7*, 654–660.

Segraves, R. T. (2010b). Considerations for a better definition of male orgasmic disorder in DSM-V. *The Journal of Sexual Medicine, 7*, 690–695.

Segraves, R. T. (2010c). Considerations for an evidence-based definition of premature ejaculation in the DSM-V. *The Journal of Sexual Medicine, 7*, 672–679.

Shifren, J. L., Johannes, C. B., Monz, B. U., Russo, P. A., Bennett, L., & Rosen, R. (2009). Help-seeking behavior of women with self-reported distressing sexual problems. *Journal of Women's Health, 18*, 461–468.

Sills, T., Wunderlich, G., Pyke, R., Segraves, R. T., Leiblum, S., Clayton, A., et al. (2005). The Sexual Interest and Desire Inventory – Female (SIDI-F): Item response analyses of data from women diagnosed with hypoactive sexual desire disorder. *The Journal of Sexual Medicine, 2*, 801–818.

Smith, J. F., Caan, B. J., Sternfeld, B., Haque, R., Quesenberry, C. P., Quinn, V. P., et al. (2009). Racial disparities in erectile dysfunction among participants in the California Men's Health Study. *The Journal of Sexual Medicine, 6*, 3433–3439.

Spanier, G. B. (1976). Measuring dyadic adjustment: New scales for assessing the quality of marriage and similar dyads. *Journal of Marriage and Family, 38*, 15–28.

Spector, I. P., Carey, M. P., & Steinberg, L. (1996). The Sexual Desire Inventory: Development, factor structure, and evidence of reliability. *Journal of Sex & Marital Therapy, 22*, 175–190.

Sullivan, M. J. L., Bishop, S. R., & Pivik, J. (1995). The Pain Catastrophizing Scale: Development and validation. *Psychological Assessment, 7*, 524–532.

Tiefer, L. (1991). Historical, scientific, clinical, and feminist criticisms of "the human sexual response cycle" model. *Annual Review of Sex Research, 2*, 1–23.

U.S. Census Bureau. (2011). *Statistical abstract of the United States* (130th ed.). Washington, DC: U.S. Census Bureau. http://www.census.gov/statab/www/

Weeks, G. R., & Cross, C. (2004). The intersystem model of psychotherapy: An integrative systems approach. *Guidance and Counseling, 19*, 57–64.

Wiederman, M. W., Maynard, C., & Fretz, A. (1996). Ethnicity in 25 years of published sexuality research: 1971–1995. *Journal of Sex Research, 33*, 339–342.

World Health Organization. (2011). *Sexual health*. Retrieved August 29, 2011, from www.who.int/topics/sexual_health/en/

14 Assessing Eating Pathology in Hispanic Americans

Marisol Perez and Cortney S. Warren

Eating disorders are one of the most common yet damaging psychiatric problems experienced by young women in the United States today, with rates in men on the rise (Ricciardelli, Mccabe, Williams, & Thompson, 2007). Furthermore, eating disorders are pernicious and debilitating disorders characterized by a persistent course, comorbidity with other psychiatric disorders, medical complications, and elevated mortality (Thompson & Stice, 2001). Historically, eating disorders were considered "culture-bound syndromes" occurring in Western societies, among White women from higher socioeconomic status (Bruch, 1973). Since the early 1990s, extensive research has indicated that eating disorders occur in Hispanic Americans (Alegria et al., 2007; Dolan, 1991). A recent epidemiological study on minority mental health constituting a nationally representative sample of Hispanic adults residing in the United States that sampled 2,554 Hispanics (1,127 men, 1,427 women) indicated that lifetime prevalence rates for each eating disorder diagnosis as defined by *Diagnostic and Statistical Manual of Mental Disorders, Text Revision* (DSM-IV-TR; American Psychiatric Association, 2000), were 0.03% for men and 0.12% for women with anorexia nervosa, 1.34% for men and 1.91% for women with bulimia nervosa, and 1.55% for men and 2.31% for women with binge eating disorder (Alegria et al.).

In addition, comparable rates of eating disorder symptoms between Hispanic and Caucasian Americans have been found by numerous researchers. For example, Hispanic adolescent girls and women have endorsed abnormal eating attitudes above clinical cutoffs at levels comparable with Caucasian American girls (Fischer, Pastore, Schneider, Pegler, & Napolitano, 1994; le Grange, Telch, & Agras, 1997; Pumariega, 1986). Hispanic women report weight control behaviors such as vomiting, laxatives, diuretics, and diet pills at similar rates to Caucasian women (Cachelin, Veisel, Barzegarnazari, & Streigel-Moore, 2000; Crago & Shisslak, 2003; Regan & Cachelin, 2006), and some research suggests that binge eating may occur at higher rates among Hispanic American women when compared to other ethnicities (Fitzgibbons et al., 1998; Smith & Krejci, 1991). The same pattern of findings holds true for males as well; Hispanic males report comparable or higher levels of normative and

M. Perez, Ph.D. (✉)
Department of Psychology, Texas A&M University, 230 Psychology Building,
College Station, TX 77843-4235, USA
e-mail: marisol.perez00@gmail.com

C.S. Warren, Ph.D.
Department of Psychology, University of Nevada, 4505 Maryland Parkway,
Box 455030, Las Vegas, NV 89154-5030, USA
e-mail: cortney.warren@unlv.edu

L.T. Benuto (ed.), *Guide to Psychological Assessment with Hispanics*,
DOI 10.1007/978-1-4614-4412-1_14, © Springer Science+Business Media New York 2013

Table 14.1 Summary of assessments reviewed

Assessment	Language	What is assessed	Normative data
Eating Disorder Examination	English/ Spanish	AN, BN, BED, EDNOS, eating concerns, shape concerns, weight concerns, dietary restraint	Yes, Hispanic American adults
Structured Interview for Anorexic and Bulimic Eating Disorders	English/ Spanish	AN, BN, BED, EDNOS, depression, anxiety, general psychopathology, sexuality and social integration, substance abuse, and atypical binges	Yes, Mexican American women only
Body Shape Questionnaire	English/ Spanish	General satisfaction with weight and body shape	Yes for Hispanic American adult men and women
Eating Attitudes Test	English/ Spanish	Dieting, bulimia and food preoccupation, oral control	Yes, Hispanic American girls and Puerto Rican adults
Eating Disorder Examination Questionnaire	English/ Spanish	Derived from eating disorder examination, same subscales as above	Yes, Hispanic American girls and adult women, Spanish adult women
Eating Disorders Inventory	English	Drive for thinness, body dissatisfaction, bulimia, emotional dysregulation, low self-esteem, and other key risk factors	Yes, Hispanic American boys and girls, college women
Sociocultural Attitudes Towards Appearance Questionnaire	English	Information, pressure, internalization-general, internalization-athletic	Yes, Hispanic American men and women

extreme weight control behaviors than their White counterparts (see Ricciardelli et al., 2007 for a review). In addition, some research has found Hispanic males to report more binge eating (Croll, Neumark-Sztainer, Story, & Ireland, 2002; Neumark-Sztainer et al., 2002) and comparable levels of body dissatisfaction compared to Caucasian Americans (Warren, 2008).

Given these data, it is essential for researchers and clinicians to consider multicultural factors in the assessment, conceptualization, and treatment of eating pathology in Hispanic Americans. To make accurate assessments, researchers must evaluate the conceptual equivalence of constructs, create psychometrically stabile assessment instruments, and evaluate them for cross-cultural equivalence. Simultaneously, clinicians must use sound judgment in selecting appropriate assessment instruments and interpreting the results. Consequently, this chapter aims to (1) review some key cultural considerations relevant to evaluating eating pathology in Hispanic Americans, (2) provide descriptions of existing assessment instruments used to evaluate eating pathology, and (3) discuss current limitations of the assessment literature for Hispanic American clients. The table above provides a summary of the assessments reviewed (Table 14.1).

Cultural Considerations

In addition to evaluating the core diagnostic symptoms of eating pathology, at least three important additional factors should be considered when assessing Hispanic clients for eating disorders: acculturation, acculturative stress, and endorsement of mainstream American values and ideals of appearance as perpetuated by the media. Acculturation is broadly defined as the basic process through which an individual is immersed in a new social environment and, consequently, learns and adopts the behaviors, attitudes, beliefs, or values of a new, dominant culture (Berry, 2003; Paukert, Pettit, Perez, & Walker, 2006). A second, related construct is acculturative stress, defined as the inherent stress associated with adaptation to a new culture (Berry, Kim, Minde, & Mok, 1987). A third, interrelated risk factor for the development of eating disorders for the Hispanic population is exposure and internalization of appearance-based messages depicted in mainstream US media (Miller & Pumariega, 2001). All three of these factors related to the experience of American culture have been found to relate to eating pathology in association studies (Ayala, Mickens, Galindo, & Elder, 2007; Cachelin et al., 2000; Gordon, Castro, Sitnikov, & Holm-Denoma, 2010; Joiner & Kashubeck, 1996; Perez, Voelz, Pettit, & Joiner, 2002; Pumariega, 1986; Warren, 2008; Warren, Castillo, & Gleaves, 2010; Warren, Frampton, Lask, & Bryant-Waugh, 2005).

The Decision-Making Process

How well we understand eating disorders is influenced by how precisely we can capture and assess the symptoms, risk factors, and psychological correlates of eating disorder pathology. In addition, assessments are used to detect severity, clinically meaningful changes in treatment, treatment goal attainment, and recovery (Anderson, Lavender, & DeYoung, 2010). Thus, assessments provide crucial information that directly impacts the treatment of individuals suffering from eating disorders.

The decision-making process of choosing the right assessment is guided by the need and skill of the clinician or researcher. Structured interview schedules can assist in obtaining diagnoses, severity, general functioning, related psychopathology, and history of eating disorder symptoms. An advantage to interviews is it allows the opportunity for the interviewer to clarify concepts and inquire further on symptoms when there is uncertainty. For this reason, structured interviews are generally thought to be more valid than other assessments. However, structured interviews require clinical skill, knowledge to score, and can be time consuming. Paper-and-pencil questionnaires designed from structured clinical interviews can provide current diagnostic information, severity, and functioning. Although these instruments are quicker and require less clinical skill, they do not provide as rich information as structured interviews. Finally, there are paper-and-pencil questionnaires that can be used to assess eating disorder attitudes, thoughts, and behaviors, along with related psychopathology. Although some of these instruments cannot be used to derive diagnoses, they can highlight individuals at risk for the development of eating disorders.

The following section will discuss the clinical interviews and self-report questionnaires and screeners most frequently used in assessing eating disorders. In addition, the psychometric information available for Hispanics will be discussed. For each measure, validity, reliability, utility, cutoff scores, and Spanish translations of each measure will be discussed. Since eating disorders can occur at young ages as well, a discussion of appropriate age ranges, and if child versions exist, will also be included. Very few studies have established norms for Hispanic Americans for assessments in eating pathology; thus, a thorough literature search on PsycINFO and Medline was conducted looking for studies that reported means and standard deviations specific to Hispanic Americans for the assessments discussed. In addition, individual searches were conducted for the following journals: *Hispanic Journal of Behavioral Sciences*, *Cultural Diversity and Ethnic Minority Psychology*, *International Journal of Eating Disorders*, *Body Image: An International Journal of Research*, and *Eating Behaviors*.

Clinical Interviews

There are two clinical interviews specific to the assessment of eating disorders that have been used for Hispanic samples and translated to Spanish: the Eating Disorder Examination (EDE) and the Structured Interview for Anorexic and Bulimic Disorders (SIAB-EX).

Eating Disorder Examination (EDE)

The EDE is the most frequently used clinical interview for eating disorders among older adolescents and adults. It is a semi-structured interview designed for use by professionals trained in the art of clinical interviewing, knowledgeable in the assessment of eating disorders, and trained on using the EDE (Fairburn, Cooper, & O'Connor, 2008). The EDE takes between 45 min and 1 h and 15 min to complete and can be scored to yield four eating disorder diagnoses: anorexia nervosa, bulimia nervosa, binge eating disorder, and eating disorder NOS. The interview focuses on the past 28 days prior to assessment and inquires on the frequency of key eating disorder behaviors such as meal frequency, overeating, and a variety of weight control behaviors. In addition, there are four subscale scores on eating disorder psychopathology, consisting of eating concern, shape concern, weight concern, and dietary restraint. All items on the EDE are rated on a 7-point Likert scale with higher scores indicating higher pathology. The subscale scores and global scores are averaged. The most recent version of the EDE (16.0D; Fairburn et al.) has made some improvements that are relevant to assessing Hispanic clients. For example, there are now two scores that can be generated from dietary restraint: the original score which reflects dietary restraint for the purposes of influencing weight and shape and a new score which reflects dietary restraint for the purposes of gaining sense of control. Since previous researchers have found that only a small percentage of Hispanics report body dissatisfaction (Alegria et al., 2007), it is recommended that interviewers consider scoring dietary restraint both ways. The most recent version of the EDE also includes a module for binge eating disorder, the most frequent eating disorder found among Hispanics (Alegria et al.). The EDE has demonstrated overall good psychometric properties, but no research has been conducted examining the psychometric properties specific for Hispanic samples in the United States. Among non-Hispanic samples, the interrater reliability has been found to be above .75 for items and subscales (Rosen, Vara, Wendt, & Leitenberg, 1990; Wilson & Smith, 1989). Internal consistency of the subscales has ranged from .68 to .92 for individuals with eating disorders (Cooper, Cooper, & Fairburn, 1989).

The EDE has been translated to Spanish. The Spanish language version of the EDE (S-EDE) was developed by Grilo, Lozano, and Elder (2005) with excellent interrater reliability for the S-EDE subscales and binge eating and consistent with the English version. The authors describe a detailed and thorough translation process, where a bilingual psychologist translated the EDE from English to Spanish, then a second bilingual psychologist back translated from Spanish to English, and discrepancies were discussed and resolved. Next, the final Spanish interview was presented to a committee of bilingual psychologists who discussed language choices to make the interview compatible across the diverse Hispanic cultures.

Currently, there are no studies that have produced norms for the EDE among Hispanic American samples. Below is a table with means and standard deviations for the global scores, and each of the subscales of the EDE, along with a description of the sample found through a search of the literature (Table 14.2).

Table 14.2 Norms for the EDE in means (standard deviations) among Hispanic American samples

References	Global	Restraint	Eating	Shape	Weight	Sample
Chui, Safer, Bryson, Agras, and Wilson (2007)	–	3.66(0.85)	2.96(1.58)	4.02(1.46)	3.74(1.35)	25 Hispanics with bulimia nervosa
Elder, Paris, Añez, and Grilo (2008)	0.97(1.1)	0.97(1.2)	0.36(0.8)	1.44(1.5)	1.05(1.3)	61 individuals from community with Spanish version
	2.33(1.0)	2.20(1.4)	1.31(1.2)	3.26(1.2)	2.54(1.1)	16 individuals from community with subjective loss of control over eating with Spanish version

A child version of the EDE has been created and is appropriate for children between the ages of 8 and 14 years (Bryant-Waugh, Cooper, Taylor, & Lask, 1996). This child version has demonstrated adequate reliability and validity (Bryant-Waugh et al., 1996; Wade, Byrne, & Bryant-Waugh, 2008; Watkins, Frampton, Lask, & Bryant-Waugh, 2005), but no research to date has examined this child version among Hispanic American samples.

Structured Interview for Anorexic and Bulimic Eating Disorders (SIAB-EX)

The SIAB-EX is a structured clinical interview for the assessment of eating disorders and other related psychopathology that can be used to assess symptomatology currently (i.e., within the past 3 months) or life history (Fichter, Herpertz, Quadflieg, & Herpertz-Dahlmann, 1998). It is designed for use by professionals knowledgeable in eating disorders and structured clinical interviews. The SIAB-EX takes between 30 and 60 min to complete and is appropriate for the assessment of individuals between the ages of 12 and 65 years. Most items are scored on a 5-point Likert scale, ranging from 0 to 4 with higher scores indicating greater pathology. Items in the interview can be used to derive eating disorder diagnoses consistent with DSM-IV or ICD-10, and algorithms are provided for each. In addition, the SIAB-EX assesses depression and anxiety and has subscales consisting of body image and slimness ideal, general psychopathology, sexuality and social integration, bulimic symptoms, inappropriate compensatory behaviors to counteract weight gain, fasting and substance abuse, and atypical binges. The SIAB-EX has demonstrated good psychometric properties, but no research has been conducted examining the psychometric properties specific for Hispanic samples in the United States. Among non-Hispanic samples, the interrater reliability has been found to range from .80 to .96 for current and past history items and subscales (Fichter et al., 1998; Fichter & Quadflieg, 2001). Internal consistency of the subscales has ranged from .78 to .91 for individuals with eating disorders (Fichter et al.). In addition, authors have demonstrated convergent and discriminant (construct) validity of the SIAB-EX (Fichter & Quadflieg). The SIAB-EX was translated to Spanish by the authors; all materials available in English are available in Spanish. However, there are no psychometric or normative data available for the Spanish versions among Hispanic Americans. In addition, the process of translation is unknown. There is one study that provided means and standard deviations for three of the SIAB-EX subscales administered to English-speaking Mexican American women, and this information is provided below (Kuba & Harris, 2001) (Table 14.3).

Table 14.3 Norms for the SIAB-EX in means (standard deviations) among Hispanic American samples

Reference	Body image and slimness	Sexuality and social integration	Bulimic symptoms	Sample
Kuba and Harris (2001)	0.52 (0.57)	0.41 (0.45)	0.42 (0.45)	115 Mexican American women

Self-Report Questionnaires

Paper-and-pencil self-report questionnaires can assess the symptoms, risk factors, and psychological correlates of eating disorder pathology. Although clinical interviews are considered the gold standard for information gathering, self-report assessments have numerous benefits. For example, self-report questionnaires can provide a lot of information in a short period of time, be more cost effective, and often require less expertise than clinical interviews to score. In addition, one study found that among individuals suffering from eating disorders, participants were more forthcoming when anonymity increased (Keel, Crow, Davis, & Mitchell, 2002). Although numerous self-report questionnaires and screening tools exist to assist clinicians and researchers to identify eating pathology and its correlates, only those most frequently used with Hispanic Americans will be reviewed.

Body Shape Questionnaire (BSQ)

The BSQ is a 34-item measure that is used to assess general satisfaction with one's body shape and weight (Cooper, Taylor, Cooper, & Fairburn, 1987). The BSQ is appropriate for older adolescents and adults. Items are scored on a 6-point scale ranging from 1 (*never*) to 6 (*always*) and summed to yield a total dissatisfaction score ranging from 34 to 204, with higher scores indicating more body dissatisfaction. It is easy to administer and score. Psychometric evaluations of the original BSQ indicate high internal consistency and test-retest reliability estimates for both the original 34-item version and shorter screener versions (Rosen, Jones, Ramirez, & Waxman, 1996; Warren et al., 2008). Among Hispanic American samples, the BSQ has had internal consistency coefficients ranging from 0.83 to 0.97 (Warren et al., 2008, 2010). Additionally, the BSQ has been found to have invariant factor structure when comparing Caucasians and Hispanic Americans (Warren et al., 2008). The BSQ was translated to Spanish (Raich et al., 1996) and has been used in Spain, Mexico, and South America. Scores of the Spanish version of the 34-item BSQ generally have high internal consistency, with Cronbach's alphas at around .95, and good concurrent validity with other eating disorder measures among samples from Spain (Raich et al.).

A search of the literature revealed six studies that have published means and standard deviations for Hispanic Americans on the BSQ. All of these studies used the English version of the measure (Table 14.4).

Eating Attitudes Test (EAT)

The EAT is a screener that primarily assesses the symptoms of anorexia nervosa such as symptoms associated with extreme weight loss and restriction (Garner & Garfinkel, 1979; Garner, Olmstead, Bohr, & Garfinkel, 1982), with the most commonly used version being a 26-item version. Individuals rate the frequency that they have engaged in particular behaviors over the past month on a 6-point Likert-type

Table 14.4 Norms for BSQ in means (standard deviations) among Hispanic Americans

References	BSQ total score	Sample
Franko and George (2008)	98.40 (34.30)	28 college women
Hrabosky and Grilo (2007)	87.90 (45.02)	53 women from community sample
Warren et al. (2005)	91.30 (33.76)	100 Mexican American women
Warren (2008)	61.05 (25.11)	91 males
Warren et al. (2008)	96.33 (26.16)	151 college women
Warren, Castillo, and Gleaves (2010)	22.36 (8.82)	94 college women

Table 14.5 Norms for EAT in means (standard deviations) among Hispanic Americans

References	Total score	Sample
Erickson and Gerstle (2007)	12.00 (9.08)	82 Hispanic girls 8–12 year old; child version
Joiner and Kashubeck (1996)	12.78 (10.99)	120 Mexican Americans 12–18 year old
Pumariega (1986)[a]	18.20 (12.70)	138 Hispanic girls 16–18 year old
Reyes-Rodriguez et al. (2010)	28.67 (10.74) 6.64 (4.92) 24.83 (12.23) 5.36 (4.26)	188 Puerto Rican women met clinical cutoff; Spanish version 1,236 Puerto Rican women did not meet clinical cutoff; Spanish version 46 Puerto Rican men met clinical cutoff; Spanish version 663 Puerto Rican men did not meet clinical cutoff; Spanish version
Reyes-Rodriguez et al. (2011)	6.60 (7.00)	722 Puerto Rican men; Spanish version
Vander Wal (2004)	11.34 (10.10)	65 Hispanic girls 9–12 year old; child version

[a]This is a 40-item version

scale from *always* to *never* with total scores ranging from 0 to 78, higher scores indicating greater pathology. Individuals who score above a cutoff score of 20 are endorsing clinically significant pathology and should be followed with a clinical interview. The EAT is appropriate with adolescents 12–18 years of age and adults. The EAT consists of three subscales: dieting, bulimia and food preoccupation, and oral control. The EAT has been found to have strong psychometric properties (Garner et al.). Scoring for the EAT was originally done on a 0–3 scale (i.e., scored 0 0 0 1 2 3); however, other researchers have scored it on the original 1–6 scale as described by Wells, Coope, Gabb, and Pears (1985), which has shown to yield good internal consistency (McVey, Davis, Tweed, & Shaw, 2004) that is comparable to the original 0–3 scoring method developed by Garner and colleagues. Among Hispanic Americans, good internal consistency coefficients have been found, ranging from .85 for adolescent samples (Joiner & Kashubeck, 1996) to .89 for adult women (Bettendorf & Fischer, 2009). With regard to factor structure, there was one study on female Hispanic Americans of Mexican descent that found a five-factor structure a better fit to the data than the original three subscales reported (Rutt & Coleman, 2001). Yet, a second study that assessed measurement invariance found a four-factor model best fit Caucasians and Hispanic Americans (Belon et al., 2011). The EAT has been translated to Spanish. The Spanish version has also yielded strong psychometric properties. Internal consistency scores are .89 for adult men and women (Reyes-Rodriguez et al., 2010). The Spanish version also uses a clinical cutoff score of 20.

A search of the literature revealed five studies that reported means and standard deviations for the EAT among Hispanic Americans. One study, which used the Spanish version, divided their large sample into four groups: women who met clinical cutoff, women who did not meet clinical cutoff, men who met clinical cutoff, and men who did not meet clinical cutoff scores. Thus, the data for this study is presented separately in the table above (Table 14.5).

A child version of the EAT, 26 items, has been created and is appropriate for ages 8–13 years, with a similar cutoff score of 20 (Maloney, McGuire, & Daniels, 1988). Among Hispanic American girls, the internal consistency scores range from .78 to .82 (Erickson & Gerstle, 2007; Vander Wal & Thomas, 2004). It should be noted that one study assessed the psychometric properties of the child version of the EAT and found the sensitivity of the EAT for girls 8–9 years old to be questionable (Erickson & Gerstle).

Eating Disorder Examination Questionnaire (EDE-Q)

The EDE-Q is a 21-item questionnaire that assesses eating disorder symptoms that an individual has experienced over the past 28 days (Fairburn & Beglin, 2008). Derived from the Eating Disorder Examination Interview (discussed above), EDE-Q items are rated on a 7-point scale and consists of a global score and four subscales: dietary restraint, eating concern, weight concern, and shape concern. A score of 4 or higher on the global or subscale scores is clinically significant. The EDE-Q comes with algorithms for deriving DSM-IV-TR diagnoses of anorexia nervosa, bulimia nervosa, binge eating disorder, and eating disorder NOS. The EDE-Q has demonstrated good psychometric properties. Among Hispanic American women, internal consistency scores range from .70 to .92 for the subscales (Arriaza & Mann, 2001; Hrabosky & Grilo, 2007). Among a sample of multiethnic high school athlete girls, including 103 Hispanic Americans, 7–10 day test-retest intraclass correlation coefficients were 0.84–0.92, and internal consistency ranged from 0.92 to 0.96 for global and subscale scores (Pernick et al., 2006). However, it should be noted that the factor structure of the EDE-Q has yielded inconsistent results (Byrne, Allen, Lampard, Dove, & Fursland, 2010). The EDE-Q has been translated into several languages, including Spanish. Grilo and colleagues (2005) describe the process of translation of the EDE-Q involving one bilingual psychologist translating the EDE-Q from English to Spanish, followed by a second bilingual psychologist conducting a back translation from Spanish to English, and a committee of bilingual psychologists reviewing the measure for language choices. Elder and Grilo (2007) compared the Spanish language questionnaire (S-EDE-Q) with the Spanish version of the interview (S-EDE). The short-term test-retest reliability (5–14 days) of the questionnaire was examined in a Spanish-speaking Hispanic women sample with coefficients ranging from 0.71 to 0.85 for the global and subscale scores (Elder & Grilo).

There has been no single study that has provided norms for the EDE-Q for Hispanic American samples. Below is a list of studies that have provided means and standard deviations for the global and subscales among Hispanic Americans for both the EDE-Q and S-EDE-Q (Table 14.6).

Eating Disorder Inventory (EDI)

The EDI has been found to be the most frequent measure used in clinical practice in a sample of 480 eating disorder professionals (Anderson & Paulosky, 2004). It is a self-report questionnaire that consists of three subscales designed to assess key risk factors of eating disorders including drive for thinness, bulimia, and body dissatisfaction (Garner, 2004). The original EDI was first published in 1983 with 64 items (Garner). It was later revised in 1991 and again in 2004 (Garner). The authors of the EDI preserved the original items in each revision to allow researchers to compare data across revisions. The most current revision has 91 items, and in addition to assessing key risk factors, it includes important clinically relevant subscales, including low self-esteem, personal alienation, interpersonal insecurity, interpersonal alienation, interoceptive deficits, emotional dysregulation, perfectionism, asceticism, and maturity fears. Total scores range from 0 to 364 with higher scores indicating greater eating disorder

Table 14.6 Norms for the EDE-Q in means (standard deviations) among Hispanic Americans

References	Global	Restraint	Eating	Shape	Weight	Sample
Arriaza and Mann (2001)	–	1.41(1.44)	0.71(1.01)	2.58(1.44)	2.23(1.44)	52 college women
	–	1.27(1.42)	0.72(0.99)	2.45(1.42)	2.06(1.48)	38 college women
Elder and Grilo (2007)	1.74(1.32)	1.50(1.59)	1.07(1.28)	2.45(1.81)	1.93(1.47)	77 community sample Spanish version
Franko and George (2008)		1.90 (1.60)		3.30 (1.50)	2.70 (1.60)	28 college women
Hrabosky and Grilo (2007)	–	1.40(1.44)	1.20(1.21)	2.88(1.71)	2.35(1.64)	53 community sample
Pernick et al. (2006)	1.63(1.13)	1.31(1.25)	0.90(0.99)	2.32(1.52)	1.96(1.49)	103 high school athletes
Villarroel, Penelo, Portell, and Raich (2006)	1.30(1.19)	1.29(1.33)	0.66(0.97)	1.75(1.50)	1.51(1.41)	708 college women from Spain

Table 14.7 Norms for EDI in means (standard deviations) among Hispanic Americans

References	Bulimia	Body dissatisfaction	Drive for thinness	Sample
Cashel et al. (2003)	1.74 (2.87)	12.90 (7.96)	6.48 (6.70)	31 college women
Franko and George (2008)		12.80 (7.50)	6.60 (6.50)	28 college women
Gordon et al. (2010)	13.17 (5.76)	30.73 (10.24)	21.96 (9.12)	75 women 17–49 year old
Joiner and Kashubeck (1996)		10.18 (8.37)		120 Mexican Americans 12–18 year old
Rhea (1999)	2.28 (3.06)	10.74 (7.05)	6.71 (5.40)	235 athletes 13–19 year old
Stein et al. (2010)	1.40 (2.20)	8.60 (6.80)	5.20 (5.20)	66 Mexican American college women
Xanthopoulos et al. (2011)		9.40 (7.80)		184 boys and girls grades 4–6

pathology. It is appropriate for individuals 13 years of age and older. Profile analysis can be conducted with this measure in addition to inconsistency responding, which is appealing to practitioners. However, this measure is copyrighted and available for purchase through Psychological Assessment Resources, Inc. The EDI has extensive psychometric research supporting its reliability and validity. The reliability for the clinical scales tends to range between .90 to .97 and .80s to .90s for all the other scales (Garner). The EDI has also demonstrated great test-retest stability, with intervals ranging as short as 1 day, with all scales having coefficients higher than .95 (Garner). There is also evidence that the 12 subscale scores are nonoverlapping (Garner). The psychometric proprieties of the EDI among Hispanic American samples are strong as well, with internal consistency scores ranging from .64 to .91 for adults (Bettendorf & Fischer, 2009; Joiner & Kashubeck, 1996; Stein, Corte, & Ronis, 2010) and .62 to.83 for adolescent samples (Rhea, 1999; Xanthopoulos et al., 2011). There have been no studies in the United States on Hispanic American samples, using a Spanish version of the EDI.

A search of the literature revealed seven studies that have published means and standard deviations for the three main scales: bulimia, body dissatisfaction, and drive for thinness of the EDI. It should be noted that two studies, Cashel, Cunningham, Landeros, Cokley, and Muhammed (2003) and Rhea (1999), also provided means and standard deviations for the other subscales of the EDI as well (Table 14.7).

Sociocultural Attitudes Towards Appearance Questionnaire (SATAQ)

The SATAQ was designed to measure the degree of recognition and acceptance of Western socially and culturally endorsed standards of appearance. The original SATAQ was first published in 1995 and included two subscales: awareness which assesses if an individual knows what the ideal standard

Table 14.8 Norms for SATAQ in means (standard deviations) among Hispanic Americans

References	Awareness[a]	General internalization	Sample
Blow et al. (2010)		3.09 (0.80)	95 women
		2.76 (0.90)	68 males
Cashel et al. (2003)	21.48 (3.89)	26.48 (7.51)	31 college women
Cordero (2011)		26.56 (9.07)	283 college women
Warren (2008)	40.14 (5.88)	31.38 (6.70)	91 males
Warren, Castillo, and Gleaves (2010)	40.46 (6.11)	34.10 (6.81)	94 college women
Warren et al. (2005)	40.53 (6.23)	33.90 (7.03)	100 Mexican American women

[a]This subscale was eliminated in the third revision of the SATAQ

of beauty is for Western cultures and internalization which assesses internalization of the standards (Heinberg, Thompson, & Stormer, 1995). Since the original publication, the measure has been revised twice with the most recent version published in 2004 expanding the measure to include four subscales: information which measures awareness and dependence on the media for information about appearance, pressure which measures the perceived pressures from the media to modify one's appearance, internalization-general which measures internalization of thin-ideal body types, and internalization-athletic which measures internalization of athletic or fit body types (Thompson, van den Berg, Roehrig, Guarda, & Heinberg, 2004). The most recent version is a 30-item scale with participants responding to items on a 5-point Likert scale ranging from 1 (definitely disagree) to 5 (definitely agree). Subscale scores range from 9 to 45 for the information and internalization-general scales, 7–35 for the pressure scale, and from 5 to 25 for internalization-athletic scale, with higher scores indicating greater problematic behaviors or beliefs. The SATAQ has excellent psychometric properties with internal consistency estimates above .90s for college women and individuals suffering from eating disorders (Calogero, Davis, & Thompson, 2004; Thompson et al., 2004). Among Hispanic Americans, internal consistency estimates range from .82 to .93 for adult women (Blow, Taylor, Cooper, & Redfearn, 2010; Cashel et al., 2003; Cordero, 2011; Warren et al., 2005, 2008) and .81 to .87 for adult men (Blow et al., 2010; Warren, 2008). The SATAQ is currently available only in English and all studies on Hispanic Americans have used English versions. There have been no specific studies conducted that established norms on the SATAQ for Hispanic Americans. However, a search of the literature did yield six studies that provided mean and standard deviation information for the scale (Table 14.8).

Conclusions

There are several important issues to consider when assessing Hispanic Americans with eating pathology. First, the ability of the DSM-IV-TR diagnostic criteria to capture the illness presentation of Hispanics has been questioned (Franko, 2007). Recent epidemiological studies have brought to light several problematic diagnostic criteria (Alegria et al., 2007). For Hispanics with lifetime anorexia nervosa, only a minority 6% reported fear of gaining weight (Criteria B, DSM-IV) and only 8% reported body dissatisfaction (Criteria C, DSM-IV; Alegria et al.). For Hispanics with lifetime bulimia nervosa, the frequency and simultaneity of the bingeing and purging dramatically decreased the number of Hispanics meeting criteria for the disorder (Criteria C, DSM-IV; Alegria et al.). For these reasons, Hispanic Americans tend to be classified as eating disorder NOS. This also highlights an important issue with structured clinical interviews used in treatment and for epidemiological research.

For time efficiency, structured clinical interviews employ skip rules; however, the screener items for eating disorders section are often questions related to body dissatisfaction. Given that only a minority of Hispanics endorses body dissatisfaction, structured clinical interviews with skip rules may miss the majority of Hispanics with eating disorders. Thus, it is important that when assessing Hispanic clients all questions be administered without skip rules or supplemental questions be added. In addition, time should be taken to assess any stereotypes a Hispanic client may have toward eating disorders. Some Hispanic individuals believe that eating disorders is a "White thing" and when asked questions using language consistent with eating disorders will trigger denial responses. For example, when asked about vomiting or purging, the individual will deny engaging in behaviors, but will endorse the question "Does food ever come out of your mouth?" Thus, it is important that the assessor understand the individual's belief system and tailor the questions appropriately.

When reviewing the data on paper-and-pencil questionnaires, it is clear that more research is needed in this area. Basic research on the psychometric properties of these measures with Hispanic Americans are needed such as internal consistency, test-retest reliability, factor structure, and validity. Given that these measures are used to describe eating pathology among Hispanic Americans, measurement invariance studies need to be performed to ensure that items have the same meanings across ethnic groups. For all measures, normative data specific to Hispanic Americans are needed as well.

In summary, this chapter has attempted to provide a thorough review of the literature on select clinical interviews and paper-and-pencil questionnaires related to eating pathology in Hispanic Americans and to provide the relevant information for researchers and practitioners to assist their decision making process when using assessments. This literature review was not exhaustive, and there are several other paper-and pencil-questionnaires that were not covered.

References

Alegria, M., Woo, M., Cao, Z., Torres, M., Meng, X., & Striegel-Moore, R. (2007). Prevalence and correlates of eating disorders in Latino in the United States. *International Journal of Eating Disorders, 40*, S15–S21. doi:10-1002/eat.

American Psychiatric Association. (2000). *Diagnostic and statistical manual of mental disorders* (Revised 4th ed.). Washington, DC: Author.

Anderson, D. A., Lavender, J. M., & De Young, K. P. (2010). The assessment process: Refining the clinical evaluations of patients with eating disorders. In M. Maine, B. H. McGilley, & D. W. Bunnell (Eds.), *Treatment of eating disorders: Bridging the research–practice gap* (pp. 71–87). San Diego, CA: Elsevier Academic Press. doi:10.1016/B978-0-12-375668-8.10005-1.

Anderson, D. A., & Paulosky, C. A. (2004). A survey of the use of assessment instruments by eating disorder professionals in clinical practice. *Eating and Weight Disorders, 9*, 238–241.

Arriaza, C. A., & Mann, T. (2001). Ethnic differences in eating disorder symptoms among college students: The confounding role of body mass index. *Journal of American College Health, 49*, 309–315.

Ayala, G. X., Mickens, L., Galindo, P., & Elder, J. P. (2007). Acculturation and body image perception among Latino youth. *Ethnicity and Health, 12*(1), 21–41. doi:10.1080/13557850600824294.

Belon, K. E., Smith, J. E., Bryan, A. D., Lash, D. N., Winn, J. L., & Gianini, L. M. (2011). Measurement invariance of the eating attitudes test-26 in Caucasian and Hispanic women. *Eating Behaviors, 12*, 317–320. doi:10.1016/j.eatbeh.2011.07.007.

Berry, J. W. (2003). Conceptual approaches to acculturation. In K. M. Chun, P. B. Organista, & G. Marín (Eds.), *Acculturation: Advances in theory, measurement, and applied research* (pp. 17–37). Washington, DC: American Psychological Association.

Berry, J. W., Kim, U., Minde, T., & Mok, D. (1987). Comparative studies of acculturative stress. *International Migration Review, 21*, 491–511. doi:10.1177/136346158802500203.

Bettendorf, S. K., & Fischer, A. R. (2009). Cultural strengths as moderators of the relationship between acculturation to the mainstream U.S. society and eating- and body-related concerns among Mexican American women. *Journal of Counseling Psychology, 56*, 430–440. doi:10.1037/a0016382.

Blow, J. A., Taylor, T., Cooper, T. V., & Redfearn, C. K. (2010). Correlates of weight concern and control in a Hispanic college student sample. *Eating Behaviors, 11*, 6–10. doi:10.1016/j.eatbeh.2009.08.001.

Bruch, H. (1973). *Eating disorders: Obesity, anorexia nervosa and the person within*. New York: Basic Books.

Bryant-Waugh, R., Cooper, P. J., Taylor, C. L., & Lask, B. D. (1996). The use of the eating disorder examination with children: A pilot study. *International Journal of Eating Disorders, 19*, 391–397.

Byrne, S. M., Allen, K. L., Lampard, A. M., Dove, E. R., & Fursland, A. (2010). The factor structure of the eating disorder examination in clinical and community samples. *International Journal of Eating Disorders, 43*, 260–265. doi:10.1002/eat.20681.

Cachelin, F. M., Veisel, C., Barzegarnazari, E., & Streigel-Moore, R. H. (2000). Disordered eating, acculturation, and treatment-seeking in a community simple of Hispanic, Asian, black, and white women. *Psychology of Women Quarterly, 24*, 244–253. doi:10.1111/j.1471-6402.2000.tb00206.x.

Calogero, R. M., Davis, W. N., & Thompson, J. K. (2004). The sociocultural attitudes towards appearance questionnaire (SATAQ-3): Reliability and normative comparisons of eating disordered patients. *Body Image: An International Journal of Research, 1*, 193–198. doi:10.1016/j.bodyim.2004.01.004.

Cashel, M. L., Cunningham, D., Landeros, C., Cokley, K. O., & Muhammed, G. (2003). Sociocultural attitudes and symptoms of bulimia: Evaluating the SATAQ with diverse college groups. *Journal of Counseling Psychology, 50*, 287–296. doi:10.1037/0022-0167.50.3.287.

Chui, W., Safer, D. L., Bryson, S. W., Agras, W. S., & Wilson, G. T. (2007). A comparison of ethnic groups in the treatment of bulimia nervosa. *Eating Behaviors, 8*, 485–491. doi:10.1016/j.eatbeh.2007.01.005.

Cooper, Z., Cooper, P. J., & Fairburn, C. G. (1989). The validity of the eating disorder examination and its subscales. *The British Journal of Psychiatry, 154*, 807–812.

Cooper, P. J., Taylor, M. J., Cooper, Z., & Fairburn, C. G. (1987). The development and validation of the body shape questionnaire. *International Journal of Eating Disorders, 6*, 485–494.

Cordero, E. D. (2011). Self esteem, social support, collectivism, and the thin ideal in Latina undergraduates. *Body Image: An International Journal of Research, 8*, 82–85. doi:10.1016/j.bodyim.2010.11.006.

Crago, M., & Shisslak, C. M. (2003). Ethnic differences in dieting, binge eating, and purging behaviors among American females: A review. *Eating Disorders, 11*, 289–304. doi:10.1080/10640260390242515.

Croll, J., Neumark-Sztainer, D., Story, M., & Ireland, M. (2002). Prevalence and risk and protective factors related to disordered eating behaviours among adolescents: Relationship to gender and ethnicity. *Journal of Adolescent Health, 31*, 166–175. doi:10.1016/S1054-139X(02)00368-3.

Dolan, B. (1991). Cross-cultural aspects of anorexia and bulimia: A review. *International Journal of Eating Disorders, 10*, 67–78. doi:10.1002/1098-108X(199101)10:1<67::AID-EAT2260100108>3.0.CO;2-N.

Elder, K. A., & Grilo, C. M. (2007). The Spanish language version of the eating disorder examination questionnaire: Comparison with the Spanish language version of the eating disorder examination and test-retest reliability. *Behaviour Research and Therapy, 45*, 1369–1377. doi:10.1016/j.brat.2006.08.012.

Elder, K. A., Paris, M., Jr., Añez, L. M., & Grilo, C. M. (2008). Loss of control over eating is associated with eating disorder psychopathology in a community sample of Latinas. *Eating Behaviors, 9*, 501–503. doi:10.1016/j.eatbeh.2008.04.003.

Erickson, S. J., & Gerstle, M. (2007). Developmental considerations in measuring children's disordered eating attitudes and behaviors. *Eating Behaviors, 8*, 224–235. doi:10.1016/j.eatbeh.2006.06.003.

Fairburn, C. G., & Beglin, S. (2008). Eating disorder examination questionnaire (EDE-Q6). In C. G. Fairburn (Ed.), *Cognitive behavior therapy and eating disorders*. New York: Guilford Press.

Fairburn, C. G., Cooper, Z., & O'Connor, M. E. (2008). Eating disorder examination (EDE 16.0D). In C. G. Fairburn (Ed.), *Cognitive behavior therapy and eating disorders* (pp. 265–308). New York: Guilford Press.

Fichter, M. M., Herpertz, S., Quadflieg, N., & Herpertz-Dahlmann, B. (1998). Structured interview for anorexic and bulimic eating disorders for DSM-IV and ICD-10: Updated (third) revision. *International Journal of Eating Disorders, 24*, 227–249.

Fichter, M. M., & Quadflieg, N. (2001). The structured interview for anorexic and bulimic eating disorders for DSM-IV and ICD-10 (SIAB-EX): Reliability and validity. *European Psychiatry, 16*, 38–48.

Fischer, M., Pastore, D., Schneider, M., Pegler, C., & Napolitano, B. (1994). Eating attitudes in urban and suburban adolescents. *International Journal of Eating Disorders, 16*, 67–74. doi:10.1002/1098-108X(199407)16:1<67::AID-EAT2260160107>3.0.CO;2-I.

Fitzgibbon, M. L., Spring, B., Avelone, M. E., Blackman, L. R., Pingitore, R., & Stolley, M. R. (1998). Correlates of binge eating in Hispanic, black, and white women. *International Journal of Eating Disorders, 24*, 43–52. doi:10.1002/(SICI)1098-108X(199807)24:1<43::AID-EAT4>3.0.CO;2-0.

Franko, D. L. (2007). Race, ethnicity, and eating disorders: Considerations for DSM-V. *International Journal of Eating Disorders, 40*, S31–S34. doi:10.1002/eat.

Franko, D. L., & George, J. B. E. (2008). A pilot intervention to reduce eating disorder risk in Latina women. *European Eating Disorders Review, 16*, 436–441. doi:10.1002/erv.891.

Garner, D. M. (2004). *EDI-3: Eating disorder inventory-3 professional manual*. Lutz, FL: Psychological Assessment Resources, Inc.

Garner, D. M., & Garfinkel, P. E. (1979). The eating attitudes test: An index of the symptoms of anorexia nervosa. *Psychology Medicine, 9*, 273–279.

Garner, D. M., Olmstead, M. P., Bohr, Y., & Garfinkel, P. E. (1982). The eating attitudes test: Psychometric features and clinical correlates. *Psychological Medicine, 12*, 871–878.

Gordon, K. H., Castro, Y., Sitnikov, L., & Holm-Denoma, J. M. (2010). Cultural body shape ideals and eating disorder symptoms among white, Latina, and black college women. *Cultural Diversity and Ethnic Minority Psychology, 16*, 135–143. doi:10.1037/a0018671.

Grilo, C. M., Lozano, C., & Elder, K. A. (2005). Inter-rater and test-retest reliability of the Spanish language versi6n of the eating disorder examination interview: Clinical and research implications. *Journal of Psychiatric Practice, 11*, 231–240. doi:10.1097/00131746-200507000-00003.

Heinberg, L. J., Thompson, J. K., & Stormer, S. (1995). Development and validation of the sociocultural attitude towards appearance questionnaire (SATAQ). *International Journal of Eating Disorders, 17*, 81–89. doi:10.1002/1098-108X(199501)17:1<81::AID-EAT2260170111>3.0.CO;2-Y.

Hrabosky, J. I., & Grilo, C. M. (2007). Body image and eating disordered behavior in a community sample of Black and Hispanic women. *Eating Behaviors, 8*, 106–114. doi:10.1016/j.eatbeh.2006.02.005.

Joiner, G. W., & Kashubeck, S. (1996). Acculturation, body image, self-esteem, and eating-disorder symptomatology in adolescent Mexican-American women. *Psychology of Women Quarterly, 20*, 419–435. doi:10.1111/j.1471-6402.1996.tb00309.x.

Keel, P. K., Crow, S., Davis, T. L., & Mitchell, J. E. (2002). Assessment of eating disorders: Comparison of interview and questionnaire data from a long-term follow-up study of bulimia nervosa. *Journal of Psychosomatic Research, 53*, 1043–1047. doi:10.1016/S0022-3999(02)00491-9.

Kuba, S. A., & Harris, D. J. (2001). Eating disturbances in women of color: An exploratory study of contextual factors in the development of disordered eating in Mexican American women. *Health Care for Women International, 22*, 281–298.

le Grange, D., Telch, C. F., & Agras, W. S. (1997). Eating and general psychopathology in a sample of Caucasian and ethnic minority subjects. *International Journal of Eating Disorders, 21*, 285–293. doi:10.1002/(SICI)1098-108X(199704)21:3<285::AID-EAT9>3.0.CO;2-G.

Maloney, M. J., McGuire, J. B., & Daniels, S. R. (1988). Reliability testing of a children's version of the eating attitude test. *Journal of the American Academy of Child and Adolescent Psychiatry, 27*, 541–543. doi:10.1097/00004583-198809000-00004.

McVey, G. L., Davis, R., Tweed, S., & Shaw, R. F. (2004). Evaluation of a school-based program designed to improve body image satisfaction, global self-esteem, and eating attitudes and behaviors: A replication study. *International Journal of Eating Disorders, 36*, 1–11. doi:10.1002/eat.20006.

Miller, M. N., & Pumariega, A. J. (2001). Culture and eating disorders: A historical and cross-cultural review. *Psychiatry: Interpersonal and Biological Processes, 64*, 93–110. doi:10.1521/psyc.64.2.93.18621.

Neumark-Sztainer, D., Croll, J., Story, M., Hannan, P. J., French, S. A., & Perry, C. (2002). Ethnic/racial differences in weight-related concerns and behaviours among adolescent girls and boys: Findings from project EAT. *Journal of Psychosomatic Research, 53*, 963–974. doi:10.1016/S0022-3999(02)00486-5.

Paukert, A. L., Pettit, J. W., Perez, M., & Walker, R. L. (2006). Affective and attributional features of acculturative stress among ethnic minority college students. *Journal of Psychology: Interdisciplinary and Applied, 140*, 405–419. doi:10.3200/JRLP.140.5.405-419.

Perez, M., Voelz, Z. R., Pettit, J. W., & Joiner, T. E. (2002). The role of acculturative stress and body dissatisfaction in predicting bulimic symptomatology across ethnic groups. *International Journal of Eating Disorders, 31*, 442–454. doi:10.1002/eat.10006.

Pernick, Y., Nichols, J. F., Ruah, M. J., Kern, M., Ji, M., Lawson, M. J., et al. (2006). Disordered eating among a multi-racial/ethnic sample of female high-school athletes. *Journal of Adolescent Health, 38*, 689–695. doi:10.1016/j.jadohealth.2005.07.003.

Pumariega, A. J. (1986). Acculturation and eating attitudes in adolescent girls: A comparative and correlational study. *Journal of the American Academy of Child and Adolescent Psychiatry, 25*, 276–279. doi:10.1016/S0002-7138(09)60238-7.

Raich, R. M., Mora, M., Soler, A., Avila, C., Clos, I., Zapater, L., et al. (1996). Adaptaci6n de un instrumento de evaluaci6n de la insatisfacci6n corporal [Adaptation of a body dissatisfaction measure]. *Clinical y Salud, 7*, 51–66.

Regan, P. C., & Cachelin, F. M. (2006). Binge eating and purging in a multiethnic community sample. *International Journal of Eating Disorders, 39*, 523–526. doi:10.1002/eat.20268.

Reyes-Rodriguez, M. L., Franko, D. L., Matos-Lamourt, A., Bulik, C. M., Von Holle, A., Camara-Fuentes, A. R., et al. (2010). Eating disorder symptomatology: Prevalence among Latino college freshmen students. *Journal of Clinical Psychology, 66*, 666–679. doi:10.1002/jclp. 20684.

Reyes-Rodriguez, M. L., Sala, M., Von Holle, A., Unikel, C., Bulik, C. M., Camara-Fuentes, L., et al. (2011). A description of eating disorder behaviors in Latino males. *Journal of American College Health, 59*, 266–272. doi:10.1080/07448481.2010.502205.

Rhea, D. J. (1999). Eating disorder behaviors of ethnically diverse urban female adolescent athletes and non-athletes. *Journal of Adolescence, 22*, 379–388. doi:0140-1971/99/030379.

Ricciardelli, L. A., McCabe, M. P., Williams, R. J., & Thompson, J. K. (2007). The role of ethnicity and culture in body image and disordered eating among males. *Clinical Psychology Review, 27*, 582–606. doi:10.1016/j.cpr2007.01.016.

Rosen, J. C., Jones, A., Ramirez, E., & Waxman, S. (1996). Body shape questionnaire: Studies of validity and reliability. *International Journal of Eating Disorders, 20*, 315–319. doi:10.1002/(SICI)1098-108X(199611)20:3<315::AID-EAT11>3.0.CO;2-Z.

Rosen, J. C., Vara, L., Wendt, S., & Leitenberg, H. (1990). Validity studies of the eating disorder examination. *International Journal of Eating Disorders, 9*, 519–528. doi:10.1002/1098-108X(199009)9:5<519::AID-EAT2260090507>3.0.CO;2-K.

Rutt, C. D., & Coleman, K. J. (2001). The evaluation of a measurement model for the body image questionnaire and the eating attitudes test in a Hispanic population. *Hispanic Journal of Behavioral Sciences, 23*, 153–170. doi:10.1177/0739986301232003.

Smith, J. E., & Krejci, J. (1991). Minorities join the majority: Eating disturbances among Hispanic and Native American youth. *International Journal of Eating Disorders, 10*, 179–186. doi:10.1002/1098-108X(199103)10:2<179::AID-EAT226010020 6>3.0.CO;2-S.

Stein, K. F., Corte, C., & Ronis, D. L. (2010). Personal identities and disordered eating behaviors, in Mexican American women. *Eating Behaviors, 11*, 197–200. doi:10.1016/j.eatbeh.2010.02.001.

Thompson, J. K., & Stice, E. (2001). Thin-ideal internalization: Mounting evidence for a new risk factor for body-image disturbance and eating pathology. *Current Directions in Psychological Science, 10*, 181–183. doi:10.1111/1467-8721.00144.

Thompson, J. K., van den Berg, P., Roehrig, M., Guarda, A., & Heinberg, L. (2004). The sociocultural attitudes towards appearance questionnaire-3 (SATAQ-3): Development and validation. *International Journal of Eating Disorders, 35*, 293–304. doi:10.1002/eat.10257.

Vander Wal, S. V. (2004). Eating and body image concerns among average-weight and obese African American and Hispanic girls. *Eating Behaviors, 5*, 181–187. doi:10.1016/j.eatbeh.2004.01.007.

Vander Wal, S. V., & Thomas, N. (2004). Predictors of body image dissatisfaction and disturbed eating attitudes and behaviors in African American and Hispanic girls. *Eating Behaviors, 5*, 291–301. doi:10.1016/j.eatbeh.2004.04.001.

Villarroel, A. M., Penelo, E., Portell, M., & Raich, R. M. (2006). Screening for eating disorders in undergraduate women: Norms and validity of the Spanish version of the eating disorder examination questionnaire (EDE-Q). *Journal of Psychopathology and Behavioral Assessment, 33*, 121–128. doi:10.1007/s10862-009-9177-6.

Wade, T. D., Byrne, S., & Bryant-Waugh, R. (2008). The eating disorder examination: Norms and construct validity with young and middle adolescent girls. *International Journal of Eating Disorders, 41*, 551–558. doi:10.1002/eat.20526.

Warren, C. S. (2008). The influence of awareness and internalization of Western appearance ideals on body dissatisfaction in Euro-American and Hispanic males. *Psychology of Men and Masculinity, 9*(4), 257–266. doi:10.1037/a0012472.

Warren, C. S., Castillo, L. G., & Gleaves, D. H. (2010). The sociocultural model of eating disorders in Mexican American women: Behavioral acculturation and cognitive marginalization as moderators. *Eating Disorders: The Journal of Treatment and Prevention, 18*, 43–57. doi:10.1080/10640260903439532.

Warren, C. S., Cepeda-Benito, A., Gleaves, D. H., Moreno, S., Rodriguez, S., Fernandez, M. C., et al. (2008). English and Spanish versions of the body shape questionnaire: Measurement equivalence across ethnicity and clinical status. *International Journal of Eating Disorders, 41*, 265–272. doi:10.1002/eat.20492.

Warren, C. S., Gleaves, D. H., Cepeda-Benito, A., del Carmen Fernandez, M., & Rodriguez-Ruiz, S. (2005). Ethnicity as a protective factor against internalization of a thin ideal and body dissatisfaction. *International Journal of Eating Disorders, 37*(3), 241–249. doi:10.1002/eat.20102.

Watkins, B., Frampton, I., Lask, B., & Bryant-Waugh, R. (2005). Reliability and validity of the child version of the eating disorder examination: A preliminary investigation. *International Journal of Eating Disorders, 38*, 183–187.

Wells, J. E., Coope, P. A., Gabb, D. C., & Pears, R. K. (1985). The factor structure of the eating attitudes test with adolescent schoolgirls. *Psychological Medicine: A Journal of Research in Psychiatry and the Allied Sciences, 15*, 141–146. doi:10.1017/S0033291700021000.

Wilson, G. T., & Smith, D. (1989). Assessment of bulimia nervosa: An evaluation of the eating disorder examination. *International Journal of Eating Disorders, 8*, 173–179. doi:10.1002/1098-108X(198903)8:2<173::AID::EAT22600 80206>3.0.CO;2-V.

Xanthopoulos, M. S., Borraidale, K. E., Hayes, S., Sherman, S., Vander Veur, S., Grundy, K. M., et al. (2011). The impact of weight, sex, and race/ethnicity on body dissatisfaction among urban children. *Body Image: An International Journal of Research, 8*, 385–389. doi:10.1016/j.bodyim.2011.04.011.

15 Assessing for Personality Disorders in the Hispanic Client

Saul G. Alamilla and James V. Wojcik

Assessing for Personality Disorders in the Hispanic Client

The worldview of nondominant culture members influences behaviors that are then understood and interpreted by dominant culture members including clinicians. The risks of insensitive or biased assessment for personality disorders (PDs) include the risk of inaccurate diagnostic decisions that overstate apparent deviance, as well as missing important clinical information that might direct effective intervention, placement, or hiring and employment decisions. Those assumptions may include decisions about diagnostic categorization such as assigning a personality disorder diagnosis (Alarcon, Foulks, & Vakkur, 1998; Dana, 1993). Further complicating the diagnostic task, immersion in and participation with Latino/a culture also varies, and the individual of concern may be more or less immersed with their ethnocultural group. This may influence the amount of information the individual is comfortable sharing, the method in which they experience an interview or respond to a testing task, their beliefs about mental health and mental illness, their social alienation from mainstream dominant culture, and their willingness to accept various forms of intervention (Kim, 2007). Traditional healing methods may also be expected, and deviation from those methods may be met with disbelief and cause further alienation. Thus, for both the assessment of PD and the assessment of the cultural factors, multiple sources of information, and competence at evaluating this information, are essential (Buffenstein, 1997; Hays, 2001; Millon, 2011).

Clinical practice emphasizes individual personality pathologies on dimensions that are assumed to be relatively evenly distributed among the population of concern. There is a broad assumption that personality qualities being measured are relatively universal, or etic (Triandis, 1994). The clinician focuses on individual treatment or assignment of a quality that is assumed to reside in that individual. This individualistic clinical bias (i.e., individualistic fallacy) has been a source of concern among

We thank Steven R. Smith, Ph.D., for his comments on an earlier draft of this manuscript.

S.G. Alamilla, Ph.D. (✉)
Department of Psychology, Kennesaw State University, 1000 Chastain Road Northwest, MD 2202, Kennesaw, GA 30144, USA
e-mail: salamil1@kennesaw.edu

J.V. Wojcik, Ph.D.
Canvas Health, 7066 Stillwter Blvd. N., Oakdale, MN 55128, Oakdale, MN 55128, USA
e-mail: jwojcik@canvashealth.org

L.T. Benuto (ed.), *Guide to Psychological Assessment with Hispanics*,
DOI 10.1007/978-1-4614-4412-1_15, © Springer Science+Business Media New York 2013

psychologists and other mental health professionals and has prompted calls for efforts to attend to social and cultural contexts (American Psychiatric Association [APA], 2000; American Psychological Association [APA], 2003). Knowledge of culture and contextual factors is essential to engaging clients or examinees in the assessment process, as well as understanding their responses, making accurate attributions regarding their meaning, and obtaining valid measurement. Collecting, understanding, integrating, and reporting assessment data require knowledge of sociocultural factors (APA, 2000; Dana, 1993). Divergence of worldviews and values between examiners and examinees or clients can result in misunderstanding, misclassification, and iatrogenic treatment.

PD assessment may occur in a number of settings (Alarcon et al., 1998), such as hospitals, outpatient settings, forensic settings, criminal court, and family court, resulting in variations in the quality and amount of information available for the task and the critical nature of decision-making (Millon, 2011). Each of these contexts provides a different level of information and referral question. In other words, assessment settings and contexts will differ with respect to the nature and purpose of assessment, which may further complicate cross-cultural issues in the assessment process.

In many clinical settings, individuals seek relief from stress and have a vested interest in accurately describing their problems. In the case of PDs, however, individuals are more likely to not see themselves as having a problem, or being a problem, even when they or those around them are significantly distressed (Westen & Shedler, 2007). Based on current conceptualizations of PDs, deviation from expected cultural behavior is such that individuals with PDs causes stress to those around them, despite their conviction that their feelings or behaviors are justified. Their own description of the problem will inherently contain significant subjectivity biases (Westen & Shedler, 2007).

This chapter will therefore provide an overview of relevant demographic and important sociocultural information for Latino/a Americans in the context of personality (disorder) assessment and present a discussion of the range of clinical tools and strategies used to assess and diagnose PDs, as well as recommendations for assessing Latino/as. This chapter will review specific psychological tests and interview schedules and discuss their potential utility in personality (disorder) assessment among Latino/a clients. The following measures are reviewed: Minnesota Multiphasic Personality Inventory-2 (MMPI-2; Butcher, Dahlstrom, Graham, Tellegen, & Kaemmer, 1989), Personality Assessment Inventory (PAI; Morey, 1991), and Millon Clinical Multiaxial Inventory-III (MCMI-III). The following interview schedules are also reviewed: Shedler-Westen Assessment Procedure (SWAP; Westen & Shedler, 2007) and Hare Psychopathy Checklist Revised (PCL-R; Hare, 2003; Hare, Clark, Grann, & Thornton, 2000) as examples of additional tools to consider with Latino/as. Although interview schedules such as the Structured Clinical Interview for DSM-IV Personality Disorders (SCID-II; First, Gibbon, Spitzer, Williams, & Benjamin, 1997) are used frequently in the assessment of PDs in clinical and research settings, their use with Latino/as has been understudied.

Overview of U.S. Latino/a Population

Latino/as are the fastest growing ethnocultural group in the U.S. (U.S. Census Bureau, 2010). Current official census estimates have the U.S. Latino/a population at 50,478,000 (Passel & Cohn, 2011). This represents an increase from 2006 official estimates of 44.3 million or 14.8% of the total U.S. population (U.S. Census Bureau, 2006). Some projections indicate that by 2050, the U.S. Latino/a population will increase to 29% (Passel & Cohn, 2008).

According to 2008 U.S. Census estimates, the majority of U.S. Latino/as were of Mexican background (66%), 9% were of Puerto Rican background, 3.4% were of Cuban background, 3.4% were of Salvadoran background, and 2.8% were of Dominican background (U.S. Census Bureau, 2010).

Previous estimates indicated that 7.2% of Latino/as were from Central America, 5.5% were from South America, and 6.7% reported *other Hispanic or Latino* background (U.S. Census Bureau, 2007). Almost half of Latino/as were foreign-born (47%). Notably, 76% of Latino/as 5 years or older spoke Spanish at home.

Socioeconomically, U.S. Latino/as face many challenges. Among Latino/as aged 25 or older, only 62% had at least a high school education and 13% a bachelor's degree or higher. The poverty rate among Latino/as was 23.2%, while 30.7% of Latino/as lacked health insurance (U.S. Census Bureau, 2010). These challenges are compounded by current economic factors and trends, which have adversely affected Latino/as (Pew Research Center, 2011).

There is substantial diversity within the U.S. Latino/a population (Casas, Alamilla, Ortega, & Cabrera, in press; Gloria & Segura-Herrera, 2004). For instance, Latino/as differ with respect to several factors such as ethnic and racial ancestry, ethnic and racial identity, country of origin, size, nativity rates, geographical concentration and immigration history, acculturation and assimilation, socioeconomic status, and, as recent epidemiological data suggest, mental and chemical health (Alegria et al., 2007, 2008; Casas et al., in press; Gonzalez, Tarraf, Whitfield, & Vega, 2010; Kim, Soliz, Orellana, & Alamilla, 2009; Pew Hispanic Center/Kaiser Family Foundation, 2002; U.S. Census Bureau, 2006).

Sociocultural Considerations in Assessing the Latino/a Client

Latino/as represent a heterogeneous group of individuals from various racial, ethnic, and cultural backgrounds (Casas et al., in press; Gloria & Segura-Herrera, 2004). Such distinctions are important, and the use of the term *Latino/a* or *Hispanic*[1] is not meant to convey a homogenous group. Despite such differences, Latino/as differ from other ethnic/racial groups, such as European and African Americans, on a broad range of social dimensions and factors. For instance, compared to European and African Americans, Latino/as possess more conservative social values (e.g., morality), place a strong value on familism, and adhere to fatalism (Pew Hispanic Center/Kaiser Family Foundation, 2002).[2] Thus, despite their diversity, Latino/as do not represent a "hodgepodge of distinct national origin groups" (Pew Hispanic Center/Kaiser Family Foundation, 2002, p. 6). The following sociocultural variables are helpful in understanding and assessing Latino/as. As such, they should be considered when completing assessments with this population.

Acculturation and Enculturation

Acculturation and enculturation are useful for understanding the psychosocial functioning of Latino/as (Kim et al., 2009). Psychological acculturation "refers to changes in an individual who is a participant in a culture-contact situation—a person who is being influenced directly by the external culture and by the changing culture of which the individual is a member" (Berry, 2003, p. 19). Psychological acculturation thus describes individual changes in knowledge, behaviors, values, and cultural identity (Kim & Abreu, 2001) resulting from intercultural contact and/or socialization to the cultural norms of another society. Psychological enculturation refers to the process by which individuals are socialized

[1] Although Latino/as may share a general, basic cultural system (Marin & Marin, 1991), there are substantial within-group differences among Latino/as. The adoption of self-referential racial or ethnic labels (e.g., *Latino/a, Hispanic, Chicana/o, Boricua*) among subgroups and individuals varies as a function of generation status, geographic region, nationality, socioeconomic status, and personal preference (Gloria & Segura-Herrera, 2004) as well as context (e.g., Brewer, 1991; Sellers et al., 1998).

[2] Yet there are likely to be within and between group as well as generational differences.

to traditional or indigenous cultural norms (Herskovits, 1948). Psychological enculturation thus describes individual processes or changes resulting from (re)socialization to indigenous cultural norms, that is, values, behaviors, attitudes, or worldviews (Kim, 2007). Psychological acculturation and enculturation refer to complex changes and processes encompassing several domains and dimensions.

Acculturation and enculturation do not represent opposite ends of one continuum but rather separate co-occurring processes, and not all dimensions change at the same time or rate (Kim & Abreu, 2001; also see Alegria, Chap. 10, this volume). Cultural values, cultural identity, and ethnic identity may be the most resistant and last to change (Keefe & Padilla, 1987; Kim, Atkinson, & Yang, 1999; Liebkind, 2006). Of particular relevance to the psychosocial functioning and mental health of Latino/as are pan-Latino/a values such as familism (centrality of the family) and fatalism (Pew Hispanic Center/Kaiser Family Foundation, 2002). These coincide with traditional Latino/a values identified by Kim et al. (2009). Kim et al. identified the following Latino/a values dimensions: cultural pride, simpatía (congeniality), familismo (familism), and espiritismo (spirituality).[3] Cultural values and scripts such as simpatía may be common to several Latino/a subgroups (Kim et al., 2009; Ramirez-Esparza, Gosling, & Pennebaker, 2008), although they may be more pronounced among certain groups (e.g., Latino/as from Mexico) and stronger in earlier generations.

Acculturation and enculturation have important implications for the assessment of Latino/as (see Alegria, Chap. 10, this volume). For one, acculturation and enculturation are useful for assessing individual and within-group differences as well as the mental health and psychosocial functioning of Latino/as (Atkinson, 2004; Kim & Abreu, 2001; Kim et al., 2009). Some research has suggested the role of acculturation and enculturation as moderating variables between psychosocial variables and mental health outcomes (e.g., Alamilla, 2010; Alamilla, Kim, & Lam, 2010; Cervantes & Acosta, 1992; Cuellar, Siles, & Bracamontes, 2004). It is important to keep in mind that acculturation and enculturation are integrally tied to culture, and culture influences experience, meaning, and expression of psychological symptoms as well as course and outcomes of psychopathology (Chiriboga, Yuri, Banks, & Giyeon, 2007; Marsella & Yamada, 2007; U.S. Department of Health and Human Services [USDHHS], 2001).

Mental Health Burdens and Risk Factors

As a whole, Latino/as shoulder a disproportionate number of health burdens and risk factors relative to their European American counterparts (Alegria et al., 2008). The growing mental health disparities literature continues to document support for the Latino/a health paradox (Alegria et al., 2007, 2008; Gonzalez et al., 2010), which holds that although low socioeconomic status is associated with poorer health outcomes, the health of Latino/as in low socioeconomic strata is better than that of European Americans in the same socioeconomic strata, and the health of Latino/a immigrants is better than that of U.S.-born Latino/as, but Latino/as' health declines over time (Alegria et al., 2007).[4] The mental health risk factors confronting Latino/as (and other ethnocultural groups) consist of experiences of racism and discrimination, poverty, adjustment/adaptation issues, disparities in health and mental health services (USDHHS, 2001), and inadequate health insurance (U.S. Department of Health and Human Services, 2004). Consideration of these factors is important to the accurate assessment of Latino/as, as a means of minimizing the individualistic fallacy, and avoiding faulty overgeneralizations.

---

[3] Although these values dimensions were initially developed from a larger pool of theoretical pan-Latino/a values, their representativeness remains to be addressed as they have thus far only been validated with college students primarily of Mexican heritage.

[4] As important, within-group differences have been found for specific subgroups and for type of disorder (Alegria et al., 2008).

Of particular relevance is the issue of disparities and bias in mental health services. Influential reports support the notion of statistical[5] or non-intentional forms of discrimination in health settings (e.g., Balsa & McQuire, 2001; Smedley et al., 2003). Even in the context of mental health, rater bias or misdiagnosis cannot be ruled out (Chavira et al., 2003). For instance, Chavira et al. could not rule out the role of misdiagnosis and clinical bias in the case of higher endorsement rates of schizotypal personality disorer (STPD) criteria among African Americans. Whether "taste" or "statistical discrimination," conscious or unconscious, intentional or unintentional, it is likely that subtle forms of prejudice and racism are fundamentally at work. Despite their advanced training, health service providers are also susceptible to contemporary racism:

> It is reasonable to assume, however, that the vast majority of healthcare providers find prejudice morally abhorrent and at odds with their professional values. But healthcare providers, like other members of society, may not recognize manifestations of prejudice in their own behavior. While there is no direct evidence that provider biases affect the quality of care for minority patients, research suggests that healthcare providers' diagnostic and treatment decisions, as well as their feelings about patients, are influenced by patients' race or ethnicity. (Smedley, Stith, & Nelson, 2003, pp. 10–11)

And negative experiences with health care providers during the clinical encounter may diminish a patient's preference for optimal treatment(s), thereby increasing health disparities (Smedley et al., 2003). Language and communication barriers are likely to compound misunderstanding and misdiagnosis.

To summarize, the literature discussed above strongly suggests the importance of taking into account acculturation, enculturation, nativity or generation status, ethnicity/race, socioeconomic status, demographic variables, type of disorder, and various structural factors in understanding the health of Latino/as as these are associated with mental health risk and protective factors (Alegria et al., 2008; Marsella & Yamada, 2007; USDHHS, 2001). In addition to considering the role of ethnicity or race when assessing Latino/as, assessors should also consider the role of acculturation and enculturation as Latino/as may be differentially immersed in their respective cultural groups. Considering each in the assessment of Latino/as can aid in the interpretation of assessment results. For instance, considering the differential protective effect associated with nativity for certain disorders can provide clinicians with a more nuanced and accurate understanding of their Latino/a client's functioning. As further examples, persons who are in the immigration process or new to a society or social setting, and especially those who are not fluent in the language of the dominant culture, may experience substantial stress and perceived to be socially alienated and to employ strong defensive measures that may make them appear schizoid or avoidant. Persons from cultures that hold specific religious beliefs and rituals outside of the dominant culture may be thought to demonstrate a schizotypal disorder. Persons in hostile social settings may adopt protective behavior which makes them appear antisocial. Persons under substantial social stress, including immigration, may display the emotional instability of borderline personality. Clinicians will also need to be cognizant of the potential for unconscious and subtle forms of prejudice which may result in unintentional forms of discrimination as these can result in negative patient experiences and clinical encounters, which can further result in health disparities (Smedley et al., 2003).

Psychopathology and Mental Health Among Latino/as

Relatively few studies have documented the epidemiology of personality disorders (PDs) or shed light on the cross-cultural aspects of PDs for Latino/as. An older study, the Epidemiological Catchment Area study (Robins et al., 1984) focused on three PDs (antisocial personality disorder, ASD; borderline

[5] Balsa and McGuire (2001) define taste discrimination as intentional and statistical discrimination as unintentional. These are akin to conscious versus unconscious discrimination, respectively.

personality disorder, BPD; and histrionic personality disorder, HPD) and found that rates differed as a function of race/ethnicity, disorder, and SES (Chavira et al., 2003). Although DSM conceptualizations and descriptions of Axis I and II disorders support a supposition that Axis II disorders underlie and influence the expression of the Axis I clinical disorders (APA, 2003), sociocultural factors appear to play an important role in both Axis I and II disorders (Chavira et al., 2003; Marsella & Yamada, 2007; Shiraev & Levy, 2010; USDHHS, 2001).

Using data from the Collaborative Longitudinal Personality Disorder Study (CLPS), Chavira et al. (2003) compared the relative proportion of four PDs (schizotypal, STPD; BPD; avoidant, AVPD; and obsessive-compulsive, OCPD) among a clinical sample of African Americans ($n=65$), European Americans ($n=433$), and Latino/a Americans ($n=56$) from several cities in the northeast. Chavira et al. found that Latino/as were more likely to be diagnosed with BPD than African Americans and European Americans. African Americans were more likely to have STPD than European and Latino/a Americans, using diagnoses from structured interviews. No significant ethnic/racial differences were found for AVPD or OCPD. Interestingly, ethnic differences were found for BPD criterion 1 (intense anger), BPD criterion 2 (affective instability), and BPD criterion 9 (unstable relationships), with Latino/as endorsing disproportionately more criteria. African Americans had disproportionately more criteria of endorsement for criterion 9. African Americans also had disproportionately higher rates of several STPD criteria: social anxiety, no close friends, odd beliefs, and paranoia, relative to European Americans, and higher rates of social anxiety and odd beliefs relative to Latino/a Americans. Gender-specific analyses revealed that Latino/a American men had disproportionately more BPD diagnoses than European American men. African American women had disproportionately more STPD diagnoses than European and Latino/a American women. No gender effects were found for AVPD or OCPD. Plausible explanations for BPD differences for Latino/as are acculturation and acculturation-related problems. Another possible explanation offered by the authors was diagnostic bias. No information was presented for generation status.

Perez-Benitez et al. (2010) used data from the CLPS to examine ethnic differences in adverse childhood experiences as well as lifetime traumatic events and current and lifetime prevalence rates of major depressive disorder (MDD), posttraumatic stress disorder (PTSD), substance use disorder, and BPD among 708 participants. Controlling for educational level and employment status, results indicated that European Americans reported higher rates of neglect, verbal/emotional abuse, and traumatic events (e.g., serious accidents, injury/fear of injury) compared to African and Latino/a Americans. It is not clear whether this finding was due to objectively higher rates for European Americans or differences in reporting. No interactions were found between risk factors and proportion of participants from different ethnic groups with a disorder: That is, there was no evidence in support of greater vulnerability to disorders for ethnocultural groups, after controlling for type of event, ethnicity, educational level, and employment status. However, Latino/as constituted a relatively small proportion of the sample ($n=94$; 13%), and results were not disaggregated for Latino/a subgroups. No information was presented for generation status.

Although the literature on the epidemiology of personality disorders among Latino/as and other ethnocultural populations is scarce, the current evidence suggests that Latino/as in certain clinical settings may present with certain disorders (or for specific criteria on certain disorders; e.g., BPD) relative to other disorders. A study by Ansell et al. (2010) also found that BPD was more prevalent relative to other disorders among a sample of Latino/as with substance use problems in an outpatient setting.[6] However, results from these studies are not generalizable to the larger Latino/a population—and do not provide evidence regarding the prevalence of these personality disorders among the general U.S. Latino/a population. Furthermore, previous studies have not found any evidence of differences in rates of certain personality disorders among Latino/as (e.g., ASD; Robins et al., 1984).

[6] Both studies included nonrepresentative clinical samples of Latino/as from the northeast.

It is possible that sociocultural factors as well as bias (i.e., misdiagnosis) played a role in the higher rates of BPD diagnoses among Latino/as (Chavira et al., 2003). For instance, Chavira et al. noted the possible role of acculturation and acculturation difficulties. From a sociocultural perspective, the primary clinical features of BPD, namely, unstable self-image or sense of self, possessing contradictory feelings or ideas, poor affect regulation or requiring involvement of another person to help regulate affect, and, to some extent, unstable, chaotic, or unstable relationships (APA, 2000; Westen & Shedler, 2007), appear particularly vulnerable to sociocultural factors and cross-cultural differences in self-construals, self-organization, cognition, affect, and interpersonal behavior (Kitayama, Duffy, & Uchida, 2007; Marsella & Yamada, 2007; Tov & Diener, 2007). For instance, collectivist and interdependent cultures, such as Latino/a culture, may promote intersubjective emotional experiences, wherein emotions are experienced intersubjectively and may dissipate outside the context in which they are originally experienced (Tov & Diener, 2007).

Summary

Evidence from the epidemiology literature on personality and psychiatric disorders points to disparities for certain psychiatric disorders and role of sociocultural factors in these disparities. For instance, several studies demonstrate support for the Latino/a health paradox, in that Latino/a immigrants are generally less likely to have a mood, anxiety, or substance use disorder relative to their U.S.-born Latino/a and European American counterparts. U.S.-born, English-language-proficient, and third-generation Latino/as generally have increased rates of any psychiatric disorder (Alegria et al., 2007, 2008; Gonzalez et al., 2010). Evidence from health research also indicates disparities in rates of diabetes and in provision and quality of medical care (Smedley et al., 2003). The disparities literature underscores the importance of nativity, ethnicity, SES, demographic variables, type of disorder (Alegria et al., 2008), level of impairment (Gonzalez et al., 2010), and sociocultural and contextual variables in understanding the mental health of Latino/as. While the prevalence of certain disorders (e.g., obsessive-compulsive personality disorder, OCPD) is unknown for Latino/as, their prevalence may be moderated by demographic and psychiatric characteristics (Ansell et al., 2010).

Taken together, the research findings have important implications for personality disorder assessment among Latino/as. For one, the findings implicate the preponderance of psychosocial factors in the overall mental health of Latino/as (e.g., Alegria et al., 2007, 2008; Breslau et al., 2011)—the importance of which cannot be understated in the assessment of Latino/as. Cumulative adversities and health burdens are believed to account for disparities in the health status of ethnocultural groups (Myers, 2009). Thus, considering these factors and sociocultural factors is critical in reducing the individualist fallacy and viewing behavior as not only reflecting internal, innate, and dispositional characteristics but as response(s) to psychosocial stressors and adversities, social alienation, cultural mistrust, discrimination, and perhaps hostile sociopolitical environment (consider current anti-immigration sentiment). While examiners will need to be attuned to the larger sociocultural context and potential for bias (mis- or overdiagnosis), examiners will also need to be attuned to true signals of problems (Iwamasa, Larranee, & Merritt, 2000), thereby avoiding underdiagnosing, provision of inappropriate treatment, and further disparities.

Personality, Personality Disorder, and Personality Assessment

The perspective adopted throughout the chapter is that sociocultural factors, as well as the context of evaluation, impact the psychosocial functioning and mental health of Latino/as, are intimately tied to conceptions and classification systems of normative personality functioning, and impact the assessment process. The authors' perspective is that personality assessment should entail a careful consideration of relevant sociocultural factors, use of multiple psychometrically sound and culturally valid testing tools, and diverse sources of information. In this manner, personality assessment can be used to accurately understand and describe—and not merely diagnose—Latino/a clients.

PD defines a broad class of psychopathology that describes the persistently deviant interaction of the individual in a social context (APA, 2000). As such, personality disorders perhaps are the most important class of disorders to be considered from a social and cultural context. These disorders are specifically defined by homogeneous categories in the diagnostic and statistical manual of American psychiatry (APA, 2000). Further, these disorders are both important clinically and essential in the understanding of the individual's functional failures (Millon, 2011). Understanding these problems has been a major mission of psychology and psychiatry over the past century, and while there are some recurring themes in the writings of clinicians and scholars in the area, it clearly is a difficult task to define and measure these disorders in a reliable and meaningful way (Westen & Shedler, 1999a, 1999b, 2007).

While the diagnosis of PDs in homogeneous categories in the diagnostic and statistical manual of American psychiatry is recognized as a problem for a quality of human behavior so clearly dimensional (Alarcon et al., 1998; Millon, 2011; Westen & Shedler, 2007), PDs are defined as enduring patterns of internal experience and behavior that deviate markedly from the expectations of the individual's culture, are pervasive and inflexible, have onset (or stable presence that may allow diagnosis) in adolescence or early adulthood, are stable over time, and lead to distress and/or impairment (APA, 2000). Beginning with DSM-III, personality disorders were structured to be the foundational context for Axis I disorders and given specific criteria to qualify for diagnosis. PD was not intended to be seen as a disease entity but a context of the individual's stress that then shapes the expression of illness and behavior (Millon, 2011).

There are a variety of complex conceptual problems with PDs among clinicians, researchers, and epidemiologists. Westen and Shedler (1999a, 1999b) described nine categories of needed improvements in the efforts to understand, diagnose, and predict PDs in any person or population. These include the discrete and dichotomous categories of disorder and the numerous diagnostic requirements of which only a subset are required, allowing any two individuals with the same diagnosis to have very different behaviors or symptoms. Further, the descriptions and criteria for the diagnoses were shaped by the limitations of information that could be collected by the interview method of diagnosis, limiting the criteria that could improve discrimination of a disorder. Finally, DSM criteria fail to account for ways that adaptive personality attributes might compensate for less adaptive personality qualities.

Despite the homogeneous categories of PD diagnosis, personality and PDs are increasingly described by clinicians and researchers in a conceptual framework, ranging from normal personality to abnormal personality style to personality disorder, in a manner that reflects difficulties in human adaptation (Millon, 2011). Future diagnostic classifications of PDs are expected to have more dimensional than categorical structure, resolving some of these diagnostic dilemmas. This definition is expected to change as of the release of the fifth edition of DSM, expected in 2013.

The DSM-IV-TR (APA, 2000), which is still in use at the time of this volume and defines the approach to diagnosis at the present time, lists ten defined personality disorders, organized into three clusters. Cluster A of the personality disorder grouping includes behavior patterns considered to be odd and eccentric. This category includes paranoid, schizoid, and schizotypal personality disorders. Cluster B of this grouping, dramatic and emotional, contains disorders of borderline, histrionic, and narcissistic personality. Cluster C contains anxious and fearful, avoidant, dependent, and obsessive-compulsive disorders. Combinations of these personality disorders are possible, both within and across the clusters. Each of these disorders may have special meaning and importance in a cultural context. This is also important given the experience of immigration, social discrimination, economic hardship, and other adversities and health burdens discussed earlier. However, little is known about the cross-cultural prevalence and expression of these disorders. Persons who find themselves in conflict with social institutions may have been unaware of or unable to avoid the attention of authority, or may have been more noticed because of their relative visible differences from the dominant culture members, and more frequently identified as engaged in deviant or illegal behavior. They may have been engaged in behaviors and relationships that are considered normative in their native culture. However, in an adopted country, the dominant culture enforces its own normative behavior. DSM-IV has attempted to account for this; for example, the description of paranoid personality disorder recognizes the increased for frequency of social disruption and misunderstanding that is likely because of unfamiliarity of social norms, or in response to perceived injustices of the dominant culture. DSM also notes that some ethnocultural groups may have cultural norms that might be misunderstood as a paranoid personality disposition. It contains the caveat that these diagnoses are not to be made in situations where the behavior or relationship of concern is endorsed or native to the person's culture (APA, 2000).

Personality and PDs are predicted to exist across cultures. Evidence from cross-cultural studies of mental illness and personality concordance supports that personality has both adaptive and maladaptive elements, and that persistent extremes of personality reflect disorder across cultures. Terraciano and McCrae (2006) wrote that the Five Factor Model of personality (FFM) has been found to successfully describe patterns of personality across cultures, and to demonstrate that despite the reliability of differences across the aggregate personality patterns of cultures, the range of individual differences between individuals in a given culture is much greater. Further, patterns of personality as portrayed by the FFM are relevant to the patterns of and vulnerability to both Axis I disorders, such as depression or anxiety disorders, as well as Axis II PDs (Bagby, Costa, Widiger, Ryder, & Marshal, 2005; Dyce & OConnor, 1998). Despite the apparent cross-cultural applicability of the FFM, some research has suggested that the FFM does not completely describe personality in all cultures, there are interpersonal dimensions relevant to collectivistic cultures not captured by the FFM (Cheung et al., 2001).

Tools for Measurement of Personality and PDs

Assessment of PDs in most health care settings comes from two major categories of measurement. Self-report inventories such as the MMPI, MCMI, PAI, and NEO-PI-R form one major category. Structured clinical interviews such as the SCID-II (First et al., 1997) form the second major category. Further assessment also is possible from interviews with family, and detailed observation in clinical settings such as hospitalization or other institutional settings, or outpatient therapy. Clinical records from arrest histories may also contribute to these determinations. As an important third category, data is also gleaned from the manner in which the client interacts with the assessor. Despite the method of measurement, assessors utilize a great degree of clinical observation, judgment, and inference when assessing personality disorders (Westen & Shedler, 2007). The last category of information is organized into an assessment tool, the Shedler-Westen Assessment Procedure (SWAP; Westen & Shedler, 2007), described below, as well as being commonly integrated in less formal assessment as practiced alongside the structures of DSM (Westen & Shedler, 1999a, 1999b).

Use of tests and structured interviews to diagnose personality disorders may not provide equivalent results (Millon, 2011). In a comparison of eight studies using both psychological testing and structured interviews, Perry (1992) found low reliability of overall diagnostic agreement between any two instruments (Table 15.1). Diagnostic concordance was lower between self-report questionnaire and interview methods, while reliability between interview methods was improved. Thus, while methods for making personality disorder diagnoses may have high reliability, the diagnoses they yield are not significantly

Table 15.1 Measures and interview schedules for the assessment of personality disorders in adults

Test name	Original language	Type of assessment	Country of norms	Age range (years)
Minnesota Multiphasic Personality Inventory-2 (MMPI-2)	English; multiple versions in Spanish; multiple other languages	Personality and personality disorder, psychological functioning	U.S. (no specific norms for U.S. Latino/a population), Mexico, Chile, Argentina, Spain	18 and older
Personality Assessment Inventory (PAI)	English; available in Spanish	Personality problems and clinical syndromes	U.S. (no specific norms for U.S. Latino/a population)	18–89
Millon Clinical Multiaxial Inventory (MCMI-III)	English, Spanish, Dutch, Portuguese, Chinese	Personality and personality disorder, psychiatric symptoms	U.S.	18 and older
Shedler-Westen Assessment Procedure (SWAP)	English and 21 other languages	Personality and personality disorder	U.S.	18 and older
Hare Psychopathy Checklist Revised (PCL-R)	English, European Spanish, Chilean Spanish, Portuguese, 11 other languages	Psychopathy	N/A	18 and older
Diagnostic Interview Schedule (DIS-IV)	English	DSM psychiatric symptoms	N/A	18 and older
Diagnostic Interview for DSM-IV Personality Disorders (DIPD-4)	English	DSM personality disorders	N/A	18 and older
Structured Interview for DSM-III Personality Disorders (SIPD)	English	DSM personality disorders	N/A	18 and older
Structured Clinical Interview for DSM-IV Personality Disorders (SCID-II)	English	DSM personality disorders	N/A	18 and older
Spanish-Language Version of the Diagnostic Interview for DSM-IV Personality Disorders (S-DIPD-IV)	Spanish	DSM personality disorders	N/A	18 and older

comparable across methods. Structured interviews even vary compared with checklists used by clinicians, such as the International Diagnostic Checklist for the assessment of DSM-III-R and ICD 10 (IDCL-P) (Bronisch & Mombour, 1994).

Assessment Measures

Personality assessment and underlying theories of mental health are based on Western-European culture and worldviews (Butcher, Cabiya, Lucio, & Garrido, 2007; Dana, 1997; Marsella & Yamada, 2007). Not surprisingly, the history of personality assessment with Latino/as has been controversial and replete with accounts of the inappropriate use and interpretation of (translated) instruments, potential bias, and scarcity of instruments specific to Latino/as (Cervantes & Acosta, 1992; Iwamasa et al., 2000).

The focus of this section is on commonly used objective measures of personality (i.e., norm-referenced, standardized tests that possess psychometric information) and interview schedules for Latino/as. Measures are discussed in terms of their construct validity, predictive validity, content validity, face validity, internal consistency (internal consistency reliability), temporal stability (test-retest reliability), equivalence, and potential bias for Latino/as, where available. While important in personality assessment for ethnocultural populations, non-pathology measures such as the California Psychological Inventory will not be reviewed. Similarly, although self-report questionnaires and checklists are often used in the assessment of psychopathology and psychosocial functioning (e.g., Symptom Checklist-90-R; Gass, 2000), these will not be reviewed as they are the subject of previous chapters and works.

Although evaluating the validity and reliability of an instrument is important, it is especially important to evaluate the equivalence and potential bias (i.e., freedom from cultural bias) of an instrument for Latino/as and other ethnocultural populations. This is particularly relevant for measures that have been translated and/or adapted for use with Latino/as. Cultural bias may be avoided when the following are present: conceptual equivalence, functional equivalence, linguistic equivalence, and psychometric equivalence (Helms, 1997; Kwan, Gong, & Maestas, 2010; Puente & Agranovich, 2004). Conceptual equivalence is concerned with the extent to which constructs have similar meanings, definitions, and manifestations across cultures (Kwan et al., 2010). Functional equivalence is concerned with the extent to which a given phenomenon (trait, behavior) serves the same function across cultures (Kwan et al., 2010). Linguistic equivalence is present when the language used in an instrument has the same meaning for different cultural groups and is concerned with the wording of translated and/or adapted tests and can be assessed with translation and back-translation (Helms, 1997; Kwan et al., 2010; Puente & Agranovich, 2004). Psychometric equivalence is concerned with the extent to which a scale measures the same thing at the same level for different cultural groups (Helms, 1997; Kwan et al., 2010; Puente & Agranovich, 2004). Different ways of assessing psychometric equivalence depend on the specific theoretical and analytical questions but can be achieved through comparisons of scale scores, distributions, and factor structure (Kwan et al., 2010).

Bias, when a test measures different things in different groups, can occur at the level of items or composite scores involving several measures. Although assessing test bias has been problematic and controversial, statistical measures used to infer test bias have been proposed (Nunnally & Bernstein, 1994). Intercept and slope bias are based on the Cleary rule (Cleary, 1968), which concerns differences in the consequences of using a test rather than in the test itself (Nunnally & Bernstein, 1994). The Cleary rule states that a test is fair if its regression equation for two different groups is the same (Nunnally & Bernstein, 1994). Intercept bias indicates an intercept difference between members of two groups, which indicates that performance on the criterion systematically differs for the two groups at a given level of the test (Nunnally & Bernstein, 1994). In other words, bias is present because members from the two groups will have different criterion scores despite having similar test scores. Slope bias indicates differential validity, that is, performance on the criterion is predicted less well for members of one group. Both intercept and slope bias can be investigated through the use of moderated multiple regression (Nunnally & Bernstein, 1994).

Statistical evidence of the relative performance on test items of ethnocultural groups and European Americans is necessary but not sufficient in determining bias (Hambleton, Swaminathan, & Rogers, 1991). Determining whether a test is biased requires an inference that goes beyond the empirical evidence (Hambleton et al., 1991). Hambleton et al. distinguish the empirical evidence from the inference of test bias through *differential item functioning* (DIF). One definition of DIF is "an item shows DIF if individuals having the same ability, but from different groups, do not have the same probability of getting the item right" (as cited in Hambleton et al., 1991). We believe that the utility of an instrument depends not only on presence of validity and reliability but on the absence of cultural and test bias.

In general, there is a dearth of research on commonly used personality measures for Latino/as. Research on equivalence and test bias is virtually nonexistent for Latino/as. A search using *PsycINFO*, *PsycARTICLES*, *MEDLINE*, and *Psychology and Behavioral Sciences Collection* with the terms such as *validity, reliability*, *factorial invariance*, *measurement invariance, test bias*, *item bias*, *cultural bias, intercept bias,* and *slope bias* resulted in surprisingly few peer-reviewed studies for Latino/as and commonly used personality measures.

Minnesota Multiphasic Personality Inventory-2

The MMPI-2 (Butcher et al., 1989) is one of the most widely used measures of personality and psychological functioning (Gass, 2000). The MMPI-2 contains 567 items and 11 validity scales (*Cannot Say, L, F, K, F-K Index, Fb, F(p), FBS, S, VRIN, TRIN*), 10 basic clinical scales (*Scale 1, Hs; Scale 2, D; Scale 3, Hy; Scale 4, Pd; Scale 5, Mf; Scale 6, Pa; Scale 7, Pt; Scale 8, Sc; Scale 9, Ma;* and *Scale 0, Si*), 10 restructured clinical (RC) scales, 15 content scales, and 12 supplementary scales. Subscales are available for several scales. Response options consist of *True, False*. In 2010, a shorter version of the MMPI, the MMPI-RF, was introduced as an alternative. As it is new and little research has yet been developed for it, it will not be further discussed here. Numerous Spanish translations of the MMPI-2, international and national, with accompanying norms are available.[7] An adolescent version for use with English and Spanish-speaking Latino/a populations is also available (Butcher et al., 2007).

Although the MMPI-2 sought to improve the representation of ethnocultural groups in the normative sample over the MMPI, only 2.8% of the normative sample was Latino/a (Whitworth & Unterbrink, 1994). Nevertheless, the English language version of the MMPI-2 is widely used with Latino/as in the USA (Butcher et al., 2007). Available research on the validity and reliability of the MMPI-2 for Latino/as is scarce. Nevertheless, available research suggests minimal differences between Latino/a Americans and European Americans. For instance, Hall, Bansal, and Lopez (1999) conducted a meta-analysis of published studies comparing MMPI-2 scale differences between Latino/as (and ethnocultural groups) and European Americans and found few significant differences between these two groups.[8] Although Latino/as had higher scores on all three validity scales (*Scales L, F, & K*), they had lower scores on all 10 clinical scales (*1, 2, 3, 4, 5, 6, 7, 8, 9, & 0*). However, effect sizes were small, with the exception of differences for Scale *L* and *5*. A rather robust finding was observed for Latino

[7] However, there are no norms available for the Spanish versions in the USA (Butcher et al., 2007).

[8] Hall et al. examined the results of 13 studies—all of which included only male participants. Importantly, most samples were comprised primarily of Mexican Americans in inpatient settings.

and European American males on *Scale 5* (Masculinity/Femininity), with Latinos endorsing more traditionally masculine gender roles.

Whitworth and Unterbrink (1994) compared scores on the MMPI-2 clinical and content scales of Mexican American and European American college students.[9] Results indicated that Mexican Americans scored significantly higher on two validity scales (*L* & *F*) and four clinical scales (*D, Pd, Sc,* & *Ma*). Mexican American participants also scored significantly higher on 13 of the 15 content scales; however no significant differences were found on the Low Self-Esteem and Social Discomfort scales. All observed differences were relatively small, and it should be pointed out none of the Mexican Americans participants scores were in the clinically elevated range. None of the observed differences appear to be explained by SES (student self-report of parent's educational attainment and occupation) differences. It is interesting to note that the Mexican American participants were less acculturated (with respect to language preference, ethnic loyalty, entertainment preferences, and friendship preferences) relative to the European American participants; no differences were found with respect to SES.

Using different Spanish versions of the MMPI-2, Cabiya and colleagues (2000) reported mean validity and clinical scale scores among a sample of Puerto Rican, Mexican, and U.S. Latino/a college students. The authors administered the Chilean version (Rissetti, Himmel, & Gonzalez-Moreno, 1996) to Puerto Rican participants, Mexican version (Lucio & Reyes-Lagunes, 1994; Lucio, Reyes-Lagunes, & Scott, 1994) to Mexican participants, and U.S.-Spanish translation (Garcia-Peltoniemi & Azan-Chaviano, 1993) for U.S. Latino participants. With the exception of the *Mf* scale, mean scores for all scales were within one standard deviation (SD=10; $M=50$) for the three groups, which the authors suggest as promise for the adaption of the MMPI-2 in Latin America. However, valid comparisons were rendered difficult due to grossly unequal sample sizes for the three groups (Mexicans, $n=1{,}920$; Puerto Ricans, $n=290$; U.S. Latino/as, $n=28$). Additionally, different methodological and analytic approaches are necessary for determining the adaptability of the MMPI-2 for use in Latin America.

The MMPI-2 Hispania (Garcia-Peltoniemi & Azan Chaviano, 1993) was developed for use with Latino/as in the USA who do not speak or understand English well and is widely used in the U.S., Puerto Rico, and even Argentina (Butcher et al., 2007). U.S. norms are used with the MMPI-2 Hispania. While the MMPI-2 has been used in several Latin American countries, the most commonly used Spanish version of the MMPI-2 is the Mexican version (Lucio & Reyes-Lagunes, 1994) (see Butcher et al. for a review of this and other international Spanish versions of the MMPI-2). Butcher et al. cited research demonstrating the validity, clinical utility, and reliability of the MMPI-2 Hispania.[10] Examples of the former have involved comparisons between Latino/as and European American patients in different clinical settings. An example of the latter was studies (Cruz-Niemiec, 2004; Velasquez, Callahan, Reimann, & Carbonell, 1998) that demonstrated the comparability of the temporal stability (1-week test-retest reliability and 6-month test-retest reliability) of the MMPI-2 Hispania and MMPI-2 among a sample of bilingual Latino/as.

One peer-reviewed study (Fantoni-Salvador & Rogers, 1997) examined the clinical utility and concurrent validity of a Spanish version of the MMPI-2 (Butcher et al., 1989) with Latino/a patients receiving services in various mental health settings, for a variety of clinical problems (depressive disorders, anxiety disorders, schizophrenia, alcohol dependence). Forty-eight Mexican Americans, 40 Puerto Ricans, and 17 "Latin Americans" were included in the study. Most participants were first and second generation and socioeconomically disadvantaged (81% had family incomes below the poverty level). All participants were orally administered select MMPI-2 scales. Results from this study demonstrated concordance between MMPI-2 code types for depression and schizophrenia and diagnoses

[9] This study was not included in Hall et al.'s review.

[10] These consisted of unpublished studies (conference presentations and/or unpublished doctoral dissertations).

obtained using the Spanish version of the Diagnostic Interview Schedule (DIS). No correspondence was found for MMPI-2 code types for anxiety disorders or alcohol dependence. Whereas the sensitivity of MMPI-2 scales was good for *Scale 2* (D) and *Scale 8* (Sc), specificity for these scales was less so. Results varied for the different substance abuse scales. The Addiction Acknowledgment Scale (AAS) demonstrated good clinical utility, whereas the MacAndrew Alcoholism Scale (MAC) and Addiction Potential Scale (APS) demonstrated at best modest clinical utility (as evidenced by their combined sensitivity and specificity). The authors reported modest concurrent validity for the clinical scales, as evidenced by scale correlations with DIS symptoms for specific disorders. Although specific findings were not reported, the authors reported within-group differences for the MAC.

In summary, very few peer-reviewed studies have examined the validity, reliability, equivalence, or bias of MMPI-2 scales for Latino/as. Nevertheless, the available evidence suggests few and relatively small differences between Latino/a Americans and European Americans on MMPI-2 scales. For instance, one major study (Hall et al., 1999) failed to find any differences between Latinos and European American males on various MMPI-2 scales. Consistent differences appear to hold only for validity scales and *Scale 5, Mf*, for Latino/as, and it is possible that sociocultural factors are partly responsible for these differences (Butcher et al., 2007). Yet the absence of significant differences does not necessarily indicate a lack of test bias (Hall et al., 1999).

It is imperative that future research address potential issues of equivalence and bias of MMPI-2 scales for Latino/as. Research that better addresses the functional, conceptual, and linguistic equivalence of the MMPI-2 for Latino/as is needed. For instance, more stringent tests of the functional equivalence of the MMPI-2 are needed, especially with community samples of Latino/as. Such research may use mixed methods designs and additional outcome measures necessary to address the question of whether given traits or behaviors serve a similar function in two ethnocultural groups. As few studies have examined the effects of acculturation, enculturation, ethnic identity, or other important sociocultural variables as well as within-group differences on the MMPI-2 (Hall et al., 1999),[11] future research should address these variables.

Although there is limited research on the content or supplementary scales for Latino/as, clinicians may consider utilizing them in addition to the clinical scales to inform their assessment work with Latino/as. These scales may provide alternate (non-pathological and strength-based) perspectives into personality and psychosocial functioning, which may be helpful in reducing a biased and skewed understanding of Latino/as (Sam, 2006). Another strength of the MMPI-2 is the availability of several translated (Spanish) versions and corresponding norms (see Butcher et al., 2007 for more information).

The Personality Assessment Inventory

The Personality Assessment Inventory (PAI; Morey, 1991) is a 344-item self-administered inventory of adult personality problems and clinical syndromes used extensively in clinical settings. The PAI is comprised of 22 nonoverlapping full scales: 4 validity scales (Inconsistency, ICN; Infrequency, INF; Negative Impression Management, NIM; Positive Impression Management, PIM), 11 clinical scales (Somatic Complaints, SOM; Anxiety, ANX; Anxiety-Related Disorders, ARD; Depression, DEP; Mania, MAN; Paranoia, PAR; Schizophrenia, SCZ; Borderline Features, BOR; Antisocial Features, ANT; Alcohol Problems, ALC; Drug Problems, DRG), 5 treatment consideration scales (Aggression, AGG; Suicidal Ideation, SUI; Stress, STR; Nonsupport, NON; Treatment Rejection, RXR), and 2 interpersonal scales (Dominance, DOM; Warmth, WRM) (Morey & Hopwood, 2008). All items are rated on a 4-point Likert-

[11] Only one study in Hall et al.'s review assessed acculturation.

type scale, ranging from 1 (*false, not at all true*) to 4 (*very true*). There are Spanish and adolescent versions (PAI-A) available from Psychological Assessment Resources (PAR).

Although the PAI has evidenced good psychometric properties (i.e., convergent and discriminant validity, internal consistency, and test-retest reliability) as well as content validity (Morey, 1991; Morey & Hopwood, 2008), virtually no studies have examined the psychometric properties of the PAI with Latino/a or other ethnocultural groups. As such, research on the validity, reliability, bias, or use of the PAI with Latino/as and ethnocultural groups is extremely limited. According to the test manual, differences of about one standard error of measurement were found in PAI scores for ethnic/racial groups (Morey, 1991). Rather marked differences were found between European Americans, African Americans, and *Other* racial groups on the Paranoia scale—the latter groups scored on average seven *T*-score points higher than European Americans (Morey, 1991). Although raw score means and standard deviations needed to convert raw scores to *T*-scores with reference to African Americans in the normative sample are included in the test manual (Morey & Hopwood, 2008), such data is not provided for Latino/as.

Results from an unpublished study of Latino/a (mostly Mexican American) and European American college students found that Latino/as had higher scores on several PAI scales (Alamilla, Ryan, Smith, & Kim, 2009). Based on descriptive statistics and distributions, Latino/as also had higher scores on several PAI scales compared to the standardization sample. Compared to European Americans, Latino/as had higher scores on the ANX, ARD, DEP, PAR, SCZ, BOR, AGG, and STR scales. Effect sizes, based on partial eta-squared, were moderate (Ferguson, 2009). Importantly, some of the differences were statistically moderated by behavioral and cultural identity dimensions of acculturation and enculturation (ARSMA-II scores; Cuellar, Arnold, & Maldonado, 1995).

Alterman et al. (1995) examined the reliability and concurrent validity of PAI scores among low SES African American and Latino/a American methadone maintenance patients. Their results revealed moderate to good internal reliability for several PAI scales for the entire sample, with the exception of the DRG and three nonclinical scales, and similar scale intercorrelations with those observed in the standardization sample. Modest support for the concurrent validity of PAI scales was established through correlations with the Diagnostic Interview Schedule (DIS; Robins, Helzer, Croughan, & Ratcliff, 1981) and Addiction Severity Index (ASI; McLellan et al., 1985). The authors also found significant ethnicity/race differences. Latino/as, particularly males, reported more symptomatology than African Americans on the SOM, ANX, DEP, ALC, and SUI scales. Because subjects were not matched, nor specific subgroup information provided, it is difficult to attribute these differences to ethnicity or race alone. Furthermore, because acculturation and enculturation were not measured, it is difficult to know to what extent these differences were due to sociocultural factors. No significant gender differences were found for any of the scales. Compared with the standardization sample, subjects had higher scores on all PAI scales, differed from the clinical standardization sample on 11 scales, and differed from a drug-dependent sample on three scales.

One study compared socially desirable responding between Latino/as and European Americans on the PAI (Hopwood, Flato, Ambwani, Garland, & Morey, 2009). The authors found that Latino/as scored significantly higher on the Defensiveness Indicator (DEF) composite score, a composite of several PAI indicators, and Cashel Discriminant Function (CDF) score, a composite of six PAI scale scores used to discriminate between individuals instructed to fake good and honest responders (Hopwood et al., 2009). Latino/a enculturation was positively associated with PIM and DEF scores, suggesting the possible role of cultural factors. Analyses comparing Latino/as and European Americans on the PAI Mean Clinical Elevation, an index of the average clinical elevation in the PAI, found no significant differences. No differences were found in internal reliability coefficients, and the authors did not find any evidence of scale bias.

Rogers, Flores, Ustad, and Sewell (1995) examined the "usefulness" of the PAI Spanish Edition (Morey, 1991) among a sample of mostly monolingual and bilingual Spanish-speaking Latino/as (most were Mexican American; some were Central American). The PAI English version was also examined with a sample of bilingual subjects. All participants were receiving intensive outpatient services for chemical health problems and co-occurring emotional problems in a community mental health center setting targeting first and second generation immigrants. Internal consistency reliability estimates were mostly poor for the validity scales but varied from poor to good for the clinical scales. Internal consistency reliability estimates for treatment scales also ranged from poor to good. Internal consistency reliability estimates were mostly poor for the interpersonal scales. Internal consistency coefficients for the clinical, treatment, and interpersonal scales were lower for the two samples than for the "non-White" standardization sample (Rogers et al., 1995). Test-reliability estimates for all scales showed a similar pattern for the Spanish version and ranged from acceptable to good ($M\ r = .79$). The temporal stability of the Spanish version was also less than that of the English version (Rogers et al.). Unfortunately, the (moderating) effects of nativity, ethnic/racial identification, acculturation, or enculturation were not tested.

In a follow-up study, Fantoni-Salvador and Rogers (1997) examined the clinical utility and concurrent validity of the PAI Spanish version with Latino/a patients receiving services in various mental health settings for a variety of clinical problems (depressive disorders, anxiety disorders, schizophrenia, alcohol dependence).[12] All participants were orally administered select PAI scales. Sensitivity was strong for the DEP and SCZ, whereas specificity was modest. The Alcoholism Scale (ALC) evidenced good clinical utility (as evidenced by its sensitivity and specificity). Concurrent validity, as evidenced by scale correlations with DIS symptoms for specific disorders, for clinical scales varied, with the ANX and ARD demonstrating at best modest concurrent validity and the DEP and SCZ demonstrating moderate concurrent validity. The ALC demonstrated good concurrent validity. No within-group differences were found for any of the scales.

Very few studies have examined the validity, reliability, equivalence, or potential bias of the PAI among Latino/as. As with the MMPI-2, more research is needed on the equivalence and potential bias of the PAI for Latino/as. Although one study (Hopwood & Moser, 2011) failed to find evidence for the factorial invariance of a superordinate two-factor internalizing and externalizing structure for Latino/as and European Americans, no analyses were carried out for the original PAI measurement model (i.e., manifest variables, first-order factors, or second-order factors). Some studies have found evidence of differences among Latino/as and European Americans on select scales. Yet this research should be replicated with different and diverse Latino/a samples. According to the test manual, 78.8% of the clinical standardization sample was European American, 12.6% was African American, and 8.6% was *Other* (Morey, 1991). As Latino/as comprise approximately 14.8% of the total U.S. population (U.S. Census Bureau, 2006)—yet at most comprise no more than 8.6% of the PAI standardization sample—it is imperative that researchers continue to examine the appropriateness of the PAI for Latino/as.

Little information is known about the actual development and psychometric properties of the PAI-Spanish, as there is virtually no research on this measure. Another potential limitation of the PAI is the absence of norms for Spanish-speaking U.S. Latino/as well as those living in Latin America. As such, research and clinical applications of the Spanish version of the PAI appear to be limited.

A positive feature of the PAI is its inclusion of non-pathological features of personality in the Structural Summary, such as self-concept, interpersonal style, and perception of one's environment (Morey & Hopwood, 2008).

[12] These authors also examined selected MMPI-2 scales. Refer to previous section for brief background information for this study.

The Millon Clinical Multiaxial Inventory-III

The Millon Clinical Multiaxial Inventory (MCMI-III) was developed as a part of the DSM-III process and first published in 1987 (Millon, 1997). It has since gone through two major revisions, with the latest edition, the MCMI-III, published in 1994, with each revision corresponding to a furtherchange in the DSM (Millon, Millon, Davis, & Grossman 2009). The MCMI-III consists of 175 items scored into twenty-four scales: I. eleven Clinical Personality Patterns scales: Schizoid, Avoidant, Depressive (Melancholic), Dependent, Histrionic, Narcissistic, Antisocial, Sadistic, Compulsive, Negativistic, and Masochistic; II. three Severe Personality Pathology scales: Schizotypal, Borderline, and Paranoid; III. seven Clinical Syndrome Scales: Anxiety, Somatoform, Bipolar (Manic), Dysthymia, Alcohol Dependence, Drug Dependence, and Posttraumatic Stress Disorder; IV. three Severe Clinical Syndrome scales: Thought Disorder, Major Depression, and Delusional Disorder; V. three Modifying Indices, and a Validity scale. The personality scales are grouped into two levels of severity, the Clinical Personality Patterns scales and Severe Personality scales. The Axis I scales represent clinical conditions frequently seen in clinical settings. These also are grouped into two levels of severity, the Clinical Syndrome scales and the Severe Syndrome scales. Finally, the three Modifying Indices, Disclosure, Desirability, and Debasement, assess response tendencies and influence the scoring of scales revealing specific Axis I conditions or personality patterns. The MCMI is available in Spanish from Pearson assessments.

The original MCMI was normed on a sample of 998 male and female adults with a wide variety of clinical disorders. Of 293 males, 246 (84%) were White, 25 (8.5%) were Black, and 13 (4.4%) were Hispanic. Of 307 females, 272 (88.6%) were White, 27 (8.8%) were Black, and 4 (1.3%) were Hispanic. A cross-validation sample of 197 males and 201 females contained only 3 Hispanic males (1.5%) and 5 Hispanic females (2.5%).

Use of the MCMI across cultural or other groupings makes the assumption that the rate of prevalence of a disorder is the same as in the normative sample or requires an adjustment to the scores.[13] Even in the U.S., where the MCMI was normed, few studies comparing racial groups have been published. Those available have focused on the comparison of European Americans and African Americans but have found no significant racial bias in the MCMI-I or MCMI-II (Craig, 2008). Although Millon references culture as important, no scale adjustments for non-European American populations have been published.

Research on the validity, reliability, or cultural validity of the MCMI with Latino/a populations is limited. One study (Sugihara & Warner, 1999) compared profiles of 60 Mexican American male batterers in a Texas court system with those of 45 Mexican American non-batterers from a community setting. The authors found that 35% of the batterers and 45% of the non-batterers of the Mexican American sample had higher base rate scores on the Desirability Index, suggesting that social desirability might be a common response set among this sub-population. The batterers in the court system scored significantly higher on the Schizoid, Avoidant, Dependent, Depressive, Negativistic, Self-Defeating, Schizotypal, Borderline, and Paranoid scales, while the non-batterers scored significantly higher on the Histrionic and Compulsive scales. The batterer population also scored significantly higher on the Anxiety, Somatoform, Bipolar Manic, Dysthymia, Alcohol Dependent, and PTSD Axis I scales, and on the Posttraumatic, Thought Disorder, Major Depression, and Delusional Disorder scales. The authors concluded that Mexican American batterers were not likely to match the stereotype of *machismo* but rather

[13] Unlike the normalized standard score transformations commonly used in psychological tests, the MCMI inventory uses actuarial base rate data. This avoids the implicit assumption of *T*-scores that the prevalence rates of all disorders are equal, for example, assuming there are equal numbers of persons manifesting depression as schizophrenia.

likely to have a fear of relating to others and to withdraw from social interactions. They suggested these results to be useful in the treatment of these persons.

Ghafoori and Hierholzer (2010) used the MCMI-III and measures of combat trauma to compare 24 Hispanic, 60 White, and 12 Black veterans and found the Hispanic veterans more likely to qualify for a Cluster A PD diagnosis compared to non-Hispanic veterans, but not more likely to qualify for Cluster B PDs. The level of combat exposure, PTSD symptom level, or demographic variables did not account for the PD prediction. They considered that acculturation factors, which were not measured, may have been the critical variables in this result.

In an unpublished doctoral dissertation, Gross (2011) compared the performance of Hispanic American sexual offenders with European American sexual offenders on select MCMI-III scales, the Desirability, Thought Disorder, and Dependent Scales, and found no statistically significant differences between the two groups. Despite the lack of significant differences, it is not known whether the results would have changed with the examination of key sociodemographic and sociocultural factors.

Very few peer-reviewed studies have examined the validity or psychometric properties of the Spanish version of the MCMI-III for Latino/as. Results from an unpublished dissertation (Rossi, 2003) demonstrated the comparability between the English and Spanish translations of the MCMI-III among bilingual college students, as evidenced by moderate correlations between the English and Spanish versions of the MCMI-III and MMPI-2 for Latino/a participants, fairly comparable (6 week) test-retest reliability coefficients for the Spanish and English versions of the MCMI-III and MMPI-2 for Latino/a participants, and few "major" significant scale score differences between Latino/a Americans and European Americans on the English version of the MCMI-III. However, a major problem of this study was its use of the MMPI-2 as a criterion. Additionally, this study was limited by its use of college students and small sample size ($n=50$).

The MCMI-III represents a relevant instrument for diagnosis of PDs in Latino/as, as it does for other cultural and ethnic groups, but requires a full research program to clarify the potential biases and errors that may be incurred by its use. The examiner is encouraged to use the MCMI only in the context of other corroborating information, especially in light of general limitations of the MCMI. These consist of an imbalance between true and false items, with the vast majority of items keyed in the "true" direction; relative weakness in assessing minor personality pathology and those with psychotic disorders; perception that the Histrionic, Narcissistic, and Compulsive scales are more likely to detect personality styles rather than disorders; poor convergent validity with standard psychiatric rating schedules across many of its scales; the speculative nature of the personality disorder subtypes; the modest size of the normative sample, which underrepresents ethnocultural groups; and the few validation studies and limited research on the measure compared with some other scales (Craig, 1999, 2008). (For a critique of the MCMI in forensic settings, see Ackerman & Kane, 2011).

Interview Schedules

Two instruments are now reviewed as examples of structures guiding clinicians and researchers in using a broad range of collateral information to organize judgments and classifications. These are the SWAP and Hare PCL-R.

The Shedler-Westen Assessment Procedure (SWAP)

The SWAP (Westen & Shedler, 2007) was developed to challenge and refine DSM and other concepts of personality disorders and develop a more meaningful assessment process for PDs. They observed that clinicians across theoretical frameworks listened carefully to the narrative accounts of their patients' lives and relationships and observed the patients' interactions with them in their therapeutic encounters in the consulting room, and built these careful observations into hypotheses about the patients' characteristic interpersonal problems. The SWAP method then combined these clinical observations with psychometric methods and algorithms to generate predictions and diagnostic conclusions.

SWAP is primarily a research psychometric instrument at the present time, although efforts are underway to bring it to greater presence in clinical practice. It consists of a clinician-report Q-sort for assessing personality and personality pathology. The SWAP-200 yields a 0–7 score for each of 200 items derived from sources such as the DSM PD criteria, clinical and empirical literature on personality pathology, research on normal traits and psychological health, and previous research with pilot versions of the instrument. The instrument is available on an Excel program to enable researchers and clinicians to use the algorithms developed by the authors. The authors granted requests to translate the instrument into several languages including Spanish.

The SWAP generates a wide range of scales with multiple clinical applications. The scores can be expressed as *T*-scores and graphed as a profile, resembling an MMPI-2™ profile. Using appropriate cutoffs, clinicians can read a likely DSM-IV personality diagnosis from the PD profile. Personality Disorder Scores (PD Scores) measure the similarity or match between a patient and offer a DSM-IV-referenced personality description for each personality disorder. The Personality Health Index (PHI) utilizes information from the complete SWAP data set to provide an overall measure of personality health and to measure personality change in psychotherapy. SWAP factor scores (12 scales for adults, 11 for adolescents) can be used to supplement PD scores.

The SWAP is likely to continue to influence research into PDs, and should be seriously considered in cross-cultural PD research. While the SWAP may lack efficiency compared to self-report or structured interview methods, it most closely approximates the understanding of how PDs are recognized and understood in a person. The approach adopted by SWAP is expected to be visible in future versions of PD diagnostic systems, including the DSM-5. However, at present time, there is insufficient evidence regarding the appropriateness of the SWAP for Latino/as.

The Hare Psychopathy Checklist Revised (PCL-R)

The PCL-R (Hare, 2003; Hare et al., 2000) is a 20-item scale for assessment of psychopathy in research, clinical, and forensic settings. It uses trained clinician ratings from a semi-structured interview, as well as historical behavior from collateral interviews and file review. The PCL-R measures two factors: the first, Interpersonal and Affective Problems, and a second factor reflecting Impulsive and Antisocial Behavior and Unstable Lifestyle. The Hare PCL-R has become a frequently used instrument in the prediction of violence risk, treatment response, civil commitment for psychopathic sex offenders, and in research on antisocial behavior and related problems. It is frequently used as an adjunct to other psychological instruments such as the MMPI.

Hare et al., 2000) asserted that the reliability, total scores, and differences in mean scores of the PCL across racial groups studied were not significantly different, and that in a survey of findings from several other countries, including England and Sweden, the PCL-R retained the ability to predict recidivism, violence, and treatment outcome with considerable cross-cultural generalizability (Hare et al., 2000).

Sullivan, Abramowitz, Lopez, and Kosson (2006), comparing 83 Latino inmates with matched samples of African Americans and European Americans, found the PCL-R to provide a reliable and valid measure of psychopathy (related to the presence of ASPD) in Latinos, finding similar patterns of psychopathy emerging between Latino and European American inmates across other measures of psychopathy and related constructs, between psychopathy and alcohol and substance abuse ratings, and trait anxiety scores. Latino and European American groups were also similar in the relationships between PCL-R measured psychopathy and criminal behavior, psychopathy and age, and between psychopathy and intelligence.

However, it is important to point out that ASPD is vulnerable to bias in the rater or diagnostician (Alarcon et al., 1998). Broad criticisms of the definitions of ASPD given the cross-cultural variability of human behavior were described in Dingies, Mera, and Vi (1997). They observed that such concepts as a lack of remorse may be particularly variable across cultures and situations, and ASPD may be understood differently in dominant culture-non-dominant culture interactions. Irresponsibility is a further culturally vulnerable concept. They particularly challenged the assumption that the frequency of arrest rates among different racial and ethnic minorities reflected in any way the frequency of ASPD in that population. While Dingies et al. accepted the likely existence of ASPD in most or all ethnic groups in America, they rejected the sufficiency of DSM criteria to define it. While the standardization efforts of the PCL-R are an effort to reduce challenges to validity of the ASPD diagnosis, the definitions of psychopathy contained in the PCL-R remain imperfect and potentially culturally invalid. The PCL-R may be an appropriate instrument for Latino/as when caution regarding the source data is used, but that may be more difficult than clinicians are aware of.

Structured Clinical Interviews

There are numerous interview schedules used to make PD diagnoses, in clinical practice and research, such as the Diagnostic Interview Schedule (DIS-IV; Robins et al., 1981), Diagnostic Interview for DSM-IV Personality Disorders (DIPD-4; Zanarini, Frankenburg, Sickel, & Yong, 1996), and Structured Interview for DSM-III Personality Disorders (SIPD) among others.

The Structured Clinical Interview for DSM-IV Personality Disorders (SCID-II; First et al., 1997) is a semi-structured interview for making DSM-IV Axis II (PD) diagnoses. Using this interview to evaluate PD takes 30–60 min for a trained interviewer, who need not be a mental health professional. It is available in clinical and research versions, and a Spanish version is available. As this is an interview, appropriate Spanish fluency would be essential. Patient versions of the SCID-II are also available. However, given the absence of research for Latino/as with these measures, examiners should consider their potential merits with regard to their potential limitations for Latino/as.

Of particular relevance is the Spanish-Language Version of the Diagnostic Interview for DSM-IV Personality Disorders (S-DIPD-IV; Grilo, Anez, & McGlashan, 2003). Grilo et al. examined the psychometric properties of the S-DIPD-IV among a sample of adult monolingual Latino/a patients, many of whom were in treatment for substance abuse problems. Cross- and back-translation procedures were used to ensure linguistic equivalence. Interrater reliability estimates for the S-DIPD-IV for 10 DSM-IV PDs were adequate to good (mean kappa = .83) and were comparable to those reported for the DIPD-IV, with the exception for PPD (kappa = .38). Interestingly, 65.3% of the patients met criteria for at least one PD, with the most common being BPD (33.7%), followed by OCPD (31.6%) and APD (31.6%). No gender differences were found in the number of PD diagnoses, with the exception for ASPD (a greater proportion of males were diagnosed with ASPD). Criteria sets for each of the PDs were stronger within each PD versus between PDs, suggesting good discriminant validity and internal consistency of PD criteria (acceptable Cronbach's alpha coefficients and intercriterion correlations were reported), with the exception of Cluster A PDs (none of Cronbach's alpha coefficients were greater than .70). Cluster A PDs evidenced significant overlap with other PD criteria, whereas two (HPD & DPD) evidenced some, and six (BPD, ASPD, NPD, APD, & OCPD) evidenced no overlap with other PD criteria.

Summary/Conclusion

A glaring omission in the available research concerns the cultural validity, equivalence, and potential bias of measures for Latino/as. The use of tests with populations or groups for whom they were not validated poses potential ethical and professional issues (APA, 2002, 2003; Fantoni-Salvador & Rogers, 1997). Psychologists "...are encouraged not to use instruments that have not been adapted for the target population, and they are also encouraged to use both pilot tests and interviews to determine the cultural validity of their instruments" (APA, 2003, p. 389). The extant research has also failed to include basic sociodemographic and cultural variables such as nativity, generation status, acculturation, enculturation, and SES. As mentioned in previous sections, Latino/as are an incredibly diverse group (Alegria et al., 2008, 2009; Casas et al., in press)—and findings obtained with one Latino/a group may not generalize to others. Additionally, the available research suffers from small and non-representative samples (e.g., Fantoni-Salvador & Rogers, 1997; Rogers et al., 1995). Especially in the case of translated tests with little research, research is needed to determine the effects of language on outcomes. One study regarding the Latino/a health paradox found that language used played a role in self-rated health of Latino/as (Viruell-Fuentes, Morenoff, Williams, & House, 2011).

Recommendations

Clinical

Consistent with published guidelines and ethical standards (APA, 2002, 2003), psychologists need to be aware of the limitations of instruments in all facets and components of the assessment process. Assessing the empirical evidence of a measure with regard to equivalence and bias is of paramount importance. Unfortunately, given the dearth of research, assessors and consumers of personality assessments should at least consider the available research on the validity, including content validity, and reliability of a measure for Latino/as. In the absence of well-validated measures for use with Latino/as, it is not acceptable to use measures whose psychometric properties are questionable or unknown (e.g., ad hoc assessments or assessments that have not been validated) (APA, 2002, 2003).

In the absence of research, clinicians ought to be aware that bias, broadly defined, can occur at different points during and at different levels of the assessment process: at the level of items, scales, during the interview, and interpretation of findings (e.g., individualistic and decontextualized interpretation of client's symptoms, behaviors). As such, clinicians should consider sociocultural factors in the interpretation of these assessment measures when used with Latino/a clients (APA, 2003). Cultural formulation models should be considered with Latino/a clients.

In essence, cultural formulation models call attention to the importance and consideration of sociocultural factors that could influence various aspects of the assessment process (APA, 2000; Cuellar & Gonzalez, 2000; Dana, 2000). These consist of (a) the cultural identity of client, and we would argue, other dimensions of acculturation and enculturation; (b) cultural explanations of an individual's illness or behavior pattern; (c) cultural factors vis-à-vis a client's psychosocial environment and functioning, including the assessment of strengths and non-pathological personality traits in addition to psychosocial stressors; (d) impact of cultural differences in the client-clinician relationship; and (e) overall cultural assessment for diagnosis, interpretation of results, or provision of care. In addition, socioeconomic status should be independently considered: "...without measuring all relevant SES dimensions, ethnic differences in health variables cannot be considered independent from SES" (Perez-Benitez et al., 2010, p. 595). Clinicians may wish to consult guidelines for using cultural formulation in practice (e.g., Mezzich, Caracci, Fabrega, & Kirmayer, 2009).

Despite limited clinical measures of acculturation and enculturation, or guidelines for the use of these constructs in assessment (see Kohatsu, Concepcion, & Perez, 2010 for incorporating acculturation in counseling practice), clinicians can use extant published acculturation and enculturation measures along with qualitative interview data based on these measures. Acculturation and enculturation can be used to determine the use of appropriate norms and in interpreting results (Cervantes & Acosta, 1992). Examiners may also deem it necessary to qualify findings based on estimated degree of acculturation and enculturation. For instance, an elevated score on an odd beliefs or psychotic thinking scale as a result of adherence to traditional/indigenous spiritual beliefs (i.e., enculturation) should be interpreted and handled accordingly. Factoring in acculturation and enculturation as well as specific sociocultural factors in the assessment of PD symptoms and criteria appears particularly relevant because the meaning and function of symptom(s) are likely to differ for individuals and PDs (Westen & Shedler, 2007), and PD dimensions do not appear to be culturally neutral. In the case of BPD, for instance, key features such as cohesiveness and consistency of the self and affect regulation are influenced by culture (Kitayama et al., 2007; Tov & Diener, 2007).

Test results by themselves are insufficient in making a diagnosis (Sattler, 2001); clinicians need to gather a wealth of information (Westen & Shedler, 2007). However, communication between the client and clinician as well as differences inherent in cross-cultural assessment are other potential sources of bias or misdiagnosis (either under- or overdiagnosis) (Zayas, Cabassa, Perez, & Howard, 2005). For example, one study found that more Latinos were diagnosed as having BPD relative to African and European American men (Casteneda & Franco, 1985). It was hypothesized that misdiagnosis was the result of linguistic factors (the patients were Spanish speaking) as well as misunderstanding among clinicians of culturally appropriate behavior (Casteneda & Franco, 1985). Thus, the obligation is always on the clinician to understand both the degree of maladaptive behavior and the degree of difference beyond that of the individual's native cultural expectations before offering a diagnosis of personality disorder (APA, 2000, 2003; Sue, Arredondo, & McDavis, 1992). Importantly, clinicians may be another source of error in diagnosis (Smedley et al., 2003; Pieterse & Miller, 2010), and they need to be aware of the ways in which their biases may lead to diagnostic errors (e.g., Balsa & McGuire, 2001).

Given the many issues (e.g., assessing immigrants or monolingual Spanish speakers) not addressed in the present chapter, the reader is referred to other sources on other practical considerations, such as the use of culturally competent interpreters, when assessing Latino/as (Judd et al., 2009) and the forthcoming monograph section on psychological testing and assessment section with Latino/a Americans by the Council of National Psychological Associations for the Advancement of Ethnic Minority Issues (CNPAAEMI).

Research

Research on the validity and reliability, item bias, test bias, or ethnic/racial differences on widely used measures for Latino/as is alarmingly scarce. Consistent with published guidelines, researchers are called on to present the reliability, validity, and equivalence data for use of instruments across diverse populations (APA, 2003). In light of the dearth of research for Latino/as, and other ethnocultural groups, research should prioritize establishing all forms of equivalence and testing for item and test bias for the major assessments for various Latino/a groups (Helms, 1997; Kwan et al., 2010; Puente & Agranovich, 2004). Contemporary and more robust approaches such as factorial invariance analysis and DIF should be used to address potential issues of psychometric equivalence and bias while also addressing important sociocultural factors. In the absence of this research, it is unclear whether the development of norms is needed for Latino/as at this point. However, the reader is encouraged to consult suggestions for the use of separate norms, where applicable (e.g., Butcher et al., 2007).

Another promising area of research is to determine the extent to which the assessment process and diagnosis in particular are influenced by sociocultural factors as well as individual clinician characteristics. That is to say, how do the latter influence critical points in the assessment process and cognitive decision-making? Or influence what further questions clinicians seek, ask? How is certain sociocultural information used in a biased way, either in favor of or against the client (Iwamasa et al., 2000)? What sociocultural information is more salient? How is nonverbal communication influenced by sociocultural factors and individual clinician characteristics? How does multicultural supervision change the clinician's perceptions of a client's or examinee's behavior and test results? Do cultural formulation models or guidelines as well as approaches like the SWAP improve diagnostic accuracy and treatment outcomes? This line of research will benefit from mixed methods and from cognitive science perspectives.

References

Ackerman, M. J., & Kane, A. W. (2011). *Psychological experts in divorce actions* (5th ed.). New York: Aspen.

Alamilla, S. G. (2010). *Examining the moderating effects of enculturation and color-blind racial ideology on the relationship between racism-related stress and psychological distress among Latino/as.* Unpublished doctoral dissertation, University of California, Santa Barbara, CA.

Alamilla, S. G., Cartnal, R., Kim, B. S. K., & Smith, S. R. (2009, August). *Cultural validity of the personality assessment inventory for Latino/as.* Poster session presented at the annual meeting of the American Psychological Association, Toronto, ON, Canada.

Alamilla, S. G., Kim, B. S. K., & Lam, A. N. (2010). Acculturation, enculturation, perceived racism, minority status stressors, and psychological symptomatology among Latino/as. *Hispanic Journal of Behavioral Sciences, 32*(1), 55–76.

Alarcon, R. D., Foulks, E. F., & Vakkar, M. (1998). *Personality disorders and culture: Clinical and conceptual interactions.* New York: Wiley.

Alegria, M., Canino, G., Shrout, P. E., Woo, M., Duan, N., Vila, D., et al. (2008). Prevalence of mental illness in immigrant and non-immigrant US Latino groups. *American Journal of Public Health, 165*, 359–369.

Alegria, M., Mulvaney-Day, N., Torres, M., Polo, A., Cao, Z., & Canino, G. (2007). Prevalence of psychiatric disorders across Latino subgroups in the United States. *American Journal of Public Health, 97*, 68–75.

Alterman, A. I., Zaballero, A. R., Lin, M. M., Siddiqui, N., Brown, L. S., Rutherford, M. J., et al. (1995). Personality assessment inventory (PAI) scores of lower- socioeconomic African American and Latino methadone maintenance patients. *Assessment, 2*(1), 91–100.

American Psychiatric Association. (2000). *Diagnostic and statistical manual of mental disorders* (4th ed., Rev.). Washington, DC: Author.

American Psychological Association. (2002). *Ethical principles of psychologists and code of conduct.* Washington, DC: Author.

American Psychological Association. (2003). Guidelines on multicultural education, training, research, practice, and organizational change for psychologists. *American Psychologist, 58*(5), 377–402.

Ansell, E. B., Pinto, A., Crosby, R. D., Becker, D. F., Anez, L. M., Paris, M., et al. (2010). The prevalence and structure of obsessive-compulsive personality disorder in Hispanic psychiatric outpatients. *Journal of Behavior Therapy and Experimental Psychiatry, 41*, 275–281.

Atkinson, D. R. (2004). *Counseling American minorities* (6th ed.). Boston: McGraw Hill.

Bagby, R. M., Costa, P. T., Widiger, T. A., Ryder, A. G., & Marshall, M. (2005). DSM-IV personality disorders and the five-factor model of personality: A multi-method examination of domain- and facet-level predictions. *European Journal of Personality, 19*, 307–324.

Balsa, A. I., & McGuire, T. G. (2001). Statistical discrimination in health care. *Journal of Health Economics, 20*, 881–907.

Berry, J. W. (2003). Conceptual approaches to acculturation. In K. M. Chun, P. B. Organista, & G. Marin (Eds.), *Acculturation: Advances in theory, measurement, and applied research* (pp. 17–37). Washington, DC: American Psychological Association.

Breslau, J., Borges, G., Tancredi, D., Saito, N., Kravitz, R., Hinton, L., et al. (2011). Migration from Mexico to the United States and subsequent risk for depressive and anxiety disorders: A cross-national study. *Archives of General Psychiatry, 68*(4), 428–433.

Brewer, M. B. (1991). The social self: On being the same and different at the same time. *Personality and Social Psychology Bulletin, 17*, 475–482.

Bronisch, T., & Mombour W. (1994). Comparison of a diagnostic checklist with a structured interview for the assessment of DSM-III-R and ICD-10 personality disorders. *Psychopathology, 27*(6):312–320.
Buffenstein, A. (1997). Personality disorders. In T. Wen-Shing & J. Streltzer (Eds.), *Culture and psychopathology: A guide to clinical assessment*. Philadelphia: Brunner/Mazel.
Butcher, J. N., Cabiya, J., Lucio, E., & Garrido, M. (2007). *Assessing the Hispanic client using the MMPI-2 and MMPI-A*. Washington, DC: American Psychological Association.
Butcher, J. N., Dahlstrom, W. G., Graham, J. R., Tellegen, A., & Kaemmer, B. (1989). *Minnesota multiphasic personality inventory-2 (MMPI-2): Manual for administration and scoring*. Minneapolis, MN: University of Minnesota Press.
Cabiya, J. J., Lucio, E., Chavira, D. A., Castellanos, J., Gomez, F. C., & Velasquez, R. J. (2000). MMPI-2 scores of Puerto Rican, Mexican, and U.S. Latino college students: A research note. *Psychological Reports, 87*, 266–268.
Casas, J. M., Alamilla, S. G., Ortega, S., & Cabrera, A. P. (in press). The browning of the U.S.: Latina/os from generalizations to specifics: A mental health perspective. In G. Harvette (Ed.), *Psychological treatment of ethnic minority populations*. New York: Oxford University Press.
Casteneda, R., & Franco, H. (1985). Sex and ethnic distribution of borderline personality disorder in an inpatient sample. *The American Journal of Psychiatry, 142*, 1202–1203.
Cervantes, R. C., & Acosta, F. X. (1992). Psychological testing for Hispanic Americans. *Applied and Preventive Psychology, 1*, 209–219.
Chavira, D. A., Grilo, C. M., Shea, M. T., Yen, S., Gunderson, J. G., Morey, L. C., et al. (2003). Ethnicity and four personality disorders. *Comprehensive Psychiatry, 44*, 483–491.
Cheung, F. M., Leung, K., Zhang, J. X., Sun, H. F., Gan, Y. Q., Song, W. Z., et al. (2001). Indigenous Chinese personality constructs: Is the five-factor model complete? *Journal of Cross-Cultural Psychology, 32*(4), 407–433.
Chiriboga, D. A., Yuri, J., Banks, S., & Giyeon, K. (2007). Acculturation and its effect on depressive symptom structure in a sample of Mexican American elders. *Hispanic Journal of Behavioral Sciences, 29*(1), 83–100.
Cleary, T. A. (1968). Test bias: Prediction of grades of Negro [sic] and white students in integrated colleges. *Journal of Educational Measurement, 5*, 115–124.
Craig, R. J. (1999). *Interpreting personality tests: A clinical manual for the MMPI-2, MCMI- III, CPI-R, and 16PF*. New York: Wiley.
Craig, R. J. (2008). Millon clinical multi-axial inventory-III. In R. P. Archer & S. R. Smith (Eds.), *A guide to personality assessment: Evaluation, application, and integration*. New York: Routledge.
Cruz-Niemiec, R. (2004). *Factores de tiempo y genero sexual asociados al MMPI-2, Version Hispana, con una muestra de hombres y mujeres Puertoriquenos/as*. Unpublished doctoral dissertation, Albizo University, San Juan, Puerto Rico.
Cuellar, I., Arnold, B., & Maldonado, R. (1995). Acculturation Rating Scale for Mexican Americans-II: A revision of the original ARSMA scale. *Hispanic Journal of Behavioral Sciences, 17*, 275–304.
Cuellar, I., & Gonzalez, G. (2000). Cultural identity description and cultural formulation for Hispanics. In R. H. Dana (Ed.), *Handbook of cross-cultural and multicultural personality assessment* (pp. 605–621). Mahwah, NJ: Lawrence Erlbaum Associates.
Cuellar, I., Siles, R. I., & Bracamontes, E. (2004). Acculturation: A psychological construct of continuing relevance for Chicana/o psychology. In R. J. Velasquez, L. M. Arellano, & B. W. McNeill (Eds.), *The handbook of Chicana/o psychology and mental health* (pp. 23–42). Mahwah, NJ: Lawrence Erlbaum Associates.
Dana, R. H. (1993). *Multicultural assessment perspectives for professional psychology*. Needham Heights, MA: Allyn & Bacon.
Dana, R. H. (1997). Multicultural assessment and cultural identity: An assessment-intervention model. *World Psychology, 3*(1–2), 121–141.
Dana, R. H. (2000). Psychological assessment in the diagnosis and treatment of ethnic group members. In J. F. Aponte (Ed.), *Psychological intervention and cultural diversity* (2nd ed., pp. 59–74). Needham Heights, MA: Allyn & Bacon.
Dingies, N., Mera, M. M., & Vi, G. M. (1997). Cross-cultural perspectives in antisocial behavior. In D. M. Stoff, J. Breiling, & J. D. Maser (Eds.), *Handbook of antisocial behavior*. New York: Wiley.
Dyce, J. A., & OConnor, B. P. (1998). Personality disorders and the five factor model: A test of facet-level predictions. *Journal of Personality Disorders, 12*, 31–45.
Fantoni-Salvador, P., & Rogers, R. (1997). Spanish versions of the MMPI-2 and PAI: An investigation of concurrent validity with Hispanic patients. *Assessment, 4*(1), 29–39.
Ferguson, C. J. (2009). An effect size primer: A guide for clinicians and researchers. *Professional Psychology: Research and Practice, 40*, 532–538.
First, M. B., Gibbon, M., Spitzer, R. L., Williams, J. B. W., & Benjamin, L. S. (1997). *Structured clinical interview for DSM-IV personality disorders*. Washington, DC: American Psychiatric Association.
Garcia-Peltoniemi, R., & Azan-Chaviano, A. (1993). *MMPI-2: Inventario Multifascio de la Personalidad de Minnesota*. Minneapolis, MN: University of Minnesota Press.

Gass, C. S. (2000). Assessment of emotional functioning with the MMPI-2. In G. Groth-Marnat (Ed.), *Neuropsychological assessment in clinical practice* (pp. 457–532). New York: Wiley.

Ghafoori, B., & Hierholzer, R. W. (2010). Personality patterns among Black, White, and Hispanic combat veterans. *Psychological Trauma: Theory, Research, Practice, and Policy, 2*(1), 12–18.

Gloria, A. M., & Segura-Herrera, T. A. (2004). ¡Somos! Latinas and Latinos in the United States. In D. R. Atkinson (Ed.), *Counseling American minorities* (6th ed., pp. 279–299). Boston: McGraw Hill.

Gonzalez, H. M., Tarraf, W., Whitfield, K. E., & Vega, W. A. (2010). The epidemiology of major depression and ethnicity in the United States. *Journal of Psychiatric Research, 44*, 1043–1051.

Grilo, C. M., Anez, L. M., & McGlashan, T. H. (2003). The Spanish- language version of the diagnostic interview for DSM–IV personality disorders: Development and initial psychometric evaluation of diagnosis and criteria. *Comprehensive Psychiatry, 44*(2), 154–161.

Gross, G. D. (2011). MCMI-III desirability, thought disorder, and dependent scores of Hispanic American sexual offenders: Implications for interpretation. *Dissertation Abstracts International: Section B: The Sciences and Engineering, 71*(12-B), 724.

Hall, G. C., Bansal, A., & Lopez, I. R. (1999). Ethnicity and psychopathology: A meta-analytic review of 31 years of comparative MMPI/MMPI-2 research. *Psychological Assessment, 11*(2), 186–197.

Hambleton, R. K., Swaminathan, H., & Rogers, H. J. (1991). *Fundamentals of item response theory*. Newberry Park, CA: Sage.

Hare, R. D. (2003). *Manual for the revised psychopathy checklist* (2nd ed.). Toronto, ON, Canada: Multi-Health Systems.

Hare, R. D., Clark, D., Grann, M., & Thornton, D. (2000). Psychopathy and the predictive validity of the PCL-R: An international perspective. *Behavioral Sciences & the Law, 18*(5), 623–645.

Hays, P. A. (2001). *Addressing cultural complexities in practice: A framework for clinicians and counselors.* Washington, DC: American Psychological Association.

Helms, J. E. (1997). The triple quandary of race, culture, and social class in standardized cognitive ability testing. In D. P. Flanagan, J. L. Genshaft, & P. L. Harrison (Eds.), *Contemporary intellectual assessment: Theories, tests, and issues* (pp. 517–532). New York: Guilford.

Herskovits, M. J. (1948). *Man and his works: The science of cultural anthropology*. New York: Knopf.

Hopwood, C. J., Flato, C. G., Ambwani, S., Garland, B. H., & Morey, L. C. (2009). A comparison of Latino and Anglo socially desirable responding. *Journal of Clinical Psychology, 65*, 769–780.

Hopwood, C. J., & Moser, J. S. (2011). Personality assessment inventory internalizing and externalizing structure in college students: Invariance across sex and ethnicity. *Personality and Individual Differences, 50*, 116–119.

Iwamasa, G. Y., Larranee, A. L., & Merritt, R. D. (2000). Are personality disorder criteria ethnically biased?: A card-sort analysis. *Cultural Diversity and Ethnic Minority Psychology, 6*(3), 284–296.

Judd, T., Capetillo, D., Carrion-Baralt, J., Marmol, L. M., San Miguel-Montes, L., Navarrete, M. G., et al. (2009). Professional considerations for improving the neuropsychological evaluation of Hispanics: A National Academy of Neuropsychology education paper. *Archives of Clinical Neuropsychology, 24*, 127–135.

Keefe, S. E., & Padilla, A. M. (1987). *Chicano ethnicity*. Albuquerque, NM: University of New Mexico Press.

Kim, B. S. K. (2007). Acculturation and enculturation. In F. T. L. Leong, A. G. Inman, A. Ebreo, L. Yang, L. Kinoshita, & M. Fu (Eds.), *Handbook of Asian American psychology* (2nd ed., pp. 141–158). Thousand Oaks, CA: Sage.

Kim, B. S. K., & Abreu, J. M. (2001). Acculturation measurement: Theory, current instruments, and future directions. In J. G. Ponterotto, J. M. Casas, L. A. Suzuki, & C. M. Alexander (Eds.), *Handbook of multicultural counseling* (2nd ed., pp. 394–424). Thousand Oaks, CA: Sage.

Kim, B. S. K., Atkinson, D. R., & Yang, P. H. (1999). The Asian values scales: Development, factor analysis, validation, and reliability. *Journal of Counseling Psychology, 46*, 342–352.

Kim, B. S. K., Soliz, A., Orellana, B., & Alamilla, S. G. (2009). Latino/a values scale: Development, reliability, and validity. *Measurement and Evaluation in Counseling and Development, 42*(2), 71–91.

Kitayama, S., Duffy, S., & Uchida, Y. (2007). Self as cultural mode of being. In S. Kitayama & D. Cohen (Eds.), *Handbook of cultural psychology* (pp. 136–174). New York: Guilford Press.

Kohatsu, E. L., Concepcion, W., & Perez, P. (2010). Incorporating levels of acculturation in counseling practice. In J. G. Ponterotto, J. M. Casas, L. A. Suzuki, & C. M. Alexander (Eds.), *Handbook of multicultural counseling* (3rd ed., pp. 343–356). Thousand Oaks, CA: Sage.

Kwan, K. L. K., Gong, Y., & Maestas, M. (2010). Language, translation, and validity in the adaptation of psychological tests for multicultural counseling. In J. G. Ponterotto, J. M. Casas, L. A. Suzuki, & C. M. Alexander (Eds.), *Handbook of multicultural counseling* (3rd ed., pp. 397–412). Thousand Oaks, CA: Sage.

Liebkind, K. (2006). Ethnic identity and acculturation. In D. L. Sam & J. W. Berry (Eds.), *The Cambridge handbook of acculturation psychology* (pp. 78–96). New York: Cambridge University Press.

Lucio, E., & Reyes-Lagunes, I. (1994). The Mexican version of the MMPI-2 in Mexico and Nicaragua: Translation, adaption, and demonstrated equivalency. In J. Butcher (Ed.), *International adaptions of the MMPI-2* (pp. 265–283). Minneapolis, MN: University of Minnesota Press.

Lucio, E., Reyes-Lagunes, I., & Scott, R. L. (1994). MMPI-2 for Mexico: Translation and adaptation. *Journal of Personality Assessment, 63*, 105–116.

Marin, G., & Marin, B. V. (1991). *Research with Hispanic populations*. Newberry Park, CA: Sage.
Marsella, A. J., & Yamada, A. M. (2007). Culture and psychopathology: Foundations, issues, and directions. In S. Kitayama & D. Cohen (Eds.), *Handbook of cultural psychology* (pp. 797–818). New York: Guilford.
McLellan, A. T., Luborsky, L., Cacciola, J., Griffith, J., Evans, F., Barr, H. L., et al. (1985). New data from the Addiction Severity Index: Reliability and validity in three centers. *The Journal of Nervous and Mental Disease, 173*, 412–423.
Mezzich, J. E., Caracci, G., Fabrega, H., & Kirmayer, L. J. (2009). Cultural formulation guidelines. *Transcultural Psychiatry, 46*(3), 383–405.
Millon, T. (1997). *Millon clinical multiaxial inventory manual*. Minneapolis, MN: National Computer Systems.
Millon, T. (2011). *Disorders of personality: Introducing a DSM/ICD spectrum from normal to abnormal*. Hoboken, NJ: Wiley.
Millon, T., Millon, C., Davis, R. D., & Grossman, S. (2009). *Millon clinical multiaxial inventory-III manual* (4th ed.). Minneapolis, MN: NCS Pearson.
Morey, L. C. (1991). *The personality assessment inventory: Professional manual*. Lutz, FL: Psychological Assessment Resources.
Morey, L. C., & Hopwood, C. J. (2008). The personality assessment inventory. In R. P. Archer & S. R. Smith (Eds.), *A guide to personality assessment: Evaluation, application, and integration* (pp. 167–212). New York: Routledge.
Myers, H. F. (2009). Ethnicity and socioeconomic status-related stresses in context: An integrative review and conceptual model. *Journal of Behavioral Medicine, 32*, 9–19.
Nunally, J. C., & Bernstein, I. H. (1994). *Psychometric theory* (3rd ed.). New York: McGraw Hill.
Passel, J. S., & Cohn, D. (2008). *U.S. population projections: 2005–2050*. Washington, DC: Pew Research Center.
Passel, J. S., & Cohn, D. (2011). *How many Hispanics? Comparing new census counts with latest census estimates*. Washington, DC: Pew Hispanic Center.
Perez-Benitez, C. I., Yen, S., Shea, M. T., Edelen, M. O., Markowitz, J. C., McGlashan, T. H., et al. (2010). Ethnicity and trauma and psychiatric disorders: Findings from the Collaborative Longitudinal Study of Personality Disorders. *Journal of Clinical Psychology, 66*(6), 583–598.
Perry, J. C. (1992). Problems and considerations in the valid assessment of personality disorders. *The American Journal of Psychiatry, 149*(12), 1645–1653.
Pew Hispanic Center/Kaiser Family Foundation. (2002). *2002 national survey of Latinos*. Washington, DC: Author. Retrieved October 9, 2009, from http://pewhispanic.org/files/reports/15.pdf.
Pew Research Center. (2011). *Wealth gaps rise to record highs between Whites, Blacks and Hispanics*. Washington, DC: Pew Research Center. http://pewsocialtrends.org/2011/07/26/wealth-gaps-rise-to-record-highs-between-whites-blacks-hispanics/.
Pieterse, A. L., & Miller, M. J. (2010). Current considerations in the assessment of adults: A review and extension of culturally inclusive models. In J. Ponterotto, L. A. Suzuki, C. Alexander, & J. M. Cases (Eds.), *Handbook of multicultural counseling* (3rd ed., pp. 649–666). Thousand Oaks, CA: Sage.
Puente, A. E., & Agranovich, A. V. (2004). The cultural in cross-cultural neuropsychology. In G. Goldstein, S. R. Beers, & M. Hersen (Eds.), *Comprehensive handbook of psychological assessment, Vol. 1: Intellectual and neuropsychological assessment* (pp. 321–332). Hoboken, NJ: Wiley.
Ramirez-Esparza, N., Gosling, S. D., & Pennebaker, J. W. (2008). Paradox lost: Unraveling the puzzle of simpatia. *Journal of Cross-Cultural Psychology, 39*, 703–715.
Rissetti, F. J., Himmel, E., & Gonzalez-Moreno, J. A. (1996). Use of the MMPI-2 in Chile. In J. N. Butcher (Ed.), *International adaptations of the MMPI-2: Research and clinical applications* (pp. 221–251). Minneapolis, MN: University of Minnesota Press.
Robins, L. N., Helzer, J. E., Croughan, J., & Ratcliff, K. S. (1981). National Institute of Mental Health diagnostic interview schedule: Its history, characteristics, and validity. *Archives of General Psychiatry, 38*(4), 381–389.
Robins, L. N., Helzer, J. E., Weissman, M. M., Orvaschel, H., Gruenberg, E., Burke, J. D., et al. (1984). Lifetime prevalence of specific psychiatric disorders in three sites. *Archives of General Psychiatry, 41*, 949–958.
Rogers, R., Flores, J., Ustad, K., & Sewell, K. W. (1995). Initial validation of the Personality Assessment Inventory-Spanish version with clients from Mexican American communities. *Journal of Personality Assessment, 64*(2), 340–348.
Rossi, L. E. (2003). Comparability of the English and Spanish translations of the MMPI-2 and MCMI-III. *Dissertation Abstracts International: Section B: The Sciences and Engineering, 63*(10-B), 4961.
Sam, D. L. (2006). Acculturation: Conceptual background and core components. In D. L. Sam & J. W. Berry (Eds.), *The Cambridge handbook of acculturation psychology* (pp. 11–26). New York: Cambridge University Press.
Sattler, J. M. (2001). *Assessment of children: Cognitive applications* (4th ed.). San Diego, CA: Sattler.
Sellers, R. M., Smith, M. A., Shelton, J. N., Rowley, S. A. J., & Chavous, T. M. (1998). The multidimensional model of racial identity: A reconceptualization of African American racial identity. *Personality and Social Psychology Review, 2*(1), 18–39.
Shiraev, E. B., & Levy, D. A. (2010). *Cross-cultural psychology: Critical thinking and contemporary applications* (4th ed.). Boston: Allyn & Bacon.

Smedley, B. D., Stith, A. Y., & Nelson, A. R. (2003). *Unequal treatment: Confronting racial and ethnic disparities in healthcare*. Washington, DC: National Academies Press.

Sue, D. W., Arredondo, P., & McDavis, R. J. (1992). Multicultural counseling competencies and standards: A call to the profession. *Journal of Counseling and Development, 70*, 477–483.

Sugihara, Y., & Warner, J. A. (1999). Mexican-American male batterers on the MCMI-III. *Psychological Reports, 85*, 163–169.

Sullivan, E. A., Abramowitz, C. S., Lopez, M., & Kosson, D. S. (2006). Reliability and construct validity of the psychopathy checklist-revised for Latino, European American, and African American male inmates. *Psychological Assessment, 18*(4), 382–392.

Terraciano, A., & McCrae, R. R. (2006). Cross-cultural studies of personality traits and their relevance to psychiatry. *Epidemiologia e Psichiatria Sociale, 15*(3), 176–184.

Tov, W., & Diener, E. (2007). Culture and subjective wellbeing. In S. Kitayama & D. Cohen (Eds.), *Handbook of cultural psychology* (pp. 691–713). New York: Guilford.

Triandis, H. C. (1994). *Culture and social behavior*. New York: McGraw Hill.

U.S. Census Bureau. (2006). *U.S. Hispanic population: 2006*. Retrieved from http://www.census.gov/population/www/socdemo/hispanic/files/Internet_Hispanic_in_US_2006.pdf on 11 Apr 2011.

U.S. Census Bureau. (2007). *The American Community–Hispanic: 2004*. Retrieved December 3, 2008, from http://www.census.gov/prod/2007pubs/acs-03.pdf.

U.S. Census Bureau. (2010). *Facts for features. Hispanic heritage month*. Retrieved April 22, 2011, from http://www.census.gov/newsroom/releases/archives/facts_for_features_special_editions/cb10-ff17.html.

U.S. Department of Health and Human Services. (2001). *Mental health: Culture, race, and ethnicity-a supplement to mental health: A report of the Surgeon General*. Rockville, MD: U.S. Department of Health and Human Services, Substance Abuse and Mental Health Services Administration, Center for Mental Health Services.

U.S. Department of Health and Human Services. (2004). *The burden of chronic diseases and their risk factors: National and state perspectives*. Atlanta, GA: Centers for Disease Control and Prevention.

Velasquez, R. J., Callahan, W. J., Reimann, J., & Carbonell, S. (1998, August). *Performance of bilingual Latinos on an English-Spanish MMPI-2*. Paper presented at the 106th annual convention of the American Psychological Association, San Francisco.

Viruell-Fuentes, E. A., Morenoff, J. D., Williams, D. R., & House, J. S. (2011). Language of interview, self-rated health, and the other Latino health puzzle. *American Journal of Public Health, 101*, 1306–1313.

Westen, D., & Shedler, J. (1999a). Revising and assessing axis II, part I: Developing a clinically and empirically valid assessment method. *The American Journal of Psychiatry, 156*, 258–272.

Westen, D., & Shedler, J. (1999b). Revising and assessing axis II, part II: Toward an empirically and clinically useful classification of personality disorders. *The American Journal of Psychiatry, 156*, 273–285.

Westen, D., & Shedler, J. (2007). Personality diagnosis with the Shedler-Westen assessment procedure (SWAP): Integrating clinical and statistical measurement and prediction. *Journal of Abnormal Psychology, 116*(4), 810–822.

Whitworth, R. H., & Unterbrink, C. (1994). Comparison of MMPI-s clinical and content scales administered to Hispanic and Anglo-Americans. *Hispanic Journal of Behavioral Sciences, 16*(3), 255–264.

Zanarini, M. C., Frankenburg, F. R., Sickel, A. E., & Young, L. (1996). *The diagnostic interview for DSM-IV personality disorders*. Belmont, MA: McLean Hospital.

Zayas, L. H., Cabassa, L. J., Perez, M. C., & Howard, M. O. (2005). Clinician-patient ethnicity in psychiatric diagnosis: A pilot study with Hispanics. *Journal of Ethnic & Cultural Diversity in Social Work, 14*(1), 93–109.

Assessment of Dementia in the Hispanic Client: A Neuropsychological Perspective

16

Lorraine T. Benuto and Brian D. Leany

Relevant Statistics

With an astounding 62.9% of Hispanics aged 85 and older exhibiting dementia-related symptoms (Alzheimer's Association, 2011) and a substantial portion of Hispanics speaking Spanish only, the need for psychometrically sound measures designed to assess for cognitive impairment in this cohort is essential. In fact, norms for ethnic minority non-English-speaking populations are rare (Ardila, Rodríguez-Menéndez, & Rosselli, 2002; Dick, Teng, Kempler, Davis, & Taussig, 2002; Mahurin, Espino, & Holifield, 1992), calling to question current assessment practices. Given that the Hispanic population in the United States is projected to grow substantially (mirroring past trends, e.g., U.S. Census Bureau, 2002) and that Hispanics are eight times more likely to experience dementia due to common health-related risk factors (e.g., hypertension, diabetes, stroke: Crisostomo, Butler, Webster, & Moran, 2002), it seems necessary to critically evaluate the current assessment practices employed to assess for cognitive impairment in the Hispanic client and to develop guidelines for assessing cognitive impairment with this group.

What About the Issue of Language?

When addressing assessment of the Hispanic client, two central themes always emerge. The first and probably most obvious issue is that of language. We are often challenged in finding an assessment measure that is available in Spanish and that is applicable to a broad range of linguistic variability. For example, if we broadly consider IQ assessment, we can clearly see that language is a significant portion of intellectual functioning, and, thus, the WAIS has a normative sample that encompasses a broad range of English language proficiency. We would therefore expect to have a similar range of language proficiency represented in the normative sample for any Spanish-language-based assessment.

L.T. Benuto, Ph.D. (✉)
Department of Psychology, Victims of Crime Treatment Center, University of Nevada,
Reno MS 0296, Reno, NV 89557, USA
e-mail: dr.benuto@gmail.com

B.D. Leany, Ph.D.
California Department of Corrections and Rehabilitation, Adult Division, California Correctional
Health Care Services, Sacramento, CA, USA
e-mail: leanyb@gmail.com

L.T. Benuto (ed.), *Guide to Psychological Assessment with Hispanics*,
DOI 10.1007/978-1-4614-4412-1_16, © Springer Science+Business Media New York 2013

The second challenge is that of ethnic and cultural differences among Hispanics. While Hispanic culture shares a language that can be understood in spite of regional differences, we want to ensure that there are also not culturally unique values that bias the measure and interpretation of the assessment. In this chapter, we aim to address both of these themes from an evidence-based perspective.

How to Assess for Dementia

The American Psychological Association (2011) has created guidelines for the evaluation of dementia and age-related cognitive decline. They emphasize the importance of the clinical interview as well as the administration of standardized psychological and neuropsychological tests. In particular, the guidelines call for the use of a brief mental status examination (although the APA stresses that such tests may generate adequate sensitivity to dementia but may not have reasonable specificity) and also for comprehensive neuropsychological evaluations for dementia and cognitive change including tests that assess multiple cognitive domains, i.e., memory, attention, perceptual and motor skills, language, visuospatial abilities, reasoning, and executive functions (and in certain instances measures of mood and personality may be relevant). This chapter offers a summary of the individual tests designed to assess the various domains mentioned above (see Table 16.1) as they pertain to the Hispanic client, although readers are advised to see the Chap. 22 of this book on "Neuropsychological Assessment with Hispanic Clients" for a more detailed overview of relevant neuropsychological assessment measures and batteries that can be used to arrive at a diagnosis of dementia (but are not necessarily specific to the assessment of dementia) with the Hispanic client. Instead, the majority of this chapter focuses on measures used to screen for dementia, assessment measures and batteries specifically designed to assess for dementia, and a neuropsychological assessment battery specifically designed for use with minority clients. We also provide relevant guidelines specific to the Hispanic client.

Differential Diagnosis

The DSM-IV-TR (American Psychiatric Association, 2000) classifies the various dementias as follows: dementia of the Alzheimer's type, vascular dementia, dementia due to other general medical conditions, substance-induced persisting dementia, dementia due to multiple etiologies, and dementia not otherwise specified. Leaders in the field have indicated that DSM-IV-TR's approach to dementia is outdated and have proposed an alternate model of dementia with an emphasis on the differential diagnosis of dementia (Weintraub, 2011), and Fig. 16.1 offers a visual depiction of the differential diagnosis of dementia (adapted from Weintraub). The measures discussed in this chapter (and the Chap. 22 on "Neuropsychological Assessment of Hispanics Clients" in this book) are aimed at assessing for cognitive impairment in various domains (i.e., memory, attention, perceptual and motor skills, language, visuospatial abilities, reasoning, and executive functions) and performance on the tests that assess these domains can help establish which type of dementia diagnosis is the most likely. Furthermore, certain assessment measures can also aid in the differential diagnosis of dementia (e.g., the CVLT-II), although we do not expect that the actual approach to the differential diagnosis of dementia requires adaption for the Hispanic client.

Measures of Mood and Personality

As with any assessment, at times it is important and necessary to rule out alternative diagnoses that could potentially explain the symptoms at hand. Thus, it is important that the clinician keep in mind and formulate and test hypotheses regarding alternate explanations for the presenting concern. This can

Table 16.1 Cognitive domains and selected relevant assessments measures

Domain assessed	Assessment name	Recommendation(s) and/or relevant research findings	Relevant references
Memory and learning			
	Wechsler Memory Scales	The previously revised version (WMS-R) and selected portions of the WMS-III have been translated with normative data and incorporated into other Spanish-language batteries	See Chap. 22 of this book
	WRAML-2	This assessment may be appropriate for use with Hispanic individuals, but one may wish to consider the limited normative information available for level of language proficiency	See Chap. 22 of this book
	California Verbal Learning Test	There is either limited or nonexistent data on the translated version of this measure	Harris, Cullum, and Puente (1995) and Wilke et al. (2004)
	Hopkins Verbal Learning and Memory (HVLT)	Utilize corrected percentile and *T*-scores or apply the correction formulas from Cherner et al. (2007)	Cherner et al. (2007)
	Spanish English Verbal Learning Test (SEVLT)	Utilize most recent norms from 2002 study	Gonzalez, Mungas, and Haan (2002)
	Test of Memory and Learning-2 (TOMAL-2)	Little information is available regarding the TOMAL-2's generalizability toward Hispanic populations	NA
	Biber-Figure Learning Test Extended (BLFT-E)	Test is nonverbal and therefore may be without the influences of language or acculturation seen in other neuropsychological assessments	NA
	Benton Judgment of Line Orientation	No modifications required	Rey et al. (1999)
	Digit span	Utilize normative data for Hispanics that corresponds to their language ability	Boone, Victor, Wen, Razani, and Pontón (2007), Gasquoine, Croyle, Cavazos-Gonzalez, and Sandoval (2007), and Wheeler (2010)
(*Visuospatial memory*)	Rey-Osterreith Complex Figure Drawing Task	Utilize age- and education-corrected norms	Peña-Casanova et al. (2009)
(*Semantic memory*)	Animal Naming Test/Sem-Flu	Some research has found better performance on this test for English speakers when compared to Spanish speakers. Results may need to be accordingly interpreted with caution	Carrión-Baralt, Meléndez-Cabrero, Beeri, Sano, & Silverman (2009)
Attention			
	Conners' Continuous Performance Test-II (CPT-2)	There appears to be minimal research on this measure with Hispanics, although some literature has indicated that ethnicity does not appear to impact test results	Conners, Epstein, Angold, and Klaric (2003)
	Stroop Color-Word Interference Task	Support diagnostic decisions with evidence from additional tests	Peña-Casanova et al. (2009)
	Digit span	Discussed under memory and learning	See above

(continued)

Table 16.1 (continued)

Domain assessed	Assessment name	Recommendation(s) and/or relevant research findings	Relevant references
Perceptual and motor skills			
	Trails	Support diagnostic decisions with evidence from additional executive functioning or perceptual motor coordination tests	Menon, Hall, Hobson, Johnson, and O'Bryant (2011), Boone et al. (2007), and Carrión-Baralt et al. (2009)
	Physiological tasks	We do not expect statistically significant differences in bilateral grip strength or more pronounced cogwheel rigidity among cultures, races, or ethnicities	See Chap. 22 of this book
Language			
	Boston Naming Test (MBNT-S)	The MBNT-S is able to differentiate non-demented and moderately demented individuals	Marquez de la Plata et al. (2009)
	Texas Naming Test (TNT)	Utilize for superior item discrimination	Marquez de la Plata et al. (2009)
(*Verbal fluency*)	F-A-S	Utilize *P*, *S*, and *R* for Spanish speakers, and examine data both with and without age-/education-corrected norms in conjunction with supporting evidence from other language-based measures	Jacobs et al. (1997)
(*Verbal fluency*)	Animal Naming Test/ Sem-Flu	Discussed under memory and learning	See above
Visuospatial			
(*Visuospatial memory*)	Tower of London (TOLDX)	Statistical differences did not appear to be clinically relevant	Peña-Casanova et al. (2009)
(*Visuospatial memory*)	Rey-Osterreith Complex Figure Drawing Task	Discussed under memory and learning	See above
(*Visuospatial reconstruction*)	Biber-Figure Learning Test Extended	Discussed under memory and learning	See above
(*Visuospatial memory and reconstruction*)	Clock Drawing Test (CDT)	Research has indicated that the CDT offers a rapid, culturally unbiased and cost-effective means of assessing for impairment in executive control function	Royall et al. (2003)
(*Visuospatial organization*)	Benton Judgment of Line Orientation	Discussed under memory and learning	See above
Reasoning			
	WAIS-IV subtests	See Chap. 6 of this book on "IQ Testing and the Hispanic Client"	NA
Executive functioning			
	Clock Drawing Test	Discussed under memory and learning	See above
	CLOX1	Adjustment of scores across age. Utilize appropriate normative data	La Rue, Romero, Ortiz, Liang, and Lindeman (1999)
	CLOX2	None required	NA
	Trails	Discussed under perceptual and motor skills	See above
	Wisconsin Card Sorting Task	Differentiate groups based on level of acculturation	Coffey, Marmol, Schock, and Adams (2005)
	Stroop Color-Word Interference Task	Discussed under attention	See above
	Tower of London (TOLDX)	Discussed under visuospatial	See above

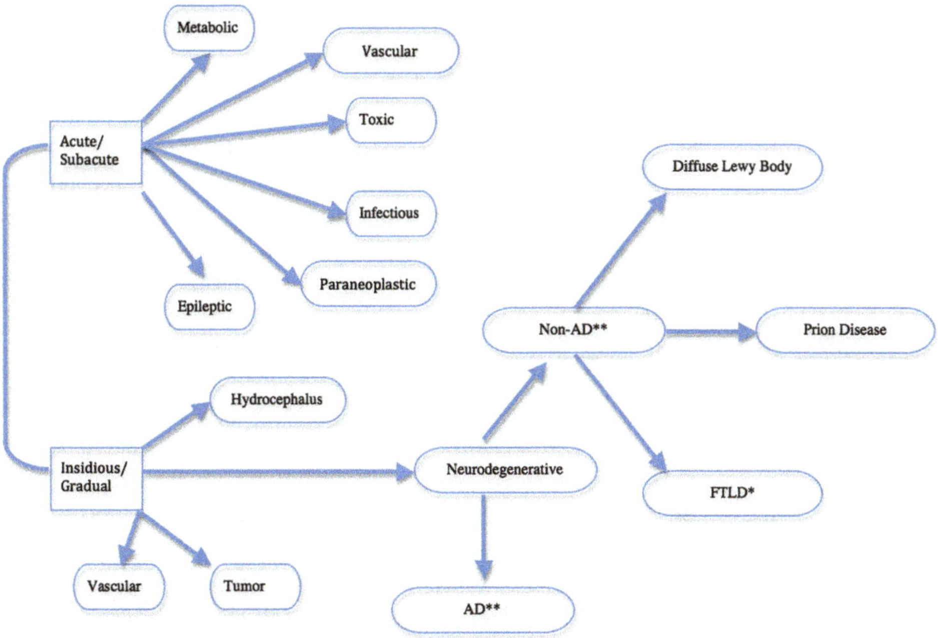

Fig. 16.1 Differential diagnosis of dementia (*AD* Alzheimer's disease, *FLTD* frontotemporal lobar degeneration) (Adapted from Weintraub, 2011)

be done by administering psychological tests that are useful in differentiating between cognitive impairment and other diagnoses (e.g., Test of Memory Malingering to rule out feigning; the California Verbal Learning Test-2 can be useful in differentiating between cognitive impairment and depression; the Millon Clinical Multiaxial Inventory-III can help to determine the presence of a personality disorder). An expansive discussion of such tests is beyond the scope of this chapter, and details regarding specific measures can be found in the chapters that are specific to the differential diagnoses in question.

Assessment Components

The Clinical Interview

The clinical interview allows the clinician to decide what course the assessment process should take and is very important to psychological assessment in general. In the context of the psychological assessment of dementia, the clinical interview carries equal importance and should serve to meet several goals. First, during the clinical interview, the clinician should seek to establish rapport. This may be particularly key in the assessment of dementia as individuals experiencing age-related cognitive decline may be embarrassed by this process and reluctant or resistant to discussing (or accepting) that it is happening. Second, the clinical interview will serve as a foundation for (informally) assessing mental status. During the clinical interview, the clinician can note the client's grooming, coherence, thought processes, judgment, insight, etc. Third, one of the main goals of the clinical interview should be to establish the presenting concern (including the onset of symptoms, course of symptoms, preexisting mental health or physical conditions, premorbid functioning, family history of dementia or other mental health conditions, current use of medications, substance use/abuse/dependence history, psychosocial history, etc.) with special attention being paid to activities of daily living and instrumental activities of daily living and any changes therein. Because there are several medical conditions that can mimic the symptoms associated with cognitive decline, it is important that these conditions be ruled out and that the client be referred for a general medical evaluation (this also can aid in the differential diagnosis of the dementias). During the clinical interview, the client's language proficiency can also be assessed (i.e., is the client fluent in English, are they bilingual) with goal being to determine in what language the assessment should be conducted.

In addition to conducting a clinical interview with the client, collaterals should also be contacted. Collaterals may include family members, the client's partner, friends, or anyone else who has substantial contact with the client and might be able to provide information about the client's current functioning and symptoms, as well as information about the client's premorbid functioning. Collaterals may also be useful informants in terms of the accuracy of the client's report.

This book offers ample discussion regarding the approach clinicians may wish to have when working with the Hispanic client. Suffice to say, it is important to remember that Hispanics have been known to distrust the medical system and cultural characteristics such as *marianismo* and *machismo* (which both emphasize the importance of the caretaking role) could make it difficult for the client to accept and/or discuss any dementia-related symptoms they are experiencing, e.g., forgetfulness and difficulty managing finances. Thus, the clinician is advised to be warm and empathetic, although certainly the cultural considerations mentioned above may not be specific to the Hispanic client and may in fact apply to clients presenting with cognitive decline in general.

Evaluating Mental Status

The assessment of mental status can come in many forms, i.e., via observation of the client in the clinical setting or alternatively via formal assessment. Typically, the clinician is called upon to observe and note the client's general appearance and behavior, mood and affect, perception, and thought including content and form (Groth-Marnat, 2003). The alternative is to formally complete a mental status examination (which are most commonly used to screen for cognitive impairment) of which there are many. These assessments are designed to assess domains of status (such as attention, concentration, judgment, and insight) based on a structured or semi-structured approach, often with normative criteria to determine impairment or functional performance in each of the various domains. These assessments tend to act as screens for cognitive impairment with the goal being to identify when further testing is needed. Formal assessments will be discussed below and reviewed within the context of the Hispanic client.

Screening for Dementia

While the APA guidelines (APA, 2011) call for the use of a brief mental status examination to screen for dementia, they stress that while such tests may generate adequate sensitivity to dementia, they may not have reasonable specificity. Therefore, the tests discussed below may be used as a means to screen for dementia and to help the health provider determine whether or not additional testing is necessary. In this section, we review several screens and discuss their utility with the Hispanic client. It is important to note that other tests exist, but only those most relevant to Hispanics are discussed here (e.g., the Cognitive Abilities Screening Instrument is a well-researched screen for cognitive decline but the majority of research on it has been conducted with Euro-Americans and Asians).

Table 16.2 Mini-mental state examination and Latinos (Adapted from Ramírez et al., 2006)

Item	Finding	References
"Season"	More difficult for Hispanics	Escobar et al. (1986), Valle et al. (1991), and Marshall et al. (1997)
State recall	More difficult for Hispanics	Escobar et al. (1986), Valle et al. (1991), and Teresi et al. (1995)
Repeat/recall three objects	Less difficult for Hispanics	Jones and Gallo (2002)
Serial 7s	More difficult for Hispanics	Escobar et al. (1986) and Hohl, Grundman, Salmon, Thomas, & Thal (1999)
"World" spelled backward	More difficult for Hispanics	Escobar et al. (1986) and Hohl et al. (1999)
"No ifs, ands, or buts"	Less difficult for Hispanics	Escobar et al. (1986), Marshall et al. (1997), and Teresi et al. (1995)
"Close your eyes"	Item is a poor discriminator for Hispanics	Teresi et al. (1995)
Sentence completion	Item is less discriminating of Spanish speakers	Escobar et al. (1986) and Teresi et al. (1995)

Mini-Mental State Examination

The mini-mental state examination is a brief test that is used to screen for cognitive impairment. According to the Psychological Assessment Resources website (PAR, n.d.), more recently a second edition of this test has become available (the *MMSE-2: Standard Version [MMSE-2:SV]*) and a briefer version of the MMSE-2:SV has been developed (*MMSE-2: Brief Version [MMSE-2:BV]*). There is also an extended version of the test (the *MMSE-2: Expanded Version [MMSE-2:EV]) that is more sensitive* to subcortical dementia and to changes associated with aging. There are various Spanish-translated versions of the MMSE-2 available (i.e., Spanish for the United States, Spanish for Latin America, and European Spanish). However, it is important to note that on the Psychological Assessment Resources website (PAR, n.d.) where the MMSE is sold, there is a clause that reads as follows:

> Users of non-English language versions of the MMSE-2 should base the clinical interpretation of MMSE-2 scores upon locally collected standardization data and/or clinical patient data. PAR does not endorse use of the U.S. population-based MMSE-2 norms for interpreting the MMSE-2 scores of patients who do not match the demographic characteristics of the MMSE-2 standardization sample. Clinical use of the raw score cutoff ranges for the MMSE-2 should be based on the scientific literature on the MMSE/MMSE-2 in the native language in which it is being used.
>
> Thus, as the MMSE-2: SV is based on, and equivalent to, the original MMSE for the purpose of this chapter, relevant literature to the original MMSE will be discussed. This is done in light of the recent publication date of the second edition of the MMSE and the lack of research on the norms for the Spanish version.

The MMSE consists of 30 items, which together assess capacity in terms of orientation, attention, memory, recall, language, and ability to follow written and verbal commands (Ramírez, Teresi, Holmes, Gurland, & Lantigua, 2006), and scores range from 0 to 30 with a score of less than 24, suggesting cognitive impairment (Royall et al., 2003). Research has indicated that MMSE scores are affected by age, education, and cultural background (Tombaugh & McIntyre, 1992). Specific to Hispanics, Ramírez and colleagues (2001) have summarized extant literature and found that the MMSE underestimates the cognitive capacities of Latinos and that relatively higher false-positive ratios have been observed for this group. There also appear to be some issues with regard to specific items on the MMSE (Teresi, Holmes, Ramirez, Gurland, & Lantigua, 2001); see Table 16.2 for details. In addition to the above, various items on the MMSE are impacted by education, although this is not specific to Hispanics. In terms of translations, there are also some issues related to certain items (e.g., “No ifs, ands, or buts.”) resulting in different cultural and idiomatic nuances (Ramírez et al.). For example, in a previous study, Mungas, Marshal, Weldon, Haan, and Reed (1996) showed that the mini-mental state exam (MMSE) had differential validity for detecting dementia across African Americans, Hispanics, and Caucasians when standard cut-offs, based on Caucasian samples, were used. These studies suggest that there are some items that have a linguistically sensitive component that changes the ability of the assessment to discriminate impairment from functioning (see Table 16.2). It may be the dropping of an *s* from the end of a word that discriminates this status in English, but a direct translation to Spanish somehow removes this discriminate ability from the assessment. Thus, while our overall goal is to encourage the use and adaptation of measures in the absence of an appropriately standardized measure, one must be cognizant of this possibility and interpret such measures with caution. A superior method would be to collect data for regional norms and to develop and share linguistically appropriate alternatives with the community.

Mini-Cog

The Mini-Cog (which consists of a clock drawing task and 3-item recall) was developed as a brief test for discriminating demented from non-demented persons and has been found to be an effective screen for dementia. In the original study examining the Mini-Cog's effectiveness, the sample consisted of 129 participants who met criteria for probable dementia based on informant interviews and 120 participants with no history of cognitive decline. The *Mini-Cog* had the highest sensitivity (99%) when compared to the MMSE and the Cognitive Abilities Screening Instrument (CASI) and correctly classified the greatest percentage (96%) of participants with probable dementia. Perhaps most relevant to this chapter, its diagnostic value was not influenced by education or language (Borson, Scanlan, Brush, Vitaliano, & Dokmak, 2000). In fact, Thombaben (2010) discusses how the clients age, level of education and literacy, and ethnic background do not negatively influence the results of the screening. Finally, research specifically aimed at examining the use of the Mini-Cog with individuals from ethnic minority groups (including Hispanics) has indicated that the Mini-Cog detects clinically significant cognitive impairment as well as or better than the MMSE in multiethnic elderly individuals, is easier to administer to non-English speakers, and is less biased by low education and literacy (Borson, Scanlan, Watanabe, Tu, & Lessig, 2005). In sum, the Mini-Cog may serve as a useful and easy to administer tool in screening for dementia with Hispanics.

The Cognistat a.k.a. the Neurobehavioral Cognitive Status Examination (NCSE)

The Cognistat is a brief mental status examination that consists of several subtests that assess language functioning, attentional processing, recent verbal memory, constructional praxis, mental calculations, judgment, and verbal concept formation (Drane et al., 2003) and can be administered online (Cognistat, n.d. a) or by a clinician in the traditional paper and pencil format. The Cognistat has been criticized for its lack of a composite impairment score and a high frequency of false-positives (Drane & Osato, 1997; Oehlert et al., 1997) and researchers have called for the development of better norms that are stratified by age and education (Drane et al.). A review of extant literature has not yielded any studies specific to Hispanics, although according to the Cognistat website (Cognistat, n.d. b), a Spanish version of the test is available for purchase, but research on this version seems to be lacking. All in all, given the availability of this measure in Spanish, some research that supports its superiority to the MMSE (in English-speaking samples, e.g., Roper, Bieliauskas, & Peterson, 1996) clinicians may wish to use this measure as a cognitive screen, although because the Mini-Cog does not require socio-demographic adjustments and there is extensive research on the MMSE, both these may be superior screening tools.

Screening for Dementia in the Hispanic Client

Here we have reviewed three screening tools (the MMSE, the Mini-Cog, and the Cognistat) that can be administered when dementia is suspected. These tools all have various strengths and weaknesses, which should be evaluated when determining which is most appropriate for use (factors to consider include the training of the administrator, language of the client, etc.). Ultimately, it is important to keep in mind that a positive screen simply indicates the need for further assessment, and assessment measures that seek to evaluate several domains should be employed. An examination of the scientific literature on such measures follows.

Assessment of Specific Domains

As described above, the APA (2011) has indicated that multiple cognitive domains (i.e., memory, attention, perceptual and motor skills, language, visuospatial abilities, reasoning, and executive functions) should be assessed when dementia is suspected. Table 16.1 offers a summary of these domains and relevant assessment measures as well as information as to how these measures can be used and interpreted with the Hispanic client. Readers are encouraged to see the "Neuropsychological Assessment with Hispanic Clients" (Chap. 22) in this book for a detailed overview of the measures summarized in Table 16.1.

Batteries Specific to the Assessment of Dementia and the Hispanic Client

The CERAD

While there are many approaches to the assessment of dementia, a relatively large movement was made by the National Institute on Aging (NIA) in 1986 to establish the Consortium to Establish a Registry for Alzheimer's Disease (CERAD). This movement aimed to develop standardized, reliable, and valid assessments of Alzheimer's Disease (AD) for use by all Alzheimer Disease Centers (ADCs) established by the NIA (Fillenbaum et al., 2008). Standardized diagnostic criteria and assessment instruments were used in a large study where subjects were examined at entry and, annually thereafter, to observe the natural progression of AD, and ultimately autopsy examination of the brain was included to obtain neuropathologic confirmation of the clinical diagnosis. This resulted in a battery of tests known as the CERAD Battery (which will be described in greater detail below), which has been translated into many languages, including Spanish.

What Is the Spanish-Language CERAD?

The Spanish-language CERAD is a translated version of the original CERAD with some additional cultural modifications. The Spanish-language CERAD Neuropsychological Battery consists of seven subtests (Fillenbaum, Kuchibhalta, Henderson, Clark, & Taussig, 2007), and details regarding each subtest can be found in Table 16.3.

Research on the CERAD with Hispanics

As indicated above, the CERAD Neuropsychological Battery has been translated into Spanish (including directions for administration) using established guidelines for forward and backward translation and reconciliation (Fillenbaum et al., 2007) and has been researched with Hispanics over the last several years (e.g., Carrión-Baralt et al., 2009; Fillenbaum et al., 2007; Krueger, Wilson, Bennett, & Aggarwal, 2009; Marquez de la Plata et al., 2009; Mungas, Reed, Farias, & DeCarli, 2005). It is

Table 16.3 Original CERAD neuropsychological battery subtests (Fillenbaum et al., 2007)

Subtest	Authors	Subtest description	Range of scores
Verbal Fluency	–	Number of animals named in a 60-s time period	0+
15-item Boston Naming Test	Kaplan, Goodglass, and Weintraub (1978)	This is a modified version of the Boston Naming Test whereby 15 of the 60 items from the original BNT were selected to represent words of high, medium, and low frequency in the English language (a translation into Spanish was used)	0–15
Mini-Mental State Examination	Folstein, Folstein, and McHugh (1975)	A brief screen of cognitive function Note: Spelling of "world" ("mundo" in Spanish) is used as a substitution to subtraction of serial 7 s	0–30
10-item Word List Learning Task	–	Ten common nouns are presented consecutively and read aloud by the participant over three trials with a different order for each trial. After each presentation, the participant is asked to recollect the nouns that he/she read	0–10 for each presentation or 0–30 for all three presentations combined
Constructional Praxis	Rosen, Mohs, and Davis (1984)	Participants are asked to copy a circle, diamond, overlapping rectangles, and a cube	0–11
Word List Recall	–	Participants are asked to recall the nouns from the 10-item Word List Learning Task	0–10
Word List Recognition	–	Participants are asked to identify which of 20 nouns (ten of which are from the 10-item Word List Learning Task) they were presented with previously	0–10

important to note that the initial translation was back-translated by five bilingual psychologists with Spanish as spoken in North, Central, and South America and in Puerto Rico. The battery was also checked to ensure appropriate use in Spain with careful attention paid to ensure that all terms used would have the same meaning, familiarity, and level of difficulty for Spanish speakers coming from geographically different areas (Fillenbaum et al.). These procedures are considered outstanding and are best described as high-quality translation procedures.

A search using the PsycINFO database with the search terms "CERAD" or "Consortium to Establish a Registry for Alzheimer's Disease" and "Spanish" or "Latino" or "Hispanic" yielded five relevant results. Below, a review of these studies will be provided as well as guidelines regarding the use of the CERAD with the Hispanic client who is suspected to have dementia of the Alzheimer's type.

Fillenbaum et al. (2007). Fillenbaum and colleagues examined the Spanish-language CERAD with a sample of 140 Alzheimer's Disease (AD) patients contrasted with 88 non-demented controls. Findings indicate that performance was rarely affected by demographic characteristics for either group. The authors report that caution should be exercised when applying their findings due to the higher education and younger age of the control subjects. Nonetheless, data did suggest that the Spanish-language CERAD neuropsychology measures may be able to distinguish cognitively normal persons from those with mild AD as well as between successive stages of decline. Specifically, they report Word List Recall is more sensitive at an early stage, reaching floor rapidly; verbal fluency, Boston Naming Test, and MMSE show a consistent decline over a wide range; and the Word List Recognition does not reach floor until later stages of the disease.

In terms of ethnic group comparisons, this study clearly demonstrates that Spanish-speaking cognitively normal people who have completed grade school perform comparable to both other minorities (e.g., African Americans) and the majority (i.e., non-Latino White groups) with a comparable level of education. It is important to note that the researchers from this study stress that the norms presented from their research should be considered site specific and treated with caution because of a restriction of range based on higher educated and younger age for controls, but their findings are promising. The study suggests that the Spanish-language CERAD is a good measure of decline over time, in particular due to the fact that some measures showed rapid floor effects in early stages of decline, with others measuring a consistent decline over time and still others that avoid reaching floor effects until later stages of the dementia. They further go on to suggest that the use of all the measures in the CERAD could differentiate gradients of impairment on a spectrum from non-impaired to severe.

Carrion-Baralt et al. (2008). Carrión-Baralt et al. evaluated the neuropsychological performance of non-demented nonagenarians residing in Puerto Rico with an English-speaking sample from New York. The CERAD neuropsychological assessment was administered to 81 subjects in Spanish. Results indicated that education was a significant predictor of performance, and when sex and education were controlled for, only a significant difference between the Puerto Rico and New York samples on the Trail-Making Tests was identified (with better scores for the New York sample).

Marquez de la Plata et al. (2009). The naming subtest of the CERAD is an abridged and modified version of the BNT, which Marquez de la Plata et al. examined in a comparison study (in conjunction with the Texas Naming Test) with demented and non-demented participants across three countries (United States, Colombia, and Spain). Marquez de la Plata et al. discuss how the Spanish translation of the CERAD naming subtest is commonly used with Spanish speakers without normative data on Spanish speakers to base interpretive conclusions. Subjects in this study were administered three different naming tests: the Texas Naming Test (a Spanish naming test developed using depicted objects that are relevant and familiar to Spanish speakers), the Modified Boston Naming Test-Spanish (which consists of 30 items adapted from the original 60-item BNT—norming information on this test is discussed in the "Neuropsychology Assessment with Hispanic Clients," Chap. 22), and the CERAD naming test. Results indicated that all three Spanish naming tests differentiated non-demented and moderately demented individuals although the results suggested that the TNT may be a superior test for use with Spanish speakers (as evidenced by its greater Cronbach's alpha). Likewise, the item difficulty index appeared to be highest for all three tests in Spain. This finding may be the result of the higher education level among the Spaniards in this study, as education is known to influence performance on naming tests. These results suggest the CERAD is too easy to accurately assess naming ability among Spanish speakers with dementia, as even the most difficult CERAD items can be correctly identified by 72 and 86% of individuals with dementia in Colombia and Spain, respectively. The relative lack of increasing item difficulty seems to render the CERAD too easy and may negatively impact its ability to assess confrontation naming among mildly impaired individuals.

Kruegar et al. (2009). In a similar study, Kruegar and colleagues selected, adapted (for Spanish speakers), and administered a battery of cognitive tests (used in cognitive aging studies of English speakers) to 66 older Latinos. The CERAD version of the Boston Naming Test was included as part of this battery. Results from this study suggest that the BNT loads on similar factors of semantic memory suggesting a neuropsychological invariability exists for this test across cultures of Anglo-Americans and Hispanics (Mexican and Puerto Rican).

What to Do when Using the CERAD with Hispanics?

We have reviewed the research on the CERAD with Hispanics. Certainly, the CERAD is one of the most extensively researched assessment batteries specific to the assessment of AD. In the context of

Hispanics, a few studies have supported this battery as useful in the assessment of AD in the Hispanic client, suggesting that this assessment probably is a reasonable battery for use with the Hispanic client when AD is suspected (although this may not be ideal for use when other types of dementia are suspected or when a differential diagnosis is required). In the studies we reviewed, it seems that consistent with other ethnic groups (including the non-majority), education (and in some cases sex) can act as a confounder and should be appropriately controlled for. The biggest caveats come with regard to the naming subtest of the CERAD as some research findings have indicated that this subtest may not be sensitive enough to detect AD. Below, additional testing batteries as well as assessment measures commonly used to assess for dementia will be reviewed.

The SENAS

What Is the SENAS?

The Spanish and English Neuropsychological Assessment Scales (SENAS) were created to provide psychometrically sound assessment measures for older English- and Spanish speakers using extensive test development procedures (beginning in 1996; Mungas, Reed, Haan, & González, 2005) with large samples (Mungas, Reed, Crane, Haan, & González, 2004; Mungas, Reed, & Farias et al., 2005; Mungas, Reed, Marshall, & Gonzalez, 2000) guided by item response theory (Hambleton & Swaminathan, 1985; Hambleton, Swaminathan, & Rogers, 1991). The SENAS is not specific to the detection and diagnosis of dementia but is designed to be a Spanish-language-based neuropsychological assessment battery to measure functioning and impairment in a variety of neurocognitive domains associated with dementia and is therefore discussed in this chapter.

The SENAS consists of 13 original scales and also three scales (which were added later) that assess executive function. The entire SENAS battery takes approximately 4 h to administer, although a smaller subset of the scales can be used which takes approximately 2 h to administer (Mungas, 2006). See Table 16.4 for descriptions of the various subtests. The SENAS can be obtained from Dr. Mungas free of charge along with norms for the scales that include adjustments for effects of education, language proficiency, age, and sex. For a breakdown and description of the various subscales, please see Table 16.4.

Research on the SENAS with Hispanics

Extensive research on the SENAS has been conducted and the culmination of nearly 20 years of research has provided extensive support for the SENAS as a psychometrically viable assessment battery for use with both English- and Spanish-speaking Hispanics. In fact several well-conducted studies have demonstrated that the SENAS is a viable assessment battery for differentiating between normal cognition and cognitive impairment and non-demented and demented elderly Hispanics and Whites (Mungas, Reed, & Farias et al., 2005). This battery is also applicable for use with multiethnic (Whites, African Americans, English-speaking Hispanics, and Spanish-speaking Hispanics) and bilingual (Spanish and English) older adults (Mungas et al., 2011). Nonetheless, a few caveats are in order. Research has generally indicated that beyond ethnicity, other socioeconomic factors (e.g., sex, age, education) can impact cognitive test results. The SENAS is not exempt from such an impact. In fact, Mungas, Reed, & Haan et al. (2005) have found that education and language have strong influences on SENAS scores and largely explain group differences in mean scale scores,

Table 16.4 The SENAS subtests (Mungas, Widaman, Reed, & Farias, 2011)

Subtest	Domain(s) assessed	Test description
Verbal Conceptual Thinking	Abstract/conceptual thinking	The subject is presented with six words, five of which belong to a common category, and asked to identify which word does not belong
Non-verbal Conceptual Thinking	Capacity for abstract/ conceptual thinking	The subject is presented with six designs, of which five are similar in form, follow a consistent sequence, or form a consistent pattern, and asked to identify the outlier
Verbal Attention Span	Fixed attention span	The subject is asked to repeat a string of digits (one per second). Some items contain nonrandom sequences of digits (so as to facilitate chunking of information and create gradients of item difficulty)
Visual Attention Span	Fixed attention span	Subjects observe a series of spots (nine spots on a stimulus page) in sequence and are asked to point to the same series in the same sequence (some items contain nonrandom sequences of spots)
Object Naming	Ability to retrieve verbal information from semantic memory store	Subjects are shown color pictures and asked to name specific objects (all words have similar frequency of usage in the Spanish and English languages)
Picture Association	Ability to access and utilize semantic memory of nonverbal information	Subjects are shown color pictures of stimulus objects and 6–12 potential associates are asked to point to the one associate that is most related with the stimulus (seeds with fruits, tools with associated objects, and household goods)
Word List Learning – Version I	Ability to learn and recall verbal information	A standard word list learning task format using a list of 15 common items (from five semantic categories) purchased from a grocery store. Five learning trials and a delayed recall free trial included at a rate of one word per second and order fixed across trials
Word List Learning – Version II	Ability to learn and recall verbal information, with different format	A standard word list learning test with 15 different common items (five exemplar words from three categories) with three words presented on trial 1 with three new words each trial until all are given at a rate of one word per second and immediate recall (delayed free recall is tested after a distractor procedure)
Spatial Configuration Learning	Ability to learn and recall visual-spatial information	Participants match the color chosen by the examiner during each trial (12 different-colored regions on an unlabeled map). Order of item recall testing varies across trials, and after a distractor procedure, delayed recall is tested the same way (format similar to Word List Learning II)
Verbal Comprehension	Ability to understand and carry out auditory-verbal commands	Uses pictures of scenes and objects as stimuli. Subjects are given commands that vary in semantic and syntactic complexity and involve pointing to objects in the stimuli
Verbal Expression	Ability to verbally express ideas and to reason verbally	Subjects are asked questions to which they respond verbally where 2–3 specific response elements correspond to individual items (objective guidelines are provided to guide scoring)
Pattern Recognition	Ability to discriminate black and white designs	A stimulus design is presented with six target alternatives (one that is identical to the stimulus) and must indicate which target is the same as the stimulus
Spatial Localization	Ability to accurately perceive and reproduce spatial relationships	The subject is presented a page with a stimulus (top half, a dog burying a bone by a doghouse and tree) and a target area (bottom half, gridded for scoring) where they point to the perceived buried bone (stimuli changes for increased difficulty)
Category Fluency	Executive function	This is a traditional verbal fluency task in which the examinee is asked to name as many animals as possible (in 60 s), scores are separated between the first and last half of the task

(continued)

Table 16.4 (continued)

Subtest	Domain(s) assessed	Test description
Phonemic Fluency	Executive function	The examinee is asked to name as many words (in 60 s each sound) as possible that begin with specific sounds ("F" and "L"). Total correct responses in the first 30 s and the last 60 s are recorded
Working Memory	Executive function	This is a composite measure derived from three tasks: Digit Span Backward (two trials, must repeat number sequence of 2–8 digits backward), Visual Span Backward (two trials, must point to dots presented in reverse ranging from 2 to 7), and a new List Sorting Task (presented with a list of fruits and animals, in part 1 are asked to repeat from smallest to largest and in part 2 asked to repeat fruit first then animals from smallest to largest)

while age, with the exception of the verbal memory domain, has weak effects (although acculturation in Hispanics was largely accounted for by education and language use). Thus, the interpretation of SENAS scores must be informed by effects related to education and language fluency (hence the excel adjustments provided by Dr. Mungas). Nonetheless, there is demonstrated equivalent validity in Hispanics and Caucasians with respect to concurrent measures of cognition and independent function.

What to Do When Using the SENAS with Hispanics?

In sum, the SENAS is a useful tool that has been extensively researched with Hispanics. Its availability in both English and Spanish and the rigorous development procedures that were employed to ensure cultural fairness make it an excellent assessment measure for assessing for cognitive impairment in the Hispanic client. Furthermore, the SENAS can be used as is (given the above), i.e., further cultural modifications are not necessary. Other strengths of this test include its easy and flexible administration (depending on the referral question a partial battery could be administered), its availability for use (any clinician can e-mail Dr. Mungas for a copy of the scales), and the norm adjustments that have been created for effects of education, language proficiency, age, and sex.

Other Psychological Tests Useful in the Assessment of Dementia

So far we have presented the various domains set forth in the guidelines created by the APA (2011) and offered an overview of how these domains can be assessed and used with the Hispanic client. We have also discussed two useful assessment batteries for use with the Hispanic client. One was specific to the assessment of Alzheimer's disease (the CERAD), whereas the second one (the SENAS) was good for the assessment of dementia and also for detecting cognitive impairment with the Hispanic client. The remainder of this chapter will consist of a review of other assessment measures that are relevant to the assessment of dementia.

Montreal Cognitive Assessment (MoCA)

The Montreal Cognitive Assessment (MoCA) assesses for mild cognitive impairment (MCI) and the suggested normal range for the MoCA is 26–30 points with a 1-point education correction for those individuals who have less than 12 years of education (Nasreddine et al., 2005). It is freely available in multiple languages on the Internet, and there one can find references to research for its use related to a broad spectrum of cognitive disorders (e.g., Parkinson's, Alzheimer's dementia, and HIV-related dementia). The MoCA covers several domains including attention, orientation, language, verbal memory, visuospatial, and executive function and is available free of charge at http://www.mocatest.org/ in several languages (including Spanish). The original normative sample for the MoCA was Canadian; however, subsequently Rossetti, Lacritz, Cullum, and Weiner (2011) obtained normative data from an ethnically diverse population-based sample of which 11% was Hispanic. The authors did not make ethnic comparisons but did find that the majority of the participants (62%) scored below the cutoff of <26 (even with the one-point education correction). Performance was most impaired for the items of cube drawing, delayed free recall (<4/5 words), sentence repetition, placement of clock hands, abstraction items, and verbal fluency (<11 words in 1 min). Limited research on the Spanish version of this measure exists. Strutt and Scott (2011) found differential performance for older Spanish speakers, and they examined the influence of education, which was separated by either less than 6 years or from 6 to 13 years. Results from this study indicated poorer performance for those with less than 6 years of education that appeared to be predominantly in the domain of visuospatial-executive performance. Thus, the MoCA may be useful to implement as a screen but in most cases will require substantial follow-up assessment procedures before a diagnosis can be reached.

Mattis Dementia Rating Scale (MDRS; Mattis, 1988)

The MDRS (Mattis, 1988) consists of 36 tasks divided into five subscales (attention, initiation/perseveration, construction, conceptualization, and memory; the maximum total score is 144) and has thus far been mostly used with English-speaking samples with a few exceptions (Arnold, Cuellar, & Guzman, 1998; Hohl et al., 1999; Lyness, Hernandez, Chui, & Teng, 2006; Taussig, Henderson, & Mack, 1992). Initially, Taussig et al. administered the Dementia Rating Scale (among other measures, e.g., the WAIS-R, MMSE) to two groups of Spanish- and English-speaking participants: one group met criteria for probable AD, and the other group were normal controls. Results indicated that all Spanish-language neuropsychological tests differentiated between the control group and those with mild to moderate AD (although Taussig and colleagues did not discuss what procedures they used to translate the MDRS). Later, Jacobs et al. (1997) administered the oddities and identities subtest of the MDRS to a group of English and Spanish speakers (a Spanish-translated version of the MDRS was administered to the Spanish-speaking participants) matched for age and education as part of a neuropsychological battery. Results from this study revealed that Spanish speakers scored lower on the battery than English speakers and specifically on the identities and oddities subtest of the MDRS (and also on other tests) despite the language-free nature of this subtest.

Subsequently, Arnold and colleagues (1998) used rigorous translation procedures to generate a Spanish Adaptation of the MDRS (MDRS-SA) that was appropriate for use with individuals from diverse linguistic backgrounds (i.e., those from Florida, Puerto Rico, Cuba, Mexico, Texas, Central America, and South America). Results indicated that when education, acculturation, and gender were controlled for, the MDRS-SA was effective at discriminating between those who were neurologically impaired and those who were not both across all scales and with the total score ($p < .05$). However, these results suggested that although there was a statistically significant difference between impaired and non-impaired individuals (as well as an ability to correctly classify the individuals clinically), there was a larger amount of variability in the Spanish sample than the English sample (nearly double), suggesting that more data needs to be collected to establish acceptable norms. It is also important to note that due to the sensitivity of this test and to maximize correct detection of impairment, collaborative use of other sources of patient data are essential (although this is not specific to Hispanics or to the Spanish version of this test).

Hohl and colleagues (1999) also examined the utility of a translated version of the MDRS although they did not employ the rigorous procedures employed in the Arnold study (they simply translated the MDRS directly with one modification—instead of having participants repeat "bee-key-gee" and "be-ba-bo," they had them repeat "si-ti-mi" and "si-sa-su"). Results from their study indicated that while mild to moderate demented Hispanics scored similarly to their non-Hispanic counterparts, those Spanish-speaking participants who were severely impaired obtained considerably lower scores than the non-Hispanic group. Hohl and colleagues suggest that this discrepancy might reflect a cultural bias in the test or educational differences in the groups. Most recently, Hernandez, Chui, and Teng (2006) administered the MDRS-SA (the same version used in the Arnold study) and MMSE to Spanish- and English-speaking participants matched on education, age, and gender. Results indicated that despite this match, Spanish-speaking normal controls scored lower than their English-speaking counterparts (which they cite is consistent with the norms published by Mattis (1988)), although this was mostly accounted for by scores on certain tasks (e.g., conceptualization subscale identities and oddities task which was also a finding in the Jacobs et al., 1997 study). They conclude that norms specific to Spanish-speaking individuals are necessary. However, they further suggest that to screen for dementia, the MDRS Memory subscale and the MMSE are as good as utilizing the entire MDRS. Thus, one could expect to achieve equivalent measures of performance using only the MDRS Memory subscale and MMSE rather than administering the entire MDRS. In sum, the MDRS may be useful in the assessment of dementia with Hispanic clients, although in the absence of good normative data, the interpretations of test results should be made with caution.

Summary and Overview of Recommendations

A review of extant literature has indicated that there are different approaches to assessing dementia. With regard to the Hispanic client, we followed APA's recommendations for assessment and discussed the various domains that should be assessed when dementia is suspected as part of a comprehensive assessment battery. The interested reader has also been referred to the Chap. 22 on "Neuropsychological Assessment with Hispanic Clients" in this book for a more detailed overview of several measures that assess memory, attention, perceptual and motor skills, language, visuospatial abilities, reasoning, and executive functions (Table 16.1 offers a nice overview of these measures). While the number of assessments available to Hispanics is comparably smaller to that of their English counterparts, quality measures with good normative data and sound psychometric properties exist. When using these measures, one should keep in mind the consistent findings of influence of demographic variables such as age, education, and language abilities. Again, the authors encourage the translation and or development of new measures for areas where there is a need. The overarching goal is to step away from the all to common practice of identifying problem areas or deficits in assessment domains without offering solutions. That said, we remind the readers that in translating or adapting existing measures, we need to be cognizant of the potential nuances in language and culture that may skew measurement and interpretation.

In addition to this review, we also reviewed and discussed at length assessment batteries and individual tests specific to dementia and the Hispanic client. This review has revealed that as is the case

Table 16.5 Summary of measures reviewed

Type of assessment	Test name	Language availability	Useful to assess for	Research and recommendations
Screening	*Mini-Mental State Examination*	English and Spanish	Cognitive decline	Fairly extensive research has been conducted and a summary of this research can be found in Table 16.1
	Mini-Cog	English and Spanish[a]	Cognitive decline	Research has indicated that the Mini-Cog may serve as a useful and easy to administer tool in screening for dementia with Hispanics, and it does not does not require sociodemographic adjustments
	Cognistat	English and Spanish	Cognitive decline	Despite that this measure is available in Spanish, research on its use with Hispanics appears to be absent
Batteries	*CERAD*	English and Spanish	Alzheimer's disease	A few studies have supported this battery as useful in the assessment of AD in the Hispanic client although education and sex may need to be controlled for
	SENAS	English and Spanish	Cognitive impairment	The SENAS is a useful tool that has been extensively researched with Hispanics; no further cultural modifications are necessary, and norms with relevant adjustments exist
Individual tests	*Montreal Cognitive Assessment (MoCA)*	English and Spanish	Cognitive impairment	Little research has been conducted on the Spanish version of the MoCA, which may be useful as a screen but requires substantial follow-up assessment procedures before a diagnosis can be reached
	Mattis Dementia Rating Scale	English and Spanish[b]	Dementia	In the absence of good normative data, the interpretations of test results should be made with caution

[a]This test is primarily nonverbal
[b]Various Spanish translations exist

for other ethnic groups, demographic information about the client (even in the absence of ethnic minority status) must be taken into account when results are being interpreted. Namely, sociodemographic factors such as age, gender, and education can impact test performance. Furthermore, English and Spanish-language proficiency can also carry an impact on test performance. Thus, while clinicians and researchers alike are encouraged to keep the above factors in mind when interpreting results, our review of the literature has produced several assessment options that are likely to lead to a reliable diagnosis (particularly those that have adjustments to sociocultural factors), and for those assessment measures where an "interpret results with caution" clause was warranted, we recommend collateral contacts and results from additional assessment measures be used as a means for either confirming or disconfirming a test result (Table 16.5).

References

Alzheimer's Association. (2011). *2011 Alzheimer's disease facts and figure*. Retrieved from www.alz.org/downloads/Facts_Figures_2011.pdf

American Psychiatric Association. (2000). *Diagnostic and statistical manual of mental disorders* (4th ed., text rev.). Washington, DC: APA.

American Psychological Association. (2011). *Guidelines for the evaluation of dementia and age-related cognitive change*. Retrieved from www.apa.org/pi/aging/resources/dementia-guidelines.pdf

Ardila, A., Rodríguez-Menéndez, G., & Rosselli, M. (2002). Current issues in neuropsychological assessment with Hispanics/Latinos. In R. Ferrao (Ed.), *Minority and cross-cultural aspects of neuropsychological assessment* (pp. 151–180). Lisse, the Netherlands: Swets & Zeitlinger Publishers.

Arnold, B. R., Cuellar, I., & Guzman, N. (1998). Statistical and clinical evaluation of the Mattis dementia rating scale-Spanish adaptation: An initial investigation. *Journal of Gerontology: Psychological Science, 53*(6), 364–369.

Boone, K., Victor, T. L., Wen, J., Razani, J., & Pontón, M. (2007). The association between neuropsychological scores and ethnicity, language, and acculturation variables in a large patient population. *Archives of Clinical Neuropsychology, 22*(3), 355–365. doi:10.1016/j.acn.2007.01.010.

Borson, S., Scanlan, J., Brush, M., Vitaliano, P., & Dokmak, A. (2000). The mini-cog: A cognitive 'vital signs' measure for dementia screening in multi-lingual elderly. *International Journal of Geriatric Psychiatry, 15*(11), 1021–1027. doi:10.1002/1099-1166(200011)15:11<1021::AID-GPS234>3.0.CO;2-6.

Borson, S., Scanlan, J. M., Watanabe, J., Tu, S., & Lessig, M. (2005). Simplifying detection of cognitive impairment: Comparison of the mini-cog and mini-mental state examination in a multiethnic sample. *Journal of the American Geriatrics Society, 53*(5), 871–874. doi:10.1111/j.1532-5415.2005.53269.x.

Carrión-Baralt, J. R., Meléndez-Cabrero, J., Beeri, M. S., Sano, M., & Silverman, J. M. (2009). The neuropsychological performances of nondemented Puerto Rican nonagenarians. *Dementia and Geriatric Cognitive Disorders, 27*, 353–360.

Carrión-Baralt, J. R., Schnaider-Beeri, M., Melendez-Cabrero, J., Rodriguez-Ubinas, H., Sano, M., & Silverman, J. M. (2008). P3-285: Impact of APOE e4 on very late life cognition. *Alzheimer's & Dementia: The Journal of the Alzheimer's Association, 4*(4), T606.

Census Bureau, U. S. (2002). *Hispanic population in the United States: March 2002*. Washington, DC: GPO.

Cherner, M. M., Suarez, P. P., Lazzaretto, D. D., Fortuny, L., Mindt, M., & Dawes, S. S. (2007). Demographically corrected norms for the Brief Visuospatial Memory Test-revised and Hopkins Verbal Learning Test-revised in monolingual Spanish speakers from the U.S.-Mexico border region. *Archives of Clinical Neuropsychology, 22*(3), 343–353. doi:10.1016/j.acn.2007.01.009.

Coffey, D. M., Marmol, L., Schock, L., & Adams, W. (2005). The influence of acculturation on the Wisconsin Card Sorting Test by Mexican Americans. *Archives of Clinical Neuropsychology, 20*(6), 795–803.

Cognistat. (n.d. a). *Pioneers in brain fitness cognistat cognitive assessment: About the exam*. Retrieved from http://www.cognistat.com/about-exam-faq

Cognistat. (n.d. b). *Pioneers in brain fitness cognistat cognitive assessment: Languages & translations & international distributors*. Retrieved from http://www.cognistat.com/languages-translations-international-distributors

Conners, C., Epstein, J. N., Angold, A., & Klaric, J. (2003). Continuous performance test performance in a normative epidemiological sample. *Journal of Abnormal Child Psychology: An Official Publication of the International Society for Research in Child and Adolescent Psychopathology, 31*(5), 555–562. doi:10.1023/A:1025457300409.

Crisostomo, P. R., Butler, K. A., Webster, J. R., & Moran, M. B. (2002). Prevalence of cognitive impairment in an urban Hispanic community population. *Journal of the American Geriatrics Society, 50*(5), 977–978.

Dick, M. B., Teng, E. L., Kempler, D., Davis, D. S., & Taussig, I. (2002). The cross-cultural neuropsychological test battery (CCNB): Effects of age, education, ethnicity, and cognitive status on performance. In F. Ferraro & F. Ferraro (Eds.), *Minority and cross-cultural aspects of neuropsychological assessment* (pp. 17–41). Lisse, Netherlands: Swets & Zeitlinger Publishers.

Drane, D. L., & Osato, S. S. (1997). Using the neurobehavioral cognitive status examination as a screening measure for older adults. *Archives of Clinical Neuropsychology, 12*, 139–143.

Drane, D. L., Yuspeh, R. L., Huthwaite, J. S., Klingler, L. K., Foster, L. M., Mrazik, M., et al. (2003). Healthy older adult performance on modified version of the Cognistat (NCSE): Demographic issues and preliminary normative data. *Journal of Clinical and Experimental Neuropsychology, 25*(1), 133–144. doi:10.1076/jcen.25.1.133.13628.

Escobar, J. L., Burnam, A., Karno, M., Forsythe, A., Landsverk, J., & Golding, J. M. (1986). Use of the Mini-Mental State Exami- nation (MMSE) in a community population of mixed ethnicity. *Journal of Nervous and Mental Disease*, 174, 607–614.

Fillenbaum, G. G., Kuchibhalta, M., Henderson, V. W., Clark, C. M., & Taussig, I. M. (2007). Comparison of performance on the CERAD neuropsychological battery of Hispanic patients and cognitively normal controls at two sites. *Clinical Gerontologist, 30*(3), 1–22.

Fillenbaum, G. G., van Belle, G., Morris, J. C., Mohs, R. C., Mirra, S. S., Davis, P. C., et al. (2008). Consortium to establish a registry for Alzheimer's disease (CERAD): The first twenty years. *Alzheimer's & Dementia, 4*(2), 96–109.

Folstein, M.F., Folstein, S. E., & McHugh, P.R. (1975), "Mini-mental state". A practical method for grading the cognitive state of patients for the clinician. *Journal of Psychiatric Reserves, 12*(3), 189–198.

Gasquoine, P., Croyle, K. L., Cavazos-Gonzalez, C., & Sandoval, O. (2007). Language of administration and neuropsychological test performance in neurologically intact Hispanic American bilingual adults. *Archives of Clinical Neuropsychology, 22*(8), 991–1001. doi:10.1016/j.acn.2007.08.003.

Gonzalez, H. M., Mungas, D., & Haan, M. N. (2002). A Verbal Learning and Memory Test for English- and Spanish-speaking older Mexican-American adults. *The Clinical Neuropsychologist, 16*(4), 439–451.

Groth-Marnat, G. (2003). *Handbook of psychological assessment* (4th ed.). Hoboken, NJ: Wiley.

Hambleton, R. K., & Swaminathan, H. (1985). *Item response theory: Principles and applications*. Toronto, Canada: Wiley.

Hambleton, R. K., Swaminathan, H., & Rogers, H. J. (1991). *MMSS: Fundamentals of item response theory*. Newbury Park, CA: Sage Publications.

Harris, J. G., Cullum, C. M., & Puente, A. E. (1995). Effects of bilingualism on verbal learning and memory in Hispanic adults. *Journal of the International Neuropsychological Society, 1*, 10–16.

Hernandez et al. (2006),à the in-text citation needs to be changed to Lyness, Hernandez, Chui, & Teng, 2006

Hohl, U., Grundman, M., Salmon, D. P., Thomas, R. G., & Thal, L. J. (1999). Mini-mental state examination and Mattis dementia rating scale performance differs in Hispanic and non-Hispanic Alzheimer's disease patients. *Journal of the International Neuropsychological Society, 5*(4), 301–307. doi:10.1017/S1355617799544019.

Jacobs, D. M., Sano, M., Albert, S., Schofield, P., Dooneief, G., & Stern, Y. (1997). Cross-cultural neuropsychological assessment: A comparison of randomly selected, demographically matched cohorts of English- and Spanish-speaking older adults. *Journal of Clinical and Experimental Neuropsychology, 19*(3), 331–339.

Jones, R.N. & Gallo, J.J. (2002). Education and sex differences in the Mini-Mental State Examination: Effects of Differential Item Functioning. *Journal of Gerontology, 57B*, 548–558.

Kaplan et al. (1978) should be Kaplan, Goodglass, and Weintraub (1983) and the reference for that is: Kaplan, E., Goodglass, H., & Weintraub, S. (1983). Boston Naming Test. Philadelphia: Lea & Febiger.

Krueger, K. R., Wilson, R. S., Bennett, D. A., & Aggarwal, N. T. (2009). A battery of tests for assessing cognitive function in older Latino persons. *Alzheimer Disease and Associated Disorders, 23*(4), 384–388.

La Rue, A., Romero, L. J., Ortiz, I. E., Liang, H., & Lindeman, R. D. (1999). Neuropsychological performance of Hispanic and non-Hispanic older adults: An epidemiologic survey. *The Clinical Neuropsychologist, 13*(4), 474–486. doi:10.1076/1385-4046(199911)13:04;1-Y;FT474.

Lyness, S. A., Hernandez, I., Chui, H. C., & Teng, E. L. (2006). Performance of Spanish speakers on the Mattis dementia rating scale (MDRS). *Archives of Clinical Neuropsychology, 21*, 827–836.

Mahurin, R. K., Espino, D. V., & Holifield, E. B. (1992). Mental status testing in elderly Hispanic populations: Special concerns. *Psychopharmacology Bulletin, 28*(4), 391–399.

Marshall, S.C., Mungas, D., Weldon M. et al. Differential item functioning in the Mini-Mental State Examination in English-and Spanish-speaking older adults. *Psychology Aging*, 12, 718–725.

Marquez de la Plata, C., Arango-Lasprilla, J. C., Alegret, M., Moreno, A., Tárraga, L., Lara, M., et al. (2009). Item analysis of three Spanish naming tests: A cross-cultural investigation. *NeuroRehabilitation, 24*, 75–85.

Mattis, S. (1988). *Dementia Rating Scale (DRS)*. Odessa, FL: Psychological Assessment Resources.

Menon, C., Hall, J., Hobson, V., Johnson, L., & O'Bryant, S. E. (2011). Normative performance on the executive clock drawing task in a multi-ethnic bilingual cohort: A project FRONTIER study. *International Journal of Geriatric Psychiatry*. doi:10.1002/gps.2810.

Mungas, D. (2006). Neuropsychological assessment of Hispanics elders: Challenges and psychometric approaches. In G. Yeo & D. Gallagher-Thompson (Eds.), *Ethnicity and the dementias* (2nd ed., pp. 71–86). New York: Routledge/Taylor & Francis Group.

Mungas, D., Marshal, S. C., Weldon, M., Haan, M., & Reed, B. R. (1996). Age and education correction of mini-mental state examination for English- and Spanish-speaking elderly. *Neurology, 46*(3), 700–706.

Mungas, D., Reed, B. R., Crane, P. K., Haan, M. N., & González, H. (2004). Spanish and English neuropsychological assessment scales (SENAS): Further development and psychometric characteristics. *Psychological Assessment, 16*(4), 347–359.

Mungas, D., Reed, B. R., Farias, S. T., & DeCarli, C. (2005). Criterion-referenced validity of a neuropsychological test battery: Equivalent performance in elderly Hispanics and non-Hispanic whites. *Journal of the International Neuropsychological Society, 11*, 620–630.

Mungas, D., Reed, B. R., Haan, M. N., & González, H. (2005). Spanish and English neuropsychological assessment scales: Relationship to demographics, language, cognition, and independent function. *Neuropsychology, 19*(4), 466–475.

Mungas, D., Reed, B. R., Marshall, S. C., & Gonzalez, H. C. (2000). Development of psychometrically matched English and Spanish language neuropsychological tests for older persons. *Neuropsychology, 14*(2), 209–223.

Mungas, D., Widaman, K. F., Reed, B. R., & Farias, S. T. (2011). Measurement invariance of neuropsychological tests in diverse older persons. *Neuropsychology, 25*(2), 260–269.

Nasreddine, Z. S., Philips, N. A., Bédirian, V., Charbonneau, S., Whitehead, V., Collin, I., et al. (2005). The Montreal cognitive assessment, MoCA: A brief screening tool for mild cognitive impairment. *Journal of the American Geriatrics Society, 53*(4), 695–699.

Oehlert, M., Hass, S. D., Freeman, M. R., Williams, M. D., Ryan, J. J., & Sumerall, S. W. (1997). The neurobehavioral cognitive status examination: Accuracy of the "screen-metric" approach in a clinical sample. *Journal of Clinical Psychology, 53*, 733–737.

Peña-Casanova, J., Blesa, R., Aguilar, M., Gramunt-Fombuena, N., Gómez-Ansón, B., Oliva, R., et al. (2009). Spanish multicenter normative studies (NEURONORMA project): Methods and sample characteristics. *Archives of Clinical Neuropsychology, 24*(4), 307–319.

Ramírez, M., Teresi, J. A., Holmes, D., Gurland, B., & Lantigua, R. (2006). Differential item functioning (DIF) and the mini-mental state examination (MMSE): Overview, sample, and issues of translation. *Medical Care, 44*(11), S95–S106.

Ramírez, M., Teresi, J. A., Silver, S., Holmes, D., Gurland, B., & Lantigua, R. (2001). Cognitive assessment among minority elderly: Possible test bias. *Journal of Mental Health and Aging, 7*(1), 91–118.

Rey, G. J., Feldman, E., Rivas-Vazquez, R., Levin, B. E., & Bentin, A. (1999). Neuropsychological development and normative data on Hispanics. *Archives of Clinical Neuropsychology, 14*, 593–601.

Roper, B. L., Bieliauskas, L. A., & Peterson, M. R. (1996). Validity of the mini-mental state examination and the neurobehavioral cognitive status examination in cognitive screening. *Neuropsychiatry, Neuropsychology, and Behavioral Neurology, 9*(1), 54–57.

Rosen, W.G., Mohs, R.C., & Davis, K.L. (1984). A new rating scale for Alzheimer's diseases. *American Journal of Psychiatry, 14*, 1356–1364.

Rossetti, H. C., Lacritz, L. H., Cullum, M., & Weiner, M. F. (2011). Normative date of the Montreal cognitive assessment (MoCA) in a population based sample. *Neurology, 77*(13), 1272–1275.

Royall, D. R., Espino, D. V., Polk, M. J., Verdeja, R., Vale, S., Gonzales, H., et al. (2003). Validation of a Spanish translation of the CLOX for use in Hispanic samples: The Hispanic EPESE study. *International Journal of Geriatric Psychiatry, 18*(2), 135–140. doi:10.1002/gps.804.

Strutt, A. & Scott, B. (2011). Misclassification of Cognitive Impairment on the MOCA with Spanish-Speaking Older Adults. Retrieved from: http://acn.oxfordjournals.org/content/26/6/470.abstract

Taussig, M., Henderson, V. W., & Mack, W. (1992). Spanish translation and validation of a neuropsychological battery: Performance of Spanish- and English-speaking Alzheimer's disease patients and normal comparison subjects. *Clinical Gerontologist, 11*(3–4), 95–108.

Teresi, J., Golden, R., Cross, P. et al. (1995). Item bias in cognitive screening measures: Comparison of elderly White, Afro-Americans, Hispanic, and high and low education subgroups. *Journal of Clinical Epidemiology, 48*, 473–483.

Teresi, J. A., Holmes, D., Ramirez, M., Gurland, B. J., & Lantigua, R. (2001). Performance of cognitive tests among different racial/ethnic and education groups: Findings of differential item functioning and possible item bias. *Journal of Mental Health and Aging, 7*(1), 79–89.

Thombaben, M. (2010). A simple tool to screen clients for cognitive impairment. *Home Health Care Management Practice, 22*, 448.

Tombaugh, T. N., & McIntyre, N. J. (1992). The mini-mental state examination: A comprehensive review. *Journal of the American Geriatrics Society, 40*(9), 922–935.

Valle, R., Hough, R., Kolody, B., Cook-Gait, H., Figueroa, G., Jimenez, R., & Atkinson, J.H. (1991). The validation of the Blessed Mental Status Test and the Mini-Mental Status Examination with an Hispanic population. In *Final report to the National Institute of Mental Health, Grunt #ROI MH43390-01*.

Weintraub, S. (2011). *Neuropsychology of aging and dementia*. Retrieved from people.bu.edu/abudson/06-03-09SwPRESENT.pdf

Wheeler, D. K. (2010). *Digit span with a linguistically diverse Latina/Latino population: A cross-language study*. ProQuest Dissertations and Theses, Fielding Graduate University. Retrieved from http://search.proquest.com/docview/855633123?accountid=452

Assessing Psychosis in Hispanics

17

Veronica Cardenas, Paula Helu, Denisse Tiznado, and Jennifer Ho

Assessing Psychosis in Hispanic Patients

What Is Psychosis?

Psychosis is characterized by a series of symptoms indicating impairment in the perception of reality. Delusions (strongly held beliefs despite disconfirming evidence) and hallucinations (perceptions that occur in the absence of a stimulus and that are not perceived by others) are the primary criteria for diagnosing psychosis. There are various conditions that can cause either brief (i.e., 1 month or less) or more enduring and debilitating symptoms of psychosis such as a general medical condition, substance use, a mood disorder, or schizophrenia. The symptoms of schizophrenia are continual for a minimum of 6 months or more. According to the DSM-IV-TR (American Psychiatric Association, 2000), there are five types of schizophrenia (i.e., paranoid, disorganized, catatonic, undifferentiated, residual), and symptoms are classified into positive symptoms (i.e., delusions, hallucinations, disorganized behavior and speech) and negative symptoms (i.e., restricted emotional expression, restricted initiation in goal-directed behavior). Additionally, a diagnosis of schizophrenia requires impairment in one or more areas of functioning, work, self-care, or interpersonal relationship. A diagnosis of psychosis not otherwise specified (NOS) includes the presence of psychotic symptoms that do not meet the criteria for any specific psychotic disorder due to inadequate or contradictory information to make a specific diagnosis. As indicated above, there are other disorders during which psychosis can manifest itself including during mood episodes associated with major depressive disorder or bipolar disorder.

What Are the Challenges in Assessing Psychosis?

The assessment and diagnosis of psychosis is a complex task that is further confounded by factors introduced by culturally diverse populations. Hispanics are certainly not immune from experiencing a psychotic disorder, although how it presents or is expressed, what it is labeled, and how distressing

V. Cardenas, Ph.D. (✉) • P. Helu, M.S. • D. Tiznado, B.S. • J. Ho, B.A.
Department of Psychiatry, University of California – San Diego,
MC 09939500 Gilman Drive, La Jolla, CA 92093-0680, USA
e-mail: vcardenas@ucsd.edu

L.T. Benuto (ed.), *Guide to Psychological Assessment with Hispanics*,
DOI 10.1007/978-1-4614-4412-1_17, © Springer Science+Business Media New York 2013

it is can vary across individuals and across cultures. Valid assessment of psychosis in Hispanics should take cultural variables into consideration, including ethnic, socioeconomic, and religious factors. The following section will discuss specific challenges and considerations for assessment and diagnosis of psychosis in Hispanics.

With the birth of cross-cultural psychiatry in 1977, culture and ethnicity have taken a lead role in specialty interdisciplinary journals. The research that emerged during this period encouraged mental health professionals to realize the importance of considering factors relating to a subject's cultural background to accurately identify illness and disorder, without overlooking what could be considered "culture-specific phenomena" (Lopez & Guarnaccia, 2000). Thus, a new scientific consciousness developed, with a mission to provide culturally sensitive assessment, diagnosis, and treatment. Emerging from this new school of thought, the *Diagnostic and Statistical Manual-IV-TR* (DSM-IV-TR) (known as the primary guide for diagnosing mental health conditions) was revised and enriched with cultural materials that were incorporated in various sections (APA, 2000). These additions brought forward a new model of practice that considered diagnosis without cultural assessment unethical. Currently, mental health professionals working with Hispanics and other culturally diverse populations are expected to demonstrate cultural competency and awareness as standard practice. This awareness is called *counselor personal awareness* and refers to a mental health professional's awareness of their own biases, values, and stereotypes and an attempt to see the situation from a patient's perspective (White Kress, Eriksen, Rayle, & Ford, 2005). Overdiagnosis of psychosis (or other mental health conditions) and oftentimes ethnic discrimination (by reporting lower functional capacity) can result.

In particular, religion and spirituality have received widespread attention within the context of psychosis in Hispanics. Hispanic religious culture, most commonly Catholicism, is rich in references to the supernatural. Catholicism praises imagery of apparitions, encounters with spirits (with influences from indigenous cultures). Moreover, many Hispanics believe in the supernatural power of *curanderos* (folk healers) and shamans, who channel their energy from the realm of the magical and godly and are believed to change form and become possessed by souls of the past. A large number of Hispanics currently hold these beliefs, which may have clinical significance when trying to decipher whether an individual has psychosis or if he/she is engaging in a cultural practice. This has important relevance here as it is a defining difference between Hispanics and the normative Caucasian population on which psychosis-related diagnostic criteria were based. However, it is important to note that not all Hispanics are highly religious and that is critical to keep in mind the degree of acculturation and religiosity of the patient when making clinical judgments. Nonetheless, when assessing and diagnosing psychosis in Hispanics, it is possible to confuse the endorsement of certain symptoms as indicators of psychosis (e.g., hallucinations or delusional thought content), when in fact they are expressions of culture and/or religion. This has the potential to pose a major problem as ignoring the role of culture could result in overdiagnosing psychosis (or other mental health conditions), which can lead to increased discrimination, the administration of unnecessary treatment, etc.

Language is an additional important cultural consideration that must be accounted for in the assessment of psychosis. It is estimated that 29 % of Latinos living in the United States have language barriers in communicating in English with their healthcare providers (Pew Hispanic Center/Kaiser Family Foundation, 2002). Because most assessment and diagnostic tools are available in English only, a lack of English comprehension on the part of the patient jeopardizes the validity of the conclusions and inferences that can be made from these tools. Thus, to conduct valid clinical assessment, diagnostic and assessment tools should be presented in a patient's preferred language. Another relevant factor in the valid assessment of psychosis in Hispanics and other diverse populations is that normative data are predominantly representative of highly educated, higher SES, Caucasian populations. Recent studies with a focus on culturally valid assessment suggest that these norms are not representative of Hispanic populations and therefore may not be applicable. In an effort to increase validity and provide accurate diagnoses from a multicultural perspective, many assessment tools have indexes and scales specific to certain ethnic groups to ensure higher diagnostic accuracy.

Assessment Tools Used to Assess for Psychosis

MMPI-2

The Minnesota Multiphasic Personality Inventory-2 (MMPI-2) has been widely used as a tool to aid in the diagnosis of schizophrenia (Ben-Porath, Butcher, & Graham, 1991). Past research has found that the MMPI-2 is able to successfully differentiate schizophrenia from diagnoses such as major depression (Ben-Porath et al.) and bipolar disorder (Bagby et al., 2005). Specifically, an elevation on Scale 8 is thought to indicate schizophrenia (although this scale is consistently cited as difficult to interpret) as is an elevation on the Schizophrenia Proneness Scale (Bolinskey, Gottesman, & Nichols, 2003). The validity and reliability of the MMPI-2 among Caucasians has been established in many different studies. However, studies have reported mixed findings regarding the validity and reliability of the MMPI-2 in Hispanic patients (the reader is encouraged to view the chapter for a thorough review of the use of the MMPI-2 with Hispanics). For example, Velasquez, Gonzales, Butcher, and Castillo-Canez (1997) found that the validity and clinical scales fell within half a standard deviation of one another and differences in scores were of little consequence. Alternatively, a meta-analysis by Hall, Bansal, and Lopez (1999) suggested that the MMPI-2 does not portray African-Americans and Latinos as more pathological than Caucasians. However, concerns are still raised as to whether the use of the MMPI-2 with Hispanics may exaggerate psychopathology because it fails to take culture, ethnicity, and assimilation into account (Whitworth & McBlaine, 1993).

A central issue in the valid use of the MMPI-2 in Hispanics involves normative data. The MMPI-2 was normed in 1989 to include a representative sample of the US population (Butcher, Dahlstrom, Graham, Tellegen, & Kaemmer, 1989). A stratified sample based on the 1980 US Census consisted of 2,600 community-dwelling respondents, of which 12 % were Hispanics. Although this sample was representative of the US population in the 1980s, the US Hispanic population has since changed dramatically. Therefore, caution should be used when using these norms to interpret Hispanic MMPI-2 scores. Moreover, different studies have investigated the different MMPI-2 scales in both healthy controls and patient groups. Past research has found small significant differences between Caucasian and Hispanic undergraduate students, suggesting acceptable validation of the MMPI-2 in the Hispanic population (Whitworth & McBlaine, 1993; Whitworth & Unterbrink, 1994). However, important considerations need to be taken when assessing Hispanics using the MMPI-2.

Velasquez et al. (1997) presented a list of considerations when using the MMPI-2 with Hispanic patients. These included understanding of the specific reasons for assessment, the role of acculturation, the patient's environment and language preferences, the patient's motivation toward the assessment, and the mental status. The *Multifasico de la Personalidad-2-Minnesota, Version Hispana,* translated by Garcia-Peltoniemi and Azan Chaviano (1993), is considered to be the "official" US Spanish translation of the MMPI-2. There is also the *Inventario Multifasico de la Personalidad de Minnesota-2 Español,* translated by Lucio and Reyes-Lagunes for use in Mexico (Lucio, Reyes-Lagunes, & Scott, 1994). The *Inventario Multifasico de la Personalidad de Minnesota-2 Español* was validated with a college student sample in Mexico. The authors found few differences between MMPI-2 scores between scores from the normative Mexican sample and the US normative sample (Lucio et al.). This translated version has also been found to have construct validity, in that it significantly discriminated between college students and a psychiatric sample in Mexico (Lucio-G, Palacios, Duran, & Butcher, 1999). Later, normative data for the *Inventario Multifasico de la Personalidad de Minnesota-2 Español* was published (Lucio, Ampudia, Duran, Leon, & Butcher, 2001). Psychometric data is also available for other Spanish-speaking countries including Chile (Rissetti, Himmel, Gonzalez-Moreno, Cusullo, & Butcher, 1996), Spain (Avila-Espada & Jimenez-Gomez, 1996), Peru (Scott & Pampa, 2000), and Argentina (Casullo & Samartino, 1996).

In summary, there are mixed findings regarding the validity of the MMPI-2 and whether or not it overpathologizes Hispanics. Nonetheless, there is ample evidence to suggest that the MMPI-2 is a useful tool in both the evaluation of psychosis (Ben-Porath et al., 1991; Wetzler, Khadivi, & Moser, 1998) and in terms of general use with Hispanics (multiple sets of normative data exists). Therefore, the MMPI-2 can be used when psychosis is suspected in the Hispanic patient. However, it is recommended that other assessment strategies be incorporated (e.g., reliable collateral contacts, a clinical interview, record review, administration of additional tests).

MCMI-III

The Millon Clinical Multiaxial Inventory-III (Millon, 1994; Millon, Millon, Davis, & Grossman, 2006) is a self-report measure that can aid in the diagnosis of various psychological disorders. Key scales to consider with this measure with regard to psychosis are the *Thought Disorder* and *Delusional Disorder* scales. The MCMI-III has been translated to Spanish, and while there are no Hispanic norms available, this measure can be useful in identifying psychosis particularly with Hispanics. Research with Hispanics has indicated that this measure is able to differentiate between dysthymic disorder, major depressive disorder, bipolar disorder, and schizophrenia (e.g., Castañeda, Kjenslie, & Steil, 2006; by Kjenslie, Castañeda, & Velasquez, 2006). Because this measure is discussed extensively in Chap. 5 on "Assessing Personality Using Self-Report Measures with Hispanic Clients" of this book, readers are encouraged to see that chapter for a more detailed overview of this measure. In sum, it does appear that the MCMI-III can serve as a useful tool when psychosis is suspected in the Hispanic client.

Rorschach

The Rorschach Comprehensive System is used as a guide to interpret the answers participants give regarding their perception of ten different images (i.e., ink blots). This guide is available in English, Spanish, and Portuguese. As the images used to prompt responses and descriptions from the participants do not consist of verbal or written items, it is the guide to interpret the responses and the scoring parameters that have been translated into Spanish. Despite that the interpretation guide has been translated to Spanish, the indexes and scores cannot be considered valid unless they have been normalized for cultural and ethnic minorities, for example, Hispanics (Garb, Wood, Nezworski, Grove, & Stejskal, 2001). Studies of normativity exist for Spanish-speaking populations in Barcelona, Madrid, and Valencia (Campo, 2000; Font & Saiz, 1996; Fuster, Sifre, Barriuso, Lobato, & Martinez, 1997; Sangro, 1997). In these studies, the partial results indicate that there is a dire need to establish normative data for Spanish-speaking populations as research has clearly shown that there are significant differences between the non-US groups and the subjects reflected in Exner's studies (1986, 1993) whose results have been used to establish the norms in the Rorschach Comprehensive System (Sangro). A review of the problems as they relate to the lack of normative data for the Rorschach Comprehensive System follows.

Trying to interpret what certain ratios and scores within the Rorschach scoring system represent for Hispanics in the United States has been met with questioning and doubt (Constantino, Flanagan, & Malgady, 1995). Generally speaking, a number of issues emerge when we examine the literature on normative data and ethnic minority groups with this test. Specifically, there is insufficient normative data for most ethnic minorities, and there is a lack of studies dedicated to analyzing and validating parallel results for diverse populations. This raises concerns specific to the Rorschach Comprehensive System, which acts as a guide for evaluating results from the Rorschach suggesting that this may not be the best option to evaluate minority ethnic groups in the United States (Garb et al., 2001).

Several index scores in the comprehensive system strongly differ when evaluated outside of the United States, which might indicate that the interpretation of these perceptions can be different depending on the cultural context. Garb et al. (2001) discussed an example provided by Rodriguez-Sutil, Ortiz, Canovas, Moreno Garcia, and Scott (1994) whereby t F+% and X+% are usually different in children with learning disabilities in the United States vs. those who present high reading scores, but they are not different in Spanish children presenting opposing polar scores on the reading measures (Rodríguez-Sutil, Calonge, & Scott, 1992). Therefore, Garb et al. concluded that interpreting the results for children in Spain using the comprehensive system norms can result in misdiagnosing of pathology. This calls to light the importance of being culturally sensitive when assessing Latinos in the United States.

An additional reason why the validity and normativity of the Rorschach (as well as other projective assessments) is often questioned is the possibility of test results being affected by the assessor's interpretive inferences (i.e., bias, personalization, fantasy) (Dana, 1966). As concluded by Dana (1993), "The Rorschach and the Exner Comprehensive versions are not recommended for routine cross-cultural applications" (p. 160).

In sum, one of the most significant limitations (relevant to this chapter) of the Rorschach is the lack of normative data to guide the evaluator in interpreting results from Hispanics and other ethnic minorities. The bulk of empirical data pertaining to this assessment is dedicated to the interpretation from a dominant ethnic framework (Garb et al., 2001) and does not take cultural factors into consideration or establish norms for diverse populations. However, the reader is invited to view the chapter specific to the Rorschach for a more detailed overview of this test as a general assessment measure with the Hispanic patient. A discussion on how this test pertains to the assessment of psychosis follows.

When interpreting the responses of participants in minority groups in the Rorschach, overpathologizing may occur (Dana, 1993). This is particularly a problem if a Eurocentric framework is used to interpret the responses instead of the participants, and it also becomes problematic when the person assessing and the participant are from different ethnocultural backgrounds, especially if the subject and evaluator speak a different language (Weiner, 1998).

The comprehensive system describes index SCZI as an indicator of processes related to schizophrenia. However, there are no studies to date that indicate that this test has incremental validity related to diagnosing schizophrenia (i.e., does it provide us with additional information that cannot be otherwise gleaned from other assessment tools, e.g., a clinical interview and MMPI-2 scores). As concluded by Garb et al. (2001), "Although the Rorschach can be used to identify schizophrenia, there are usually easier, more effective ways to make this diagnosis" (p. 434).

There are few studies that evaluate norms in children of different ethnic backgrounds (e.g., Krall et al., 1983; Raspantini, Fernandes, & Pasian, 2011), although studies specific to the Rorschach as a means of diagnosing psychosis (or schizophrenia) in Hispanics are absent. Thus, given the overall lack of research on the Rorschach with Hispanics and that there are superior methods of assessing psychosis, the Rorschach is not recommended as a useful assessment tool for the diagnosis of psychosis in Hispanics.

Positive and Negative Syndrome Scale (PANSS)

The Positive and Negative Syndrome Scale (PANSS) was created to address the limitations of other tools that have been developed to assess the severity of positive and negative symptoms of schizophrenia (Kay, Fiszbein, Vital-Herne, & Fuentes, 1990). It is composed of three scales: one with seven items used to rate severity of positive symptoms, a second scale with another seven items to rate behavior that characterizes negative symptomatology, and lastly a third scale of general psychopathology composed of 16 items to evaluate other behaviors. It has been described as one of the measures used more often in schizophrenia research (Barrio et al., 2003).

The PANSS was translated to Spanish under the supervision of the team that developed and standardized it. They followed protocol from the Royal Academy of Spain to ensure language was accurate and used internationally (Kay et al., 1990). Initial research on translated versions of the PANSS (conducted both in the United States and abroad) has shown valid application across different cultures. However, as reported by Barrio et al. (2003), there are no studies that evaluate the ethnic effects of using the PANSS in patients with a severe mental illness. Nonetheless, the overall internal consistency of the PANSS has been found to be acceptable across ethnic groups, and research has identified significant (yet weak) correlations between the positive and negative scale scores across ethnic groups (although when the general scale score was partialled out, this difference disappeared for all ethnic groups) (Barrio et al.).

Further results from the Barrio et al. (2003) study described above indicated that Latinos scored higher in somatic concerns than both Caucasians and African-Americans. However, this may be an underrepresentation of the level of somatic concerns experienced by Latinos in general as the sample was generally highly acculturated. It is also important to note that their Latino sample was highly composed of individuals of Mexican origin, and, therefore, the findings may not be applicable to all Latinos. Overall, the results of their study showed no significant ethnic differences in all three scales of the PANSS, and they attributed those minor disparities to the way each ethnicity expresses illness (Barrio et al.).

UCSD Performance-Based Skills Assessment (UPSA)

Although most tools developed to assess psychosis have been designed to identify symptoms and diagnose, other types of tools seek to approach assessment from a well-rounded perspective by measuring functional capacity. Many patients who suffer from schizophrenia or psychosis NOS, even when following a strict medication regime, may present a significant decrease in everyday functioning that reduces their quality of life (Green, 1996). Moreover, research has found that if 40 % of the clinical symptomatology was eliminated from patients, there would only be an average of an 8 % improvement in employment rates (Meesters et al., 2010), calling to light the importance of not only assessing symptoms but also functional capacity.

The UCSD Performance-Based Skills Assessment (UPSA; Patterson, Goldman, McKibbin, Hughs, & Jeste, 2001) uses role-play tasks to examine five areas of everyday functioning including household chores, communication, finance, transportation, and planning recreational activities. Patients are asked to plan a trip to the beach, write a check, read a bus route map, complete a shopping list, and call a doctor to reschedule an appointment. It typically takes about 30 min to administer and includes several props such as grocery items, maps, and a telephone. The UPSA has shown excellent reliability as well as strong convergent validity and good criterion validity with real-world outcome measures (Mausbach, Moore, Bowie, Cardenas, & Patterson, 2009). Also available is the UPSA-Brief, which includes only the communication and finance sections of the original UPSA.

The UPSA-Brief and UPSA show high levels of convergence in predicting real-world functional outcomes (Mausbach, Harvey, Goldman, Jeste, & Patterson, 2007). Past research has found that participants who preferred to take the UPSA test in Spanish scored significantly lower than healthy controls (Jeste et al., 2005; Patterson et al., 2005), but these comparisons were made without understanding how Hispanic healthy controls performed on the test. This issue could lead to potential problems when interpreting Hispanic UPSA scores because they could be perceived as functioning poorer than English-speaking participants.

Patterson and colleagues (2005) tested middle-aged to older adults who were Mexican-American and monolingual in Spanish and had a diagnosis of schizophrenia or schizoaffective disorder. Participants were randomized to one of two treatment groups: a culturally tailored skills-based training intervention called Programa de Entrenamiento para el Desarrollo de Aptitudes para Latinos (PEDAL) and a support group conducted in Spanish. The culturally adapted Spanish version of the UPSA was used for assessment (Jeste et al., 2005). They hypothesized and reported that individuals in the tailored treatment condition showed greater improvements in functional capacity, as indicated by a higher UPSA score.

Jeste and colleagues (2005) conducted a regression comparison between Anglo-Americans and Mexican-Americans. This group predicted that level of acculturation would be a significant predictor of UPSA scores in Mexican-American participants. However, because they showed that this cultural variable was significantly related to UPSA scores, this finding suggested that the UPSA is not measuring the same construct across different racial and ethnic groups. However, because this study had a small sample size, further studies should investigate this relationship with a larger sample size, and possibly in different racial/ethnic groups.

Historically, individuals who are Mexican-Americans tend to have lower levels of education than Anglo-Americans in the United States. Because of unequal status in education, the UPSA may be measuring disparate English reading comprehension rather than functional capacity in Mexican-Americans. The Planning of Recreational Activities and Communication sections, for instance, are highly dependent on being able to read and understand written language. Thus, an individual who is Mexican-American may struggle more with the task due to lower reading abilities as opposed to an individual who is Anglo-American. Consequently, UPSA scores may be particularly susceptible to bias based on race and ethnicity. More studies need to investigate the convergent and divergent validity of the UPSA across different races and ethnicities, taking SES into account.

One study conducted by Cardenas and colleagues (2008) included language preference as a measure of acculturation in a multiple regression model with the UPSA as the response variable. They reported that learning English as a second language was not a significant predictor of UPSA scores, accounting for only 4 % of the variance. This finding may suggest measure invariance of the UPSA across different languages. However, it must be noted that this study made no direct predictions about how language preference would relate to UPSA scores. Thus, more work is needed to investigate the influence of language preference on the UPSA. Moreover, findings of similar divergent validity of the UPSA across language preferences (i.e., showing that UPSA scores are not related to language and acculturation) would provide evidence for its measure invariance.

Of the three studies conducted on Spanish-speaking Mexican-American individuals with schizophrenia, there is no report on the test-retest and interrater reliabilities of the UPSA. Rather, the studies cite the reliability information as reported by previous studies on English-speaking Caucasians with schizophrenia (Patterson et al., 2001). Because the adapted Spanish version of the UPSA is an entirely different measure from the original UPSA, it cannot be assumed that the original psychometric properties apply. Moreover, because the UPSA was created for monolingual English speakers, it cannot be assumed that reliability measures of the English version of the UPSA will be the same for bilingual participants as it is for individuals who only speak English. Because English literacy is required to complete several tasks in the UPSA, differences in fluency and reading comprehension in bilingual participants may decrease test-retest reliability. Interrater reliabilities may also be affected by this difference. Thus, future studies should evaluate and report the test-retest and interrater reliability values of UPSA scores. Once these values are compared to those found in studies of other racial/ethnic groups, researchers can assess whether the UPSA is biased in Mexican-American Spanish speakers.

Cardenas and colleagues (2008) predicted and reported that individuals with higher UPSA scores should have a higher number of community activities. However, this finding seems to contradict the original predictions made by Patterson and colleagues (2001) as well as findings from the literature on schizophrenia—that UPSA scores should not relate to self-report measures of real-world functioning. Because of this discrepancy, it is unclear whether or not this study provides evidence for the criterion validity for the UPSA in Mexican-American bilingual individuals with schizophrenia. To establish criterion validity in this group, future studies should utilize more objective measures of real-world functioning, such as independent living status or proxy-rated report of community activities. Moreover, studies of criterion validity of the UPSA may be biased due to the choice of practical outcomes. Individuals of Mexican-American heritage, for example, may be more collectivist, and thus, living with one's family as an older adult is a normative trend rather than an indicator of dysfunction. Moreover, certain ethnic/racial groups may be less engaged in community activities due to socioeconomic status (SES). Thus, the unbiased evaluation of criterion validity across different racial and ethnic groups may necessitate the use of different practical criteria.

Currently, the normative data for the UPSA come from the original schizophrenia sample on which the measure was tested (Patterson et al., 2001). This group was predominantly comprised of Caucasian persons with schizophrenia, with no mention of the other racial and ethnic groups. Because these norms are far from representative of the population of individuals with schizophrenia, it is recommended that future normative studies be conducted on individuals with schizophrenia for the original UPSA. Moreover, representative population norms must be established in Spanish-speaking individuals with schizophrenia for the Spanish-adapted UPSA. Jeste and colleagues (2005) provided the norms for Spanish-speaking Mexican-Americans with schizophrenia on the Spanish-adapted UPSA as well as for bilingual Mexican-Americans with schizophrenia on the original UPSA. However, these norms are based on a very small sample. Thus, it is recommended that future studies include a larger sample to establish cultural-specific norms on the UPSA.

The UPSA has strong convergent validity in the literature. However, few studies have reported on its internal consistency in different groups. A strength is that several studies have performed preliminary studies on its validity in different cultural groups. Although results are mixed, there is evidence that it may be valid in individuals of different gender, race, and linguistic abilities. Moreover, two studies have used the UPSA on other clinical groups, including bipolar disorder, mild cognitive impairment, and Alzheimer's. The results of these studies suggest possible utility of the UPSA in these clinical groups.

No studies have been conducted on children's performance on the UPSA. Patterson and colleagues (2001) specifically stated that the UPSA was developed for use in middle-aged to older adults with schizophrenia living in a community facility. Because the UPSA tests skills that are specific to tasks that adults must complete for daily living, it would be invalid to use in children. Functional capacity in children may be an entirely different construct altogether because they are highly functional despite not being able to perform chores, manage/count money, pay bills, communicate effectively, use public transportation, and plan recreational activities. Clearly, another measure would be more appropriate to assess functional capacity in children.

Jeste and colleagues (2005) provided the norms for Spanish-speaking Mexican-Americans with schizophrenia on the Spanish-adapted UPSA. However, these norms are based on a small sample that is specific to Hispanics of Mexican origin. These norms may or may not apply to other

Hispanic ethnic groups. Thus, future studies should administer the Spanish-adapted UPSA to more ethnically diverse Hispanic groups to establish norms. In the meantime, there is ample research to suggest that the UPSA is a useful tool that can help with the assessment of Hispanics where psychosis is suspected.

Summary and Recommendations

Assessing for psychosis and schizophrenia can be challenging in and of itself, and assessing for psychosis and schizophrenia in Hispanics can be challenging due to the cultural characteristics of this group. Cultural practices such as religion and spirituality may be difficult to disentangle from symptom presentation. However, through the practice of cultural competence and valid assessment (selecting appropriate assessment measures and norms, obtaining reliable collateral contacts, conducting a thorough clinical interview, and reviewing medical and mental health records), an accurate diagnosis can be obtained. Other issues that we have discussed in this chapter include the issue of language and normative data for the measures that we covered. Certainly, from the data we presented, it seems that the MMPI-2, the PANSS, the UPSA, and, to some extent, the MCMI-II can serve as useful assessment measures that can be administered to the Hispanic patient. However, interpretation of assessment results may vary depending on cultural idiosyncrasies of the patient (e.g., language proficiency, level of acculturation, and SES). Clinicians should also be mindful of issues related to differential diagnosis, specifically differentiating between psychosis and mood disorders (the MMPI-2 may serve as a useful tool for this) and malingering (see the Chap. 7 of this book on "Assessing Effort and Malingering with the Hispanic Client").

References

Avila-Espada, A., & Jimenez-Gomez, F. (1996). The Castilian version of the MMPI-2 in Spain: Development, adaptation, and psychometric properties. In J. N. Butcher (Ed.), *International adaptations of the MMPI-2: Research and clinical applications* (pp. 305–328). Minneapolis, MN: University of Minnesota Press.

Bagby, R., Marshall, M., Basso, M., Nicholson, M. R., Bacchiochi, R. A., Miller, J., et al. (2005). Distinguishing bipolar depression, major depression, and schizophrenia with the MMPI-2 clinical and content Scales. *Journal of Personality Assessment, 84*(1), 89–95.

Barrio, C., Yamada, A., Atuel, H., Hough, R. L., Yee, S., Berthot, B., et al. (2003). A tri-ethnic examination of symptom expression on the positive and negative syndrome scale in schizophrenia spectrum disorders. *Schizophrenia Research, 60*(2–3), 259–269.

Ben-Porath, Y. S., Butcher, J. N., & Graham, J. R. (1991). Contribution of the MMPI-2 content scales to the differential diagnosis of schizophrenia and major depression. *Psychological Assessment: A Journal of Consulting and Clinical Psychology, 3*(4), 634–640.

Bolinskey, P. K., Gottesman, I., & Nichols, D. S. (2003). The schizophrenia proneness (SzP) scale: An MMPI-2 measure of schizophrenia liability. *Journal of Clinical Psychology, 59*(9), 1031–1044.

Butcher, J. N., Dahlstrom, W. G., Graham, J. R., Tellegen, A., & Kaemmer, B. (1989). *Minnesota multiphasic personality inventory-2: Manual for administration and scoring*. Minneapolis, MN: University of Minnesota Press.

Campo, V. (2000). The SCZI index and the normative sample of Barcelona (1993). *Rorschachiana, 24*(1), 28–38.

Garcia, R.E., Azan, A.A.(1993). Inventario multifasico de la personalidad-2 Minnesota: Version Hispana. Minneopolis, MN: University of Minnesota Press.

Cardenas, V., Mausbach, B. T., Barrio, C., Bucardo, J., Jeste, D., & Patterson, T. (2008). The relationship between functional capacity and community responsibilities in middle-aged and older Latinos of Mexican origin with chronic psychosis. *Schizophrenia Research, 98*(1–3), 209–216.

Castañeda, G., Kjenslie, T. A., & Steil, A. K. (2006). *MCMI-III and Latino psychiatric outpatients: Implications for international research*. Washington, DC: American Psychological Association, 2006 Conference Abstract. Database: Psych Extra.

Casullo, M. M., & Samartino, L. (1996). Studies of the MMPI-2 in Argentina. In J. N. Butcher (Ed.), *International adaptations of the MMPI-2: Research and clinical applications* (pp. 252–264). Minneapolis, MN: University of Minnesota Press.

Constantino, G., Flanagan, R., & Malgady, R. (1995). The history of the Rorschach: Overcoming bias in multicultural projective assessment. *Rorschachiana, 20*, 148–171.

Dana, R. (1966). Eisegesis and assessment. *Journal of Projective Techniques & Personality Assessment, 30*, 215–222.

Dana, R. H. (1993). *Multicultural assessment perspectives for professional psychology*. Boston: Allyn & Bacon.

Exner, J. E. (1986). Some research data comparing schizophrenics with borderline and schizotypal personality disorders. *Journal of Personality Assessment, 50*(3), 455–471.

Exner, J. E. (1993). *The Rorschach: A comprehensive system: Vol. 1. Basic foundations* (3rd ed.). New York: Wiley.

Font, J., & Saiz, J. (1996). Estudio de validación del índice de deterioro del yo (Eh Vera Campo de W. Perry y D. Viglione) en pacientes melancólicos y esquizofrénicos. *Revista de la Sociedad Española del Rorschach y Métodos Proyectivos, 9*, 26–35.

Fuster, J., Sifre, S., Barriuso, I., Lobato, E., & Martinez, M. (1997). Comparacion de una muestra de poblacion normal valenciana con la muestra barcelonesa. *Revista de la Sociedad Espanola del Rorschach y Metados Proyectivos, 10*, 58–66.

Garb, H. N., Wood, J. M., Nezworski, M., Grove, W. M., & Stejskal, W. J. (2001). Toward a resolution of the Rorschach controversy. *Psychological Assessment, 13*(4), 433–448. doi:10.1037/1040-3590.13.4.433.

Green, M. F. (1996). What are the neurocognitive deficits in schizophrenia? *The American Journal of Psychiatry, 153*(3), 321–330.

Hall, G., Bansal, A., & Lopez, I. R. (1999). Ethnicity and psychopathology: A meta-analytic review of 31 years of comparative MMPI/MMPI-2 research. *Psychological Assessment, 11*(2), 186–197.

Jeste, N. D., Moore, D. J., Goldman, S., Bucardo, J., Davila-Fraga, W., Golshan, S., et al. (2005). Predictors of everyday functioning among older Mexican Americans vs. Anglo-Americans with schizophrenia. *The Journal of Clinical Psychiatry, 66*(10), 1304–1311.

Kay, S. R., Fiszbein, A., Vital-Herne, M., & Fuentes, L. S. (1990). The positive and negative syndrome scale – Spanish adaptation. *The Journal of Nervous and Mental Disease, 178*(8), 510–517.

Kjenslie, T. A., Castañeda, G., & Velasquez, R. J. (2006). *MCMI-III performance of Latino and Euro-American outpatients: Role of culture*. Washington, DC: American Psychological Association, 2006 Conference Abstract. Database: Psych Extra.

Krall, V., Sachs, H., Lazar, B., Rayson, B., Crowe, G., Novar, L., et al. (1983). Rorschach norms for inner city children. *Journal of Personality Assessment, 47*, 155–157.

Lopez, S. R., & Guarnaccia, P. J. (2000). Cultural psychopathology: Uncovering the social world of mental illness. *Annual Review of Psychology, 51*, 571–598.

Lucio, E., Ampudia, A., Duran, C., Leon, I., & Butcher, J. N. (2001). Comparison of the Mexican and American norms of the MMPI-2. *Journal of Clinical Psychology, 57*(12), 1459–1468.

Lucio, E., Reyes-Lagunes, I., & Scott, R. L. (1994). MMPI-2 for Mexico: Translation and adaptation. *Journal of Personality Assessment, 63*(1), 105–116.

Lucio-G, M. E., Palacios, H., Duran, C., & Butcher, J. N. (1999). MMPI-2 with Mexican psychiatric inpatients: Basic and content scales. *Journal of Clinical Psychology, 55*(12), 1541–1552.

Mausbach, B. T., Harvey, P. D., Goldman, S. R., Jeste, D. V., & Patterson, T. L. (2007). Development of a brief scale of everyday functioning in persons with serious mental illness. *Schizophrenia Bulletin, 33*(6), 1364–1372.

Mausbach, B. T., Moore, R., Bowie, C., Cardenas, V., & Patterson, T. L. (2009). A review of instruments measuring recovery in those diagnosed with psychosis. *Schizophrenia Bulletin, 35*(2), 307–318.

Meesters, P. D., Stek, M. L., Comijs, H. C., de Haan, L., Patterson, T. L., Eikelenboom, P., et al. (2010). Social functioning among older community-dwelling patients with schizophrenia: A review. *The American Journal of Geriatric Psychiatry, 18*(10), 862–878.

Millon, T. (1994). *The Millon clinical multiaxial inventory-III*. Minneapolis, MN: NCS Pearson.

Millon, T., Millon, C., Davis, R., & Grossman, S. (2006). *Manual for the Millon clinical multiaxial inventory-III* (3rd ed.). Minneapolis, MN: NCS Pearson.

Patterson, T. L., Bucardo, J., McKibbin, C. L., Mausbach, B. T., Moore, D., Barrio, C., et al. (2005). Development and pilot testing of a new psychosocial intervention for older Latinos with chronic psychosis. *Schizophrenia Bulletin, 31*(4), 922–930. doi:sbi036 [pii] 10.1093/schbul/sbi036.

Patterson, T. L., Goldman, S., McKibbin, C. L., Hughs, T., & Jeste, D. V. (2001). UCSD performance-based skills assessment: Development of a new measure of everyday functioning for severely mentally ill adults. *Schizophrenia Bulletin, 27*(2), 235–245.

Pew Hispanic Center/Kaiser Family Foundation. (2002, December). *2002 National survey of Latinos: Summary of findings*. Menlo Park, CA: Henry J. Kaiser Foundation.

Raspantini, R., Fernandes, S., & Pasian, S. (2011). The Rorschach in Brazilian children: Normative data from a 9- to 11-year-old nonpatient sample. *Rorschachiana, 32*(2), 199–222.

Rissetti, F. J., Himmel, E., Gonzalez-Moreno, J. A., Cusullo, M. M., & Butcher, J. N. (1996). *Spanish adaptations for Latin America and Spain International adaptations of the MMPI-2: Research and clinical applications* (pp. 221–325). Minneapolis, MN: University of Minnesota Press.

Rodríguez-Sutil, C., Calonge, I., & Scott, R. (1992). Academic learning problems and Rorschach indices: A Spanish replication. *Perceptual and Motor Skills, 74*, 771–778.

Rodriguez-Sutil, C., Ortiz,P. Canovas, C.P., Moreno Garcia, M.C., Scott, R. (1994). Perceptual accuracy as measured by the Rorschach: Are American norms applicable for cross-cultural assessment? Perceptual and Motor Skills, 78, 1287–1290.

Sangro, F. (1997). Location tables, form quality, and popular responses in a Spanish sample of 470 subjects. *Rorschachiana, 22*(1), 38–66.

Scott, R. L., & Pampa, W. M. (2000). The MMPI-2 in Peru: A normative study. *Journal of Personality Assessment, 74*(1), 95–105.

The American Psychiatric Association: *Diagnostic and Statistical Manual of Mental Disorders*, Fourth Edition, Text Revision, Washington, DC, American Psychiatric Association, 2000.

Velasquez, R. J., Gonzales, M., Butcher, J. N., & Castillo-Canez, I. (1997). Use of the MMPI-2 with Chicanos: Strategies for counselors. *Journal of Multicultural Counseling and Development, 25*(2), 107–120.

Weiner, I. B. (1998). *Principles of Rorschach interpretation*. Mahwah, NJ: Erlbaum.

Wetzler, S., Khadivi, A., & Moser, K. R. (1998). The use of the MMPI-2 for the assessment of depressive and psychotic disorders. *Assessment, 5*(3), 249–261.

White Kress, V. E., Eriksen, K. P., Rayle, A. D., & Ford, S. J. W. (2005). The DSM-IV-TR and culture: Considerations for counselors. *Journal of Counseling and Development, 83*(1), 97–104.

Whitworth, R. H., & McBlaine, D. D. (1993). Comparison of the MMPI and MMPI-2 Administered to Anglo- and Hispanic-American University students. *Journal of Personality Assessment, 61*(1), 19–27. doi:10.1207/s15327752jpa6101_2.

Whitworth, R. H., & Unterbrink, C. (1994). Comparison of MMPI-2 clinical and content scales administered to Hispanic and Anglo-Americans. *Hispanic Journal of Behavioral Sciences, 16*(3), 255–264. doi:10.1177/07399863940163004.

18 Assessing Sleep Disorders in the Hispanic Patient

Jose S. Loredo

Cultural Considerations

The evaluation of sleep disorders in Hispanics living in the USA presents three unique problems: (1) the dearth of basic and clinical sleep research in Hispanic populations, (2) the potential cultural and anatomical differences among the various Hispanic groups that could affect their predisposition to sleep disorders, and (3) the individual patient's degree of acculturation to the US lifestyle.

Most of the basic and clinical sleep research has been done in non-Hispanic whites of European descent and, to a lesser degree, in African Americans (Loredo et al., 2010). Most of the published human sleep research in Spanish-speaking populations has been done outside the USA. A quick search in PubMed showed 530 articles from Spain, 162 articles from South America (with a large representation from Brazil), and 147 articles from Mexico. Very little sleep research has been done in Hispanics living in the USA. A PubMed search of the English-language human sleep research using the terms "sleep research in Hispanics, Latinos, Mexican Americans, Chicanos, and Puerto Ricans" yielded 92 articles from 1975 to 2011. The Sleep Heart Health Study is currently the largest completed study in the USA dedicated only to sleep research. Of the more than 6,000 participants, only 4.3% were Hispanic (Baldwin et al., 2001; Quan et al., 1997), and, to date, only a few ethnic subgroup analyses have included Hispanics (Baldwin et al., 2010; O'Connor et al., 2003; Redline et al., 2004; Young et al., 2002). The current findings support the conclusion that racial/ethnic differences may affect sleep patterns, sleep quality, the prevalence of sleep disorders, and health-related quality of life (Baldwin et al., 2010; Loredo et al., 2010; Roberts, Roberts, & Chen, 2000). Therefore, the available bulk of sleep research findings from whites or African Americans may be difficult to generalize to other ethnic minorities, such as Hispanics, living in the USA.

Hispanics or Latinos comprised 16.3% of the US population in 2010, making them the largest minority group in the USA. They are also the fastest growing population with a 43% increase in numbers from 2000 to 2010 (Ennis, Rios-Vargas, & Albert, 2011). Hispanics are a diverse group, immigrating from all Latin American countries (63% Mexico, 9% Puerto Rico, 4% Cuba, and 24%

J.S. Loredo, M.D., M.S., MPH, FCCP, FAASM (✉)
Division of Pulmonary and Critical Care Medicine, Director of the UCSD Sleep Medicine Center, San Diego School of Medicine, University of California, 200 West Arbor Dr., San Diego, CA 92103, USA
e-mail: jloredo@ucsd.edu

L.T. Benuto (ed.), *Guide to Psychological Assessment with Hispanics*, DOI 10.1007/978-1-4614-4412-1_18, © Springer Science+Business Media New York 2013 from Central and South America and other Spanish-speaking countries) (Ennis et al.). Their ancestral origins include various combinations of Native American/Indian, African, and European white. However, Hispanics are bound by a common language and Spanish heritage. There is very little research looking at the differences in sleep health between various Hispanic groups. So far, sleep research has mostly viewed Hispanics as a homogenous block without considering the racial and cultural differences that could affect their knowledge about sleep health or the prevalence of common sleep disorders. Also, most of the sleep research in Hispanics has primarily involved Mexican Americans (Baldwin et al., 2010; O'Connor et al., 2003; Quan et al., 2003; Redline et al., 2004; Young et al., 2002).

For example, Will et al. reported baseline cephalometric differences in Hispanics and blacks who suffered from obstructive sleep apnea as compared to their non-Hispanic white counterparts. The authors theorized that cephalometric differences may affect the prevalence and surgical treatment of obstructive sleep apnea in minorities (Will et al., 1995). Short and long sleep durations have emerged as significant risk factors for health, especially cardiovascular health (Cappuccio, Cooper, D'Elia, Strazzullo, & Miller, 2011; Sabanayagam & Shankar, 2010). In the 1990 National Health Interview Survey, Hispanics (excluding Mexican Americans) and African Americans reported short sleep duration more often than whites. Mexican Americans reported longer sleep duration than whites, but the difference was not significant after controlling for socioeconomic characteristics (Hale & Do, 2007). In a 2008 survey that included all 50 states and US territories, Puerto Rico was among the five states reporting the lowest habitual sleep duration. However, Hispanics overall reported fewer days of insufficient sleep duration than whites or blacks (Centers for Disease Control and Prevention [CDC], 2009). Based on these findings, it is possible that Hispanics with an African ancestry may have a greater predisposition to obstructive sleep apnea or habitual short sleep duration than their Hispanic counterparts of Native American/Indian or European ancestry.

Other research has suggested that Hispanics may differ in their attitude toward medical therapies. Cherniack EP et al. reported that Hispanics are more likely than whites or African Americans to use alternative remedies than over-the-counter or prescription medications (Cherniack et al., 2008). This is not surprising, since herbal remedies such as valerian are commonly used in Mexican traditional medicine for the treatment of insomnia and anxiety (Herrera-Arellano et al., 2001). Another study has shown a higher risk of hypersomnia in Mexican, Central American, and African American youth as compared to Anglos (Roberts et al., 2000). The available sleep data from Hispanics suggest that the various Hispanic communities in the USA may differ in their sleep health. Potential sleep health differences among Hispanic groups should be taken into consideration when assessing sleep disorders.

We have long known that the level of acculturation to the USA is associated with changes in the health status of Hispanics, but the reasons for these changes have not been clear. Among Hispanic immigrants and their descendants living in the USA, several studies have documented an increase in obesity (Hazuda, Haffner, Stern, & Eifler, 1988; Khan, Sobal, & Martorell, 1997; Pawson, Martorell, & Mendoza, 1991; Sundquist & Winkleby, 2000), diabetes (Hazuda et al., 1988; Samet, Coultas, Howard, Skipper, & Hanis, 1988; Stern et al., 1991), cardiovascular disease (Crespo, Loria, & Burt, 1996; Goslar et al., 1997; Stern, Rosenthal, Haffner, Hazuda, & Franco, 1984; Sundquist & Winkleby, 1999), and psychiatric disorders (Alderete, Vega, Kolody, & Aguilar-Gaxiola, 2000; Burnam, Hough, Karno, Escobar, & Telles, 1987) with increasing acculturation. These negative health outcomes have been attributed to changes in diet (Bermudez, Falcon, & Tucker, 2000; Elder et al., 1991; Otero-Sabogal, Sabogal, Perez-Stable, & Hiatt, 1995), increases in alcohol use (Caetano & Mora, 1988; Markides, Krause, & Mendes de Leon, 1988) and tobacco use (Marin, Perez-Stable, & Marin, 1989; Palinkas et al., 1993), limited access to health services (Roberts & Lee, 1980; Solis, Marks, Garcia, & Shelton., 1990; Wells, Golding, Hough,

Burnam, & Karno, 1988), low socioeconomic status (Hazuda et al., 1988; Winkleby, Fortmann, & Rockhill, 1993), and the stress associated with sociocultural change and change in social status (Alderete et al., 2000; Burnam et al., 1987; Espino & Maldonado, 1990).

Much less is known about the effects of acculturation on the sleep of Hispanics. However, a study of middle-aged and elderly Hispanic women from Los Angeles showed that acculturation negatively affected the sleep habits of middle-aged but not elderly women (Cantero, Richardson, Baezconde-Garbanati, & Marks, 1999). A study of adolescent Hispanic men (ages 11–19) suggested that higher levels of acculturation were associated with fewer hours of sleep per night (Ebin et al., 2001). In 2004, Roberts, Lee, Hemandez, and Solari evaluated the prevalence of insomnia in 5,118 ninth-grade Hispanic students living in the Rio Grande Valley of Texas. Students who identified themselves as "Mexican" rather than "Mexican American" were at lower risk for insomnia. However, acculturation was not a significant risk factor after multivariate analysis. More recently, better sleep in Mexican-born US immigrants as compared to Mexican Americans and the overall US population was suggested as the explanation for the Hispanic paradox (better cardiovascular health in Hispanics) (Seicean, Neuhauser, Strohl, & Redline, 2011).

In summary, the few research studies on the sleep health of Hispanics suggest that acculturation to the US lifestyle negatively impacts the sleep health practices of Hispanics, especially younger Hispanics.

Another cultural consideration in the Hispanic patient is "la siesta," typically a postprandial nap in the early afternoon (Dinges, 1989). Approximately 60–80% of Mexicans and people from Ecuador practice *la siesta* more than 4 days/week (Webb & Dinges, 1989). An early afternoon nap may be of cardiovascular benefit in healthy adults (Naska, Oikonomou, Trichopoulou, Psaltopoulou, & Trichopoulos, 2007); however, a daytime nap may also be a marker for insufficient or poor sleep quality the previous night (Partinen & Guilleminault, 1990) and has been associated with increased cardiovascular disease, especially in those who take daily siestas longer than 1 h (Campos & Siles, 2000; Stang et al., 2007). *La siesta* also contradicts common sleep hygiene recommendations in patients having difficulty with insomnia or circadian rhythm disorders.

There are a number of other cultural factors to consider when evaluating sleep disorders in Hispanic patients. These include the prevalence of common sleep disorders (such as obstructive sleep apnea, restless legs syndrome, and insomnia) in the various Hispanic groups and their attitudes toward sleep (such as the significance of snoring, knowledge about sleep disorders, and knowledge of sleep as a healthy activity). However, there are almost no published peer-reviewed studies on these culturally important topics. Two large NIH-sponsored studies of sleep in Hispanics have recently completed recruitment; these promise better information regarding the prevalence of sleep apnea and other sleep disorders in US Hispanics.

The Sleep Health and Knowledge in U.S. Hispanics study, which completed recruitment in 2010, is a population-based evaluation of 1,754 Hispanics of Mexican descent and 1,913 non-Hispanic whites in the San Diego area. This project included an extensive telephone survey to gather information on sleep health, medical and psychiatric diseases, quality of life, and knowledge about sleep health through various validated instruments. In addition, an overnight home polysomnogram and anthropometric measurements were performed in a subpopulation of the participants to assess the prevalence of sleep apnea, other sleep disorders, and risk factors (Loredo et al., 2010).

The Hispanic Community Health Study/Study of Latinos is a multicenter longitudinal study of the health of 16,000 US Hispanics, including Hispanics of Mexican, Cuban, Puerto Rican, and Central American and South American descent. This study completed recruitment in 2011 (Sorlie et al., 2010). Sleep evaluations include an unattended overnight sleep screening using Type 3 sleep recorders and a sleep questionnaire to assess risk of snoring and insomnia.

Brief History of Sleep Evaluation in Hispanics

Sleep has been a part of human behavior, as well as that of most multicellular organisms, since their appearance on earth. However, only recently has sleep been recognized as an important factor in health and disease. In humans, short sleep duration and sleep deprivation have been linked to organ dysfunction, reduced immune function, and impaired learning, mood, and daytime functioning (Bonnet, 2005; Everson, 1993; Faraut, Boudjeltia, Vanhamme, & Kerkhofs, 2012). However, now both short and long sleep duration, as well as poor sleep quality, have been associated with increased morbidity and mortality (Kripke, Garfinkel, Wingard, Klauber, & Marler, 2002; Kripke, Simons, Garfinkel, & Hammond, 1979).

The work of French scientist Henri Pieron is commonly regarded as the beginning of the modern approach to sleep research. In his book published in 1913, *Le Probleme Physiologique du Sommeil*, Pieron was the first to examine sleep from a physiologic perspective. However, evaluation of the brain as the source of sleep started years before this. Electrical brain activity was first discovered in animals in England in 1875 (Caton, 1875), and in humans in 1929, when the electroencephalogram was described in Germany (Berger, 1929).

What we now know as non-REM sleep was described in the USA in 1937 (Loomis, Harvey, & Hobart, 1937). In 1953, Dr. Nathaniel Kleitman and one of his students, Dr. Eugene Aserinsky, made the landmark discovery of rapid eye movement (REM) during sleep (Aserinsky & Kleitman, 1953). In 1957, Dement and Kleitman described the human non-REM sleep stages and repeating REM sleep cycles throughout the night (Dement & Kleitman, 1957), which has been the basis for the polysomnogram and for most of what we have learned about sleep in the last 55 years (Shepard et al., 2005). In 1996, the American Medical Association recognized sleep medicine as a new medical specialty.

According to PubMed archives, the earliest sleep research in a Hispanic population in the USA was an article entitled "Working with Latinos and the Use of Dream Analysis" published in 1982 (Maduro, 1982). In 1990, a survey of adult Hispanic Americans showed a high prevalence of snoring, suggesting that obstructive sleep apnea was probably common in Hispanics (Schmidt-Nowara, Coultas, Wiggins, Skipper, & Samet, 1990). In 1997, Kripke et al. performed overnight oximetry in 355 subjects, including 44 Hispanics. The authors estimated that 16.3% of Hispanics had ≥20 transient oxyhemoglobin desaturation events/hour of sleep (comparable to having moderate sleep apnea) compared to 4.9% of non-Hispanic whites. However, the Sleep Heart Health Study in 2003, which included the largest number of Hispanic participants so far (296 Hispanics), showed that although Hispanics had a higher prevalence of snoring than white, black, American Indian, and Asian-Pacific Islanders, their prevalence of sleep apnea as measured by polysomnography was not different than that of other ethnic groups (O'Connor et al., 2003).

Sleep research involving Hispanics is still in its early stages. The Sleep Health and Knowledge in U.S. Hispanics project and the Hispanic Community Health Study/Study of Latinos promise to significantly advance our knowledge on a number of sleep-related issues including the prevalence of common sleep disorders and the appropriateness of polysomnography, home sleep studies, and sleep-related questionnaires in Hispanic populations (Loredo et al., 2010; Sorlie et al., 2010).

Most Frequently Used Assessment Measures for Diagnosing Sleep Disorders

All currently available tools to assess sleep and sleep disorders were developed in English-speaking whites of European descent. Available sleep tests range from the overnight attended laboratory-based polysomnogram to self-administered questionnaires to assess sleepiness. Most of the sleep assessment questionnaires have been translated into Spanish. However, due to the diversity of Hispanic cultures, most authors have felt the need to adapt the translation to their target Hispanic population. A case in point is the Pittsburgh Sleep Quality Index (PSQI) which has been translated into Spanish by various authors and validated in Spanish-speaking populations in Spain (Royuela & Macias, 1997), Colombia (Escobar-Cordoba & Eslava-Schmalbach, 2005), and Mexico (Jiménez-Genchi, Monteverde-Maldonado, Nenclares-Portocarrero, Esquivel-Adame, & de la Vega-Pacheco, 2008), each translation varying slightly from each other.

A description of the most commonly used tools to evaluate sleep disorders follows.

Clinical History and Physical Examination

The history and physical examination remains the most important assessment of the patient presenting with sleep complaints. Most patients will present to the primary care practitioner or the sleep specialist complaining of fatigue, lack of energy, tiredness, sleepiness, or not getting enough sleep. However, most symptoms of sleep disorders are nonspecific, and primary care providers do not routinely screen for them (Senthilvel, Auckley, & Dasarathy, 2011). Also, patients will frequently minimize their complaints, which are perceived as embarrassing or even a sign of laziness (Dement, Carskadon, & Richardson, 1978). Therefore, the clinician must have a high degree of suspicion and ask specific questions that will elicit the information necessary to develop a reasonable differential diagnosis.

It is not sufficient to ask the patient if he/she is sleepy, since most will answer "no." Instead, the provider must ask specific questions about falling asleep in inappropriate circumstances. The clinical history also provides important clues as to the severity of the symptoms, which will allow the practitioner to make immediate recommendations (e.g., falling asleep while driving and the decision to temporarily suspend driving privileges). All efforts should be made to determine when the symptoms started, what makes them better, and what makes them worse.

It is helpful to evaluate predisposing factors including family history of sleep disorders, potential precipitating factors, and perpetuating factors, which usually include maladaptive behaviors. Common precipitating factors include a new stressful situation, weight gain, onset of a medical or psychiatric diagnosis, and a change in sleep habits or in sleep hygiene.

Chronic insomnia is often associated with stress (Yang, Chou, & Hsiao, 2011), depression (Berk, 2009), menopausal symptoms (Joffe, Massler, & Sharkey, 2010), chronic pain (Louie, Tektonidou, Caban-Martinez, & Ward, 2011), poor sleep hygiene (Gellis & Lichstein, 2009), and use of stimulants or alcohol before bedtime (Jefferson et al., 2005).

Obstructive sleep apnea is strongly associated with obesity (Yu & Berger, 2011), diabetes (Schober, Neurath, & Harsch, 2011; Tassone et al., 2003), cardiovascular disease (Drager, Polotsky, & Lorenzi-Filho, 2011), stroke (Yaggi et al., 2005), nasal obstruction (Georgalas, 2011), and atrial fibrillation and other arrhythmias (Gami & Somers, 2008).

Restless legs syndrome and periodic limb movement during sleep can be associated with iron and ferritin deficiencies (Wang, O'Reilly, Venkataraman, Mysliwiec, & Mysliwiec, 2009), diabetes and peripheral neuropathy (Merlino et al., 2007), kidney failure (Araujo et al., 2010), and pregnancy (Neau et al., 2010).

REM sleep behavior disorder is primarily a condition of elderly men who act out violent or action-packed dreams, often injuring themselves or their bed partners. In up to 85% of cases, this disorder is associated with the presence or future development of neurodegenerative conditions such as Parkinson's disease and multiple system atrophy (Frenette, 2010).

New onset narcolepsy can be associated with stressful life events during the year prior to diagnosis (Orellana et al., 1994) and, in rare cases, with head trauma (Ebrahim, Peacock, & Williams, 2005).

An assessment of the patient's wake-sleep habits over a typical 24-h day is essential to uncover sleep hygiene issues, maladaptive behavior that could be perpetuating insomnia, and circadian rhythm sleep disorders. However, even in the best clinical hands, the sleep history is insufficient to make a definitive diagnosis except in restless legs syndrome, insomnia, or circadian rhythm disorders. In the case of obstructive sleep apnea, the sensitivity and specificity of the clinical evaluation is generally low (Hoffstein & Szalai, 1993; Rowley, Aboussouan, & Badr, 2000); therefore, a high degree of suspicion and referral to the sleep laboratory is required to make the diagnosis.

The physical evaluation for the sleep disorders patient centers around the examination of the head and neck. Anatomical findings that may contribute to sleep-disordered breathing include partial nasal obstruction due to a deviated nasal septum, allergic rhinitis, overbite, retrognathia, long face syndrome (Cistulli, Gotsopoulos, & Sullivan, 2001), macroglossia with scalloping (Weiss, Atanasov, & Calhoun, 2005), high Mallampati score(Liistro et al., 2003), short, thick neck (circumference ≥16 in. for women and ≥17 in. for men), and central obesity (Katz, Stradling, Slutsky, Zamel, & Hoffstein, 1990; Young, Skatrud, & Peppard, 2004). Physical evaluation of the conjunctive to screen for anemia is important when restless legs syndrome or periodic limb movements during sleep are among the differential diagnoses. Examination of the heart and lungs is also important since sleep-disordered breathing is strongly associated with hypertension and heart disease.

The sensitivity and specificity of the sleep medicine history and physical in the Hispanic patient has not been researched. Certainly, an accurate subjective clinical evaluation may be problematic if there is a language and/or cultural barrier between the practitioner and the patient. Furthermore, cultural attitudes to sleep and sleep complaints may play a role in the evaluation of sleep disorders in the Hispanic patient. However, clinical research in these important areas is lacking. Insufficient knowledge of sleep as a health factor may also play a role in the current health disparities in Hispanics living in the USA (Loredo et al., 2010). Currently, there is no peer-reviewed published research evaluating the sleep health knowledge of Hispanics. The only published work so far has been in abstract form, which showed that Hispanics of Mexican descent living in San Diego County had a large and significant deficit in their knowledge of common sleep disorders including obstructive sleep apnea, restless legs syndrome, and insomnia as compared to non-Hispanic whites (Sell et al., 2009). Despite the paucity of clinical research evaluating cultural issues in the Hispanic sleep patient, it is reasonable to recommend that, insofar as possible, a culturally competent practitioner should elicit the clinical history.

Subjective Evaluation of Sleepiness, Sleep Quality, and Risk for Sleep Disorders

There are a number of questionnaires used in sleep medicine to gather clinical and research data. This section will describe those questionnaires that are commonly used in clinical sleep medicine and some that have been used specifically in Hispanic populations for research purposes.

The Epworth Sleepiness Scale (*ESS*) is perhaps the most commonly used questionnaire in both the clinical and research setting (Johns, 1991). It assesses the propensity of a patient to fall asleep inappropriately during the course of daily activities. The ESS is composed of eight questions in which the subject is asked to rate the likelihood of falling asleep in real-life situations (0 = no chance of falling asleep, 1 = slight chance, 2 = moderate chance, 3 = high chance): while sitting and reading, watching television, sitting inactive in a public place, as a passenger in a car for 1 h, lying down to rest in the afternoon when circumstances permit, sitting and talking to someone, sitting quietly after lunch without alcohol, and in a car while stopped for a few minutes in traffic. Composite scores of 10 or greater (maximum 24) indicate the presence of significant excessive daytime somnolence and the need for further clinical investigation (Benbadis, 1998). The ESS has been used as a self-administered questionnaire and in telephone surveys. It has been translated into Spanish and has been validated in normal subjects and obstructive sleep apnea patients in Spain. The reliability and validity of the Spanish version questionnaire was felt to be equivalent to that of the original instrument (Chiner, Arriero, Signes-Costa, Marco, & Fuentes, 1999; Ferrer et al., 1999). The ESS was used in 296 Hispanic subjects in the Sleep Heart Health Study in the USA and showed no difference in excessive daytime sleepiness between whites and Hispanics, despite Hispanics having a higher prevalence of snoring (O'Connor et al., 2003).

The Stanford Sleepiness Scale (*SSS*) measures how alert a patient feels at any given time of the day (Hoddes & Zarcone, 1972). The SSS can be administered multiple times during the day and is more commonly used for research purposes. Some sleep laboratories administer the SSS before each multiple sleep latency test nap (an objective measure of daytime sleepiness performed in the laboratory) to correlate subjective and objective sleepiness. In the SSS, the patient is asked to rate his/her level of alertness from 1 to 7 (1 = feeling active, vital, alert, or wide awake; 2 = functioning at high levels, but not at peak, able to concentrate; 3 = awake, but relaxed, responsive but not fully alert; 4 = somewhat foggy, let down; 5 = foggy, losing interest in remaining awake, slowed down; 6 = sleepy, woozy, fighting sleep, prefer to lie down; 7 = no longer fighting sleep, sleep onset soon, having dream-like thoughts). A score higher than 3 when the patient is supposed to be alert is considered an indication of excessive sleepiness. The SSS has been validated in normal populations and was found to be sensitive to deficits in alertness resulting from partial sleep deprivation (Herscovitch & Broughton, 1981). The SSS has not been used in Spanish-speaking populations.

The Pittsburgh Sleep Quality Index (*PSQI*) is a self-rated questionnaire designed to measure subjective sleep quality over the past month for the psychiatric clinical practice and for research (Buysse, Reynolds, Monk, Berman, & Kupfer, 1989). The PSQI differentiates between good and poor sleepers with a global score of subjective sleep quality (poor sleepers have a PSQI global score ≥5) but can also be divided into seven-subscales evaluating various aspects of sleep quality: subjective sleep quality, sleep latency, sleep duration, sleep efficiency, sleep disturbances, use of sleep medication, and daytime dysfunction. This instrument can be used for initial assessment and for ongoing comparative measurements across all health care settings. The PSQI has been validated with a reliability coefficient (Cronbach's alpha) of 0.83 for its seven components. Numerous studies have used the PSQI and support its validity and reliability in many languages and situations (Aloba, Adewuya, Ola, & Mapayi, 2007; Beck, Schwartz, Towsley, Dudley, & Barsevick, 2004; Burkhalter et al., 2010; Cole et al., 2006; Doi et al., 2000; Kotronoulas, Papadopoulou, Papapetrou, & Patiraki, 2011; Shochat, Tzischinsky, Oksenberg, & Peled, 2007; Tsai et al., 2005). The PSQI has been translated into Spanish by various authors and validated in Spanish-speaking populations in Spain (Royuela & Macias, 1997), Colombia (Escobar-Cordoba & Eslava-Schmalbach, 2005), and Mexico (Jiménez-Genchi et al., 2008). Each translation varies slightly in order to adapt its content to the specific Hispanic population being studied. For example, in question 5c, the word bathroom can be translated as "baño," "servicio," "escusado," or "sanitario" depending on the population in question. We used the PSQI to measure subjective sleep quality in 1,445 Hispanics of Mexican descent and 1,693 non-Hispanic whites in San Diego County participating in the Sleep Health and Knowledge in U.S. Hispanics study (Loredo et al., 2010). We used the Spanish translation by Royuela and Macias and made minor changes to some of the expressions to adapt the instrument to a telephone interview format and to the Mexican American population in San Diego. We found no difference in subjective sleep quality between Hispanics of Mexican descent and non-Hispanic whites (Soler, Bardwell, Ancoli-Israel, Palinkas, & Loredo, 2009). However, factor analyses suggested that for English- and Spanish-speaking Hispanics, a five-subscale PSQI global score (subjective sleep quality, sleep duration, sleep disturbance, daytime dysfunction, and sleep latency) was better for assessing sleep quality (unpublished data currently under review).

The Functional Outcomes of Sleep Questionnaire (*FOSQ*) measures the impact of sleepiness on a patient's daily life (Weaver et al., 1997). The FOSQ is composed of 30 questions evaluating the impact of sleepiness or tiredness on the subject's ability to perform everyday activities. Each question is rated by the subject as no difficulty, little, moderate, or extreme difficulty. The FOSQ provides a global assessment of sleep-related daytime function and a subscale score in five different domains: activity level, vigilance, intimacy, productivity, and social outcome. The FOSQ is widely used primarily for research in healthy and diseased populations. It has been translated into Spanish and validated in research patients in Spain (Mar et al., 2005; Vidal et al., 2007). The reliability of the Spanish version of the FOSQ was high (Cronbach's alpha >0.9), and the authors concluded that the Spanish version of the FOSQ was conceptually equivalent to the original FOSQ (Ferrer et al., 1999). The Spanish version of the FOSQ has not been validated in Hispanics living in the USA.

Questionnaires used to assess preoperative risk for obstructive sleep apnea. The Berlin questionnaire (Netzer, Stoohs, Netzer, Clark, & Strohl, 1999), the STOP (Chung et al., 2008a), and the American Society of Anesthesiologists checklist (ASA) (Gross et al., 2006) have been validated and used clinically, primarily to screen surgical patients into high or low risk of obstructive sleep apnea (Chung et al., 2008b). The *Berlin questionnaire* uses ten questions assessing the frequency and severity of snoring, witnessed apneas, fatigue and excessive daytime sleepiness, and the presence of arterial hypertension (Netzer et al.). The *STOP questionnaire* uses four yes/no questions related to the presence of Snoring, Tiredness during daytime, Observed apneas, and high blood Pressure (STOP) (Chung et al., 2008a). The *ASA checklist* assesses three screening categories including physical characteristics predisposing to obstructive sleep apnea, history of upper airway obstruction during sleep, and presence of somnolence or fatigue (Gross et al.). In a review of the available literature (ten studies, $n = 1{,}484$ patients) on screening questionnaires for obstructive sleep apnea, the group sensitivity and specificity for patients with obstructive sleep apnea was low at 72 and 61%, respectively (Abrishami, Khajehdehi, & Chung, 2010). None of these obstructive sleep apnea risk assessment questionnaires have been translated or validated in Spanish-speaking populations.

The Sleep Habits questionnaire was designed specifically for the Sleep Heart Health Study in which the questionnaire was available in English and Spanish (Quan et al., 1997). The Sleep Habits questionnaire collects information on sleep habits, symptoms associated with abnormal sleep patterns, and previous therapy for sleep-disordered breathing. However, this instrument does not lend itself to validation since it does not produce a numerical risk score. The Sleep Habits questionnaire so far has only been used for research purposes. The questionnaire was administered to approximately 300 Hispanic participants in the Sleep Heart Health Study (Baldwin et al., 2010, 2001; O'Connor et al., 2003; Quan et al., 1997; Redline et al., 2004; Young et al., 2002), to 16,000 Hispanic participants in the Hispanic Community Health Study/Study of Latinos (Sorlie et al., 2010), and to 1,754 Hispanics of Mexican descent in San Diego County in the Sleep Health and Knowledge in U.S. Hispanics study (Loredo et al., 2010).

The four diagnostic questions of the International Restless Legs Syndrome Study Group (Allen et al., 2003; Walters, 1995) were designed to diagnose restless legs syndrome (RLS), also known as Ekbom syndrome. Restless legs syndrome is a sensorimotor disorder of sleep-wake motor regulation rather than a true sleep disorder (Hening, 2002). However, up to 80% of RLS patients also suffer from periodic limb movement during sleep, which can significantly interfere with sleep continuity. The symptoms of RLS can range from infrequent and mild to irresistible and constant. The four diagnostic RLS questions are descriptive of the symptoms: Do you have an urge (a sensation) to move the legs? Does the urge come usually while resting? Does the urge appear only in the evening? Does the urge resolve when you stand up and walk? The four diagnostic RLS questions have been translated into Spanish and validated in Spain. However, examples of sensations were added to the questionnaire to ensure its understanding by patients from different parts of Spain (García-Borreguero, Lahuerta-Dal Ré,

Table 18.1 Sleep questionnaires available and validated in Spanish for the assessment of the Hispanic patient

Test name	Original language	Type of assessment	Country of norms	Age range
The Epworth Sleepiness Scale (ESS)	English	Excessive daytime sleepiness score. Likelihood of dozing off in eight real-life situations	Australia	Adults
The Pittsburgh Sleep Quality Index (PSQI)	English	Sleep quality over the past month. Global score and seven-subscale scores: sleep quality, latency, duration, efficiency, disturbances, sleep medication, and daytime dysfunction	USA	Adults
The Functional Outcomes of Sleep Questionnaire (FOSQ)	English	Impact of sleepiness on performance of everyday activities. Global score and subscale scores in five domains: activity level, vigilance, intimacy, productivity, and social outcome	USA	Adults
The Sleep Habits questionnaire (Sleep Heart Health Study)	English	Collects information on sleep habits, symptoms of abnormal sleep, therapy for sleep-disordered breathing	USA	Adults
The four diagnostic questions of the International Restless Legs Syndrome Study Group	English	Diagnosis of restless legs syndrome	International	Adults

Albares, Zaragoza, & de Gracia, 2009). The four RLS diagnostic questions have been used in 1,754 English- and Spanish-speaking Hispanics of Mexican descent in San Diego County in the Sleep Health and Knowledge in U.S. Hispanics study (Loredo et al., 2010; Sawanyawisuth et al., 2009). Results from the RLS questions in this project are currently under peer review (Sawanyawisuth et al., 2012) (Table 18.1).

Objective Physiologic Evaluation of Sleep

Nighttime and daytime physiologic measurements of sleep have been designed to evaluate sleep disorders and for research purposes in normal populations. These studies are normally performed in the sleep laboratory setting, requiring highly trained sleep technicians and significant supporting infrastructure. More recently, with the miniaturization of sleep recording equipment, home sleep testing has emerged that allows the patient to sleep in his/her natural surroundings, which may improve access to testing and therapy for obstructive sleep apnea at a potential cost savings (Mulgrew, Fox, Ayas, & Ryan, 2007; Pietzsch, Garner, Cipriano, & Linehan, 2011). Nighttime sleep studies have been divided into four levels (1–4) to denote the extent of physiologic parameters measured.

Polysomnography (Type 1) is the most extensive physiologic measurement of sleep for adults and children (Aurora et al., 2011; Kushida et al., 2005). Polysomnography (Type 1) is performed in the laboratory with an attendant sleep technician. It will normally include four electroencephalogram derivations, an electrooculogram, a measurement of nasal-oral airflow by pressure transducer and thermistor, respiratory effort at the abdomen and chest using piezoelectric bands or respiratory inductance plethysmography bands, an electromyogram at the submental and tibialis anterior muscles, a snoring microphone, a position sensor, an electrocardiogram, pulse oximetry, and videotaping of the sleeping patient. In expert hands, it takes approximately 30–45 min to properly apply the recording equipment and to instruct the patient. It also requires time-consuming manual scoring by a trained polysomnography technician and interpretation of the data by a competent clinician. Some have developed algorithms to automatically score polysomnography data, but manual scoring is still considered more accurate, especially for abnormal sleep (Jensen, Sorensen, Leonthin, & Jennum, 2010). Polysomnography can detect abnormal sleep architecture, sleep fragmentation, some seizure activity during sleep, snoring and abnormal breathing patterns, arrhythmias, abnormal muscle tone and limb movements during sleep, transient and prolonged oxygen desaturations during sleep, and complex behavior during sleep. Polysomnography is indicated in the evaluation of the sleepy patient or those who present with abnormal behavior during sleep (Aurora et al.). Polysomnography has been used extensively for clinical purposes and in research studies. It has been used for research purposes involving healthy Hispanic subjects (Rao, Hammen, & Poland, 2009) and Hispanics with sleep disorders (O'Connor et al., 2003). There is very little research using polysomnography to characterize normal sleep in Hispanics; most reports have included very few subjects, and their results have been inconsistent. Some have found more REM sleep in healthy and depressed Mexican Americans than whites, African Americans, or Asians (Poland et al., 1999; Rao et al., 2009), and Hispanic children living in Arizona had less deep sleep than their white counterparts regardless of socioeconomic status (Quan et al., 2003). However, the Sleep Heart Health Study evaluated nearly 300 Hispanics and found no difference in sleep architecture between Hispanics and whites (Redline et al., 2004). Based on the current sleep research, there is no indication that Type 1 sleep studies for the Hispanic patient should be modified.

Polysomnography (*Type 2*) is the same procedure as Type 1 studies, but this study is an unattended exam performed at the subject's home using portable equipment (Campbell & Neill, 2011). Normally, the technician comes to the patient's home and applies the equipment. The technician then returns in the morning to remove the equipment. There are a number of portable polysomnography recorders on the market that are battery powered and can be worn by the patient, avoiding the necessity of being tethered to a bedside monitor. Type 2 studies have more loss of electrodes during the course of the night, but redundancy in the montage makes up for this (Campbell & Neill). Type 2 sleep studies have been used in Hispanic populations for research purposes in the Sleep Heart Health Study (O'Connor et al., 2003; Redline et al., 2004), in the Sleep Health and Knowledge of U.S. Hispanics study (Loredo et al., 2010), and in Hispanic children (Quan et al., 2003).

Unattended portable sleep recordings (*Type 3*) primarily measure cardiorespiratory physiology during sleep (Collop et al., 2007). These studies utilize compact portable recorders that are worn by the patient and, in most cases, self-applied. Type 3 studies must measure three physiologic parameters, including nasal and oral airflow via thermistor and/or pressure transducer, chest and/or abdominal respiratory effort, and pulse oximetry (Collop et al.). Heart rate is usually derived from the pulse oximetry. The number of physiologic parameters measured varies among the various Type 3 recorders. Some, in addition to the required parameters, also include sensors to detect snoring, leg movements, and position during sleep. Type 3 studies do not measure sleep quantity or quality. The total time the patient is in bed wearing the equipment is usually assumed to be the total sleep time, which, by its nature, may underestimate respiratory disturbance indices (Ghegan, Angelos, Stonebraker, & Gillespie, 2006). The American Academy of Sleep Medicine recommends that Type 3 studies allow for display of raw data and the capability of manual scoring (Collop et al.). Type 3 studies are primarily recommended to diagnose obstructive sleep apnea in patients with a high likelihood of having the condition, and they should be performed only in conjunction with a comprehensive sleep evaluation (Collop et al.). Type 3 sleep recordings were performed successfully in 16,000 adult Hispanics to screen for obstructive sleep apnea in the Hispanic Community Health Study/Study of Latinos (Sorlie et al., 2010).

Unattended portable sleep recordings (*Type 4*) are single physiologic parameter recordings. Most of these recordings measure overnight oximetry (Chesson, Berry, & Pack, 2003), but some have measured other parameters including peripheral arterial tonometry (Ayas, Pittman, MacDonald, & White, 2003; Pittman et al., 2004) and pulse transit time (Huang et al., 2011). The routine use of Type 4 studies to diagnose obstructive sleep apnea is not recommended due to their diagnostic variability depending on the equipment used, the method of analysis, and the patient population (Chesson et al.). However, clinicians commonly use Type 4 recordings (overnight oximetry) for a variety of purposes, including screening studies for sleep-disordered breathing, to evaluate suspected hypoxemia during sleep and to prescribe supplemental oxygen, or to determine efficacy of oxygen therapy or correction of oxygen desaturation during continuous positive airway pressure (CPAP) or bi-level positive airway pressure (BPAP) therapy (Ramsey, Mehra, & Strohl, 2007). Despite the extensive use of overnight oximetry in clinical medicine, there is no standardized approach to data presentation or to the interpretation and discussion of its indications (Ramsey et al.). Overnight oximetry has been used for research purposes in Hispanic populations to screen for sleep-disordered breathing (Schmidt-Nowara et al., 1990).

Actigraphy is not a sleep recording. However, it is often used to assess sleep duration and pattern in healthy children and adults and in patients suspected of sleep disorders. It is primarily used in clinical research, but it is increasingly being used in clinical practice (Morgenthaler et al., 2007a). Actigraphy utilizes a wristwatch-like device that records wrist or hand movements. Periods of no movement correlate with sleep, even in patients with obstructive sleep apnea (Dick et al., 2010). Clinically, actigraphy is used primarily to evaluate circadian rhythm sleep disorders or patterns of sleep in insomniacs and to assess habitual total sleep duration over a number of days (Morgenthaler et al., 2007b). Actigraphy has been used in research to measure physical activity in Hispanic children and adults (Kelly et al., 2010; Ruiz, Gesell, Buchowski, Lambert, & Barkin, 2011), and it is currently being used to measure habitual sleep duration and sleep patterns in 2,000 subjects participating in the Hispanic Community Health Study/Study of Latinos (Sorlie et al., 2010).

Studies to Objectively Evaluate Excessive Daytime Sleepiness

The multiple sleep latency test (*MSLT*) is a physiologic measurement of daytime sleepiness currently in widespread clinical and research use (Carskadon & Dement, 1977; Sullivan & Kushida, 2008). The MSLT measures sleep latency every 2 h in 4–5 nap periods throughout the day; in addition, it also tests for sleep onset rapid eye movement (REM) sleep periods important in the diagnosis of narcolepsy. A polysomnogram is normally done the night before the MSLT to rule out any sleep disorders that would confound the test and to ensure that the patient has had at least 6 h of sleep to avoid a false positive MSLT. Typically, the first nap starts at 8:00 a.m. The patient is allowed 20 min to fall asleep; if sleep occurs, the patient is allowed to sleep for 15 min, at which time the nap is interrupted. Sleep onset REM is scored if REM sleep occurs within the first 15 min of sleep (Carskadon et al., 1986). Normal sleep latency ranges from 10 to 20 min after lights out (Richardson, Carskadon, Orav, Dement, 1982). A mean sleep latency of ≤5 min is considered pathological and correlates with poor daytime performance (Afifi & Carskadon, 2005; Carskadon & Dement, 1985). The most recent international classification of sleep disorders in 2005 designated a mean sleep latency of ≤8 min as the diagnostic cutoff for pathologic hypersomnolence (American Academy of Sleep Medicine, 2005). Currently, the MSLT is considered the best objective measure of excessive daytime somnolence (Littner et al., 2005).

The maintenance of wakefulness test (*MWT*) is a physiologic measurement of daytime sleepiness that challenges to patient to remain awake for 40 min while comfortably sitting semi-recumbent in bed in a dimly lit room (Littner et al., 2005). The test is repeated four times every 2 h during the day. No use of stimulants or extraordinary measures to stay awake is allowed. The MWT is indicated as a complementary study in the assessment of individuals in whom the inability to remain awake constitutes a safety issue. It is also used to assess response to treatment in patients with narcolepsy, obstructive sleep apnea, or idiopathic hypersomnolence, especially when documentation is required by their employment (Sullivan & Kushida, 2008). An average sleep latency of ≤8 min constitutes an abnormal MWT. The significance of a sleep latency between 8 and 40 min is unclear. Staying awake during the entire 440-min trials provides the strongest objective evidence of a patient's ability to stay awake. For both the MSLT and the MWT, there have been no large, multicenter, prospective studies to establish normative values. Cutoff values have been derived from smaller studies with various methodological differences (Sullivan & Kushida). The MWT has not been used as a research tool in Hispanic populations.

Recommendations

The scarcity of clinical sleep research in Hispanic populations is a major deficiency in our ability to make recommendations for assessing sleep disorders in the Hispanic patient. Most of the sleep research has been performed in non-Hispanic whites and, to a lesser extent, in African Americans; generalization to other racial/ethnic groups may not always be appropriate. Also, the cultural variability among Hispanics, based on their country of origin and the level of acculturation to the US lifestyle, may affect their understanding, their knowledge about sleep as a health issue, and their acceptance and attitude toward sleep disorders testing. However, based on the available data, a few recommendations can be made.

Insofar as possible, the history and physical evaluation of the Hispanic sleep patient should be performed in his/her language of choice by a culturally competent clinical practitioner. The use of questionnaires to gather sleep data, even when available and validated in Spanish, may have to be adjusted to the local Hispanic population's idioms and attitudes as long as the primary message is not changed. Based on the current sleep research, there is no indication that laboratory-based or home sleep studies need to be modified for the Hispanic patient. However, it is recommended that the sleep laboratory provide culturally competent personnel that will address the patient in his/her language of choice to properly introduce the sleep recording, which may be viewed as invasive in some cases.

More clinical research is needed to better understand the sleep health, sleep health knowledge, sleep attitudes, risk factors for sleep disorders, and prevalence of these disorders in Hispanic populations living in the USA. Current ongoing research promises to shed more light on these deficiencies (Loredo et al., 2010; Sorlie et al., 2010).

References

Abrishami, A., Khajehdehi, A., & Chung, F. (2010). A systematic review of screening questionnaires for obstructive sleep apnea. *Canadian Journal of Anaesthesia, 57*, 423–438.

Afifi, L. K. C., & Carskadon, M. (2005). MSLT. In C. Kushida (Ed.), *Sleep deprivation: Clinical issues, pharmacology, and sleep loss effects*. New York: Informa Health Care.

Alderete, E., Vega, W. A., Kolody, B., & Aguilar-Gaxiola, S. (2000). Lifetime prevalence of and risk factors for psychiatric disorders among Mexican migrant farmworkers in California. *American Journal of Public Health, 90*, 608–614.

Allen, R. P., Picchietti, D., Hening, W. A., Trenkwalder, C., Walters, A. S., & Montplaisi, J. (2003). Restless legs syndrome diagnosis and epidemiology workshop at the National Institutes of Health; International Restless Legs Syndrome Study Group. Restless legs syndrome: Diagnostic criteria, special considerations, and epidemiology: A report from the restless legs syndrome diagnosis and epidemiology workshop at the National Institutes of Health. *Sleep Medicine, 4*, 101–119.

Aloba, O. O., Adewuya, A. O., Ola, B. A., & Mapayi, B. M. (2007). Validity of the Pittsburgh Sleep Quality Index (PSQI) among Nigerian university students. *Sleep Medicine, 8*, 266–270.

American Academy of Sleep Medicine. (2005). *International classification of sleep disorders: Diagnostic and coding manual* (2nd ed.). Westchester, IL: American Academy of Sleep Medicine.

Araujo, S. M., de Bruin, V. M., Nepomuceno, L. A., Maximo, M. L., Daher Ede, F., Correia Ferrer, D. P., et al. (2010). Restless legs syndrome in end-stage renal disease: Clinical characteristics and associated comorbidities. *Sleep Medicine, 11*, 785–790.

Aserinsky, E., & Kleitman, N. (1953). Regularly occurring episodes of eye mobility and concomitant phenomena during sleep. *Science, 118*, 273–274.

Aurora, R. N., Zak, R. S., Karippot, A., Lamm, C. I., Morgenthaler, T. I., Auerbach, S. H., et al. (2011). American Academy of Sleep Medicine. Practice parameters for the respiratory indications for polysomnography in children. *Sleep, 34*, 379–388.

Ayas, N. T., Pittman, S., MacDonald, M., & White, D. P. (2003). Assessment of a wrist-worn device in the detection of obstructive sleep apnea. *Sleep Medicine, 4*, 435–442.

Baldwin, C. M., Ervin, A. M., Mays, M. Z., Robbins, J., Shafazand, S., Walsleben, J., et al. (2010). Sleep disturbances, quality of life, and ethnicity: The Sleep Heart Health Study. *Journal of Clinical Sleep Medicine, 6*, 176–183.

Baldwin, C. M., Griffith, K. A., Nieto, F. J., O'Connor, G. T., Walsleben, J. A., & Redline, S. (2001). The association of sleep-disordered breathing and sleep symptoms with quality of life in the Sleep Heart Health Study. *Sleep, 24*, 96–105.

Beck, S. L., Schwartz, A. L., Towsley, G., Dudley, W., & Barsevick, A. (2004). Psychometric evaluation of the Pittsburgh Sleep Quality Index in cancer patients. *Journal of Pain and Symptom Management, 27*, 140–148.

Benbadis, S. R. (1998). Daytime sleepiness: When is it normal? When to refer? *Cleveland Clinic Journal of Medicine, 65*, 543–549.

Berger, H. (1929). Über das elektroenkephalogramm des menschen. *Archiv für Psychiatrie und Nervenkrankheiten, 97*, 6–26.

Berk, M. (2009). Sleep and depression—Theory and practice. *Australian Family Physician, 38*, 302–304.

Bermudez, O. I., Falcon, L. M., & Tucker, K. L. (2000). Intake and food sources of macronutrients among older Hispanic adults: Association with ethnicity, acculturation, and length of residence in the United States. *Journal of the American Dietetic Association, 100*, 665–673.

Bonnet, M. H. (2005). Acute sleep deprivation. In M. H. Kryger, T. Roth, & W. Dement (Eds.), *Principles and practice of sleep medicine* (4th ed., pp. 51–66). Philadelphia: Saunders.

Burkhalter, H., Sereika, S. M., Engberg, S., Wirz-Justice, A., Steiger, J., & De Geest, S. (2010). Structure validity of the Pittsburgh Sleep Quality Index in renal transplant recipients: A confirmatory factor analysis. *Sleep and Biological Rhythms, 8*, 274–281.

Burnam, M. A., Hough, R. L., Karno, M., Escobar, J. I., & Telles, C. A. (1987). Acculturation and lifetime prevalence of psychiatric disorders among Mexican Americans in Los Angeles. *Journal of Health and Social Behavior, 28*, 89–102.

Buysse, D. J., Reynolds, C. F., III, Monk, T. H., Berman, S. R., & Kupfer, D. J. (1989). The Pittsburgh Sleep Quality Index: A new instrument for psychiatric practice and research. *Journal of Psychiatric Research, 28*, 193–213.

Caetano, R., & Mora, M. E. (1988). Acculturation and drinking among people of Mexican descent in Mexico and the United States. *Journal of Studies on Alcohol, 49*, 462–471.

Campbell, A. J., & Neill, A. M. (2011). Home set-up polysomnography in the assessment of suspected obstructive sleep apnea. *Journal of Sleep Research, 20*(1 Pt 2), 207–213.

Campos, H., & Siles, X. (2000). Siesta and the risk of coronary heart disease: Results from a population-based, case-control study in Costa Rica. *International Journal of Epidemiology, 29*(3), 429–437.

Cantero, P. J., Richardson, J. L., Baezconde-Garbanati, L., & Marks, G. (1999). The association between acculturation and health practices among middle-aged and elderly Latinas. *Ethnicity & Disease, 9*, 166–180.

Cappuccio, F. P., Cooper, D., D'Elia, L., Strazzullo, P., & Miller, M. A. (2011). Sleep duration predicts cardiovascular outcomes: A systematic review and meta-analysis of prospective studies. *European Heart Journal, 32*, 1484–1492.

Carskadon, M. A., & Dement, W. C. (1977). Sleepiness and sleep state on a 90-min schedule. *Psychophysiology, 14*, 127–133.

Carskadon, M. A., & Dement, W. C. (1985). Sleep loss in elderly volunteers. *Sleep, 8*, 207–221.

Carskadon, M. A., Dement, W. C., Mitler, M. M., Roth, T., Westbrook, P. R., & Keenan, S. (1986). Guidelines for the multiple sleep latency test (MSLT): A standard measure of sleepiness. *Sleep, 9*, 519–524.

Caton, R. (1875). The electric currents of the brain. *British Medical Journal, 2*, 278.

Centers for Disease Control and Prevention (CDC). (2009). Perceived insufficient rest or sleep among adults—United States, 2008. *Morbidity and Mortality Weekly Report, 58*, 1175–1179.

Cherniack, E. P., Ceron-Fuentes, J., Florez, H., Sandals, L., Rodriguez, O., Palacios, J., et al. (2008). Influence of race and ethnicity on alternative medicine as a self-treatment preference for common medical conditions in a population of multi-ethnic urban elderly. *Complementary Therapies in Clinical Practice, 14*, 116–123.

Chesson, A. L., Jr., Berry, R. B., & Pack, A. (2003). American Academy of Sleep Medicine; American Thoracic Society; American College of Chest Physicians. Practice parameters for the use of portable monitoring devices in the investigation of suspected obstructive sleep apnea in adults. *Sleep, 26*, 907–913.

Chiner, E., Arriero, J. M., Signes-Costa, J., Marco, J., & Fuentes, I. (1999). Validación de la versión Española del test de somnolencia Epworth en pacientes con síndrome de apnea de sueño. *Archivos de Bronconeumología, 35*, 422–427.

Chung, F., Yegneswaran, B., Liao, P., Chung, S. A., Vairavanathan, S., Islam, S., et al. (2008a). STOP questionnaire: A tool to screen patients for obstructive sleep apnea. *Anesthesiology, 108*, 812–821.

Chung, F., Yegneswaran, B., Liao, P., Chung, S. A., Vairavanathan, S., Islam, S., et al. (2008b). Validation of the Berlin questionnaire and American Society of Anesthesiologists checklist as screening tools for obstructive sleep apnea in surgical patients. *Anesthesiology, 108*, 822–830.

Cistulli, P. A., Gotsopoulos, H., & Sullivan, C. E. (2001). Relationship between craniofacial abnormalities and sleep-disordered breathing in Marfan's syndrome. *Chest, 120*, 1455–1460.

Cole, J. C., Motivala, S. J., Buysse, D. J., Oxman, M. N., Levin, M. J., & Irwin, M. R. (2006). Validation of a 3-factor scoring model for the Pittsburgh Sleep Quality Index in older adults. *Sleep, 29*, 112–116.

Collop, N. A., Anderson, W. M., Boehlecke, B., Claman, D., Goldberg, R., Gottlieb, D. J., et al. (2007). Portable Monitoring Task Force of the American Academy of Sleep Medicine. Clinical guidelines for the use of unattended portable monitors in the diagnosis of obstructive sleep apnea in adult patients. Portable Monitoring Task Force of the American Academy of Sleep Medicine. *Journal of Clinical Sleep Medicine, 3*, 737–747.

Crespo, C. J., Loria, C. M., & Burt, V. L. (1996). Hypertension and other cardiovascular disease risk factors among Mexican Americans, Cuban Americans, and Puerto Ricans from the Hispanic Health and Nutrition Examination Survey. *Public Health Reports, 111*(Suppl 2), 7–10.

Dement, W. C., Carskadon, M. A., & Richardson, G. (1978). Excessive daytime sleepiness in the sleep apnea syndrome. In C. Guilleminault & W. C. Dement (Eds.), *Sleep apnea syndromes* (pp. 23–46). New York: Alan R. Liss.

Dement, W. C., & Kleitman, N. (1957). Cyclic variations in EEG during sleep and their relation to eye movements, body motility and dreaming. *Electroencephalography and Clinical Neurophysiology, 9*, 673–690.

Dick, R., Penzel, T., Fietze, I., Partinen, M., Hein, H., & Schulz, J. (2010). AASM standards of practice compliant validation of actigraphic sleep analysis from SOMNOwatch™ versus polysomnographic sleep diagnostics shows high conformity also among subjects with sleep disordered breathing. *Clinical Physics and Physiological Measurement, 31*, 1623–1633.

Dinges, D. F. (1989). Napping patterns and effects in human adults. In D. F. Dinges & R. J. Broughton (Eds.), *Sleep and alertness. Chronobiologicals, behavioral, and medical aspects of napping* (pp. 171–204). New York: Raven.

Doi, Y., Minowa, M., Uchiyama, M., Okawa, M., Kim, K., Shibui, K., et al. (2000). Psychometric assessment of subjective sleep quality using the Japanese version of the Pittsburgh Sleep Quality Index (PSQI-J) in psychiatric disordered and control subjects. *Psychiatry Research, 97*, 165–172.

Drager, L. F., Polotsky, V. Y., & Lorenzi-Filho, G. (2011). Obstructive sleep apnea: An emerging risk factor for atherosclerosis. *Chest, 140*, 534–542.

Ebin, V. J., Sneed, C. D., Morisky, D. E., Rotheram-Borus, M. J., Magnusson, A. M., & Malotte, C. K. (2001). Acculturation and interrelationships between problem and health-promoting behaviors among Latino adolescents. *Journal of Adolescent Health, 28*, 62–72.

Ebrahim, I. O., Peacock, K. W., & Williams, A. J. (2005). Posttraumatic narcolepsy—Two case reports and a mini review. *Journal of Clinical Sleep Medicine, 1*, 153–156.

Elder, J. P., Castro, F. G., de Moor, C., Mayer, J., Candelaria, J. I., Campbell, N., et al. (1991). Differences in cancer-risk-related behaviors in Latino and Anglo adults. *Preventive Medicine, 20*, 751–763.

Ennis, S. R., Rios-Vargas, M., & Albert, N. G. (2011). *The Hispanic population: 2010. 2010 census briefs* (Report No. C2010BR-04). U.S. Census Bureau, U.S., Department of Commerce Economics and Statistics Administration. Retrieved from http://www.census.gov/prod/cen2010/briefs/c2010br-04.pdf.

Escobar-Cordoba, F., & Eslava-Schmalbach, J. (2005). Validación colombiana del índice de calidad de sueño de Pittsburgh. *Revista de Neurologia, 4*, 150–155.

Espino, D. V., & Maldonado, D. (1990). Hypertension and acculturation in elderly Mexican Americans: Results from 1982–1984 Hispanic HANES. *Journal of Gerontology, 45*, M209–M213.

Everson, C. A. (1993). Sustained sleep deprivation impairs host defense. *American Journal of Physiology, 265*(5 Pt 2), R1148–R1154.

Faraut, B., Boudjeltia, K. Z., Vanhamme, L., & Kerkhofs, M. (2012). Immune, inflammatory and cardiovascular consequences of sleep restriction and recovery. *Sleep Medicine Reviews, 16*, 137–149.

Ferrer, M., Vilagut, G., Monasterio, C., Montserrat, J. M., Mayos, M., & Alonso, J. (1999). Measurement of the perceived impact of sleep problems: The Spanish version of the functional outcomes sleep questionnaire and the Epworth sleepiness scale. *Medicina Clinica, 113*, 250–255.

Frenette, E. (2010). REM sleep behavior disorder. *Medical Clinics of North America, 94*, 593–614.

Gami, A. S., & Somers, V. K. (2008). Implications of obstructive sleep apnea for atrial fibrillation and sudden cardiac death. *Journal of Cardiovascular Electrophysiology, 19*, 997–1003.

García-Borreguero, D., Lahuerta-Dal Ré, J., Albares, J., Zaragoza, S., & de Gracia, M. (2009). Validated translation to Spanish of the evaluation questionnaire of patients with restless legs syndrome. *Neurología, 24*(10), 823–834.

Gellis, L. A., & Lichstein, K. L. (2009). Sleep hygiene practices of good and poor sleepers in the United States: An internet-based study. *Behavior Therapy, 40*, 1–9.

Georgalas, C. (2011). The role of the nose in snoring and obstructive sleep apnoea: An update. *European Archives of Oto-Rhino-Laryngology, 268*, 1365–1373.

Ghegan, M. D., Angelos, P. C., Stonebraker, A. C., & Gillespie, M. B. (2006). Laboratory versus portable sleep studies: A meta-analysis. *The Laryngoscope, 116*, 859–864.

Goslar, P. W., Macera, C. A., Castellanos, L. G., Hussey, J. R., Sy, F. S., & Sharpe, P. A. (1997). Blood pressure in Hispanic women: The role of diet, acculturation, and physical activity. *Ethnicity & Disease, 7*, 106–113.

Gross, J. B., Bachenberg, K. L., Benumof, J. L., Caplan, R. A., Connis, R. T., Cote, C. J., et al. (2006). Practice guidelines for the perioperative management of patients with obstructive sleep apnea: A report by the American Society of Anesthesiologists Task Force on Perioperative Management of Patients with Obstructive Sleep Apnea. *Anesthesiology, 104*, 1081–1093.

Hale, L., & Do, D. P. (2007). Racial differences in self-reports of sleep duration in a population-based study. *Sleep, 30*, 1096–1103.

Hazuda, H. P., Haffner, S. M., Stern, M. P., & Eifler, C. W. (1988). Effects of acculturation and socioeconomic status on obesity and diabetes in Mexican Americans. The San Antonio Heart Study. *American Journal of Epidemiology, 128*, 1289–1301.

Hening, W. A. (2002). Restless legs syndrome: A sensorimotor disorder of sleep/wake motor regulation. *Current Neurology and Neuroscience Reports, 2*, 186–196.

Herrera-Arellano, A., Luna-Villegas, G., Cuevas-Uriostegui, M. L., Alvarez, L., Vargas-Pineda, G., Zamilpa-Alvarez, A., et al. (2001). Polysomnographic evaluation of the hypnotic effect of *Valeriana edulis* standardized extract in patients suffering from insomnia. *Planta Medica, 67*, 695–699.

Herscovitch, J., & Broughton, R. (1981). Sensitivity of the Stanford sleepiness scale to the effects of cumulative partial sleep deprivation and recovery oversleeping. *Sleep, 4*, 83–91.

Hoddes, E. D. W., & Zarcone, V. (1972). The development and use of the Stanford sleepiness scale (SSS). *Psychophysiology, 9*, 150.

Hoffstein, V., & Szalai, J. P. (1993). Predictive value of clinical features in diagnosing obstructive sleep apnea. *Sleep, 16*, 118–122.

Huang, H., Ye, J. Y., Li, Y. R., Wang, X. Y., Zhang, Y. H., Wang, J. Y., et al. (2011). Pulse transit time for quantifying inspiratory effort in patients with obstructive sleep apnea. *Journal for Oto-Rhino-Laryngology and Its Related Specialties, 73*, 53–60.

Jefferson, C. D., Drake, C. L., Scofield, H. M., Myers, E., McClure, T., Roehrs, T., et al. (2005). Sleep hygiene practices in a population-based sample of insomniacs. *Sleep, 28*, 611–615.

Jensen, P. S., Sorensen, H. B., Leonthin, H. L., & Jennum, P. (2010). Automatic sleep scoring in normals and in individuals with neurodegenerative disorders according to new international sleep scoring criteria. *Journal of Clinical Neurophysiology, 27*, 296–302.

Jiménez-Genchi, A., Monteverde-Maldonado, E., Nenclares-Portocarrero, A., Esquivel-Adame, G., & de la Vega-Pacheco, A. (2008). Reliability and factorial analysis of the Spanish version of the Pittsburgh Sleep Quality Index among psychiatric patients. *Gaceta Médica de México, 144*, 491–496.

Joffe, H., Massler, A., & Sharkey, K. M. (2010). Evaluation and management of sleep disturbance during the menopause transition. *Seminars in Reproductive Medicine, 28*, 404–421.

Johns, M. (1991). A new method for measuring daytime sleepiness: The Epworth sleepiness scale. *Sleep, 14*, 540–545.

Katz, I., Stradling, J., Slutsky, A. S., Zamel, N., & Hoffstein, V. (1990). Do patients with obstructive sleep apnea have thick necks? *American Review of Respiratory Disease, 141*(5 Pt 1), 1228–1231.

Kelly, E. B., Parra-Medina, D., Pfeiffer, K. A., Dowda, M., Conway, T. L., Webber, L. S., et al. (2010). Correlates of physical activity in black, Hispanic, and white middle school girls. *Journal of Physical Activity and Health, 7*, 184–193.

Khan, L. K., Sobal, J., & Martorell, R. (1997). Acculturation, socioeconomic status, and obesity in Mexican Americans, Cuban Americans, and Puerto Ricans. *International Journal of Obesity and Related Metabolic Disorders, 21*, 91–96.

Kotronoulas, G. C., Papadopoulou, C. N., Papapetrou, A., & Patiraki, E. (2011). Psychometric evaluation and feasibility of the Greek Pittsburgh Sleep Quality Index (GR-PSQI) in patients with cancer receiving chemotherapy. *Supportive Care in Cancer, 19*, 1831–1840.

Kripke, D. F., Ancoli-Israel, S., Klauber, M. R., Wingard, D. L., Mason, W. J., et al. (1997). Prevalence of sleep-disordered breathing in ages 40–64 years: A population-based survey. *Sleep, 20*, 65–76.

Kripke, D. F., Garfinkel, L., Wingard, D. L., Klauber, M. R., & Marler, M. R. (2002). Mortality associated with sleep duration and insomnia. *Archives of General Psychiatry, 59*, 131–136.

Kripke, D. F., Simons, R. N., Garfinkel, L., & Hammond, E. C. (1979). Short and long sleep and sleeping pills. Is increased mortality associated? *Archives of General Psychiatry, 36*, 103–116.

Kushida, C. A., Littner, M. R., Morgenthaler, T., Alessi, C. A., Bailey, D., Coleman, J., Jr., et al. (2005). Practice parameters for the indications for polysomnography and related procedures: An update for 2005. *Sleep, 28*, 499–521.

Liistro, G., Rombaux, P., Belge, C., Dury, M., Aubert, G., & Rodenstein, D. O. (2003). High Mallampati score and nasal obstruction are associated risk factors for obstructive sleep apnoea. *The European Respiratory Journal, 21*, 248–252.

Littner, M. R., Kushida, C., Wise, M., Davila, D. G., Morgenthaler, T., Lee-Chiong, T., et al. (2005). Standards of Practice Committee of the American Academy of Sleep Medicine. Practice parameters for clinical use of the multiple sleep latency test and the maintenance of wakefulness test. *Sleep, 28*, 113–121.

Loomis, A. L., Harvey, E. N., & Hobart, G. A. (1937). Cerebral states during sleep as studied by human brain potentials. *Journal of Experimental Psychology, 21*, 127–144.

Loredo, J. S., Soler, X., Bardwell, W., Ancoli-Israel, S., Dimsdale, J. E., & Palinkas, L. A. (2010). Sleep health in U.S. Hispanic population. *Sleep, 33*, 962–967.

Louie, G. H., Tektonidou, M. G., Caban-Martinez, A. J., & Ward, M. M. (2011). Sleep disturbances in adults with arthritis: Prevalence, mediators, and subgroups at greatest risk. Data from the 2007 National Health Interview Survey. *Arthritis Care and Research, 63*, 247–260.

Maduro, R. J. (1982). Working with Latinos and the use of dream analysis. *The Journal of the American Academy of Psychoanalysis and Dynamic Psychiatry, 10*, 609–628.

Mar, J., Rivero-Arias, O., Durán-Cantolla, J., Alonso-Alvarez, M. L., Gaminde, I., & de la Torre-Muñecas, G. (2005). Effect on quality of life of nCPAP treatment in patients with obstructive sleep apnea. *Medicina Clinica, 125*, 611–615.

Marin, G., Perez-Stable, E. J., & Marin, B. V. (1989). Cigarette smoking among San Francisco Hispanics: The role of acculturation and gender. *American Journal of Public Health, 79*, 196–198.

Markides, K. S., Krause, N., & Mendes de Leon, C. F. (1988). Acculturation and alcohol consumption among Mexican Americans: A three-generation study. *American Journal of Public Health, 78*, 1178–1181.

Merlino, G., Fratticci, L., Valente, M., Del Giudice, A., Noacco, C., Dolso, P., et al. (2007). Association of restless legs syndrome in type 2 diabetes: A case-control study. *Sleep, 30*, 866–871.

Morgenthaler, T., Alessi, C., Friedman, L., Owens, J., Kapur, V., Boehlecke, B., et al. (2007). Standards of Practice Committee; American Academy of Sleep Medicine. Practice parameters for the use of actigraphy in the assessment of sleep and sleep disorders: An update for 2007. *Sleep, 30*, 519–529.

Morgenthaler, T. I., Lee-Chiong, T., Alessi, C., Friedman, L., Aurora, R. N., Boehlecke, B., et al. (2007). Standards of Practice Committee of the American Academy of Sleep Medicine. Practice parameters for the clinical evaluation and treatment of circadian rhythm sleep disorders. An American Academy of Sleep Medicine report. *Sleep, 30*, 1445–1459.

Mulgrew, A. T., Fox, N., Ayas, N. T., & Ryan, C. F. (2007). Diagnosis and initial management of obstructive sleep apnea without polysomnography: A randomized validation study. *Annals of Internal Medicine, 146*, 157–166.

Naska, A., Oikonomou, E., Trichopoulou, A., Psaltopoulou, T., & Trichopoulos, D. (2007). Siesta in healthy adults and coronary mortality in the general population. *Archives of Internal Medicine, 167*, 296–301.

Neau, J. P., Marion, P., Mathis, S., Julian, A., Godeneche, G., Larrieu, D., et al. (2010). Restless legs syndrome and pregnancy: Follow-up of pregnant women before and after delivery. *European Journal of Neurology, 64*, 361–366.

Netzer, N. C., Stoohs, R. A., Netzer, C. M., Clark, K., & Strohl, K. P. (1999). Using the Berlin questionnaire to identify patients at risk for the sleep apnea syndrome. *Annals of Internal Medicine, 131*, 485–491.

O'Connor, G. T., Lind, B. K., Lee, E. T., Nieto, F. J., Redline, S., Samet, J. M., et al. (2003). Variation in symptoms of sleep-disordered breathing with race and ethnicity: The Sleep Heart Health Study. *Sleep, 26*, 74–79.

Orellana, C., Villemin, E., Tafti, M., Carlander, B., Besset, A., & Billiard, M. (1994). Life events in the year preceding the onset of narcolepsy. *Sleep, 17*(8 Suppl), S50–S53.

Otero-Sabogal, R., Sabogal, F., Perez-Stable, E. J., & Hiatt, R. A. (1995). Dietary practices, alcohol consumption, and smoking behavior: Ethnic, sex, and acculturation differences. *Journal of the National Cancer Institute. Monographs* (18), 73–82.

Palinkas, L. A., Pierce, J., Rosbrook, B. P., Pickwell, S., Johnson, M., & Bal, D. G. (1993). Cigarette smoking behavior and beliefs of Hispanics in California. *American Journal of Preventive Medicine, 9*, 331–337.

Partinen, M., & Guilleminault, C. (1990). Daytime sleepiness and vascular morbidity at seven-year follow-up in obstructive sleep apnea patients. *Chest, 97*, 27–32.

Pawson, I. G., Martorell, R., & Mendoza, F. E. (1991). Prevalence of overweight and obesity in US Hispanic populations. *American Journal of Clinical Nutrition, 53*, 1522S–1528S.

Pietzsch, J. B., Garner, A., Cipriano, L. E., & Linehan, J. H. (2011). An integrated health-economic analysis of diagnostic and therapeutic strategies in the treatment of moderate-to-severe obstructive sleep apnea. *Sleep, 34*, 695–709.

Pittman, S. D., Ayas, N. T., MacDonald, M. M., Malhotra, A., Fogel, R. B., & White, D. P. (2004). Using a wrist-worn device based on peripheral arterial tonometry to diagnose obstructive sleep apnea: In-laboratory and ambulatory validation. *Sleep, 27*, 923–933.

Poland, R. E., Rao, U., Lutchmansingh, P., McCracken, J. T., Lesser, I. M., Edwards, C., et al. (1999). REM sleep in depression is influenced by ethnicity. *Psychiatry Research, 88*, 95–105.

Quan, S. F., Goodwin, J. L., Babar, S. I., Kaemingk, K. L., Enright, P. L., Rosen, G. M., et al. (2003). Sleep architecture in normal Caucasian and Hispanic children aged 6–11 years recorded during unattended home polysomnography: Experience from the Tucson Children's Assessment of Sleep Apnea Study (TuCASA). *Sleep Medicine, 4*, 13–19.

Quan, S. F., Howard, B. V., Iber, C., Kiley, J. P., Nieto, F. J., O'Connor, G. T., et al. (1997). The Sleep Heart Health Study: Design, rationale, and methods. *Sleep, 20*, 1077–1085.

Ramsey, R., Mehra, R., & Strohl, K. P. (2007). Variations in physician interpretation of overnight pulse oximetry monitoring. *Chest, 132*, 852–859.

Rao, U., Hammen, C. L., & Poland, R. E. (2009). Ethnic differences in electroencephalographic sleep patterns in adolescents. *Asian Journal of Psychiatry, 2*, 17–24.

Redline, S., Kirchner, H. L., Quan, S. F., Gottlieb, D. J., Kapur, V., & Newman, A. (2004). The effects of age, sex, ethnicity, and sleep-disordered breathing on sleep architecture. *Archives of Internal Medicine, 164*, 406–418.

Richardson, G. S., Carskadon, M. A., Orav, E. J., & Dement, W. C. (1982). Circadian variation of sleep tendency in elderly and young adult subjects. *Sleep, 5*(Suppl), S82–S94.

Roberts, R. E., & Lee, E. S. (1980). Medical care use by Mexican-Americans: Evidence from the human population laboratory studies. *Medical Care, 18*, 267–281.

Roberts, R. E., Lee, E. S., Hemandez, M., & Solari, A. C. (2004). Symptoms of insomnia among adolescents in the lower Rio Grande Valley of Texas. *Sleep, 27*, 751–760.

Roberts, R. E., Roberts, C. R., & Chen, I. G. (2000). Ethnocultural differences in sleep complaints among adolescents. *The Journal of Nervous and Mental Disease, 188*, 222–229.

Rowley, J. A., Aboussouan, L. S., & Badr, M. S. (2000). The use of clinical prediction formulas in the evaluation of obstructive sleep apnea. *Sleep, 23*, 929–938.

Royuela, A., & Macias, J. A. (1997). Propiedades clinimetricas de la versi6n castellana del cuestionario de Pittsburgh. *Vigilia-Sueño, 9*, 81–94.

Ruiz, R., Gesell, S. B., Buchowski, M. S., Lambert, W., & Barkin, S. L. (2011). The relationship between Hispanic parents and their preschool-aged children's physical activity. *Pediatrics, 127*(5), 888–895.

Sabanayagam, C., & Shankar, A. (2010). Sleep duration and cardiovascular disease: Results from the National Health Interview Survey. *Sleep, 33*, 1037–1042.

Samet, J. M., Coultas, D. B., Howard, C. A., Skipper, B. J., & Hanis, C. L. (1988). Diabetes, gallbladder disease, obesity, and hypertension among Hispanics in New Mexico. *American Journal of Epidemiology, 128*, 1302–1311.

Sawanyawisuth, K., Bardwell, W. A., Palinkas, L. A., Ancoli-Israel, S., Dimsdale, J. E., & Loredo, J. S. (2009). Ethnic differences in the prevalence and predictors of restless leg syndrome between non-Hispanic whites and Hispanics of Mexican descent. *Sleep, 32*(Abstract Supplement), A299.

Sawanyawisuth, K., Palinkas, L. A., Ancoli-Israel, S., Dimsdale, J. E., & Loredo, J. S. (2012) Ethnic differences in the prevalence and predictors of restless legs syndrome between Hispanics of Mexican descent and non-Hispanic whites in San Diego County: a population based study. *Journal of Clinical Sleep Medicine*.

Schmidt-Nowara, W. W., Coultas, D. B., Wiggins, C., Skipper, B. E., & Samet, J. M. (1990). Snoring in a Hispanic-American population. Risk factors and association with hypertension and other morbidity. *Archives of Internal Medicine, 150*, 597–601.

Schober, A. K., Neurath, M. F., & Harsch, I. A. (2011). Prevalence of sleep apnoea in diabetic patients. *The Clinical Respiratory Journal, 5*, 165–172.

Seicean, S., Neuhauser, D., Strohl, K., & Redline, S. (2011). An exploration of differences in sleep characteristics between Mexico-born US immigrants and other Americans to address the Hispanic Paradox. *Sleep, 34*, 1021–1031.

Sell, R. E., Bardwell, W., Palinkas, L., Ancoli-Israel, S., Dimsdale, J., & Loredo, J. S. (2009). Ethnic differences in sleep-health knowledge. *Sleep, 32*(Abstract Supplement), A392.

Senthilvel, E., Auckley, D., & Dasarathy, J. (2011). Evaluation of sleep disorders in the primary care setting: History taking compared to questionnaires. *Journal of Clinical Sleep Medicine, 7*, 41–48.

Shepard, J. W., Jr., Buysse, D. J., Chesson, A. L., Jr., Dement, W. C., Goldberg, R., Guilleminault, C., et al. (2005). History of the development of sleep medicine in the United States. *Journal of Clinical Sleep Medicine, 1*, 61–82.

Shochat, T., Tzischinsky, O., Oksenberg, A., & Peled, R. (2007). Validation of the Pittsburgh Sleep Quality Index Hebrew translation (PSQI-H) in a sleep clinic sample. *Israel Medical Association Journal, 9*, 853–856.

Soler, X., Bardwell, W., Ancoli-Israel, S., Palinkas, L., & Loredo, J. S. (2009). Ethnic differences in sleep quality, depression and anxiety. *American Journal of Respiratory and Critical Care Medicine, 179*, A2115.

Solis, J. M., Marks, G., Garcia, M., & Shelton, D. (1990). Acculturation, access to care, and use of preventive services by Hispanics: Findings from HHANES 1982–1984. *American Journal of Public Health, 80*(Suppl), 11–19.

Sorlie, P. D., Avilés-Santa, L. M., Wassertheil-Smoller, S., Kaplan, R. C., Daviglus, M. L., Giachello, A. L., et al. (2010). Design and implementation of the Hispanic Community Health Study/Study of Latinos. *Annals of Epidemiology, 20*, 629–641.

Stang, A., Dragano, N., Poole, C., Moebus, S., Möhlenkamp, S., Schmermund, A., et al. (2007). Daily siesta, cardiovascular risk factors, and measures of subclinical atherosclerosis: Results of the Heinz Nixdorf Recall Study. *Sleep, 30*, 1111–1119.

Stern, M. P., Knapp, J. A., Hazuda, H. P., Haffner, S. M., Patterson, J. K., & Mitchell, B. D. (1991). Genetic and environmental determinants of type II diabetes in Mexican Americans. Is there a "descending limb" to the modernization/diabetes relationship? *Diabetes Care, 14*, 649–654.

Stern, M. P., Rosenthal, M., Haffner, S. M., Hazuda, H. P., & Franco, L. J. (1984). Sex difference in the effects of sociocultural status on diabetes and cardiovascular risk factors in Mexican Americans. The San Antonio Heart Study. *American Journal of Epidemiology, 120*, 834–851.

Sullivan, S. S., & Kushida, C. A. (2008). Multiple sleep latency test and maintenance of wakefulness test. *Chest, 134*, 854–861.

Sundquist, J., & Winkleby, M. A. (1999). Cardiovascular risk factors in Mexican American adults: A transcultural analysis of NHANES III, 1988–1994. *American Journal of Public Health, 89*, 723–730.

Sundquist, J., & Winkleby, M. (2000). Country of birth, acculturation status and abdominal obesity in a national sample of Mexican-American women and men. *International Journal of Epidemiology, 29*, 470–477.

Tassone, F., Lanfranco, F., Gianotti, L., Pivetti, S., Navone, F., Rossetto, R., et al. (2003). Obstructive sleep apnoea syndrome impairs insulin sensitivity independently of anthropometric variables. *Clinical Endocrinology, 59*, 374–379.

Tsai, P. S., Wang, S. Y., Wang, M. Y., Su, C. T., Yang, T. T., Huang, C. J., et al. (2005). Psychometric evaluation of the Chinese version of the Pittsburgh Sleep Quality Index (CPSQI) in primary insomnia and control subjects. *Quality of Life Research, 14*, 1943–1952.

Vidal, S., Ferrer, M., Masuet, C., Somoza, M., Martínez Ballarín, J. I., & Monasterio, C. (2007). Spanish version of the Functional Outcomes of Sleep Questionnaire: Scores of healthy individuals and of patients with sleep apnea-hypopnea syndrome. *Archivos de Bronconeumología, 43*, 256–261.

Walters, A. S. (1995). International Restless Legs Syndrome Study Group. Toward a better definition of the restless legs syndrome. *Movement Disorders, 10*, 634–642.

Wang, J., O'Reilly, B., Venkataraman, R., Mysliwiec, V., & Mysliwiec, A. (2009). Efficacy of oral iron in patients with restless legs syndrome and a low-normal ferritin: A randomized, double-blind, placebo-controlled study. *Sleep Medicine, 10*, 973–975.

Weaver, T. E., Laizner, A. M., Evans, L. K., Maislin, G., Chugh, D. K., Lyon, K., et al. (1997). An instrument to measure functional status outcomes for disorders of excessive sleepiness. *Sleep, 20*, 835–843.

Webb, W. B., & Dinges, D. F. (1989). Napping patterns and effects in human adults. In D. F. Dinges & R. J. Broughton (Eds.), *Sleep and alertness. Chronobiological, behavioral, and medical aspects of napping* (pp. 247–266). New York: Raven.

Weiss, T. M., Atanasov, S., & Calhoun, K. H. (2005). The association of tongue scalloping with obstructive sleep apnea and related sleep pathology. *Archives of Otolaryngology – Head & Neck Surgery, 133*, 966–971.

Wells, K. B., Golding, J. M., Hough, R. L., Burnam, M. A., & Karno, M. (1988). Factors affecting the probability of use of general and medical health and social/community services for Mexican Americans and non-Hispanic whites. *Medical Care, 26*, 441–452.

Will, M. J., Ester, M. S., Ramirez, S. G., Tiner, B. D., McAnear, J. T., & Epstein, L. (1995). Comparison of cephalometric analysis with ethnicity in obstructive sleep apnea syndrome. *Sleep, 18*, 873–875.

Winkleby, M. A., Fortmann, S. P., & Rockhill, B. (1993). Health-related risk factors in a sample of Hispanics and whites matched on sociodemographic characteristics. The Stanford Five-City Project. *American Journal of Epidemiology, 137*, 1365–1375.

Yaggi, H. K., Concato, J., Kernan, W. N., Lichtman, J. H., Brass, L. M., & Mohsenin, V. (2005). Obstructive sleep apnea as a risk factor for stroke and death. *The New England Journal of Medicine, 353*, 2034–2041.

Yang, C. M., Chou, C. P., & Hsiao, F. C. (2011). The association of dysfunctional beliefs about sleep with vulnerability to stress-related sleep disturbance in young adults. *Behavioral Sleep Medicine, 9*, 86–91.

Young, T., Shahar, E., Nieto, F. J., Redline, S., Newman, A. B., Gottlieb, D. J., Walsleben, J. A., Finn, L., Enright, P., Samet, J. M., & Sleep Heart Health Study Research Group. (2002). Predictors of sleep-disordered breathing in community-dwelling adults: The Sleep Heart Health Study. *Archives of Internal Medicine, 162*, 893–900.

Young, T., Skatrud, J., & Peppard, P. E. (2004). Risk factors for obstructive sleep apnea in adults. *Journal of the American Medical Association, 291*, 2013–2016.

Yu, J. C., & Berger, P. III. (2011). Sleep apnea and obesity. *South Dakota Journal of Medicine* (Spec No), 28–34.

19 Assessing Somatoform Disorders with the Hispanic Client

Irene M. Bravo and Carmen S. Roca

More than 150 years have elapsed since Briquet's (1859) treaty on hysteria, identifying a syndrome with a variety of somatic symptoms. These "idiopathic somatic complaints and syndromes" (ISCS; Escobar & Gureje, 2007, p. 841) have been found at similar rates cross-culturally. ISCS are usually related to stress but, particularly, to depression. Symptoms of depression or anxiety are often masked comorbid conditions observed in the somatoform disorders (Kessler et al., 1996; Rodríguez et al., 2004), although post-traumatic stress (PTSD) symptoms predict somatic complaints significantly better than depression or anxiety (Andreski, Chilcoat, & Breslau, 1998; Escalona, Achilles, Waitzkin, & Yager, 2004). Nevertheless, the somatoform disorders are considered a discrete diagnostic category, unrelated to other types of disorders (Hiller & Janca, 2003). Overall, somatization has decreased substantially in loose, individualistic societies, such as the USA, where individuals express their psychological distress directly (Askew & Keyes, 2006), but not in Hispanics (Angel & Guarnaccia, 1989; Hiller & Janca, 2003). Indeed, Hispanics are likely to seek medical assistance more often than non-Hispanics for symptoms with no organic etiologies (Angel & Guarnaccia, 1989; Askew & Keyes, 2006; Hiller & Janca, 2003). This propensity to express psychological distress as symptoms of medical conditions has the potential to muddle or obstruct assessment and diagnostic accuracy, not to mention incapacitation, increased health care costs, and therapeutic failure (Escobar et al., 1998).

Although the mortality rate of Hispanics in the USA is lower than that of non-Hispanics, Hispanics consider their health to be poorer (Finch, Hammer, Reindl, & Vega, 2002). Stress may be verbalized as "nervios" or in similar linguistic terms often grouped as "idioms of distress" (Escobar & Gureje, 2007, p. 843). Hispanics are overly diagnosed with major depression when compared to other ethnic groups (Minsky, Vega, Miskimen, Gara, & Escobar, 2003), albeit often undiagnosed at depression screenings, when symptoms of "subjective" depression are voiced, a combination of somatic and subclinical symptoms of depression (Caplan et al., 2010). Hispanics also may present co-occurring "ataques de nervios" with "unexplained neurological symptoms" (UNS; Interian et al., 2005). This

I.M. Bravo, Ph.D. (✉)
Psychology Department, Carlos Albizu University, 2173 N.W. 99th Avenue, Miami, FL 33172, USA
e-mail: ibravo@albizu.edu

C.S. Roca, Ph.D.
Carlos Albizu University, 2173 N.W. 99th Avenue, Miami, FL 33172, USA
e-mail: croca@albizu.edu

L.T. Benuto (ed.), *Guide to Psychological Assessment with Hispanics*,
DOI 10.1007/978-1-4614-4412-1_19, © Springer Science+Business Media New York 2013

Table 19.1 Tests available in Spanish to assess somatoform disorders

Test name	Original language	Type of assessment	Country of norms
CIDI	English	Diagnostic interview	Spain, Puerto Rico
DIS	English	Diagnostic interview	Spain, Peru, Puerto Rico
SCAN	English	Diagnostic interview	Spain
SDS	English	Somatoform diagnoses	Spain
PHQ-15	English	Screening	USA
GHQ	English	Screening	USA, Spain, El Salvador
SCL-90-R	English	Severity index	USA, Argentina, Mexico
BSI-18	English	Severity index	USA, Spain
BSI-21	English	Severity index	Italian immigrants
IAS	English	Hypochondriasis severity	Spain, USA
MPQ	English	Pain severity	Spain, Mexico, Costa Rica
			Argentina, Panama, Chile
MMPI, MMPI-2	English	Hypochondriasis	Cuba, Argentina,
		Hysteria	Chile, Mexico, Peru,
		Somatic complaints	Puerto Rico, Spain
BIRS	English	Body image	USA
ASI	English	Associated symptoms	Spain, USA,
			Puerto Rico
NS	English	Associated symptoms	USA

CIDI Composite International Diagnostic Interview, *DIS* Diagnostic Interview Schedule, *SCAN* Schedules for Clinical Assessment in Neuropsychiatry, *SDS* Somatoform Disorders Schedule, *PHQ-15* Patient Health Questionnaire, Somatic, *GHQ* General Health Questionnaire, *SCL-90-R* Symptom Checklist-90-Revised, *BSI-18* Brief Symptom Inventory-18, *BSI-21* Bradford Somatic Inventory, *IAS* Illness Attitude Scales, *MPQ* McGill Pain Questionnaire, *MMPI, MMPI-2* Minnesota Multiphasic Personality Inventory, *BIRS* Body Image Rating Scale, *ASI* Anxiety Sensitivity Inventory, *NS* Nervios Scale

functional, indirect manifestation of affective distress is frequently observed in tight, collectivistic cultures (Askew & Keyes, 2006), where the opinions of friends and family members are valued, and mental health problems are often ignored, hidden, or condemned.

Complicating matters further is the finding that Hispanics are a heterogeneous group, and their clinical presentation varies by gender, country of origin, and acculturation level. Studies show that, in general, females are overrepresented in the somatoform disorders, except in the diagnosis of hypochondriasis (Escobar, Burnham, Karno, Forsythe, & Golding, 1987). Puerto Rican Americans report a higher number of somatic complaints than Mexican Americans (Angel & Guarnaccia, 1989; Canino, Rubio-Stipec, Canino, & Escobar, 1992), and Cuban Americans tend to minimize their symptoms (Jackson, 2006). Because studies assessing Hispanics often group information on Central and South Americans as "other Hispanics," specific information on these Hispanic subgroups is scant, though their reported level of somatization is higher when compared to non-Hispanics (Aragona et al., 2005). Last, as Hispanics become acculturated, their level of somatization and mortality also increase (Finch et al., 2002). When compared to other Hispanic groups, immigrants from Central and South America, Cuba, and Mexico have better health outcomes than US-born Hispanics, especially Puerto Ricans, whose health status is poorer than that of any other Hispanic subgroup (Cho, Parker Frisbie, Hummer, & Rogers, 2004). In general, acculturated Hispanics are at a higher risk for psychiatric disorders or substance abuse than less acculturated Hispanics (Ortega, Rosenheck, Alegría, & Desai, 2000).

Epidemiological studies, such as the Epidemiologic Catchment Area (ECA), National Comorbidity Survey (NCS), and the Mexican American Prevalence and Services Survey (MAPSS), have focused almost exclusively on the mental health of Mexican immigrants and Mexican Americans. These studies show lower prevalence rates of mental disorders in Mexican born as opposed to US-born Mexican Americans. In particular, the ECA study reported similar rates of psychiatric disorders in Mexican Americans and non-Hispanic White Americans, except for substance abuse and major depressive episodes found at a higher rate in non-Hispanic Whites (Sue & Chu, 2003). Conversely, information derived from the ECA and the Puerto Rican Epidemiologic Survey revealed a specific somatic symptom cluster, very similar to *ataque de nervios*, only found in Puerto Rican participants, composed of "abdominal pain, nausea, vomiting, excessive gas, dyspnea, chest pain, palpitations, unusual spells, amnesia, paralysis, dizziness, fainting and muscle weakness" (Escobar & Gureje, 2007, p. 844).

Assessment of Somatoform Disorders

Widely used nosologies, such as the Diagnostic and Statistical Manual of Mental Disorders, Fourth Edition (DSM-IV) and the International Classification of Disease (ICD-10), utilize similar symptom clusters to describe the somatoform disorders (SFDs, i.e., somatization, undifferentiated somatoform, conversion, pain, hypochondriasis, and body dysmorphic). However, it has been forcefully argued (Escobar & Gureje, 2007) that these categories do not capture the most commonly endorsed symptoms of clients with somatic complaints. Indeed, the somatic symptom disorders work group of the proposed DSM-V recognizes the existence of significant overlap among some of the current SFDs (e.g., somatization, hypochondriasis, undifferentiated somatoform, and pain) and proposes their reclassification into a *complex somatic symptom disorder* (http://www.dsm5.org/proposedrevision/Pages/SomaticSymptomDisorders.aspx) American Psychiatric Association (2010).

Assessment of Somatoform Disorders in Hispanics

The assessment of somatoform disorders in Hispanics is complicated by either the nonexistence or translation of appropriate psychological tests. Cross-cultural nuances in test translation may mar appropriate construct meanings; test administration instructions may be inconsistently adhered to, and test items may be improperly translated (van de Vijver & Hambleton, 1996). The method of back-translation is often used to ameliorate these problems (Brislin, 1970). This method requires that a fully bilingual individual translates the test, a second person back-translates it to its original language, and a third individual resolves any word discrepancies. The back-translation method has been modified and improved by the World Health Organization (WHO), recommending groups of translators that are culturally sensitive bilingual and monolingual native experts of the country in which the test will be used (Sartorius & Janca, 1996). Although this procedure improves translation accuracy, it does not guarantee complete test equivalency (Shrout et al., 2008).

Global epidemiological studies generally focus on counting physical complaints unexplained by medical syndromes (Escobar & Gureje, 2007). The instruments used in these studies include the Symptom Checklist-90-Revised (SCL-90-R), the General Health Questionnaire (GHQ), the Diagnostic Interview Schedule (DIS), and the Composite International Diagnostic Interview (CIDI) (Escobar & Gureje). In this chapter, we will review these instruments but also other well-established self-report inventories and questionnaires used to screen, diagnose, or assess symptom severity in Hispanics with somatoform symptoms. Although somatization is observed in children and adolescents (e.g., separation anxiety disorder and other disorders), the inclusion of child somatization measures is beyond the scope of this chapter.

Diagnostic Instruments

The most widely used instruments in diagnosing DSM-IV and ICD-10 disorders are the Structured Clinical Interview for DSM-IV (SCID) and the Composite International Diagnostic Interview (CIDI). Although there is a SCID available in Spanish, its somatoform disorders section has not been translated (http://www.masson.es) Masson, S.A. Spanish, 2011. See Table 1 for a list of all tests reviewed in this chapter that have been translated into Spanish.

The Composite International Diagnostic Interview

The Composite International Diagnostic Interview (CIDI) is a validated (see review, Sartorius & Janca, 1996), international research instrument of the World Health Organization with a structured, somatoform module assessing 41 upsetting but medically unsubstantiated symptoms (Aragona et al., 2005). Lay interviewers administer the CIDI. Worldwide field trials of the CIDI (Wittchen, 1994; Wittchen et al., 1991) report Kappas of the somatization module at $\kappa=0.67$ (Wittchen et al.) and Kappas of joint studies at $\kappa=0.74$ (somatization), $\kappa=0.68$ (pain disorder), and $\kappa=0.71$ (hypochondriasis) (Wittchen). Comparably, an international multisite study (Simon, Gater, Kisely, & Piccinelli 1996; $N=5{,}438$ at 15 sites) administered an abridged CIDI somatoform module (23 validated items) as a "current somatic symptom scale" (p. 483), reporting no statistical differences in somatization among sites but showing a correlation between somatization and anxiety (*r*. 40), depression (*r*. 32), and general distress (*r*. 42, anxiety and depression). Somatic complaints and general distress were assessed in the context of each country's level of development, resulting in a slight elevation of symptoms in less developed countries. In this study, fewer years of formal education across sites were related to having higher somatic symptoms (r. $-.18$, $p<.001$) (Simon et al.). It is worth noting that the percentage of Hispanics attaining a bachelors' degree in the USA is lower (11%) than that of African Americans (17%), Whites (30%), and Asian Americans (49%) (U.S. Census Bureau, 2003). However, in another large study (Villaseñor & Waitzkin, 1999), the Spanish CIDI's somatoform module inaccurately identified somatic symptoms in new primary care clients ($N=1{,}456$; Central American, Mexican, Chicano, non-Latino White). The authors concluded that the distortions were due to language discrepancies of clients and providers, poor identification of cultural syndromes, and clients' inability to seek alternative health care due to financial reasons (Villaseñor & Waitzkin). This study questions the validity of previous CIDI studies identifying a higher number of somatic symptoms in Hispanics when compared to non-Hispanic Whites or other ethnic groups. Nonetheless, in a recent randomized study, the Spanish CIDI was compared to its original English version in participants selected from the National Latino and Asian American Study (NLAAS). The two versions of the CIDI demonstrated equivalency in the administered clusters, with the exception of generalized anxiety disorder (GAD), which was diagnosed more frequently in the bilingual group tested in English than in the bilingual group tested in Spanish (Shrout et al., 2008). This is yet another study lending support to the notion that higher acculturation relates to higher psychopathology in Hispanics. To strengthen the somatoform module of the CIDI, the Somatoform Disorders Schedule (SDS) was constructed to assess DSM-IV/ICD-10 diagnoses for somatoform disorders, hypochondriasis and neurasthenia (Janca, Isaac, Costa, & Silva, 1993). The SDS has adequate reliability; Kappas of $\kappa=0.87$ (inter-rater reliability), and $\kappa=0.72$ (test-retest reliability) (World Health Organization [WHO], 1993, www.who.org), but no Spanish translation or validation studies exist for the SDS (A. Janca, October 11, 2011, personal communication).

Similar Diagnostic Instruments

Other instruments used for diagnostic purposes are the Diagnostic Interview Schedule (DIS; Robins, Helzer, Croughan, & Ratcliff, 1981) and the Schedules for Clinical Assessment in Neuropsychiatry (SCAN; WHO, 1994).

The Diagnostic Interview Schedule

The Diagnostic Interview Schedule (DIS) is a validated, lay-administered structured interview of the National Institutes of Mental Health (NIMH), used to identify mental health disorders in epidemiological studies. Several DIS Spanish translations exist; the first translation was conducted in California by Karno, Burnam, Escobar, Hough, and Eaton (1983). A DIS version comparable to Karno's et al. (1983) was adapted in Puerto Rico, and it was validated in a psychiatric and community sample ($N=189$) (Bravo, Canino, & Biro, 1987). Later, the factor structure of the Spanish DIS was validated in Puerto Rico ($N=1,513$) and compared to participants in Los Angeles ($N=1,113$ Mexican American and $N=975$ Anglo-American). The Cronbach's reliability coefficient of the somatization factor was reported at $\alpha=.72$ (Puerto Rico), $\alpha=.58$ (Los Angeles' Anglo-Americans), and $\alpha=.62$ (Los Angeles' Mexican Americans) (Rubio-Stipec, Shrout, Bird, Canino, & Bravo, 1989). Although this factor analysis clearly identified a somatization factor in the Puerto Rican sample, it did not replicate in Los Angeles. This finding is plausibly related to a lower somatization in the Los Angeles group or to true cultural differences between the groups (Rubio-Stipec et al., 1989). The DIS's somatization module has been criticized for having overly restrictive diagnostic criteria. Thus, several methods have been identified to assess somatization. The Bucholz method, based on DSM-IV criteria, requires the presence of eight symptoms in four body sites (four pain, two gastrointestinal, one sexual, and one pseudoneurological). Based on DSM-III criteria, Escobar's abridged method is more flexible. Of a total number of 13 symptoms, females must endorse only six and males four of these symptoms. Last, Kroenke proposed a multisomatoform cluster comprised of three unsubstantiated medical symptoms to reach somatization criteria and one unsubstantiated medical symptom to meet the undifferentiated somatoform criterion. Comparing these methods in a group of family practice clients ($N=172$), the Bucholz method was superior in identifying clients with somatization problems but not better than the DIS (Lynch, McGrady, Nagel, & Zsembik, 1999).

The Schedules for Clinical Assessment in Neuropsychiatry

The Schedules for Clinical Assessment in Neuropsychiatry (SCAN) is a WHO semi-structured interview used in epidemiological studies that requires professional training and administration by a psychiatrist or a psychologist. The SCAN allows clinicians to use their clinical judgment in assessing all available client information, together with the client's present and lifetime symptoms, to formulate a DSM-IV/ICD-10 diagnosis. The somatization section is moderately short, covering health-related and somatoform symptoms (Sartorius & Janca, 1996). The SCAN is available in Spanish, and it was validated in Spain by J. López-Ibor as part of an international multisite field trial. To assess reliability, each translated version was compared to both ICD-10 categorizations and its original English version (see Wing et al., 1990). The SCAN covers the essential somatoform disorders' symptom clusters, with standard probe questions, excluding organic etiologies (Hiller & Janca, 2003).

Screening Instruments

Screening instruments are often useful in providing preliminary information about various mental disorders or in supporting diagnoses in both clinical and research settings. These measures are especially helpful when time and other constraints do not permit the use of semi-structured, diagnostic interviews. Two of the most often used somatization measures in Spanish are the Patient Health Questionnaire (PHQ; Spitzer, Kroenke, & Williams, 1999) and the General Health Questionnaire (GHQ; Goldberg & Williams, 1988).

The Patient Health Questionnaire

The Patient Health Questionnaire (PHQ; Spitzer et al., 1999) assesses Axis I mental health disorders in medical patients. Its somatization module, the PHQ-15, evaluates the presence of 15 common somatic complaints in the last month. Similar Cronbach's reliability coefficients (α=.89) were found for Hispanic and non-Hispanic groups, but convergence with the CIDI was higher in the non-Hispanic (r=0.68) than in the Hispanic group (r=.44). The authors concluded that, among Hispanics, the PHQ-15 captured clinical distress but not other symptom clusters (decreased function and unsubstantiated symptoms) reported by the non-Hispanic group (Interian, Allen, Gara, Escobar, & Díaz-Martínez, 2006).

The General Health Questionnaire

The General Health Questionnaire (GHQ-60; Goldberg & Hiller, 1979) is a self-report, screening questionnaire that detects psychiatric disorders. The original version included 60 items, but abridged versions exist in English (GHQ-30; GHQ-28; GHQ-12) and in Spanish (GHQ-28; Gibbons, Flores de Arévalo, & Mónico, 2004; Gili, Ferrer, Roca, & Bernardo, 2000; GHQ-12; Sánchez-López & Dresch, 2008). The GHQ-28 was validated in several Spanish studies with mixed results (see Molina et al., 2006). These findings prompted Molina et al. to reanalyze the original GHQ's 60 items in Spain, adhering to Goldberg and Hiller's (1979) original methodology, to extract reliable and valid items strongly endorsed by the Spanish population. The internal consistency of each of the final four extracted factors was equivalent: Cronbach's α=.80, .83, .76, and .87, for each of Goldberg's factors, and Cronbach's α=.82, .85, .78, and .88 for Molina et al.'s sample in Spain. The authors concluded that all abridged, translated versions of the scale should prioritize the scale's factor structure, grouping items by type of symptomatology and not by the number of items contained in each factor. More recently, Sánchez-López and Dresch (2008) validated a briefer, 12-item GHQ in Spain, reporting three factors that measure successful coping, self-esteem, and stress. The internal consistency of the Spanish scale was reported at an acceptable level, Cronbach's reliability coefficient α=.76 (.76 men and .75 women), albeit slighter lower than the reliability coefficients reported for other international versions of the scale (German, Australian, Iranian, and Arabic) (Sánchez-López & Dresch). Other studies (see Katerndahl, Amodei, Larme, & Palmer, 2002) have reported excellent reliability (Cronbach's α>.80) and construct validity for the GHQ-12 with English-speaking Hispanics.

Instruments of Severity Ratings

Spanish-translated symptom severity measures of the somatoform disorders include the Symptom Checklist-90-Revised (SCL-90-R; Derogatis, 1994), its abridged version, the Brief Symptom Inventory-18 (BSI-18; Derogatis, 2000), the 21-item Bradford Somatic Inventory (BSI-21; Mumford et al., 1991), the Illness Attitude Scales (IAS; Kellner, Abbott, Winslow, & Pathak, 1987), the long and short forms of the McGill Pain Questionnaire (SF-MPQ; Melzack, 1987), and the Minnesota Multiphasic Personality Inventory-2 (Butcher, Dahlstrom, Graham, Tellegen, & Kaemmer, 1989).

The Symptom Checklist-90-Revised

The Symptom Checklist-90-Revised (SCL-90-R; Derogatis, 1994) contains 90 items, grouped into nine clusters of symptoms that produce distress. The clusters capture symptoms of somatization, obsessive-compulsive, interpersonal sensitivity, depression, anxiety, hostility, phobic anxiety, paranoid ideation, and psychoticism. A Spanish version of the SCL-90-R (Bonicatto, Dew, Soria, & Seghezzo, 1997), originally validated in Argentina, was administered to a normative sample in Mexico (Cruz Fuentes, López Bello, Blas García, González Macías, & Chávez Balderas, 2005). The SCL-90-R somatization factor had a very good internal consistency: Cronbach's $\alpha=.85$. As expected, mean somatization scores were higher for females ($M=0.73$, SD = 0.61) than for males ($M=0.43$, SD = 0.43). When compared to the Argentinean normative group, the Mexican sample endorsed a higher number of somatic complaints (Mexico mean scores: $M=.69$ females, $M=.49$ males; Argentina mean scores: $M=.55$ females, $M=.35$ males (Cruz Fuentes et al., 2005). The SCL-90-R also showed excellent reliability (Cronbach's $\alpha>.80$) and construct validity in English-speaking Hispanics in the USA (Katerndahl et al., 2002).

The Brief Symptom Inventory-18

The Brief Symptom Inventory-18 (BSI-18; Derogatis, 2000) is a much briefer version of the original BSI's 53 items derived from the SCL-90-R, assessing the same nine areas of psychological distress. The abridged BSI-18, however, is simple and easy to administer, focusing on only three of the most ubiquitous psychiatric problems, i.e., depression, anxiety, and somatization. The normative data of the BSI-18 shows stable Cronbach's reliability coefficients of $\alpha=.74$ (somatization), $\alpha=.79$ (anxiety), $\alpha=.84$ (depression), and $\alpha=.89$ (global severity index) (Derogatis). The best fit for the BSI-18 in Spain was a four-factor model, comprised of somatization, depression, general anxiety, and panic (Andreu et al., 2008). The authors reported that the BSI-18 in Spanish is valid, captures therapeutic change well, and it has good internal consistency and test-retest reliability.

The 21-Item Bradford Somatic Inventory

The 21-item Bradford Somatic Inventory (BSI-21; Mumford et al., 1991) has been widely used in international research studies, and it has been translated into Spanish and several other languages (Canino et al., 1992). Using the BSI-21 to evaluate immigrants' level of somatization in Italy, the mean score of the Hispanic group (Central and South Americans; $M=15.15$, SD=9.64) was significantly higher ($p<.012$) than the mean scores of all other immigrant comparison groups (Africans $M=11.44$, SD=9.17; Asians $M=10.18$, SD=7.75; and Caucasians $M=11.54$, SD=8.70) (Aragona et al., 2005). The high level of somatization found in this study was similar to the highest somatization rate reported by WHO for Hispanics when compared to other ethnic groups (Gureje, Simon, Ustun, & Goldberg, 1997). The BSI-21 cutoff score of 14 discriminated psychiatric from nonpsychiatric cases, with .75 specificity and .87 sensitivity (Aragona et al.).

The Illness Attitude Scales

The Illness Attitude Scales (IAS; Kellner et al., 1987) is a self-report questionnaire that measures the attitudes, symptom perception, and beliefs toward illness of hypochondriacal patients. The IAS contains seven scales composed of three items, each measuring "worry about illness, concern about pain, health habits, hypochondriacal beliefs, thanatophobia, disease phobia, bodily preoccupation, and treatment experience" (Kellner et al., p. 21). The IAS has several Spanish translations. In a validation study of the Somatosensory Amplification Scale (SSAS) (Martínez, Belloch, & Botella, 1999) in Spain, the Spanish IAS internal consistency was reported at Cronbach's $\alpha=.87$, $\alpha=.91$, and $\alpha=.90$ in clients with hypochondriasis, panic, and controls, respectively (Martínez et al.). Another IAS Spanish translation was transformed from a Likert scale to a categorical format (yes or no) in a sample of mostly Cuban American, depressed, and nondepressed elderly clients in South Florida (Bravo & Arrufat, 2005). The original scale consisted of 28 items; one of the items (item 28) was removed, as it assessed the frequency of different types of treatments received. The reported Cronbach's reliability coefficients of the original, Likert scale version ranged from $\alpha=.62$ to 1.00 (Kellner et al.). The

Spanish-translated, categorically reformatted version's internal consistency (Cronbach's α=.83) was comparable to its equivalent English version (Cronbach's α=.84) (Bravo & Arrufat). Frazier and Waid (1999) also reported adequate internal consistency (Cronbach's α=.76) for this IAS version in spite of removing the Health Worries subscale. Although this IAS version was initially validated with older adults, it is easy to administer and appropriate to use with younger adults endorsing hypochondriacal concerns.

The Long and Short Forms of the McGill Pain Questionnaire

The long and short forms of the McGill Pain Questionnaire (SF-MPQ; Melzack, 1987) are frequently used measures to assess sensations and feelings of pain. Pain severity is indicated in a 4-point Likert scale from no pain to severe pain. The short form of the scale is congruent with its original version (*r* .77 to .93) for both the full scale and the subscales. Several Spanish translations of the MPQ have been validated. One of these versions (Lázaro, Bosch, Torrubia, & Baños, 1994) was cross-validated in Spain (*N*=282) and other Latin American countries (*N*=205; Mexico, Costa Rica, Panama, and Argentina) on participants with acute or chronic pain. All countries reported equivalent correlations, with most of the MPQ descriptors deemed appropriate and easy to understand (Lázaro et al., 2001). However, a validation study in Chile (Boyle, Fernández, & Ortet, 2003) reported psychometric complexity, item confusion, and overlap between the MPQ affective and evaluative components. Similar psychometric difficulties were reported in US Hispanic participants who were less likely to endorse severity ratings for *throbbing* pain or bodily sensations described as *gnawing* or *aching* but were more likely to endorse *tiring-exhausting* and *sickening* feelings (Zinke, Lam, Norman Harden, & Fogg, 2010). These discrepancies were attributed to linguistic problems due to lower educational level in the Hispanic group (Hispanics: less than high school to high school; non-Hispanic Whites: college and postgraduate). Notwithstanding, the internal consistency of the scale was reported at Cronbach's α=.90 for Hispanics and Cronbach's α=.89 for non-Hispanic Whites (Zinke et al.).

The Minnesota Multiphasic Personality Inventory-2's

The Minnesota Multiphasic Personality Inventory-2's (MMPI-2; Butcher et al., 1989) original version (MMPI) was first translated to Spanish in 1951 by Alfonso Bernal del Riesgo in Cuba (Butcher, Cabiya, Lucio, & Garrido, 2007). Since then, the MMPI, MMPI-2, and MMPI-A have had numerous translations, and it has been extensively validated in several Spanish-speaking countries, such as Argentina, Chile, Cuba, Mexico, Perú, Puerto Rico, and Spain (Butcher et al., 2007). The translated clinical scales are essentially equivalent to the original English version (Butcher et al., 2007). Two of the MMPI-2 scales can be used to assess somatoform symptoms, i.e., scale 1: hypochondriasis (*Hs*), measuring elusive, indistinct bodily complaints and unrealistic health worries; and scale 3: hysteria (*Hy*), assessing poor insight, unawareness, and exaggerated stress responses (Hiller & Janca, 2003). It is recommended that the MMPI-2 content scales also be interpreted, as the Health Concerns (*HEA*) scale comprises a great number of somatic complaints in diverse body sites (Butcher, Graham, Williams, & Ben-Porath, 1990). Although the MMPI-2 is widely used, the somatization items have been judged to be "loose" (Hiller & Janca, p. 173). Hiller and Janca state that scales 1 and 3 (*Hs* and *Hy*) encompass multiple symptoms not restricted to the somatoform disorders. Conversely, the Health Concerns (*HEA*) content scale is more accurate, as it contains items that exclusively endorse somatic complaints (Hiller & Janca). In general, Hispanics may be more likely to interpret their emotional discomfort as health or somatic concerns, slightly elevating the Hypochondriasis (*Hs)* or Health Concerns (*HEA*) scales (Garrido & Velasquez, 2005). In terms of validity, it is essential to consider that the Hispanic client may have elevations on the *F* (Infrequency) scale, due to stress, cultural, or linguistic reasons, and on the *L* (Lie) scale, in an effort to preserve a positive image. These elevations require a close examination of the *VRIN* (Variable Response Inconsistency) and *TRIN* (True Response

Inconsistency) to assess if the Hispanic client clearly understands the meaning of the test's items (Butcher et al., 2007). In comparing the US clinical and nonclinical norms of the MMPI-2 to populations in other Spanish-speaking countries, no significant differences were found in Cuba, but they were found for Mexican clients in treatment settings (*Hs*, $F=7.5$, $p \leq .001$; *Hy*, $F=5.7$, $p \leq .001$; and *HEA*, $F=3.93$, $p \leq .01$; Díaz, Jurado, Lucio, & Cuevas, 2003). Because of these and other discrepancies (see Butcher et al., 2007 for a thorough review), specific norms were developed for the MMPI-2 in Mexico. Problems of acculturation may occlude MMPI-2 results in Puerto Ricans living in the US mainland when compared to Puerto Ricans residing in the island (Butcher et al., 2006). However, the MMPI-2 differentiates well between clinical and nonclinical samples in Puerto Rico (Cabiya, 1996). The MMPI-2 also was adapted in Chile, with no significant differences from normative samples in the USA (Rissetti, Himmel, & González, 1996). This MMPI-2 Chilean version was readapted successfully in Argentina (Casullo, Samartino, Brenella, Marquez, & Dupertuis, 1996). In Peru, the MMPI-2 norms were very close to the American population (Scott & Pampa, 2000), although the *F* scale resembled the results found in Mexican women. Last, the Castilian translation of the MMPI-2 in Spain showed equivalency to US normative samples (Avila-Espada & Jimenez-Gómez, 1996).

Instruments Validated with English-Speaking Hispanics

In addition to instruments available in Spanish, other measures written in English have been used with English-speaking Hispanics in the USA. The measures reviewed in this chapter include the Body Image Rating Scale (BIRS: Mayville, Gipson, & Katz, 1998), an instrument used to evaluate the prevalence of body dysmorphic disorder (BDD), and a nonverbal, culture-free test to detect body dissatisfaction and body distortion (Fallon & Rozin, 1985).

The Body Image Rating Scale

The Body Image Rating Scale (BIRS: Mayville et al., 1998) allows for both screening and severity assessment of BDD. The BIRS evaluates affective, cognitive, and behavioral correlates of BDD; rules out eating and gender identity disorders; and arrives at DSM-IV diagnostic criteria for BDD. In a comparison of adolescents from 19 different ethnic groups (including Hispanics), a significant difference ($p=.0006$) was reported for gender, with females ($M=61.33$, SD=20.13) endorsing more symptoms of BDD than males ($M=52.30$, SD=19.39). In general, African Americans were more satisfied (F (6, 450)=4.06, $p=.0006$) with their bodies than all other ethnic groups (Mayville, Katz, Gipson & Cabral, 1999); no significant differences were found for Hispanics. The scale's internal validity was reported at coefficient $\alpha=.93$ and its test-retest reliability at r .86. Convergent validity with the Body Dysmorphic Disorder Examination Self-Report scale was r .86 (Mayville et al., 1998).

Nonverbal Assessment of Body Image

The nonverbal assessment of body image is a culture-free test that provides a measure of body dissatisfaction and body distortion (Fallon & Rozin, 1985). This assessment uses two, nine-drawing sets of human figures organized from very slender to corpulent. Each set is composed of figures of one gender; same sex drawings are administered first followed by opposite sex drawings. Clients select three figures: (1) one that matches their own body, (2) an ideal figure, and (3) a figure they consider would be attractive to the opposite sex. After selecting the three figures of the first set, clients are presented with the second set of opposite sex figures, selecting the one they consider most attractive (Fallon & Rozin). The Hispanic participants' body image was compared to their Caucasian and African American counterparts (Demarest & Allen, 2000). A significant difference in body dissatisfaction was found for females (F (1,108)=14.3, $p<.0001$) but not for ethnicity, with the

Caucasian women being most dissatisfied. When compared to the women's expressed preferences, men of all ethnic groups had the distorted view that women prefer male figures with the bulkiest bodies (Demarest & Allen).

Measuring Associated Symptoms

Some associated somatoform symptoms in Hispanics include cultural syndromes, such as *ataque de nervios, nervios,* or *decaimiento* that seem to be captured by measures such as the Anxiety Sensitivity Index (Peterson & Reiss, 1992) and the Nervios Scale (Hinton, Lewis-Fernández, & Pollack, 2009).

Anxiety Sensitivity Index

The *Anxiety Sensitivity Index* (ASI; Peterson & Reiss, 1992) measures "fear of fear" or the appraisal that fearful feelings can have negative bodily, social, or psychological consequences. The Spanish ASI (Sandín, Chorot, & McNally, 1996), validated in Spain, has a reported internal consistency of Cronbach's $\alpha = .91$ for individuals with anxiety disorders and of Cronbach's $\alpha = .80$ for controls (Sandín et al.). Anxiety sensitivity has been found to be the best predictor of hypochondriacal concerns (when compared to trait anxiety and depression) in non-Hispanic, depressed young adults (Otto, Pollack, Sachs, & Rosenbaum, 1992). This finding was replicated in a group of depressed, older Cuban immigrants (Bravo & Silverman, 2001). In comparing the internal consistency of the ASI with Hispanics and non-Hispanic Whites, the ASI's Cronbach's reliability coefficients were reported at $\alpha = .91$ and $\alpha = .92$, respectively (Bravo & Silverman). The ASI also was used to investigate *ataque de nervios* in Puerto Rico (Cintrón, Carter, & Sbrocco, 2005). Participants were divided in three groups: (1) at least one *ataque de nervios,* (2) no *ataque de nervios* and low anxiety sensitivity, and (3) no *ataque de nervios* and high anxiety sensitivity. Participants who scored high on anxiety sensitivity (HAS) scored at similar levels than those who had experienced *ataques de nervios* (ADN) (ASI's HAS group $M = 38.3$, SD = 6.9; ASI's ADN group $M = 30.5$, SD = 12.86 at $p = \text{ns}$), and both groups differed significantly from participants with low anxiety sensitivity. All groups had the same level of trait anxiety. Interestingly, participants with high anxiety sensitivity and those with history of *ataque de nervios* had elevated scores on the Beck Anxiety Inventory (BAI) but not on trait anxiety (State-Trait Anxiety Inventory, State version, STAI-S). This finding is congruent with Hinton, Chong, Pollack, Barlow, and McNally's (2008) report of a significant association between *ataque de nervios* and anxiety sensitivity and with previous findings (Bravo & Silverman, 2001; Otto et al., 1992) identifying anxiety sensitivity as a better predictor of hypochondriacal concerns and panic-like symptoms than trait anxiety.

Nervios Scale

Nervios Scale (Hinton et al., 2009). The Spanish Nervios Scale is brief, composed of only three items that assess the presence of *nervios* and severity of *ataque de nervios,* in the last month. The inter-rater reliability of the scale was reported at r .92 and its test-retest reliability (after 1 week) at r .86 (Hinton et al.). In a group of Hispanic women (half Dominican, half Puerto Rican) receiving Culturally Appropriate Cognitive Behavioral Therapy (CA-CBT) or Applied Muscle Relaxation (AMR) for PTSD, the Nervios Scale captured treatment effects (CA-CBT: Pre $M = 2.3$, SD 0.7; Post $M = 1.2$ SD 0.5, F/U: $M = 1.3$, SD 0.6, $p < .01$, es = 1.8 and AMR: Pre $M = 2.1$, SD 0.6; Post $M = 1.8$ SD 0.7, F/U: $M = 1.9$, SD 0.7, es = 0.4) adequately (Hinton, Hofmann, Rivera, Otto, & Pollack, 2011). Assessing for the presence of *nervios* (Salgado de Snyder, Díaz-Pérez, & Ojeda, 2000) in Mexican rural adults ($N = 942$), 15.5% of the sample endorsed suffering from *nervios* (104 of 501 women or 20.8% and 42 of 441 males or 9.5%). Women endorsing *nervios* had lower education ($t = 2.7$, $p < .01$)

than their counterparts. The authors concluded that *nervios* may occur more frequently in women of lower education residing in rural settings.

Summary and Recommendations

The diagnostic instruments reviewed in this chapter include the Composite International Diagnostic Interview (CIDI), the Diagnostic Interview Schedule (DIS), and the Schedules for Clinical Assessment in Neuropsychiatry (SCAN). These are highly reliable diagnostic instruments well validated in international studies. The CIDI and DIS can be administered by lay interviewers, but not the SCAN, whose administration is restricted to WHO trained physicians or psychologists. Although these research instruments are frequently used in epidemiological studies, it may not be parsimonious to use them in clinical practice. The Somatoform Disorders Schedule (SDS) derived from the CIDI may be a viable clinical alternative (Janca et al., 1995). However, it has not yet been translated into Spanish (A. Janca, October 11, 2011, personal communication).

Screening instruments such as the Patient Health Questionnaire's somatization section (PHQ-15) and the General Health Questionnaire (GHQ) are available in Spanish and can be used in clinical settings or when time does not allow the use of structured interviews. The reliability of the PHQ-15 in Spanish is very good, although convergent validity with the CIDI is relatively low, when compared to non-Hispanic groups. The GHQ has several Spanish versions (its briefest version is the GHQ-12), and it is a reliable and well-validated instrument, although its reliability is slightly lower when compared to other language versions.

Several well-validated, reliable, and widely used instruments exist in Spanish and can be used in clinical and research settings to assess symptom severity, such as the Symptom Checklist-90-Revised (SCL-90-R), its abridged version, the BSI-18, the 21-item Bradford Somatic Inventory (BSI-21), the Illness Attitude Scales (IAS), the McGill Pain Questionnaire (MPQ), and the MMPI-2. In validating the SCL-90-R in Argentina and Mexico, Mexican participants exhibited higher somatization. The BSI-18 was validated in Spain, and the BSI-21 detected higher somatization in Italy's Hispanic immigrants when compared to immigrants of other nationalities. In terms of hypochondriasis, a reliable instrument validated in Spain and with older Hispanics in USA is the Illness Attitude Scales (IAS). The modified Spanish IAS is a checklist amenable to use with adults of all ages endorsing hypochondriacal concerns. The Spanish McGill Pain Questionnaire (MPQ) is widely used and has been validated in Spain and Latin America with similar results. However, psychometric complexity and interpretative problems have been reported both in Chile and in English-speaking Hispanics in the USA. The MMPI-2 has been adapted successfully in several Spanish-speaking countries. In general, the Health Concerns content scale captures the essence of somatic complaints better than the Hypochondriasis and Hysteria clinical scales.

Other reliable and valid instruments have been used with English-speaking Hispanics, such as the Body Image Rating Scale, to assess body dysmorphic disorder. A nonverbal, culture-free screener that detects body dissatisfaction and body distortion also has been validated in a variety of cultural groups, including Hispanics. Last, instruments that measure somatoform associated symptoms include the Anxiety Sensitivity Index, a widely used and reliable instrument that correlates highly with the presence of *ataque de nervios,* and Nervios Scales that simply ask about the presence or history of having had *ataque de nervios.*

In general, assessing the somatoform disorders using translated measures for Spanish-speaking Hispanics requires certain special considerations. Although well-validated diagnostic tools exist in Spanish, some authors (Villaseñor & Waitzkin, 1999) consider that the high number of somatic complaints found in Hispanics, as reported in cross-cultural studies, may be a function of client-physician language barriers, financially limited access to health care, and medically unidentified cultural syndromes. Thus, it is recommended that reliable, well-validated, and carefully translated measures be used with Hispanics, and that they be administered by culturally sensitive clinicians, mindful about idioms of distress, culture-bound syndromes, and cultural differences among Hispanics.

Acknowledgement The authors would like to thank Yamilka Gonzalez, Assistant Librarian at Carlos Albizu University, Miami Campus, for her help in obtaining the literature reviewed in this chapter.

References

American Psychiatric Association. (2010). *DSM-5 development*. Retrieved from http://www.dsm5.org/proposedrevision/Pages/SomaticSymptomDisorders.aspx.

Andreski, P., Chilcoat, H., & Breslau, N. (1998). Post-traumatic stress disorder and somatization symptoms: A prospective study. *Psychiatry Research, 79*, 131–138.

Andreu, Y., Gald6n, M. J., Dura, E., Ferrando, M., Murgui, S., García, A., et al. (2008). Psychometric properties of the Brief Symptom's Inventory-18 (BSI-18) in a Spanish sample of outpatients with psychiatric disorders. *Psicothema, 20*, 844–850.

Angel, R., & Guarnaccia, P. J. (1989). Mind, body, and culture: Somatization among Hispanics. *Social Science & Medicine, 28*(12), 1229–1238.

Aragona, M., Tarsitani, L., Colosimo, F., Martinelli, B., Raad, H., Maisano, B., et al. (2005). Somatization in primary care: A comparative survey of immigrants from various ethnic groups in Rome, Italy. *International Journal of Psychiatry in Medicine, 35*, 241–248.

Askew, R. A., & Keyes, C. L. M. (2006). Stress and somatization: A sociological perspective. In D. Johns (Ed.), *Stress and its impact on society* (pp. 117–132). Hauppauge, NY: Nova.

Avila-Espada, A., & Jimenez-G6mez, F. (1996). The Castilian versi6n of the MMPI-2 in Spain: Development, adaptation, and psychometric properties. In J. N. Butcher (Ed.), *International adaptations of the MMPI-2: Research and clinical applications* (pp. 305–328). Minneapolis, MN: University of Minnesota Press.

Bonicatto et al., 1997. Bonicatto, S., Dew, M.A., Soria, J.J., & Seghezzo, M.E. (1997). Validity and reliability of Symptom Checklist '90 (SCL90) in an Argentine population sample. Social Psychiatry and Psychiatric Epidemiology, 32, 332–338.

Boyle, G. J., Fernández, E., & Ortet, G. (2003). The McGill Pain Questionnaire – MPQ: Linguistic and statistical consideration. *Revista de Psicología de la Universidad de Chile, 12*(1), 111–119.

Bravo, I. M., & Arrufat, O. (2005). The illness attitude scales: Adaptation and translation into Spanish for use with older adults. *Journal of Applied Gerontology, 24*, 355–371.

Bravo, M., Canino, G. J., & Biro, H. (1987). El DIS en Español: Su traducci6n y adaptaci6n en Puerto Rico. *Acta Psiquiátrica y Psicológica de América Latina, 33*, 27–42.

Bravo, I. M., & Silverman, W. K. (2001). Anxiety sensitivity, anxiety, and depression in older patients and their relation to hypochondriacal concerns and medical illnesses. *Aging & Mental Health, 5*, 349–357.

Briquet, P. (1859). *Traité clinique et Thérapeutique de l'Hystérie*. Paris: Baillière.

Brislin, R. W. (1970). Back-translation for cross-cultural research. *Journal of Cross-Cultural Psychology, 1*(3), 185–216.

Butcher, J. N., Cabiya, J., Lucio, E., & Garrido, M. (2007). *Assessing Hispanic clients using the MMPI-2 and MMPI-A*. Washington, DC: American Psychological Association.

Butcher, J. N., Dahlstrom, J. R., Graham, J. R., Tellegen, A., & Kaemmer, B. (1989). *Minnesota Multiphasic Personality Inventory (MMPI-2): Manual for administration and scoring*. Minneapolis, MN: University of Minnesota Press.

Butcher, J. N., Graham, J. R., Williams, C. L., & Ben-Porath, Y. S. (1990). *Development and use of the MMPI-2 content scales*. Minneapolis, MN: University of Minnesota Press.

Cabiya, J. J. (1996). Use of the MMPI and the MMPI-2 in Puerto Rico. In J. N. Butcher (Ed.), *International adaptations of the MMPI-2: Research and clinical applications* (pp. 284–304). Minneapolis, MN: University of Minnesota Press.

Canino, I. A., Rubio-Stipec, M., Canino, G., & Escobar, J. I. (1992). Functional somatic symptoms: A cross-ethnic comparison. *The American Journal of Orthopsychiatry, 62*, 605–612.

Caplan, S., Alvidrez, J., Paris, M., Escobar, J. I., Dixon, J. K., Desai, M. M., et al. (2010). Subjective versus objective: an exploratory analysis of Latino primary care patients with self-perceived depression who do not fulfill primary care evaluation of mental disorders patient health questionnaire criteria for depression. *Primary Care Companion Journal of Clinical Psychiatry, 12*(5).

Casullo, M. M., Samartino, L. G., Brenella, M. E., Marquez, M. A., & Dupertuis, D. G. (1996). Studies of the MMPI-2 in Argentina. In J. N. Butcher (Ed.), *International adaptations of the MMPI-2: Research and clinical applications* (pp. 252–264). Minneapolis, MN: University of Minnesota Press.

Cho, Y., Parker Frisbie, W., Hummer, R. A., & Rogers, R. G. (2004). Nativity, duration of residence, and the health of Hispanic adults in the United States. *International Migration Review, 38*, 184–211.

Cintrón, J. A., Carter, M. M., & Sbrocco, T. (2005). *Ataques de nervios* in relation to anxiety sensitivity among island Puerto Ricans. *Culture, Medicine and Psychiatry, 29*, 415–431.

Cruz Fuentes, C. S., López Bello, L., Blas García, C., González Macías, L., & Chávez Balderas, R. A. (2005). Datos sobre la validez y confiabilidad de la Symptom Check List 90 (SCL 90) en una muestra de sujetos mexicanos. *Salud Mental, 28*(1), 72–81.

Demarest, J., & Allen, R. (2000). Body image: Gender, ethnic, and age differences. *The Journal of Social Psychology, 140*, 465–472.

Derogatis, L. R. (1994). *Manual for the symptom checklist 90-revised.* Minneapolis, MN: Pearson Assessments.

Derogatis, L. R. (2000). *Brief Symptom Inventory (BSI)-18: Administration, scoring, and procedures manual.* Minneapolis, MN: NCS Pearson.

Díaz, A., Jurado, M., Lucio, G. E., & Cuevas, M. (2003). Detection of treatment dropout in university students. *Psiquiatría, 19*, 1–9.

Escalona, R., Achilles, G., Waitzkin, H., & Yager, J. (2004). PTSD and somatization in women treated at a VA primary care clinic. *Psychosomatics, 45*, 291.

Escobar, J. I., Burnham, M. A., Karno, M., Forsythe, A., & Golding, J. M. (1987). Somatization in the community. *Archives of General Psychiatry, 44*, 713–718.

Escobar, J. I., Gara, M., Silver, R. C., Waitzkin, H., Holman, A., & Compton, W. (1998). Somatization disorder in primary care. *The British Journal of Psychiatry, 173*, 262–266.

Escobar, J. I., & Gureje, O. (2007). Influence of cultural and social factors on the epidemiology of idiopathic somatic complaints and syndromes. *Psychosomatic Medicine, 69*(9), 841–845.

Fallon, E., & Rozin, P. (1985). Sex differences in perceptions of desirable body shape. *Journal of Abnormal Psychology, 94*, 102–105.

Finch, B. K., Hammer, R. A., Reindl, M., & Vega, W. A. (2002). The validity of self-rated health among Latino(a)s. *American Journal of Epidemiology, 155*, 755–759.

Frazier, L. D., & Waid, L. D. (1999). Influences on anxiety in later life: The role of health status, health perceptions and health locus of control. *Aging & Mental Health, 3*, 213–220.

Garrido, M., & Velasquez, R. J. (2005). Interpretation of Latino/Latina MMPI-2 profiles: Review and application of empirical findings and cultural-linguistic considerations. In J. N. Butcher (Ed.), *MMPI-2: The practitioner's handbook* (pp. 477–504). Washington, DC: American Psychological Association.

Gibbons, P., Flores de Arévalo, H., & Mónico, M. (2004). Assessment of the factor structure and reliability of the 28 item version of the General Health Questionnaire (GHQ-28) in El Salvador. *International Journal of Clinical and Health Psychology, 4*, 389–398.

Gili, M., Ferrer, V., Roca, M., & Bernardo, M. (2000). Psychiatric disorders and medical comorbidity in a community epidemiological study. *Psicothema, 12*, 131–135.

Goldberg & Hillier, 1979. Goldberg, D.P., & Hillier, V. F. (1979). A scaled version of the General Health Questionnaire. Psychological Medicine, 9, 139–145.

Goldberg, P., & Williams, P. (1988). *A user's guide to the General Health Questionnaire.* Windsor, UK: NFER-Nelson.

Gureje, O., Simon, G. E., Ustun, T. B., & Goldberg, D. P. (1997). Somatization in cross-cultural perspective: A World Health Organization study in primary care. *The American Journal of Psychiatry, 154*, 989–995.

Hiller, W., & Janca, A. (2003). Assessment of somatoform disorders: A review of strategies and instruments. *Acta Neuropsychiatrica, 15*, 167–179.

Hinton, D. E., Chong, R., Pollack, M. H., Barlow, D. H., & McNally, R. J. (2008). *Ataque de nervios*: Relationship to anxiety sensitivity and dissociation predisposition. *Depression and Anxiety, 25*, 489–495.

Hinton, D. E., Hofmann, S. G., Rivera, E., Otto, M. W., & Pollack, M. H. (2011). Culturally adapted CBT (CA-CBT) for Latino women with treatment-resistant PTSD: A pilot study comparing CA-CBT to applied muscle relaxation. *Behaviour Research and Therapy, 49*, 275–280.

Hinton, D. E., Lewis-Fernández, R., & Pollack, M. H. (2009). A model of the generation of *ataque de nervios*: The role of fear of negative affect and fear of arousal symptoms. *CNS Neuroscience and Therapeutics, 15*, 264–275.

Interian, A., Allen, L. A., Gara, M. A., Escobar, J. I., & Díaz-Martínez, A. M. (2006). Somatic complaints in primary care: Further examining the validity of the Patient Health Questionnaire (PHQ-15). *Psychosomatics, 47*(5), 392–398. Retrieved from http://psy.psychiatryonline.org.

Interian, A., Guarnaccia, P. J., Vega, W. A., Gara, M. A., Like, R. C., Escobar, J. I., et al. (2005). The relationship between *ataque de nervios* and unexplained neurological symptoms: A preliminary analysis. *The Journal of Nervous and Mental Disease, 193*(1), 32–39.

Jackson, Y. (2006). *Encyclopedia of multicultural psychology*. Thousand Oaks, CA: Sage Publications, Inc.

Janca, A., Burke, J.D. Jr., Isaac M. et al. (1995) The World Health Organization Somatoform Disorders Schedule. A preliminary report on design and reliability. *European Psychiatry, 10*, 373–378.

Janca, A., Isaac, M., Costa, E., Silva, J.A. (1995). World Health Organization International Study of Somatoform Disorders -background and rationale. *European Journal of Psychiatry, 9*, 100–110.

Karno, M., Burnam, M. A., Escobar, J. I., Hough, R. L., & Eaton, W. W. (1983). Development of the Spanish-language version of the National Institute of Mental Health Diagnostic Interview Schedule. *Archives of General Psychiatry, 40*, 1183–1188.

Katerndahl, D. A., Amodei, N., Larme, A. C., & Palmer, R. (2002). Psychometric assessment of measures of psychological symptoms, functional status, life events, and context for low income Hispanic patients in a primary care setting. *Psychological Reports, 91*(3,Pt2), 1121–1128.

Kellner, R., Abbott, P., Winslow, W. W., & Pathak, D. (1987). Fears, beliefs, and attitudes in *DSM-III* hypochondriasis. *The Journal of Nervous and Mental Disease, 174*, 20–25.

Kessler, R. C., Nelson, C. B., McGonagle, K. A., Liu, J., Swartz, M., & Blazer, D. G. (1996). Comorbidity of DSM-III-R major depressive disorder in the general population: Results from the US National Comorbidity Survey. *The British Journal of Psychiatry, 30*(Suppl), 17–30.

Lázaro, C., Bosch, F., Torrubia, R., & Baños, J. E. (1994). The development of a Spanish questionnaire for assessing pain: Preliminary data concerning reliability and validity. *European Journal of Psychological Assessment, 10*, 145–151.

Lázaro, C., Caseras, X., Whizar-Lugo, V. M., Wenk, R., Baldioceda, F., Bernal, R., Ovalle, A., Torrubia, R., & Baños, J. E. (2001). Psychometric properties of a Spanish version of the McGill Pain Questionnaire in several Spanish-speaking countries. *The Clinical Journal of Pain, 17*(4), 365–374.

Lynch, D. J., McGrady, A., Nagel, R., & Zsembik, C. (1999). Somatization in family practice: Comparing 5 methods of classification. *Primary Care Companion: Journal of Clinical Psychiatry, 1*, 85–89.

Martínez, M. P., Belloch, A., & Botella, C. (1999). Somatosensory amplification in hypochondriasis and panic disorder. *Clinical Psychology & Psychotherapy, 6*, 46–53.

Masson, S. A. *Spanish (SCID-I and SCID-II)* 2011. Retrieved from the internet http://www.scid4.org/trans.html.

Mayville, S., Gipson, M., & Katz, R. (1998, April). *Body image rating scale.* Poster presented at the annual meeting of the Western Psychological Association, Albuquerque, NM.

Mayville, S., Katz, R. C., Gipson, M. T., & Cabral, K. (1999). Assessing the prevalence of body dysmorphic disorder in an ethnically diverse group of adolescents. *Journal of Child and Family Studies, 8*, 357–362.

Melzack, R. (1987). The short-form McGill Pain Questionnaire. *Pain, 30*(2), 191–197.

Minsky, S., Vega, W., Miskimen, T., Gara, M., & Escobar, J. (2003). Diagnostic patterns in Latino, African American, and European American psychiatric patients. *Archives of General Psychiatry, 60*, 637.

Molina, J. D., Andrade-Rosa, C., González-Parra, S., Blasco-Fonecilla, H., Real, M. A., & Pintor, C. (2006). The factor structure of the General Health Questionnaire (GHQ): A scaled version for general practice in Spain. *European Psychiatry, 21*, 478–486.

Mumford, D. B., Bavington, J. T., Bhatnagar, K. S., Hussain, Y., Mirza, S., & Naraghi, M. M. (1991). The Bradford Somatic Inventory: A multi-ethnic inventory of somatic symptoms reported by anxious and depressed patients in Britain and the Indo-Pakistan Subcontinent. *The British Journal of Psychiatry, 158*, 379–386.

Ortega, A. N., Rosenheck, R., Alegría, M., & Desai, R. A. (2000). Acculturation and the lifetime risk of psychiatric and substance use disorders among Hispanics. *The Journal of Nervous and Mental Disease, 188*(11), 728–735.

Otto, M. W., Pollack, M. H., Sachs, G. S., & Rosenbaum, J. F. (1992). Hypochondriacal concerns, anxiety sensitivity, and panic disorder. *Journal of Anxiety Disorders, 6*, 93–104.

Peterson, R. A., & Reiss, S. (1992). *Anxiety sensitivity index manual* (2nd ed.). Worthington, OH: International Diagnostic Systems.

Rissetti, F., Himmel, E., & González, H. A. (1996). Use of the MMPI-2 in Chile. In J. N. Butcher (Ed.), *International adaptations of the MMPI-2: Research and clinical applications* (pp. 221–251). Minneapolis, MN: University of Minnesota Press.

Robins, I. N., Helzer, J. E., Croughan, J., & Ratcliff, K. S. (1981). The NIMH Diagnostic Interview Schedule: Its history, characteristics and validity. *Archives of General Psychiatry, 38*, 381–389.

Rodríguez, B. F., Weisberg, R. B., Pagano, M. E., Machan, J. T., Culpepper, L., & Keller, M. B. (2004). Frequency and patterns of psychiatric comorbidity in a sample of primary care patients with anxiety disorders. *Comprehensive Psychiatry, 45*, 129–137.

Rubio-Stipec, M., Shrout, P. E., Bird, H., Canino, G., & Bravo, M. (1989). Symptom scales of the diagnostic interview schedule: Factor results in Hispanic and Anglo samples. *Psychological Assessment, 1*, 30–34.

Salgado de Snyder, V. N., Díaz-Pérez, Ma de J., & Ojeda, V. D. (2000). The prevalence of *nervios* and associated symptomatology among inhabitants of Mexican rural communities. *Culture, Medicine and Psychiatry, 24*, 453–470.

Sánchez-López, M. del P., & Dresch, V. (2008). The 12-item General Health Questionnaire (GHQ-12): Reliability, external validity and factor structure in the Spanish population. *Psicothema, 20*, 839–843.

Sandín, B., Chorot, P., & McNally, R. J. (1996). Validation of the Spanish version of the anxiety sensitivity index in a clinical sample. *Behaviour Research and Therapy, 34*, 283–290.

Sartorius, N., & Janca, A. (1996). Psychiatric assessment instruments developed by the World Health Organization. *Society of Psychiatry and Psychiatric Epidemiology, 31*, 55–69.

Scott, R. L., & Pampa, W. M. (2000). The MMPI-2 in Peru: A normative study. *Journal of Personality Assessment, 74*, 95–105.

Shrout, P. E., Alegría, M., Canino, G., Guarnaccia, P. J., Vega, W. A., & Cao, Z. (2008). Testing language effects in psychiatric epidemiological surveys with randomized experiments: Results from the national Latino and Asian American study. *American Journal of Epidemiology, 168*, 345–352.

Simon, G., Gater, R., Kisely, S., & Piccinelli, M. (1996). Somatic symptoms of distress: An international primary care study. *Psychosomatic Medicine, 58*, 481–488.

Spitzer, R. L., Kroenke, K., & Williams, J. B. (1999). Validation and utility of a self-report version of prime MD: the PHQ Primary Care Study (Primary Care Evaluation of Mental Disorders-Patient Health Questionnaire). *Journal of the American Medical Association, 282*, 1737–1744.

Sue, S., & Chu, J. Y. (2003). The mental health of ethnic minority groups: Challenges posed by the supplement to the Surgeon General's report on mental health. *Culture, Medicine and Psychiatry, 27*, 447–465.

U.S. Census Bureau. (2003). *Annual social and economic supplement. Current population survey*. Washington, DC: Author.

van de Vijver, F., & Hambleton, R. K. (1996). Translating tests: Some practical guidelines. *European Psychologist, 1*, 89–99.

Villaseñor, Y., & Waitzkin, H. (1999). Limitations of a structured psychiatric diagnostic instrument in assessing somatization among Latino patients in primary care. *Medical Care, 37*(7), 637–646.

Wing, J. K., Babor, T., Brugha, T., Burke, J., Cooper, J. E., Giel, R., et al. (1990). SCAN: Schedules for clinical assessment in neuropsychiatry. *Archives of General Psychiatry, 47*, 589–593.

Wittchen, H. U. (1994). Reliability and validity studies of the WHO-Composite International Diagnostic Interview (CIDI): A critical review. *Journal of Psychiatric Research, 28*, 57–84.

Wittchen, H. U., Robins, L. N., Cottler, L. B., Sartorius, N., Burke, J. D., Regier, D., & participants in the multicentre WHO/ADAMHA field trials. (1991). Cross-cultural feasibility, reliability and sources of variance of the Composite International Diagnostic Interview (CIDI). *The British Journal of Psychiatry, 159*, 645–653.

World Health Organization. (1993, June). *World Health Organization (WHO) international study of somatoform disorders: Study protocols and instruments*. Geneva, Switzerland: Author. Retrieved from the internet http://www.whqlibdoc.who.int/hq/1994/MNH_MND_94.1.pdf.

WHO, 1994. World Health Organization (WHO) (1994). Schedules for Clinical Assessment in Neuropsychiatry (SCAN). Washington, DC: American Psychiatric Press.

Zinke, J. L., Lam, C. S., Harden, R. N., & Fogg, L. (2010). Examining the cross-cultural validity of the English short-form McGill Pain Questionnaire: Using the matched moderated regression methodology. *The Clinical Journal of Pain, 26*, 153–162.

20 Assessing Developmental Learning and Communication Disorders in Hispanic Children: A Neuropsychological Perspective

Mónica Rosselli, Esmeralda Matute, and Alfredo Ardila

According to the *Etymology Dictionary* (2011), the term Hispanic refers to a group of people who trace their origins back to Spain (*Hispania*). In the USA, however, this word is used more generally to refer to people from Iberian or Latin American backgrounds who share common cultural elements, such as surnames, customs, and the Spanish language, which in most Hispanic countries is the official one, though some sectors of those populations may also speak a native language. Thus, it is not uncommon to find significant bilingual populations, for example, Spanish/Quechua or Spanish/Aymara in Peru and Bolivia, Spanish/Guaraní in Paraguay, and Spanish/Nahuatl in Mexico.

The USA is now the second largest Spanish-speaking country in the world, after Mexico (U.S. Census Bureau, State and County Quick Facts, 2011), as it is estimated that 18.7% of the American population is bilingual, and that Hispanics represent approximately 75% of this group (U.S. Census Bureau, 2004). This ethnic group is linguistically diverse, as some members speak Spanish or English almost exclusively (i.e., are virtually monolingual), while the majority speak both languages, though with varying degrees of fluency. In most cases, especially when children are descendants of first-generation immigrants, the primary household language is Spanish, with exposure to English coming in the school setting. There is an enormous variation in the level of proficiency in the two languages among Hispanic children, such that one of the first problems that researchers involved in clinical assessments of this group face consists in deciding which language to use. On some occasions, English is the preferred, or dominant, language, but in others it is Spanish; while often both are used to a similar extent. If the language selected is Spanish, the evaluator faces the additional difficulty of the many idiomatic variations that exist among Spanish speakers in terms of vocabulary, phonology, grammar, and even pragmatics, all of which can deeply affect the ecological validity of their assessments.

M. Rosselli, Ph.D. (✉)
Department of Psychology, Charles E. Schmidt College of Science, Florida Atlantic University, 3200 College Avenue, Davie, FL 33314, USA
e-mail: mrossell@fau.edu

E. Matute, Ph.D.
Neuroscience Institute, University of Guadalajara, Francisco de Quevedo 180, Guadalajara 44130, Mexico
e-mail: ematute@cencar.udg.mx

A. Ardila, Ph.D.
Department of Communication Sciences and Disorders, Florida International University, 11200 SW 8th Street, AHC3-431B, Miami, FL 33199, USA
e-mail: ardilaa@fiu.edu

L.T. Benuto (ed.), *Guide to Psychological Assessment with Hispanics*,
DOI 10.1007/978-1-4614-4412-1_20, © Springer Science+Business Media New York 2013

The Hispanic (and Latin American) population in the USA is growing rapidly; indeed, it is estimated that by the year 2050, one-fourth of all North Americans will be Hispanic, while with respect to the younger generations, it is expected that approximately one-third of all people under 19 years of age will be Hispanic by that year (U.S. Census Bureau, 2010).

With the increase in the number of Hispanic children and youths in the USA, schools can predict a corresponding rise in Hispanics with special needs, including individuals who suffer developmental disorders. This, in turn, will require assessment practices that are cross-culturally competent, which entails understanding Hispanic cultures and comprehending the attitudes and beliefs that go hand in hand with such testing. Furthermore, it will become increasingly important to have a broad knowledge of the tests that are available for use with Hispanic children.

Developmental learning and communication disabilities are relatively common disorders during childhood and adolescence. Often, reading, writing, mathematics, and language disorders are included in these two umbrella categories. Perhaps the most widely used classification system for learning and communication developmental disabilities is the one offered by the American Psychiatric Association in its *Diagnostic and Statistical Manual of Mental Disorders* (*DSM-IV-TR*) (APA, 2000), as for all cases of developmental disorders, the *DSM-IV*'s diagnostic criteria include the failure to perform adequately on "individually standardized measures" of reading accuracy or comprehension, mathematical ability, writing skills, and language related to disorders in reading, mathematics, writing, and communication, respectively. Performance on such tests may well be "substantially below that expected given a person's chronological age, measured intelligence, and age-appropriate education." Also, these criteria give strong weight to academic test scores, but fail to define more clearly the underlying cognitive difficulties. Despite such drawbacks, those disabilities are thought to be related to dysfunctions in the way that children perceive, process, organize, integrate, store, or retrieve information. Significantly, certain specific cognitive mechanisms underlying these learning disabilities have been identified. For example, children with reading disorders (dyslexia) frequently present metalinguistic disabilities, low vocabulary size, and defects in their phonological abilities, whereas children with mathematical disorders (dyscalculia) present some combination of primary deficits in the appreciation of magnitudes and working memory. These cognitive deficits can be identified through neuropsychological testing; therefore, including neuropsychological data in assessments of children with learning disorders provides supplementary cognitive information that may facilitate cognitive interventions. While the subgroups of learning difficulties have been classified on the basis of neuropsychological assessments, including low linguistic functioning, limited abstract thinking, low sequencers, and poor body awareness and control, most categorizations of these phenomena are still grounded on the presence of verbal *vs*. nonverbal problems.

This chapter analyzes variables related to the complex assessment of learning and communication disorders in Hispanic children, including characteristics of the Spanish language and the influence of bilingualism. It also reviews the instruments that are available in English and Spanish for carrying out assessments of these children.

Learning Disabilities in Hispanic/Latino Children

Linguistic factors can have an impact on the idiosyncrasies of childhood and developmental disorders. In particular, developmental disorders in both oral (dysphasia, developmental language disorder, or specific language impairment) and written language (dyslexia or reading disorder) are affected by the characteristics of the individual's language. Like every other language in the world, Spanish has particular phonological, lexical, and grammatical characteristics and a writing system also marked by distinctive features.

Due to the size of the Spanish-speaking population worldwide (approximately 500 million people; etymology dictionary), procedures for assessing developmental language impairments have never been unified, a reflection, at least in part, of the great diversity and heterogeneity that characterize the different Spanish-speaking nations (Ardila, 2009).

Several papers have examined the specific characteristics of oral and reading disorders in Spanish populations (e.g., Aguilar-Mediavilla, Sanz-Torrent, & Serra-Ravento, 2007; Anderson & Lockowit, 2009; Davies, Cuetos, & Glez-Seijas, 2007; Jackson-Maldonado, 2011; Jimenez Gonzalez & Hernandez Valle, 2000; Jiménez, Rodríguez, & Ramirez, 2009; Matute & Leal, 2003; Matute, Rosselli, & Ardila, 2010; Serrano & Deflor, 2008). As one might well expect, both commonalities and contrasts can be found among the difficulties described in oral and written languages between Spanish and other languages.

In children who speak Spanish – or other Latin-based languages – certain problems have been identified in relation to developmental language disorders (Bortilini, Caselli, Deevy, & Leonard, 2002; Jackson-Maldonado, 2011; Paradis, 2010). They include an increased use of verbs in the infinitive, a reduced frequency in the use of auxiliary verbs, shorter utterance length, and difficulties in noun-adjective agreement. Hence, it is likely that such difficulties arise from the specific grammatical features of those languages.

The prevalence of dyslexia varies in different languages as a result of the complexity (irregularity) of their respective writing systems (Lindgren, De Renzi, & Richman, 1985; Paulesu et al., 2001). Thus, for instance, studies have shown that dyslexia is less prevalent in Spanish than English (Matute et al., 2010), perhaps due to the transparent nature of the former's writing system. In fact, the transparency/opacity of writing systems has been proposed as a major variable affecting the level of difficulty in learning to read (e.g., Ziegle & Goswami, 2005). A transparent language is one in which there is a straightforward correspondence between phonemes and graphemes; Italian, Spanish, and Russian are examples of transparent languages. It has been estimated that reading skills develop more quickly in Spanish than English due to the differences between the respective orthography systems of these two languages (Goswami, 2002; Ziegle & Goswami, 2005).

However, there are reports indicating that the deficits in phonological processing that underlie dyslexia may also be observed in Spanish-speaking children, despite this language's shallow orthography. Although during the initial school years errors in reading precision and slowness in reading are observed in Spanish-speaking dyslexic children, in older ones, the sole distinguishing characteristic of dyslexia is a decrease in reading speed (Davies et al., 2007; Defior & Serrano, 2011; Goswami et al., 2010; Jimenez Gonzalez & Hernandez Valle, 2000; Jiménez et al., 2009; Matute & Leal, 2003; Serrano & Deflor, 2008).

Given that Hispanic children living in the USA are frequently bilingual, it is important to note that in bilinguals, dyslexia can affect reading ability differently in each language (Karanth, 1992). Furthermore, upon taking into account the transparency of the Spanish reading system that contrasts with the opacity of its English counterpart (Spencer, 2000), it is easy to understand that English is usually the language more acutely affected in Spanish/English bilingual children who experience difficulties in reading.

In addition to linguistic variables, environmental variables can also affect the development of cognitive skills (Molfese & Molfese, 2002; Samuelsson & Lundberg, 2003). Socioeconomic conditions vary greatly from one Spanish-speaking country to another. In Mexico, for example, 44% of the population lives below the poverty line (i.e., income below $2 USD/day), while in the USA, this percentage is only 12% (Wikipedia, 2011). In addition, there is great socioeconomic and educational disparity across ethnic groups in the USA. For example, Hispanic Americans frequently have lower SES and attain lower levels of education than Euro-Americans. For this reason, the number of books and amount of other reading materials may be quite limited in the homes of a significant number of

Hispanic children. Also, on average, students from low-SES settings have fewer opportunities to practice literacy and mathematics at the preschool level than children from more advantaged conditions (Roberts & Bryant, 2011).

Bilingualism and Learning Disorders

Assessing bilingual children represents a special challenge in neuropsychology. First, it is important to bear in mind that such children are often thought to suffer learning difficulties simply because their mastery of both of the languages to which they are exposed may be incomplete (Baker, 2000). Indeed, suspicions of learning impairments are a major reason for referrals to neuropsychological evaluation. Two types of potential misclassifications of bilingual children have been described (Genesee, Paradis, & Crago, 2004): (1) "mistaken identity": due to their slow progress in learning the second language, normally developing bilingual children may be placed in classrooms with pupils who require special education programs, and (2) "missed identity": the problems of bilingual, language-impaired children may easily be overlooked because their slow development is seen simply as a natural consequence of the task of learning a second language and the time required to master it. In both cases, diagnostic errors result from such inappropriate assessments of the child's language and cognitive abilities.

The knowledge of one or both of the languages that a particular bilingual child uses may have be narrower or broader, but insufficient knowledge of either language can result in defective communication, regardless of the specific language selected. Furthermore, comparisons of bilingual children clearly show that there is enormous heterogeneity in their respective degrees of bilingualism, and that specific patterns of bilingualism are dynamic phenomena that can change in accordance with such factors as time, increased schooling, new environmental conditions, etc.

Therefore, selecting the most appropriate language is a major concern when testing bilingual children. Obviously, testing children in the language in which they have lower proficiency will yield inaccurate measurements of both their language use and their general intellectual ability. An inappropriate selection of the testing language often occurs because there are no bilingual professional/technicians capable of carrying out neuropsychological testing in Spanish/English bilingual children. A second area that can prove problematic is the selection of the testing instruments to be used. In this sense, the relative scarcity of instruments developed specifically for evaluating Spanish/English bilingual children (e.g., Systematic Analysis of Language Transcripts, or SALT; Bilingual Spanish/English Version) is an unfortunate reality. Some batteries originally developed for monolingual Spanish children have been used with Spanish/English bilingual populations, for instance, the *Evaluación Neuropsicológica Infantil* (Matute, Rosselli, Ardila, & Ostrosky, 2007; Rosselli, Ardila, Navarrete, & Matute, 2010). The consequences of selecting an inadequate testing language include errors in estimates of participants' language ability *and* their wider intellectual level. Ideally, in any neuropsychological evaluation, children should be allowed to use their best language and cognitive resources. Bilingual subjects should thus be tested by a bilingual evaluator and should be given every opportunity to express themselves in both languages. Bilinguals perform significantly higher when the conditions established leave them free to use both languages than when testing is restricted to the dominant one.

Bilingual children with specific language impairments constitute a particular subtype of the general bilingual population. It is to be expected that in any subgroup of children – bilinguals or monolinguals – a certain percentage will manifest specific defects in language development (Tomblin et al., 1997), but this does not mean that bilingualism is the cause of their impairments. For some time now, clinicians have asked themselves whether bilingualism increases the percentage of children with specific language impairments, and whether using two languages intensifies the verbal difficulties that such population sectors may experience. During one period, the recommendation was that bilingualism be avoided at all cost in children with specific language impairments, but this approach is simply inapplicable when dealing with social bilingualism, because in those circumstances the child is unavoidably exposed to two languages, and so will necessarily achieve some degree of bilingualism. This is the type of situation seen, for instance, in Hispanic children living in Miami. Research carried out over the past decade has demonstrated that this popular belief (i.e., that bilingualism is inconvenient in children with specific language impairments) is, in fact, unfounded (Paradis, 2003). The truth is that those children will present language impairments in both languages, just as they would have presented in only one if they had been exposed to a monolingual environment. Indeed, bilingual children with specific language impairments do not acquire language more slowly than monolingual children with similar impairments. Moreover, despite their language difficulties, such bilingual children are capable of using grammatical code-switching (Gutiérrez-Clellen, Simon-Cereijido, & Leone, 2009).

Cognitive Assessment Tools for Hispanic Children

This section describes the tests that have been developed in various Spanish-speaking countries (including the USA) to evaluate cognitive strengths and deficits in developmental learning and communication disorders in Hispanic children. It begins with a description of tests developed in Spanish based on normative data from Spanish-speaking samples outside the USA, followed by an overview of tests that have been adapted for use in Spanish from earlier English versions using norms obtained from Hispanic children living in the USA and/or children in other Spanish-speaking countries. Table 20.1 lists the tests discussed in this section.

Tests Developed in Spanish and Normed Outside the USA

Neuropsychological Batteries

Evaluación Neuropsicológica Infantil – ENI (Child Neuropsychological Assessment) (Matute et al., 2007)

This battery was developed to assess Spanish-speaking children between 5 and 16 years of age. It includes nine neuropsychological domains: constructional abilities, memory (coding and delayed recall), sensory perception (visual, auditory, and tactile), oral language (repetition, expressive language, receptive language), metalinguistic awareness (awareness of phonemes, words, orthography), spatial abilities, attention, concept formation and reasoning, and executive functions. Descriptions of these tasks and examples of the items included are provided in Table 20.2.

The ENI also contains items that assess three academic areas, reading, writing, and arithmetic, and includes a self-administered questionnaire designed to be answered by the child's parents, or caregiver, which gathers personal data and the reasons for consultations. It also contains a structured questionnaire that inquires into the child's developmental and clinical history. Finally, this battery provides an assessment of soft neurological signs.

The original standardization of the ENI was based on a sample of 789 children (350 boys, 439 girls) from different socioeconomic levels in Manizales, a medium-sized city in Colombia, and two cities in Mexico: Guadalajara and Tijuana. It is important to note that Tijuana is right on the Mexico/US border and that Guadalajara is in the state of Jalisco, an area long characterized by a high rate of migration to the USA. Thus, a significant percentage of Hispanic children in the aforementioned standardization sample have roots in Jalisco (CONAPO, 2011), like many Mexican immigrants in the USA.

Table 20.1 Tests available in Spanish for the assessment of Hispanic children

Test name	Original language	Type of assessment	Country of norms	Age range (years)
Evaluación Neuropsicológica Infantil	Spanish	Neuropsychological battery: memory; language; perception; attention; constructional, spatial, conceptual, and executive functions	Mexico, Colombia, USA	6–16
NEUROPSI Atencion y Memoria	Spanish	Memory and attention battery	Mexico	6–85
CUMANIN	Spanish	Screening battery	Spain	3–6
ECOFÓN	Spanish	Phonological awareness	Mexico	7–11
LEE	Spanish	Reading and writing skills		
Batería-R	English	Intelligence index, cognitive abilities, and academic achievement	USA, Mexico, Puerto Rico, Costa Rica, Spain, Argentina, and Peru	2–90
WISC-IV	English	Intelligence IQ, perceptual reasoning index	USA, Mexico, Spain, and Argentina	6–16
Preschool language scale	English and Spanish	Comprehension and expression	USA	2–6
Expressive one-word picture vocabulary test – Spanish-bilingual	English and Spanish	Vocabulary	USA	4–12
Receptive one-word picture vocabulary test – Spanish-bilingual	English and Spanish	Receptive vocabulary	USA	4–12
ROCF	French	Constructional, visual perceptual integration, visuomotor	Mexico and Colombia	4–15

Various types of validity and reliability indexes are reported, and *inter-rater reliability* coefficients for those ENI subtests that require a degree of interpretation were calculated. They ranged from 0.858 for written narrative coherence to 0.987 for complex figure recovery. These high coefficients of inter-rater reliability indicate that the standardized instruction presented in the ENI manual assures a consistent scoring of tests across examiners. *Stability coefficients* were also considered, using a retesting method with an average retest interval of 7.8 months and an average coefficient of 0.508.

The *External Validity* of the ENI was difficult to obtain because there are so few neuropsychological batteries in Spanish. The *Content Validity* of some of the ENI subtests was probed using subtests from the WISC *Escala de Inteligencia Wechsler para Niños* (Wechsler, 1984) and the *Batería Woodcock Psicoeducativa en Español* (Woodcock, 1982). Correlations with the WISC subtests ranged from 0.54 to 0.69 (see the ENI manual for details). These rather low correlations are not unexpected because, in contrast to the WISC, the ENI is not an intelligence test and was not developed under the g-factor theoretical construct. Higher correlations (range: 0.65–0.72) were found between the memory and perceptual subtests of the ENI and the corresponding tasks in the *Batería* (Matute et al., 2007).

The ENI has been tested in diverse groups of children with neurodevelopmental disorders, such as dyslexia (De los Reyes Aragón et al., 2008), dyscalculia (Rosselli & Matute, 2005; Rosselli, Matute, Pinto, & Ardila, 2006), attention deficit hyperactivity disorder (ADHD, Ramos-Loyo, Michel Taracena, Sánchez-Loyo, Matute, & González-Garrido, 2011), 15q overgrowth syndrome (Gutiérrez-Franco et al., 2010), del(3) (p26) syndrome (Rivera, Domínguez, & Matute, 2006),

Table 20.2 Subtest description of the *Evaluación Neuropsicológica Infantil* (ENI)

Cognitive domain	Area	Subtests	Description	Item example	Scoring
1. Constructional abilities		Stick construction	Make 4 designs using toothpicks		Two points for each figure made correctly
	Graphic abilities	Copying simple figures	Copy 6 simple figures		Two points for each correct design
		Drawing a human figure	Draw a human figure by command		Total body parts (i.e., head + eyes + hair + …)
		Copying a complex figure	Copy a complex geometrical figure	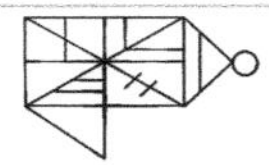	Total number of elements drawn correctly
2. Memory	Verbal coding	Word learning	9–12 word list (animals, fruits, and body parts) in four consecutive trials		Total number of words in the 4 trials
		Story recall	Recall of a story containing 15 story points		Number of story points recalled
	Visual coding	Figure learning	9–12 geometric figures in four consecutive trials	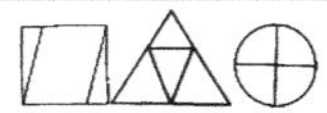	Total number of figures in the 4 trials
	Verbal 30-min delayed recall	Delayed word recall	Free recall	Words are recalled spontaneouly	Total number of words remembered for each recall condition
			Cue recall	Words are recalled by categories (animals, fruits, and body parts)	Total number of words remembered in the three categories
			Recognition	Recognition from a 18/24 word list	Number of words identified
		Delayed story recall	Story points recall of the story presented	Story points are recalled spontaneously	Number of story points recalled
	Visual 30-min delayed recall	Delayed figure recall	Free recall	Figures are recalled spontaneouly	Number of designs drawn spontaneously
			Cue recall	Recall of figures by categories (triangles, squares, and circles)	Total of figures drawn in the three categories
			Recognition	Recognition of figures from among 18/24 figures	Number of figures identified
		Delayed complex figure recall		Complex figure drawn spontaneously	Number of elements drawn

(continued)

Table 20.2 (continued)

Cognitive domain	Area	Subtests	Description	Item example	Scoring
3. Perceptual abilities	Tactile perception		Recognition of objects placed in each hand out of child's view	Common objects are placed in each hand one by one	Number of objects recognized by each hand
	Visual perception	Superimposed figures	Recognition of 3 overlapping figures	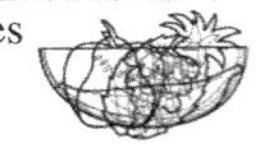	Number of objects identified in the 3 figures
		Blurry images	Recognition of photographs with increasing degrees of clarity	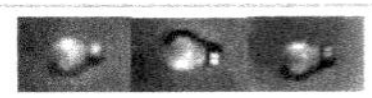	Two points are given when a picture is recognized at the lowest degree of clarity
		Visual closure	Identification of incomplete drawings		Number of drawings identified
		Facial expressions	Recognition of facial expressions		Number of facial expressions identified
		Object integration	Integrate parts to make up an object	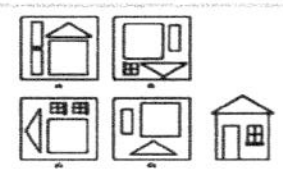	Number of correct answers
	Auditory perception	Musical notes	Same or different decision on recorded piano notes	8 pairs of notes are presented	Number of pairs identified as same or different
		Environmental sounds	Identification of environmental sounds presented on a tape recording	E.g., rooster, frog, train, etc.	Number of sounds identified correctly
		Phonemic perception	Decision on similarities and differences of pair of words	E.g., dado-dedo, quiso-guiso	Number of pairs correctly identified as same or different

4. Oral language	Repetition	Repetition	Eight syllables presented orally one by one	E.g., bi, pro, clin	Number of syllables repeated correctly
			Eight words presented orally one by one	E.g., sol, campana	Number of words repeated correctly
			Nonwords presented orally	E.g., bul, fampina	Number of nonwords repeated correctly
			Sentences presented orally		Number of words repeated correctly
	Expression	Naming	Name 15 objects that are presented on a card	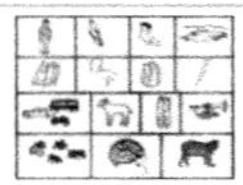	
		Narrative coherence	The examiner reads a story, and the child must retell it		Two measures are taken: coherence degree and utterance length
	Comprehension	Images pointing	Point on command to 15 images of objects		Number of objects pointed out correctly
		Oral commands	Follow oral commands given in increasing order of difficulty	E.g., señala un avión azul y un cohe verde	
		Discourse comprehension	Eight questions must be answered about a story presented previously		Number of correct answers
5. Metalinguistic awareness	Phonemic awareness	Phonemic blending	Forming words from oral spelling (using the sound of the letters)	E.g.,/s/a/l/	Number of words formed correctly
		Phoneme counting	Counting the phonemes in words	E.g., brinco	Number of correct answers
	Orthographic awareness	Spelling	Spelling of words		Number of words spelled correctly
	Word awareness	Word counting	Counting the words in sentences		Number of correct answers

(continued)

Table 20.2 (continued)

Cognitive domain	Area	Subtests	Description	Item example	Scoring
6. Spatial abilities	Spatial-verbal abilities	Right-left Comprehension	Understand oral commands that involve distinguishing right and left	A doll is moved on a map	Number of commands followed correctly
		Right-left expression	Describe right and left directions on a map	A doll is moved on a map	Number of commands uttered correctly
		Different angled pictures	Recognition of the angle from which drawings of 2 objects are seen (right, left, front, back, above)	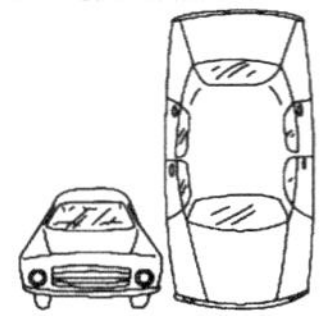	Number of correct answers
	Spatial-nonverbal abilities	Line orientation	Identification of a target line within a group of lines with different spatial orientation		Number of correct answers
		Coordinates	Trace a route using visual directions on a 6 x 6 array of one-cm squares		Number of lines placed correctly
7. Attention	Visual attention	Picture cancellation	Cancellation of large rabbits in an array of small and large ones		Number of rabbits cancelled correctly
		Letter cancellation (paradigm AX)	Select all the "X"s that are followed by the letter "A"		Number of letters cancelled correctly
	Auditory attention	Digits forward	Repetition of oral digits sets of 3–8 digits		Maximum number of digits repeated in a series
		Digits backward	Repeating digits backward, sets of 2–7		Maximum number of digits repeated backward in a series
8. Conceptual formation and reasoning		Verbal reasoning	Similarities between two concepts		Two points are given for each abstract response
		Matrices	Identification of a missing part on a logical array	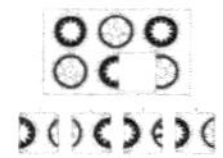	Number of correct answers
		Arithmetical problems	Word problems		Number of correct answers

9. Executive functions	Fluency	Verbal fluency	Semantic: recall animals and fruits	Number of words correctly uttered in each category
			Phonemic fluency: identify as many words as possible that begin with/m/	Number of correct words
		Graphic fluency	Graphic semantic: draw different meaningful figures	Number of correct designs
			Graphic non-semantic: draw geometric figures with four lines that connect 5 dots in a square in a 35-square matrix	Number of correct designs
	Cognitive flexibility	Sorting cards	Categorize sorting cards based on color, number, and form	Number of correct answers, errors, failure to maintain the set, categories completed, perseverance in responding
	Planning and organizing	Pyramid of Mexico	The child must use three blocks to reproduce the requested constructions as quickly as possible with the minimum number of moves	Total number of correct constructions, constructions performed with the minimum of moves, number of moves in the correct constructions

Table 20.3 Means and standard deviations for the ENI memory subsets in three groups of atypically developed children and a matched control

Subtest	Dyslexia		DD		DD and RD		Control	
	N=20		*N*=13		*N*=17		*N*=20	
	M	SD	*M*	SD	*M*	SD	*M*	SD
Digits forward	5.2	.95	5.3	1.2	5.0	1.2	5.7	.8
Digits backward	3.3	.73	3.6	.27	3.4	.3	5.1	.3
Sentence repetition	4.1	.58	4.9	.9	4.6	1.1	5.8	1.1
Word learning	30.5	6.83	32.5	3.7	30.9	5.1	32.5	4.1
Story recall	7.0	1.7	8.3	1.9	7.1	2.6	9.0	2.3
Naming	9.2	2.9	10.3	1.7	8.9	2.7	10.6	1.3
Visual memory	29.2	7.36	31.0	5.7	26.6	6.3	33.0	6.6

DD developmental dyscalculia, *DD* and *RD* developmental dyscalculia and reading disorder combined

girls with congenital adrenal hyperplasia (Inozemtseva, Matute, & Juárez, 2008), and children born to mothers with gestational diabetes (Bolaños, Ramírez, & Matute, 2007). Table 20.3 compares the performance on seven memory subtests of 20 children with dyslexia, 17 with dyscalculia and dyslexia, 13 with dyscalculia, and 40 controls (adapted from Rosselli, Matute, Pinto, et al., 2006; Medrano, Matute, & Zarabozo, 2007). In this case, all children involved were monolingual Mexicans.

In typical Spanish-speaking pediatric populations, multivariate analyses of the ENI subtests have been conducted that include examining the interaction between scores and sociodemographic variables (Matute et al., in press; Pinto-Dussán, Aguilar-Mejía, & Gómez-Rojas, 2010; Rosselli, Ardila, Matute, & Inozemtseva, 2009). Developmental age and gender patterns have been described in the general profile of the ENI (Ardila, Rosselli, Matute, & Inozemtseva, 2011) and for specific domains, such as memory, language (Inozemtseva et al., 2010), reading (Canet-Juric, Urquijo, Richards, & Burin, 2009; González Reyes, Matute, Inozemtseva, Guajardo-Cárdenas, & Rosselli, 2011; Matute et al., 2008; Rosselli, Matute, & Ardila, 2006), and executive functions (Ardila, Rosselli, Matute, & Guajardo, 2005; Matute, Rosselli, Ardila, & Morales, 2004).

More recently, additional normative data for the ENI were collected from 108 bilingual Hispanics living in the states of Florida and Colorado. That sample was divided into five age groups (5–6, 7–8, 9–10, 11–12, and 13–14 years). Analyses of these data showed that language ability scores were lower in the bilingual Hispanic children compared to the Mexican/Colombian children in the standardization sample, though nonverbal and executive functioning abilities were similar in the two groups. More specifically, differences were evident in expressive language measures and in the metalinguistic awareness domain (Rosselli et al., 2010). A post hoc comparison of this group with a monolingual Spanish-speaking group demonstrated differences in writing skills. Table 20.4 compares the means and standard deviations for this bilingual group (*N*=108) with a group of Mexican/Colombian (*N*=217) monolinguals selected from the standardization sample; the two groups were matched by age and educational level. No children in this sample suffered learning disabilities or neurological or psychiatric disorders. As these scores come from normally developed children from Mexico, Colombia, and the USA, they may prove useful in establishing the gold standard for comparisons of tests applied to monolingual Hispanic children with neurodevelopmental disabilities.

NEUROPSI *Atención y Memoria* (NEUROPSI Attention and Memory) (Ostrosky-Solis et al., 2003)
This test was designed to assess orientation, attention and concentration, immediate and delayed verbal and visual memory, and executive functions, including working memory. The norms were obtained from 950 individuals in Mexico City, aged 6–85. The sample included 199 typically

Table 20.4 Mean test scores and standard deviations (in parenthesis) in typically developed monolingual (Mono) and bilingual (Bi) groups in the different ENI subtests

		Age groups				
		5–6	7–8	9–10	11–12	13–14
Measures		*N*=44/17	*N*=39/24	*N*=40/25	*N*=48/22	*N*=46/13
Constructional abilities						
Stick construction (8)	Mono	2.2 (1.5)	4.1 (1.7)	5.0 (1.3)	5.5 (1.3)	5.4 (1.3)
	Bi	3.4 (1.8)	5.2 (1.9)	5.8 (1.5)	6.5 (1.4)	7.7 (0.4)
Copying simple figure (8)	Mono	5.4 (1.9)	7.7 (2.2)	8.5 (1.9)	9.4 (1.1)	10.0 (1.3)
	Bi	5.8 (2.3)	7.7 (2.3)	9.2 (1.8)	9.7 (2.1)	10.6 (1.9)
Drawing a human figure (20)	Mono	11.2 (1.9)	12.9 (2.9)	13.5 (2.0)	14.1 (2.5)	15.6 (2.5)
	Bi	11.3 (2.7)	13.5 (3.4)	14.0 (2.5)	15.0 (2.4)	15.8 (1.9)
Copying a complex figure (12/15)	Mono	6.5 (2.6)	10.4 (1.6)	12.4 (2.3)	13.7 (1.5)	14.3 (0.7)
	Bi	7.2 (2.9)	8.8 (2.1)	12.1 (2.7)	13.6 (1.7)	13.3 (1.8)
Verbal memory coding						
Word learn (36/48)	Mono	20.6 (6.1)	24.4 (4.8)	30.9 (6.7)	32.6 (6.8)	33.9 (6.1)
	Bi	17.5 (5.2)	20.6 (7.1)	27.5 (6.7)	28.6 (7.5)	31.3 (5.0)
Story recall (15)	Mono	4.2 (2.0)	7.4 (2.5)	8.4 (2.2)	8.9 (2.4)	9.9 (2.1)
	Bi	3.1 (1.9)	5.2 (2.6)	6.2 (2.7)	7.7 (3.1)	9.5 (1.4)
Visual memory coding						
Visual learn (36/48)	Mono	11.9 (5.0)	17.5 (7.5)	28.3 (8.9)	30.5 (10.9)	32.6 (8.3)
	Bi	11.9 (6.8)	18.2 (5.8)	27.0 (7.6)	29.4 (5.7)	32.5 (6.1)
Verbal memory recall						
Free recall (12)	Mono	4.8 (2.2)	6.6 (1.4)	9.0 (1.9)	9.2 (2.2)	9.7 (2.1)
	Bi	3.7 (2.1)	5.2 (2.7)	7.9 (2.6)	8.0 (3.0)	8.6 (1.7)
Cue recall (12)	Mono	4.6 (2.5)	6.5 (1.9)	8.7 (2.1)	9.2 (2.4)	10.0 (2.0)
	Bi	3.9 (2.2)	5.3 (1.9)	7.8 (2.6)	8.0 (2.9)	9.0 (1.3)
Recognition (18/24)	Mono	15.2 (3.0)	16.8 (1.3)	23.1 (1.2)	22.7 (2.0)	23.3 (1.4)
	Bi	14.8 (2.4)	16.9 (1.4)	22.0 (1.9)	21.9 (2.7)	22.3 (1.2)
Story recall (15)	Mono	3.4 (2.2)	6.5 (2.7)	8.3 (2.3)	8.6 (2.3)	9.1 (2.3)
	Bi	2.7 (1.7)	4.2 (2.4)	5.8 (2.5)	7.0 (3.7)	9.0 (2.4)
Visual memory recall						
Free recall (12)	Mono	3.3 (2.1)	6.1 (2.0)	9.0 (2.4)	9.4 (2.5)	9.8 (2.3)
	Bi	4.0 (2.1)	5.7 (1.7)	7.7 (2.3)	8.7 (2.2)	9.7 (2.4)
Cue recall (12)	Mono	3.8 (2.3)	6.0 (2.2)	9.3 (2.0)	9.6 (2.5)	10.0 (2.2)
	Bi	3.8 (2.4)	5.8 (1.9)	8.0 (3.7)	9.2 (1.5)	10.3 (1.8)
Recognition (18/24)	Mono	15.8 (2.7)	17.2 (1.6)	23.5 (1.4)	23.2 (1.6)	23.5 (1.1)
	Bi	16.4 (2.0)	18.2 (2.3)	23.0(1.7)	23.7 (0.6)	23.6 (0.6)
Complex figure (12/15)	Mono	3.5 (2.91)	8.1 (2.72)	9.1 (3.24)	10.8 (2.45)	11.7 (1.91)
	Bi	4.5 (3.40)	6.9 (3.21)	8.7 (2.96)	10.7 (2.65)	12.1 (2.06)
Visual perception						
Superimposed figures (16)	Mono	7.2 (2.4)	9.9 (2.7)	12.2 (1.8)	12.6 (1.8)	13.7 (1.9)
	Bi	7.9 (2.2)	10.0 (2.0)	11.0 (1.9)	12.1 (2.4)	14.0 (1.4)
Blurry images (10)	Mono	5.4 (1.4)	6.0 (1.3)	6.5 (1.2)	7.2 (1.5)	7.7 (1.5)
	Bi	6.4 (1.4)	6.7 (1.0)	8.0 (1.4)	7.5 (1.5)	8.0 (1.5)
Visual closure (8)	Mono	2.4 (1.4)	3.8 (1.4)	5.1 (1.5)	5.2 (1.5)	5.7 (1.6)
	Bi	3.5 (1.2)	4.6 (1.5)	4.9 (1.4)	5.9 (1.1)	6.0 (1.4)

(continued)

Table 20.4 (continued)

		Age groups				
		5–6	7–8	9–10	11–12	13–14
Measures		*N*=44/17	*N*=39/24	*N*=40/25	*N*=48/22	*N*=46/13
Facial expressions (8)	Mono	6.0 (1.3)	6.8 (1.1)	7.3 (0.8)	7.3 (0.9)	7.2 (0.9)
	Bi	6.1 (1.2)	6.7 (1.2)	7.0 (1.2)	7.1 (1.0)	7.3 (1.1)
Object integration (8)	Mono	2.5 (1.4)	3.6 (1.4)	4.1 (1.5)	4.7 (1.6)	4.6 (1.7)
	Bi	2.2 (1.3)	3.2 (2.0)	3.8 (1.9)	4.7 (1.3)	5.7 (1.4)
Auditory perception						
Musical notes (8)	Mono	4.4 (1.6)	4.3 (1.7)	5.1 (1.8)	5.7 (1.9)	5.9 (1.6)
	Bi	4.7 (2.3)	4.9 (1.6)	6.3 (1.6)	6.1 (1.8)	5.9 (1.8)
Environmental sounds (8)	Mono	4.3 (1.4)	5.2 (1.3)	6.0 (1.1)	6.1 (1.2)	6.5 (1.0)
	Bi	3.7 (1.5)	5.3 (1.2)	5.6 (1.3)	6.3 (0.8)	6.8 (1.1)
Phonemic perception (20)	Mono	17.3 (3.3)	18.8 (1.6)	19.3 (1.1)	19.3 (0.9)	19.5 (0.7)
	Bi	16.5 (4.3)	18.3 (1.5)	18.6 (1.2)	17.9 (4.4)	18.2 (3.7)
Oral language						
Repetition						
Syllables (8)	Mono	6.2 (1.6)	6.9 (1.1)	7.5 (0.8)	7.2 (1.0)	7.4 (0.8)
	Bi	6.4 (1.9)	7.2 (1.2)	7.3 (0.85)	7.5 (0.6)	7.6 (0.4)
Words (8)	Mono	6.2 (1.2)	6.9 (1.4)	7.3 (0.8)	7.1 (1.2)	7.3 (0.8)
	Bi	6.9 (0.9)	7.1 (1.0)	7.5 (0.8)	7.3 (1.1)	7.9 (0.2)
Nonwords (8)	Mono	6.2 (1.2)	6.9 (1.4)	7.3 (0.8)	7.1 (1.2)	7.3 (0.8)
	Bi	6.9 (0.9)	7.1 (1.0)	7.5 (0.8)	7.3 (1.1)	7.9 (0.2)
Sentences (8)	Mono	3.8 (1.1)	4.8 (1.2)	5.8 (1.2)	6.1 (1.0)	6.4 (1.2)
	Bi	3.3 (1.3)	3.6 (0.6)	4.3 (1.1)	4.5 (1.2)	6.5 (1.3)
Expression						
Naming (15)	Mono	7.0 (2.7)	8.8 (3.4)	11.1 (2.8)	11.7 (2.2)	12.3 (1.6)
	Bi	8.4 (2.4)	9.5 (3.1)	11.1 (2.7)	11.9 (1.7)	13.6 (1.1)
Narrative coherence (7)	Mono	1.6 (1.0)	3.1 (1.1)	4.2 (1.5)	4.7 (1.3)	5.1 (1.0)
	Bi	1.6 (1.3)	3.1 (2.4)	3.3 (1.4)	4.5 (2.0)	6.0 (1.0)
Utterance length ++	Mono	27.1 (27.4)	90.7 (76.4)	133.8 (61.6)	141.9 (59.6)	154.8 (2.2)
	Bi	20.9 (20.4)	57.1 (55.8)	66.2 (48.6)	87.3 (60.5)	116.8 (42.9)
Comprehension						
Image pointing (15)	Mono	13.5 (2.1)	14.5 (1.4)	15.0 (0.0)	14.9 (0.3)	14.9 (0.2)
	Bi	13.0 (1.8)	13.95 (1.1)	14.5 (0.8)	14.8 (0.4)	14.9 (0.2)
Following oral commands (10)	Mono	7.7 (1.5)	9.0 (0.9)	9.4 (0.6)	9.5 (0.6)	9.7 (0.4)
	Bi	7.9 (1.0)	8.3 (0.8)	9.0 (0.8)	9.5 (0.5)	9.9 (0.1)
Discourse comprehension (8)	Mono	3.1 (1.2)	4.2 (1.4)	5.3 (1.6)	5.7 (1.4)	6.4 (1.2)
	Bi	2.5 (1.6)	3.0 (1.5)	4.0 (1.0)	5.0 (2.0)	6.3 (1.1)
Metalinguistic awareness+						
Phonemic blending (8)	Mono	0.8 (1.6)	2.9 (2.5)	3.7 (2.3)	4.7 (2.5)	5.1 (2.3)
	Bi	2.3 (2.1)	3.3 (2.4)	4.3 (1.8)	4.5 (2.1)	5.7 (2.0)
Spelling ++ (8)	Mono	1.0 (1.7)	5.0 (1.6)	6.0 (1.5)	6.6 (1.1)	7.3 (0.7)
	Bi	2.2 (2.1)	3.4 (1.8)	4.5 (1.3)	5.3 (1.6)	6.8 (1.4)
Phoneme counting (8)	Mono	1.5 (2.3)	5.8 (1.8)	6.6 (1.4)	6.6 (1.6)	7.1(1.0)
	Bi	2.5 (2.6)	3.7 (3.0)	5.5 (2.4)	6.2 (2.3)	7.4 (1.6)
Word counting (8)	Mono	1.5 (2.1)	5.1 (2.1)	6.0 (1.7)	6.1 (1.4)	7.0 (1.0)
	Bi	1.8 (2.2)	4.0 (2.3)	5.4 (1.5)	6.5 (2.0)	7.1 (1.1)

(continued)

Table 20.4 (continued)

Measures		Age groups 5–6 N=44/17	7–8 N=39/24	9–10 N=40/25	11–12 N=48/22	13–14 N=46/13
Verbal spatial abilities						
Right-left comprehension (8)	Mono	4.2 (2.2)	6.1 (1.6)	6.7 (1.2)	6.5 (1.5)	6.7 (1.0)
	Bi	2.7 (1.6)	3.9 (2.5)	5.2 (1.8)	6.0 (1.9)	7.6 (0.4)
Right-left expression (8)	Mono	3.3 (2.0)	5.9 (1.8)	6.9 (1.0)	6.8 (1.6)	7.2 (0.6)
	Bi	2.5 (1.8)	3.9 (2.4)	5.3 (2.6)	6.2 (2.2)	7.9 (0.2)
Nonverbal spatial abilities						
Different angled pictures (8)	Mono	4.6 (2.4)	5.9 (2.1)	6.4 (2.3)	6.8 (1.6)	7.3 (1.6)
	Bi	4.0 (2.7)	5.0 (2.6)	6.6 (1.9)	6.8 (1.9)	7.6 (1.1)
Line orientation (8)	Mono	3.4 (2.2)	5.7 (1.4)	7.0 (1.3)	7.3 (0.9)	7.6 (0.6)
	Bi	2.4 (2.6)	5.8 (2.1)	6.0 (2.5)	7.2 (1.0)	7.9 (0.2)
Nonverbal attention						
Picture cancellation (44)	Mono	10.4 (4.7)	16.6 (5.5)	24.0 (6.5)	28.3 (8.4)	34.0 (6.9)
	Bi	12.7 (5.6)	17.2 (4.8)	23.2 (7.4)	26.6 (12.6)	32.4 (13.3)
Letter cancellation (82)	Mono	11.1 (5.6)	17.3 (6.2)	26.3 (7.1)	31.8 (7.0)	40.9 (8.2)
	Bi	10.8 (6.9)	19.1 (5.4)	31.4 (19.3)	29.8 (14.8)	38.9 (19.5)
Verbal attention						
Digits forward (8)	Mono	4.1 (1.3)	5.1 (0.9)	5.6 (1.1)	5.8 (0.9)	6.1 (1.1)
	Bi	3.7 (1.7)	3.8 (1.0)	4.0 (1.8)	4.6 (1.0)	5.0 (2.3)
Digits backward (7)	Mono	1.8 (1.2)	3.3 (0.9)	3.9 (0.9)	3.9 (0.9)	4.4 (1.3)
	Bi	2.3 (1.2)	2.8 (0.7)	3.3 (1.6)	3.5 (1.2)	3.7 (2.6)
Concept formation						
Similarities (16)	Mono	3.9 (2.2)	5.7 (2.5)	7.6 (2.1)	8.5 (2.5)	10.3 (2.3)
	Bi	3.4 (2.5)	5.3 (2.3)	6.6 (3.3)	9.1 (2.6)	12.1 (1.5)
Matrices (8)	Mono	1.9 (1.7)	3.5 (1.74)	4.6 (2.1)	5.2 (2.3)	5.6 (1.61)
	Bi	1.91 (1.3)	2.5 (1.9)	4.2 (2.7)	5.4 (2.0)	7.1 (0.8)
Arithmetical problems (8)	Mono	1.1 (1.0)	3.3 (1.2)	4.6 (1.4)	5.1 (1.3)	5.5 (1.1)
	Bi	0.8 (0.8)	2.9 (1.2)	4.0 (1.5)	5.0 (1.2)	7.7 (0.9)
Executive functioning						
Verbal fluency						
Semantic fluency (fruits)	Mono	7.0 (2.7)	9.3 (2.2)	11.4 (3.0)	13.2 (2.7)	14.5 (2.2)
	Bi	5.8 (2.4)	6.3 (2.8)	8.2 (2.7)	9.4 (2.3)	13.2 (2.9)
Semantic fluency (animals)	Mono	9.3 (3.5)	12.8 (4.2)	15.6 (3.9)	16.2 (4.4)	19.4 (3.7)
	Bi	9.0 (3.6)	10.4 (3.9)	13.0 (3.8)	13.9 (4.4)	17.0 (3.2)
Phonemic fluency	Mono	2.5 (2.2)	6.1 (3.1)	7.5 (3.3)	9.5 (2.8)	11.4 (3.0)
	Bi	3.7 (2.1)	4.8 (2.7)	5.9 (1.8)	8.1 (4.7)	10.0 (3.9)
Nonverbal fluency						
Graphic semantic fluency (35)	Mono	9.0 (3.5)	11.4 (4.5)	17.1 (6.2)	17.9 (6.7)	21.7 (5.9)
	Bi	7.6 (4.3)	10.0 (4.0)	10.2 (3.8)	12.5 (8.3)	15.5 (4.8)
Graphic non-semantic (35)	Mono	3.3 (2.8)	5.5 (3.9)	10.4 (5.4)	11.4 (5.5)	13.4 (5.8)
	Bi	3.0 (2.9)	5.6 (3.7)	6.8 (4.7)	10.1 (5.7)	10.8 (5.4)
Cognitive flexibility						
Card-sorting errors	Mono	25.8 (5.6)	16.9 (8.9)	15.0 (7.8)	11.4 (7.3)	11.0 (6.4)
	Bi	23.6 (7.2)	16.3 (7.7)	16.3 (10.6)	10.0 (6.3)	8.3 (3.5)

(continued)

Table 20.4 (continued)

		Age groups				
		5–6	7–8	9–10	11–12	13–14
Measures		*N*=44/17	*N*=39/24	*N*=40/25	*N*=48/22	*N*=46/13
Card-sorting categories	Mono	1.1 (0.7)	2.2 (0.9)	2.2 (0.8)	2.5 (0.7)	2.5 (0.5)
	Bi	1.6 (0.8)	2.1 (0.9)	1.9 (0.9)	2.7 (0.5)	2.8 (0.6)
Pyramid of Mexico correct	Mono	8.2 (2.7)	9.9 (2.3)	10.7 (0.6)	10.7 (0.5)	10.6 (0.6)
	Bi	8.2 (3.2)	9.3 (2.3)	10.0 (2.3)	10.6 (0.5)	10.7 (0.4)

Maximum scores when appropriate are indicated in parenthesis adjacent to the name of the corresponding measure

developed children divided into five age groups: 6–7, 8–9, 10–11, 12–13, and 14–15 years (Ostrosky-Solis et al., 2007). The manual includes standard scores for each age group – mean = 100, standard deviation of 15 – for three domains: (1) attention and executive function, (2) memory, and (3) attention and memory. Additionally, scaled scores are provided for each task with a mean of 10 and a standard deviation of 3. The profile that can be generated shows strong and weak areas. Table 20.5 presents the means and standard deviations for the different subtests of the NEUROPSI Attention and Memory battery across three age groups (adapted from Ostrosky-Solis et al., 2007). These data are especially useful when testing monolingual Spanish children.

Factor analysis revealed a total of 6 factors: Factor I included the category formation test, visual search, semantic and phonological verbal fluency, and design fluency; Factor II contained the following tasks: logic memory, immediate and delayed recall, immediate and delayed recall of verbal paired associates, and motor functions; Factor III involved word list encoding, word list free recall, word list cue recall, and a word list recognition trial; Factor IV utilized items that assess time orientation, digit detection, mental control, and immediate and delayed faces recall; Factor V employed digit forward span, digit backward span, spatial forward span, and spatial backward span; and, finally, Factor VI focused on place and person orientation. With regard to age effects on children, the age ranges at which the highest performance level was reached varied across factors: the first areas to mature were related to memory functions (Factors II and III), at 6–7 or 8–9 years. The highest performance for functions tested in Factors IV and V was attained at 10–11 years. The last area to reach the highest performance level was related to Factor I, at 14–15 years (Ostrosky-Solis et al., 2007).

The validity of the NEUROPSI Attention and Memory in screening for attention problems was tested in 61 6–10-year-old children previously diagnosed with ADHD (Flores, 2009). This attention and memory battery has also been used to assess children/adolescents with cerebral palsy ranging in age from 5 to 18. Significant variations in attention/memory scores appeared in children with different subtypes of cerebral palsy: those with the athetosis type performed better, followed by the mixed group and, finally, the spastic group, which underperformed the other two (Ramírez-Flores & Ostrosky-Solís, 2009).

Cuestionario de Madurez Neuropsicológica Infantil – CUMANIN (Child Neuropsychological Maturity Questionnaire – Portellano Pérez, Mateos Mateos, Martínez Arias, Tapia Pavón, & Granados García-Tenorio, 2000)

CUMANIN was developed to assess neuropsychological development in children aged 3–6.5 years (36–78 months). Tasks are grouped in 13 scales: gross and fine motor skills, repetition, expressive language, receptive language, spatial abilities, visuoperception, visual memory, rhythm, verbal fluency, attention, laterality (hand, eye, foot), reading, and spelling. The last two are used only with children over 61 months. CUMANIN was developed in Spain and normed on a sample of 803 Spanish children, 51% males and 49% females. Preliminary studies with special populations have been con-

Table 20.5 Means and (standard deviations) for the NEUROPSI Attention and Memory subsets in three groups of typically developed Mexican children (Maximum scores are in parenthesis)

		6–9	10–13	14–15
		n=68	*n*=80	*n*=25
Orientation	Time (4)	3.2(0.9)	3.2(0.9)	3.9(0.3)
	Place (2)	1.8(0.45)	2.0(0.15)	2.0(0.0)
	Person (1)	1(0.0)	1.0(0.0)	1.0(0.0)
Attention and concentrations	Digit forward span (9)	4.65(0.85)	5.5(0.9)	5.8(1.0)
	Digit detection (10)	5.1(1.6)	8.85(1.15)	9.3(0.9)
	Mental control (3)	1.05(1.3)	1.55(1.25)	1.7(1.3)
	Spatial forward span (9)	4.8(0.9)	5.5(0.9)	5.8(1.0)
	Visual search (24)	11.55(4.4)	15.65(3.85)	18.0(3.2)
Executive functions	Category formation test (25)	13.5(4.45)	16.5(4.2)	17.6(5.6)
	Semantic verbal fluency	14.6(4.5)	17.5(3.45)	19.7(4.3)
	Phonological verbal fluency	8.1(2.5)	11.35(3.25)	15.0(6.0)
	Design fluency (35)	8.0(3.6)	12.35(4.45)	15.7(6.3)
	Motor functions (20)	17.4(2.15)	18.65(1.25)	19.1(1.1)
	Stroop (time)	67.7(21.7)	47.35(11.95)	36.8(15.0)
	Stroop (correct)	32.4(4.15)	34.5(1.6)	35.1(1.6)
Working memory	Digit backward span (8)	3.05(0.8)	3.75(0.85)	3.9(0.9)
	Spatial backward span (8)	4.05(0.9)	5.0(0.85)	5.4(1.0)
Immediate memory	Word list (12)	5.95(1.55)	7.0(1.4)	7.5(1.6)
	Verbal paired associates (12)	7.05(2.25)	8.6(2.0)	8.2(1.5)
	Logical memory (16)	6.85(2.7)	9.1(2.15)	9.9(2.6)
	Rey-Osterreith Complex Figure (36)	27.8(5.0)	31.5(4.15)	34.4(2.8)
	Faces (4)	2.61(1.0)	3.45(0.8)	3.6(0.7)
Delayed memory	Word list (free recall) (12)	6.35(1.95)	7.85(1.8)	8.1(2.2)
	Word list (cued recall) (12)	6.35(1.8)	8.05(1.75)	8.2(1.9)
	Word list (recognition) (12)	9.7(1.8)	10.65(1.55)	10.2(2.2)
	Verbal paired associates (12)	8.45(2.45)	10.15(1.95)	10.2(1.8)
	Logical memory (16)	6.3(2.6)	8.6(2.1)	9.6(2.5)
	Rey-Osterreith Complex Figure (36)	16.9(5.9)	20.2(5.65)	24.6(5.4)
	Faces (2)	0.9(1.05)	1.3(1.0)	1.4(0.8)

ducted with low-birth-weight children, youngsters with Down's syndrome, and learning-disabled children, all in Spain. This instrument was also adapted for use in Chile with a sample of 243 infants aged 36–72 months at private and public educational institutions (Urzua, Ramos, Alday, & Alquinta, 2010) and a group of two hundred and sixty-one 43–78-month-old urban children in Lima, Peru (Guerrero Leiva, 2011).

Reading and Writing Tests

Evaluación de la conciencia fonológica (ECOFÓN – Phonological Awareness Assessment)

ECOFÓN was designed to assess phonological awareness in Spanish-speaking children aged 7–11 in the second to sixth grades of elementary school (Matute, Montiel, Hernández-Ramírez, & Gutiérrez-Bugarín, 2006). This test is sensitive to reading disabilities and involves three phonological levels and ten tasks. The syllabic awareness level comprises two tasks: syllabic segmentation in words and syllabic counting in words, whereas the intra-syllabic level includes two tasks: rhyme detection in words and initial phoneme detection in words. Finally, six tasks are included at the phonemic level: phoneme suppression within a word, phonemic decoding in words, phonemic decoding in nonwords, phoneme substitution in words, phoneme blending in words, and phonemic blending in nonwords.

This metalinguistic awareness test was standardized using a sample of 119 children (50% males) from private and public schools in Guadalajara, Mexico. All children had scores ≥50 on the Raven Matrices. Reliability was verified by analyzing test-retest stability. Norms are provided according to age or school grade. ECOFÓN has been shown to be useful in detecting children with reading difficulties, as the performances achieved on this battery and in reading tests correlated significantly (Montiel & Matute, 2007).

LEE. Test de Lectura y Escritura en Español (LEE. Spanish Reading and Writing Test) (Defior et al., 2006)

The aim of LEE is to assess reading and writing abilities in relation to expected achievement levels according to school grade. A qualitative analysis makes it possible to detect the error type, attain a precise diagnosis, and develop therapy programs. Nine tests are included: phonemic segmentation, reading letters, reading words, reading pseudowords, word and phrase comprehension, prosody, text comprehension, writing words, and writing pseudowords. Norms were obtained from a representative sample of 400 schoolchildren enrolled in the first to fourth grades of primary school at public and private institutions in Buenos Aires, Argentina, and Granada, Spain. Norms are provided separately for each country. Two types of validity were considered: (1) convergent and (2) discriminating. The test showed appropriate internal consistency according to the split and test-retest stability methods.

Tests Translated to Spanish and Normed Outside the USA

Test Batteries

Batería Woodcock-Muñoz-Revisada (Batería-R) (Woodcock & Munoz, 1998)

The Batería-R is the Spanish version of the Woodcock-Johnson Psychoeducational Battery-Revised (WJ-R) and is composed of the *Batería Woodcock-Munoz pruebas de habilidad cognitiva-revisada* (Batería-R COG – cognitive battery) and the *Batería Woodcock-Munoz pruebas de aprovechamiento-revisada* (Batería-R APR –achievement battery). The cognitive battery includes 21 memory tests for names, memory for sentences, visual matching, incomplete words, visual closure, picture vocabulary, analysis-synthesis, visual auditory learning, memory for words, cross out, sound blending, picture recognition, oral vocabulary, concept formation, delayed recall for names, delayed recall-visual-auditory learning, numbers reversed, sound patterns, spatial relations, listening comprehension, and verbal analogies. The achievement battery includes eighteen subtests: letter-word identification, passage comprehension, calculation, applied problems, dictation, writing samples, science, social studies, humanities, word attack, reading vocabulary, quantitative concepts, proofreading, writing fluency, punctuation, spelling, usage, and handwriting.

The cognitive items are clustered in 4 groups: broad cognitive ability, cognitive factors, scholastic aptitude, and oral language. Cognitive ability represents the Horn–Cattell theory of intelligence (g) and measures different domains of general intelligence, such as fluid reasoning (Gf), comprehensive knowledge (Gc), visual processing (Gv), auditory processing (Ga), processing speed (Gs), long-term retrieval (Glr), and, finally, short-term retrieval (Gsm). The achievement battery is clustered into basic and broad reading, reading comprehension, mathematical abilities (basic and reasoning), writing abilities, general knowledge, and skills. Woodcock and Munoz-Sandoval (2001) suggest that the Batería-R can provide useful information for neuropsychological assessments as it evaluates aspects of different processes, running from basic (i.e., attention) to more complex ones (i.e., reasoning to problem solving).

Norms are based on 6,359 English speakers aged 24 months to 90 years and subsequently recalibrated on 2,000 Spanish speakers in six countries (Mexico, Puerto Rico, Costa Rica, Spain, Argentina,

Peru) and five US states (Arizona, California, Florida, New York, Texas). Norms on the Batería-R were "equated" with the WJ-R through item response theory. Specifically, where subtest items had nonverbal content, norms from the WJ-R were used, whereas when subtests used verbal prompts and required verbal responses, items were translated from English to Spanish by native Spanish speakers from several countries, all of whom adopted an iterative cross-checking process until a consensus was reached. The new items that emerged in Spanish were integrated into the item difficulty rankings of the existing English items.

All items (those translated from English plus new items developed in Spanish) were recalibrated with a sample of 2,000 Spanish-speaking individuals. The external validity of the cognitive battery in English has shown a high correlation (0.64) with the WAIS-R Full-Scale IQ, though external validity with the WISC or any one of the Spanish versions of this intelligence test has been reported.

Both strengths and weaknesses have been observed in the Batería-R. The major strength is that it is one of the most comprehensive, adequately validated, and normed intelligence test available for use with Spanish speakers in several Latin America countries and the USA (Schrauf & Navarro, 2005). However, questions have been raised as to just how suitable the Batería-R norms (obtained largely outside the USA) are for Hispanic-American children, many of whom are better characterized as bilingual. The high number of verbal subtests compared to the low number of nonverbal tasks in the Batería-R is another limitation on the cognitive assessment of children with learning disabilities, especially those affected by visuospatial defects. The final weakness of this battery is the lack of validation of its nonverbal tests in the Spanish sample, which was based on the erroneous assumption that visuospatial and nonverbal tests are culturally and educationally fair or at least fairer than verbal tests, a supposition that has since been refuted (see Rosselli & Ardila, 2003 for a review).

Wechsler Intelligence Scale for Children (WISC-IV, Wechsler, 2004)

This battery aims to assess intellectual abilities in children and adolescents aged 6–16. It provides a full IQ score plus scores on four indexes: verbal comprehension, perceptual reasoning, working memory, and processing speed. Compared to the WISC-III, it places less emphasis on crystallized knowledge (Information is now a supplemental test to the full IQ score) by accentuating the contribution of fluid reasoning (matrix reasoning, picture concepts), working memory (letter-number sequencing), and processing speed (coding and symbol search). Whereas the WISC-IV FSIQ is comprised of subtests that encompass these four index scores, the earlier WISC-III FSIQ included only one measure of processing speed and one of working memory. Also, the WISC-IV maintains ten subtests from the WISC-III while adding five additional ones (picture concepts, letters and numbers, symbol search, word reasoning, cancellation). The WISC-FSIQ scores allow the evaluator to assign the child's scores to intellectual groups that range from very high (gifted) to very low (mentally retarded). Also, pattern analyses have helped clinicians characterize the cognitive profiles of children with developmental disorders.

The WISC-IV Spanish edition was translated from English and adapted to Spanish taking into consideration cultural issues. A panel of scholars that included native Spanish speakers worked together to minimize the dialectic and regional differences that exist among the various Hispanic nations that were to be included in the standardization sample. The resulting scores were equated to the WISC-IV norms so that Hispanic children could be measured and compared to English norms.

The original WISC-IV in Spanish was standardized on a nationally stratified sample of 851 children selected on the basis of data from the 2000 US Census to represent the Hispanic population in the USA in terms of age, sex, gender, parental education, parental race/ethnicity, geographic area, and disability status. The WISC-IV Spanish norms were developed on the basis of 500 of those individuals and obtained from the four major geographic regions identified in the aforementioned census (northeast, south, midwest, west). Puerto Rico was included in the South region. Norms for the

WISC-IV are available for Mexican (Wechsler, 2007), Argentinean (Wechsler, 2010), and Spanish (Wechsler, 2005) children. The Mexican standardization was performed on a sample of 1,234 children and adolescents from urban and rural areas in 11 states. The norms of the Argentinean WISC-IV are from a sample group based in Buenos Aires. Finally, the Spanish standardization (in Spain) was conducted with a sample of 1,590 children and adolescents representative of that country's population.

Few studies have addressed the use of the WISC-IV in learning disabilities. Recently, for example, De Clercq-Quaegebeur et al. (2010) found that the working memory index of the WISC-IV in French is deficient in tests on children with dyslexia compared to the other three indexes (verbal comprehension, perceptual reasoning, and processing speed). Those authors found marked deficiencies in the digit span and letter-number sequence tasks and, though to a lesser degree, also in coding. San Miguel Montes, Allen, Puente, and Neblina (2010), meanwhile, found that the WISC-IV Spanish letter-number sequencing subtest successfully distinguished 35 Puerto Rican children with neurological dysfunction – including nine with different types of learning disabilities – from a normal control group. These results suggest that the inclusion of a WM index in IQ tests has made this assessment tool more suitable for the evaluation of learning disabilities, although additional research is required.

Language

Preschool Language Scale – Fourth Edition Spanish – PLS-4 (Zimmerman, Steiner, & Pond, 2002)

The Preschool Language Scale – Fourth Edition Spanish – PLS-4 is an individually administered test used to identify monolingual or bilingual Spanish-speaking children who have a language disorder or delay (Zimmerman et al., 2002). It is not a translation of the English version; instead, the test tasks and sub-items of both versions were codeveloped. PLS-4 Spanish is composed of two scales: auditory comprehension and expressive communication, together with a total language score. The test includes three supplemental assessments: a language sample checklist, the articulation screener, and the caregiver questionnaire.

The sample was formed according to the Hispanic population as it is portrayed in the US Census. The PLS-4 Spanish standardization sample included 1,188 children (613 female, 575 male), aged 2 days to 6 years and 11 months. The caregiver's education level was used as an SES indicator. Four groups based on years of schooling were considered: (1) 0–11 years, (2) 12 years (diploma or GED), (3) 1–3 years of college or technical school, and (4) 4 years or more of college. The sample included children from different countries of origin according to the Spanish dialect spoken in their households; 81.2% were from Mexico. Also, 61 children in the sample reported previously identified developmental conditions or having received earlier diagnoses. Exposure to Spanish was also considered during sample selection. The reliability of PLS-4 Spanish was estimated using test-retest reliability, internal consistency, and inter-rater reliability.

Expressive One-Word Picture Vocabulary Test – Spanish-Bilingual Edition (Brownell, 2001a)

The Expressive One-Word Picture Vocabulary Test – Spanish-Bilingual Edition (EOWPVT-SBE) provides an assessment of an individual's combined Spanish and English speaking vocabulary. This test is individually administered. The standardization edition was applied to 1,150 bilingual individuals in testing conducted in 50 cities in 17 states across the USA. The demographic criteria for inclusion required potential subjects to speak at least some Spanish and be aged 4–12 years. Standard scores, confidence intervals, percentile ranks, and age equivalents are provided. Three types of validity were considered: (1) content validity, (2) criterion-related validity, and (3) construct validity. Standard scores from 105 children who had been identified as receiving special education or speech-language services were examined. Only the articulation disorder group showed no differences in performance when compared to the entire sample.

Table 20.6 Comparison of the performance of two groups of Latin American children on the ROCF

Colombian sample (Ardila & Rosselli, 2003)			Mexican sample (Galindo & Cortes, 2003)		
Age group	Copy	Immediate recall ratio	Age group	Copy	3-min recall ratio
5–6	14.5 (7.9)	8.4 (6.2) 57%	–	–	–
7–8	22.0 (8.8)	13.9 (7.3) 63%	8–9	17.6 (3.2)	10.6 (4.0) 60%
9–10	24.6 (6.1)	17.0 (6.3) 70%	10–12	21.4 (5.0)	12.0 (4.4) 56%
11–12	27.9 (4.7)	19.4 (5.2) 69%	13–15	22.9 (4.1)	14.3 (4.9) 62%

The ratio memory score equals memory/copy

Receptive One-Word Picture Vocabulary Test – Spanish-Bilingual Edition (Brownell, 2001b)

The Receptive One-Word Picture Vocabulary Test – Spanish-Bilingual Edition (ROWPVT-SBE) is also administered individually. It is intended for use with children who speak Spanish and English at varying levels of proficiency. The ROWPVT-SBE is an adaptation of the Receptive One-Word Picture Vocabulary Test (ROWPVT; Brownell, 2000). The EOWPVT-SBE and ROWPVT-SBE were co-normed. Standard scores, confidence intervals, percentile ranks, and age equivalents are all given. Three types of validity were considered: (1) content validity, (2) criterion-related validity, and (3) construct validity. Reliability was analyzed by considering internal consistency and temporal stability. As with the EOWPVT-SBE, the ROWPVT-SBE was also tested on four exceptional groups: (1) mentally retarded, (2) expressive/receptive language disorder, (3) learning disabled, and (4) articulation disorder. Only the latter group showed no differences when compared to a group of typical children.

Nonverbal Test with Norms for Spanish-Speaking Children

Rey-Osterrieth Complex Figure (ROCF)

This test is one of the most common neuropsychology instruments used to assess constructional abilities, visual perceptual organization, and visual memory. The test includes two complex figures: the standard complex figure with 18 perceptual units and a maximum score of 36 and a simpler complex figure that has only nine perceptual units and a maximum score of 18. The standard ROCF is commonly used with adults and children over 8, whereas the second is appropriate for younger children, ages 4–8 (Galindo & Cortes, 2003). Normative data for Spanish-speaking children are available for both types of tests.

Galindo and Cortes (2003) administered the standard ROCF to 2,250 Mexican children ranging in age from 8 to 15 years (50% females). The administration procedure was of the standard "copy everything you see on the card" type, with a 3-min immediate recall: "on this blank paper draw everything you can remember from the figure you just copied." Rosselli and Ardila (2003) followed a similar procedure to obtain norms from a sample of 233 Colombian children aged 5–12. No gender effects were seen. A summary of the results from these two studies appears in Table 20.6. The results from the Colombia sample are higher than those reported for the Mexican group, a finding that may be due to the fact that half of the Colombian sample came from a high SES group, whereas the Mexican sample was probably a more homogeneous mid-SES group. The means and standard deviations by age range and SES group are presented in Ardila and Rosselli (2003).

Norms for the Spanish population on the simpler version of ROCF are available in Rey (1997). Also, Galindo and Cortes (2003) provide norms for this ROCF for younger children in a sample of 750 Mexicans aged 4–8 years. The means for copying/memory the figure at ages 4, 5, 6, 7, and 8 are 5.8/3.63 (sd = 2.9/2.13), 8.6/6.4 (sd = 2.2/2.3), 9.9/7.2 (sd = 2.2/2.4), 11.3/8.2 (1.9/2.3), and 11.8/8.8 (sd = 1.7/2.2), respectively.

Recommendations

Neuropsychological assessment of Hispanic children with possible learning and communication disorders is complex and requires not just a solid background in the neurometrics of cognitive developmental disorders, but also an understanding of cross-cultural issues of assessment. Tests should be selected on the basis of the children's cultural background. Tests developed in Spanish are best employed to assess monolingual Hispanic children or those who recently immigrated to the USA but whose preferred language is still Spanish. Bilingual children should be assessed by a bilingual examiner, and responses in both languages should be accepted when calculating verbal scores; also, whenever available, norms determined for bilingual populations should be used. Tests in Spanish that are simple translations of earlier English instruments must be interpreted with great care, since the act of translating by no means rules out cultural bias (Table 20.7). Finally, it is important to note that Hispanic children with emerging bilingualism and blended cultural backgrounds are usually not included in norm samples and, therefore, tend not to be represented in most US standardizations.

Table 20.7 Other tests available in Spanish. Most of them are English translations

Global cognitive assessment
AMPE-F Aptitudes Mentales Primarias Equivalente. Secadas, F. (1989). Madrid: TEA Ediciones
BTI Batería TEA Inicial. García, J.E. Arribas, D. Uriel, E. J. (2006). Madrid: TEA Ediciones
DAS Escala de Aptitudes Diferenciadas Elliot (1990)
Escala de Alexander. ALEXANDER, W.P. (1978). Madrid: TEA Ediciones
K-ABC Batería de evaluación de Kaufman para niños. Kaufman, A. y Kaufman, N. (1997). Madrid: TEA Ediciones
MSCA Escalas McCarthy de Aptitudes y Psicomotricidad para niños. McCarthy, D. (1996). Madrid: TEA Ediciones
Intelligence
K-BIT Test breve de inteligencia de Kaufman, 4 a 90 años. Kaufman, A. y Kaufman N. (1990) Madrid: TEA Ediciones
TIG Test de inteligencia general (S. dominós) Formas 1 y 2 (10 y 14)C/U. Cordero, A. (1994) Madrid: Estudios TEA
Laterality
HPL Test de homogeneidad y preferencia lateral de 4–10 años. Gómez Castro, J. L. y Ortega López, M. J. Madrid: TEA Ediciones
Language
ITPA Test Illinois de aptitudes psicolingüísticas. Kirk S.A., McCarthy J.J., Kirk W.K. (1989) 2da. Edicion. Madrid: TEA Ediciones
BLOC, Batería del Lenguaje Objetivo y Criterial. Puyuelo, M., Wiig, E., Renom, J. y Solanas, A. (1997). Barcelona: Masson, S.A
CDI – Inventarios MacArthur-Bates del Desarrollo de Habilidades Comunicativas. Jackson-Maldonado D., Thal, D. J., Fenson, L., Marchman, V. A., Newton, T. et al., (2005). México: Manual Moderno
Attention
AGL, Atención Global Local. Blanca, M.J., Zalabardo, C., Rando,B., López-Montiel D., y Luna R. (2005). Madrid: TEA Ediciones
Escala de Connners. Conner, K. (1997) New York: Multi-Health Systems, Inc.
EDAH Evaluación del trastornos por déficit de atención con hiperactividad. Farré-Riba, A. y Narbona, J. (2003) Madrid: TEA Ediciones
Smith, A. (2002). *SDMT Test de símbolos y dígitos*. Madrid, España, TEA Ediciones S.A. (Spain norms)
Reading and writing
EDAF Evaluación de la discriminación auditiva y fonológica. Brancal, M., Ferrer, A., Alcantud, F. y Quiroga, M. (1998) Barcelona: Lebón
ECL Evaluación de la comprensión lectora de 6 a 9 años. Cruz, M. V. (1999) Madrid: TEA Ediciones
PROLEC Batería de Evaluación de los Procesos Lectores de los Niños de Educación Primaria. Cuetos, F., Rodríguez, B., y Ruano, E.(1996). Madrid, Spain: TEA Ediciones

(continued)

Table 20.7 (continued)

TALE Test de análisis de la lectoescritura. Cervera, M. y Toro, J. (1980). Madrid: Visor Libros
Learning
ACRA, Estrategias de Aprendizaje. Román, J.M. y Gallego S. (1994) Madrid: TEA Ediciones
TAVECI, Test de Aprendizaje Verbal España-Complutense Infantil. Benedet MJ, Alejandre M.A., y Pamos de la Hoz A. (2001) Madrid: TEA Ediciones
Razonamiento no verbal/Coordinación visomotora
Test Guestáltico Visomotor. Bender L. (1998) México: Paidós
Test de matrices progresivas. Infantil. Raven J.C. (1997) Buenos Aires: Paidós
Porteus, S.D. (2001). *Laberintos de Porteus*. Madrid, España, TEA Ediciones S.A. (Spain norms)
Smith, A. (2002). *SDMT Test de símbolos y dígitos*. Madrid, España, TEA Ediciones S.A. (Spain norms)
Memoria
MAI Memoria auditiva inmediata 7–13 años. Cordero A. (1997) Madrid: TEA Ediciones
MY Test de memoria nivel I, II, III 7–8 años 8–10 años 14–18 años. Yuste, C. (1994) 4ta. Edicion, Madrid: TEA Ediciones

References

Aguilar-Mediavilla, E., Sanz-Torrent, M., & Serra-Ravento, M. (2007). Influence of phonology on morpho-syntax in Romance languages in children with specific language impairment (SLI). *International Journal of Language & Communication Disorders, 42*, 325–347.

American Psychiatric Association. (2000). *Diagnostic and statistical manual of mental disorders* (text rev.). Washington, DC: Author.

Anderson, R., & Lockowit, A. (2009). How do children ascribe gender to nouns? A study of Spanish-speaking children with and without specific language impairment. *Clinical Linguistics & Phonetics, 23*, 489–506.

Ardila, A. (2009). Características de la Población Hispanohablante: Sociedad, Lengua y Cultura. *Glosas. Academia Norteamericana de la Lengua Española, 9*, 2–20.

Ardila, A., & Rosselli, M. (2003). Education effects on ROCF performance. In J. A. Knight & E. Kaplan (Eds.), *The handbook of Rey-Osterrieth complex figure usage: Clinical and research applications*. Lutz, FL: Psychological Assessment Resources.

Ardila, A., Rosselli, M., Matute, E., & Guajardo, S. (2005). The influence of parents' education on the development of their children's executive functions. *Developmental Neuropsychology, 28*, 539–560.

Ardila, A., Rosselli, M., Matute, E., & Inozemtseva, O. (2011). Gender differences in cognitive development. *Developmental Psychology, 47*(4), 984–990.

Baker, C. (2000). *The care and education of young bilinguals: An introduction for professionals*. Clevedon, UK: Multilingual Matters.

Bolaños, M. L., Ramírez, M. L., & Matute, E. (2007). Características neuropsicológicas de niños escolares nacidos de madres con diabetes gestacional. *Revista Neuropsicología, Neuropsiquiatría y Neurociencias, 7*(1–2), 107–123.

Bortilini, U., Caselli, M. C., Deevy, P., & Leonard, L. (2002). Specific language impairment in Italian: The first steps in the search for a clinical marker. *International Journal of Language & Communication Disorders, 37*, 77–93.

Brownell, R. (2000). *Receptive one-word picture vocabulary test* (3rd ed.). Novato, CA: Academic Therapy Publications.

Brownell, R. (2001a). *Expressive one-word picture vocabulary test – Spanish-bilingual version*. Novato, CA: Academic Therapy Publications.

Brownell, R. (2001b). *Receptive one-word picture vocabulary test – Spanish-bilingual edition*. Novato, CA: Academic Therapy Publications.

Canet-Juric, L., Urquijo, S., Richards, M. M., & Burin, D. (2009). Predictores cognitivos de niveles de comprensión lectora médiante análisis discriminante. *Journal of Psychological Research, 2*, 99–111.

CONAPO. (2011). www.conapo.gob.mx/index.php?option=com_content&view=article&id=324&Itemid=251. Accessed September 23, 2011.

Davies, R., Cuetos, F., & Glez-Seijas, R. M. (2007). Reading development and dyslexia in a transparent orthography: A survey of Spanish children. *Annals of Dyslexia, 57*, 179–198.

De Clercq-Quaegebeur, M., Casalis, S., Lemaitre, M. P., Bourgois, B., Getto, M., & Vallée, L. (2010). Neuropsychological profile on the WISC-IV of French children with dyslexia. *Journal of Learning Disabilities, 43*(6), 563–574.

De los Reyes Aragón, C., Lewis Harb, S., Mendoza Rebolledo, C., Neira Meza, D., León Jacobus, A., & Peña Ortiz, D. (2008). Estudio de prevalencia de dificultades de lectura en niños escolarizados de 7 años de Barranquilla (Colombia). *Psicología desde el Caribe, 22*, 37–49.

Defior, S., Fonseca, L., Gottheil, B., Aldrey, A., Rosa, G., Pujals, M., et al. (2006). *LEE. Test de Lectura y Escritura en Español*. Buenos Aires, Argentina: Paidós.

Defior, S. & Serrano, F. (2007). Dislexia en español: bases para su diagnóstico y tratamiento. In: E. Matute, S. Guajardo (Coords.). Dislexia: Definición e intervención en hispanohablantes. Guadalajara, México: Universidad de Guadalajara. pp. 73–88.

Etymology Dictionary. www.ethnologue.com. Accessed September 20, 2011.

Flores, L. (2009). Características de comorbilidad en los diferentes subtipos de trastorno por deficit de atención con hiperactividad. *Psicothema, 21*(1), 592–597.

Galindo, G., & Cortes, J. F. (2003). The ROCF and the complex figure for children in Spanish speaking populations. In J. A. Knight & E. Kaplan (Eds.), *The handbook of Rey-Osterrieth complex figure usage: Clinical and research applications*. Lutz, FL: Psychological Assessment Resources.

Genesee, F., Paradis, J., & Crago, M. B. (2004). *Dual language development and disorders: A handbook on bilingualism and second language learning*. Baltimore: Brookes.

González Reyes, A. L., Matute, E., Inozemtseva, O., Guajardo-Cárdenas, S., & Rosselli, M. (2011). Influencia de la edad en medidas usuales relacionadas con tareas de lectura en escolares hispanohablantes. *Revista de Neuropsicología, Neuropsiquiatría y Neurociencia, 11*(1), 51–65.

Goswami, U. (2002). Phonology, reading development, and dyslexia: A cross-linguistic perspective. *Annals of Dyslexia, 52*, 141–163.

Goswami, U., Wang, S., Cruz, A., Fosker, T., Mead, N., & Huss, M. (2010). Language-universal sensory deficits in developmental dyslexia: English, Spanish, and Chinese. *Journal of Cognitive Neuroscience, 23*, 325–337.

Guerrero Leiva, M. K. (2011) Adaptación del cuestionario de madurez neuropsicológica infantil-CUMANIN en una población urbana de Lima. *Revista Psicológica Herdiana*, 66–75. Retrieved July 12, 2012 from http://www.upch.edu.pe/fapsi/rph/NUMERO/Guerrero.pdf.

Gutiérrez-Clellen, V. F., Simon-Cereijido, G., & Leone, A. E. (2009). Code-switching in bilingual children with specific language impairment. *International Journal of Bilingualism, 13*, 91–109.

Gutiérrez-Franco, M. A., Madriaga-Campos, M. L., Vásquez-Velásquez, A. I., Matute, E., Guevara-Yañez, R., & Rivera, H. (2010). A girl with the 15q overgrowth syndrome and dup (15) (q24q26.3) including telomeric sequences. *The Korean Journal of Laboratory Medicine, 30*, 501–507.

Inozemtseva, O., Matute, E., González Reyes, A. L., Guajardo Cárdenas, S., Rosselli, M., & Ruíz Sánchez, E. A. (2010). Influencia de la edad en la ejecución de tareas relacionadas con el lenguaje en escolares. *Revista de Neuropsicología, Neuropsiquiatría y Neurociencia, 10*(1), 9–21.

Inozemtseva, O., Matute, E., & Juárez, J. (2008). Learning disabilities spectrum and sexual dimorphic abilities in congenital adrenal hyperplasic girls. *Child Neurology, 23*(8), 862–869.

Jackson-Maldonado, D. (2011). La identificación del trastorno específico de lenguaje en niño hispano-hablantes por medio de pruebas formales e informales. *Neuropsicología, Neuropsiquiatría y Neurociencias, 11*(1), 33–50.

Jimenez Gonzalez, J. E., & Hernandez Valle, I. (2000). Word identification and reading disorders in the Spanish language. *Journal of Learning Disabilities, 33*, 44–60.

Jiménez, J. E., Rodríguez, C., & Ramírez, G. (2009). Spanish developmental dyslexia: Prevalence, cognitive profile, and home literacy experiences. *Journal of Experimental Child Psychology, 103*, 167–185.

Karanth, P. (1992). Developmental dyslexia in bilingual-biliterates. *Reading and Writing, 4*, 297–306.

Lindgren, S. D., De Renzi, E., & Richman, L. C. (1985). Cross-national comparisons of developmental dyslexia in Italy and the United States. *Child Development, 56*, 1404–1417.

Matute, E., Chamorro, Y., Inozemtseva, O., Barrios, O., Rosselli, M., & Ardila, A. (2008). Efecto de la edad en una tarea de planificación y organización ('pirámide de México') en escolares. *Revista de Neurologia, 47*(2), 61–70.

Matute, E., & Leal, F. (2003). Los llamados "errores ortográficos" en niños hispanohablantes con problemas del aprendizaje de la lectoescritura. In *Introducción al estudio del español desde una perspectiva multidisciplinaria* (pp. 549–570). Guadalajara, México: Universidad de Guadalajara.

Matute, E., Montiel, T., Hernández-Ramírez, C., & Gutiérrez-Bugarín, M. (2006). *ECOFÓN Evaluación de la conciencia fonológica (Phonological awareness assessment)*. Guadalajara, México: Universidad de Guadalajara.

Matute, E., Montiel, T., Pinto, N., Rosselli, M., Ardila, A., & Zarabozo, D. (2012). Comparing cognitive performance in illiterate and literate children. *International Review of Education*, 1–19.

Matute, E., Rosselli, M., & Ardila, A. (2010). Trastorno de la lectura. In M. Rosselli, E. Matute, & A. Ardila (Eds.), *Neuropsicología del desarrollo infantil* (pp. 161–180). Mexico City, Mexico: Manual Moderno.

Matute, E., Rosselli, M., Ardila, A., & Morales, G. (2004). Verbal and nonverbal fluency in Spanish-speaking children. *Developmental Neuropsychology, 26*(2), 647–660.

Matute, E., Rosselli, M., Ardila, A., & Ostrosky, F. (2007). *ENI: Evaluación Neuropsicológica Infantil*. Mexico City, Mexico: Manual Moderno.

Medrano, A. P., Matute, E., Zarabozo. D. (2007). Características neuropsicológicas de niños hispanohablantes con trastorno de la lectura. In: E. Matute, S. Guajardo (Coords.). Dislexia: Definición e intervención en hispanohablantes. Guadalajara, México: Universidad de Guadalajara. pp. 73–88.

Molfese, V., & Molfese, D. (2002). Environmental and social influences on reading skills as indexed by brain and behavioral responses. *Annals of Dyslexia, 52*, 121–140.

Montiel, T., & Matute, E. (2007). Relación entre conciencia fonológica y aprendizaje de la lectura en escolares. *Revista Neuropsicología, Neuropsiquiatría y Neurociencias, 7*, 19–20.

Ostrosky-Solis, F., Gomez-Perez, M. E., Matute, E., Rosselli, M., Ardila, A., & Pineda, D. (2003). *Neuropsi Atención y Memoria (NEUROPSI attention and memory)*. Mexico City, Mexico: American Book Store S.A. de C.V.

Ostrosky-Solis, F., Gomez-Perez, E. M., Matute, E., Rosselli, M., Ardila, A., & Pineda, D. (2007). Neuropsi attention and memory: A neuropsychological test battery in Spanish with norms by age and educational level. *Applied Neuropsychology, 14*(3), 156–170.

Paradis, J. (2003). Bilingual children with specific language impairment: Theoretical and applied issues. *Applied PsychoLinguistics, 28*, 551–564.

Paradis, J. (2010). The interface between bilingual development and specific language impairment. *Applied PsychoLinguistics, 31*, 227–252.

Paulesu, E., Démonet, J. F., Fazio, F., McCrory, E., Chanoine, V., Brunswick, N., et al. (2001). Dyslexia: Cultural diversity and biological unity. *Science, 291*, 2165–2167.

Pinto-Dussán, M. C., Aguilar-Mejía, O. M., & Gómez-Rojas, J. D. (2010). Estrés psicológico como possible factor de riesgo prenatal para el desarrollo de dificultades cognoscitivas: Caracterización neuropsicológica de una muestra Colombiana. *Universitas Psychologica, 9*(3), 749–759.

Portellano Pérez, J. A., Mateos Mateos, R., Martínez Arias, R., Tapia Pavón, A., & Granados García-Tenorio, M. J. (2000). *Cuestionario de Madurez Neuropsicológica Infantil – CUMANIN*. Madrid, Spain: TEA Ediciones, S.A.

Ramírez-Flores, M., & Ostrosky-Solís, F. (2009). Atención y memoria en pacientes con parálisis cerebral infantil. *Revista Neuropsicología, Neuropsiquiatría y Neurociencias, 9*(1), 55–64.

Ramos-Loyo, J., Michel Taracena, A., Sánchez-Loyo, L. M., Matute, E., & González-Garrido, A. A. (2011). Relación entre el funcionamiento ejecutivo en pruebas neuropsicológicas y en el contexto social en niños con TDAH. *Revista de Neuropsicología, Neuropsiquiatría y Neurociencia, 11*(1), 1–16.

Rey, A. (1997). *Test de copia de una figura compleja. Adaptación Española*. Madrid, Spain: TEA.

Rivera, H., Domínguez, M. A., & Matute, E. (2006). Follow-up of an intelligent odd-mannered teenager with del(3)(p26). *Genetic Counseling, 17*(4), 401–405.

Roberts, G., & Bryant, D. (2011). Early mathematics achievement trajectories: English-language learner and native English-speaker estimates, using the early childhood longitudinal survey. *Developmental Psychology, 47*(4), 916–930.

Rosselli, M., & Ardila, A. (2003). The impact of culture and education on non-verbal neuropsychological measurements: A critical review. *Brain and Cognition, 52*, 326–333.

Rosselli, M., Ardila, A., Matute, E., & Inozemtseva, O. (2009). Gender differences and cognitive correlates of mathematical skills in school-aged children. *Child Neuropsychology, 15*, 216–231.

Rosselli, M., Ardila, A., Navarrete, G., & Matute, E. (2010). Performance of Spanish/English bilingual children on a Spanish-Language neuropsychological battery: Preliminary normative data. *Archives of Clinical Neuropsychology, 25*, 218–235.

Rosselli, M., & Matute, E. (2005). Neuropsychologie de la dyscalculie développementale: Derniers résultats de recherche en Amérique du Nord. In A. Van Hout & C. Meljac (Eds.), *Troubles du calcul et dyscalculies chez l'enfant* (pp. 175–185). Paris: Masson.

Rosselli, M., Matute, E., & Ardila, A. (2006). Predictores neuropsicológicos de la lectura en español. *Revista de Neurologia, 42*(4), 202–210.

Rosselli, M., Matute, E., Pinto, N., & Ardila, A. (2006). Memory abilities in children with subtypes of dyscalculia. *Developmental Neuropsychology, 30*(3), 801–818.

Samuelsson, S., & Lundberg, I. (2003). The impact of environmental factors on components of reading and dyslexia. *Annals of Dyslexia, 53*, 2001–2217.

San Miguel Montes, L. E., Allen, D. N., Puente, A. E., & Neblina, C. (2010). Validity of the WISC–IV Spanish for a clinically referred sample of Hispanic children. *Psychological Assessment, 22*, 465–469.

Schrauf, R. W., & Navarro, E. (2005). Using existing tests and scales in the field. *Field Methods, 17*, 373–393.

Serrano, F., & Deflor, D. (2008). Dyslexia speed problems in a transparent orthography. *Annals of Dyslexia, 58*, 81–95.

Spencer, K. (2000). Is English a dyslexic language? *Dyslexia, 6*(2), 152–162.

Tomblin, J. B., Records, N. L., Buckwalter, P., Zhang, X., Smith, E., & O'Brien, M. (1997). Prevalence of specific language impairment in kindergarten children. *Journal of Speech and Hearing Research, 40*(6), 1245–1260.

United States Census Bureau. (2004). *United States population*. Washington, DC: US Census Bureau.

United States Census Bureau. (2010). *United States population*. Washington, DC: US Census Bureau.

Urzua, A., Ramos, M., Alday, C., & Alquinta, A. (2010). Madurez neuropsicológica en preescolares: Propiedades psicométricas del test CUMANIN. *Terapia psicológica, 28*(1), 13–25.

U.S. Census Bureau, State. (2011). State and County QuickFacts. Retrieved, September 20, 2011, from http://quickfacts.census.gov/qfd/states/12000.html.

Wechsler, D. (1984). *WISC-RM Escala de inteligencia revisada para nivel escolar*. Mexico City, Mexico: Manual Moderno. (Adaptado y estandarizado para México por Gómez Palacio MM, Padilla ER, Roll S).

Wechsler, D. (2004). *WISC-IV, Escala de Inteligencia Wechsler para niños*. San Antonio, TX: Harcourt Assessment Inc.

Wechsler, D. (2005). *WISC-IV, Escala de Inteligencia Wechsler para niños Spanish version*. San Antonio, TX: Harcourt Assessment Inc.

Wechsler, D. (2007). *WISC-IV Escala Wechsler de inteligencia para niños-IV: Manual de aplicación* (G. Padilla Sierra, Trans.). Mexico City, Mexico: Editorial El Manual Moderno.

Wechsler, D. (2010). *Wechsler Intelligence Scale for Children 4ª ed. (WISC-IV). Manual Técnico de Interpretación* (M. E. Brenlla, A. Taborda, & C. Barbenza, Trans.). Buenos Aires, Argentina: Paidos. (Edic. Orig.: Harcourt Assessment)

Wikipedia. (2011). *Poverty in Mexico*. Retrieved September 21, 2011, from http://en.wikipedia.org/wiki/Poverty_in_Mexico

Woodcock, R. W. (1982). *Bateria Woodcock Psicoeducativa en Español*. Chicago: Riverside Publishing.

Woodcock, R. W., & Munoz, A. F. (1998). *Batería Woodcock-Muñoz-Revisada (Batería-R)*. Chicago: Riverside Publishing.

Woodcock, R. W., & Munoz-Sandoval, A. F. (2001). The Bateria-R in neuropsychological assessment. In M. O. Ponton & J. L. Carrion (Eds.), *Neuropsychology and the Hispanic patient*. Mahwah, NJ: LEA.

Ziegle, J. C., & Goswami, U. (2005). Reading acquisition, developmental dyslexia and skilled reading across languages: A psycholinguistic grain size theory. *Psychological Bulletin, 131*, 3–29.

Zimmerman, I. L., Steiner, V. G., & Pond, R. E. (2002). *Preschool language scale, Fourth edition Spanish*. San Antonio, TX: The Psychological Corporation.

School-Based Assessment with Latina/o Children and Adolescents

21

Manuel X. Zamarripa and Eunice Lerma

Latino children today comprise the largest student ethnic minority group in the USA (U.S. Census Bureau, 2010). In some of the largest cities in the country, Latina/o children and adolescents are the majority of the student population. Additionally, Latina/o immigrants (primarily Mexican) are no longer just settling in the southwestern states but are increasing in numbers in the US southern states (e.g., Georgia, Tennessee, Virginia) (Pew Hispanic, 2010). As Latina/o families increase in numbers in our schools, knowledge of cultural factors and accurate assessment procedures becomes ever important.

Currently, the Latina/o population in the USA is approximately 50.5 million, according to the Census Bureau (2010). 23.1% of this number is under the age of 18 (Pew Hispanic Center, 2011a, 2011b). In terms of school completion, the Latina/o dropout rate is at twice the national average (21%) (Pew Hispanic Center, 2011a, 2011b). One aspect contributing to this situation is a historical lack of full inclusion of Latina/os in the US educational system (San Miguel & Valencia, 1998). Also, Latina/os are considered a high-risk group for depression, anxiety, and substance abuse with higher rates of mental illness among US-born and long-term residents compared to Latina/o immigrants (Sue et al, 2003). This factor may become more relevant as Latino birth rate has surpassed immigration as the primary cause in the increase of Latina/os in the country (Pew Hispanic Center, 2011a, 2011b). More specifically, there is little research that informs us of whether and the extent to which stressors may affect Spanish and English speakers differently or how these may impact healthy development of these youth (Cervantes & Cordova, 2011).

Latina/o cultural values or behaviors may also impact both education and mental health in schools when these values and/or behaviors are not understood or recognized by school personnel. This may include school counselors, school psychologists, or any mental health professional working inside or within the school to conduct psychological and educational assessments. In fact, utilizing mainstream assessment instruments or procedures with Latina/o students without taking cultural considerations into account has been related to inaccurate assessment results (Acevedo-Polakovich et al., 2007).

M.X. Zamarripa, Ph.D. (✉)
Department of Counseling & Educational Psychology, Texas A&M-Corpus Christi,
6300 Ocean Drive, Corpus Christi, TX 78412, USA
e-mail: manuel.zamarripa@tamucc.edu

E. Lerma, Ph.D.
Department of Educational Psychology and Leadership Studies, 80 Fort Brown,
Brownsville, Texas 78520, USA
e-mail: aeunice_star@msn.com

L.T. Benuto (ed.), *Guide to Psychological Assessment with Hispanics*,
DOI 10.1007/978-1-4614-4412-1_21, © Springer Science+Business Media New York 2013

This chapter will review the research and literature currently available regarding the assessment of Latina/o students in a school context. This will necessarily include a discussion of cultural factors and values associated with this population as well as the cultural factors inherent in the assessment context and process. In a school context, it is often more appropriate to discuss the "identification" of students experiencing emotional or behavior disturbance or disorders. This identification is the end result of a compilation of assessment procedures including standardized tests, formal and informal interviews, checklists, and observations (McCloskey, Hess, & D'Amato, 2003). Behavioral checklists appear to lend themselves to a multicontext assessment as information can be gathered from the school and home environment. Discussion of tests that have been used specifically with Latina/o students and those commonly used that are available in Spanish will also be included.

Brief History and Overview of Latina/o US Education and Assessment

Although the necessity of taking culture into consideration in assessment and testing has been recognized by the profession (e.g., APA Guidelines on Multicultural Education, Training, Research, Practice, and Organizational Change for Psychologists, 2003; Reynolds and Kamphaus, 1992), the inappropriateness of "standard" tests and testing procedures was recognized as early as the 1930s. Psychologist George I. Sánchez was the first known scholar to publish research findings on the importance of incorporating culture in the assessment process for Latina/o children. In a series of three publications, Sánchez (1932a, 1932b, 1934a, 1934b) impressively outlined the shortcomings of testing procedures when applied to children of Mexican descent.

Sánchez devoted much of his work toward the constructive changes of the educational system and to equivalent educational opportunities for every individual. One of his earliest published works focused on the intelligence testing of Spanish-speaking children in the southwest USA. He challenged IQ test results that indicated Spanish-speaking children were inherently intellectually inferior to English-speaking White American children. He noted that environmental and linguistic factors were significantly related to IQ scores, and, thus, test results would not show accurate results when administered to bilingual children if these factors were not taken into consideration (Murillo, 1977).

He criticized those that disregarded the importance of these fundamental facts, especially bilingual and cultural factors, while interpreting intelligence testing results. Sánchez claimed that the facts of genetics and heredity were being distorted in order to champion the dominance of one "race" over another. His main argument was that instruments were only useful if they provided assistance to the increasing educational needs of the pupil, which could only be provided with proper interpretation (Murillo, 1977). The Binet test use of vocabulary for bilingual students was highly criticized by Sánchez. The English vocabulary was inappropriate for Spanish-speaking students and clearly an invalid as a measure of intelligence. Simple translation from English into Spanish was also an inaccurate way of assessing intelligence of bilingual children. In his recommendations, he suggested that the school system was to address the needs of the bilingual students (Murillo).

The research and practice of focusing specifically on Latina/o assessment has been sorely lacking since the work of Sanchez and has only increased over the last two decades (Puente & Puente, 2009). Currently, however, most psychological or behavioral tests published in the USA have no Spanish translations (Puente & Puente), and problems with norm-referenced instruments are known and well documented. Laing and Kamhi (2003) discuss what they view as the most common problems with norm-referenced tests: content bias, linguistic bias, and disproportionate representation in normative samples. Content bias reflects the notion that all children have been exposed to the same life experiences such as similar concepts and vocabulary. Linguistic bias can refer to a disparity between the language or dialect used by the examiner, the language or dialect used by the child, and the language or dialect that is expected in the child's responses.

The third problem of representative samples of diverse students for standardizing tests has also been recognized, and some test developers have made efforts to increase the amount of culturally diverse students in their normative sample. When Latina/os are included in standardization samples, test authors often use Census Bureau statistics. However, general best practice is to oversample under-represented populations (Puente & Puente, 2009). The issue of representative sampling is more than the inclusion of Latinos in general. Cuellar (1998) notes that most representative samples do not account for gender, ethnicity (Mexican, Puerto Rican, Cuban, etc.), geography, education, or acculturation. In fact, the area of most concern with attempts to include Latino representation is that Spanish-dominant bicultural participants with elementary level education, who make up a significant portion of Latina/os in the USA, rarely are included in norm groups. In fact, Schon, Shaftel, and Markhaml (2008, p. 169) have indicated, "Tests are devised by and represent mainstream middle-class culture. Students with little exposure to mainstream culture in the United States may do poorly on these types of assessments."

Cultural Considerations in the Assessment Process

Cultural considerations affect the assessment of Latina/o students on several levels. This may include not only the cultural values of the clients/students, but also cultural aspects of the examiner and cultural and social environment where the assessment takes place. Although the student population in our country is increasingly multicultural, school psychologists performing assessments on Latina/o students are overwhelmingly monocultural (Loe & Miranda, 2005). Further, it has been reported that psychologists express a lack of competence in determining client acculturation and in properly incorporating the clients' cultural characteristics in the assessment process (Fisher & Chambers, 2003). Even school psychologists (in fact an astounding 70% of school psychologists) who conduct bilingual psychoeducational assessments describe their training regarding bilingual assessment and cultural diversity as inadequate (Ochoa, Rivera, & Ford, 1997). The use of reliable and valid cultural indexes has been noted as necessary for accurate understanding of cultural factors' effects on test results (Cuellar, 1998). Examples of such indexes are those measuring linguistic abilities, ethnic identity (MEIM, Phinney, 1992), and acculturation (ARSMA-II, Cuellar, Arnold, & Maldonado, 1995).

Examiners should be prepared for Latina/o children, parents, and community to respond to them as members of the educational system with which there is a long history of interactions that were potentially marked by misunderstanding and mistrust (Schon et al., 2008). Examiners may need to make particular efforts to establish credibility before receiving the Latina/o member's trust and full cooperation. Ideally, examiners should have a history of visible involvement and participation in support of the community; this will be discussed a bit further in the section on school context below (Quintana, Castillo, & Zamarripa, 2000).

Language

When assessing Spanish-speaking or bilingual Latina/o students, the issue of language becomes a central consideration. As discussed earlier with Sanchez' (1932a) groundbreaking research, it is now understood in the field that assessing a Spanish-speaking in English brings into question the validity of test results and any subsequent interpretation of such results (Schon et al., 2008). In fact, the errors on the test are more likely an indication of the degree to which the child understands English. For students who are bilingual, the Spanish versions of some cognitive tests (e.g., WISC-IV Spanish, Wechsler, 2005; Bateria III Woodcock-Munoz, Muoz-Sandoval et al., 2007) are normed on Spanish-speaking students and thus may not be a comparable norming group. A bilingual framework is not the same as a monolingual Spanish-speaking framework (Cuellar, 1998; Schon et al., 2008).

Additionally, Spanish-speaking students learning English in US schools may exhibit two different types of language proficiency (Cummins, 1984). Basic interpersonal communication skills (BICS) have to do with being able to converse in social settings, most often in informal situations, where language and its meaning can be gathered from the particular situation context. Cognitive academic language proficiency (CALP) refers to the language skills of being able to comprehend academic language and concepts. Collier (1989) reported that students may be adept at BICS within 2 years while CALP develops in 5–7 years. Thus, assessing test readiness in a particular language must go beyond the child or adolescent being able to converse with the examiner in English. The use of several methods to determine the language of assessment is necessary. This may include a formal instrument such as the Woodcock-Munoz Language Survey-Revised (Woodcock & Muñoz-Sandoval, 2005) as well reviewing the child's schools work and teacher and parent interviews in both school and home environments.

Familismo

In addition to the issue of language in the assessment of Latina/o students, there are at least two other cultural characteristics mental health professionals should be aware of when testing and interpreting the results of such tests with this school population. The cultural orientation values of familismo and personalism are variables that will often impact the assessment process. Zayas (1992) describes familismo as a sense of obligation among family members with a responsibility to care for all members, especially elderly and children. It can also be defined as a sense of obligation to and connectedness with one's immediate family. Extended family network such as grandparents, aunts, uncles, cousins, and godparents are also part of the person's obligation and connectedness (Unger et al., 2002). This may necessitate that the examiner include more than just the parents when obtaining information about the child who may be able to provide a more holistic picture of the child's behaviors and emotions (Quintana et al., 2000). Latina/o family relationships often play a significant role in the social and cognitive performance of Latina/o youth and children (Belsky & MacKinnon, 1994) and thus can affect the assessment process.

Personalismo

Personalismo refers to Latina/os' desire to form relationships in a warm and emotional manner. It also refers to behaviors and actions that demonstrate a direct interest in and concern for others. This significance is congruent with values inherent in psychotherapy and has been identified as a value in the Latino/a culture that merits consideration in the assessment (Cuellar, Arnold, & Gonzalez, 1995; Santiago-Rivera, Arredondo, & Gallardo-Cooper, 2002). Zayas, Evans, Mejia, and Rodriguez (1997) encouraged counselors (and by implication, psychologists and other mental health professionals) to incorporate a personal style of relating to others, specifically behaviors that promote personal relationships. It is important to build a sense of personal closeness with Latina/o student examinees.

Cultural Context of the School

Cultural context of the school setting is an important consideration while conducting school-based psychological assessments. Bias occurs in the schools as in any other institution; this is why examiners must evaluate the degree to which this bias affects a student's experience in the school environment. Cultural differences between school environments and Latina/o students may be a difficulty in the assessment process. US culture, in general, is often less tolerant of "undercontrolled" behavioral problems when compared to other cultures. Schools are a reflection of US societal values, and, thus, the examiner should be aware of the potential cultural conflict between school norms and those of the Latina/o community (Quintana et al., 2000). In fact, some parents may consciously or unconsciously react to what may be interpreted as pressure to conform to school cultural norms by not cooperating in various ways with the school system. Adolescents in particular may respond behaviorally, making concerted efforts to show their solidarity with their cultural background by actively retaining those cultural and linguistic differences that more distinguish them from the dominant school culture and populations (Davidson, 1996). This may reach the extent of displaying noncompliant behavior with school rules or policies.

Acculturation and Acculturative Stress

Acculturation refers to changes in cultural patterns, such as values and behaviors that are a result of contact between two distinct cultures (Berry, Trimble, & Olmedo, 1986; Gordon, 1978). When an individual engages in the process of acculturation within a host culture distinct from his or her own, the tension experienced is known as acculturative stress (Berry & Kim, 1988). Acculturative stress, although related to other types of stress, appears to be distinct source of stress in the lives of Latina/o children (Suarez-Morales, Dillon, & Szapocznik, 2007).

Suarez-Morales et al. (2007) have indicated that US-born Latina/o children reported higher levels of stress relating to perceived discrimination than their foreign-born peers. In addition, Gil, Vega, and Dima (1994) found that US-born Latina/o adolescents who were more unacculturated were more likely to internalize negative self-images and a minority status. Thus, US-born students and immigrant students may have their distinct experiences of acculturative stress.

As Latina/o children and adolescents experience the acculturative process, acculturative stress may result from issues of language conflict, perceived discrimination, and deciding whether to adhere to protective behaviors or values that are culturally prescribed (e.g., familismo, cultural pride) (Vega, Zimmerman, Gil, Warheir, & Apospori, 1993). The negative effects of acculturative stress can most readily be seen in relation to decreases in self-esteem and increases in acting out behavior, although it is also suggested to indirectly affect academic performance as well (Schwartz, Zamboanga, & Jarvis, 2007). However, these difficulties due to acculturative stress may not be interpreted through the majority of the standard assessment instruments (Fouad & Arredondo, 2007).

O'Bryon and Rogers (2010) study of bilingual school psychologists found that when assessing students in the process of learning English, 84.1% assess acculturation, 11.6% do not, and 4.3% did not respond. The majority of the respondents (85%) reported using interviews to assess acculturation, while 41.3% used questionnaires, 32.9% used other instruments (e.g., observations, record review), and 55% used multiple methods (O'Bryon & Rogers). It is crucial for all examiners to assess the Latina/o examinee's level and degree of acculturation as part of any assessment procedure where academic and psychological decisions will result. The most widely used instrument with Latina/os to assess acculturation is the ARSMA-II (Cuellar, Arnold, & Maldonado, 1995). It measures both European American and Mexican American orientations on separate subscales that result in several possible, multidimensional acculturative types (e.g., integrated, separated, assimilated, and marginalized). Both cultural orientation subscales have internal reliabilities of .86 and .88, respectively. Construct validity was demonstrated with a sample of 379 Mexican Americans from representing various generational status (i.e., 1–5).

The Assessment Context and Process

As mentioned, school norms and climate can be crucial players in the assessment process for this population. In particular, power relationships in the school must be incorporated as data regarding the overall assessment given that Latina/o students will be referred for testing via these processes (Castillo, Quintana, & Zamarripa, 2000). This highlights the need for examiners to be aware of the underlying assumptions that may initial the assessment process. More specifically to the actual assessment, competency regarding appropriate test-taking behavior is crucial. For example, additional time may be required to develop the appropriate rapport with a Latina/o examinee in order for assessment results to be accurate (Quintana et al., 2000).

Castillo et al. (2000) recommend that evaluators consider the impact of the relationship between the Latina/o community and the school or the conceptualization of the behavior problem of the child, the assessment process, and the motivation to seek treatment.

Additionally, a thorough psychosocial interview conducted prior to selecting and implementing assessment procedures is foundational, as this information will necessarily guide the selection of appropriate measures and interpreting assessment results (Acevedo-Polakovich et al., 2007).

Common Tests in School Assessment

The remainder of this chapter will focus on the most commonly used tests and procedures in school-based assessments. Given the increasing Latina/o population, the continuously revised editions of many instruments, and the importance of reporting the most recent research available, there was a concerted effort to include empirical studies not more than 10–15 years old. Attempts were made to include studies focusing or prominently featuring Latina/o children and adolescents. For some, no studies with school-aged Latina/os currently exist, however, based on available information recommendations are made regarding use with Latina/o students. Finally, those instruments translated in Spanish were included and discussed (Table 21.1).

Cognitive Assessments

WISC-IV (Wechsler, 2003)

The WISC-IV is an individually administered intelligence test designed for examinees aged 6 years 0 months to 16 years 11 months and is the most commonly used intelligence test for children (San Miguel Montes, Allen, Puente, & Neblina, 2010). In particular, the English versions of the Wechsler Scales are most commonly used with culturally and linguistically diverse students (McCloskey & Athanasiou, 2000). As stated earlier, it is important to take caution with test interpretation as results may be more indicative of lack of English language proficiency rather than cognitive or academic performance (Schon et al., 2008).

The standardization sample (2,200) was guided by the 2000 Census data in its inclusion of examinees in terms of age, gender, race, ethnicity, parent education level, and four geographical regions.

Table 21.1 Common tests used with Hispanic children in schools

Test name	Spanish version available	Spanish version test name	Assessment category	Age range (years)
WISC-IV	Yes	N/A	Cognitive	6–16.11
Woodcock-Johnson III	Yes	Batería III Woodcock-Muñoz	Cognitive and educational achievement	2–90
Achenbach System of Empirically Based Assessment	Yes (several versions)	N/A	Rating scales – behavior and emotion	1.5–5; 6–18
Behavior Assessment System for Children – Parent Report System (BASC)	Yes	El Sistema	Rating scales – behavior and emotion	2–18
Schedule for Affective Disorders and Schizophrenia for School-Age Children (K-SADS)	No	N/A	Clinical interview	6–18

Coefficients for subtest coefficients range from .70s or .80s, with index coefficients between .84 and .95. The FSIQ reliability coefficient was at or above .91 for each age group. The WISC-IV was tested with an oversample of African Americans and Latina/os; however, there is little detail reported regarding item bias related to comparison groups (ethnic, gender, and special populations) and sample sizes (Maller, 2003).

Although the WISC-IV is arguably the most widely used English intelligence tested, there is a lack of empirical research focused on determining the strengths and limitations of utilizing this test with Latina/o children and adolescents in a school setting. The norm sample does have some oversampling of Latina/os, and the psychometric properties are strong, overall. Still, more research is needed that specifically focuses on Latina/o children. Until that time, the results of this assessment can reasonably be accepted by examiners; however, any and all cultural data that is gathered must be taken into account when interpreting test results.

WISC-IV Spanish Edition (Wechsler, 2005)

Relative to the discussion earlier regarding acculturation, the WISC-IV Spanish edition is designed to be used with children who are currently in the process of learning English and consequently is most appropriate for Spanish-speaking children in the US educational system. This is intended as a translation of the English WISC-IV and, thus, is not a distinct test itself. Exploratory and confirmatory factor analysis for the core and supplemental subtests was found to be consistent with that of the WISC-IV (Wechsler, 2005).

The WISC-IV Spanish reliability sample (500) was stratified by parent education level based on the 2001 US Census. In order to attempt to best represent the diversity of Latina/os participants were grouped according to parents countries/region of origin which included Mexico, Cuba, Puerto Rico, Central/South America, and the Dominican Republic. Given this representation, the Spanish manual does not include how or if there were attempts to address cultural validity (Clinton, 2007).

Empirical studies focusing on the use of the WISC-IV Spanish edition with Latina/o students are severely limited. Oakland and Harris (2009) conducted a study the effect of test-taking behaviors of Latina/os on the WISC-IV Spanish edition. Children in the standardization sample had 5 or fewer years of experience in US schools. Overall, participants in the study exhibited typical test-taking behaviors. This may be related to the fact that the examiner was Spanish-speaking and the test was in the child's first language. "Counterproductive" test-taking behaviors that were detected were higher for males than females and for older rather than younger children. More specifically, relationships between test-taking behaviors and full-scale IQ scores were most noted in the 13–16-year age group. Special attention may be warranted for this group given that these participants had less than 5 years in the USA after having come to the country later in their childhood (Oakland & Harris, 2009).

Although focusing on a more specific group of Latina/o children, San Miguel Montes et al. (2010) found that for a clinical population with brain dysfunction, there appears to be criterion validity support for the WISC-IV Spanish. The study included a sample of 35 bilingual (Spanish-dominant) children primarily with diagnoses of learning disabilities and attention deficit/hyperactivity disorder. To date, these appear to be the only two peer-reviewed empirical articles that prominently feature the WISC-IV Spanish with a Latina/o sample.

The Woodcock-Johnson III (WJ III)

The Woodcock-Johnson III (Woodcock, McGrew, & Mather, 2001) is the most recent version of the Woodcock-Johnson batteries of cognitive abilities (WJ III COG) and educational/academic achievement (WJ III ACH). This replaces the Woodcock-Johnson Psycho-Educational Battery-Revised (WJ-R), published in 1989. The WJ III, along with the WISC-IV, is often used in school-based psychological assessment. It is designed to be used with children as young as 2 years of age to adults to age 90. Internal consistency reliability estimates are reported in the .80s and .90s for individual tests.

The WJ III ACH includes the basic interpersonal communication skill (BICS) scores and the cognitive academic language proficiency (CALP) scores that are helpful when assessing students who are not native English speakers and can be particularly useful with Latina/o students who are in the process of learning English as their second language. Cizek (2001) points to the renorming of the WJ III from the WJ-R as one of the most significant differences between the two editions. The sample included 8,818 (5,926 children and adolescents) who matched US demographics with regard to geographic region, community size, gender, race, Hispanic origin, and type of school or college (Cizek). This included English language learning who had attended at least 1 year in English language classes.

Empirical studies focusing specifically on Latina/o students with the Woodcock-Johnson are limited. Frisby and Osterlind (2007) investigated the test-session behavior of Latina/os and Whites taking the WJ III; however, this included children and adults. The results indicated that test-taking behaviors were generally consistent between both groups. Given that the focus was not on children and not specifically for a school context, the conclusions may have little relevance for school-based psychological assessment. Related to the argument that lower cognitive and academic achievement test scores for Latina/o students are a result of cultural conflicts that can lead examinees to misunderstand test directions, provide the wrong answers, or perform correctly, but beyond task time limits.

De Von Figueroa-Moseley, Ramey, Keltner, and Lanzi (2006) studied the effects of parenting behaviors on the cognitive development of three Latino subgroups (Mexican American, Puerto Rican, Salvadoran). The authors report that there was a significant relationship between parent responsiveness and higher academic achievement as well as significant differences between subgroups on scores for the Letter Work and Applied Problems subtests of the WJ-R (1989). While this study utilized the WJ (albeit the WJ-R version), the authors did relate the use of this assessment to their study topic of population. Only once was it mentioned that the WJ could be administered in Spanish, but this was not discussed extensively not directly tied to the results.

Although there is limited research on the use of the WJ with a Latina/o school population, its use is widespread, and its psychometric properties make it an attractive choice for school-based assessments. The inclusion of the BICS and CALP is a distinctive feature when considering use with Latina/o students in the process of learning English. The use of the WJ III is recommended assuming the examiner will also collect and use other cultural data when interpreting results.

Batería III Woodcock-Munoz (2005)

The Bateria III Woodcock-Munoz (Bateria III) (Muñoz-Sandoval, Woodock, McGrew, Mather, & Schrank, 2005) is the Spanish-language version of the Woodcock-Johnson III (WJ III; Woodcock et al., 2001; 15:281). It is meant to be a translation of the WJ III with all the tests being translated or adapted from the WJ III. In Doll and LeClair's (2007) review of the WJ III, they highlight that the Bateria III is not standardized as its own instrument, but that it was administered to 1,413 participants primarily from the USA, Mexico, and Costa Rica. Reliability coefficients for the cognitive abilities subtests (pruebas de habilidades cognitivas) ranged from .80 to .93 and for the achievement subtests (pruebas de aprovechamiento) from .77 to .98. Overall, the psychometric properties are highly comparable to the WJ III with evidence of its construct validity demonstrated via analyses utilizing the calibration sample data reported above (Olivarez & Boroda, 2007).

A point of concern regarding the small calibration sample is that it does not consider differences in language exposure and dialects that exist in different regions (Olivarez & Boroda, 2007). Although, not a substitute for this deficiency, the Bateria III does offer two interpretive features regarding language proficiency assessment. There is an oral language performance on instructional situations using CALP measures, and there is a Comparative Language Index (CLI) for direct comparisons of Spanish and English language proficiencies within a single index (Olivarez & Boroda).

Perhaps because the publication of this newest version is relatively new, there are no empirical studies where the Bateria III is prominently featured in its use for psychological assessment for Latina/o students in a school context. Although it is arguably the most widely used assessment (cognitive and achievement) with Latina/o students, current references involve its use primarily for academic preparedness (language or reading ability) (e.g., Hughes, Zhang, & Hill, 2006; Wilson & Hughes, 2006). Given the demonstrated construct validity and other psychometric properties, the Bateria III is a recommended assessment instrument given that results are interpreted within its limitations and that other cultural data is gathered and utilized in psychological assessment of Latina/o students.

Rating Scales

Achenbach System of Empirically Based Assessment

The Achenbach System of Empirically Based Assessment (ASEBA) is a series of several checklists designed to identify children at high risk of emotional and/or behavioral disorders, who therefore warrant further assessment (Achenbach & Rescorla, 2000; Achenbach et al., 2008). The ASEBA is cited as the most extensively used and researched rating scale of children's internalizing and externalizing emotions (Casas, Furlong, Alvarez, & Wood, 1998). The forms are self-administered or administered by lay interviewers and are available in two versions for children (ages 1.5–5 and 6–18). Parents complete the Child Behavior Checklist (CBCL/1 1/2–5, CBCL/6–18), teachers complete the Teacher Report Form (TRF/6–18), adults in other school or caregiving settings complete the Caregiver-Teacher Report (C-TRF), and youth aged 11–18-years old complete the Youth Self-Report (YSR). Subscales for the YSR and CBCL/6–18 are subsumed under groupings called competence, syndrome, and DSM-oriented (based on the *Diagnostic and Statistical Manual of Mental Disorders, 4th Edition*; American Psychiatric Association, 1994) (Flanagan, 2004).

Content validity is based on prior research with the scales. Criterion-related validity of the CBCL/6–18, YSR, and TRF is based on multiple regression analyses and indicates that 2–33% of the variance on individual scales is accounted for by referral status (Flanagan, 2004). Construct validity was determined by correlations with similar instruments. Achenbach et al. (2008) state that comparisons of scale scores, psychometrics, and correlates are available for diverse populations and that data and responses from hundreds of thousands of respondents from diverse groups have culminated in comparable results for many populations.

Internal consistencies for empirically based syndromes in US samples are reported as follows: CBCL .83, TRS .85, and YSR .79 (Achenbach et al., 2008).

Empirical studies that focus exclusively on Latina/o youth and the ASEBA are not extensive. Although, there is little research explicitly on applicability and appropriateness of the ASEBA with Latina/o children and adolescents, several authors have utilized these scales when investigating clinical issues in this population. In terms of use with various subgroups of Latina/os, Vega, Khoury, Zimmerman, and Gil (1995) compared total problem scores on the TRF among Cuban, Puerto Rican, Nicaraguan, and Colombian youth and found no significant differences. However, this was based on the 1983 version of CBCL (Achenbach & Edelbrock, 1983). Glover, Pumariega, Holzer, Wise, and Rodriguez (1999) utilized the 1991 Youth Self-Report version (YSR) to study anxiety symptomatology with Mexican American youth. The researchers found the YSR acceptable for use in the study but noted that the resulting high scores on anxiety levels are either evidence of similar reports with Mexican American adults or a culturally related bias in the reporting of anxiety symptoms (Glover et al., 1999). The 1991 Parent Report Form and the Teacher Report Form were used in determining the distinctiveness of the inattentive type and the combined type of attention deficit hyperactivity disorder with a sample of 26 Puerto Rican children in San Juan, Puerto Rico (Bauemeister et al., 2005). The results led the authors to conclude that the ADHD construct was supported for this specific population and additionally stated their reason for use of the ASEBA was that it had been culturally adapted for use in Puerto Rico. Alpha coefficients for the study sample ranged from .51 to .97 (Bauemeister et al.).

Dominguez de Ramirez and Shapiro (1998) is the only study reviewed here that utilized an ASEBA version and specifically focused on a school context. The researchers compared White teacher's ratings of ADHD for nonreferred Latina/o (primarily Puerto Rican – US east coast) and White children between ages 6 and 11. They used multiple objective instruments including the 1991 TRS (Achenbach). The results were that White teachers' scores rated Latina/o similar to or lower than White students. The authors did not report any reliability data for the TRS with respect to their study but expressed confidence in the use of this instrument with Latina/o children.

With regard to the Spanish versions of the ASEBA, Casas et al. (1998) stated that after a search for empirical studies, of forty only four could be considered validation studies. Further, only two of the four were conducted in the USA. In their effort to examine the validity of then (1998) three Spanish versions, Casas et al. found a number of items that could have significantly different meaning in English and thus warranted further analysis.

More recently, Gross, Fogg, and Young (2006) examined the equivalence of the English and Spanish (Achenbach & Rescorla, 2000) versions of the CBCL for the 1.5–5 age group. They also included family SES. Latina/o parents represented 46.8% of the 682 sample with 218 (32%) considered low-income and 101 (14.8%) middle/upper class. The authors concluded that there were no significant scale score differences between Latino parents who filled out the Spanish version and Latino parents who filled out the English version.

In general, the ASEBA's long research and practice history with diverse populations (Achenbach et al., 2008) make it a viable choice for use with Latina/o children and adolescents. However, an increase in empirical studies with both English and Spanish versions with Latina/os is warranted given the limited empirical studies available and given the fact that the ASEBA has been updated in 2001. Culturally responsive examiners must still make efforts and including other culturally relevant data when conducting school-based psychological assessment with this population.

Behavior Assessment System for Children-Parent Report System (BASC)

The BASC is a standardized instrument used in public schools and clinical settings for over two decades to identify behavioral and emotional disorders in children and adolescents (McCloskey et al., 2003). The BASC is now in its second edition (BASC–2; Reynolds & Kamphaus, 2004) which is a revision of the original BASC, published in (Reynolds and Kamphaus, 1992). It is composed of three rating scales, one for teachers (Teacher Rating Scales, or TRS), one for parents (Parent Rating Scales, or PRS), and a self-report scale (Self-Report of Personality, or SRP). Additionally, there is a Structured Developmental History (SDH) form and a Student Observation System (SOS) for observing classroom behavior.

The updated norms were collected between 2002 and 2004, which include more than 13,000 cases between ages 2 and18. There was an attempt to reflect the racial and ethnic demographics of the country for the general norms. However, the clinical samples were not similarly matched demographically (Stein, 2007). Reliability coefficients were relatively strong for all scales (e.g., low-mid .90s) with validity data involving mostly correlational studies with other reputable measures of parent, teacher, and self-report standardized instruments (Stein).

McCloskey et al. (2003) conducted a series of analyses on the Spanish version of the BASC (1992), referred to as El Sistema, to determine its appropriateness with Latina/o children. Scores of 55 parents of Latina/o children were compared with scores from the standardization sample. Overall, the results of their analyses showed that correlation data were strongly similar to the BASC (1992) with the example of four scales included in the Behavior Symptom Index (Withdrawal, Attention, Hyperactivity, and Atypicality). It was concluded that, given the general compatibility with the English version, parents in the study sample had a reasonable understanding of translated questions (McCloskey et al.). In terms of the sample, a significant limitation was that it was taken from one city in the southwest and all parents were from a low SES background limiting the generalizability to a larger Latina/o population.

In this 2003 study, McCloskey, Hess, and D'Amato stated that there were no studies to date at that time that addressed the Spanish translation of the BASC (1992). Presently, we found only McCloskey et al.'s study that addresses the 1992 El Sistema and no studies that address Spanish translations of the BASC-2. In addition, no empirical studies prominently featuring Latina/os with the BASC-2 were encountered in the literature. Again, given the current data on both the BASC and BASC-2, it is reasonable to suggest that continued use of these measures with a Latina/o student population is appropriate with necessary steps to include important cultural and linguistic data.

Clinical Interview

Schedule for Affective Disorders and Schizophrenia for School-Age Children (K-SADS)

The clinical interview is a necessary component in school-based psychological assessment, and the K-SADS (Puig-Antich & Chambers, 1978) is the most widely used semi-structured interview for children and adolescents (6–18 years) according to Klein, Dougherty, and Olino (2005). It is also the least structured of the semi-structured interviews and therefore requires the greatest amount of clinical training and experience. Although originally developed in the 1970s, there are currently several versions that are now compatible with DSM-IV criteria. Information is gathered from both parent and child with administration time ranging from 35 min to 2.5 h each (Klein et al., 2005). Based on more recent versions, interrater reliability appears to be strong for depressive disorders (Klein et al.).

There are two versions: the K-SADS-P (present state) and the K-SADS-E (epidemiologic). The most recent update by Ambrosini and Dixon in 1996 of the K-SADS-P is the K-SADS-P IVR to correspond to the DSM-II and DSM-IV. The K-SADS-E has two editions: the K-SADS-E updated in 1995 and DSM-IV compatible (Orvaschel, Puig-Antich, Chambers, Tabrizi, & Johnson, 1982) and the K-SADS-P/L updated in 1996 (Kaufman et al., 1996).

Administration is similar for all versions and varies due to some format differences. Test-retest reliability is reported to range from .63 to .90 depending on diagnostic category (Ambrosini, 2000).

Semi-structured interviews depend greatly on clinical judgment, and the results are particularly influenced by the examiner's culture sensitivity and responsiveness. The above discussion regarding the cultural context of the assessment process and the perceived role of mental health professionals by some in ethnic minority communities should be present in the mind of the examiner during semi-structured interview with Latina/o children and adolescent in a school context. To date, there are no studies utilizing the K-SADS that focus explicitly on this population. Further, there is little research on the use of the K-SADS with culturally diverse populations in the USA. Given this situation, it is recommended that the use of the K-SADS with Latina/os be used with heightened attention to cultural considerations and results should be interpreted with caution.

Conclusion and Recommendations

It appears that for key, commonly used assessments, there are some Spanish language versions. This is a significant move forward in their field; however, as discussed, some of these translations do not use overrepresentation and do not necessarily include differences in cultural values. The authors strongly encourage examiners to also give heed to the particular Latina/o subgroup with whom they are working, along with the knowledge that there are regional differences in Spanish use and dialect that can occur within and accurse Latina/o subgroups. Finally, it can be argued that the validity of any school-based assessment with Latina/o children and adolescents may be called into question without some careful measure of acculturation. This relates not only to an immigrant child learning English but may also contextualize the results for a third-generation Latina/o whose adherence to his/her cultural values may place that child at odds with a school culture where he/she may still feel much discrimination. Thus, it remains important to obtain data from multiple informants, including the child, parents, and teachers. Ortiz and Ochoa (2005b, p. 156) state, "The validity of results obtained in the assessment of diverse individuals may therefore be improved if two important and interrelated pieces of information can be obtained: (1) the individual's level of acculturation as compared to age-related peers, and (2) the degree to which performance on a stand-alone test or a test from a battery is contingent upon possession of culture-specific knowledge."

References

Acevedo-Polakovich, I. D., Reynago-Abiko, G., Garriott, P. O., Derefinko, K. J., Wimsatt, M. K., Gudonis, L. C., et al. (2007). Beyond instrument selection: Cultural considerations in the psychological assessment of U.S. Latinas/os. *Professional Psychology: Research and Practice, 38*, 375–384.

Achenbach, T. M., Becker, A., Dopfner, M., Heiervang, E., Roessner, V., Steinhausen, V. H., & Rothenberger, A. (2008). Multicultural assessment of child and adolescent psychopathology with ASEBA and SDQ instruments: Research findings, applications, and future directions. *Journal of Child Psychology and Psychiatry, 49*(3), 251–275.

Achenbach, T. M., & Edelbrock, C. (1983). *Manual for the child behavior checklist and revised child behavior profile*. Burlington, VT: Department of Psychiatry, University of Vermont.

Achenbach, T. M., & Rescorla, L. A. (2000). *Manual for the ASEBA preschool forms & profiles*. Burlington, VT: Research Center for Children, Youth, & Families, University of Vermont.

Ambrosini, P. J. (2000). Historical development and present status of the schedule for affective disorders and schizophrenia for school-age children (K-SADS). *Journal of the American Academy of Child and Adolescent Psychiatry, 39*, 49–58.

American Psychiatric Association. (1994). *Diagnostic and statistical manual of mental disorders* (4th ed.). Washington, DC: American Psychiatric Association.

American Psychological Association. (2003). Guidelines on multicultural education, training, research, practice, and organizational change for psychologists. *American Psychologist, 58*, 377–402.

Bauemeister, J. J., Matos, M., Reina, G., Salas, C. C., Martínez, J. V., Cumba, E., & Barkley, R. A. (2005). Comparison of the DSM-IV combined and inattentive types of ADHD in a school-based sample of Latino/Hispanic children. *Journal of Child Psychology and Psychiatry, 46*(2), 166–179.

Belsky, J., & MacKinnon, C. (1994). Transition to school: Developmental trajectories and school experiences. *Early Education and Development, 5*, 106–119.

Berry, J. W., & Kim, U. (1988). Acculturation and mental health. In P. R. Dasen, J. W. Berry, & N. Sartorius (Eds.), *Health and cross-cultural psychology* (pp. 207–236). Newbury Park, CA: Sage.

Berry, J. W., Trimble, J., & Olmedo, E. (1986). Assessment of acculturation. In W. Lonner & J. W. Berry (Eds.), *Field methods in cross-cultural research*. Newbury Park, CA: Sage.

Casas, J., Furlong, M. J., Alvarez, M., & Wood, M. (1998). *Que dice? Initial analyses examining three Spanish translations of the CBCL*. Retrieved from ERIC database (ED432866).

Castillo, E. M., Quintana, S. M., & Zamarripa, M. X. (2000). Cultural and linguistic issues. In E. S. Shapiro, T. R. Kratochwill, E. S. Shapiro, & T. R. Kratochwill (Eds.), *Conducting school-based assessments of child and adolescent behavior* (pp. 274–308). New York: Guilford Press.

Cervantes, R. C., & Cordova, D. (2011). Life experiences of Hispanic adolescents: Developmental and language considerations in acculturation stress. *Journal of Community Psychology, 39*(3), 336–352.

Cizek, G. J. (2001). Review of the Woodcock-Johnson(r) III. In *The fourteenth mental measurements yearbook*. Available from http://www.unl.edu/buros/

Clinton, A. (2007). Test Review: Wechsler, D. (2005). "Wechsler Intelligence Scale for Children-Four Edition Spanish." San Antonio, TX: Psychological Corporation. *Journal of Psychoeducational Assessment, 25*(3), 285–292.

Collier, V. P. (1989). How long? A synthesis of research on academic achievement in a second language. *TESOL Quarterly, 23*(3), 509–31.

Cuellar, I. (1998). Cross-cultural clinical psychological assessment of Hispanic Americans. *Journal of Personality Assessment, 70*, 71–86.

Cuellar, I., Arnold, B., & Gonzalez, G. (1995). Cognitive referents of acculturation: Assessment of cultural constructs in Mexican-Americans. *Journal of Community Psychology, 23*, 339–356.

Cuellar, I., Arnold, B., & Maldonado, R. (1995). Acculturation rating scale for Mexican Americans-II: A revisión of the original ARSMA scale. *Hispanic Journal of Behavioral Sciences, 17*, 275–304.

Cummins, J. (1984). *Bilingualism and special education: Issues in assessment and pedagogy*. San Diego, CA: College-Hill.

Davidson, A. L. (1996). *Making and molding identity in schools*. Albany, NY: SUNY Press.

De Von Figueroa-Moseley, C., Ramey, C. T., Keltner, B., & Lanzi, R. G. (2006). Variations in Latino parenting and their efforts on child cognitive behavioral developmental outcomes. *Hispanic Journal of Behavioral Sciences, 28*(1), 102–114.

Doll, B., & LeClair, C. (2007). Review of the Batería III Woodcock-Muñoz. In *The seventeenth mental measurements yearbook*. Available from http://www.unl.edu/buros/.

Dominguez de Ramirez, R., & Shapiro, E. S. (1998). Teacher ratings of attention deficit hyperactivity disorder symptoms in Hispanic children. *Journal of Psychopathology and Behavioral Assessment, 20*, 275–293.

Fisher, J. M., & Chambers, E. (2003). Multicultural counseling ethics and assessment competencies: Directions for counselor education programs. *Journal of Applied Rehabilitation Counseling, 34*(2), 17–21.

Flanagan, R. (2004). Review of the Achenbach system of empirically based assessment. In *The sixteenth mental measurements yearbook*. Available from http://www.unl.edu/buros/.

Fouad, N. A., & Arredondo, P. (2007). *Becoming culturally oriented: Practical advice for psychologists and educators*. Washington, DC: American Psychological Association.

Frisby, C. L., & Osterlind, S. J. (2007). Hispanic test-session behavior on the Woodcock Johnson psychoeducational battery-Third edition. *Journal of Psychoeducational Assessment, 25*(3), 257–270.

Gil, A. G., Vega, W. A., & Dima, J. M. (1994). Acculturative stress and personal adjustment among Hispanic adolescent boys. *Journal of Community Psychology, 22*, 43–54.

Glover, S. H., Pumariega, A. J., Holzer, C. E., Wise, B. K., & Rodriguez, M. (1999). Anxiety symptomatology in Mexican-American adolescents. *Journal of Child and Family Studies, 8*(1), 47–57.

Gross, D., Fogg, L., & Young, M. (2006). The equivalence of the child behavior checklist 1 1/2–5 across parent race/ethnicity, income level, and language. *Psychological Assessment, 18*(3), 313–323.

Hughes, J. N., Zhang, D., & Hill, C. R. (2006). Peer assessments of normative and individual teacher–student support predict social acceptance and engagement among low-achieving children. *Journal of School Psychology, 43*, 447–463.

Kaufman, J., Birmaher, B., Brent, D., Rao, U., Flynn, C., Moreci, P., Williamson, D., & Ryan, N. (1996). Schedule for affective disorder and schizophrenia for school-age children-present and lifetime version (K-SADS-PL): Internal reliability and validity data. *Child and Adolescent Psychiatry, 36*(7), 980–988.

Klein, D. N., Dougherty, L. R., & Olino, T. M. (2005). Toward guidelines for evidence-based assessment of depression in children and adolescents. *Journal of Clinical Child and Adolescent Psychology, 34*(3), 412–432.

Laing, S. P., & Kamhi, A. (2003). Alternative assessment of language and literacy in culturally and linguistically diverse populations. *Language, Speech, and Hearing Services in Schools, 34*, 44–55.
Loe, S. A., & Miranda, A. H. (2005). An examination of ethnic incongruence in school-based psychological services and diversity-training experiences among school psychologist. *Psychology in the Schools, 42*(4), 419–432.
Maller, S. J. (2003). Review of Wechsler intelligence scale for children-Fourth edition. In *The fifteenth mental measurements yearbook*. Available from http://www.unl.edu/buros/.
McCloskey, D., & Athanasiou, M. S. (2000). Assessment and intervention practices with second language learners among school psychologists. *Psychology in the Schools, 37*(3), 209–225.
McCloskey, D. M., Hess, R. S., & D'Amato, R. C. (2003). Evaluating the utility of the Spanish version of the behavioral assessment system for children-parent report system. *Journal of Psychoeducational Assessment, 21*, 325–337.
Muñoz-Sandoval, A. F., Woodock, R. W., McGrew, K. S., Mather, N., & Schrank, F. A. (2005). *Bateria III Woodcock-Muñoz*. Itasca, IL: Riverside.
Murillo, N. (1977). The works of George I. Sanchez: An appreciation. In J. L. Martinez (Ed.), *Chicano psychology* (pp. 1–10). New York: Academic.
O'Bryon, E. C., & Rogers, M. R. (2010). Bilingual school psychologists' assessment practices with English language learners. *Psychology in the Schools, 47*(10), 1018–1034.
Oakland, T., & Harris, J. G. (2009). Impact of test-taking behaviors on full-scale IQ scores from the Wechsler intelligence scale for children–IV Spanish Edition. *Journal of Psychoeducational Assessment, 27*(5), 366–373.
Ochoa, S. H., Rivera, B., & Ford, L. (1997). An investigation of school psychology training pertaining to bilingual psychoeducational assessment of primarily Hispanic students: Twenty-five years after Diana vs. California. *Journal of School Psychology, 35*, 329–349.
Olivarez, A., & Boroda, A. (2007). Review of the Bateria III Woodcock-Munoz. In *The seventeenth mental measurements yearbook*. Available from http://www.unl.edu/buros/.
Ortiz, S. O., & Ochoa, S. H. (2005). Conceptual measurement and methodological issues in cognitive assessment of culturally and linguistically diverse individuals. In R. L. Rhodes, S. H. Ochoa, & S. O. Ortiz (Eds.), *Assessing culturally and linguistically diverse students: A practical guide* (pp. 153–167). New York: Guilford Press.
Orvaschel, H., Puig-Antich, P., Chambers, W., Tabrizi, M. A., & Johnson, R. (1982). Retrospective assessment of prepubertal major depression with the Kiddie-SADS-E. *Journal of American Academic Child Psychiatry, 21*, 392–397.
Pew Hispanic Center. (2011a). *Hispanics account for more than half of the nation's growth in past decade*. Retrieved August 25, 2011, from http://pewhispanic.org/reports/report.php?ReportID=140.
Pew Hispanic Center. (2011b). *Latino teens staying in high school: A challenge for all generations*. Retrieved August 25, 2011, from http://pewhispanic.org/files/factsheets/7.3.pdf.
Phinney, J. S. (1992). The multigroup ethnic identity measure: A new scale for use with diverse groups. *Journal of Adolescent Research, 7*(2), 156–76.
Puente, A. E., & Puente, A. N. (2009). The challenge of measuring abilities and competencies in Hispanics/Latinos. In E. L. Grigorenko & E. L. Grigorenko (Eds.), *Multicultural psychoeducational assessment* (pp. 417–441). New York: Springer Publishing Co.
Puig-Antich, J., & Chambers, W. (1978). *The schedule for affective disorders and schizophrenia for school-age children (Kiddie-SADS)*. New York: New York State Psychiatric Institute.
Quintana, S. M., Castillo, E. M., & Zamarripa, M. X. (2000). Assessment of ethnic and linguistic minority children. In E. Shapiro, T. R. Kratochwill, E. Shapiro, & T. R. Kratochwill (Eds.), *Behavioral assessment in schools: Theory, research, and clinical foundations* (2nd ed., pp. 435–463). New York: Guilford Press.
Reynolds, C. R., & Kamphaus, R. W. (1992). *Behavior assessment system for children: Manual*. Circle Pines, MN: American Guidance.
Reynolds, C. R., & Kamphaus, R. W. (2004). *Behavior assessment system for children (BASC-2)* (2nd ed.). Circle Pines, MN: AGS.
San Miguel, G., & Valencia, R. R. (1998). From the treaty of Guadalupe Hidalgo to Hopwood: The educational plight and struggle of Mexican Americans in the southwest. *Harvard Educational Review, 68*(3), 353–412.
San Miguel Montes, L. E., Allen, D. N., Puente, A. E., & Neblina, C. (2010). Validity of the WISC–IV Spanish for a clinically referred sample of Hispanic children. *Psychological Assessment, 22*(2), 465–469.
Sánchez, G. I. (1932a). Group differences and Spanish-speaking children-A critical review. *Journal of Applied Psychology, 16*, 549–558.
Sánchez, G. I. (1932b). Scores of Spanish-speaking children on repeated tests. *Journal of Genetic Psychology, 40*, 223–231.
Sánchez, G. I. (1934a). Bilingualism and mental measures: A word of caution. *Journal of Applied Psychology, 18*, 465–772.
Sánchez, G. I. (1934b). The implications of basal vocabulary to the measurement of the abilities bilingual children. *Journal of Social Psychology, 5*, 395–402.
Santiago-Rivera, A., Arredondo, P., & Gallardo-Cooper, M. (2002). *Counseling Latinos and la familia*. Thousand Oaks, CA: Sage Publications.

Schon, J., Shaftel, J., & Markhaml, P. (2008). Contemporary issues in the assessment of culturally and linguistically diverse learners. *Journal of Applied School Psychology, 24*(2), 163–189.

Schwartz, S. J., Zamboanga, B. L., & Jarvis, L. H. (2007). Ethnic identity and acculturation in Hispanic early adolescents: Mediated relationships to academic grades, prosocial behaviors, and externalizing symptoms. *Cultural Diversity and Ethnic Minority Psychology, 13*, 364–373.

Stein, S. (2007). Review of the behavior assessment system for children, Second Edition. In *The seventeenth mental measurements yearbook*. Available from http://www.unl.edu/buros/.

Suarez-Morales, L., Dillon, F. R., & Szapocznik, J. (2007). Validation of the acculturative stress inventory for children. *Cultural Diversity and Ethnic Minority Psychology, 13*, 216–224.

Sue, D. W., Arredondo, P., & McDavis, R. J. (1992). Multicultural competencies and standards: A call to the profession. *Journal of Counseling and Development, 70*, 477–486.

Unger, J. B., Ritt-Olson, A., Teran, L., Huang, T., Hoffman, B. R., & Palmer, P. (2002). Cultural values and substance use in a multiethnic sample of California adolescents. *Addiction Research and Theory, 10*, 257–279.

U.S. Census Bureau. (2010). *The Hispanic population: 2010*. Retrieved August 25, 2011, from http://www.census.gov/prod/cen2010/briefs/c2010br-04.pdf.

Vega, W. A., Khoury, E. L., Zimmerman, R. S., & Gil, A. G. (1995). Cultural conflicts and problem behaviors of Latino adolescents in home and school environments. *Journal of Community Psychology, 23*(2), 167–179.

Vega, W. A., Zimmerman, R., Gil, A., Warheir, G., & Apospori, E. (1993). Acculturative strain theory: Its application in explaining drug use behavior among Cuban and Non-Cuban Hispanic youth. In M. De La Rosa (Ed.), *Drug abuse among minority youth: Advances in research and methodology*. Rockville, MD: National Institute of Drug Abuse.

Wechsler, D. (2003). *Wechsler intelligence scale for children* (4th ed.). San Antonio, TX: Psychological Corporation.

Wechsler, D. (2005). *Wechsler intelligence scale for children* (4th ed.). San Antonio, TX: Harcourt Assessment (Spanish).

Wilson, V. L., & Hughes, J. N. (2006). Retention of Hispanic/Latino students in first grade: Child, parent, teacher, school, and peer predictors. *Journal of School Psychology, 44*(1), 31–49.

Woodcock, R. W., McGrew, K. S., & Mather, N. (2001). *Woodcock-Johnson III*. Itasca, IL: Riverside Publishing.

Woodcock, R. W., & Muñoz-Sandoval, A. F. (2005). *Woodcock-Muñoz language survey revised*. Itasca, IL: Riverside Publishing.

Zayas, L. H. (1992). Childrearing, social stress and child abuse: Clinical considerations with Hispanic families. *Journal of Social Distress and the Homeless, 1*, 291–309.

Zayas, L. H., Evans, M. E., Mejia, L., & Rodriguez, O. (1997). Cultural-competency training for staff serving Hispanic families with a child in psychiatric crisis. *Families in Society, 78*, 405–412.

Neuropsychological Assessment with Hispanic Clients

22

Brian D. Leany, Lorraine T. Benuto, and Nicholas S. Thaler

Introduction

Neuropsychological assessment is recommended when we suspect an organic deficit or insult (either congenital or acquired, as in the case of stroke, traumatic brain injury, dementia, fetal alcohol syndrome, pervasive developmental disorder, or toxin exposure to name a few) has impacted expected functional performance for an individual, or when we wish to rule out such deficits or insults. These assessments take on a holistic approach in that we attempt to identify the region of the brain that is impacted, identify the extent of the insult, ascertain the spared functioning, and predict prognosis through a multimodal/multidomain assessment.

The comprehensive neuropsychological evaluation allows us to make predictions about prognosis as well as make recommendations for possible intervention and rehabilitation. Because we have long since abandoned the eugenic notion of inherent intellectual and cognitive differences among cultures, ethnicity, and races, we assume when conducting neuropsychological assessment with the Hispanic client an absence of any underlying cognitive or intellectual differences specific to ethnicity. This assumption can also be seen in research that investigates the invariable components of cognitive functioning (e.g., those processes that seem to be measurably consistent across race, ethnicity, and culture), rather than looking for discrepancies. Further, this research supports a greater level of homogeny and ubiquity for basic neuropsychological traits (Siedlecki et al., 2010). Thus, it seems that the quality of the test in regard to its appropriateness toward Hispanic clients relies on the quality of its translation and its ability to generalize

B.D. Leany, Ph.D. (✉)
California Department of Corrections and Rehabilitation, Adult Division, California Correctional Health Care Services, High Desert State Prison, PO Box 750, Susanville, CA 96127, USA
e-mail: leanyb@gmail.com

L.T. Benuto, Ph.D.
Department of Psychology, Victims of Crime Treatment Center, University of Nevada, Reno MS 0296, Reno, NV 89557, USA
e-mail: dr.benuto@gmail.com

N.S. Thaler, M.A.
Department of Psychology, University of Nevada, 4505S. Maryland Pkwy, Box 455030, Las Vegas, NV 89154-5030, USA
e-mail: nick.thaler@gmail.com

L.T. Benuto (ed.), *Guide to Psychological Assessment with Hispanics*,
DOI 10.1007/978-1-4614-4412-1_22, © Springer Science+Business Media New York 2013

to multiple Hispanic microcultures (e.g., Mexican, Puerto Rican, and Dominican). It was in this vein that Artioli I Fortuny and colleagues (Artioli I Fortuny & Mullaney, 1997; Artioli I Fortuny et al., 2005) described lapses in this area (quality and accuracy of translation) and provided suggestions to address problems specific to the translation of test items for Hispanics (although these procedures can be applied for translation among many languages). While there was much debate about what specific verbiage is appropriate and how to address the process of translation and development of measures that are either direct translations or extensions of English psychological assessments, it seems that a process of translation and back-translation as well as a review by identified experts in both psychometrics and the target language is the consensus for the process. Much of the current research designed to assess cross-cultural administration of neuropsychological assessments is focused on the less measurable aspects of ethnicity and culture (e.g., the *degree* of identification with one culture versus the US culture), rather than the more empirically reliable measures of age, education, gender, years in the USA, income, etc. Some researchers suggest that proper training is almost nonexistent and would indicate that few clinicians are qualified by training to assess Hispanic clients (Echemendia, Harris, Congett, Diaz, & Puente, 1997). While this may be an overgeneralization of the data presented, it is the message that is communicated. When a psychologist is not competent in assessing this population, the impact on the Hispanic client is obviously detrimental and would seem to run contrary to the overarching goal of a helping profession.

Rather than taking a restrictive approach and portending that clinicians should invariably refer out when working with Hispanic clients whom they are not specifically trained to work with, this chapter aims to encourage competent clinicians to use the assessments that are available and provide resources for normative studies that focus on the more quantifiable variables that span race and ethnicity in an effort to improve readers' competency and knowledge as well as provide services to the Hispanic community. Thus, the normative data available for variables such as education, language ability (and to a limited extent, acculturation), age, wealth/poverty, and gender becomes paramount (Gasquoine, 1999, 2001). In a recent review of neuropsychological assessment across race and ethnicity, Gasquoine (2009) points out the problematic process of investigation that currently exists (e.g., nonoperational definitions of race and ethnicity or impossibly large groupings of ethnicity and race) that he suggests may result in false negatives or race-based substandard/extraordinary services. Therefore, rather than identify the problems we could or might encounter, or perhaps the data that we are lacking, it is the goal of this chapter to provide resources that allow one to find assessments with normative data that span the broader Hispanic culture in a manner that does not present significant differences among the various Hispanic populations. Depending on the domain being assessed, there are specific assessments designed and normed for Hispanic populations (e.g., the Escala de Inteligencia Wechsler para Adultos, now in its third edition; EIWA-III; Wechsler, 2008a), but the majority have been translations of existing measures with normative data representative of various Hispanic cultures.

Neuropsychological Assessment of the Hispanic Client from a Historical Perspective

Neuropsychological assessment lends itself to cross-cultural assessment, due to its broad range of assessment domains that, taken by face value, we would assume to be culturally neutral. In saying culturally neutral, what we are truly saying is that the same region of the brain that controls motor function in one culture or race would be the same in another. For example, the hippocampus aids in consolidating memory for individuals of African origin just as it does for those of Western European origin. Additionally, a number of tasks involved in a comprehensive neuropsychological exam include integrative tasks and purely motor-based tasks. These tasks are ones we consider to be largely culturally neutral (again, we do not expect statistically significant differences in bilateral grip-strength or more pronounced cogwheel rigidity among cultures, races, or ethnicities). Thus, the largest challenges we should face are those issues related to the assessment of linguistic-based domains, issues of communication and rapport between the examiner and the client, and the unique but relative differences in the acuity of various abilities that have allowed cultures to thrive within their environment (e.g., the differential visuospatial abilities) (Ardila & Moreno, 2001; Mulenga, Ahonen, & Aro, 2001; Pontius, 2002). The perpetual conundrum in the field of neuropsychological assessment (and much of the practice of psychological assessment in general) is the underlying need for verbal communication in even nonverbal tasks. A good number of our neuropsychological assessments are dependent upon verbal language to present the stimuli, respond to the stimuli, or both. Therefore, in order to provide an optimal measure of neuropsychological performance for Hispanics, we need to be aware of not just the availability of normative data for Hispanics, but the composition and selection of the normative group, with particular attentiveness to the normative group's dominant language.

Fixed vs. Flexible

The approach to neuropsychological assessment has traditionally been divided into two camps. On one side, there are those neuropsychologists who support a fixed battery (such as the Halstead-Reitan Neuropsychological Test Battery described later in this chapter), and on the other side are those who believe in a flexible battery approach. Initially, the flexible battery consisted of utilizing relevant portions of the Halstead-Reitan (e.g., trails to assess association cortices of visual motor integration and executive control), but today, test authors and publishers have developed batteries purposed for flexible administration. While patterns of performance on the Halstead-Reitan indicate localized areas of impairment, it does not necessarily have domain-specific implications (e.g., there is not necessarily a memory component in the Halstead-Reitan). In contrast, the flexible batteries such as the Neuropsychological Assessment Battery System (NABS), by design, incorporate specific components designed to measure executive functions, attention, language, and memory, among others.

Whether flexible or fixed, these batteries assess similar domains. The fixed battery assesses all domains as a comprehensive rule-out/rule-in for diagnostic and prognostic determinations. The flexible battery either uses a battery which contains standardized assessments that complement each other as a unified battery (such as the D-KEFS or the RBANS) or is made up of various assessments picked by the individual clinician to assess the relevant domains of a neuropsychological battery.

Recent Development Specific to Hispanics

There have been exciting developments over the last couple decades in the fields that have important implications for the neuropsychological assessment of Hispanic clients. Researchers have invested significant effort focused on developing neuropsychological assessments with better psychometric properties for this population. Many of these expansions and innovations in the field are being lead by Hispanic clinicians and their colleagues, utilizing their expertise and intimate knowledge of various Hispanic cultures, with a vested interest in improving the number and quality of resources available for these clients. The results are manifest here in this chapter and take the form of translation and extension of existing measures as well as the development of redesigned or reimagined assessment batteries. Many of the individual tests we discuss in this chapter have been studied and/or modified as part of this effort, and so often, you will see them discussed within multiple studies such as the CERAD, SENAS, and NEURONORMA projects as well as their inclusion in paradigms or batteries in their original form, where they were not intended to be used with non-Hispanic Whites or English. In order to set the stage, we will discuss briefly some of these large-scale projects here and save more specific information where appropriate, within the discussions related to their respective domains.

Spanish and English Neuropsychological Assessment Scales (SENAS; Mungas, Reed, Crane, Haan, & González, 2004)

The SENAS consists of 16 subtests (3 specific to executive functioning that were added late to 13 original scales) that were designed as a psychometrically sound assessment tool for older English- and Spanish-speaking individuals. These assessments were designed by Mungas, Haan, and Gonzalez (1996; Mungas, Reed, Haan, & González, 2005; Mungas, Reed, Marshall, & Gonzalez, 2000; Mungas et al., 2004, 2005). The entire battery takes approximately 4 h to administer, but a shorter 2-h battery has recently been developed (Mungas, 2006). The SENAS is unique in that it is completely free and can be obtained complete with demographically normed adjustments that are consistent with the recommendations of Gasquoine (1999, 2001, 2007, 2009).

Consortium to Establish a Registry for Alzheimer's Disease (CERAD)

Neuropsychological Battery (Morris et al., 1989)

The CERAD is a neuropsychological test battery with normative data developed based on participants diagnosed with Alzheimer's dementia ($n=350$) as well as normal controls ($n=250$) from a collection of medical centers across the USA (Morris et al.). This assessment battery has been adapted to Spanish and has been researched in a US bicoastal sample across Spanish-speaking cultures (Fillenbaum, Kuchibhalta, Henderson, Clark, & Taussig, 2007). This study provided data to support the further study and use of the Spanish version of the CERAD in order to differentiate Alzheimer's dementia in Spanish-speaking older adults in the USA from the unimpaired through severe cognitive impairment. Because this battery is part of the Alzheimer's Registry assessment library, it is extensively discussed in the chapter on dementia.

NEURONORMA Project (Peña-Casanova, 2009)

The NEURONORMA project is a study of neuropsychological (as well as clinical) measures developed within a multisite study of clinics dedicated to Alzheimer's detection and diagnosis as well as follow-up. The NEURONORMA project was specifically designed to collect normative and psychometric information, in order to develop profile information from a sample of 356 people across Spain. These individuals include individuals diagnosed with Alzheimer's dementia as well as mild cognitive impairment and normal controls all over 49 years of age. Tests were selected from commonly used neuropsychological tests and specific normative data for each can be found later in this chapter.

Domains

Intelligence Tests

The starting point of most neuropsychological evaluations is a clinical interview aimed to obtain historical information (e.g., a psychosocial and developmental history as well as a records review), as well as an assessment of current general intellectual capacity. Here, especially when considering a flexible battery, we can begin to formulate hypotheses regarding organic impairment through general intellectual capacity (IQ) and domain discrepancies (e.g., greater verbal performance relative to visual or general intellectual capacity). You will find a more thorough discussion of intellectual assessments in another chapter of this book. In conjunction with historical information, the intellectual assessment serves as a starting point in the decision tree of a neuropsychological evaluation. For example, a general, global impairment on an IQ assessment suggests either a developmental disability (such as mental retardation) or a global insult to the brain (through anoxia or other nonspecific trauma), and the clinician would then work to establish whether or not this was a premorbid issue or a new insult. Domain-specific problems suggest the existence of a specific developmental or learning disorder but might be more indicative of localized insults (e.g., a stroke or tumor). From the clinical interview and IQ assessment (as well as some sort of objective assessment of personality), the clinician should develop a course of action for assessment. Depending on one's theoretical perspective (and available resources), they may wish to begin the fixed battery assessment or begin to select assessment instruments that will help them assess their clinical hypothesis (through the administration of domain-specific tests that will not only support their hypothesis but also aid in ruling-out alternative explanations). The order of the items described below is not based on any recommendation for sequence of test administration but is merely presented in an order that seemed reasonable for the purpose of parsimonious explanation.

Executive Functioning

Wisconsin Card Sorting Task

The Wisconsin Card Sorting Test (WCST, Grant & Berg, 1948; Heaton, Chelune, Talley, Kay, & Curtiss, 2003) assesses the broad construct of executive functioning, as measured by the subconstructs of abstraction, problem solving, concept formation, and set-shifting/maintenance. In particular, this test has been shown to help identify impairment of functioning within the prefrontal cortex (Sullivan et al., 1993). Studies with Spanish-speaking Hispanics indicate equivalency of the assessment (when using Spanish norms) as compared to both English-speaking norms (Heaton, 2004) as well as between the manual and computerized administration (Artioli I Fortuny & Heaton, 1996). However, caution should be used, as research has shown that even Hispanics acculturated to North American culture that are assessed using the English norms may show performance that is worse than English-speaking North American participants (Coffey, Marmol, Schock, & Adams, 2005). However, these results should be interpreted with caution as the authors point out that their division of the two groups (high and low acculturation) was still relatively lesser acculturated.

While one should ensure that they are using the appropriate norms (dependent on language proficiency and acculturation), the WCST functions well for the clinician who desires to assess executive functioning for Hispanic clients including problem solving, concept formation, and abstraction and may be used in either the manual or computerized form.

Trails

The Trail Making Test (TMT) assesses timed attention, mental flexibility sequencing, and nonverbal processing speed. They consist of two parts: Part A (Trails A; see Fig. 22.1) and Part B (Trails B; see Fig. 22.2). In Trails A, there are circled numbers from 1 to 25, and the subject is asked to draw lines to connect the numbers in ascending order. This is a timed task, and the subject is given the opportunity to practice and to ensure that they understand the task prior to beginning. If the subject makes an error, the clinician immediately interjects and allows the subject to correct it. The subject is informed that they are to connect the circles as quickly as possible *without* lifting the pen or pencil

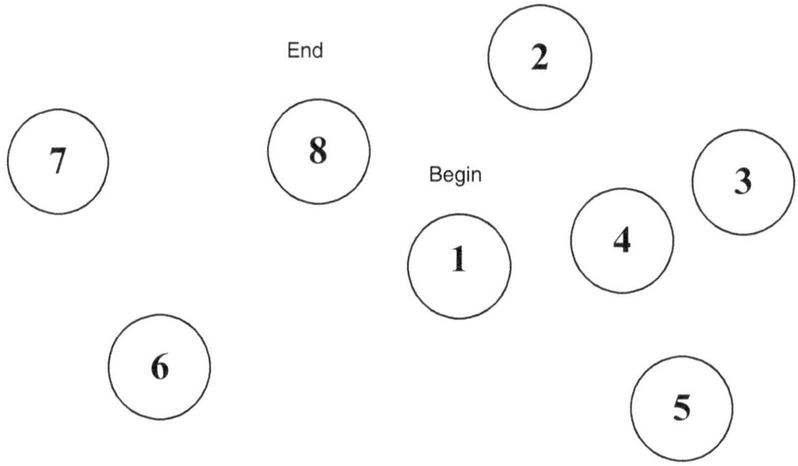

Fig. 22.1 Trails A sample

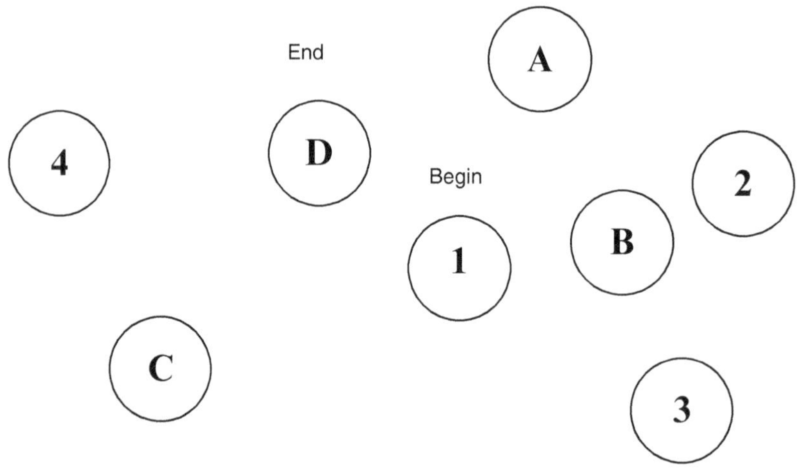

Fig. 22.2 Trails B sample

from the paper. The task is complete either once the subject finishes or after 5 min have elapsed (whichever comes first). The administration procedures are the same for Trails B although Trails B consists of circles with both numbers (1–13) and letters (A–L), and the subject is asked to connect the circles in an ascending pattern alternating between numbers and letters. The score is the number of seconds the subject required to complete each task (two scores are generated) regardless of the number of errors the subject made (Corrigan & Hinkeldey, 1987; Gaudino, Geisler, & Squires, 1995; Lezak, 2004; Reitan, 1958).

The TMT has been researched with Hispanics, and the results have been mixed. In the Menon, Hall, Hobson, Johnson, and O'Bryant (2011) study discussed within the Clock Drawing Test section of this chapter, Trails B was also administered. The normative Hispanic sample ($M=112.7$; SD=43.5) scored significantly different than the non-Hispanic White sample ($M=87.8$; SD=35.9) at the $p<.001$ level. However, it is unclear if this difference could have been best accounted for by other sociodemographic variables.

In a more thorough exploration of the association between neuropsychological scores and ethnicity, language, and acculturation variables, Boone, Victor, Wen, Razani, and Ponton (2007) included Trails A as part of a larger neuropsychological assessment battery. Differences between ethnic groups were identified between Caucasians and African Americans, but no such differences were identified between Hispanics and Caucasians, African Americans, or Asians. The same was true for English-speaking participants vs. English-as-a-second-language participants. These findings were not present with regards to Trails B.

Other differences in Trails A and B have also been found among Puerto Ricans when compared with a New York sample even after for controlling for sex and education (with better scores for the New York sample; Carrión-Baralt, 2009). Findings similar to those described above have also been found with the Color Trails Test (which provides a measure of psychomotor speed and cognitive flexibility; La Rue, Romero, Ortiz, Liang, & Lindeman, 1999). In sum, research has indicated that trails, in conjunction with other measures (discussed below) of nonverbal executive functioning, are an adequate measure of impairment of the domain of executive functioning for Hispanic clients.

Stroop Color-Word Interference Task

This Stroop Color-Word Interference Task (Golden, 1978) is a test of cognitive inhibition and set-shifting, as well as one of selective attention and processing speed. This measure is reliant on the prefrontal cortex and the anterior cingulate gyrus (Egner & Hirsch, 2005; Harrison et al., 2005; Peterson et al., 1999), which aid in attention and inhibition for competing responses. Research with older Hispanic populations on this task shows an effect of age which corresponds with a decrease in the speed with which an individual can name a color and an increase in the influence of interference effects (Peña-Casanova et al., 2009).

Drexel Tower of London

The Tower of London (TOLDX; Culbertson & Zillmer, 2001) is a modified task of the original Tower of London (Shallice, 1982), designed to assess the specific areas of executive control related to planning. It is believed that these areas also include inhibition and visuospatial memory as well as working memory and correspondingly would seem to utilize a wider range of neural cortices.

Research again showed an impact of age and education on executive functioning, but not an impact of gender, in Hispanic cohorts. The results were also compared to the normative data for Euro-American and non-Hispanic individuals and found to be roughly equivalent at the midpoints, with a variation of 1–2 points for lesser (0–5 years) or higher (13–20 years) educated individuals, suggesting that any such differences are not clinically relevant (Peña-Casanova et al., 2009).

Clock Drawing Test

Research has been conducted with Hispanics on the Clock Drawing Test, which requires the client to draw a clock with all numbers within the face of the clock and to indicate a specified time. Several renditions of this test exist. Royall et al. (2003) describe the CLOX tests and relevant procedures as follows. The first part, CLOX1, is an unprompted task that is sensitive to executive control whereas CLOX2 is a copied version and is less dependent on executive skills. Each CLOX subtest is scored on a 15-point scale, and lower CLOX scores indicate impairment (the cutpoint for CLOX1 is 10/15 and for CLOX2 is 12/15—these are representative of the 5th percentile for young adult controls; Royall, Cordes, & Polk, 1998). The CLOX has undergone forward and backward translation procedures and was piloted with a small sample of Hispanic and non-Hispanic outpatients. Results from this pilot study indicated that language had no effect on the failure rate of the test (Royall et al., 2003).

In a fairly extensive study, Royall et al. (2003) reviewed 1,309 in-home CLOX evaluations and found that a valid administration of the Spanish CLOX can be accomplished with community-based

Hispanic elder samples regardless of education or acculturation and with comparable failure rates to Anglo-American samples (despite finding considerably more Spanish language speakers than English speakers failed CLOX1 language of presentation had no significant effect on CLOX2 failure rates). These results suggest that further modifications in administration and interpretation are not necessary as these findings are similar to those observed in non-Hispanic samples. Subsequently, Royall, Espino, Polk, Palmer, and Markides (2004) found evidence that the CDT offers a rapid, culturally unbiased, and cost-effective means of assessing for impairment in executive control function, particularly with Mexican Americans.

More recently, Menon et al. (2011) have aimed to establish normative data for the CLOX in a sample of English- and Spanish-speaking Hispanic and non-Hispanic Whites. Results indicated that CLOX1 scores require adjustment by age across ethnicities (consistent with previous findings that age predicts neurocognitive functioning, e.g., Schillerstrom et al., 2007; Von Gunten et al., 2008). However, education and gender adjustments were required for CLOX1 in non-Hispanic Whites only (which contradicts previous findings that Mexican Americans' performance on various neurocognitive measures is affected by these two variables; see Heller et al., 2006). None of the demographic variables were valid predictors of CLOX2 performance, suggesting that such adjustments are not necessary for CLOX2. La Rue and colleagues (1999) also administered the Clock Drawing Test as part of a larger neuropsychological testing battery and found small ethnic differences on Clock Drawing that were strongly influenced by education. In sum, research has indicated that while the CLOX1 may be more influenced by demographic variables such as education and gender, as well as a moderate impact for language of presentation with Spanish speakers showing statistically, but not necessarily clinically poorer performance on the CLOX1, there are data for normative adjustments. Further, the CLOX2 seems to be equivalent for Hispanic and non-Hispanic Euro-Americans without adjustment. Thus, the CLOX is a valid assessment of executive functioning related to visuospatial memory and reconstruction and functions adequately as a measure of executive functioning.

Digit Span

Traditionally, it has been found that Hispanics recall, on average, fewer numbers on Digit Span than do their non-Hispanic counterparts (Kaufman, 1990). More recent research supports these earlier findings, particularly in the context of administration in English vs. Spanish (Boone et al., 2007; Gasquoine, Croyle, Cavazos-Gonzalez, & Sandoval, 2007; Wheeler, 2010), and it has been purported that these differences are a result of the differences in the phonological length of digits (e.g., Ardila, Pineda, & Rosselli, 2000). In fact, Boone and colleagues included Digit Span as part of a larger neuropsychological assessment battery and found that English-speaking participants performed better than English-as-a-second-language participants ($p = .014$) and Caucasians performed better than Hispanics ($p = .003$). Similar results were also found by La Rue and colleagues (1999). They found that education was related to scores on Digit Span (e.g., Hispanics aged 65–74 years with more than 12 years of education, Digits Forward score was $M = 6.06$; $SD = 2$) which is at the 22nd to 30th percentile compared to general age norms (Wechsler, 1987), and Hispanics 75 years and older with 6 or fewer years of school scored even lower; the mean score is only 3.48 (±1.52). In comparison, Gasquoine and colleagues (2007) found mean scores for nonimpaired Hispanics to be much more equivocal to the Digit Span norms for the English norms (English-dominant Hispanics administered in English $M = 9.7$ $SD = 2.4$, administered in Spanish $M = 8.5$ $SD = 2.5$; balanced bilinguals in English $M = 8.9$ $SD = 2.2$, in Spanish $M = 8.7$ $SD = 1.7$; and Spanish-dominant Hispanics administered Digit Span in English $M = 10.1$ $SD = 2.5$, administered in Spanish $M = 9$ $SD = 1.7$). While Gasquoine et al. found more equivocal data, they acknowledge that the sample of the study was limited and thus not necessarily generalizable to a larger population. Thus, clinicians should consider the broader research that demonstrated participants who tested in Spanish averaged shorter digit spans than those tested in English (this has also been found to be the case for Cuban American and Mexican American populations, e.g., Ardila et al., 2000, 2001; Loewenstein et al., 1994; López & Taussig, 1991). The studies suggest that it is the more complex phonological aspects of Spanish numbers (e.g., a greater number of multi-syllabic numbers) that increase demand on executive functioning and thus decrease Digit Span for Hispanic clients. Therefore, when one uses Digit Span as a measure of executive functioning, they should utilize normative data specific to Hispanic clients, appropriate to the language of administration.

Delis-Kaplan Executive Function System

The Delis-Kaplan Executive Function System (D-KEFS; Delis, Kaplan, & Kramer, 2001) is not a complete flexible battery but rather is a battery of assessments to examine various aspects of higher order executive functioning. This assessment system is valuable in that it corresponds nicely with the CVLT-II and assesses a broad range of neuropsychological abilities that are thought to be mediated by executive processes including inhibition, cognitive flexibility, verbal fluency, and sorting. The D-KEFS was also conceived to be used in a process-oriented manner in which behavioral observations factor in as much as quantifiable test data in interpreting results. The test authors endeavored to produce process scores that allow such behavioral observations that might influence test performance to be standardized and compared with normative samples. Despite the D-KEFS' broad appeal and process-oriented aesthetic, there is little information regarding its cross-cultural applicability toward Hispanic populations although a Spanish adaptation of its card-sorting subtest is available (Armengol & Moes, 2008). More adaptations are clearly warranted in consideration of the D-KEFS widespread use among clinicians.

Tests of Continuous Performance and Attention

A change in attention has been cited as the most common neuropsychological symptom associated with brain damage (Lezak, 1995), and Continuous Performance Tests (CPT) can measure not only processing speed but also focused, sustained, divided, and alternating attention characteristics in a neuropsychological evaluation (Tinius, 2003). Abnormal CPT performance has been observed in individuals with ADHD (Epstein, Conners, Sitarenios, & Erhardt, 1998), reading disabilities (Aaron, Joshi, Palmer, Smith, & Kirby, 2002; Willcutt et al., 2001), and other psychiatric conditions (Liu et al., 2002; Nelson, Sax, & Strakowski, 1998; Van den Bosch, Rombouts, & Van Asma, 1996).

Commonly Used CPTs

Commonly used CPTs include the Integrated Visual and Auditory CPT (IVA+Plus; Sandford & Turner, 1994), the Test of Variables of Attention (TOVA; Swalwell, Greenberg, & Dupuy, 2008), and the Conners' Continuous Performance Test, currently in its second (CPT-II v.5, Conners & Staff, 2000). The CPT is a test predominantly designed to test attention as it relates to attention deficit/hyperactivity disorder (ADHD). While the diagnosis of ADHD is primarily a diagnosis falling into the category of childhood disorders, it is increasing in its use for adults with a prevalence rate of 5 % (Franke et al., 2011). Additionally, the test's author (Conners & Staff) has designed the test for individuals aged 6 and older to assess for other problems of attention and executive function impairment as well as working memory and motor control. While there appears to be minimal research on these measures with Hispanics, some literature has indicated that ethnicity does not appear to impact test results (Conners, Epstein, Angold, & Klaric, 2003). Of all of the measures of continuous performance discussed, only the IVA Plus is available in Spanish, but there is no corresponding research with

Spanish participants. However, in an effort to eliminate the confound of language, the TOVA uses geometric shapes rather than words or numbers. Thus, this may be a test amenable to Spanish language use, and one would reasonably expect research on this measure may demonstrate its utility with a Spanish-speaking or bilingual population.

Paced Auditory Serial Addition Test

The Paced Auditory Serial Addition Test (PASAT; Gronwall, 1977) is a continuous performance test of a different nature and is used to assess the limits of attention, processing speed, and working memory under a timed condition (which can be altered from a pace of 2 to 3 s per number) that requires that the individual sum numbers in a cumulative fashion (e.g., adding the last number presented with the current number presented). The fact that the test is paced and cumulative creates an additional requirement on the working memory and executive control system, not seen in most other tests of attention and memory (for a review of the PASAT see Tombaugh, 2006). This test is sensitive to neuropsychological impairment in the domains discussed and has been included as part of a battery to identify neuropsychological impairment in individuals diagnosed with MS (Boringa et al., 2001). While this research in MS has studied individuals who identified Spanish as their primary language, it is unclear if they were tested in English or Spanish, and an extensive review of the literature failed to identify a Spanish language version of the test (Arrondo, Sepulcre, Duque, Toledo, & Villoslada, 2010).

Memory and Learning

Wechsler Memory Scales

The Wechsler Memory Scales (WMS), currently in its fourth edition (WMS-IV; Wechsler, 2008b), is a system of assessment designed to assess of various domains of short- and long-term memory and attention. These tasks include both verbal and nonverbal assessments of both short-term memory as well as working memory. Unfortunately, neither the previous (WMS-III) nor the current versions are available in Spanish. However, the previously revised version (WMS-R) and selected portions of the WMS-III have been translated with normative data and incorporated into other Spanish language batteries (which are discussed later in this chapter). Additionally, a review of the progression of the WMS (Loring & Bauer, 2010) suggests that newer editions are not necessarily improvements and can in fact decrease the clinical accuracy and utility of the instrument. Furthermore, many of the domains assessed in the WMS are covered by other tests of memory and learning discussed here (e.g., SEVLT, BFLT-E, and ROCFT). Thus, given the lack of a comprehensive translation of the WMS for Spanish-speaking individuals, as well as the availability of relevant components of memory that are incorporated into other batteries (e.g., the Verbal/Prose Memory Test and Visual Span Test incorporated into the Batería Neuropsicológica en Español; Artiola I Fortuny, Hermosillo, & Heaton, 1999), the WMS-IV is not appropriate for use with Spanish-speaking Hispanic clients.

Wide Range Assessment of Memory and Learning

The Wide Range Assessment of Memory and Learning (WRAML; Sheslow & Adams, 1990) was originally designed as an assessment of memory and learning in children (aged 5–17 years) and is now in its second edition (WRAML-2; Sheslow & Adams, 2003). This assessment is designed to assess the broad range of memory including short- and long-term memory, as well as working memory in both verbal and nonverbal modalities. This revision now covers a greater age range than its predecessor (6–90 years). However, there is little research for this assessment that is specific to

Hispanics, and a search of EBSCO and PubMed (conducted in early 2012) yielded no evidence of a Spanish translation for the measure. While research does exist with Hispanics making up part of the sample (Burton, Mittenberg, Gold, & Drabman, 1999; Suglia, Wright, Schwartz, & Wright, 2008), this research did not necessarily examine the influence of language proficiency or ethnicity. While some research described accounting for the influence of maternal education and ethnicity, they did not specifically describe the direction or magnitude of this influence (Suglia et al., 2008). Most of the research for Hispanics either appears to be related to performance of individuals in English, whose primary or dominant language is Spanish or for Hispanics without reference to their language ability. Thus, this assessment may be appropriate for use with Hispanic individuals, but one may wish to consider the limited normative information available for level of language proficiency.

Test of Memory and Learning

The Test of Memory and Learning in its first edition (TOMAL; Reynolds & Bigler, 1996) was designed as an assessment of memory for children aged 5–19 years. Now in its second edition (TOMAL-2; Reynolds & Voress, 2007), the TOMAL-2 remains an assessment of memory though its normative sample extended its age range to 5–59 years. The TOMAL-2 is composed of 14 subtests, 8 that are core and 6 that are supplementary. Core subtests include Memory for Stories, Facial Memory, Word Selective Reminding, Visual Selective Reminding, Object Recall, Abstract Visual Memory, Digits Forward, Visual Sequential Memory, Paired Recall, and Memory for Location. Supplementary subtests include Letters Forward, Digits Backward, Letters Backward, and Manual Imitation as well as two verbal delayed recall tasks. Verbal and nonverbal as well as composite indices are calculated from the subtests. Index scores are standard scores with means of 100 and standard deviations of 15. Little information is available regarding the TOMAL-2's generalizability toward Hispanic populations. However, given that its verbal tests are highly reliant on familiarity with the English language, it is likely that clients who speak English as a second language would impact performance on these tests. Nonverbal tests may be more resilient to these factors, but research is required to corroborate these statements.

The Rey-Osterrieth Complex Figure Drawing Task (ROCFT; for a Complete Description of the Test and Scoring, See Duley et al., 1993)

The Rey-Osterrieth test is a classic neuropsychological assessment. The neuropsychologist examines not just the ability of the individual to recall and recreate a visual object from memory but also the sparing of visual location (e.g., do they put information in the correct general location), as well as sparing of perspective (are distances between objects approximately the same, differences in length maintained). This test also allows neuropsychologists to assess the cognitive processes behind the reconstruction of the figure. This can be accomplished by using multiple colored pencils or markers with a preset time limit to change colors. This process allows the clinician an opportunity to look at the order of operations for recreation (e.g., do they recreate the larger structure first and then fill in the details or vice versa). An atypical (e.g., starting with the number of holes in a circle and then drawing tangential lines to the larger structure) reconstruction may indicate odd thought processes resulting from insult to the association cortex or the frontal lobe.

As with other tests discussed in this chapter, the ROCFT was studied as part of the NEURONORMA project (with 354 Spanish-speaking participants aged 50–90), and results have demonstrated that the measure accurately examines visuospatial memory, both immediate and delayed. Also of interest is the impact of age and education. Peña-Casanova and colleagues (2009) demonstrated that while sex of the participant was not important, age and education did predict differences in performance, with those of higher education showing better performance on the task. An inverse effect was associated with age. While there did not appear to be an impact of language, one should utilize age and education corrected norms.

Verbal Learning and Memory

California Verbal Learning Test

The California Verbal Learning Test (CVLT; Delis, Kramer, Kaplan, & Ober, 1987) is a measure of declarative verbal learning and memory. Declarative memory, as opposed to procedural memory, is typically represented by tasks involving the recall of word lists presented over multiple trials. This measure is used to assess verbal learning and memory in both immediate and delayed conditions as well as free and cued recall.

There are various verbal learning and memory tests designed to assess the same processes assessed by the CVLT that exist in both English and Spanish. Two measures that have been assessed with a range of Hispanic clients are the Hopkins Verbal Learning and Memory Test (currently in its revised form, HVLT-R; Brandt & Benedict, 2001) and the Spanish English Verbal Learning Test (SEVLT; found in Mungas, Wallace, & Reed, 1998, and partially reproduced with recalculated norms in Gonzalez, Mungas, & Haan, 2002).

Spanish Verbal Learning Test

Various attempts have been made to directly translate the CVLT into a Spanish version (Harris, Cullum, & Puente, 1995; Wilkie et al., 2004), most likely to its data related to learning and memory and the assessment of mild cognitive impairment and dementia. While these translations exist, there is either limited or nonexistent data that is extensive enough to utilize them in clinical practice, and it is instead suggested that one of the aforementioned alternatives (either the SEVLT or the HVLT) is utilized instead.

Hopkins Verbal Learning Test (HVLT-R; Brandt & Benedict, 2001)

Similar to other verbal learning tests, the HVLT was designed to assess verbal learning and memory as well as aid in the detection of dementia and aphasia. Due to the large body of research showing differential performance (e.g., 85 % sensitivity and 76 % specificity for the HVLT using the suggested cutpoint of one standard deviation below; Shapiro, Benedict, Schretlen, & Brandt, 1999) on naming tests influenced by age and education. Thus, Cherner and colleagues (2007) set out to develop demographically adjusted norms for Spanish-speaking individuals and, in addition to age data, parsed education into categories of ≤6 years, 7–9 years, 10–12 years, and ≥13 years. Their results showed the expected differential performance based on education but failed to identify significant differences for age or gender. In fact, their results showed a greater than expected number of individuals misclassified as impaired, in particular for the lowest educated group studied, with 72 % of individuals in the lowest education group being classified as impaired and 24 % of the highest educated group being classified as impaired. Considering that the expected classification rate would be 16 %, even the highest group showed a rate nearly one and a half times more likely to be misclassified. Cherner and colleagues transformed the raw data using a fractional polynomial formula (found in their paper along with their norms and percentile scores) to transform the raw scores, which resulted into a distribution that more closely resembled the expected distribution.

Spanish English Verbal Learning Test (SEVLT; Gonzalez, Mungas, Reed, Marshall, & Haan, 2001)

The SEVLT is used to assess verbal learning in Spanish- and English-speaking individuals and, as the name implies, was developed as a measure to establish an assessment with comparative normative data for both Spanish and English speakers. Originally designed with a modestly large normative sample (Latino $n=689$; non-Hispanic White $n=112$), recent research (Gonzalez et al.,

2002) has expanded this normative data to include a larger sample ($n = 1{,}789$) of Latino males that were predominantly Mexican who were over age 60.

Biber Figure Learning Test-Extended

The Biber Figure Learning Test-Extended (BFLTE; Glosser, Cole, French, Saykin, & Sperling, 1997) is used as a measure of visual or nonverbal learning and memory and has been described as the visual analog of the CVLT (Glosser, Cole, Khatri, DellaPietra, & Kaplan, 2002; Tracy et al., 2001). The BFLT-E consists of 15 geometric designs constructed of simple shapes (circles, squares, and triangles), which are combined to form novel stimuli. Similar to the CVLT, the BFLT-E assesses immediate and delayed recall as well as interference and recognition. Although the CVLT and the BFLT-E are not identically matched in terms of difficulty level and item content, they can serve as relative measures of verbal and nonverbal learning (Tracy et al.). This test is easy to administer, and, in fact, the inter-tester reliability for the BLFT-E has been found to be as high as .98 (Glosser et al., 2002). The BLFT-E has also been shown to have good test-retest reliability and criterion validity (Glosser et al., 2002) as well as an ability to demonstrate sensitivity to non-language-dominant right temporal lobe functioning. In keeping with the comparison to the CVLT, the BFLT-E also includes measures of learning through trials 1–5 and scores for immediate recall, delayed recall, immediate memory, hit rate, discriminability, and total false alarm rate. While the Biber has not been specifically tested with the intent of identifying the normative properties with Hispanic- or Spanish-speaking individuals, its nonverbal nature would suggest that it lends itself well to the assessment of visual learning and memory, as well as visuospatial reconstruction, without the influences of language or acculturation seen in other neuropsychological assessments discussed in this chapter.

Benton Judgment of Line Orientation

The Benton Judgment of Line Orientation (JOL; Benton et al., 1983) serves as a measure of visuospatial organization and is considered to be a chiefly right hemisphere task (Lezak, 1995). This task requires the comparison and matching of angled line pair stimuli to a semicircle of target lines numbered 1–11. The participant is asked to choose which two lines from the semicircle are the same as the pair of the stimulus lines. There are a total of 30 items. A five-item practice trial is given with corrective feedback. Scores are based on the total correct out of 30. As part of a larger study of a Multilingual Aphasia Evaluation (MAE-S), Rey, Feldman, Rivas-Vazquez, Levin, and Bentin (1999) found that the normative data for the Benton was equivalent to that of the original English-speaking normative sample, thus suggesting that the information provided for the JOL is a valid measure of visuospatial organization for Spanish-speaking Hispanics.

Recommendations for Assessing Learning and Memory

There is not a single comprehensive measure described above that is equivalent to memory assessment systems in English (e.g., the WMS, WRAML, and TOMAL); rather there seems to be a broad range of domain-specific assessments with good normative data that would allow a clinician to create an assessment that would cover the various aspects of learning and memory in both the verbal and nonverbal domains (e.g., an amalgamation of the ROCFT, SEVLT, BFLT-E, and Digit Span) to assess for impairment or spared functioning for these domains. While there is not a single memory assessment, there are batteries discussed later in this chapter that compile measures of memory and learning, as part of a larger neuropsychological test battery that has appropriate psychometric properties and normative data for Hispanics and is available in Spanish.

Language

Naming Tests

Naming tests are typically used in the assessment of language-based disruptions to assess for things such as anomia and aphasia as well as impairments in receptive and productive language. This can be assessed via spontaneous word generation, or confrontational word retrieval, and examples of these tests are described below and often help us differentiate between semantic dementia (SD) and Alzheimer's dementia (AD; Hodges & Patterson, 1995, 1997).

Boston Naming Test

The original rendition of the Boston Naming Test (BNT; Kaplan, Gooidglass, & Weintraub, 1983) consists of 60 items. Administration of the BNT is simple; the client is presented with a series of images and asked to provide a name for each image. A search in the psycINFO database revealed that several Spanish renditions of the BNT exist (e.g., Garcia-Albea, Sanchez-Bernardos, & del Viso-Pabon, 1986; Peña-Casanova et al., 2009; Marquez de la Plata et al., 2009) and ethnic differences in performance on the original BNT have been identified with Caucasians exhibiting superior performance across ethnic groups (Boone et al., 2007). In this section, we will focus on the Modified Boston Naming Test-Spanish (MBNT-S) as a review of the literature suggests that this version of the BNT is the most generalizable to individuals from various Spanish-speaking origins (e.g., the USA, Colombia, Spain). The MBNT-S consists of 30 items from the original BNT judged and selected by experts on the basis of appropriateness for the use with Spanish speakers. Items were reordered according to difficulty, and the MBNT was normed using 300 volunteers who were mostly (70 %) monolingual and Spanish-speaking (Marquez de la Plata et al.). Marquez de la Plata and colleagues have found evidence that the MBNT-S is able to differentiate nondemented and moderately demented individuals although alternative naming tests may have superior internal consistency and a superior item discrimination pattern when compared to other tests (e.g., the Texas Naming Test discussed below).

Texas Naming Test

The Texas Naming Test (TNT) was developed by Marquez de la Plata et al. (2008) using objects that are relevant and familiar to Spanish speakers. Objects were selected based on 260 words studied in English and Spanish by various researchers (Snodgrass & Vanderwart, 1980; Cuetos et al., 1999). Administration and scoring procedures for the TNT are the same as for the BNT, and the 30 most salient and psychometrically reliable items were selected using standard item selection techniques from responses of demented and nondemented adult Spanish speakers. Order of presentation for the items is based on the level of item difficulty (Marquez de la Plata et al.). The TNT has been demonstrated to discriminate between nondemented and moderately demented individuals; to have a superior item difficulty pattern compared to other naming tests (e.g., the CERAD); a superior item discrimination pattern than the MBNT-S; and has been tested with Spanish-speaking individuals of different origins (e.g., the USA, Colombia, Spain; Marquez de la Plata et al., 2009).

Word Fluency

Commonly used measures of verbal fluency category naming tests, phonemic verbal fluency tests. These tests will be reviewed below.

F-A-S. Phonemic verbal fluency tests aim to assess for frontal lobe functions and call for the client to provide a list of words beginning with specific letters (usually F, A, and S) (Machado et al., 2009). Research has indicated slight (nonsignificant) differences in performance on F-A-S between Spanish- vs. English-speaking demented patients (La Rue et al., 1999; Lowenstein et al., 1992); sociodemographic variables have been found to impact performance on this test (sex and education: La Rue et al.), and bilingual assessment procedures (i.e., conducting an assessment in both Spanish and English) have been found to impact test performance (La Rue et al.). Additionally, in a comparison of Hispanics on the West Coast of the USA (WC; from 19 different Spanish-speaking countries and a mix of those diagnosed with Alzheimer's dementia as well as research controls; RC), with Hispanics studied from a university research center examining Alzheimer's dementia on the East Coast (EC; Described as predominantly from Puerto Rico), Fillenbaum et al. (2007) found differential performance among the groups. These results found that age and education were positively correlated with performance for the WC sample but only for those that were not diagnosed with dementia, while those individuals with dementia (WC) showed no relationship between age/education and performance on verbal fluency. Additionally, the authors found no impact for age or education on word fluency performance for the EC sample. The authors suggest that these differences could be attributed to sample size, the research intentions (e.g., the EC group was much more interested in Alzheimer's patients as they are a hospital setting more interested in treatment, while the WC sample comes from a center more focused on research and made greater efforts to include RC participants), or linguistic differences in Puerto Rican participants from those of the more diverse WC sample. There have been attempts to reduce the variability of performance not only among Hispanic ethnic groups but also between Hispanic normative date and that of English-speaking, non-Hispanic White norms using a different set of letters for Spanish speakers based upon frequency of words with the given letter in Spanish. Jacobs et al. (1997) administered a phonemic verbal fluency test to Spanish and English speakers, and English speakers were given the letters C, F, and L, and Spanish speakers were given the letters P, S, and R. With these letters, no differences were found in terms of performance in English vs. Spanish speakers.

Animal Naming Test

The Animal Naming Test is a category fluency test (Carrión-Baralt, Meléndez-Cabrero, Beeri, Sano, & Silverman, 2009) that measures impairment in verbal production, semantic memory, and language (Morris et al., 1989). Administration of this test is simple; the client is asked to verbally name as many animals as they can in a 60-s time period (Carrión-Baralt et al., 2009) and in some cases are provided with superordinate categories (e.g., animals from the farm, jungle, ocean, or house pets) to help with retrieval (Jacobs et al., 1997). This test is also sometimes referred to as the Sem-Flu (Goodglass & Kaplan, 1983). Carrion-Baralt and colleagues found this test to *not* have an association with education, sex, and age in a Hispanic sample, and they did not identify a difference in performance between Puerto Ricans and New Yorkers. However, researchers have found better performance on this test for English speakers when compared to Spanish speakers (Jacobs et al.).

Recommendations for Language Tests

As indicated above, we reviewed language tests. While there are many versions of the Boston Naming Test, the MBNT-S appears to have superior psychometric properties, and research has shown that the BNT is an effective measure in assessing Alzheimer's dementia as well as differentiating it from semantic dementia in elderly, Spanish-speaking adults (Rami et al., 2008). However, the TNT appears to have a greater degree of sensitivity for detecting even moderately demented versus nondemented patients as well as a greater item discrimination among a broad range of Hispanic cultures (Marquez de la Plata et al., 2008, 2009). Thus, when administering a flexible battery, one may wish to consider using the TNT rather than the MBNT-S and should avoid using the BNT in its unmodified form with Hispanic clients. Additionally, when using the word fluency F-A-S test, one should consider utilizing the letters C, F, and L for equivalency between Hispanic and non-Hispanic White normative performance. The Animal Naming Test may also be considered when one desires to reduce the variability of performance among Hispanic ethnic groups, but be mindful of the significantly poorer performance when compared to English, non-Hispanic White normative data.

Systems of Assessment

As discussed earlier, one can approach the neuropsychological assessment from a fixed battery approach (such as the Halstead-Reitan) or a flexible battery approach. An informal battery may contain any combination of the previously described assessments based on domains of interest or used pieces of a fixed battery based on domains of interest (e.g., Clock Drawing from the Halstead-Reitan). More recently, test publishers have developed systems of assessment that include neuropsychological assessments designed to act as a comprehensive battery that can be used as a flexible battery. The flexible battery is comprehensive in that it assesses all domains that one could expect to measure in a comprehensive neuropsychological battery. Both the fixed batteries and the flexible systems are discussed below.

Repeatable Battery for the Assessment of Neuropsychological Status

The Repeatable Battery for the Assessment of Neuropsychological Status (RBANS; Randolph, 1998) is a brief neuropsychological battery used to detect cognitive impairment in around 30 min or less. Additionally, the battery has several benefits. First, the brief time necessary for administration makes it a valuable asset to any setting that provides services to patients using insurance or managed care. Second, the RBANS can be used as a neuropsychological screening tool. Another advantage of the RBANS lies in the name. Many neuropsychological assessments or components of an assessment are considered spoiled once administered. This means that the clinician would not provide a second administration of an IQ test or redo the CVLT within a short period of time, as the artifact of learning would skew the interpretation of the information. However, the R in RBANS stands for repeatable, alluding to the fact that this assessment battery is designed with the intent of multiple administrations. This is particularly important when the clinician is looking at rate of decline or trying to evaluate the effectiveness of an intervention. Finally, the most significant advantage is the availability of the measure in multiple languages. The publishers of the RBANS indicate that it has been translated into over 30 languages. Muntal Encinas et al. (in press) have piloted a translation of the assessment in Spanish, which suggests that it has the potential to provide comparable (to English norms) normative information for Spanish-speaking Hispanics. Thus, one may wish to utilize the limited existing data for this measure or collect data of their own, interpreting the results with caution.

Neuropsychological Assessment Battery (NAB; Stern & White, 2003)

The NAB is a neuropsychological battery that has been recently developed. This system contains a screening component, can be administered as a fixed or a flexible battery, and, like the RBANS, has alternative forms available. Additionally, the sample used to develop the NAB is very robust and included over 1,400 participants who were administered all components of the battery. The NAB screening module Total Screening Score Index demonstrates a reasonable degree of validity when compared against the Modified Mini-Mental State Examination ($r=.46$), the RBANS ($r=.65$), and the Mini-Mental State Examination ($r=.55$), and the NAB's authors provide a great deal of psychometric comparisons for validity of the assessments of the full battery relative to existing measures for various neurological insults (e.g., dementia, HIV, and ADHD; White & Stern, 2003).

While the standardization sample for the battery does include Hispanics, there is not yet a version translated to Spanish. This presents a challenge for those professionals working with clients whose first or primary language is Spanish. If we consider the research by Siedlecki and colleagues (2010) and the invariable components of cognitive functioning (most likely due to the limited variability discussed in the introduction to this chapter), given the scope of the NAB, there are likely a large number of components that would appropriately classify Hispanic performance into impaired and nonimpaired domains. Currently, however, there is no normative data to support the use of this assessment battery with Hispanics.

A unique aspect of the NAB is the inclusion of a measure for Activities of Daily Living included in each of the domains. The benefit in this is that these measures have much more clinical utility and face validity in terms of describing the relationship between neuropsychological assessment and corresponding functional outcomes. Thus, research and data collection specific to language assessment that accounts for the domains of language proficiency, age, education, and socioeconomic status would be a welcome endeavor to the practice of clinical neuropsychology with Hispanic clients.

Halstead-Reitan Neuropsychological Battery (HRNB; Reitan & Wolfson, 1985)

The HRNB remains a standard fixed battery designed to assess cognitive impairment stemming from possible organic sources. Originally developed to assist in pinpointing specific lesions, its original purpose has been supplanted by modern neuroimaging techniques. Despite this, the HRNB still allows clinicians to ascertain the degree to which an organic insult impacts cognition and behavior and assesses several broad domains that overlap with those discussed above, including motor functions and cognitive flexibility, as well as basic tactile and auditory sensory functions. Studies on the HRNB have found differences in performance among Mexicans, Mexican Americans, and Anglo-Americans based on level of acculturation. These differences are primarily found in subtle components of the Tactile Performance Test (TPT) and the Seashore Rhythm Test (SRT). This is to say that the overall tests did not show a significant difference for acculturation but aspects of them (e.g., adaptive motor learning showed a sensitivity to acculturation, but performance did not). Further, while the differences found are statistically significant, the authors concede that the differences never exceed half a standard deviation and thus would likely not be clinically significant. Thus, regardless of the statistically significant difference, in clinical application, the Halstead-Reitan would not inappropriately identify a Hispanic client as being impaired, when they were not.

NEUROPSI

The NEUROPSI is a test of attention and memory that is written in Spanish with corresponding normative data. The test consists of nine domains (orientation, attention and concentration, executive functions, working memory, and immediate and delayed verbal and visual memory) in an effort to comprehensively measure common neurocognitive domains, with test design and normative data designed from the ground-up from a Spanish-speaking sample (Ostrosky-Solı's et al., 2003). Many of these domains contain assessments that are discussed elsewhere in this chapter (e.g., the ROCFT for assessing visual memory and Digit or Spatial Span tasks to assess verbal and nonverbal working memory, respectively). However, there are unique tests to assess attention and inhibition such as the Conflicting Instruction test, which asks the individual to make a response (e.g., a single pencil tap) when the examiner makes a "conflicting" response (e.g., two taps of his own pencil). Additionally, the authors developed a normative sample for this battery (Ostrosky-Solı's et al., 2007) that includes a wide range for the variables of age (6–85 years old) and education (0–22 years), which we have consistently identified as factors influencing performance on neurocognitive tests, and the results found by the authors for this variable were particularly interesting. Ostrosky-Solı's and colleagues (2007) found statistically significant interactions for these variables on the domains of contextual executive memory and place/person orientation. Further, the interactions between age and education were only seen in the age ranges of 16–30 and 31–55. Thus, the benefits of these factors for the aforementioned domains did not occur outside of these age ranges, and the protective factor that education provided deteriorated after age 56.

Thus, while this battery shows some of the same differential performance based on demographic variables of age and education, these appear to be offset by the size and scope of the normative data and the wide range of neurocognitive domains covered by the battery, which appears to serve its stated goal of providing a battery that contains normative data accounting for the impact of age and education through the span of development.

Batería Neuropsicológica en Español (Artiola I Fortuny, Hermosillo, & Heaton, 1999)

The Neuropsychological Test Battery in Spanish is a battery designed for adults aged 18–65. This battery was developed by Artiola I Fortuny and colleagues to account for the demographic variables identified in Heaton, Grant, and Matthews's (1991) normative corrections for English-speaking neuropsychological test performance. Thus, the test is designed to assess the domains of attention, executive functioning, learning, and memory, using eight subtests (Visual Memory Test, Verbal/Prose Memory Test, Wisconsin Test, Word Learning Test, Stroop Test, Digit Span Test, Visual Span Test, Letter [PMR] Fluency Test), which include both verbal and nonverbal domains. The normative sample is large and includes a range of individuals from the Mexico Border region of the USA as well as samples from Spain. Thus, the normative sample includes a broad range of age and education as well as linguistic diversity. This test, while not as exhaustive a battery as the HRNB, has a good normative sample of Hispanic ethnic groups. Additionally, it collected this data for many of the common neurocognitive domains assessed and seems a reasonable alternative for those clinicians seeking a briefer and more focused neuropsychological assessment.

Montreal Cognitive Assessment (MOCA; Nasreddine et al., 2003; http://www.mocatest.org/)

The MOCA is a brief cognitive screening measure that can be utilized to detect mild cognitive impairment. It is freely available in multiple languages on the internet, and there one can find references to research for its use related to a broad spectrum of cognitive disorders (e.g., Parkinson's, Alzheimer's dementia, and HIV-related dementia). While there is a great deal of research available for the screening and the measure is available in a great number of languages including Spanish, there is little research specifically related to Hispanics.

Some of the limited research available for Hispanics (Rossetti, Lacritz, Cullum, & Weiner, 2011) is that conducted with multiethnic samples. This data shows mean scores ($M=23.4$, SD=4.0) that are below the cutoff for impairment (26). Eleven percent of the sample were Hispanic, and performance was most impaired for the items of cube drawing, delayed free recall (<4/5 words), sentence repetition, placement of clock hands, abstraction items, and verbal fluency (<11 words in 1 min). Similarly, Strutt and Scott (2011) found differential performance for older Spanish speakers. This study examined the influence of education, which was separated by either less than 6 years or from 6 to 13 years, and found poorer performance for those with less than 6 years of education that appeared to be predominantly in the domain of visuospatial-executive performance. While the assessment of dementia is covered extensively in another chapter, the MOCA may be useful in screening for mild cognitive impairment and with the appropriate normative considerations serve as an indicator for further cognitive assessment.

Malingering and Effort

While not always the primary consideration, a comprehensive neuropsychological assessment should necessarily include the evaluation of effort and malingering. Assessment of malingering and effort is important because a competent and comprehensive evaluation should not only identify diagnosis, but also needs to rule out potential treatment interfering problems, as well as confounds of invalid responses. To be clear, effort suggests that one may not be responding in a manner that necessarily reflects what is truly occurring. A lack of effort may occur for any number of reasons but suggests less than optimal performance due to fatigue or indifference. Malingering, however, implies the purposeful presentation of symptoms for the purpose of gaining access to some secondary incentive beyond that of adopting the sick role. Thus, if we fail to assess effort and intention, we have the potential to cause harm to the client and also secondary harm to those who are involved with the client (e.g., friends, family, and coworkers). Malingering is specifically covered elsewhere in this book and so will not be described in detail. It is only brought up here because of its import to a comprehensive battery, and the additional fact that many neuropsychological tests (or components of them) are also measures of malingering and effort are incorporated into neuropsychological test measures (e.g., reliable Digit Span and the Word Fluency Tests and Controlled Oral Word Association Test). Thus, when conducting a neuropsychological assessment, one wants to be aware of the measures of psychological assessment that are also used to assess for effort and malingering, as well as their psychometric properties related to the Hispanic client.

Recommendations

As discussed, there are several challenges to the competent neuropsychological assessment of the Hispanic client (in comparison to the non-Hispanic, English-speaking client). Echemendia et al. (1997) discuss the more practically logistical issue of a lack of Hispanic neuropsychologists as well as a lack of training for neuropsychologists with Hispanic clientele. However, the limited number of assessments available for the Spanish-speaking client also challenges us, as well as corresponding normative data. Additionally, Gasquoine (1999, 2001) and Gasquoine et al. (2007) discuss the challenge and complexity of measuring all of the variables relevant to identifying culture and ethnicity and instead recommend a more psychometrically sound approach toward quantifying variables related to language proficiency, duration of residency in the USA, educational attainment, and economic status. In fact, other studies (Acevedo et al., 2001) found that for Spanish speakers, education is the most influential variable related to neuropsychological performance. As we saw with the comparison of a neuropsychological assessment consisting of purely English assessments adapted to Spanish, the performance between Hispanic cultures (those from the Mexican Border Region of the USA and those from Spain) showed nearly equivalent performance, with any differences disappearing as education level increased (Artioli I Fortuny, Heaton, & Hermosillo, 1998). Again, this suggests that the more important variables for consideration consist of those related to SES such as education and wealth.

To this end, we discussed the efforts to move toward a more culturally equivalent battery of neuropsychological assessment that relies on these variables of education level of English proficiency or bilingualism (in English and Spanish). Similar to the Heaton norms (1991) for common neuropsychological assessment to account for age and education, the goal of these assessment measures and corresponding normative scales is to account for individual differences, in this case, due to linguistic and cultural factors. The number of measures designed for Spanish-speaking clients is expanding as is the (re)development of normative data for extensions of existing measures. Such efforts also generalize with intellectual assessment, which may have an even greater reliance on verbal knowledge and vocabulary within the dominant culture (see chapter on intelligence in this book). This chapter discussed a summary of measures that are being used in the field of neuropsychology as well as relevant normative data for those measures as a resource for practicing clinicians in the field. Additionally, a supplementary but unstated goal is to encourage those working in the field to aid in the collection of data and development of norms. Ultimately, the guiding principal should be to provide competent services for our clients within the guidelines of the APA and to avoid passing the buck, so to speak, when it comes to our Hispanic clients.

References

Aaron, P. G., Joshi, R. M., Palmer, H., Smith, N., & Kirby, E. (2002). Separating genuine cases of reading disability from reading deficits caused by predominantly inattentive ADHD behavior. *Journal of Learning Disabilities, 35*, 425–435, 447.

Acevedo, A., Loewenstein, D. A., Barker, W. W., Harwood, D. G., Luis, C., Bravo, M., et al. (2001). Category fluency test: Normative data for English and Spanish-speaking elderly. Journal of the International Neuropsychological Society, 6, 760–769.

Anez, L. M., Paris, M., Jr., Bedregal, L. E., Davidson, L., & Grilo, C. M. (2005). Application of cultural constructs in the care of first generation Latino clients in a community mental health setting. *Journal of Psychiatric Practice, 11*(4), 221–230.

Archer, R. P., Buffington-Vollum, J. K., Stredny, R. V., & Handel, R. W. (2006). A survey of psychological test use patterns among forensic psychologists. *Journal of Personality Assessment, 87*(1), 84–94.

Ardila, A., & Moreno, S. (2001). Neuropsychological test performance in Aruaco Indians: An exploratory study. *Journal of the International Neuropsychological Neuropsychology Society, 7*, 510–515; *14*(2), 74.

Ardila, A., Pineda, D., & Rosselli, M. (2000). Correlation between intelligence test scores and executive function measures. *Archives of Clinical Neuropsychology, 15*(1), 31–36.

Armengol, C., & Moes, E. (2008, July 2–5). *Spanish adaptation of the D-KEFS card sorting test Mexican Norms*. The International Neuropsychological Society, Sociedad de Neuropsicología de Argentina, Joint Mid-Year Meeting, Buenos Aires, Argentina.

Arrondo, G., Sepulcre, J., Duque, B., Toledo, J., & Villoslada, P. (2010). Narrative speech is impaired in multiple sclerosis. *European Neurological Journal, 2*(1), 11–40.

Artiola, L., Hermosillo, D., Heaton, R., & Pardee, R. E. (1999). *Manual de normas y procedimientos para la bateria neuropsicologica en espanol*. Tucson, AZ: mPress.

Artiola L. F., Hermosillo Romo, D., Heaton, R., Roy, E. (1999). *Batería Neuropsicológica en Español*. Tucson, AZ: III.m Press.

Artioli I Fortuny, L., Garolera, M., Hermosillo Romo, D., Feldman, E., Fernandez Barillas, H., Keefe, R., et al. (2005). Research with Spanish-speaking populations in the United States: Lost in the translation a commentary and a plea. *Journal of Clinical and Experimental Neuropsychology, 27*, 555–564.

Artioli I Fortuny, L., & Heaton, R. K. (1996). Standard versus computerized administration of the Wisconsin Card Sorting Test. *The Clinical Neuropsychologist, 10*(4), 419–424.

Artioli I Fortuny, L., Heaton, R. K., & Hermosillo, D. (1998). Neuropsychological comparisons of Spanish-speaking participants from the U.S.–Mexico border region versus Spain. *Journal of the International Neuropsychological Society, 4*, 363–379.

Artioli I Fortuny, L., & Mullaney, H. A. (1997). Neuropsychology with Spanish speakers language use and proficiency issues for test development. *Journal of Clinical and Experimental Neuropsychology, 19*, 615–622.

Benton, A., Hamsher, K., Varney, N., & Spreen, O. (1983). *Contributions to neuropsychological assessment: A clinical manual. New York: Oxford University Press.*

Boone, K. B., Victor, T. L., Wen, J., Razani, J., & Ponton, M. (2007). The association between neuropsychological scores and ethnicity, language, and acculturation variables in a large patient population. *Archives of Clinical Neuropsychology, 22*, 355–365. doi:10.1016/j.acn.2007.01.010.

Boringa, J. B., Lazeron, R. H., Reuling, I. E., Adèr, H. J., Pfennings, L., Lindeboom, J., et al. (2001). The brief repeatable battery of neuropsychological tests: normative values allow application in multiple sclerosis clinical practice. *Multiple Sclerosis, 7*(4), 263–267.

Brandt, J., & Benedict, R. (2001). *Hopkins verbal learning test-revised.* Lutz, FL: Psychological Assessment Resources, Inc.

Broner, N., Franczak, M., Dye, C., & McAllister, W. (2001). Knowledge transfer, policymaking and community empowerment: A consensus model approach for providing public mental health and substance abuse services. *Psychiatric Quarterly, 72*(1), 79–102.

Burton, B. D., Mittenberg, W., Gold, S., & Drabman, R. (1999). A structural equation analysis of the wide range assessment of memory and learning in a clinical sample. *Child Neuropsychology, 5*(1), 34.

Carrión-Baralt, J. R., Meléndez-Cabrero, J., Beeri, M. S., Sano, M., & Silverman, J. M. (2009). The neuropsychological performances of nondemented Puerto Rican nonagenarians. *Dementia and Geriatric Cognitive Disorders, 27*, 353–360.

Cherner, M., Suarez, P., Lazzaretto, D., Artiola I Fortuny, L., Monica Rivera Mindt, Dawes, S., et al. (2007). Demographically corrected norms for the Brief Visuospatial Memory Test-revised and Hopkins Verbal Learning Test revised in monolingual Spanish speakers from the U.S.–Mexico border region. *Archives of Clinical Neuropsychology, 22*, 343–353.

Coffey, D. M., Marmol, L., Schock, L., & Adams, W. (2005). The influence of acculturation on the Wisconsin Card Sorting Test by Mexican Americans. *Archives of Clinical Neuropsychology, 20*(6), 795–803.

Cognistat. (n.d.) a. *Pioneers in brain fitness cognistat cognitive assessment: About the exam.* Retrieved from: http://www.cognistat.com/about-exam-faq.

Conners, C., Epstein, J. N., Angold, A., & Klaric, J. (2003). Continuous Performance Test performance in a normative epidemiological sample. *Journal of Abnormal Child Psychology: An Official Publication of The International Society for Research in Child and Adolescent Psychopathology, 31*(5), 555–562. doi:10.1023/A:1025457300409.

Conners, C. K., & Staff, M. H. S. (Eds.). (2000). *Conners' Continuous Performance Test II: Computer program for windows technical guide and software manual.* North Tonawanda, NY: Multi-Health Systems.

Correa, A. A. (2010). *Validation of the Spanish Sirs: Beyond linguistic equivalence in the assessment of malingering among Spanish speaking clinical populations.* Master of Science thesis, University of North Texas.

Corrigan, J. D., & Hinkeldey, M. S. (1987). Relationships between parts A and B of the Trail Making Test. *Journal of Clinical Psychology, 43*(4), 402–409.

Cuetos, F., Ellis, A., & Alvarez, B. (1999). Naming times for the Snodgrass and Vanderwart pictures in Spanish. *Behavior Research Methods, Instruments, & Computers, 31*, 650–658.

Culbertson, W. C., & Zillmer, E. A. (2001). *Tower of London. Drexel University. TOLDX.* North Tonawanda, NY: Multi-Health Systems.

David, B., Otis, D., & Price, B. T. (2004). The use of restraint and seclusion in different racial groups in an inpatient forensic setting. *The Journal of the American Academy of Psychiatry and the Law, 32*, 163–168.

Delis, D. C., Kaplan, E., & Kramer, J. H. (2001). *D-KEFS executive function system: Examiners manual.* San Antonio, TX: Psychological Corporation.

Delis, D. C., Kramer, J. H., Kaplan, E., & Ober, B. A. (1987). *California verbal learning test.* New York: Psychological Corporation.

Duley, J. F., Wilkins, J., Hamby, S., Hopkins, D., Burwell, R., & Barry, N. (1993). Explicit scoring criteria for the Rey-Osterrieth and Taylor complex figures. *The Clinical Neuropsychologist, 7*(1), 29–38.

Echemendia, R. J., Harris, J. G., Congett, S. M., Diaz, M. L., & Puente, A. E. (1997). Neuropsychological training and practices with Hispanics: A national survey. *The Clinical Neuropsychologist, 11*, 229–243.

Egner, T., & Hirsch, J. (2005). The neural correlates and functional integration of cognitive control in a Stroop task. *NeuroImage, 24*, 539–547.

Epstein, J. N., Conners, C. K., Sitarenios, G., & Erhardt, D. (1998). Continuous performance test results of adults with Attention Deficit Hyperactivity Disorder. *The Clinical Neuropsychologist, 12*, 155–168.

Fass, T. L., Heilbrun, K., DeMatteo, D., & Fretz, R. (2008). The LSI-R and the Compas: Validation data on two risk-needs tools. *Criminal Justice and Behavior, 35*, 1094–1107. doi:10.1177/0093854808320497.

Fillenbaum, G. G., Kuchibhalta, M., Henderson, V. W., Clark, C. M., & Taussig, I. M. (2007). Comparison of performance on the CERAD neuropsychological battery of Hispanic patients and cognitively normal controls at two sites. *Clinical Gerontologist, 30*(3), 1–22.

Franke, B., Faraone, S. V., Asherson, P., Buitelaar, J., Bau, C. H., Ramos- Quiroga, J. A., et al. (2011). The genetics of attention deficit/hyperactivity disorder in adults, a review. *Molecular Psychiatry*. doi:10.1038/mp. 2011.138.

Frederick, R. I. (2000). A personal floor effect strategy to evaluate the validity of performance on memory tests. *Journal of Clinical and Experimental Neuropsychology, 22*(6), 720–730.

Frederick, R. I., & Bowden, S. C. (2009). Evaluating constructs represented by symptom validity tests in forensic neuropsychological assessment of traumatic brain injury. *The Journal of Head Trauma Rehabilitation, 24*(2), 105–122.
Garb, H. N., Wood, J. M., Nezworski, M. T., Grove, W. M., & Stejskal, W. J. (2001). Toward a resolution of the Rorschach controversy. *Psychological Assessment, 13*(4), 433–448.
Garcia-Albea, J. E., Sanchez-Bernardos, M. L., & del Viso-Pabon, S. (1986). Test de Boston para el diagnostic de la afasia: Adaptación española [Boston Naming Test for aphasia diagnosis: Spanish version]. In H. Goodglass & E. Kaplan (Eds.), La evaluación de la afasia y de trastornos relacionados [*Assessment of aphasia and related disorders*] (Carlos Wernicke, Trans., 2nd ed., pp. 129–198). Madrid, Spain: Editorial Medica Panamericana.
Gasquoine, P. G. (1999). Variables moderating cultural and ethnic differences in neuropsychological assessment: The case of Hispanic Americans. *The Clinical Neuropsychologist, 13*(3), 376–383.
Gasquoine, P. G. (2001). Research in clinical neuropsychology with Hispanic American participants: A review. *The Clinical Neuropsychologist, 15*, 2–12.
Gasquoine, P. G. (2009). Race-norming of neuropsychological tests. *Neuropsychological Review, 19*, 250–262.
Gasquoine, P. G., Croyle, K. L., Cavazos-Gonzalez, C., & Sandoval, O. (2007). Language of administration and neuropsychological test performance in neurologically intact Hispanic American bilingual adults. *Archives of Clinical Neuropsychology, 22*, 991–1001. doi:10.1016/j.acn.2007.08.003.
Gaudino, E. A., Geisler, M. W., & Squires, N. K. (1995). Construct-validity in the Trail Making Test—What makes Part B harder? *Journal of Clinical and Experimental Neuropsychology, 17*, 529–535.
Glosser, G., Cole, L. C., French, J. A., Saykin, A. J., & Sperling, M. R. (1997). Predictors of intellectual performance in adults with intractable temporal lobe epilepsy. *Neuropsychology, 3*, 252–259.
Glosser, G., Cole, L., Khatri, U., DellaPietra, L., & Kaplan, E. (2002). Assessing nonverbal memory with the Biber Figure Learning Test—Extended in temporal lobe epilepsy patients. *Archives of Clinical Neuropsychology, 17*(1), 25–35.
Golden, C. J. (1978). *Stroop color and word test. A manual for clinical and experimental uses*. Wood Dale, IL: Stoelting Company.
Gonzalez, H. M., Mungas, D., & Haan, M. N. (2002). A verbal learning and memory test for English- and Spanish-speaking older Mexican-American adults. *The Clinical Neuropsychologist, 16*(4), 439–451.
Gonzalez, H. M., Mungas, D., Reed, B. R., Marshall, S., & Haan, M. N. (2001). A new verbal learning and memory test for English- and Spanish-speaking older people. *Journal of the International Neuropsychological Society, 7*, 544–555.
Goodglass, H., & Kaplan, E. (1983). *The assessment of aphasia and related disorders* (2nd ed.). Philadelphia: Lea and Febiger.
Graham, J. R., Naglieri, J. A., & Weiner, I. B. (Eds.). (2003). *Handbook of psychology: Assessment psychology* (10th ed.). New Jersey, NY: Wiley.
Grant, D. A., & Berg, E. A. (1948). A behavioural analysis of degree of reinforcement and ease of shifting to new responses in a Weigl-type card-sorting problem. *Journal of Experimental Psychology, 38*, 404–411.
Greenberg, A. D., & Dupuy, T. R. (2008). *TOVA 7.3 user's manual*. Los Alamitos, CA: TOVA Company.
Gronwall, D. M. (1977). Paced auditory serial-addition task: A measure of recovery from concussion. *Perceptual & Motor Skills, 44*, 367–373.
Harris, J. G., Cullum, C. M., & Puente, A. E. (1995). Effects of bilingualism on verbal learning and memory in Hispanic adults. *Journal of the International Neuropsychological Society, 1*, 10–16.
Harris, G. T., Rice, M. E., & Camilleri, J. A. (2004). Applying a forensic actuarial assessment (the Violence Risk Appraisal Guide) to nonforensic patients. *Journal of Interpersonal Violence, 19*(9), 1063–1074. doi:10.1177/0886260504268004.
Harrison, B. J., Shaw, M., Yu¨cel, M., Purcell, R., Brewer, W. J., Strother, S. C., et al. (2005). Functional connectivity during Stroop task performance. *NeuroImage, 24*, 181–191.
Heaton, R. K., et al. (2004). *Revised comprehensive norms for an expanded Halstead-Reitan battery: Demographically adjusted neuropsychological norms for African Americans and Caucasian adults*. Lutz, Fl: Psychological Assessment Resources, Inc.
Heaton, R. K., Chelune, G. J., Talley, J. L., Kay, G. G., & Curtiss, G. (2003). *Computerised Wisconsin Card Sort Task version 4 (WCST)*. Odessa, FL: Psychological Assessment Resources.
Heaton, R. K., Grant, I., & Matthews, C. G. (1991). *Comprehensive norms for an expanded Halstead–Reitan battery*. Odessa, FL: Psychological Assessment Resources.
Heller, P. L., Briones, D. F., Schiffer, R. B., Guerrero, M., Royall, D. R., Wilcox, J. A., et al. (2006). Mexican-American ethnicity and cognitive function: Findings from an elderly southwestern sample. *The Journal of Neuropsychiatry and Clinical Neurosciences, 18*(3), 350–355.
Hicks, J. W. (2004). Ethnicity, race, and forensic psychiatry: Are we color-blind? *The Journal of the American Academy of Psychiatry and the Law, 32*, 21–33.
Hill, C. D., Rogers, R., & Bickford, M. E. (1996). Predicting aggressive and socially disruptive behavior in a maximum security forensic psychiatric hospital. *Journal of Forensic Sciences, 41*(1), 56–59.
Hodges, J. R., & Patterson, K. (1995). Is semantic memory consistently impaired early in the course of Alzheimer's disease? Neuroanatomical and diagnostic implications. *Neuropsychologia, 33*, 441–459.
Hodges, J. R., & Patterson, K. (1997). Semantic memory disorders. *Trends in Cognitive Sciences, 1*, 68–72.

Jacobs, D. M., Sano, M., Albert, S., Schofield, P., Dooneief, G., & Stern, Y. (1997). Cross-cultural neuropsychological assessment: A comparison of randomly selected, demographically matched cohorts of English- and Spanish-speaking older adults. *Journal of Clinical and Experimental Neuropsychology, 19*(3), 331–339. doi:10.1080/01688639708403862.

Judd, T., Capetillo, D., Carrion-Baralt, J., Marmol, L. M., San Miguel-Montes, L., Navarrete, M. G., et al. (2009). Professional considerations for improving the neuropsychological evaluation of Hispanics: A National Academy of Neuropsychology education paper. *Oxford Journals: Archives of Clinical Neuropsychology, 24*, 127–135.

Kaplan, E., Gooidglass, H., & Weintraub, S. (1983). *Boston naming test*. Philadelphia: Lea and Febiger.

Kaufman, A. S. (1990). *Assessing adolescent and adult intelligence*. Boston: Allyn & Bacon.

La Rue, A., Romero, L. J., Ortiz, I. E., Liang, H., & Lindeman, R. D. (1999). Neuropsychological performance of Hispanic and non-Hispanic older adults: An epidemiologic survey. *The Clinical Neuropsychologist, 13*(4), 474–486. doi:10.1076/1385-4046(199911)13:04;1-Y;FT474.

Laffon, L. L. (2009). *Detecting feigning in a correctional setting: A comparison of multiple measures*. Doctor of Psychology dissertation, Pacific University Common Knowledge School of Professional Psychology Theses, Dissertations and Capstone Projects.

Lezak, M. (2004). *Neuropsychological assessment*. New York: Oxford University Press.

Lezak, M. D. (1995). *Neuropsychological assessment* (3rd ed.). New York: Oxford University Press.

Liu, S. K., Chiu, C.-H., Chang, C.-J., Hwang, T.-J., Hwu, H.-G., Chen, W.-J., et al. (2002). Deficits in sustained attention in schizophrenia and affective disorders: Stable versus state-dependent markers. *The American Journal of Psychiatry, 159*, 975–982.

López, S. R., & Taussig, I. (1991). Cognitive-intellectual functioning of Spanish-speaking impaired and nonimpaired elderly: Implications for culturally sensitive assessment. *Psychological Assessment: A Journal of Consulting and Clinical Psychology, 3*(3), 448–454. doi:10.1037/1040-3590.3.3.448. Loring & Bauer, 2010.

Loring, D. W., & Bauer, R. M. (2010). Testing the limits: Cautions and concerns regarding the new Wechsler IQ and Memory scales. *Neurology, 74*(8), 685–690.

Loving, J. L. (2002). Treatment planning with the Psychopathy Checklist-Revised (PCL-R). *International Journal of Offender Therapy and Comparative Criminology, 46*, 281–293. doi:10.1177/0306624x02463003.

Lowenstein, D. A., Ardila, A., Rosselli, M., Hayden, S., Duara, R., Berkowitz, N., et al. (1992). A comparative analysis of functional status among Spanish- and English-speaking patients with dementia. *Journal of Gerontology, 47*(6), 389–394.

Lyons, J. S., Griffin, G., Quintenz, S., Jenuwine, M., & Shasha, M. (2003). Clinical and forensic outcomes from the Illinois mental health juvenile justice initiative. *Psychiatric Services, 54*(12), 1629–1634. http://ps.psychiatryonline.org.

Machado, T. H., Fichman, H. C., Santos, E. L., et al. (2009). Normative data for healthy elderly on the phonemic verbal fluency task—FAS. *Neuropsychology, 3*(1), 55–60.

Marquez de la Plata, C., Arango-Lasprilla, J. C., Alegret, M., Moreno, A., Tárraga, L., & Lara, M. (2009). Item analysis of three Spanish naming tests: A cross-cultural investigation. *NeuroRehabilitation, 24*, 75–85.

Marquez de la Plata, C. D., Hart, T., Hammond, F. M., Frol, A. B., Hudak, A., & Harper, C. R. (2008). Impact of age on long-term recovery from traumatic brain injury. *Archives of Physical Medicine and Rehabilitation, 89*(5), 896–903.

McCann, R. A., & Ball, E. M. (2000). DBT with an inpatient forensic population: The CMHIP forensic model. *Cognitive and Behavioral Practice, 7*, 447–456.

Menon, C., Hall, J., Hobson, V., Johnson, L., & O'Bryant, S. E. (2011). Normative performance on the executive clock drawing task in a multi-ethnic bilingual cohort: A project FRONTIER study. *International Journal of Geriatric Psychiatry*, 1099–1116.

Monahan, J., Steadman, H. J., Robbins, P. C., Silver, E., Appelbaum, P. S., Grisso, T., et al. (2000). Developing a clinically useful actuarial tool for assessing violence risk. *The British Journal of Psychiatry, 176*, 312–319. doi:10.1192/bjp. 176.4312.

Morris, J. C., Heyman, A., Mohs, R. C., Hughes, J. P., van Belle, G., Fillenbaum, G., et al. (1989). The Consortium to Establish a Registry for Alzheimer's Disease (CERAD). Part 1. Clinical and neuropsychological assessment of Alzheimer's disease. *Neurology, 39*, 1159–1165.

Mulenga, K., Ahonen, T., & Aro, M. (2001). Performance of Zambian children on the NEPSY: A pilot study. *Developmental Neuropsychology, 20*, 375–384.

Mungas, D. (2006). Neuropsychological assessment of Hispanics elders: Challenges and psychometric approaches. In G. Yeo, D. Gallagher-Thompson, G. Yeo, & D. Gallagher-Thompson (Eds.), *Ethnicity and the dementias* (2nd ed., pp. 71–86). New York: Routledge/Taylor & Francis Group.

Mungas, D., Reed, B. R., Crane, P. K., Haan, M. N., & González, H. (2004). Spanish and English Neuropsychological Assessment Scales (SENAS): Further development and psychometric characteristics. *Psychological Assessment, 16*(4), 347–359.

Mungas, D., Marshal, S. C., Weldon, M., Haan, M., & Reed, B. R. (1996). Age and education correction of mini-mental state examination for English- and Spanish-speaking elderly. *Neurology, 46*(3), 700–706.

Mungas, D., Reed, B. R., Haan, M. N., & González, H. (2005). Spanish and English neuropsychological assessment scales: Relationship to demographics, language, cognition, and independent function. *Neuropsychology, 19*(4), 466–475.

Mungas, D., Reed, B. R., Marshall, S. C., & Gonzalez, H. C. (2000). Development of psychometrically matched English and Spanish language neuropsychological tests for older persons. *Neuropsychology, 14*(2), 209–223.
Mungas, D., Wallace, R., & Reed, B. R. (1998). Dimensions of cognitive ability in dementia: Differential sensitivity to degree of impairment in Alzheimer's disease. *The Clinical Neuropsychologist, 12*, 129–142.
Muntal Encinas, S., et al. (in press). Traducción y adaptación espanola de la batería neuropsicológica Repeatable Battery for the Assessment of Neuropsychological Status (RBANS) forma A en una muestra piloto. *Neurología.* doi:10.1016/j.nrl.2011.07.006.
Naglieri, J. A., Winsler, A., & Booth, A. L. (2004). Comparison of Hispanic children with and without limited English proficiency on the Naglieri Nonverbal Ability Test. *Psychological Assessment, 16*(1), 81–84. doi:10.1037/1040-3590.16.1.81.
Nasreddine, Z. S., et al. (2003). Sensitivity and specificity of the Montreal Cognitive Assessment (MoCA) for detection of mild cognitive deficits. *Canadian Journal of Neurological Science, 30*(2). Presented at Canadian Congress of Neurological Sciences Meeting, Quebec City, Quebec, June 2003.
Nelson, E. B., Sax, K. W., & Strakowski, S. M. (1998). Attentional performance in patients with psychotic and nonpsychotic major depression and schizophrenia. *The American Journal of Psychiatry, 155*, 137–139.
Nieberding, R. J., Gacono, C. B., Pirie, M., Bannatwne, L. A., Viglione, D. J., Cooper, B., et al. (2003). MMPI-2 based classification of forensic psychiatric outpatients: An exploratory cluster analytic study. *Journal of Clinical Psychology, 59*(9). doi:907-920. 10.1002/jclp. 10192.
Olson, C. L., Acosta, L. P., Hochberg, N. S., Olveda, R. M., Jiz, M., McGarvey, S. T., et al. (2009). Anemia of inflammation is related to cognitive impairment among children in Leyte, the Philippines. *PLOS Neglected Tropical Disease, 3*(10), E3. doi:10.1371/journal.pntd.0000533.
Osterrieth, P. A. (1944). Le test de copie d'une figure complexe [The complex figure test]. *Archives de Psychologie, 30*, 206–356.
Ostrosky-Solı's, F., Go'mez-Pe'rez, E., Matute, E., Rosselli, M., Ardila, A., & Pineda, D. (2007). NEUROPSI attention and memory: A neuropsychological test battery in Spanish with norms by age and educational level. *Applied Neuropsychology, 14*(3), 156–170.
Ostrosky-Solı's, F., Gomez, M. E., Matute, E., Rosselli, M., Ardila, A., & Pineda, D. (2003). *NEUROPSI ATENCIO ´ N Y MEMORIA 6 a 85 a~nos* [Neuropsi attention and memory 6 to 85 years]. Mexico: American Book Store.
Patry, M. W., Magaletta, P. R., Diamond, P. M., & Weinman, B. A. (2011). Establishing the validity of the personality assessment inventory drug and alcohol scales in a corrections sample. *Assessment, 18*, 50–59..
Peña-Casanova, J., Blesa, R., Aguilar, M., Gramunt-Fombuena, N., Gómez-Ansón, B., Oliva, R., et al. (2009). Spanish multicenter normative studies (NEURONORMA project): Methods and sample characteristics. *Archives of Clinical Neuropsychology, 24*(4), 307–319.
Peña-Casanova, J., Quiñones-Úbeda, S., Gramunt-Fombuena, N., Quintana, M., Aguilar, M., Molinuevo, J., et al. (2009). Spanish Multicenter Normative Studies (NEURONORMA project): Norms for the Stroop color-word interference test and the Tower of London-Drexel. *Archives of Clinical Neuropsychology, 24*(4), 413–429.
Pontius, A. A. (2002). Impact of fear-inducing violence on neuropsychological visuospatial tests in warring hunter-gatherers: Analogies to violent Western environments. *Aggression and Violent Behavior, 7*(1), 69–84. doi:10.1016/S1359-1789(00)00037-9.
Peterson, B. S., Skudlarski, P., Gatenby, J. C., Zhang, H., Anderson, A. W., & Gore, J. C. (1999). An fMRI study of Stroop word-color interference: Evidence for cingulate subregions subserving multiple distributed attentional systems. *Society of Biological Psychiatry, 45*, 1237–1258.
Rami, L., Serradell, M., Bosch, B., Caprile, C., Sekler, A., Villar, A., et al. (2008). Normative data for the Boston Naming Test and the Pyramids and Palm Trees Test in the elderly Spanish population. *Journal of Clinical and Experimental Neuropsychology, 30*(1), 1–6.
Randolph, C. (1998). *Repeatable battery for the assessment of neuropsychological status.* San Antonio, TX: The Psychological Corporation.
Rawal, P., Romansky, J., Jenuwine, M., & Lyons, J. S. (2004). Racial differences in the mental health needs and service utilization of youth in the juvenile justice system. *The Journal of Behavioral Health Services & Research, 31*(3), 242–254.
Reitan, R. (1958). Validity of the Trail Making Test as an indication of organic brain damage. *Perceptual and Motor Skills, 8*, 271–276.
Reitan, R. M., & Wolfson, D. (1985). *The Halstead–Reitan neuropsychological battery: Theory and clinical interpretation.* Tucson, AZ: Neuropsychology Press.
Rey, G. J., Feldman, E., Rivas-Vazquez, R., Levin, B. E., & Bentin, A. (1999). Neuropsychological development and normative data on Hispanics. *Archives of Clinical Neuropsychology, 14*, 593–601.
Reynolds, C. R., & Bigler, E. D. (1996). Factor structure, factor indexes, and other useful statistics for interpretation of the Test of Memory and Learning (TOMAL). *Archives of Clinical Neuropsychology, 11*(1), 29–43.
Reynolds, C. R., & Voress, J. K. (2007). *Test of memory and learning* (2nd ed.). Austin, TX: PRO-ED.

Rossetti, H. C., Lacritz, L. H., Cullum, C. M., & Weiner, M. F. (2011). Normative data for the Montreal Cognitive Assessment (MoCA) in a population-based sample. *Neurology, 77*(13), 1272–1275.

Royall, D. R., Cordes, J. A., & Polk, M. (1998). CLOX: An executive clock drawing task. *Journal of Neurology, Neurosurgery & Psychiatry, 64*(5), 588–594. doi:10.1136/jnnp. 64.5.588.

Royall, D. R., Espino, D. V., Polk, M. J., Palmer, R. F., & Markides, K. S. (2004). Prevalence and patterns of executive impairment in community dwelling Mexican Americans: Results from the Hispanic EPESE study. *International Journal of Geriatric Psychiatry, 19*(10), 926–934. doi:10.1002/gps.1185.

Royall, D. R., Espino, D. V., Polk, M. J., Verdeja, R., Vale, S., Gonzales, H., et al. (2003). Validation of a Spanish translation of the CLOX for use in Hispanic samples: The Hispanic EPESE study. *International Journal of Geriatric Psychiatry, 18*(2), 135–140. doi:10.1002/gps.804.

Sandford, J. A., & Turner, A. (1994). *Intermediate Visual and Auditory Continuous Performance Test (Version 2.6)*. Richmond, VA: Braintrain.

Schillerstrom, J. E., Baker, P., Allman, R. M., Rungruang, B., Zamrini, E., & Royall, D. R. (2007). Clock drawing phenotypes in community-dwelling African Americans and Caucasians: Results from the University of Alabama at Birmingham Study of Aging. *Neuroepidemiology, 28*(3), 175–180. doi:10.1159/000104095.

Shallice, T. (1982). Specific impairments of planning. *Philosophical Transactions of the Royal Society of London Series B, 298*, 199–209.

Shapiro, A. M., Benedict, R. B., Schretlen, D., & Brandt, J. (1999). Construct and concurrent validity of the Hopkins Verbal Learning Test—Revised. *The Clinical Neuropsychologist, 13*(3), 348–358. doi:10.1076/clin.13.3.348.1749.

Sheslow, D., & Adams, W. (1990). *Wide range assessment of memory and learning: Administration manual*. Wilmington, DE: Jastak Assessment Systems.

Sheslow, D., & Adams, W. (2003). *Wide range assessment of memory and learning* (2nd ed.). Lutz, FL: Psychological Assessment Resources, Inc.

Siedlecki, K. L., Manly, J. J., Brickman, A. M., Schupf, N., Tang, M., & Stern, Y. (2010). Do neuropsychological tests have the same meaning in Spanish speakers as they do in English speakers? *Neuropsychology, 24*(3), 402–411. doi:10.1037/a0017515.

Snodgrass, J. G., & Vanderwart, M. (1980). A standardized set of 260 pictures: Norms for name agreement, image agreement, familiarity, and visual complexity. *Journal of Experimental Psychology: Human Learning and Memory, 6*(2), 174–215. doi:10.1037/0278-7393.6.2.174.

Stein, L. A. R., Lebeau-Craven, R., Martin, R., Colby, S. M., Barnett, N. P., Golembeske, C. Jr., et al. (2005). Use of the adolescent SASSI in a juvenile correctional setting. Retrieved from National Institute of Health. doi:101177/107319110527933.

Steinberg, A. G., Sullivan, V. J., & Loew, R. C. (1998). Cultural and linguistic barriers to mental health service access: The deaf consumer's perspective. *The American Journal of Psychiatry, 155*(7), 982–984.

Stem, S. T. (2006). *Congruence of diagnostic impressions: Comparing clinician diagnosis and personality assessment inventory diagnostic categories in an in-patient forensic population*. Doctor of Psychology. Available from Pacific University CommonKnowledge. School of Professional Psychology Theses, Dissertations and Capstone Projects. Paper 24. http://commons.pacifcu.edu/app/24. Swalwell, S. C., Sr.

Stern, R. A., & White, T. (2003). The Neuropsychological Assessment Battery (NAB): Development and psychometric properties [abstract]. *Archives of Clinical Neuropsychology, 18*, 805.

Strutt, A., & Scott, B. (2011). *Misclassification of cognitive impairment on the MOCA with Spanish-speaking older adults*. Retrieved from: http://acn.oxfordjournals.org/content/26/6/470.abstract

Suglia, S. F., Wright, R. O., Schwartz, J., & Wright, R. J. (2008). Association between lung function and cognition among children in a prospective birth cohort study. *Psychosomatic Medicine, 70*, 356–362.

Sullivan, E. V., Mathalon, D. H., Zipursky, R. B., Kersteen- Tucker, Z., Knight, R. T., & Pfefferbaum, A. (1993). Factors of the Wisconsin Card Sorting Test as a test of dorsolateral pre- frontal cortical function in schizophrenia and alcoholism. *Psychiatry Research, 46*, 175–199.

Swalwell, S., Greenberg, A., & Dupuy, T. (2008). *TOVA user manual*. Retrieved from: files.tovatest.com/documentation/7.../users_manual_7.3-4377-844.pd.

Tinius, T. P. (2003). The Integrated Visual and Auditory Continuous Performance Test as a neuropsychological measure. *Archives of Clinical Neuropsychology, 18*(5), 439–454. doi:10.1016/S0887-6177(02)00144-0.

Tombaugh, T. N. (2006). A comprehensive review of the Paced Auditory Serial Addition Test (PASAT). *Archives of Clinical Neuropsychology, 21*, 53–76.

Tracy, J. I., Mattson, R., King, C., Bundick, T., Celenza, M. A., & Glosser, G. (2001). A comparison of memory for verbal and non-verbal material in schizophrenia. *Schizophrenia Research, 50*, 199–211.

van den Bosch, R. J., Rombouts, R. P., & Van Asma, M. J. O. (1996). What determines continuous performance task performance? *Schizophrenia Bulletin, 22*, 643–651.

van den Bosch, R. J., Rombouts, R. P., & van Asma, M. O. (1997). What determines Continuous Performance Task performance? *Schizophrenia Bulletin, 23*(2), 177.

von Gunten, A., Ostos-Wiechetek, M., Brull, J., Vaudaux-Pisquem, I., Cattin, S., & Duc, R. (2008). Clock drawing test performance in the normal elderly and its dependence on age and education. *European Neurology, 60*, 73–78.

Wechsler, D. (1987). *Manual for the Wechsler memory scale-revised*. San Antonio, TX: The Psychological Corporation.

Wechsler, D. (2008a). *Escala de inteligencia wechsler para adultos, EWIA*. San Antonio, TX: Pearson.

Wechsler, D. (2008b). *Wechsler adult intelligence scale: Technical and interpretive manual* (4th ed.). San Antonio, TX: Pearson.

Wheeler, D. K. (2010). *Digit span with a linguistically diverse Latina/Latino population: A cross-language study*. Fielding Graduate University, ProQuest dissertations and theses, Retrieved from http://search.proquest.com/docview/855633123?accountid=452.

White, T., & Stern, R. A. (2003). *Psychometric and technical manual of the neuropsychological assessment battery*. Lutz, FL: Psychological Assessment Resources Inc.

Wilkie, F. L., Goodkin, K., Ardila, A., Concha, M., Lee, D., Lecusay, R., et al. (2004). HUMANS: An English and Spanish Neuropsychological Test battery for assessing HIV-1-infected individuals—Initial report. *Applied Neuropsychology, 11*(3), 121–133.

Willcutt, E. G., Pennington, B. F., Boada, R., Ogline, J. S., Tunick, R. A., Chhabildas, N. A., et al. (2001). A comparison of the cognitive deficits in reading disability and attention-deficit/hyperactivity disorder. *Journal of Abnormal Psychology, 110*, 157–172.

Wood, J. M., Garb, H. N., Lilienfeld, S. O., & Nezworski, M. T. (2002). Clinical assessment. *Annual Review of Psychology, 53*, 519–543.

23 Assessing Risk, Recidivism, and Dangerousness in Hispanics

Olga Cirlugea, Lorraine T. Benuto, and Brian D. Leany

Introduction

The assessment of risk (including both violent and sexual), recidivism, and dangerousness in adults most frequently involves predicting the probability of either an initial offense or a subsequent offense (typically criminal reoffending), either sexual or otherwise (e.g., violence and other criminal behavior). This type of assessment is extraordinarily complicated, and while certain socioeconomic variables (e.g., gender) have been studied extensively with regard to risk prediction and recidivism, such extensive research has not been conducted on ethnic differences. In fact, even where ethnic differences have been explored, research has found economic disadvantage (as exhibited by residence neighborhood) to act as a major confound (Monahan, 2002).

Assessment procedures of risk and recidivism may consist of various components including a thorough record review that may involve an evaluation of factors identified in the MacArthur Violence Risk Assessment Study (see below for an overview of this study). Risk factors when assessed can be deemed as static (those variables that cannot be changed and are most often found in actuarial-based risk assessment instruments) or dynamic factors (those that can change) (Palmer & Hollin, 2007).

Other assessment procedures may include a clinical interview, personality assessment (e.g., the MMPI-2), and the administration of specialized assessment measures. Because the MMPI-2 and the use of clinical interviews are discussed in other chapters in this book, we will turn our focus to a

O. Cirlugea, B.A. (✉)
Department of Psychology, University of Nevada, Reno MS 0296, Reno, NV 89557, USA
e-mail: olgacirlugea@gmail.com

L.T. Benuto, Ph.D.
Department of Psychology, Victims of Crime Treatment Center, University of Nevada, Reno MS 0296, Reno, NV 89557, USA
e-mail: dr.benuto@gmail.com

B.D. Leany, Ph.D.
California Department of Corrections and Rehabilitation, Adult Division, California Correctional Health Care Services, PO Box 750, Susanville, CA 96127, USA
e-mail: leanyb@gmail.com

L.T. Benuto (ed.), *Guide to Psychological Assessment with Hispanics*,
DOI 10.1007/978-1-4614-4412-1_23, © Springer Science+Business Media New York 2013

review of the specialized assessment measures often used to predict violence or recidivism, and we will discuss research relevant to the Hispanic client. In this chapter, there are two sections—one devoted to risk, recidivism, and dangerousness that is nonsexual in nature and the other section specific to the perpetration of sexual crimes.

Actuarial Versus Clinical Predictions

Within the realm of assessing risk, recidivism, and dangerousness of adults, there has been considerable discussion regarding our ability to accurately assess this, and much has been discussed on different types of predictions, namely, actuarial and statistical. Actuarial predictions are based on empirically validated relationships between client data and the condition to be predicted, while clinical predictions are based on the clinician's intuition, experience, and knowledge (Dawes, Faust, & Meehl, 1989). There has been a huge debate in the field (beginning with Meehl, 1954 and followed up by Holt in 1958) as to which method is more accurate.

Assessments such as the Violence Risk Appraisal Guide (VRAG; Harris, Rice & Quinsey, 1993) and the Historical-Clinical-Risk Management-20 (HCR-20; Webster, Douglas, Eaves, & Hart, 1997) use different aspects of actuarial and non-actuarial systems to evaluate the likeliness of reoffending. For example, the VRAG uses powerful predicators in empirical studies to build a base line and then use statistics on reliability and accuracy. A large body of research in the domain of violence risk prediction has clearly indicated that the use of clinical judgment results in poor predictive validity (Borum, 1996; Elbogen, 2002; Litwack, 2001; Quinsey, Harris, Rice, & Cormier, 1998). Therefore, in this chapter, we will discuss the use of scientifically validated, actuarial measures that have been shown to predict risk at least to some extent.

Assessing Nonsexual Risk, Recidivism, and Dangerousness

Which Measures Are the Most Reliable?

Several meta-analyses have been conducted in the name of establishing the reliability and validity of various risk assessment instruments (e.g., Gendreau, Goggin, & Law, 1997; Gendreau, Goggin, & Smith, 2002; Gendreau et al., 1996; Walters, 2006). In a quite impressive meta-analysis, Campbell, French, and Gendreau (2009) examined 88 studies from 1980 to 2006 with the main aim being to compare risk instruments and other psychological measures on their ability to predict general (primarily nonsexual) violence in adults. Within the 88 studies they examined, 70 different risk measures were reviewed, and of these measures, only instruments with reasonable effect size estimates per outcome of interest were discussed. These included the Historical-Clinical-Risk Management-20 (HCR-20; Webster et al., 1997), Level of Service Inventory–Revised (LSI-R; Andrews & Bonta, 1995), Violence Risk Appraisal Guide (VRAG; Harris, Rice & Quinsey (1993), and the Hare Psychopathy Checklist (PCL-R: Hare, 2003; Hare, Clark, Grann, & Thornton, 2000). Because this research is so impressive and inclusive, we have decided to restrict our review mostly to these measures. However, in the spirit of being thorough, we have also chosen to review the Structured Assessment of Violent Risk in Youth (SAVRY; Borum, Bartel, & Forth, 2002) as this measure is specific to adolescents, and some research on the Hispanic adolescent has been conducted. We also review the MacArthur Violence Risk Assessment Study due to the impressive data collection procedures employed and the overall emphasis on the factors identified in this study and their relationship to violence risk prediction.

Table 23.1 Risk factors identified in the MacArthur Violence Risk Assessment Study (Monahan, 2002)

Risk factor	Finding
Gender	Men were found to use substances (alcohol or street drugs) and less likely to have been compliant with psychotropic medication, prior to committing violence. Women were found to be more likely to target family members and to be violent in the home
Prior violence and criminality	Prior violence and criminality are strongly related to the post-discharge violent behavior of psychiatric patients
Childhood experiences and violence	Child physical abuse was associated with post-discharge violence as were certain parental behaviors (e.g., having parents who have excessive alcohol and drug use)
Neighborhood context	Violence by persons with mental disorders appears to be related to the high-crime neighborhoods in which they typically reside
Diagnosis	The presence of a co-occurring diagnosis of substance abuse or dependence was found associated with violence. However, a diagnosis of schizophrenia was associated with lower rates of violence than a diagnosis of depression or of bipolar disorder but higher rates of violence than the community comparison (control) group
Psychopathy	Antisocial behavior as measured by the Hare PCL:SV predicted violence
Delusions	While the presence of delusions did not predict higher rates of violence among recently discharged psychiatric patients, non-delusional suspiciousness was linked with subsequent violence
Hallucinations	While command hallucinations not elevate violence risk in and of themselves, if the voices commanded violent acts, the probability of the violent acts being committed over the subsequent year was significantly increased
Violent thoughts	Patients who reported violent thoughts during hospitalization were more likely to engage in violent acts
Anger	Patients who obtained a high score on an anger scale while hospitalized were twice as likely as those with low anger scores to engage in violent acts after discharge

MacArthur Violence Risk Assessment Study

While this description will not include a specific measure per se, it is important that we discuss this study due to its large-scale nature and also because it has established several factors that actuarially appear to predict violence risk. The MacArthur Violence Risk Assessment Study (Steadman et al., 1998) was a large-scale study conducted to develop an actuarial violence risk assessment "tool" for use with a clinical population. The authors collected data from 1,136 male and female patients recently discharged from acute psychiatric inpatient facilities (it is important to note that the experimental group did have psychiatric conditions). Methods of data collection included a research interview aimed at gathering information on demographic and historical factors, a clinical interview using the DSM-III-R checklist confirming the participant's diagnosis, and supplemental material from the patients' records. Community violence was measured upon initial discharge, 20 weeks after discharge, and 1 year post-discharge (Monahan, 2002). In addition to the psychiatric outpatient sample, the authors utilized a comparison group comprised of 519 individuals residing in the same neighborhoods as the discharged patients (Steadman et al.). Results identified several risk factors related to violence (Monahan et al. 2005), and these are outlined in Table 23.1.

Structured Assessment of Violent Risk in Youth (SAVRY)

The Structured Assessment of Violent Risk in Youth (SAVRY; Borum et al., 2002) is a 30-item instrument that assesses historical, social/contextual, and clinical/individual factors as well as protective factors with adolescents. The SAVRY was developed to assist clinical judgment, and scores on the measure are assigned ratings of low, moderate, or high violence risk. A review of the literature indicates that several authors have included Hispanics in their research on the reliability and validity of this assessment instrument. For example, Roth (2006) examined the psychometric properties of the

SAVRY in a sample of 100 incarcerated adolescent Hispanic males. Results lend support to the high concurrent validity of the SAVRY with another established clinical measure, the PCL-YV (described in a subsequent section). More recently, Vincent, Chapman, and Cook (2011) investigated the effect of racial differences on the long-term (5 years) predictive validity of the SAVRY for violent and non-violent rearrests. The authors utilized a large multicultural sample of incarcerated juvenile offenders ($n=480$) of which 23.5% were Hispanic. Results revealed that the total score of the measure predicted the time for violent rearrests. Race did not act as a moderator in this prediction. In terms of nonviolent rearrests, the SAVRY only predicted time to such rearrests for White adolescents. The authors hypothesized that the lack of predictive validity of total score with Hispanic youth for nonviolent rearrests may have been due to findings that Hispanics had greater chances of being arrested for any crimes, violent or not, than their counterparts. An additional research study conducted by McGowan, Horn, and Mellott (2011) included Hispanics in their sample (15%), which consisted of individuals in secondary educational settings. Results from this study indicated that all scales of the SAVRY except for the Historical Risks scale significantly discriminated between violent and nonviolent adolescents.

Historical-Clinical-Risk Management-20 (HCR-20)

The Historical-Clinical-Risk Management-20 (HCR-20; Webster et al., 1997) is a risk assessment instrument developed to aid in clinical decisions and guide treatment strategies. This 20-item instrument is divided into 3 subscales containing 10 historical factors, 5 clinical items, and 5 risk management items. A review of the literature indicates that there are few studies evaluating the validity and reliability of this measure with Hispanics. Specifically, Barber-Rioja, Dewey, Kopelovich, and Kucharski (2012) examined the psychometric properties of several risk assessment instruments including the HCR-20 in a sample of 131 criminal defendants who had selected mental health services over incarceration, and of the 131 participants, 30.5% were Hispanic. The authors found excellent interrater reliability as well as predictive validity of the HCR-20. Other research studies have included less-impressive percentages of Hispanics in their samples. For example, Garcia-Mansilla, Rosenfeld, and Cruise (2011) tested the predictive accuracy of the measure with a sample of 827 participants diagnosed with a serious mental disorder, of which only 18 were Hispanic (2.2%). The authors were interested in finding out whether the measure had the same predictive accuracy for women as it did for men. Results indicate that the instrument had similar predictive validity for the two genders on two of the scales (C and HC) and demonstrated a significant difference in predictive validity on the H scales. Some research in Spain (e.g., Arbach-Lucioni, Andres-Pueyo, Pomarol-Clotet, & Gomar-Sones, 2011) has also provided evidence for the clinical utility of the HCR-20 with a Spanish-speaking population.

Level of Service Inventory–Revised

The Level of Service Inventory–Revised (LSI-R; Andrews & Bonta, 1995) is a quantitative measure of risk of reconviction and need for offender populations based on social learning theory and actuarial risk factors. The LSI-R assesses 10 domains, covering both static and dynamic risk factors. According to Palmer and Hollin (2007), research on the LSI-R has been conducted with offenders who are both incarcerated and not, with men and women, and with youth and adults and has been demonstrated to be an effective predictor of reconviction (Hollin & Palmer, 2006; Kroner & Mills, 2001). While the majority of this research has not been focused on Hispanics, where Hispanics have been included, proportions of samples have been as low as low as 1.7% (Andrews & Bonta, 2003), and some research on this measure has specifically looked at ethnic differences. Specifically, Schlager and Simourd (2007) examined the use of the LSI-R with Hispanics. Their sample consisted of 446 male parolees residing in 3 halfway houses and one day reporting center, and 112 participants in this study (25%) were of Hispanic heritage. Results indicated that LSI-R had acceptable psychometric properties, although the predictive validity results were lower than previous studies on the LSI-R. Nonetheless, the authors of this study referenced research (Schlager, 2005) that has not indicated statistically significant differences in LSI-R scores between African American, Hispanic, and Caucasian offenders on the LSI-R, suggesting that it may be an appropriate measure to use with Hispanics.

Violence Risk Appraisal Guide (VRAG)

The VRAG was initially studied on a sample of 618 male offenders from a high security hospital (Harris, Rice, & Quinsey 1993), and 12 risk variables (psychopathy, a personality disorder diagnosis, early parental separation, early school difficulties, early onset of offending, history of alcohol abuse, no marital history, conditional release failure, nonviolent offending history, and injury to a victim; Quinsey et al., 1998) that correlated best with reoffending were determined by multiple regression analyses. Substantial international research has demonstrated the VRAG to have predictive accuracy regarding violence and criminal recidivism (Kröner, Stadtland, Eidt, & Nedopil, 2007), although none of this research appears to have been conducted in Latin American countries or even Spain. In fact, it does not appear that research specifically on Hispanics has been conducted, although at least a few studies have included Hispanics as part of their sample (e.g., Edens, Skeem, & Douglas, 2006; Hastings, Krishnan, Tangney, & Stuewig, 2011).

Assessing for Psychopathy

Psychopathy is often associated with antisocial personality disorder and is a chronic disturbance in an individual's relation with self, others, and their environment resulting in distress or failure to fulfill social roles and obligations (American Psychiatric Association, 2000). Currently, there is much debate as to how this disorder should be conceptualized in the DSM-V. At present, the Hare Psychopathy Checklist (PCL-R: Hare, 2003; Hare et al., 2000) is one of the most commonly used assessments for assessing for psychopathy and measures two factors—the first interpersonal and affective problems and a second factor reflecting impulsive and antisocial behavior and unstable lifestyle. The PCL-R is often cited as a measure that can be useful when an assessment calls for the assessment of risk and dangerousness.

The PCL-R (Hare, 2003; Hare et al., 2000) is a 20-item semi-structured interview and is used in research, clinical, and forensic settings. In addition to the semi-structure interview, historical behavior from collateral interviews and file review is also incorporated into assessment procedures. As discussed by Alamilla and Wojik (Chap. 15, in this book), Sullivan, Abramowitz, Lopez, and Kosson (2006) have found similar patterns of psychopathy emerging between Latino and European American inmates across other measures of psychopathy and related constructs, between psychopathy and alcohol and substance abuse ratings, and trait anxiety scores. Latino and European American groups were also similar in the relationships between PCL-R measured psychopathy and criminal behavior, psychopathy and age, and between psychopathy and intelligence. Other authors evaluating the psychometric properties of the PCL-R found evidence for the utility of the instrument with both White and Hispanic alcoholic inpatient samples (Windle & Dumenci, 1999). However, one study by Tubb (2001) showed a poor fit of the measure's 2-factor model in a sample of Hispanic inmates.

The youth version of the PCL-R, the PCL-YV, has been found to correlate highly with another clinical assessment tool, the SAVRY (discussed above), in a sample of 100 Hispanic males (Roth, 2006). Nonetheless, they discuss criticisms of the definitions of antisocial personality disorder given the cross-cultural variability of human behavior (Dinges, Atlis, & Vincent, 1997). For example, when (Walsh & Kosson, (2008) examined the effects of socioeconomic status on psychopathology and violence, he discovered that predictive power of the PCL-R was significantly stronger for the European American participants than the Latin American sample. The author cites a small Latin American sample size as well as cultural differences between the samples as possible explanations for the results.

Other measures that can aid in the assessment of psychopathy by evaluating for the presence of antisocial personality disorder include the [1]:

- Structured Clinical Interview for DSM-IV Personality Disorders (SCID-II; First, Gibbon, Spitzer, Williams, & Benjamin, 1997).
- Spanish-Language Version of the Diagnostic Interview for DSM-IV Personality Disorders (S-DIPD-IV; Grilo, Anez, & McGlashan, 2003).
- Minnesota Multiphasic Personality Inventory-2 (MMPI-2).
- Shedler-Westen Assessment Procedure (SWAP).
- Millon Clinical Multiaxial Inventory-III (MCMI-III).
- Personality Assessment Inventory.

Summary and Recommendations for Assessing Nonsexual Risk, Recidivism, and Dangerousness

As indicated at the outset of this section, the assessments of violence risk and recidivism are both extraordinarily complicated. A review of the literature has indicated that Hispanics have not been the focus of study for the assessment measures that we reviewed above (although interestingly there does appear to be substantial research on the prediction of domestic violence in Hispanics). It is also worth noting that generally speaking the verdict is still out as to the extent to which we are actually able to predict violence risk and recidivism. Therefore, the reader is cautioned to take special care when interpreting the results of the measures discussed in this section, and when the aim is to predict violence risk and recidivism in general, a means of assessing this should include MacArthur's demonstrated risk factors associated with violence.

With regard to the assessment of psychopathy, the literature indicates that one of the most pressing problems in assessing psychopathy with Hispanic clients is the culturally insensitive definition of antisocial personality disorder that fails to take into consideration the cross-cultural variability of behavior. This has serious implications for clinicians working with Hispanic clients who may as a result administer fewer correct diagnoses of psychopathy. This is also likely to have an impact on the treatment and prevention of recidivism with such clients. We recommend that clinicians be aware of the limitations of psychopathy assessment with Hispanic clients, and that they take a multi-method approach to such an assessment.

Sexual Offender Risk Assessment

Given the high rates of sex crimes in this country, accurately assessing risk of offending (or reoffending) is of utmost importance. In fact, some 234,000 offenders have been convicted of sexual assault, including rape, and are in custody or under the control of state correctional agencies (Greenfield, 1997). A review of the literature rendered few studies illustrating rates of sexual offender recidivism in Hispanics, and some have posited that this may be because Hispanic offenders who do not have legal status and

[1] Please see the chapter by Alamilla and Wojik on assessing for personality disorders for a more detailed review of these measures and relevant cultural considerations.

who are incarcerated for their crimes are often deported right after serving their sentence. However, a study of recidivism of sex offenders released from prison in 1994 showed that from an initial Hispanic prison population of 19.9% of which 41.5% were either rapists or sexual assaulters, Hispanics made up 4.1% of sex offenders who were rearrested for a sex crime (Langan, Schmitt, & Durose, 2003).

Sex offender assessments are used for a variety of reasons including for pretreatment purposes to determine treatment intensity level, to provide offense-related background and behavior, to asses for the probability of recidivism, and to call attention to treatment targets (i.e., ongoing assessments can show perpetrators' responses to treatment, posttreatment assessments can show how the offender is functioning after treatment in society, etc.). Clinicians vary in terms of their usage of various measures and the factors they assess (e.g., the STATIC-99 [Hanson & Thornton, 1999], the STABLE-2000 [Hanson & Harris, 2000]), although as a field we agree that comprehensive assessment is an integral part of the treatment and risk-assessment process, and it is important for clinicians to take a multidimensional approach when assessing for risk. Nonetheless, it is important to keep in mind that these types of assessments can be both challenging and complicated.

The most commonly used measures for assessing sexual offender risk levels in the general population include the STATIC-99, STABLE 2007, ACUTE 2007, RRASOR (Rapid Risk Assessment of Sexual Offense Recidivism), ERASOR (Estimate of Risk of Adolescent Sexual Offense Recidivism), and J-SOAP-II (Juvenile Sex Offender Assessment Protocol-II). An overview of these instruments and their relevance to the Hispanic client follows.

STATIC-99

The STATIC-99 (Hanson & Thornton, 1999) is currently the most widely used actuarial assessment instrument for predicting sex offender recidivism in individuals who have already been convicted of a sexual crime. This 10-item self-report checklist asks adult male offenders about their history of sexual and nonsexual violence, number of convictions, and victims. Scores on the STATIC-99 place individuals in one of four risk categories ranging from low to high and are only used to measure long-term risk potential, rather than aid in treatment planning or evaluating treatment effects. While the STATIC-99 has been translated to Spanish, it is important to note that language will likely have little impact here given the nature of this test i.e., the questions that make-up the STATIC-99 can be answered by a practitioner who knows the person's history (including legal history) and administration of the STATIC-99 to the client is not necessary. Nonetheless, it is important to note that the research on the STATIC-99 with Hispanics suggests that the assessment instrument is appropriate for use with Hispanic populations, although not with sexual offenders under the age of 19, as demonstrated below.

In studies focusing on the use of the STATIC-99 with minority populations, up to 50% of the samples have been comprised of Hispanics. Kilgust (2009) analyzed the use of the STATIC-99 as well as the impact of race on sentencing for sexual offenses by administering the STATIC-99 to a sample of 18 Latino males and 18 White males participating in an outpatient treatment for sexual deviancy. The author hypothesized that Latinos would score higher than Whites on the STATIC-99 and, as a result, would have higher incarceration rates and longer sentences than Whites. However, results revealed that Latinos scored similarly to Whites and that the two sample groups had comparable sentencing lengths. Other studies (e.g., Viljoen, Elkovitch, Scalora, & Ulman, 2009) have included Hispanic participants in their samples when examining the validity of the STATIC-99. Thus, in light of the inclusion of Hispanics in samples examining the psychometric properties of the STATIC-99, specific research conducted on the use of this measure with Hispanics, and the availability of a Spanish version of this measure, we recommend its use in the assessment of the Hispanic client to the extent it is recommended for use with any nonminority client.

Rapid Risk Assessment for Sexual Offender Recidivism (RRASOR)

The RRASOR, developed by Hanson (1997), is a four-factor actuarial formula used for predicting risk of sexual reoffense in adult males. Individuals are asked to report their current age, the number of prior sex offenses, the gender of the offender's victims, and the offender's familial relationship to the victims. This information is then used to generate a score from 0 to 5, which corresponds to increasing levels of risk of recidivism. The author warns that the instrument is still in its developmental stages and should only be used to place offenders into the different risk level categories. In terms of Hispanic clients, this measure is available in Spanish, and research examining its use with this population is presented below.

Kilgust (2009) compared scores on the RRASOR and mean sentence lengths for a sample of 16 Latino males and 16 White males receiving treatment for sexual perversity. The author found no statistical significance between the mean of the Latino sample versus that of the White sample and no interaction effects between race and type of crime and race and sentence length. Additionally, the difference in the scores of Whites and Latinos sex offenders on the RRASOR was not statistically significant. The results show that Whites and Latinos score similarly on measures of sexual recidivism (with Whites scoring higher [although not statistically significant] than Latinos) and experience similar sentencing lengths after having committed particularly serious crimes like sexual assault (i.e., Whites spend 27.5 months longer in prison than their Latino counterparts). These findings may be an effect of the tendency of White offenders to victimize a larger number of people during their lifetime. Due to these results and the accessibility of the measure in Spanish, we recommend that the RRASOR be used with Hispanics to the extent it is recommended for use with any nonminority client.

Estimate of Risk of Adolescent Sexual Offense Recidivism (ERASOR)

The ERASOR (Worling & Curwen, 2001) is a structured professional judgment instrument designed to determine the short-term risk of reoffending for adolescent sex offenders aged 12–18. The measure examines 25 risk factors: 9 static factors are analyzed using items that inquire about historical sexual assaults, and 16 dynamic factors assess sexual interests, attitudes and behaviors, psychosocial functioning, family/environmental functioning, and treatment. Evaluators rate these risk factors as present, partially present, not present, or unknown in order to develop a total score for the individual, which, in combination with clinical judgment, can be used to guide decision-making concerning the adolescent offender.

A review of the literature on the psychometric properties of the ERASOR indicates that research with the sole intent to examine ethnic differences or cultural properties are absent, although Hispanics have been included as participants in research studies examining the psychometric properties of the ERASOR. For example, Viljoen et al. (2009) examined professional ratings of low, moderate, or high risk of sexual reoffending on several instruments, including the ERASOR, and 4.7% of their sample was Hispanic. Data show that prediction of sexual reoffending by professionals almost reached significance when the ERASOR was used but not when the other instruments were utilized. Additionally, results demonstrated excellent interrater reliability for professional judgments utilizing the ERASOR.

Juvenile Sex Offender Assessment Protocol-II (J-SOAP-II)

The J-SOAP-II (Prentky & Righthand, 2003) is an empirically devised assessment measure designed to review risk factors associated with sexual and criminal reoffending in adolescents ages 12–18. This instrument assesses static risk of reoffending through items that measure sexual drive/preoccupations and impulsive/antisocial behavior as well as dynamic risk utilizing items that evaluate the intervention and community stability/adjustment of the offender. The J-SOAP-II is recommended for the use with both individuals who have been convicted for sexual offenses and those who have not, but have a history of sexually threatening behavior.

Specific to research on the use of the J-SOAP-II with Hispanics, Martinez et al. (2007) evaluated the utility of the J-SOAP-II administered during the initial intake session, in predicting sexual reoffending in 60 adolescents (of which 30 were Hispanic) who had completed an average of 95 treatment sessions for sexual offenses. Results indicated that the instrument had moderate to high predictive validity of reoffending and treatment outcome. Therefore, we do believe that the instrument is valuable in the assessment of sex recidivism with Hispanic clients and is recommended for use to the extent it is recommended for use with any nonminority client.

Vermont Assessment of Sex Offender Risk (VASOR)

The VASOR (McGrath & Hoke, 2001) is a two-scale assessment instrument designed to assess the probability of sexual recidivism and the nature of an offender's violence history and severity, e.g., the number of past offenses. Research has shown that the interaction between risk of reoffense and violence is an important determinant of offender's total risk level (McGrath, 1992). The instrument was developed for the use with sex offender ages 18 and older to aid in the assignment and supervision of these offenders, with scores in the "low" range indicating that the individual may be considered for community placement and treatment, and those in the "high" range would instead be recommended for incarceration.

Research examining the use of the VASOR with a Hispanic population is limited. In a 1999 study, Packard and Gordon compared the VASOR to other existing measures of sexual recidivism that have demonstrated validity and reliability such as the RRASOR. The authors discovered that the VASOR correlated highly with these measures. While their sample was not exclusively comprised of ethnic minorities, a small proportion of the sample (4%) was Hispanic. In light of their findings, McGrath, Hoke, Livingston, and Cumming (2001) recommend the use of the VASOR as a tool for sex offender placement and supervision.

Summary and Recommendations for Assessing Sexual Risk with Hispanic Clients

A review of extant literature has indicated that there are several measures that are available in Spanish and have sufficient data to make them comparable to the English versions of these measures. Furthermore, those assessment tools that consist of an evaluation of risk factors that the client may or may not have do not require specialized Spanish version of the assessment tool. Clinicians are of course encouraged to conduct clinical interviews in the language of the client's choice.

Many of the measures we reviewed have been researched in part with Hispanic samples with a few exceptions (e.g., SORAG, J-SORAG), and even with these exceptions, research study samples have not been exclusively White (meaning that inevitably Hispanics have been included as part of the sample). More detailed information regarding the measures we reviewed has been consolidated in Table 23.2. We recommend that clinicians and researchers use these measures when assessing for risk of sexual offending and/or treatment progress with the Hispanic client to the extent these measures are recommended for use with any nonminority client.

Table 23.2 Sexual offender risk assessment with Hispanics

Assessment measure	Domain(s) assessed with this measure	Researched with Hispanics?	Recommended for use with Hispanics?[a]
STATIC-99	Sexual recidivism	Kilgust (2009)	Yes
STABLE 2007	Areas of stable risk in the offender (e.g., hostility toward women)	NA	Yes
ACUTE 2007	Sexual reoffending	NA	Yes
RRASOR	Sexual recidivism	Kilgust (2009)	Yes
ERASOR	Sexual reoffending	Viljoen et al. (2009)	Yes
SORAG	Sex offender risk assessment	NA	Yes
J-SORAG	Sexual recidivism	NA	Yes
J-SOAP-II	Sexual recidivism	Martinez et al. (2007)	Yes
VASOR	Sexual recidivism, violence history, offense severity	Packard and Gordon (1999)	Yes
MnSOST-R	Sex offender recidivism	NA	Yes

[a]The measure is recommended for use with the Hispanic client to the extent it would be with any nonminority client

References

American Psychiatric Association. (2000). Diagnostic and statistical manual of mental disorders (4th ed., text rev.). Washington, DC: Author.

Andrews, D. A., & Bonta, J. (1995). *The LSI-R: Level of service inventory–revised.* Toronto, Canada: Multi-Health Systems.

Andrews, D. A., & Bonta, J. (2003). *The LSI-R: Level of service inventory–revised: U.S. norms manual supplement.* Toronto, Canada: Multi-Health Systems.

Arbach-Lucioni, K., Andres-Pueyo, A., Pomarol-Clotet, E., & Gomar-Sones, J. (2011). Predicting violence in psychiatric inpatients: A prospective study with the HCR-20 violence risk assessment scheme. *Journal of Forensic Psychiatry and Psychology, 22*(2), 203–222.

Barber-Rioja, V., Dewey, L., Kopelovich, S., & Kucharski, L. (2012). The utility of the HCR-20 and PCL:SV in the prediction of diversion noncompliance and reincarceration in diversion programs. *Criminal Justice & Behavior, 39*(4), 475–492.

Borum, R. (1996). Improving the clinical practice of violence risk assessment: Technology, guidelines, and training. *American Psychologist, 51*(9), 945–956.

Borum, R., Bartel, P., & Forth, A. (2002). Manual for the Structured Assessment for Violence Risk in Youth (SAVRY). Consultation version. Tampa: Florida Mental Health Institute, University of South Florida.

Campbell, M., French, S., & Gendreau, P. (2009). The prediction of violence in adult offenders: A meta-analytic comparison of instruments and methods of assessment. *Criminal Justice and Behavior, 36*(6), 567–590.

Dawes, R. M., Faust, D., & Meehl, P. E. (1989). Clinical versus actuarial judgment. *Science, 243*(4899), 1668–1674.

Dinges, N. G., Atlis, M. M., & Vincent, G. M. (1997). Cross-cultural perspectives on antisocial behavior. In D. M. Stoff, J. Breiling, J. D. Maser, D. M. Stoff, J. Breiling, & J. D. Maser (Eds.), *Handbook of antisocial behavior* (pp. 463–473). Hoboken, NJ: Wiley.

Edens, J. F., Skeem, J. L., & Douglas, K. S. (2006). Incremental validity analyses of the violence risk appraisal guide and the psychopathy checklist: Screening version in a civil psychiatric sample. *Assessment, 13*(3), 368–374.

Elbogen, E. B. (2002). The process of violence risk assessment: A review of descriptive research. *Aggression and Violent Behavior, 7*(6), 591–604.

First, M. B., Gibbon, M., Spitzer, R. L., Williams, J. B. W., & Benjamin, L. S. (1997). *Structured clinical interview for DSM-IV axis II personality disorders, (SCID-II).* Washington, DC: American Psychiatric Press, Inc.

Garcia-Mansilla, A., Rosenfeld, B., & Cruise, K. R. (2011). Violence risk assessment and women: Predictive accuracy of the HCR-20 in a civil psychiatric sample. *Behavioral Sciences & The Law, 29*(5), 623–633.

Gendreau, P., Goggin, C. E., & Law, M. A. (1997). Predicting prison misconducts. *Criminal Justice And Behavior, 24*(4), 414–431.

Gendreau, P., Goggin, C., & Smith, P. (2002). Is the PCL-R really the 'unparalleled' measure of offender risk? A lesson in knowledge cumulation. *Criminal Justice And Behavior, 29*(4), 397–426.

Gendreau, P., Little, T., & Goggin, C. (1996). A meta-analysis of the predictors of adult offender recidivism: What works!. *Criminology, 34*(4), 575–607.

Greenfield, L. A. (1997). *Sex offenses and offenders: An analysis of data on rape and sex* (pp. 15–24). Washington, DC: Department of Justice, Bureau of Justice Statistics.

Grilo, C. M., Anez, L. M., & McGlashan, T. H. (2003). *The Spanish-Language version of the diagnostic interview for DSM-IV personality disorders: Development and initial psychometric evaluation of diagnoses and criteria.* New Haven, CT: Yale School of Medicine.

Hanson, R. K. (1997). *The development of a brief actuarial risk scale for sexual offense recidivism* (User Report 1997–04). Ottawa, Canada: Department of the Solicitor General of Canada.

Hanson, R. K., & Harris, A. J. R. (2000). Where should we intervene? Dynamic predictors of sex offense recidivism. *Criminal Justice and Behavior, 27*, 6–35.

Hanson, R. K., & Thornton, D. (1999). *Static-99: Improving actuarial risk assessments for sex offenders* (User Report 99–02). Ottawa, Canada: Department of the Solicitor General of Canada.

Hare, R. D. (2003). *Manual for the revised psychopathy checklist* (2nd ed.). Toronto, Canada: Multi-Health Systems.

Hare, R. D., Clark, D., Grann, M., & Thornton, D. (2000). Psychopathy and the predictive validity of the PCL-R: An international perspective. *Behavioral Sciences and the Law, 18*, 623–645.

Harris, G. T., Rice, M. E., & Quinsey, V. L. (1993). Violent recidivism of mentally disordered offenders: The development of a statistical prediction instrument. *Criminal Justice and Behavior, 20*, 315–335.

Hastings, M. E., Krishnan, S., Tangney, J. P., & Stuewig, J. (2011). Predictive and incremental validity of the Violence Risk Appraisal Guide scores with male and female jail inmates. *Psychological Assessment, 23*(1), 174–183.

Hollin, C. R., & Palmer, E. J. (2006). Level of Service–Revised profile of English prisoners: Risk and reconviction analysis. *Criminal Justice and Behavior, 33*, 347–366.

Holt, R. R. (1958). Clinical and statistical prediction: A reformulation and some new data. *Journal of Abnormal and Social Psychology, 56*, 1–12.

Kilgust, A. R. (2009). *Sentencing and risk characteristics of Latino sexual offenders*. School of Professional Psychology (Paper 96). Retrieved From http://commons.pacificu.edu/spp/96.

Kroner, D. G., & Mills, J. F. (2001). The accuracy of five risk appraisal instruments in predicting institutional misconduct and new convictions. *Criminal Justice and Behavior, 28*, 471–489.

Kröner, C., Stadtland, C., Eidt, M., & Nedopil, N. (2007). The validity of the Violence Risk Appraisal Guide (VRAG) in predicting criminal recidivism. *Criminal Behaviour and Mental Health, 17*(2), 89–100.

Langan, P. A., Schmitt, E. L., & Durose, M. R. (2003). *Recidivism of sex offenders released from prison in 1994.* Washington, DC: US Department of Justice, Bureau of Justice Statistics.

Litwack, T. R. (2001). Actuarial versus clinical assessments of dangerousness. *Psychology, Public Policy, and Law, 7*(2), 409–443.

Martinez, R., Flores, J., & Rosenfeld, B. (2007). Validity of the juvenile sex offender assessment protocol-II in a sample of urban minority youth. *Criminal Justice and Behavior, 34*(10), 1284–1295.

McGowan, M. R., Horn, R. A., & Mellott, R. N. (2011). The predictive validity of the Structured Assessment of Violence Risk in Youth in secondary educational settings. *Psychological Assessment, 23*(2), 478–486.

McGrath, R. J. (1992). Five critical questions: Assessing sex offender risk. *Perspectives, 16*(3), 6–9.

McGrath, R. J., & Hoke, S. E. (2001). *Vermont assessment of sex offender risk manual.* Middlebury, VT: Author.

McGrath, R. J., Hoke, S. E., Livingston, J. A., & Cumming, G. (2001, November). The *Vermont Assessment of Sex Offender Risk (VASOR): An initial reliability and validity study.* Paper presented at the 20th Annual Research and Treatment Conference of the Association for the Treatment of Sexual Abusers, San Antonio, TX.

Meehl, P. E. (1954). *Clinical versus statistical prediction: A theoretical analysis and a review of the evidence.* Minneapolis, MN: University of Minnesota Press.

Monahan, J. (2002). The MacArthur studies of violence risk. *Criminal Behaviour & Mental Health, 12S*, 67.

Monahan, J., Steadman, H., Robbins, P., Appelbaum, P., Banks, S., Grisso, T., et al. (2005). An actuarial model of violence risk assessment for persons with mental disorders. *Psychiatric Services, 56*, 810–815.

Packard, R., & Gordon, A. (1999). *An investigation of actuarial risk scales: Concordance and factor analysis.* Paper presented at the 18th Annual Research and Treatment Conference of the Association for the Treatment of Sexual Abusers, Lake Buena Vista, FL.

Palmer, E. J., & Hollin, C. R. (2007). The level of service inventory-revised with English women prisoners: A needs and reconviction analysis. *Criminal Justice and Behavior, 34*(8), 971–984.

Prentky, R., & Righthand, S. (2003). *Youth Sex Offender Assessment Protocol-II (J-SOAPII): Manual.* Washington, DC: U.S. Department of Justice, Office of Justice Programs, Office of Juvenile Justice and Delinquency Prevention: Psychopathy and violence: The importance of factor level interactions.

Quinsey, V. L., Harris, G. T., Rice, M. E., & Cromier, C. A. (1998). *Violent offenders: Appraising and managing risk.* Washington, DC: American Psychological Association.

Roth, E. (2006). *Assessment of violence risk and psychopathy in a population of incarcerated, adolescent, Hispanic males.* Unpublished doctoral dissertation.

Schlager, M. (2005). *Assessing the reliability and validity of the Level of Service Inventory–Revised (LSI-R) on a community correction sample: Implications for corrections and parole policy*. Unpublished doctoral dissertation, Rutgers University, Newark.

Schlager, M. D., & Simourd, D. J. (2007). Validity of the Level of Service Inventory-Revised (LSI-R) among African American and Hispanic male offenders. *Criminal Justice and Behavior, 34*(4), 545–554.

Steadman, H. J., Mulvey, E. P., Monahan, J., Robbins, P., Appelbaum, P. S., Grisso, T., et al. (1998). Violence by people discharged from acute psychiatric inpatient facilities and by others in the same neighborhoods. *Archives of General Psychiatry, 55*(5), 393–401.

Sullivan, E. A., Abramowitz, C. S., Lopez, M., & Kosson, D. S. (2006). Reliability and construct validity of the psychopathy checklist-revised for Latino, European American, and African American male inmates. *Psychological Assessment, 18*(4), 382–392.

Tubb, V. A. (2001). The factor structure and psychometric proper- ties of Psychopathy Checklist Revised: Data from an Hispanic Federal inmate population. *Dissertation Abstracts International, 62*, 5426.

Viljoen, J. L., Elkovitch, N., Scalora, M. J., & Ulman, D. (2009). Assessment of reoffense risk in adolescents who have committed sexual offenses: Predictive validity of the ERASOR, PCL:YV, YLS/CMI, and Static-99. *Criminal Justice and Behavior, 36*(10), 981–1000.

Vincent, G. M., Chapman, J., & Cook, N. E. (2011). Risk-needs assessment in juvenile justice: Predictive validity of the SAVRY, racial differences, and the contribution of needs factors. *Criminal Justice and Behavior, 38*(1), 42–62.

Walsh, Z., & Kosson, D. S. (2008). Psychopathy and violence: The importance of factor level interactions. *Psychological Assessment, 20*(2), 114–120.

Walters, G. D. (2006). Risk-Appraisal Versus Self-Report in the Prediction of Criminal Justice Outcomes: A Meta-Analysis. *Criminal Justice And Behavior, 33*(3), 279–304.

Webster, C. D., Douglas, K. S., Eaves, D., & Hart, S. D. (1997). *HCR-20: Assessing risk for violence (Version 2)*. Vancouver, Canada: Simon Fraser University.

Windle, M., & Dumenci, L. (1999). The factorial structure and construct validity of the Psychopathy Checklist—Revised (PCL—R) among alcoholic inpatients. *Structural Equation Modeling, 6*(4), 372–393.

Worling, J. R. (2004). The Estimate of Risk of Adolescent Sexual Offense Recidivism (ERASOR): Preliminary psychometric data. *Sexual Abuse: A Journal of Research & Treatment, 16*(3), 235–254.

Worling, J. R., & Curwen, T. (2001). Estimate of Risk of Adolescent Sexual Offense Recidivism (ERASOR; Version 2.0). In M. C. Calder (Ed.), *Juveniles and children who sexually abuse: Frameworks for assessment* (pp. 372–397). Lyme Regis, UK: Russell Russell House Publishing.

Forensic Assessment with the Hispanic Client

24

Lorraine T. Benuto, Brian D. Leany, and Olga Cirlugea

The term "forensic assessment" includes a broad array of assessment domains. The purpose of this chapter is to evaluate some of the more common "types" of forensic assessments as they pertain to the Hispanic client. Specifically, we cover child custody evaluations, the assessment of competency and capacity, and personal injury evaluations. Within each of these, we provide a description of the typical approach to these assessments and an overview of the scientific research on each assessment with emphasis on how this research pertains to the Hispanic client. Recommendations for how to conduct the said assessments with the Hispanic client are also included. Because the field of forensic assessment is so vast, the reader will find a specific chapter on the assessment of malingering (often relevant to forensic assessment) and a separate chapter on assessing risk (including sexual risk and recidivism) and dangerousness in Hispanics.

Child Custody Evaluations and Assessing for Parenting Capacity and Conduct

Psychologists are usually called upon to give an opinion on the capacity of parents: (1) during custody proceedings following divorce, (2) when it is suspected that a child has suffered neglect or abuse and the parent is under scrutiny, and/or (3) if the parent's capacity to provide good parenting is in question due to mental health problems or learning difficulties. It is important to note that the term "parental capacity" is most typically used when it is necessary to determine whether or not the parents are able to safely parent the child(ren). The majority of this section will focus on tools used when it is necessary to determine the best interest of the child in the context of a child custody evaluation. Nonetheless, (some of) the assessment measures and procedures discussed below could be used and applied to circumstances when parental capacity must be assessed. According to Puckering

L.T. Benuto, Ph.D. (✉)
Department of Psychology, Victims of Crime Treatment Center, University of Nevada,
Reno MS 0296, Reno, NV 89557, USA
e-mail: dr.benuto@gmail.com

B.D. Leany, Ph.D.
California Department of Corrections and Rehabilitation, Adult Division, California Correctional
Health Care Services, PO Box 750, Susanville, CA 96127, USA
e-mail: leanyb@gmail.com

O. Cirlugea, B.A.
Department of Psychology, University of Nevada, Reno MS 0296, Reno, NV 89557, USA
e-mail: olgacirlugea@gmail.com

L.T. Benuto (ed.), *Guide to Psychological Assessment with Hispanics*,
DOI 10.1007/978-1-4614-4412-1_24, © Springer Science+Business Media New York 2013

(2010), such assessments should include an interview with all the actual and potential caregivers of the child; observations should be made of the parents interaction with the child including assessing the social, emotional and physical environment provided by the parent for the child; and formal tests should be administered. Collateral informants should also be interviewed, and child medical, psychological, and developmental history should be reviewed. Similar procedures should be used when attempting to determine the best interest of the child.

With regard to custody evaluation procedures, Tolle and O'Donohue (2012) have proposed the Egregious/Promotive Factors Model (EPFM) which calls for an assessment of promotive factors (factors that have been shown to enhance mental health and developmental outcomes) and egregious factors (risk factors that have been shown to be detrimental to a child's development and well-being) and uses joint custody as the default parenting plan. The factors present in either parent then influence and weigh the balance of time with one or another parent. For example, if neither parent has egregious factors, joint custody would be recommended. In line with past research regarding resilient children from divorced homes, it is apparent that involvement of both parents (i.e., involvement and regular contact with the nonresidential parent, or joint custody and adequate time with both parents) is related to better adjustment in children (Amato & Gilbreth, 1999; Lee, 2002; Menning, 2002). Of course, it is necessary to qualify that shared parenting involves low levels of conflict between parents, which is also involved in improved adjustment (Buchanan, Maccoby, & Dornbusch, 1991; Hetherington, 1999). Table 24.1 illustrates the various factors that need to be either ruled in or ruled out for each parent according to the EPFM. Therefore, assessment measures should be chosen based on their ability to help the clinician rule in or out the various egregious and promotive factors. Because the EPFM is the only evidence-based model available for child custody evaluations, we recommend its use for all clients including the administration of assessment measures that allow the assessor to rule in or out each factor.

The Hispanic Client

A literature review using 4 databases with the search terms parental, capacity, assessment, and Hispanic or Latino yielded 35 results. Generally speaking, most of these studies attested to the reliability and validity of the assessment measures typically used in parenting capacity evaluations, for example, the Alabama Parenting Questionnaire, Parenting Sense of Competence Scale, Parental Behavior Inventory, and Child Abuse Potential Inventory. As indicated above, we recommend that assessment measures be chosen to assess for each of the factors in the EPFM as the overall research on these factors and their relationship to childhood outcome is strong. The following details what assessment instruments have been researched with Hispanics broken up by which egregious or promotive factor each tool assesses.

Egregious Factors

Parent-Child Relationship

Instruments designed to assess the parent-child relationship include the Parent-child Relationship Inventory and the Parenting Stress Index-Short Form.

The Parent-child Relationship Inventory (PCRI; Gerard, 1994) is a self-report inventory designed to measure parents' attitudes toward their parenting and children. It consists of 78 items assessing parental support, satisfaction with parenting, involvement, communication, limit setting, autonomy, and role orientation and is usually administered to both parents. There are two validity scales built-in to detect whether responding is inconsistent or if the parent is portraying his or her relationship with the child in an unrealistically positive light. Support for the predictive validity, internal consistency, and test-retest reliability of the PCRI has been found (1994), and

Table 24.1 The Egregious/promotive factors model

	Factors					
Egregious factors	Parent-child relationship	Parenting skills	Environmental instability	Parent mental health	Excessive interparental conflict	
Promotive factors	Positive parenting	Parental school involvement	Promotion of interpersonal development	Promotion of mental health	Promotion of community involvement	Effective co-parenting

while this measure was validated with a mostly Caucasian sample (85.7%), Hispanics did make up a small proportion (1.5%) of the participants (1994). Further research on the PCRI (of which 20% of the sample were Hispanics) has focused on assessing the sensitivity of the PCRI to exaggeration of positive parenting in a simulated custody evaluation condition versus a research study condition (Tobin, Seals, & Vincent, 2011). Results revealed that parents of all ethnicities scored higher on the parenting subscales (communication, limit setting, and involvement) in the custody evaluation condition than the research study condition, and the custody manipulation condition produced a higher degree of social desirable responding. In terms of Hispanic clients, these results may explain elevated scores on the PCRI when the measure is administered in the context of a custody evaluation, as such settings are more likely to elicit socially desirable responding from parents of any ethnicity. While ideally research specific to the Hispanic client should be conducted with regard to the validity and reliability of the PCRI with Hispanics, of the research that does exist none has indicated any adverse reasons why this measure is not appropriate for this population. In fact, a Spanish version of this measure is available, and research on this translation indicates that the instrument is a viable alternative for assessing the parent-child relationship with the Hispanic client (Roa Capilla & del Barrio, 2001).

The Parenting Stress Index-Short Form is a 24-item tool that calls for parents to indicate to what extent they agree or disagree (possible answers range from strongly agree to strongly disagree) and is used to assess stress levels in the parent-child relationship. While the original English version of the measure has not been explicitly researched with Hispanics, a review of the research on this measure and the ethnic constellation of the samples used in said research have indicated that Hispanic participants have not been excluded. Specifically, Whiteside-Mansell et al. (2007) assessed the utility of this measure with a sample of low-income parents of preschool children in order to determine the psychometric properties of the measure as well as whether the PSI-SF is useful in clinical applications, and of their sample, 13% of the participants were Hispanic. In this study, the researchers found that the Parenting Stress Index-Short Form was able to explain relationships between parent and child outcomes and to tease apart specific aspects of stress due to parenting, providing support for its clinical utility. Results also showed that the measure had high internal consistency and was reliable and valid. Research has also been conducted on the Spanish translation of the instrument; particularly, Solis and Abidin (1991) evaluated the Spanish version of the Parenting Stress Index in a sample of 233 Hispanic mothers. The authors administered the measure to Spanish-speaking mothers to determine if the psychometric properties of this Spanish version were equivalent to those of the English version obtained using the original Caucasian validating sample. Results indicated that the internal consistency of the Spanish version was almost equal to that of the original sample. Additionally, the measure was successful in discriminating parents of children with physical and mental disabilities from those of non-disabled children in the Hispanic sample, as mothers of disabled children reported having more stress than their counterparts. These findings are consistent with existing research on the discriminant validity of the measure (e.g., Zimmerman, 1979). Thus, this measure can be used with Hispanic clients, including non-English speakers, given the availability of the PSI in Spanish and the research supporting its use.

Parenting Skills

Evaluators employ several instruments when evaluating parenting skills including the Parental Authority Questionnaire Revised, the Parent Behavior Checklist, and the Parenting Sense of Competence Scale. While the psychometric properties of latter two instruments have been investigated specifically with Hispanic samples, the Parental Authority Questionnaire lacks such research. Nevertheless, Hispanics have not been entirely left out of research with this instrument, as illustrated below.

The Parental Authority Questionnaire (PAQ; Buri, 1989) is a 30-item assessment instrument based on Baumrind's parental prototypes (permissive, authoritarian, and authoritative/flexible) and is designed to evaluate the child's perspective of parental authority. The tool is divided into three subscales reflecting the three types of parenting, each consisting of ten items. Scores for each scale are added up, and the resulting sums are taken to indicate how much authority the child perceives to be exercised by his or her parents. Varela et al. (2004) administered several assessment instruments including the Parental Authority Questionnaire to a largely Hispanics (66%) sample in order to determine the effect of acculturation on parenting styles. The authors chose a multicultural Hispanic sample with participants of Mexican descent, Mexican American, and Mexican immigrant participants. Because the initial 3-scale model produced a mediocre fit index at best, the researchers elected to run their data analysis using only the authoritarian and authoritative scales, which produced an almost perfect fit index for all ethnic samples with high internal consistency among the scales. Results indicate that Mexican immigrant and Mexican American parents employ more authoritarian parenting practices than their Mexican-descent and Caucasian non-Hispanic counterparts, suggesting that it is ethnic minority status rather than affiliation with Mexican culture that is associated with increased use of an authoritarian parenting style. Hence, evaluators interpreting scores of Hispanic parents on this questionnaire should keep in mind that parents identifying with an ethnic minority may receive elevated scores on the measure.

The Parent Behavior Checklist is a 100-item self-report inventory (PBC; Fox, 1994) that includes statements about how parents raise young children in order to identify parental expectations of children as well as parental behavior toward their children. Cardona, Nicholson, and Fox (2000) administered the PBC to a sample of 76 mothers (38 Hispanic and 38 Anglo American) with the goal of identifying differences in parenting practices and developmental expectations between the two groups. The authors found that Hispanic mothers scored higher on the discipline subscale and lower on the nurturing subscale than their Anglo American counterparts. They hypothesize that lower scores on the nurturing subscale are a result of the PBC not being an accurate measure of nurturing behavior in Hispanic mothers, that is, Hispanic mothers typically providing their children with more affective rewards and fewer material ones. Therefore, care must be taken when interpreting the scores of Hispanic parents on the different subscales of the PBC. Wong, Stewart, and Gregorich (2004) also examined the psychometric adequacy of the short form of the Parent Behavior Checklist (PBC-SF) with a sample of 196 Latino and African American parents. The shorter version of the PBC includes 32 items divided into two scales, "expectations" and "discipline." Results from this study indicate that after several items were dropped (e.g., "I praise my child for learning new things") due to the items not meeting the inter-scale correlation criteria of .30, low factorial loadings, and lack of understanding of what the questions asked on the part of the participants, both scales met the criteria for satisfactory validity and reliability. Because the PBC-SF was revised to more adequately assess parental expectations and behavior than the full-length PBC, we recommend that the shorter version of the PBC be used with Hispanics.

The Parenting Sense of Competence Scale (PSOC; Gibaud-Wallson & Wandersman, 1978a) is a 16-item questionnaire that assesses parents' self-esteem and features of reported self-confidence. Haack, Gerdes, Schneider, and Hurtado (2011) examined the psychometric and cultural properties with a sample comprised entirely of Hispanics (Haack et al., 2011). Their research included a Spanish version of the PSOC, and results from their study indicated good psychometric reliability and validity as well as cultural validity.

Environmental Instability

One of the assessment instruments used for evaluating environmental instability, which has been examined using Hispanic samples, is the Child Abuse Potential Inventory (CAP Inventory; Milner, 1986). This measure is a 160-item self-report screening tool devised for the detection of child physical abuse. This instrument contains ten scales—seven clinical ones (the primary scale being the abuse scale) and three validity scales built to identify lying, random responding, and inconsistency in responding. Rodriguez (2008) conducted a study utilizing several abuse risk measures, including the CAPI, with a sample of 90 participants. The sample consisted of 44 Hispanic participants, and 48% of the Hispanic sample was administrated the CAPI in Spanish while 52% was administered the CAPI in English. Results questioned the adequacy of the CAPI in assessing abuse risk in Hispanic parents because their scores were significantly higher than their non-Hispanic counterparts. However, no differences in disciplinary styles among the different ethnic groups were found. These findings highlight the need for further research with the CAPI with Hispanic samples in order to identify whether the measure overassesses abuse risk in this population. Due to the potentially significant consequences of overidentifying abuse risk, for example, children being taken away from their parents and placed with a foster family, we recommend that evaluators exercise caution when employing this measure with Hispanic clients and that evaluation procedures make use of multiple measures and means to assess for environmental instability.

The Home Observation for Measurement of the Environment (HOME) is an inventory developed by Bradley and Caldwell (1984) designed to reliably assess the caring environment in which the child was brought up. Different age-specific versions of this tool exist, for example, the Infant-Toddler HOME (birth to 3) and the Early Adolescent HOME (10–15). While this measure has not been explicitly researched with Hispanics, a review of the research on this measure and the ethnic makeup of the samples used in said research have indicated that Hispanic participants have been not been excluded in research conducted on the HOME. In fact, Bradley, Corwyn, McAdoo, and Garcia Coll (2001) administered four versions of the short form of the assessment tool (HOME-SF) to a sample of European, Asian, African, and Hispanic Americans and found a greater effect size for poverty status than for race, with the effects of poverty proportional for all but Asian Americans. These results indicate that poverty is a better predictor of the scores on the various versions of the HOME-SF than race. In terms of Hispanics, this suggests that economic status, not ethnicity, determines the extent to which a child will have access to resources, for example, books and quality time with a parent. The limited research on the HOME with different ethnic groups indicates that more studies should be conducted with this assessment instrument to better determine psychometric properties with Hispanics; however, the outcome of the study presented above lends support for our recommendation to utilize the measure with the Hispanic client when assessing for environmental instability.

Parent Mental Health Problems

There are numerous assessment measures for the detection of parent mental health problems, for example, the Minnesota Multiphasic Personality Inventory (MMPI-2), the Hare Psychopathy Checklist-Revised, and the Structured Interview for DSM-IV for Axis I Disorders (SCID-I). Because these assessment instruments are discussed in detail in other sections of this book, we will limit our discussion of these tools and recommend that such measures be incorporated in the child custody and parenting capacity assessment process.

Excessive Interparental Conflict

Scales measuring excessive interparental conflict encompass the Children's Perception of Interparental Conflict Scale and the Multidimensional Assessment of Interparental Conflict Scale. A review of the research on these measures and the ethnic composition of the samples used in said research have indicated that Hispanic participants have made up between 21 and 50% of the samples (McDonald & Grych, 2006; Tschann, Flores, Pasch, & Marin, 1999). In fact, the Multidimensional Assessment of Interparental Conflict Scale (MAIC; Tschann et al., 1999) was developed using a sample of 151 European American and 153 Mexican American families. The measure was administered to parents and their children, and six dimensions of interparental conflict were assessed: frequency, child-related content, intensity, conflict behavior, child involvement, and resolution. Results showed that the items performed similarly for both ethnic groups, and that the scale had similar reliability and validity properties for the two groups.

The Children's Perception of Interparental Conflict Scale (CPIC; Grych, Seid, & Fincham, 1992) is a 51-item true-false questionnaire established with the goal of assessing children's impressions of conflict between their parents. McDonald and Grych (2006) developed a new version of the scale, the Children's Perception of Interparental Conflict Scale for Younger Children (CPIC-Y), by reducing the number of items of the CPIC to 22, adding in an additional 12 items measuring parent-child relationships, and simplifying the language of the items. In order to assess the new version's psychometric properties, they administered the young children's version of the CPIC to a sample of children of which a proportion (21%) were Hispanic. The authors found excellent reliability and validity of this new, shortened version of the CPIC.

Promotive Factors

Positive Parenting

Evaluators have several tools available to assess positive parenting, including the Alabama Parenting Questionnaire, the Parent-child Relationship Inventory (described above), and the Parent Behavior Inventory. Hispanic participants have made up between 1.5 and 100% of the samples used to research these measures (Gerard, 1994; Haack et al., 2011; Robert, 2009; Weis & Toolis, 2010). A review specific to each measure follows.

The Alabama Parenting Questionnaire (APQ; Shelton, Frick, & Wootton, 1996) is a 42-item self-report questionnaire developed to measure five constructs related to parenting behaviors: positive parenting, parental involvement, poor monitoring/supervision, corporal punishment, and inconsistent discipline. When Haack et al. (2011) evaluated the psychometric and cultural properties of the Spanish version of Alabama Parenting Questionnaire on a sample composed entirely of Hispanics, the authors found evidence for the psychometric reliability and validity, as well as the cultural validity of the translation. Roberts' (2009) study also demonstrated the internal and external validity of the Alabama Parenting Questionnaire and its use with a Mexican population. In light of these findings, we recommend the use of this measure with the Hispanic client.

The Parent Behavior Inventory (PBI; Lovejoy, Weis, O'Hare, & Rubin, 1999) is a multi-method, multi-informant measure that evaluates parents' behavior toward their young children. The instrument assesses two areas of parenting behavior, hostility/coercion and support/engagement. Weis and Toolis (2010) conducted a study evaluating parenting behavior with this assessment instrument in a socioeconomically and ethnically diverse sample, 31.9% of the sample being Hispanic. The results support the factorial validity of the Parental Behavior Inventory with diverse populations.

Parental School Involvement

In addition to checking a child's academic performance, obtaining collateral contacts from teachers, and inquiring about behavioral problems in the classroom, evaluators should also use an assessment tool to assess for parental school involvement, for example, the Family Involvement Questionnaire (FIQ; Fantuzzo, Tighe, & Childs, 2000). The FIQ is a 4-point rating scale that assesses a child's primary caregiver's nature and extent of school involvement. While the measure was developed on a multicultural sample of Head Start parents, the majority of the sample was African American (57%), 29% of the participants were Caucasian, with the remaining 11% being categorized as "other ethnic backgrounds." Nonetheless, other authors have utilized this measure with Hispanics. For example,

Klimes-Dougan et al. (1992) conducted two experiments, a pilot study and expanded study, examining the school involvement of low-income caregivers in a partially Hispanic sample (42.2% in the pilot study and 61.4% in the expanded study). Caregivers were first asked to give an account of the activities available at their children's schools and then were required to indicate whether they had participated in those activities as well as to rate their involvement in parent programs. The authors found higher rates of recall and participation in school activities in the expanded study, as well as low to moderate rates of parental involvement, mothers showing a higher frequency and quantity of school involvement. Based on the research conducted with the instrument as well as the availability of the Spanish translation of the measure, we recommend the use of the FIQ with the Hispanic client with the caveat being that in some cases Hispanic parents may have to work an excessive amount (due to economic status), thus limiting the availability of the time they can dedicate to their children's school activities.

Promotion of Interpersonal Development

Multiple measures to assess promotion of interpersonal development should be used when conducting custody evaluations. Some such measures include the Child Behavior Scale, the Multidimensional Scale of Perceived Social Support, the Friendship Quality Questionnaire, and the Functional Status Questionnaire. The validity of two of these measures, the Functional Status Questionnaire (FSQ; Jette et al. 1996) and the Multidimensional Scale of Perceived Social Support (MSPSS, Zimet, Dahlem, Zimet, & Farley, 1998), has been examined with samples where Hispanics comprised the majority of participants (i.e., between 50 and 100%; Edwards, 2004; Wong et al., 2004) and will be discussed in detail below.

The FSQ is a self-administered measure that assesses physical, psychological, social, and role functions. Wong et al. (2004) examined the psychometric adequacy of the FSQ in a minority sample, half of which was Hispanic. Results indicated that the psychometric properties of the instrument were reasonable for use with Hispanics, but there was evidence of differences in the interpretation of several items between Hispanics and their comparison group, African Americans. Therefore, there were some recommendations for minor changes to accommodate different understanding of scale items by Hispanics. The authors also found that they had to drop several items on the FSQ prior to the data analysis, for example, "In the past two weeks, how often did your child react to little things by crying," due to the respondents' lack of comprehension of what the questions asked.

The other measure, the MSPSS, consists of a 7-point Likert scale that determines perceived social support in three distinct social areas: friends, family, and significant others. Participants are instructed to rate, for example, statements such as "My family really tries to help me," with higher scores indicating a higher degree of perceived social support. Edwards (2004) evaluated the psychometric properties of the MSPSS in a sample of Mexican American youth and found evidence for the adequacy of the 3-factor scale structure; additionally, results support the construct validity and internal reliability of the scale, indicating that the measure is useful in the assessment of perceived support in the target population.

Promotion of Mental Health

Assessment of parental promotion of mental health in children includes several self-esteem and autonomy measures as well as the Child's Report of Parental Behavior Inventory and the Functional Status Questionnaire (described above). Hispanics have been included in research on both of these measures and have made up between 20 and 50% of the samples in research studies examining these measures (Knight et al., 1992; Wong et al., 2004). Details of this research follow.

The Child's Report of Parental Behavior Inventory (CRPBI; Schludermann & Schludermann, 1970) is a 30-item behavior inventory grouped into three scales. Items assess five areas associated with children's perception of their parents' behavior: acceptance, rejection, inconsistent discipline, control, and hostile control. Knight et al. (1999) investigated several measures of parenting and family interactions, among which the CRPBI was included, with a minority sample which was 20% Hispanic. The authors sought to determine "the cross-ethnic equivalence of latent structures and intercorrelations among constructs" for these instruments. Results from the study support the construct validity of the different scales for the English-speaking Hispanic participants, with the exception of the rejection scale, which indicated a poor fit of the construct. In light of these findings, the authors recommend that evaluators exercise caution when using this scale with Hispanic mothers and children until further research is conducted.

Promotion of Community Involvement

The Children's Assessment of Participation and Enjoyment (CAPE; King et al., 2004; Law et al. 2004) is often used to assess promotion of community involvement. The measure was developed to identify disabled and non-disabled children's leisure activities, with a focus on five activity types drawn from empirical literature: social, recreational, skill-based, active-physical, and self-improvement activities. This instrument has not only been studied with an exclusively Hispanic sample but has also been translated into Spanish (Colon, 2008). Colon conducted a two-part study in order to first develop a culturally adapted Spanish translation of the CAPE and examined the psychometric properties of this new measure with a sample of Puerto Rican children. Preliminary results of the study demonstrated good validity and internal consistency of the Spanish version, Evaluación de Participación y Disfrute de los Niños & Preferencias de las Actividades de los Niños (EPDN/PAN), as well as support for the use of the measure with Puerto Rican children.

Effective Co-parenting

The Parenting Alliance Measure (PAM; Abidin & Konold, 1990) is a simple 20-item self-report measure developed to identify perceived alliance between parents of children under 19 years of age. The total score for the measure is indicative of the degree to which parents see themselves to be part of a cooperative relationship when caring for their children. While no validation tests have been conducted on this measure with Hispanics, Hispanics have been included in research utilizing the PAM. Specifically, Helfenbaum-Kun and Ortiz (2007) conducted a pilot study examining the effects of parenting training of fathers on child behavior and relationships. In addition to other assessment instruments, the authors administered the PAM to a predominantly Latino (85%) sample, in order to find out mothers and fathers perception about each other's parenting skills and cooperation following a parent intervention received by the fathers. Results showed a statistically nonsignificant difference in pretest and posttest scores on the measure for both mothers and fathers, indicating that the intervention did not successfully change parental perceptions of each other's parenting skills. While further research on psychometric properties of this measure with Hispanic samples is recommended, we currently have no evidence for why the PAM should not be part of the assessment of effective co-parenting with the Hispanic client.

Summary and Recommendations for Child Custody Evaluations and Assessing for Parenting Capacity and Conduct with the Hispanic Client

In addition to the assessment measures discussed above, IQ tests, administered to both children and parents, are often used as part of the child custody evaluation process. Because such assessment measures are discussed in detail in various chapters in this book, we will not elaborate on them extensively here other than to say that they should be included as part of the standard assessment battery.

In sum, a review of extant literature has indicated that for many of the measures relevant to child custody evaluations and the assessment of parental capacity, research for Hispanics (both by design and incidentally through random sampling) has been conducted (see Table 24.2 for a summary of the measures reviewed, the constructs assessed, and their relevance to the Hispanic client). Some of this research has included a wide variety of ethnic groups, while other studies have been ethnic-specific (e.g., included on Puerto Ricans in their sample) which may call into question the generalizability to other Hispanic groups. Nonetheless, except where indicated above, the majority of the research specific to Hispanics and also research that has simply not excluded Hispanic participants (i.e., Hispanics have made up a portion of the study sample despite the intention not being to examine ethnic differences) has indicated support for the use of these evidence-based assessment measures. It is worth noting that similar to other domains of assessment, the size of the Spanish-speaking population and the demands of the clinicians assessing them (Haack et al., 2011; Rodriguez, 2008) suggest that the availability of measures in Spanish remains a challenge.

Assessing Competency in Legal Proceedings

Competency is a legal concept that allows the postponement or modification of criminal proceedings (including ability to stand trial, ability for self-representation, competency to enter a plea, etc.) for defendants who are considered unable to participate in a meaningful way for their defense because of a mental or physical disorder or retardation (Roesch, Zapf, Golding, & Skeem, 1999). Individual states set the bounds of competency, and the measures most commonly used are based on pseudo-objective measures that assign point values to interview responses, record and transcript reviews, or some combination of the two. Ultimately, a cutoff score is used, and many states rely on a preponderance of the evidence (e.g., the psychological evaluation, testimony, legal representation, etc.) to determine competency. Roesch et al. (1999) provide guidelines for the assessment of competency and discuss the use of specific assessments including the Competency Assessment Instrument (CAI), the Interdisciplinary Fitness Interview (IFI), the Fitness Interview Test (FIT-R; Roesch, Webster, & Eaves, 1994), the Georgia Court Competency Test (GCCT), and the MacArthur Competence Assessment Tool-Criminal Adjudication (MacCAT-CA; Bonnie, Hoge, Monahan, & Poythress, 1996).

A review of the aforementioned literature suggests that the most challenging aspects of competency are the variability in the construct interpretation and application of the standards of competency among states, the subsequent lack of psychometrically sound measures of competency (as a result of the variable application and definition of the construct), and the sociopolitical climate (e.g., the desire of the public to consider competency if there is a perception of criminals "getting off" for feigned incompetence).

While research on the aforesaid measures and the performance of Hispanics specifically is absent, Hispanics have been included in research studies examining these measures. Additionally, the nature of the assessments (interview based) suggests that there would not be an instrumental bias against the Hispanic client. Instead, the bias would be more likely due to preconceived cultural conventions of the community. Nonetheless, some research has indicated that attorneys rate Spanish-speaking defendants as less mentally ill than the English-speaking defendant and are less likely to refer the Spanish-speaking defendant for a Competency to Stand Trial (CST) evaluation (Varela, Boccaccini, Gonzalez, Gharagozloo, & Johnoson, 2011), meaning that Hispanics may be less likely to be referred for a CST evaluation as a result of bias in the referral process. In fact, Varela and colleagues (2011) discuss how the language difference may make it difficult for a client to be active in decision-making and to voice opinions and ideas with his or her attorney. The following section will review the assessment measures mentioned above relevant to the CST evaluation process, and their relevance to the Hispanic client will be discussed.

Table 24.2 Child custody evaluation and parental capacity assessment with Hispanics

EPFM factor assessed	Measure used to assess EPFM factor	Research conducted with Hispanics	Available in Spanish	Recommended for use with this population?
Parent-child relationship	Parent-child Relationship Inventory	Yes	Yes	Yes
	Parenting Stress Index-Short Form	Yes	Yes	Yes
	Parenting Stress Index	Yes	Yes	Yes
Parenting skills	Parent Behavior Checklist	Yes	Yes	Yes[a]
	Parenting Sense of Competence Scale	Yes	Yes	Yes
	Parent Authority Questionnaire	Yes	Yes	Yes[a]
Environmental instability	The Home Observation for Measurement of the Environment	Yes	Yes	Yes
	Child Abuse Potential Inventory	Yes	Yes	Yes[b]
Excessive interparental conflict	The Children's Perception of Interparental Conflict Scale	Yes	Yes	Yes
	Multidimensional Assessment of Interparental Conflict Scale	Yes	Yes	Yes
Positive parenting	Parent Behavior Inventory	Yes	Yes	Yes
	Alabama Parenting Questionnaire	Yes	Yes	Yes
Parental school involvement	The Family Involvement Questionnaire	Yes	Yes	Yes[a]
Promotion of interpersonal development	The Multidimensional Scale of Perceived Social Support	Yes	No	Yes
	Functional Status Questionnaire	Yes	Yes	Yes[b]
Promotion of mental health	Functional Status Questionnaire	Yes	Yes	Yes[b]
	The Child's Report of Parental Behavior Inventory	Yes	Yes	Yes[b]
Promotion of community involvement	The Children's Assessment of Participation and Enjoyment	Yes	Yes	Yes
Effective co-parenting	Parenting Alliance Measure	Yes	Yes	Yes

[a]Results should be interpreted keeping in mind that factors specific to Hispanic parents (e.g., socioeconomic level) may influence the scores on these measures
[b]Results should be interpreted with caution until further research with Hispanics has been conducted

Competency to Stand Trial Assessment Instrument (CSTAI)

The CSTAI (McGarry & Associates, 1973) contains 13 items related to legal issues, and each item is scored on a 1–5 scale, ranging from "total incapacity" to "no incapacity." The CSTAI manual contains clinical examples of levels of incapacity as well as suggested interview questions. Borum and Grisso (1995) found that the CSTAI was the most commonly reported forensic instrument used in competency evaluations. However, a review of the literature has indicated limited research on the CSTAI in general, and, apparently, Hispanic-specific studies are absent.

Interdisciplinary Fitness Interview-Revised (IFI-R)

The IFI-R is a semi-structured interview and rating scale designed to take into account both legal and mental health issues and calls for an interdisciplinary approach to the assessment of competency (i.e., the use of both an attorney and a psychologist as assessors; Golding, 1993 as cited in DellaSanta-Percy, 2002–2004). Six domains relevant to current psychopathology (attention/consciousness, delusions, hallucinations, thought disorder, impaired memory, cognitive impairment, and mood and affect) and four psycholegal domains (capacity to appreciate charges/disclose pertinent fact, events and motives, courtroom demeanor and appreciating the adversarial nature of proceedings, quality of relationship with attorney, and appreciation/reasoned choice of legal options and consequences) are assessed. The psychopathology items are rated on a 3-point scale (0—symptom is absent or symptom type is present but has no bearing on this defendant's ability to stand trial; 1—symptom is present and might affect the defendant's competency but is not sufficient to prevent him or her from standing trial; and 2—symptom is present and severe enough to limit the defendant's competency). In the psycholegal section, 0 indicates minimal incapacity, 1 indicates moderate incapacity, and 2 equals substantial incapacity. A review of the literature has indicated that while more research has been conducted on the IFI-R than on the CSTAI, Hispanic-specific studies also appear to be absent.

Fitness Interview Test (FIT-R; Roesch et al., 1994)

The Fitness Interview Test-Revised (FIT-R; Roesch et al., 1994) is a structured interview that examines three main areas: (a) the ability to understand the nature or object of the proceedings or factual knowledge of criminal procedure, (b) the ability to understand the possible consequences of the proceedings or the appreciation of personal involvement in and importance of the proceedings, and (c) the ability to communicate with counsel or to participate in the defense. Questions specific to each of the 3 domains mentioned above are asked of the client, and items are rated on a 3-point scale whereby a score of 2 indicates definite or serious impairment in the defendant's ability to meet the psycholegal criteria, a score of 1 indicates possible or mild impairment, and a score of 0 indicates no impairment (Zapf, Roesch, & Viljoen, 2001). In terms of interrater reliability, research has demonstrated high levels across different professions ranging from psychiatrists to psychologists to graduate students in psychology (Viljoen, Roesch, and Zapf (2002)). The FIT-R has also been shown to have high construct validity as demonstrated by high agreement with scores on the MacArthur Competency Assessment Tool-Criminal Adjudication (Hoge, Bonnie, Poythress, & Monahan, 1999), and the FIT shows good sensitivity and negative predictive power, which suggests that it can reliably screen those individuals who are clearly fit to stand trial, before they are remanded to an inpatient facility for a fitness assessment (2001). This measure has been translated into Spanish, although a literature search did not yield any research on the translated version of this measure. Nonetheless, Hispanics have not been completely excluded from research on the FIT although they have only made up small portions of the samples used to research this measure (3.9–7.9%; Viljoen & Roesch, 2005; Viljoen, Vincent, & Roesch, 2006).

Georgia Court Competency Test (GCCT)

The GCCT was developed by Wildman et al. (1978) and consists of 21 items grouped into 6 categories: picture of court, functions, charges, helping the law, alleged crime, and consequences. Scores range from 0 to 100, and a score of 69 or less warrants further evaluation. Research has demonstrated strong interrater reliability for this measure (Nicholson, Robertson, Johnson, & Jensen, 1988), although the GCCT has been criticized as being too focused on defendant's knowledge and not enough on ability to assist with defense (Bonnie, 1992). It is apparent that research on the use of the GCCT with Hispanics may not exist as an extant review of the literature on this measure indicated that either Hispanics were not included in studies on this measure or the studies did not include demographic information on participants (e.g., Bagby, Nicholson, Rogers, & Nussbaum, 1992; Gothard, Rogers, & Sewell, 1995; Gothard, Viglione, Meloy, & Sherman, 1995; Manguno-Mire, Thompson, Shore, Croy, Artecona, & Pickering, 2007; Nicholson, Briggs, & Robertson, 1988; Nicholson et al., 1988; Rogers, Grandjean, Tillbrook, Vitacco, & Sewell, 2001; Rogers, Sewell, Grandjean, & Vitacco, 2002; Rogers, Ustad, Sewell, & Reinhardt, 1996; Springman & Vandenberg, 2009; Wildman, White, & Brandenburg, 1990).

MacArthur Competence Assessment Tool-Criminal Adjudication (MacCAT-CA; Bonnie et al., 1996)

In the administration of the MacCAT-CA, a hypothetical case (a short story about two men who get into a fight and one is subsequently charged with a criminal offense) is presented to the defendant, and competency is then rated along three axes (via 22 items): understanding of the legal system (8 items—most of which consist of 2 parts whereby the defendant's understanding is first assessed, and if it is unsatisfactory or appears to be questionable, the information is then disclosed to the defendant and his or her understanding is again assessed—this is done as a means to assess if the defendant can learn disclosed information), reasoning (8 items that ask which of two disclosed facts would be most relevant to the case), and appreciation (6 items which assess the individual's appreciation of his or her own circumstances) (Roesch et al., 1999). A review of the literature has indicated that research on the MacCAT-CA has included Hispanics as participants who have made up between 7.6 and 23% of the samples in these studies (Viljoen et al. 2007); Rogers, Grandjean, Tillbrook, Vitacco, & Sewell, 2001).

Summary and Recommendations for Assessing CST with Hispanic Clients

The literature suggests that the largest challenge in assessing CST for the Hispanic client is in overcoming a cultural predisposition by their attorneys to assume that the client is not mentally ill (Varela et al., 2011). Thus, in conducting a CST assessment, the clinician has overcome the most significant issue of this domain for their client. As indicated at the onset of this discussion, there may be some reluctance or real inability to communicate legal understanding between the client and attorney, but this is something that would be addressed as a natural function of the CST by a competent, Spanish-speaking clinician. It is also worth noting that Hispanics have only been minimally included (at best) in research on measures assessing for CST. While this does not necessarily mean that these measures are not useful with the Hispanic client, it may be necessary to interpret results with caution when using CST assessment measures with the Hispanic client.

Psychological Assessment of Capacity

Assessments regarding the mental capacity and vulnerability of adults are used in order to determine whether or not an adult is capable of making decisions regarding their own health or well-being. Historically, capacity was considered to be an all-or-none phenomenon, but more recently the field has shifted to conceptualize capacity in terms of capacities, thus distinguishing between global capacity and specific capacities (i.e., the focus is on the specific functional capacities and means of maximizing those capacities). The American Psychological Association in conjunction with the American Bar Association has put together a handbook on the assessment of older adults with diminished capacity (American Psychological Association [APA], 2008). While these guidelines are specific to older adults, there is a significant amount of information applicable to general evaluations of capacity, and, thus, it was used as a framework for this section and adapted to fit in terms of assessment of diminished capacity (not specifically in the context of older adults). The APA (2008) presents and discusses six capacities (medical consent, sexual consent, financial, testamentary, driving, and independent living capacities) and provides recommendations for the assessment of functional elements, diagnoses, psychiatric or emotional factors, cognitive underpinnings, values and preferences, and risk of harm and level of supervision.

Activities of Daily Living

In the case of functional elements, it is recommended that activities of daily living (ADLs) (e.g., grooming, toileting, eating, transferring, dressing) and the instrumental activities of daily living (IADLs) (e.g., abilities to manage finances, health, and functioning in the home and community) be assessed. As mentioned above, there are several measures of clinical functioning. However, the large majority of ADL and IADL activities of interest necessary for determining capacity in a forensic context are encompassed in the measure described in our competency section. The primary concerns for Hispanic clients here are the linguistic capabilities and cultural awareness (e.g., whether a lack of engagement in ADLs is an issue of capacity or a conscience decision based on cultural norms) of the interviewer.

Diagnoses

In terms of diagnoses and/or psychiatric or emotional facts, a review of the client's medical and psychological history can be useful in determining the client's current and past diagnoses or emotional or psychiatric complexities which may be the causative factors explaining any functional disability (Grisso, 2003). A determination of diagnoses can also be obtained by collateral contact, clinical interviewing, or the assessment of specific tests to rule in or rule out the presence of a specific diagnosis. Because the crux of this book is to provide an elaborate discussion of specific assessment measures for specific diagnoses, the reader is directed to the specific chapter they are seeking to assess for detailed information regarding specific tests.

Cognitive Underpinnings

With regard to cognitive underpinnings, to some degree, the type of assessment administered depends heavily on the specific capacity to be assessed. For example, treatment or research consent is essentially cognitive or decisional in nature, whereas driving or financial management may be a behavioral component and also rely heavily on underlying cognitive functioning (American Psychological Association, 2008; Moye & Marson, 2007). Nonetheless, a specific discussion on the factors that may require assessment follows with a discussion of specific measures that may be used to assess said factors.

Attentional Abilities

The client's ability to attend to tasks is an important first step in the completion of an assessment. An inability to do so may be indicative of a delirious state. Tasks such as digit span or coding can help to determine a baseline for attentional abilities.

Language

An ability to express a choice is a critical component of capacity assessments. Complex medical and financial decisions require the ability to read and comprehend written documents. Speech production, language comprehension, and written language skills are all components of language assessment. Impairments in object naming may be indicative of a dementia process. Impairment in language production or comprehension may be indicative of an aphasia that may be secondary to a vascular injury. A language sample can be obtained by asking an older adult to describe a scene. Language comprehension can be assessed by asking an older adult to follow commands. Object naming may be assessed by presenting an older adult with a line drawing and asking for the name of the object. A writing sample can indicate written language skills. The older adult could also be asked to read a sample and answer questions regarding the passage. If there is any indication of a frank language disturbance (i.e., Broca's aphasia), a more extensive formal assessment of language using a language-specific battery may be warranted.

Memory

Memory is a domain that may need to be assessed as disorders can impair decision-making by influencing the client's ability to recall previously learned information, integrate information across choice options, and learn new information (APA, 2008). The Wechsler Memory Scales-IV, California Learning Test, MMSE, etc., can be used to assess for memory disturbances. These tests are extensively discussed in the neuropsychological assessment and assessment of dementia chapters of this book.

Visual Perceptual Abilities

Perceptual abilities are related to both driving and financial calculations and thus can impair a person's capacity to drive and/or complete financial calculations (APA, 2008). Thus, if capacity relating to financial decision-making or driving is of concern, perceptual abilities should be assessed. This can be assessed by having the client copy figures, decipher or match patterns, and/or construct objects to samples, and all of these tasks are tasks that are conducted as part of intellectual assessments; thus, the reader should refer to the chapter on IQ assessments for details regarding the use of such measures with the Hispanic client.

Processing Speed

Slowed speed of processing can result in vulnerabilities to poor decision-making, especially in the context of coercive interactions (APA, 2008). Processing speed is most typically assessed via several subtests in the WAIS, which is discussed extensively in the chapter in IQ assessments. Other tests that may be used include the Repeatable Battery for the Assessment of Neuropsychological Status (RBANS) or Trails A from the trail-making test (see the chapter on dementia).

Executive Functioning

Executive functioning can be relevant to the assessment of capacity as it relates to the ability to plan, think flexibly, respond to feedback, and inhibit impulsive responses which are critical to effective decision-making (APA, 2008). Some common tools used to assess executive functioning include the MMSE, RBANS, and COGNISTAT, also discussed in other areas in this book.

Judgment and Reasoning

Clearly judgment and reasoning are related (at face value) to capacity. Thus, it can be important to assess a client's judgment and reasoning. The Similarities subtest of the WAIS assesses abstract reasoning and can shed light in terms of the client's thought process. In terms of assessing judgment, the Kaplan Practical Problem Solving Task or reasoning from the COGNISTAT can be useful. While there is little research related to the Kaplan Practical Problem Solving Task for Hispanic clients, the COGNISTAT exam has been translated and normed on a Spanish-speaking sample with several peer-reviewed studies of its application for this population (Bea-Muñoz & Medina-Sanchez, 2000; Drane et al., 2003; Gutiérrez, Juárez, Cantú, Hernández, & Cardiel, 2003; López, Salazar, Peña, & Mitrushina, 2003; Pino et al., 2006; Rivera-Mindt et al., 2003). The APA (2008) recommends that the psychologist examine the distinction between responses to these posed problems and the client's ability to implement them.

Summary and Recommendations for Assessing Capacity with Hispanic Clients

The guidelines set out by the (American Psychological Association [APA], 2008) provide a nice framework for assessment of capacity with Hispanic client but seem to perpetuate the confusion of competency and capacity. The guidelines do however make the important distinction of establishing clinical versus legal capacity (e.g., the identified individual has the legal capacity to enter into a contract, make a medical decision as compared to the clinical capacity to have some understanding of the specific information in a contract, but the inability to explain the long-term consequences) and identify specific domains of functioning that should be included in a capacity assessment. The various assessments available to measure the domains set forth by the APA for a comprehensive evaluation of capacity and the considerations to be made for Hispanic clients are discussed throughout this book. It is therefore reasonable to expect that the competent psychologist, given this information, could obtain an appropriate and accurate measure of these domains necessary to establish capacity or a lack thereof.

Polygraphy

Polygraphy involves the use of physiological responses to determine if a person is telling the truth. A baseline is first found by measuring physiological responses to certain questions, and a subsequent assessment is conducted. The three techniques that are most commonly used include the relevant-irrelevant technique, the comparison question technique, and the concealed information test. While some research has shown that polygraphs can be helpful in detecting deception when used by well-trained examiners (American Polygraph Association, 2000), it is important to note that evidence on the effectiveness on the use of polygraphs to assess for deception is fairly sparse (Brett, Phillips, & Beary, 1986; Phillips, 1999), and they should thus be used and interpreted with extreme caution.

The relevance of cultural issues in a test that essentially assesses for physiological changes is minimal at most. Nonetheless, a review of the literature has indicated that Hispanics have been included in research supporting (or not supporting) the validity, reliability, and usefulness of the polygraph (e.g., Elliott & McConkie, 2002; Craig & Molder, 2003), suggesting that the use of the polygraph is as appropriate for Hispanics as it is with other minority and non-minority populations.

Personal Injury

Personal injury refers to harm done to the physical well-being of a person and not their property, and litigation includes general tort law involving accidents and other injuries, the law of toxic torts, claims of sexual harassment, worker's compensation, and claims for infliction of emotional distress, either intentional or negligent (Gerbasi, 2004). There are many types of personal injury evaluations including but not limited to motor vehicle accidents, slip-and-fall cases, sexual assault resulting in a psychological disorder, work-related discrimination or harassment, physical assault, malpractice, etc. (Witt & Weitz, 2007). Psychologists can be of help in defining the nature of the injury, liability, nonfinancial loss, past financial losses, future fiscal losses, future financial costs, and mental capacity and also in explaining how the person has been affected by the injury.

A review of the literature revealed substantial research on the general topic of psychological assessment as it applies to personal injury, but a search using the terms "personal injury," "assessment," and "Hispanic" or "Latino" has no relevant results or guidelines for the assessment of the Hispanic client in the context of personal injury assessment. Nonetheless, this type of assessment is quite relevant to the Hispanic client given their high saturation in employment settings where personal injury is likely, for example, the Hispanic construction workforce numbers more than 1.4 million, comprising 15% of all construction workers in the United States (Dong & Platner, 2000), the number of Hispanic workers is growing 36% faster than other minority groups, and they have been correlated with increased injury and illness representation (Anderson, Hunting, & Welch, 2000).

Normative Standard Versus Self-Standard

Typically two types of comparisons can be made when assessing for damages as they relate to personal injury—the normative standard and the self-standard. Lanham and Misukanis (1999) provide an excellent discussion on the normative standard and self-standard of comparison, which can be used independently or simultaneously depending on the availability of records Essentially, when using the normative standard of comparison, a client's test scores are compared to the scores of others (i.e., a group of people with similar demographic factors) so that the psychologist can gather information about the client's functioning as it relates to a normative group. In contrast, when using the self-standard of comparison, the client's post-injury performance is compared with their pre-injury functioning (Lanham & Misukanis). This can be accomplished via several means but is most typically evaluated via record review and may include reviewing mental health records, medical records, work and school records, etc. (Witt & Weitz, 2007). Vanderploeg (1994) divides the methods of estimating premorbid functioning used for self-standard comparison into four basic approaches: one based on historical data reflecting past achievements, two based on an individual's post-injury test performance, and one based upon demographic information. A more detailed discussion of premorbid functioning is discussed in the chapters of intelligence and neuropsychological assessment.

The Clinical Interview

As with most assessments, the clinical interview is a central feature in the evaluation of personal injury assessment. It is important that the limits of confidentiality be made clear, the purpose of the assessment be clearly delineated to the client, and in most cases releases of information should be obtained. Collaterals should also be interviewed either via the telephone or in person to obtain corroborating information about the injured party's symptoms and adjustment history. When interviewing collaterals that may present biased information (e.g., friends and family members), it is important that the evaluator interpret the information with caution and use other information gathered in the assessment process to corroborate the information obtained. Certainly, when working with the Hispanic client, the evaluator must be cognizant of language barriers, and to avoid things being "lost in translation," the clinical interview and interviews with collaterals should be conducted in whatever language the client feels most comfortable with. In circumstances where a language barrier exists, the use of a translator may be employed.

Psychological Testing

As with all assessment procedures, it is very important that the assessment measures selected for administration be tailored to the referral question. Thus, the following overview is a broad discussion of domains that *may be* assessed but are not indicative of necessary domains.

Assessing for the Presence of a Personality Disorder

Personality is largely considered to be a set of steady and lasting characteristics shaped by both heritability and the environment. While personality disorders can create many problems (interpersonal and otherwise) for the afflicted, it is unlikely that such problems are a result of personal injury. Thus, the existence of a personality disorder should be ruled out. Extensive information regarding the measures that can be used to assess for such a disorder along with relevant considerations can be found in the associated chapter in this book.

Symptom Assessment

If we consider the common sequelae of unfavorable events in life, we can reasonably expect certain symptoms to develop into symptoms most commonly associated with anxiety and depression. This type of assessment is most relevant in cases in which there appear to be emotional damages. Thus, measures should be administered to assess for the presence of an anxiety or mood disorder. The most common anxiety and mood-based disorders that should be assessed for are depression, panic disorder (with or without agoraphobia), and PTSD (there may be others that are worthy of being assessed for depending on the individual's circumstances). Extensive information regarding the measures available to assess for depression and anxiety can be found in the associated chapters in this book.

Malingering and Effort

Because malingering and effort often come into play when assessing personal injury, it is worth noting that an extensive review of the malingering literature with relevant recommendations is included in a different chapter in this book and thus will not be discussed here.

Further Specialized Assessment

Depending on the unique circumstances of the presenting client and referral question, specialized assessment may be required. Specifically cases that involve potential neurological insult, neuropsychological assessment may be necessary.

Putting It All Together: Personal Injury and the Hispanic Client

The purpose of the forensic assessment in personal injury referrals is to establish the extent of psychological injury. Thus, baseline functioning prior to the injury should be established via the means described above and compared with present functioning. Additionally, a discussion of the evidence-based prognosis of the injury in terms of level and duration of recovery should be provided. While establishing a baseline can be difficult, we do have a good deal of information available to us for self-comparison. Knowledge of the psychometric properties (in particular normative sample characteristics) of assessments used is more paramount for accurate prognosis. Clinicians may also wish to review scientific literature on the damages suffered by the individual (e.g., trauma) and specifics regarding the course that said damages usually take on Hispanics when compared to other ethnic groups (e.g., research has indicated that Hispanic veterans, particularly Puerto Ricans, are at an increased risk for developing PTSD: Schlenger et al., 1992) so that the extent of injury can appropriately be determined.

Conclusions

The scope of forensic practice is broad, and we have accordingly covered a great deal of material related to the various specialties within this broad domain of forensic assessment. As we illustrated, forensic assessment is challenging by the nature of its intermingling of the legal system and the strong potential for influence of secondary gain. We have also discussed the additional challenges of conducting forensic assessments with Hispanic clients. The overall message we hope to convey is that there are a good deal of objective measures that are available for Hispanic clients. Additionally, one should be able to take away an understanding that many aspects of the forensic assessment rely on pseudo-objective measures largely comprised of structured and semi-structured interviews. These interviews, like most in the field of psychology, rely on the individual clinician to accurately assess their level of expertise and the expertise of those who work with them (e.g., translator qualifications if translators are utilized). Given the APA code of ethics (in particular guideline 2.01 Boundaries of Competence; American Polygraph Association, 2002), this should not be a difficult task and some might say an understood component of professional, licensed practice.

References

Abidin, R. R., & Konold, T. (1990). *Parenting alliance measure – Professional manual*. Odessa, FL: Psychological Assessment Resources.

Amato, P. R., & Gilbreth, J. G. (1999). Nonresident fathers and children's well-being: A meta-analysis. *Journal of Marriage & the Family, 61*(3), 557–573.

American Polygraph Association. (2002). *The validity and reliability of polygraph testing*. Retrieved from American Polygraph Association Online: http://www.polygraph.org.apa5.htm

American Psychological Association. (2008). *Assessment of older adults with diminished capacity*. Retrieved from www.apa.org/pi/aging/resources/guides/diminished-capacity.pdf

Anderson, J. T. L., Hunting, K. L., & Welch, L. S. (2000). Injury and employment patterns among Hispanic construction workers. *Journal of Occupational and Environmental Medicine, 42*, 176–186.

Bagby, R. M., Nicholson, R. A., Rogers, R., & Nussbaum, D. (1992). Domains of competency to stand trial: A factor analytic study. *Law and Human Behavior, 16*, 491–507.

Bea-Muñoz, M., & Medina-Sanchez, M. (2000). Perceptive and cognitive difficulties in persons with brain stroke: Detection and compensation strategies. *Rehabilitacion, 34*(6), 468–82 (Spanish).

Bonnie, R. J. (1992). The competence of criminal defendants: A theoretical reformulation. *Behavioral Sciences & the Law, 10*, 291–316.

Bonnie, R. J., Hoge, S. K., Monahan, J., & Poythress, N. G. (1996). *The MacArthur competence assessment tool – Criminal adjudication*. Unpublished manuscript.

Borum, R., & Grisso, T. (1995). Psychological test use in criminal forensic evaluations. *Professional Psychology: Research and Practice, 26*, 465–473.

Bradley, R. H., & Caldwell, B. M. (1984). The HOME inventory and family demographics. *Developmental Psychology, 20*(2), 315–320.

Bradley, R. H., Corwyn, R. F., McAdoo, H., & Garcia Coll, C. (2001). The home environments of children in the United States part I: Variations by age, ethnicity, and poverty status. *Child Development, 72*(6), 1844.

Brett, A. S., Phillips, M., & Beary, J. F., II. (1986). Predictive power of the polygraph: Can the "lie detector" really detect liars? *Lancet, 1*(8480), 544–547.

Buchanan, C. M., Maccoby, E. E., & Dornbusch, S. M. (1991). Caught between parents: Adolescents' experience in divorced homes. *Child Development, 62*(5), 1008.

Buri, J. P. (1989). *An instrument for the measurement of parental authority prototypes*. Chicago: ERIC.

Cardona, P. G., Nicholson, B. C., & Fox, R. A. (2000). Parenting among Hispanic and Anglo-American mothers with young children. *Journal of Social Psychology, 140*(3), 357–365.

Colon, W. (2008) Validity of the newly translated and culturally-adapted Spanish version of the Children's assessment of participation and enjoyment & preferences for activities of children. *Dissertation Abstracts International Section A*, 69.

Craig, R. A., & Molder, C. (2003). The use of law enforcement polygraph tests with juveniles. *Journal of Credibility Assessment and Witness Psychology, 4*(1), 63–74.

DellaSanta-Percy, C. (2002–2004). *Interdisciplinary fitness interview – IFI and IFI-R*. Retrieved from http://mysite.cdellasanta.com/pdf/ifi_research.pdf

Dong, X., & Platner, J. W. (2000). Occupational fatalities of Hispanic construction workers from 1992 to 2000. *American Journal of Indian Medicine, 45*, 45–54.

Drane, D. L., Yuspeh, R. L., Huthwaite, J. S., Klingler, L. K., Foster, L. M., Mrazik, M., & Axelrod, B. N. (2003). Healthy older adult performance on a modified version of the cognistat (NCSE): Demographic issues and preliminary normative data. *Journal of Clinical and Experimental Neuropsychology, 25*(1), 133–44.

Edwards, L. M. (2004). Measuring perceived social support in Mexican American youth: Psychometric properties of the multidimensional scale of perceived social support. *Hispanic Journal of Behavioral Sciences, 26*(2), 187–194.

Elliott, H., & McConkie, M. L. (2002). Collaborative multidisciplinary teams and polygraphs: One protocol for increasing rehabilitative integrity. *Public Administration & Management: An Interactive Journal, 7*(4), 344–366.

Fantuzzo, J., Tighe, E., & Childs, S. (2000). Family involvement questionnaire: A multivariate assessment of family participation in early childhood education. *Journal of Educational Psychology, 92*, 367–376.

Fox, R. A. (1994). *Parent behavior checklist*. Austin, TX: ProEd.

Gerard, A. B. (1994). *Parent-child relationship inventory (PCRI)*. Los Angeles, CA: Western Psychological Services.

Gerbasi, J. B. (2004). Forensic assessment in personal injury litigation. In R. I. Simon, L. H. Gold, & R. I. Simon (Eds.), *The American psychiatric publishing textbook of forensic psychiatry*. Arlington, VA: American Psychiatric Publishing, Inc.

Gibaud-Wallson, J., & Wandersman, L. P. (1978a). *Development and utility of the parenting sense of competence scale*. Paper presented at the meeting of the American Psychological Association, Toronto, ON, Canada.

Golding, S. L. (1993). *Interdisciplinary fitness interview – Revised (Training manual and interview procedure)*. Unpublished Monograph, State of Utah Division of Mental Health.

Gothard, S., Rogers, R., & Sewell, K. W. (1995). Feigning incompetency to stand trial: An investigation of the Georgia Court Competency Test. *Law and Human Behavior, 19*, 363–373. doi:10.1007/BF01499137.

Grisso, T. (2003). *Evaluating competencies: Forensic assessments and instruments* (2nd ed.). New York: Kluwer Academic/Plenum Publishers.

Grych, J. H., Seid, M., & Fincham, F. D. (1992). Assessing marital conflict from the child's perspective: The children's perception of interparental conflict scale. *Child Development, 63*, 558–572.

Gutiérrez, L., Juárez, S., Cantú, C., Hernández, H., & Cardiel, M. (2003). Alteraciones cognoscitivas y factores asociados en un grupo de pacientes con diagnóstico de lupus eritematoso generalizado. *Revista Mexicana de Neurociencia, 4*(6).

Haack, L. M., Gerdes, A. C., Schneider, B. W., & Hurtado, G. (2011). Advancing our knowledge of ADHD in Latino children: Psychometric and cultural properties of Spanish-versions of parental/family functioning measures. *Journal of Abnormal Child Psychology, 39*(1), 33–43.

Helfenbaum-Kun, E. D., & Ortiz, C. (2007). Parent-training groups for fathers of head start children: A pilot study of their feasibility and impact on child behavior and intra-familial relationships. *Child & Family Behavior Therapy, 29*(2), 47–64.

Hetherington, E. (Ed.). (1999). *Coping with divorce, single parenting, and remarriage: A risk and resiliency perspective*. Mahwah, NJ: Lawrence Erlbaum Associates Publishers. Interview Procedure (unpublished monograph), State of Utah Division of Mental Health. Retrieved from http://www.xmission.com/~sgolding/publications/ifir_manual.htm

Hoge, S. K., Bonnie, R. J., Poythress, N., & Monahan, J. (1999). *The MacArthur competence assessment tool—Criminal adjudication*. Odessa, FL: Psychological Assessment Resources.

Jette, A., Davies, A., Cleary, P., Calkins, D., Rubenstein, L., Fink, A., et al. (1986). The functional status questionnaire: Reliability and validity when used in primary care. *Journal of General Internal Medicine, 1*(6), 427.

King, G., Law, M., King, S., Hurley, P., Hanna, S., Kertoy, M., et al. (2004). *Children's assessment of participation and enjoyment (CAPE) and preferences for activities of children (PAC)*. San Antonio, TX: Harcourt Assessment, Inc.

Klimes-Dougan, B., & And, O. (1992). Two studies of low income parents' involvement in schooling. *Urban Review, 24*(3), 185–202.

Knight, G. P., & And, O. (1992). The cross-ethnic equivalence of parenting and family interaction measures among Hispanic and Anglo-American families. *Child Development, 63*(6), 1392–1403.

Lanham, R. A., & Misukanis, T. (1999). Estimating premorbid intelligence. Determining change in cognition following 768 brain injury. *Brain Injury Source, Pediatric Issue, 3*(3). Retrieved from http://www.assessmentpsychology.com/iq-estimates.htm

Law, M., King, G., King, S., Kertoy, M., Hurley, P., Rosenbaum, P., et al. (2006). Patterns of participation in recreational and leisure activities among children with complex physical disabilities. *Developmental Medicine and Child Neurology, 48*(5), 337–342.

Lee, M. (2002). A model of children's postdivorce behavioral adjustment in maternal- and dual-residence arrangements. *Journal of Family Issues, 23*(5), 672–697.

López, E., Salazar, X., Peña, R., & Mitrushina, M. (2003, October). *Datos normativos en población hispano parlante en los estados unidos con educación limitada*. Presented at the Neuropsicología-Congreso Latinoamericano Por Sociedad Latinoamericana De Neuropsicología, Montreal, QC, Canada.

Lovejoy, M., Weis, R., O'Hare, E., & Rubin, E. C. (1999). Development and initial validation of the parent behavior inventory. *Psychological Assessment, 11*(4), 534–545.

Manguno-Mire, G. M., Thompson, J. W., Shore, J. H., Croy, C., Artecona, J. F., & Pickering, J. W. (2007). The use of telemedicine to evaluate legal competence: A preliminary randomized controlled study. *The Journal of the American Academy of Psychiatry and the Law, 35*(4), 481–489.

McDonald, R., & Grych, J. H. (2006). Young children's appraisals of interparental conflict: Measurement and links with adjustment problems. *Journal of Family Psychology, 20*(1), 88–99.

McGarry, A. L., et al. (1973). Competence to stand trial and mental illness (DHEW Publication, ABM, pp. 77–103). Rockville, MD: NIMH Department of Health, Education, and Welfare.

Menning, C. L. (2002). Absent parents are more than money: The joint effect of activities and financial support on youths' educational attainment. *Journal of Family Issues, 23*(5), 648–671.

Milner, J. S. (1986). *The child abuse potential inventory* (2nd ed.). Webster, NC: Psytec.

Moye, J., & Marson, D. C. (2007). Assessment of decision-making capacity in older adults: An emerging area of practice and research. *The Journals of Gerontology: Series B: Psychological Sciences and Social Sciences, 62B*(1), P3–P11.

Nicholson, R. A., Briggs, S. R., & Robertson, H. C. (1988). Instruments for assessing competency to stand trial: How do they work? *Professional Psychology: Research and Practice, 19*, 383–394.

Nicholson, R. A., Robertson, H. C., Johnson, W. G., & Jensen, G. (1988). A comparison of instruments for assessing competency to stand trial. *Law and Human Behavior, 12*(3), 313–321.

Phillips, M. (1999). Problems with the polygraph. *Science, 286*(5439), 411. doi:10.1126/science.286.5439.411d.

Pino, O., Guilera, G., Gómez, J., Rojo, E., Vallejo, J., & Purdon, S. E. (2006). Escala breve para evaluar el deterioro cognitivo en pacientes psiquiátricos. *Psicothema, 18*(3), 447–452.

Puckering, C. (2010). Parenting capacity and conduct. In J. M. Brown, E. A. Campbell, J. M. Brown, & E. A. Campbell (Eds.), *The Cambridge handbook of forensic psychology* (pp. 242–450). New York: Cambridge University Press.

Rivera-Mindt, M., Mariana, M., Marcotte, T. D., Moore, D. J., Bentley, H., Esquivel, M. M., Lopez, Y., Grant, I., Heaton, R. K., & The HNRC Group. (2003). The functional impact of HIV-associated neuropsychological impairment in Spanish-speaking adults: A pilot study. Neuropsychology, development, and cognition. *Journal of Clinical and Experimental Neuropsychology, 25*(1), 122–132.

Roa Capilla, L., & del Barrio, V. (2001). Adaptación del Cuestionario de Crianza Parental (PCRI-M) a población española/Adaptation of the Parent-child Relationship Inventory (PCRI) to the Spanish population. *Revista Latinoamericana de Psicología, 33*(3), 329–341.

Robert, C. J. (2009). Parenting practices and child behavior in Mexico: A validation study of the Alabama Parenting Questionnaire (Doctoral dissertation). *Dissertation to the Faculty of the Graduate School of the University of Minnesota*. Retrieved from http://conservancy.umn.edu/bitstream/51024/1/Robert_umn_0130E_10269.pdf

Rodriguez, C. (2008). Ecological predictors of disciplinary style and child abuse potential in a Hispanic and Anglo-American sample. *Journal of Child and Family Studies, 17*(3), 336–352.

Roesch, R., Webster, C. D., & Eaves, D. (1994). *The fitness interview test – Revised*. Unpublished manuscript, Simon Fraser University.

Roesch, R., Zapf, P. A., Golding, S. L., & Skeem, J. L. (1999). Defining and assessing competency to stand trial. In A. K. Hess, I. B. Weiner, A. K. Hess, & I. B. Weiner (Eds.), *The handbook of forensic psychology* (2nd ed., pp. 327–349). Hoboken, NJ: Wiley.

Rogers, R., Ustad, K. L., Sewell, K. W., & Reinhart, V. (1996). Dimensions of incompetency: A factor analytic study of the Georgia Court Competency Test. *Behavioral Sciences & the Law, 14*, 323–330.

Schlenger, W. E., Kulka, R. A., Fairbank, J. A., Hough, R. L., Jordan, B. K., Marmar, C. R., & Weiss, D. S. (1992). The relevance of post-traumatic stress disorder in the Vietnam generation: A multi-method, multisource assessment of psychiatric disorder. *Journal of Trauma Stress, 5*, 333–363.

Schludermann, E., & Schludermann, S. (1970). Replicability of factors in children's report of parent behavior (CRPBI). *Journal of Psychology: Interdisciplinary and Applied, 76*(2), 239–249.

Shelton, K. K., Frick, P. J., & Wootton, J. (1996). The assessment of parenting practices in families of elementary school-aged children. *Journal of Clinical Child Psychology, 25*, 317–327.

Solis, M., & Abidin, R. R. (1991). The Spanish version parenting stress index: A psychometric study. *Journal of Clinical Child Psychology, 20*(4), 372.

Tobin, N. L., Seals, R. W., & Vincent, J. P. (2011). Response patterns on the parent–child relationship inventory in a simulated child custody evaluation. *Journal of Child Custody, 8*(4), 284–300.

Tolle, L. W., & O'Donohue, W. T. (2012). *Improving the quality of child custody evaluations: A systematic model*. New York: Springer.

Tschann, J. M., Flores, E., Pasch, L. A., & Marin, B. (1999). Assessing interparental conflict: Reports of parents and adolescents in European American and Mexican American families. *Journal of Marriage & Family, 61*(2), 269–283.

Vanderploeg, R. D. (1994). Estimating premorbid level of functioning. In R. D. Vanderploeg & R. D. Vanderploeg (Eds.), *Clinician's guide to neuropsychological assessment* (pp. 43–68). Hillsdale, NJ: Lawrence Erlbaum Associates, Inc.

Varela, J. G., Boccaccini, M. T., Gonzalez, E., Jr., Gharagozloo, L., & Johnoson, S. M. (2011). Do defense attorney referrals for competence to stand trial evaluations depend on whether the client speaks English or Spanish. *American Psychology Law Society, 35*, 501–511.

Varela, R., Vernberg, E. M., Sanchez-Sosa, J., Riveros, A., Mitchell, M., & Mashunkashey, J. (2004). Parenting style of Mexican, Mexican American, and Caucasian-Non-Hispanic families: Social context and cultural influences. *Journal of Family Psychology, 18*(4), 651–657.

Viljoen, J., Roesch, R., & Zapf, P. (2002). Interrater reliability of the fitness interview test across 4 professional groups. *The Canadian Journal of Psychiatry/La Revue Canadienne de Psychiatrie, 47*(10), 945–952.

Viljoen, J. L., Odgers, C., Grisso, T., & Tillbrook, C. (2007). Teaching adolescents and adults about adjudicative proceedings: A comparison of pre- and post-teaching scores on the MacCAT-CA. *Law and Human Behavior, 31*(5), 419–432.

Viljoen, J. L., & Roesch, R. (2005). Competence to waive interrogation rights and adjudicative competence in adolescent defendants: Cognitive development, attorney contact, and psychological symptoms. *Law and Human Behavior, 29*, 723–742.

Viljoen, J. L., Vincent, G. M., & Roesch, R. (2006). Assessing adolescent defendants' adjudicative competence: Interrater reliability and factor structure of the Fitness Interview Test-Revised. *Criminal Justice and Behavior, 33*(4), 467–487.

Weis, R., & Toolis, E. E. (2010). Parenting across cultural contexts: Assessing parenting behavior in an ethnically and socioeconomically diverse sample. *Early Child Development and Care, 180*, 849–867.

Whiteside-Mansell, L., Ayoub, C., McKelvey, L., Faldowski, R. A., Hart, A., & Shears, J. (2007). Parenting stress of low-income parents of toddlers and preschoolers: Psychometric properties of a short form of the Parenting Stress Index. *Parenting: Science and Practice, 7*(1), 27–56.

Wildman, R. W., Batchelor, E. S., Thompson, L., Nelson, F. R., Moore, J. T., Patterson, M. E., & deLaosa, M. (1978). *The Georgia court competency test: An attempt to develop a rapid, quantitative measure of fitness for trial.* Unpublished manuscript. Milledgeville, GA: Forensic Services Division, Central State Hospital.

Wildman, R. W., II, White, P. A., & Brandenburg, C. A. (1990). The Georgia Court Competency Test: The baserate problem. *Perceptual and Motor Skills, 70*, 1055–1058.

Witt, P. H., & Weitz, S. E. (2007). Personal injury evaluations in motor vehicle accident cases. *Journal of Psychiatry & Law, 35*(1), 3–24.

Wong, S. T., Stewart, A. L., & Gregorich, S. E. (2004). Measurement adequacy of parenting and children's functional status in African American and Latino families. *Journal of Nursing Measurement, 12*(1), 47–62.

Zapf, P., Roesch, R., & Viljoen, J. (2001). Assessing fitness to stand trail: The utility of the fitness interview test. *The Canadian Journal of Psychiatry/La Revue Canadienne de Psychiatrie, 46*(5), 426–432 (Revised Edition).

Zimmerman, J. L. (1979). *The relationship between support systems and stress in families with a handicapped child.* Unpublished doctoral dissertation, University of Virginia, Charlottesville, VA.

Zimet, G. D., Dahlem, N. W., Zimet, S. G., & Farley, G. K. (1988). The multidimensional scale of perceived social support. *Journal of Personality Assessment, 52*, 30–41.

Index

L.T. Benuto (ed.), *Guide to Psychological Assessment with Hispanics*,
DOI 10.1007/978-1-4614-4412-1, © Springer Science+Business Media New York 2013

R

S

Printed in the USA
CPSIA information can be obtained
at www.ICGtesting.com
CBHW060309160724
11513CB00025B/290

9 781461 444114